NORWEGIAN VENTURE

NORWEGIAN VENTURE

BATTLES FOR THE FJORDS 1940

BRITANNIA NAVAL HISTORIES OF WORLD WAR II

Britannia Museum Trust Press

First edition published by University of Plymouth Press as *Fight for the Fjords, The Battle for Norway 1940* in 2012. This revised and extended second edition published in the United Kingdom in 2024 by Britannia Museum Trust Press, Britannia Royal Naval College, Dartmouth, TQ6 0HJ, United Kingdom.

PB ISBN 978-1-917152-07-5

HB ISBN 978-1-917152-06-8

EB ISBN 978-1-917152-08-2

© Britannia Museum Trust, 2024 © The Devonshire Press™ 2024

The rights of this work have been asserted in accordance with the Crown Copyright, Designs and Patents Act 1988.

A CIP catalogue record of this book is available from the British Library.

Publisher: PWN Honeywill

Series Editors: GH Bennett, JE Harrold, R Porter and MJ Pearce

All rights reserved. No part of this publication may be reproduced, stored

in a retrieval system or transmitted in any form or by any means whether electronic, mechanical, photocopying, recording, or otherwise, without the prior written permission of BMTP. Any person who carries out any unauthorised act in relation to this publication may be liable to criminal prosecution and civil claims for damages.

Historical content courtesy of Britannia Museum, Britannia Royal Naval College, Dartmouth, TQ6 0HJ.

Cover: KMS *Bernd von Arnim* beached and scuttled in Rombaks Fjord, Norway.

Typeset in Adobe Garamond Pro 11/14pt. Printed by Print on Demand

The historical documents reproduced here appear as unedited text, apart from minor changes made to date formats and corrections to typing errors found in the original.

Unless stated images are in the public domain or Creative Commons Attribution-Share Alike 4.0 International. UK photographs are taken prior to 1957 and created by the United Kingdom Government and are in the public domain having originally been taken during Royal Navy military service. *Georg Thiele* wreck photograph by Harald Groven 1990. All other images have permission as works of individuals in private collections.

 # Britannia Royal Naval College

A majestic landmark, which towers above the harbour town of Dartmouth in Devon, Britannia Royal Naval College was designed by royal architect Sir Aston Webb to project an image of British sea power. A fine example of Edwardian architecture, the College has prepared future generations of officers for the challenges of service and leadership since 1905.

The Britannia Museum opened in 1999 to safeguard the College's rich collection of historic artefacts, art and archives and promote greater public understanding of Britain's naval and maritime heritage, as a key element in the development of British history and culture. It also aims to instil a sense of identity and ethos in the Officer Cadets that pass through the same walls as their forbears, from great admirals to national heroes to royalty.

http://www.royalnavy.mod.uk/The-Fleet/Shore-Establishments/BRNC-Dartmouth

Contents

Foreword Admiral Lord West 10
Introduction Michael Pearce and Richard Porter 12

Part I

Illustrations Michael Pearce
Photographic Narrative.. 28

Part II

Chapter I
Preliminary Events
German Plan of Invasion 106
The British Minefield and Plan 'R.4' 109
Preparations and Movements 110
German Fleet Reported at Sea 111
First Enemy Contact: Loss of the Glowworm 115
The Sinking of SS Rio de Janeiro 116
Vice-Admiral Whitworth's Movements 117
Movements of Commander-in-Chief 121

Chapter II
German Invasion of Norway
The German Landings 126
Admiral Whitworth's Encounter with the *Gneisenau* and
Scharnhorst 128
British Dispositions, Vest Fjord Area 133
Movements of Commander-in-Chief, Home Fleet 135
First Battle of Narvik 144

Operations in Vest Fjord Area 149
Movements of Commander-in-Chief, Home Fleet 154
Movements of German Naval Forces 159
Furious Aircraft Attack at Narvik 161
Second Battle of Narvik 164
Cruiser Operations 174
Submarines Activities 182
General Situation 186

Chapter III
The Allied Counter Offensive and General Employment of Naval Forces
Plans and Policy 191
Question of Direct Attack on Trondheim 195
General Employment of Home Fleet 201
Carrier and FA/A Operations 204
Employment of A/A Cruisers and Sloops 207
A/S Trawlers on Norwegian Coast 209
The Southern Area: Surface Operations 211
The Southern Area: Submarine Activities 216
The Conjunct Expeditions 217

Chapter IV
The Landings at Namsos
Operation Henry 219
Operations Maurice: First Landings 222
Naval Movements and Landing of French 226
German Air Attacks on Namsos 227
Final Reinforcements, Namsos 229

Chapter V
The Landings at Åndalsnes, Aalesund and Molde
Operation Primrose 231
Operation Sickle 235
Sickle Reinforcements 239
The Situation on Shore 243

Chapter VI
The Withdrawal from Central Norway
The Decision to Withdraw 245
Plan of the Evacuation 246
The Retreat from Åndalsnes, Molde and Aalesund 248
The Retreat from Namsos 252

Chapter VII
The Expedition to Narvik: Phase I
Inception of Operation Rupert 260
Opening Moves: Conflicting Instructions 261
Operations in Ofot Fjord 268
Changes in Squadron: Army Reinforcements 269

Chapter VIII
Operations at Bodø, Mo and Mosjoen
Object of Operations 272
The First Landings 272
Area Placed Under Narvik Command 274
German Landing at Hemnes 274
Mo and Bodø Reinforced 276
Loss of the *Chrobry* and *Effingham* 278

Chapter IX
The Expedition to Narvik: Phase II
Development of Base: Harstad Area 281
The Landing at Bjerkvik 12/13 May 284
Preparations for Assault on Narvik 288
Plan of Operations 290
The Capture of Narvik 292

Chapter X
The Retreat from Northern Norway
The Decision to Withdraw 296
Withdrawal from Mo and Bodø 297
Plan of General Withdrawal 299
The Withdrawal 301

The German Naval Sortie (Operation Juno) 309
The Sinking of the *Glorious*, *Ardent* and *Acasta* 311
British Reactions 313
Movements of Commander-in-Chief, Home Fleet 316

Chapter XI
Comment and Reflections
The Commander-in-Chief, Home Fleet's Remarks 318
System of Command 319
The Importance of Wireless Silence 321
Tactical Loading of Expeditionary Forces 323
Risks and Chances 323
The Principles of War as Applied in the Campaign 324
Conclusion 327

Appendix A Allied Warships 328
Appendix B German Warships 336
Appendix C Home Fleet 338
Appendix D Similarity of German Silhouettes 343
Appendix E Summary of Air Attacks 344
Appendix F HMS *Furious* 346
Appendix G General Auchinleck's Despatch 347
Appendix H Naval Losses 350

Endnotes 353

Part III
The German Account 379

Biographies 496

Abbreviations 499

Index 500

Time Zone minus 1 (B.S.T.) is used

Foreword

Admiral Lord West

It was a great honour to be invited to write the introduction to one of the BRITANNIA NAVAL HISTORIES OF WORLD WAR II. Our nation seems to be in denial about its reliance on the maritime and a series such as this may, in a small way, redress the balance. The truth is emblazoned in stone on the façade of the Britannia Royal Naval College…

> "It is on the Navy under the good providence of God that our wealth, prosperity and peace depend"

…and we forget that at our peril.

The Norwegian Campaign highlighted a number of lessons that still have relevance today. The invasion was highly risky for the Germans but the gamble paid off. Significantly, however, Kriegsmarine losses ensured that there was never any real possibility of the Germans invading Britain in 1940.

For the first time, air power played a major part in maritime operations with the Fleet Air Arm sinking a major warship in the early days of the campaign and the Luftwaffe causing significant loss and damage to Allied units. Many lessons were learnt about the use of carriers and operating navies against shore-based air power.

There were major intelligence failures which saved the initial German invasion forces from almost certain annihilation and were instrumental in the loss of HMS *Glorious*.

What was never in doubt was the offensive spirit of individual Royal Navy units. Whether it was Roope ramming *Hipper* in the tiny HMS *Glowworm* or Warburton-Lee leading his destroyers against the enemy at Narvik, they instilled a hesitancy and caution in German surface ship commanders, lasting the rest of the war.

I wish this series the success it deserves.

Alan West

Admiral Lord Alan West of Spithead GCB DSC PC

Introduction

Michael Pearce and Richard Porter

This title comprises two 'Naval Staff Histories' of naval operations during the Norwegian campaign of 1940, both produced under the auspices of the British Admiralty. The German account, written by the Kriegsmarine Historian, Vice Admiral Kurt Assmann, came first, in November 1948, before official British documents were released, and was based on German naval records captured by Britain in 1945 and held in the Admiralty's Naval Intelligence Department. Therefore, his account of German operations is authoritative but less accurate when dealing with detailed RN movements. The British account, issued in March 1950 as Battle Summary No 17, used definitive British official documents made available shortly before but also drew on the German records used by Vice Admiral Assmann. The two histories were printed in small numbers by the Admiralty for official purposes only. The German history was classified 'Restricted' as 'Book of Reference BR1840(1)' but the British account carried the next higher security classification as 'Confidential Book CB3305(2)', although both were de-classified many years ago. Few copies survive of these scarce and important naval history sources but the Britannia Royal Naval College archive holds both documents, which form the core of this volume of the Britannia Naval Histories of WW2, augmented by a modern introduction and a section of contemporary photographs.

It is a record of naval operations undertaken in the Spring of 1940, during the German campaign to invade and occupy Norway, in the face of a spirited defence by the small Norwegian armed forces and intervention by Britain and France. Many geographically separated and tactically unrelated actions were fought, some simultaneously, in the two months from the second week of April until the second week of June 1940, when the campaign ended with the occupation of Norway by Nazi Germany and the withdrawal of British, French and Polish forces, largely in passenger liners requisitioned as troopships.

Geographical Setting

Norway has unique geographical features which contributed significantly to its strategic importance during WW2. Indeed these features are still important today, as is demonstrated by the country being an important training area for NATO forces. The coast of Norway shows spectacular fjord development that provides safe deep-water harbours and is a consequence of the area being glaciated during a previous ice advance where glaciers filled existing river valley systems. This resulted in overdeepened glacial valleys that reach the coast, forming long arms of the sea stretching far inland between steep rocky walls. Many fjords have a terminal rock barrier at their seaward end that is usually submerged, giving the fjord a shallow threshold that acts as a breakwater, providing a calm and safe haven for ships. The development of a fjord system is also reliant upon pre-existing coastal plateaus and mountains of appropriate structure that are present in Norway. Norway is not the only area of the world to have extensive fjord development, with the coasts of Alaska and British Columbia and that of southern Chile showing equally spectacular features. But Norway is unique because of its high latitude and the fact that its coast is ice free throughout the year. The Norwegian coast is bathed in the relatively warm waters of the North Atlantic Current which keeps ports such as Narvik ice free throughout the year, even though it lies well within the Arctic Circle at approximately 68 degrees north. This relatively mild climate, unusual for ports so far north, allowed it to develop as an important port, partly to export the high quality iron-ore discovered at Kiruna in Sweden and linked to Narvik via a railway connection.

Intelligence

On 10th April 1940 Germany brought into use a new Enigma key, codenamed 'Yellow', for Luftwaffe and Army communications during the invasion of Norway. Code-breakers at Britain's Bletchley Park Government Code and Cypher School (GC&CS), broke this key within five days, subsequently producing large numbers of decrypted operational signals until the key ceased to be used after 14th May, although these decrypts yielded only limited amounts of naval intelligence. However this notable GC&CS achievement was not declassified for public release until the mid-1970s, long after these Naval Staff Histories were written. Bletchley Park produced analyses of intercepted German signal traffic in parallel with decrypted Enigma messages but, in 1940, no effective organisation existed to categorise, prioritise, disseminate or utilise information from GC&CS, as was established later. Nevertheless, so great was the fear of compromising the source of the information, that elaborate cover stories were concocted, implying that it had come from covert British intelligence agents, rather than from activities at Bletchley Park. Unfortunately, service intelligence departments at that time lacked confidence in the new organisation and often failed to pass the intelligence to those who could have acted on it.

Perhaps the most significant example of this disconnect occurred as the Norwegian campaign drew to a close, when the naval section at Bletchley Park made strenuous efforts over several days to persuade the Admiralty's Operational Intelligence Centre (OIC) that German heavy warships were en route to Norwegian waters and that a warning signal should be sent to the fleet at sea. But the OIC were not convinced and did not do so. Consequently, on 8th June, the aircraft carrier HMS *Glorious*, detached from the main RN force at her captain's request to return to Scapa Flow with just two escorting destroyers, was surprised by the battlecruisers *Scharnhorst* and *Gneisenau*; all three British ships were sunk, with the loss of more than 1,500 lives. Subsequently, the OIC began to take seriously the intelligence produced by Bletchley Park and worked more closely with them. This new partnership developed rapidly, allowing Enigma decrypts to set up the successful Battle of Cape Matapan, fought by the Mediterranean Fleet in March 1941 and then, two months later, accurate reports that the German battleship *Bismarck* was heading for France, enabled her destruction. In June 1946 GC&CS became the Government Communications Headquarters (GCHQ), moving to Eastcote in Middlesex and then to Cheltenham in the early 1950s, where it has evolved into a cornerstone of UK and western intelligence networks.

Kriegsmarine Enigma cyphers were more secure than those used by the Army and Luftwaffe and were not broken until 1st August 1941. Keeping abreast of the naval Enigma became a constant struggle for Bletchley Park during the remainder of WW2, particularly after Kriegsmarine Enigma machines were changed from three rotors to four on 1st February 1942. But by the time that the Battle of the Atlantic was at its height, eagerly awaited Enigma decrypts were acted on immediately and proved to be a decisive factor in defeating the U-boats. However, the spectacular successes of Bletchley Park were all in the future at the time of the Norwegian campaign, which was fought before regularly decrypted Enigma intercepts, code-named 'Ultra', led to new, intelligence-driven, highly informed, methods of conducting and controlling most aspects of Allied operations in the European theatre.

German naval intelligence analysts of Beobachtungsdienst (B-Dienst) were able to intercept and analyse RN signal traffic and decypher some messages in early 1940, before the highly secure British 'Type X' (or 'Typex') five-rotor cypher machine entered RN service later that year. Partial decrypts achieved by B-Dienst in March indicated that a British operation to send troops to Norway had been postponed, following the end of the Russo-Finnish 'Winter War'. Grand Admiral Raeder, head of the Kriegsmarine, argued that this gave Germany the opportunity to move against Norway first and unexpectedly; Hitler agreed and approved the invasion.

Political Background

The Nazi invasions of Norway and Denmark launched on 9th April 1940, marked the end of the 'Phoney War' and began only a month before the German 'blitzkrieg' offensive that overwhelmed Luxembourg, the Netherlands and Belgium in a matter of days and then defeated France in six weeks. The Norwegian campaign drew to a close during the desperate days of the Dunkirk evacuation, when the Allied governments were understandably preoccupied by pivotal events closer to home. Nevertheless, even when the campaign opened, the level of air and land forces committed by the Allies was inadequate for the task and the efforts of their naval forces, no matter how gallant, could not compensate for this.

Allied failures in Norway provoked profound disquiet in Britain, providing the opportunity for an angry and dissatisfied House of Commons to force the discredited Neville Chamberlain to resign as Prime Minister, allowing his replacement on 10th May by the more robust and aggressive Winston Churchill. However, in his previous appointment as First Lord of the Admiralty, Churchill had been responsible for many British naval operations in Norway, when his enthusiastic remote interference (known in the RN as 'wielding a long screwdriver') and that of the First Sea Lord, Admiral Sir Dudley Pound, added a degree of confusion to some operations.

Earlier, there had been tentative Anglo-French plans to seek Norwegian and Swedish agreement to the occupation of the Norwegian ports of Narvik, Trondheim, Bergen and Stavanger in order to deny them to Germany and block supplies of Swedish iron-ore through Narvik. Britain and France had also suggested that this action would facilitate sending vaguely specified aid via Sweden to Finland. Formerly part of the Russian Empire, Finland had been an internationally recognised independent state from 1918 but was attacked and invaded by the Soviet Union on 30th November 1939. Although British operations were imminent, a formal test of Scandinavian neutrality was avoided when Finland was forced into an unfavourable peace, signing the Treaty of Moscow on 12th March, but only after inflicting huge losses on the Red Army.

Germany had violated Norwegian neutrality in early December 1939 when *U-38* sank the British ore carrier SS *Deptford* and a Greek freighter within the three-mile limit. Both Germany and Britain did so more blatantly on 16th February 1940 when the destroyer HMS *Cossack* boarded the Kriegsmarine auxiliary *Altmark*, sheltering in Jøssingfjord, south of Stavanger, and released 299 merchant navy prisoners captured by the armoured ship *Graf Spee* during the previous year. The British Operation Wilfred to disrupt German iron-ore traffic from Narvik by mine-laying in Norwegian coastal waters, disregarded neutrality considerations but commenced only on 8th April, just as Germany's invasion began.

The scrupulously planned German invasion was personally approved by Hitler but driven by Grand Admiral Raeder, who considered it was essential to forestall any possibility of the British occupying Norway first, and to guarantee Germany's supplies of high-grade Swedish iron-ore from the mine in Kiruna that had begun production in 1898. The ore was shipped via a railway link opened in 1903, to the Norwegian port of Narvik and then by sea southwards, along the Norwegian coast. As already noted, Narvik is ice-free throughout the year, unlike the Swedish port of Lulea, also linked to Kiruna by rail, forming another supply route through the Gulf of Bothnia and across the Baltic Sea to Germany. As the Norwegian campaign came to an end, Churchill briefly championed but then cancelled Operation Paul, to disregard Swedish neutrality and mine the approaches to Lulea, using Fleet Air Arm (FAA) Fairey Swordfish fitted with long-range fuel tanks, despite the port being ice-bound in winter. Today, icebreakers keep the port of Lulea operational throughout the year, although thousands of tons of iron-ore from Kiruna continue to be exported via the rail link to Narvik.

Strategy and Tactics

Admiral Raeder accepted that invading Norway would risk the entire Kriegsmarine, already much smaller than the Royal Navy, and would require surprise, plus large scale support from the Luftwaffe, to reduce the risk to an acceptable level. The operation was planned on that basis and its initial implementation showed German co-ordination to have been effective, despite Hermann Goering's reluctance to allow anyone else to direct Luftwaffe operations. German strategic plans were largely successful overall, despite frequent disruption at a tactical level by actions that caused such significant losses of, and damage to, Kriegsmarine surface warships that its ability to operate at all, let alone effectively, was seriously curtailed for many months.

In these actions, RN personnel demonstrated single-minded determination that was recognised by the award of three Victoria Crosses (Britain's highest decoration for bravery) – two of them posthumous – and also is shown by the tenacity with which Vice Admiral William 'Jock' Whitworth, in HMS *Renown*, pursued the *Scharnhorst* and *Gneisenau* through huge seas in the early hours of 9th April, to force the last gunnery action between battlecruisers. Although largely unsupported and at a considerable disadvantage, he increased speed to commence shooting with her 15-inch (38cm) guns until mountainous seas forced a reduction to less than 23 knots to keep the *Renown*'s 'A' turret in action. She hit the *Gneisenau* three times; the first on her foretop knocked out the fire control, the second disabled her fore turret, while the third hit aft on an AA mounting. The *Renown* was hit twice in return by 28cm (11-inch) shells but suffered negligible damage. As the weather moderated around dawn, the German ships drew away northwards and, despite the heavy seas, the *Renown* briefly worked up to 29 knots in pursuit but could not regain contact.

During the morning of 8th April, as German invasion forces gathered, the destroyer HMS *Glowworm* encountered and opened fire on the heavy cruiser *Admiral Hipper*, en route to land troops in Trondheim with the destroyers *Bernd von Arnim* and *Hans Lüdemann* in company. The unequal action lasted less than an hour before the *Glowworm* was overcome by the *Hipper*'s 8-inch guns, nevertheless, before sinking, the *Glowworm* rammed the *Hipper*'s starboard side, ripping away her torpedo tubes and 40 metres of the armour belt, causing hull damage that took on 500 tonnes of water. The CO of the *Glowworm*, Lt Cdr G B Roope RN, was awarded a posthumous Victoria Cross, following accounts of the action reported by the *Glowworm*'s survivors on their release from POW camps after WW2 but also, it is said, partly on the strength of a letter written through the Red Cross by Captain Helmuth Heye of the *Admiral Hipper*.

In the early morning of 9th April, at the outset of the German campaign, unimaginative tactics forced the Kriegsmarine to re-learn the often-taught lesson that even the most powerful warships are vulnerable to coastal guns and fortifications. A strong task force, led along Oslofjord by Rear Admiral Kummetz in his flagship, the new *Hipper*-class heavy cruiser *Blücher*, with the armoured ship *Lützow* astern, approached the shore batteries and defences of Dröbak Narrows and the Oscarsborg fortress, which the Germans regarded as obsolescent and largely non-operational. But, at point-blank range, elderly 28cm (11-inch), 15cm (5.9-inch) and 57mm guns, fired on the *Blücher* from both port and starboard, rapidly inflicting extensive damage and causing serious casualties. The cruiser's steering was disabled and fierce fires spread rapidly throughout her amidships section, intensified by blazing aviation fuel that poured below decks from her wrecked Arado 196 floatplanes in the ship's burning hangar, initiating more internal explosions. The torpedo workshop was destroyed in another series of explosions, generating further fires and showers of lethal steel splinters that seriously injured many embarked troops, whose stockpiled ammunition and explosives blew up with sufficient force to blast large holes in the deck. Amidst this chaos of fires and explosions, the ship shuddered and lost all power as two torpedoes, launched from 40-year old tubes ashore, hit the turbine and boiler rooms. Finally, the ship's 10.5cm magazine amidships detonated in a colossal explosion that blew out surrounding bulkheads, increasing the already severe list until she capsized to port and sank by the bows in 90 metres (300 feet) of water, with significant loss of life. Previously, this was thought to have been 800 to 1,000 but recent Norwegian research has reassessed the figure to about 400.

In addition to her ship's company, the *Blücher* carried Gestapo officials and a large contingent of troops intended to swiftly subjugate Oslo but her sinking provided sufficient time for King Haakon VII, his government and all the Norwegian national gold reserves, to leave the capital and safely reach Britain. The old guns also badly damaged the *Lützow*, which went about with some difficulty and retraced her course down Oslofjord. Two days later, returning to Germany for repairs, the *Lützow* was torpedoed by HM submarine *Spearfish* and so seriously damaged that she was under repair for 11 months. Further south, near the mouth of Oslofjord, smaller Kriegsmarine ships supported troop landings, exchanging fire with Norwegian shore batteries on the islands of Bolaerne to the west and Rauoy to the east. In the early afternoon of 9th April, the torpedo boat or light destroyer KMS *Albatros*, seeking to avoid gunfire from Bolaerne, ran at speed across the rocks of Gyren shoal and became a total loss.

At dawn on the following day, 16 obsolescent but still effective FAA Blackburn Skua dive-bombers of 800 and 803 Naval Air Squadrons (NAS), temporarily ashore from their parent carrier HMS *Ark Royal*, flew at extreme range from RN Air Station Hatston in the Orkney Islands, to surprise and sink the German cruiser *Köenigsberg*, alongside in Bergen harbour after suffering damage from Norwegian shore batteries at

Kvarven. This notable example of accurate dive-bombing was the first time that a major warship had been sunk by air attack in war. FAA Skuas from RNAS Hatston attacked occupied Bergen again on 12th and 14th April, sinking the German supply ship *Barenfels* alongside, with her cargo of military stores intended for Narvik, and seriously damaging quays and warehouses.

Early on 9th April, ten large Kriegsmarine destroyers appeared through dense snow squalls at the mouth of Ofot Fjord, leading to the iron-ore port of Narvik. They torpedoed and sank the old Norwegian coast defence battleships *Eidsvold* and *Norge*, allowing German forces to take possession of the port. But in the early hours of the next day, five British 'H' class destroyers of the 2nd Flotilla entered the fjord in a driving snow storm to attack the Kriegsmarine destroyers and ore-carrying merchantmen, beginning the first Battle of Narvik. They sank the flotilla leader *Wilhelm Heidkamp*, the destroyer *Anton Schmitt* and 11 merchant ships, damaging three other German destroyers before five more emerged from different arms of the fjord and engaged them. The flotilla leader HMS *Hardy* was disabled and driven ashore, while HMS *Hunter* was sunk. Captain (D) of the 2nd Flotilla, Captain B A Warburton-Lee RN, commanding HMS *Hardy*, was awarded a post-humous Victoria Cross.

Two days later, a gallant but largely unsuccessful attack on German ships in Narvik was carried out in appalling weather by 17 bomb-armed Swordfish from the carrier HMS *Furious*. But the following day, on 13th April, the RN returned in greater force, with the recently modernised battleship HMS *Warspite*, flying the flag of Vice Admiral Whitworth, and nine destroyers, to fight the second battle. This resulted in the remaining eight German destroyers and their oiler, the *Jan Wellem*, being sunk or scuttled and the sinking of *U-64* by the Swordfish floatplane catapulted from HMS *Warspite*. The British surface operation was supported by the simultaneous attack of 10 bomb-armed Swordfish from HMS *Furious*, although results of the air operation were inconclusive because of poor visibility and the confusion of the surface action. The British lost two Swordfish but no ships in the second battle, however, the bows of the Tribal class destroyer HMS *Eskimo* were blown off by a torpedo from the *Georg Thiele*.

Some traditionalist RN officers, still clinging to big guns as the decisive weapon at sea, doubtless celebrated the stirring sight and sound of HMS *Warspite* steaming up Ofot Fjord, her 15-inch (38cm) guns thundering out and echoing around the precipitous rock walls. However, her huge armour-piercing shells (the only type of main-armament shells carried by RN battleships at this time) had a limited destructive effect against unarmoured destroyers. The second Battle of Narvik was an example of risking a valuable sledgehammer in order to crack a nut, as the outcome could have been very different without outstandingly competent and aggressive reconnaissance by the *Warspite*'s solitary Swordfish floatplane. This reported the positions of several German destroyers before they could launch torpedoes and flew ahead to sink *U-64* with bombs – the first U-boat to be sunk by aircraft in WW2.

Perhaps surprisingly, it was British and Allied submarines, rather than German U-boats, that had the greater influence during the Norwegian campaign, sinking the cruiser *Karlsruhe*, the minelayer and gunnery training ship *Brummer*, six escorts and at least 13 merchant ships, while severely damaging the battlecruiser *Gneisenau* and the armoured ship *Lützow*.

The pre-war Air Ministry contention that it was strategically and tactically unnecessary for the Royal Navy to develop an integral Fleet Air Arm equipped with sufficient carrier-borne aircraft of current design and performance, was comprehensively disproved by the inability of the RAF to provide adequate air cover and support for Allied operations in Norway. The limited air support available was provided by small numbers of obsolescent, low-performance naval aircraft operating from the few available aircraft carriers, or at maximum range from Orkney, plus some RAF Hawker Hurricane and Gloster Gladiator fighters flying from improvised airstrips in northern Norway, having been carried there in RN aircraft carriers. The survivors were evacuated the same way, when ten Gladiators and seven Hurricanes landed on HMS *Glorious*, despite lacking arrestor gear. Sadly, all were lost with most of their pilots, when the *Glorious* was sunk. Although courageously flown, the number of FAA and RAF aircraft available was wholly insufficient to contest the Luftwaffe's control of the air over Norway. Allied operations, ships and personnel suffered accordingly.

HMS *Suffolk* was fortunate to reach Scapa Flow, after shelling Stavanger airfield on 17th April, having shipped about 2,000 tons of water aft, following almost seven hours of accurate bombing; the promise of fighters to cover her withdrawal not being fulfilled until the afternoon, when FAA Skuas, acting as fighters, arrived to protect the damaged heavy cruiser. In addition, all five anti-submarine trawlers of the 22nd A/S Group were sunk by air attack within a week of arriving in Romsdalsfjorden on 22nd April, where they were intended to provide protection from U-boats. The consequences of insufficient air support for RN ships in Norway were compounded by the inadequate provision of ship-borne AA guns that were too few and too light, even in recently-built ships, while some types of AA weapon, such as quadruple machine gun mountings, proved to be of little use in stopping modern aircraft. Even new ships were unable to defend themselves adequately against massed attacks by dive bombers. The escort sloop HMS *Bittern*, only two years old, with a main armament of six four-inch AA guns, was overwhelmed off Namsos by unrelenting Ju87 Stuka attacks during the morning of 30th April, suffering such serious damage that she had to be scuttled. Specialised air defence ships were equally vulnerable, particularly in confined waters; the old cruiser HMS *Curlew*, refitted as an anti-aircraft ship in the late 1930s, was sunk by He111 bombers in Ofot Fjord on 26th May.

FAA Skuas provided limited air defence throughout the Norwegian campaign, destroying at least 40 aircraft, despite Luftwaffe superiority and their own restricted numbers and modest performance. They also maintained offensive operations, with more strikes on Bergen, 806 NAS sinking the minesweeper KMS *Frauenlob* on 9th May and destroying 13 oil tanks on 10th and 16th. On 13th June, following the Allied evacuation and the sinking of HMS *Glorious*, 15 Skuas of 800 and 803 NAS from HMS *Ark Royal* attacked the damaged *Scharnhorst* in Trondheim, losing eight aircraft without result. Further Skua strikes targeted other Norwegian ports in addition to Bergen, including Trondheim and Tromsø, with 5th January 1941 being their last.

Tactically, the opportunistic sinking of the isolated and unsupported HMS *Glorious* by the *Scharnhorst* and *Gneisenau* confirmed only the blindingly obvious: aircraft carriers are vulnerable to heavy guns, if armoured ships are allowed to come within range. Nevertheless, HMS *Acasta*, one of the two escorting destroyers, obtained a seriously damaging torpedo hit on the *Scharnhorst*, before sinking. As the war at sea evolved, aircraft carriers proved to be vulnerable to surface attack only when intelligence or reconnaissance failures allowed them to be taken unawares, as with HMS *Glorious*. She remains the only fleet carrier sunk in action by hostile gunfire, albeit so early in WW2 that she was not fitted with radar and carrier tactics were in their infancy. The only other operational carrier lost in this way was the USS *Gambier Bay* off Samar in the Philippines in October 1944, when Rear Admiral Sprague's escort carriers were surprised by Japanese battleships and cruisers suddenly emerging from the San Bernardino Strait, after Admiral Halsey with the main US fleet had been decoyed away, 300 miles northwards. After the Battle of Cape Engano, also in October 1944, the Japanese light carrier *Chiyoda* was finished off by gunfire from USN cruisers and destroyers but was already dead in the water, disabled by carrier aircraft.

Conclusion

The Norwegian campaign was the first of many apparently stunning successes for the German military and began a period in which it appeared invulnerable. Politically, however, the Nazis were less successful. They failed to prevent the escape of King Haakon VII, his government and Crown Prince Olav, first from Oslo, and then northwards. German special forces attempting to capture the King near Elverum were fought off by his Royal Guards, reinforced by local civilian volunteer marksmen. Eventually, on 7th June, the heavy cruiser HMS *Devonshire* evacuated him, with 460 others, from Tromsø to Britain. The King became the centre of a strong government-in-exile in London, working unceasingly towards eventual Nazi defeat as a member of the Allies, backed by the 53 tons of the Norwegian national gold and bullion reserves. This had been divided into manageable portions and smuggled north from Oslo along various clandestine routes, before being finally evacuated to Britain in three RN cruisers. The wartime partnership with Britain is still commemorated today by the annual gift of a 20 metre Norway spruce Christmas tree erected in London's Trafalgar Square.

Following Nazi occupation, the appointments of the largely unknown and unwelcome Norwegian fascist Vidkund Quisling to head the government and Josef Terboven, a committed and brutal German Nazi, as Reichskommissar, ensured that Hitler's dream of seeing a willing Norway march happily into his self-styled Aryan fold, evaporated in the heat of oppression. The Norwegian Resistance was dedicated, effective, well-organised and, often, utterly ruthless throughout the war and it began to provide Britain with vital intelligence almost immediately. As the war progressed, a steady stream of Norwegians escaped to Britain, some to serve in the country's reconstituted armed forces; others joined the Special Operations Executive (SOE), working with the Resistance to sabotage the Vemork Norsk Hydro plant in Telemark and destroy stocks of heavy water (deuterium oxide), that could have assisted Nazi Germany to develop an atomic bomb.

The most significant lesson of the Norwegian campaign, for both sides, was the lethal effectiveness of aircraft when deployed against warships lacking adequate air cover. This established that it was impracticable to conduct successful sea or land operations without air superiority over the area in dispute. Even the battleship HMS *Rodney*, flagship of the Home Fleet, flying the flag of Admiral Sir Charles Forbes, was hit on 9th April, although the bomb could not penetrate her deck armour and did little damage. The British taught the lesson that warships are vulnerable to air attack by sinking the *Köenigsberg* at Bergen and convincingly reinforced the principle against the Italian battlefleet at Taranto seven months later, but it was well understood by the Germans and, especially, by the Japanese. In the following two and a half years, the RN lost many ships to hostile shore-based aircraft and when the naval war in the Pacific began at Pearl Harbor, a year and a half later, carrier-borne air power dominated.

It quickly became obvious to the British that adequate carrier-based air support was indispensable when out of range of land-based air cover but the RN could do little to improve matters in the short term, having too few aircraft carriers and a crippling shortage of suitable carrier aircraft, until modern high-performance US naval aircraft and then escort carriers became available through lend-lease. Nevertheless, the RN had no choice but to continue to operate within easy reach of enemy land-based aircraft in home waters, the Arctic and, particularly, in the Mediterranean. In these circumstances, the pre-war Admiralty decision to build the new generation of British fleet carriers with armoured flight decks was amply justified, saving at least three of these ships from destruction by mid-1942, while the concomitant reduction in aircraft capacity was of little immediate consequence, as greater numbers of naval aircraft were not available to the RN until later in WW2.

Equipment shortages in the early years of WW2 also prevented the RN from fitting its ships with sufficient numbers of modern rapid-firing AA weapons, such as 40mm Bofors and 20mm Oerlikon guns, until later in the war. Even then, when dual-purpose medium calibre weapons firing ammunition with proximity, or VT, fuzes also became available, RN ships never became the deadly fortresses of defensive fire that characterised comparable USN ships in the latter half of WW2.

The hard fought Norwegian campaign involved Allied sea, land and air forces, all seeking the same strategic objectives but the activities of the individual services were rarely coordinated effectively. Allied tactical successes may have been locally significant and good for morale but were largely due to the gallantry and determination of 'the men on the spot', rather than to organised planning and effective direction from the top. From the beginning, operations in Norway were impeded by a lack of strategic direction and focussed orders from an overall theatre commander. The Allies suffered from poor operational command, control and coordination, with single service commanders having differing orders, separate lines of responsibility and, occasionally, unfortunate personal relationships. Allied command structures in Norway became more effective from 20th April, with the appointment of the experienced and competent Admiral of the Fleet William Boyle, 12th Earl of Cork and Orrery (known as Lord Cork) as Supreme Allied Commander, pointing the way towards the efficient and obvious concept of unity of command, exercised through a theatre or supreme commander, that became an integral part of Allied war-fighting strategy.

The Allies failed to prevent the German occupation of Norway in 1940 but the actions fought there and the consequential losses incurred by the Kriegsmarine, significantly affected the overall strategic balance of WW2 in the short term. The immediate result of the fighting in Norway was to reduce the operational strength of the Kriegsmarine surface fleet to the hastily repaired heavy cruiser *Admiral Hipper*, three light cruisers (the *Leipzig* being under repair until late 1940, having been torpedoed by HMSub *Salmon* in December 1939), a handful of destroyers and two obsolete pre-Dreadnought training battleships, apart from minor craft. The third armoured ship, *Admiral Scheer*, was in major refit, not sailing until October. Although the damage to major units was made good in due course, many of the losses, particularly in destroyers, were never entirely replaced. Most importantly, by the time that German military successes in the early Summer of 1940 had left Britain vulnerable to invasion before winter, the Kriegsmarine had insufficient strength and resources to escort and defend a cross-Channel invasion force or ensure its essential re-supply and reinforcement, even given Luftwaffe air support. In contrast, although Allied naval losses in ships and personnel were grievous, particularly the tragic sinking of HMS *Glorious*, they were at least sustainable.

Germany acquired and, in the longer-term, fortified a long coastline that enabled the deployment of capital ships as a 'fleet in being', threatening to break out into the Atlantic. It also provided bases from which those heavy ships, U-boats and large elements of the Luftwaffe, could attack convoys carrying war material to the hard-pressed Soviet Union after June 1941. The original German objective of securing supplies of high-grade Swedish iron-ore through Narvik was attained, although it was eight months before shipments via that route could recommence, owing to the ruinous levels of destruction wreaked on the port, ore facilities and railway by Allied demolitions as their forces withdrew. However, the importance of Swedish iron-ore to the German war effort diminished somewhat after France surrendered in June 1940, when the Third Reich absorbed Alsace-Lorraine, accessing large iron-ore deposits there, although this eventuality could not have been foreseen when Germany planned the Norwegian campaign.

A final ironic twist was that Britain successfully turned Nazi Germany's occupation of Norway against Hitler by convincing him, through intelligence disinformation supported by naval, FAA and commando raids on the Norwegian coast and offshore islands, that the Allies were planning to launch large-scale troop landings to wrest Norway back from German control. This pretence was actively maintained up to and beyond the Normandy landings, tying down Luftwaffe squadrons and up to 400,000 German troops that would have been invaluable to the German war effort had they been redeployed to other fronts.

Bibliography

Assmussen, John and Leon, Eric, (2012) *German Naval Camouflage*, Vol One, 1939-41, Seaforth Publishing, Barnsley.

Brice, Martin, (1971) *The Tribals*, Ian Allan, London.

Cull, Brian, (2011) *Flying Sailors at War Sept 1939 – June 1940*, Dalrymple and Verdun Publishing, Stamford.

Cumming, Anthony J, (2010) *The Royal Navy and the Battle of Britain*, Naval Institute Press, Annapolis.

Dickens, Peter, (1974) *Narvik, Battles in the Fjords*, Ian Allan, London.

Dildy, Douglas C, (2007) *Denmark and Norway 1940*, Osprey Publishing, Oxford.

Greentree, David and Campbell, David, (2018), *British Destroyer vs German Destroyer*, Osprey Publishing, Oxford.

Greentree, David, (2022) *Narvik 1940*, Osprey Publishing, Oxford.

Grove, Eric, (1993) *Sea Battles in Close-Up, World War 2*, Volume Two, Ian Allen, London.

Haarr, H Geirr (2009) *The German Invasion of Norway*, April 1940, Seaforth Publishing, Pen and Sword, Barnsley.

Haarr, H Geirr (2010) *The Battle For Norway, April – June 1940*, Seaforth Publishing, Pen and Sword, Barnsley.

Haarr, Geirr and Melien, Tor Jorgen, (2023), *The Sinking of the Blücher, The Battle of Dröbak Narrows, April 1940*, Greenhill Books, Barnsley.

Harvey, M, (1990) *Scandinavian Misadventure, The Norway Campaign 1940*, Spellmount. Tunbridge Wells.

Hinsley F H et al, (1979) *British Intelligence in the Second World War*, Vol 1, HMSO, London.

Hobbs, David, (2019) *The Dawn of Carrier Strike*, Seaforth Publishing, Barnsley.

Hobbs, David, (2022) *The Fleet Air Arm and the War in Europe 1939-1945*, Seaforth Publishing, Barnsley.

Holmes, A, (1965) *Principles of Physical Geology*. Nelson London.

Jacobsen, Alf R, (2016) *Death at Dawn, Captain Warburton-Lee VC and the Battle of Narvik, April 1940*, The History Press, Stroud, Gloucestershire.

Jarvis, Peter, (2003) *The Invasion of 1940* (Markham Memorial Lecture), Bletchley Park Trust.

Jones, Ben M.Phil., Ph.D., (2012) *The Fleet Air Arm in the Second World War*, Vol 1 1939-1941, Ashgate Publishing for the Navy Records Society

Kent, Barrie, (1993) *Signal! A History of Signalling in the Royal Navy*, Hyden House.

Kersaudy, F, (1990) *Norway 1940*. Collins London

Macintyre, Donald, (1959) *Narvik*, Evans, London.

Partridge, Major Richard T DSO RM Rtd, (1983) *Operation Skua*, The Fleet Air Arm Museum in association with Picton Publishing, Chippenham.

Pearson, Robert, (2015) *Gold Run: The Rescue of Norway's Gold Bullion From the Nazis 1940*, Casemate Books, Oxford.

Roskill, S W, (1957) *HMS Warspite*, Collins, London.

Salmon, P, (1995) *Britain and Norway in the Second World War*. HMSO London.

Smith, Michael, (2004) *Station X*, Pan Macmillan, London.

Sturtivant, Ray, (1995) *Fleet Air Arm Aircraft 1939 to 1945*, Air-Britain (Historians) Ltd, Tunbridge Wells.

Sturtivant, Ray, with Cronin, Dick, (1998) *Fleet Air Arm Aircraft, Units and Ships 1920 to 1939*, Air-Britain (Historians), Tunbridge Wells.

Symonds, Craig L, (2018), *World War II At Sea*, Oxford University Press.

Wright, Malcolm, (2014), *British and Commonwealth Warship Camouflage of WWII*, Vol One, Seaforth Publishing, Pen and Sword, Barnsley.

PART I – Illustrations

Michael Pearce

An early panoramic view of Narvik harbour, with 22 ore ships and the ore terminal in the background; this became an important facility after 1903 when the rail link opened from the Swedish iron-ore mine at Kiruna.

1. Tribal class destroyer HMS *Cossack* in 1938; rescued 299 merchant seamen from the supply ship *Altmark* on 16 February 1940, damaged at the second Battle of Narvik. Torpedoed by U-563 on 23 October 1941 and sank under tow west of Gibraltar four days later.

2. The open bridge of HMS *Cossack* in 1940, Captain Philip Vian standing to the right; a bold but irascible officer, Vian had a distinguished career, becoming Admiral of the Fleet in 1952. Lewis guns on each side of the bridge were makeshift AA weapons that may have contributed more to morale than to actual AA defence.

3. Destroyer HMS *Intrepid* shadowing the German supply ship and oiler KMS *Altmark* into Jøssingfjord as she seeks to use the neutrality of Norwegian waters to avoid interception by the RN.

4. KMS *Altmark* in Jøssingfjord, February 1940; boarded by HMS *Cossack*, 16 February, releasing 299 seaman captured from British merchant ships the previous year by the armoured ship KMS *Graf Spee*.

5. A pre-WW2 portrait of the destroyer HMS *Glowworm*; sunk by the heavy cruiser KMS *Admiral Hipper* and accompanying destroyers on 8 April but rammed the *Hipper* before sinking.

7. *Top right* HMS *Glowworm*, bows missing after ramming the *Admiral Hipper*, both banks of quintuple torpedo tubes trained to starboard but empty; she sank shortly afterwards with the loss of 109 lives.

8. *Below right* Survivors clinging to the wreckage of HMS *Glowworm* just before she sank, seen through a rangefinder on the *Admiral Hipper*, which picked up 40, although six subsequently died.

6. HMS *Glowworm*, under fire and making smoke, closes the *Admiral Hipper* before ramming her starboard side, tearing away the cruiser's torpedo tubes, 40 metres of armour belt and causing the ship to take on 500 tonnes of water, damage that required repairs in Germany.

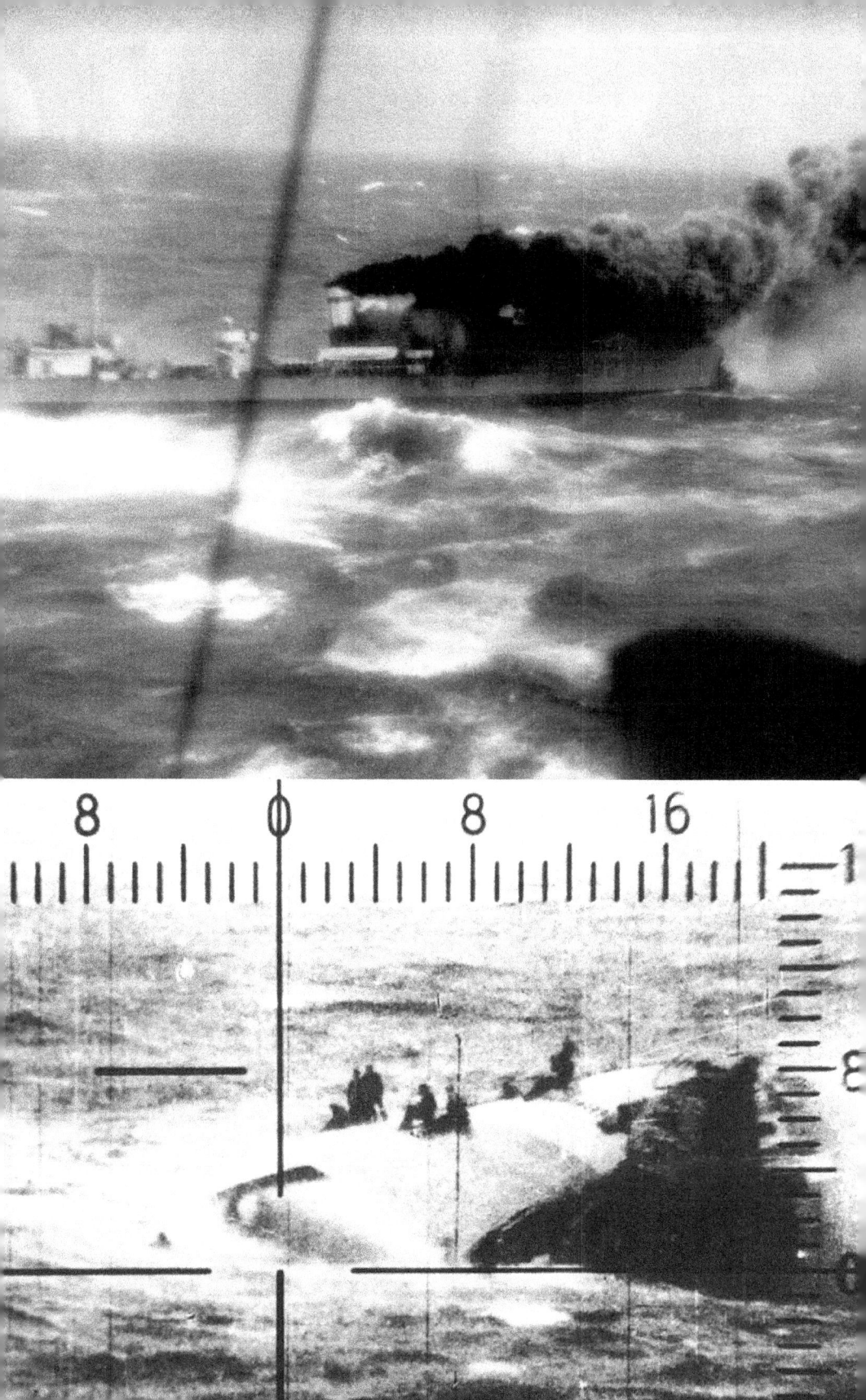

9. *Above* KMS *Admiral Hipper* dry docked at Wilhelmshaven, late April 1940, starboard side damaged below the waterline when rammed by HMS *Glowworm*; repaired hastily, allowing the ship to return to Norwegian waters.

10. *Below* KMS *Admiral Hipper*, dry docked in Brest, early 1941, after operating in the Atlantic against Allied convoys; she returned to Germany via the Denmark Strait for a seven month refit in Kiel.

11. *Right* An unusual bow view of the heavy cruiser KMS *Admiral Hipper* in Summer 1942, once more in Norwegian waters, near Trondheim.

12. Heavy cruiser KMS *Blücher* when brand new; sunk 9 April 1940 by Norwegian coastal defences at the Dröbak Narrows and Oscarsborg fortress, Oslofjord. Sister-ship of the better known *Admiral Hipper* and *Prinz Eugen*.

13. KMS *Blücher*, 9 April, burning fiercely and listing heavily to port after two torpedo hits, following multiple shell strikes from Norwegian coastal guns.

14. *Above* Survivors struggle ashore as the stern of KMS *Blücher* lifts and she sinks in Oslofjord, having capsized to port. The Kriegsmarine had declared her ready for service only four days earlier on 5 April, following structural modifications after commissioning.

15. KMS *Albatros*, a torpedo boat or light destroyer, ran at 20 knots across the Gyren Shoal near the mouth of Oslofjord on 10 April, tearing open the ship's bottom, making her a total loss. Photo shows her wreck after guns, screws and other equipment had been salvaged.

16. Blackburn Skua II L2928 of 801 NAS, flying out of RNAS Donibristle, Summer 1939; destroyed in a forced landing after engine failure in August 1943, flying with 772 NAS from Machrihanish; the pilot survived.

17. Blackburn Skua II of 803 NAS from HMS *Ark Royal* in pre-WW2 colours, June 1939. The nearest aircraft, L2889, was lost, 9 September 1940, on a strike with 801 NAS on Haugesund, Norway; both aircrew were killed.

18. Light cruiser KMS *Köenigsberg*, after her 1936 refit with a Heinkel He60c biplane floatplane on a catapult between the funnels, later replaced by an Arado Ar196.

19. KMS *Köenigsberg* after 0720 on 10 April, when first hit by 500lb semi-armour piercing bombs from FAA Skua dive bombers of 800 and 803 NAS, alongside the Skoltegrunnd Mole in Bergen.

20. KMS *Köenigsberg* burning on 10 April after at least five bomb hits from FAA Skuas. These three photos come from a series taken illicitly by a Norwegian in occupied Bergen. In the right background is the US merchant ship SS *Flying Fish*.

21. Thickening smoke pours from KMS *Köenigsberg* as her fires worsen and the ship begins to sink by the bow.

22. KMS *Köenigsberg* capsizing to port. The wreck was raised in July 1942 but not repaired, finally being scrapped at Stavanger between 1945 and 1947.

23. *Top right* FAA Skuas attacked Bergen harbour again on 12 and 14 April, sinking the German supply ship SS *Barenfels* alongside, preventing her cargo of military stores from reaching Narvik, and destroying warehouses and port facilities.

24. The 500lb SAP bombs from the Skuas detonated petrol on the quay and munitions in the after hold of the SS *Barenfels*, causing severe damage. The wreck was raised and repaired, returning to Kriegsmarine service in 1942 but was sunk again in Bergen, April 1944, by limpet mines from the RN midget submarine *X-24*.

25. Battlecruiser HMS *Renown*, completed in 1916 but comprehensively modernised 1936 to 1939, with new engines, boilers and secondary armament, increased armour and 15-inch guns given increased elevation and range. Pictured in 1944 with aircraft removed and light AA armament increased.

26. Battlecruiser or fast battleship KMS *Gneisenau* in 1939, after a funnel cap had been fitted and the former straight stem replaced by an 'Atlantic bow' to improve sea-keeping in heavy weather.

27. KMS *Gneisenau* in early Summer 1939 before embarking an Arado Ar196 catapult floatplane, replacing the biplane Heinkel He60c seen here.

28. Armoured Ship KMS *Lützow*, as KMS *Deutschland* in 1938, with a low funnel cap, Spanish Civil War neutrality patrol red, white and black national markings on 11-inch turrets and a Heinkel He60c biplane floatplane on the catapult, later replaced by an Arado Ar196.

29. KMS *Lützow*, 11/12 April, down by the stern, under tow for Kiel after being torpedoed by HMSub *Spearfish*. Centre 28cm (11-inch) gun missing from fore-turret following damage from Norwegian coastal guns at Dröbak, Oslofjord early on 9 April, when KMS *Blücher* was sunk.

30. Light cruiser KMS *Karlsruhe*, pre-WW2 aerial view showing unusual off-set triple turrets aft, sister-ship of the *Köenigsberg*. Fitted with funnel caps by the time she was torpedoed by HMSub *Truant* late on 9 April. Her well-preserved wreck rests upright in 490 metres (1,610 feet) of water off Kristiansand.

31. HMSub *Truant* hit KMS *Karlsruhe* on the starboard side amidships with one torpedo from a spread fired while the cruiser was manoeuvring. Serious flooding disabled engines and pumps and the ship was scuttled two hours later by torpedoes from KMS *Grief*.

32. HMNoS *Eidsvold*, a British-built coast defence battleship commissioned in 1901; torpedoed by the destroyer KMS *Wilhelm Heidkamp* outside Narvik harbour early on 9 April, blown in two and sank rapidly with only eight survivors.

33. HMNoS *Norge*, sister-ship of the *Eidsvold*, was at the mouth of Narvik harbour and fired unsuccessfully on KMS *Bernd von Arnim* with her 21cm (8.2-inch) and 15cm (5.9-inch) guns through heavy snow squalls; two torpedoes from the destroyer hit the *Norge* and she capsized to starboard, with 96 survivors.

34. Type 1936 destroyer KMS *Wilhelm Heidkamp* torpedoed and sank the Norwegian coast defence battleship HMNoS *Eidsvold* at Narvik. Flotilla leader of 10 large destroyers under Kommodore Friedrich Bonte, who was killed aboard as the first battle began.

35. *Below* KMS *Wilhelm Heidkamp* sinking after the first Battle of Narvik; a torpedo from HMS *Hardy* detonated her after magazine, blew off her stern, killed 81 men, and hurled the three after gun mountings into the air, one landing on her own forecastle, she capsized and sank at 0600 on 11 April.

36. Type 1936 destroyer KMS *Diether von Roeder* when brand new, from a pre-WW2 Third Reich postcard; hull numbers on Kriegsmarine destroyers indicated their flotilla positions.

37. KMS *Diether von Roeder* disabled by HMS *Hostile* at the first Battle of Narvik, three 4.7-inch shell holes in the hull are clearly visible; secured at an angle to the Post Pier, she damaged HMS *Cossack* in the second battle. Abandoned when her ammunition ran out and destroyed by detonating her depth charges.

38. Type 1936 destroyer KMS *Anton Schmitt*; hit by gunfire and a torpedo from HMS *Hunter*, then by another torpedo from HMS *Havock*, she broke in two and sank during the first Battle of Narvik.

39. Type 1934A destroyer KMS *Erich Giese*, from a pre-WW2 Third Reich postcard; seriously damaged at close range by gunfire from the Tribal class destroyer HMS *Bedouin* and in passing by other destroyers and HMS *Warspite*; ran out of ammunition and abandoned listing and burning to drift away, sank quietly after dark.

40. Type 1934A destroyer KMS *Erich Koellner*, damaged by grounding late on 11 April and positioned outside Narvik harbour during the second battle. Severely battered at close range by Tribal class destroyers HMSs *Bedouin*, *Punjabi* and *Eskimo* and hit by six 15-inch AP salvoes from HMS *Warspite*; wreck finally scuttled with a depth charge.

41. Type 1934A destroyer KMS *Bernd von Arnim* torpedoed and sank the old Norwegian coast defence battleship HMNoS *Norge* at Narvik early on 9 April and fired on HMSs *Hardy*, *Hunter* and *Havock* in the first battle. Abandoned at the end of Rombaks Fjord and scuttled by demolition and depth charges when out of ammunition after the second.

42. Type 1934A destroyer KMS *Wolfgang Zenker*, from a pre-WW2 Third Reich postcard; fought in both Battles of Narvik but scored few hits and ran out of ammunition. Abandoned at the end of Rombaks Fjord and scuttled by demolition and depth charges.

43. The scuttled wrecks of the *Bernd von Arnim* (foreground) and *Wolfgang Zenker* beached and abandoned at the end of Rombaks Fjord. Another view of the abandoned *Bernd von Arnim* appears on the cover of this volume.

44. Narvik Harbour after the first battle, three German destroyers alongside the Post Pier; nearest is the disabled *Diether von Roeder*, stern secured to the pier, bows anchored allowing her forward guns to bear on the harbour entrance, *Hans Lüdemann* in the centre with *Wolfgang Zenker* alongside her to starboard.

45. Type 1936 destroyer KMS *Hermann Künne*; damaged in collision with the sunken wreck of the *Anton Schmitt* during the first Battle of Narvik and near-missed by a Swordfish bomber from HMS *Furious* during the Second.

46. KMS *Hermann Künne* ran out of ammunition and was blown up in Rombaks Fjord by demolition charges just as HMS *Eskimo* torpedoed her, comprehensively destroying the ship.

47. The broken wreck of the *Hermann Künne* in Rombaks Fjord; although partially salvaged after WW2, the outline of the hull and some remains are still visible in shallow water in 2024.

48. KMS *Hermann Künne* burning fiercely after the impact of a torpedo from HMS *Eskimo* and detonation of scuttling charges; seen from HMS *Warspite*'s Swordfish floatplane.

49. Two destroyers alongside the Post Pier in Narvik Harbour after the first battle with *Hermann Künne* to the right and *Hans Lüdemann* to the left, both disembarking their wounded; burning and sinking merchant ships astern. Out of frame to the right, is the disabled *Diether von Roeder*.

50. Type 1936 destroyer KMS *Hans Lüdemann*; damaged by gunfire from HMSs *Havock* and *Hostile* during the first Battle of Narvik but completed temporary repairs in time for the second, when her Nos 3, 4, and 5 gun mountings were knocked out by a salvo from HMS *Eskimo*.

51. The wreck of KMS *Hans Lüdemann* in shallow water at the end of Rombaks Fjord. Scuttling charges and a depth charge had been set but failed to detonate and she was boarded by parties from HMSs *Hero* and *Icarus*; despite them wanting to tow her away as a prize, time precluded, and she was sunk by a torpedo from HMS *Hero*.

52. *Above* Narvik Harbour shortly after the first battle: the *Wolfgang Zenker* going alongside the Post Pier; the *Hans Lüdemann* the other side; the disabled *Diether von Roeder* beyond, stern-on at an angle to the Pier. Merchant ships are: (nearest to furthest) SS *Saphir*, in smoke, sinking; SS *Riverton* on fire; SS *Aachen*; SS *Cate B*; bows of sunken SS *Hein Hoyer*; SS *Bockenheim* ashore on opposite beach.

53. German SS *Bockenheim* ashore at Ankenes, opposite Narvik; beached, set ablaze and engines damaged by her crew, who mistook German destroyers for British ships on 9 April. Narvik ore terminal visible beyond and forward of funnel. Partially salvaged after WW2, the outline of the hull and some remains still visible in shallow water in 2024.

54. Type 1934 destroyer KMS *Georg Thiele* pre-WW2; damaged HMS *Hardy* so seriously as she withdrew after the first Battle of Narvik that she had to be run ashore; probably torpedoed HMS *Hunter* shortly afterwards, sinking her. Her own damage was temporarily repaired in time for the second battle.

55. KMS *Georg Thiele* defended Rombaks Fjord against several British destroyers, so the crews of *Hans Lüdemann*, *Bernd von Arnim* and *Wolfgang Zenker* could scuttle their ships and get ashore. Suffered serious damage from gunfire but managed to blow the bows off HMS *Eskimo* with her last torpedo.

56. *Above* The *Georg Thiele* was run ashore at speed after she could do no more. Her wreck remains on the rocky shore of Rombaks Fjord in 2024 and is a popular dive site. (photograph by © Harald Groven 1990).

57. Type IXB *U-64*; bombed by the Swordfish floatplane from HMS *Warspite* at the head of Herjangs Fjord 13 April and sunk, 38 survivors. Photograph shows the raised wreck in August 1957; it was scrapped at Sandnessjøen.

58. Destroyer leader HMS *Hardy* pre-WW2, an additional 4.7-inch mounting between the funnels, broad black band to top of first funnel and no pennant number, are all typical of inter-war flotilla leaders.

59. HMS *Hardy* between 1937 and 1939, taking part in the Spanish Civil War neutrality patrol with nationality markings in red, white and blue on the shield of 'B' 4.7-inch mounting.

60. The wreck of HMS *Hardy* from astern, capsized in shallow water at the head of Skjomenfjord, having drifted from Virek, where she was first beached after being disabled withdrawing from Narvik after the first battle.

61. The capsized wreck of HMS *Hardy*, ashore at her final resting place at the head of Skjomenfjord, where she was visible until broken up in the early 1960s.

62. *Above* Destroyer HMS *Hunter* pre-WW2. Torpedoed the destroyer *Anton Schmitt* but damaged withdrawing from Narvik harbour by the *Georg Thiele* and *Bernd von Arnim* with a probable torpedo hit by the *Georg Thiele*, then rammed amidships by HMS *Hotspur*, whose steering was temporarily disabled, sank shortly afterwards with 46 survivors.

63. Destroyer HMS *Havock* pre-WW2, Spanish Civil War neutrality patrol nationality markings on 'B' 4.7-inch mounting. Torpedoed the destroyer *Anton Schmitt* during the first Battle of Narvik. Wrecked on the Tunisian coast April 1942, en route to Gibraltar for repair of damage by 15-inch shells from Italian battleship *Littorio* during second Battle of Sirte.

64. Destroyer HMS *Hostile* pre-WW2, all 4.7-inch guns trained to starboard. Disabled destroyer *Diether von Roeder* at first Battle of Narvik, hit once with only minor damage. Mined and broke her back off Cape Bon 23 August 1940, en route to join Force 'H' at Gibraltar, scuttled by HMS *Hero*.

65. Destroyer HMS *Hotspur* early in WW2; an unusual view of an unofficial but effective camouflage scheme. Steering temporarily disabled during first Battle of Narvik, ramming HMS *Hunter*; converted to an escort destroyer 1943, 1948 sold to the Dominican Republic, not scrapped until 1972.

66. An early Fairey Swordfish 1, K5933, resplendent in 1930's peacetime silver; lost in mid-air collision with K5976, 30 January 1939, night flying with 825 NAS from HMS *Glorious* off Alexandria, the aircrews of both were killed.

67. A formation of Fairey Swordfish carrying 18-inch torpedoes, probably a training exercise, as the nearest aircraft is flying without a TAG (Telegraphist Air Gunner) in the rear cockpit.

68. Aircraft carrier HMS *Furious*, much altered in her long career from 1917, was fitted with a small starboard-side island during 1938-39 refit. Photograph shows appearance during Norwegian campaign, when her Swordfish carried out several strikes.

69. HMS *Ark Royal*, Britain's most modern aircraft carrier at the outbreak of WW2; in the Mediterranean when Norwegian campaign began, relieved HMS *Furious* off Norway from 25 April. Fairey Swordfish 1 from 820 NAS overhead in this pre-WW2 photograph.

70. Battleship HMS *Warspite* commissioned in 1915 but comprehensively modernised 1934-37 with new engines and boilers, increased armour and 15-inch guns given increased elevation and range. Nationality markings on 'B' turret for Spanish Civil War neutrality patrol.

71. HMS *Warspite*, late 1930s after reconstruction, showing athwartships catapult and crane installed abaft new bridge structure and funnel for operating Fairey Swordfish floatplanes, later replaced by Supermarine Walrus amphibians.

72. *Above* Fairey Swordfish 1 floatplane, V4367 of 700 NAS in 1941, being craned aboard battleship HMS *Malaya*, sister-ship of HMS *Warspite*; 690hp Bristol Pegasus III engine running. Floats were readily interchangeable with the standard wheeled undercarriage.

73. HMS *Warspite* firing on the destroyer *Erich Koellner*, hitting with six salvoes of 15-inch AP shells that went through the ship without exploding, the impact of each causing her to heel over.

74. Tribal class destroyer HMS *Bedouin*, probably March 1941 during the successful raid on the Norwegian Lofoten Islands. Heavily engaged at the second Battle of Narvik; sunk June 1942 escorting Malta convoy Operation Harpoon.

75. During the second Battle of Narvik, KMS *Georg Thiele* torpedoed the Tribal class destroyer HMS *Eskimo*, blowing away her bows. Surprisingly, the crew of 'B' mounting kept their guns in action; 'A' mounting stayed attached to the sagging remains of her bows until shipwrights from the repair ship HMS *Vindictive* removed the wreckage.

76. *Above* HMS *Eskimo* at Skjelfjorden in the Lofoten Islands after the dangling mass of steel from her damaged bows had been cut away, and her two forward 4.7-inch twin mountings hoisted out, using heavy-duty derricks aboard the captured German supply ship *Alster*. The foreshortened *Eskimo* reached the Tyne under her own steam at the end of May, for five months of repairs.

77. Destroyer HMS *Eskimo* in September 1942 escorting Arctic convoy PQ18. She was one of only four out of the RN's 16 Tribal class destroyers to survive WW2.

78. Tribal class destroyer HMS *Punjabi*, February 1942, exercising oiling with heavy cruiser HMS *Kent* at Scapa Flow. 'X' 4.7-inch mounting replaced by twin 4-inch AA May 1940 during repairs from second Battle of Narvik where she was heavily engaged. Sunk in collision with battleship HMS *King George V* 1 May 1942 in thick fog.

79. Destroyer HMS *Kimberley* at high speed, a dramatic view, cutting across the wake of another vessel; fought in the second Battle of Narvik and survived WW2, one of only two 'K' class destroyers to do so.

80. 'H' class destroyer HMS *Hero* pre-WW2; sister-ship of the five destroyers that fought the first Battle of Narvik, the *Hero* fought in the second battle, was converted to an escort destroyer in 1943 and transferred to the RCN as HMCS *Chaudiere*.

81. Destroyer HMS *Icarus* pre-WW2; fought in the second Battle of Narvik. On 10 April captured Kriegsmarine supply ship SS *Alster*, used by the RN as a repair ship at Skjelfjord, hoisting out the forward gun mountings of the damaged HMS *Eskimo* and subsequently transporting them to Britain.

82. Destroyer HMS *Foxhound* pre-WW2; one of four taking part in the second Battle of Narvik equipped with Two-Speed-Destroyer-Sweep minesweeping gear (the others being HMSs *Hero*, *Icarus* and *Forester*). Converted to an escort destroyer in 1943 and transferred to the RCN as HMCS *Qu'Appelle*.

83. Destroyer HMS *Forester* pre-WW2; assisted the damaged HMS *Cossack* during second Battle of Narvik, subsequently escorted Arctic, Atlantic and Malta convoys, surviving WW2.

84. Minelayer and gunnery training ship KMS *Brummer*, returning from landing troops in Oslo, 14 April, when HMSub *Sterlet* hit her with a single torpedo off the coast of Jutland blowing off the bows, she sank a day later. A pre-WW2 Third Reich postcard.

85. HMSub *Sterlet* torpedoed and sank KMS *Brummer* but was lost herself only three days later, on 18 April, probably depth-charged by German anti-submarine trawlers.

86. Wreck of minesweeper KMS *Frauenlob*, M134, sunk at Bergen 9 May by FAA Skua dive-bombers of 806 NAS. Salvaged and recommissioned March 1941 as patrol vessel *M534*, renamed *Jungingen*; damaged in action in the English Channel and paid off September 1943.

87. Cruiser HMS *Effingham*, heavy cruiser laid down during WW1 but not completed until 1925. Reconstructed 1937-38 under the 1930 London Naval Treaty, 7.5-inch guns replaced by nine single 6-inch, three individual mountings stepped forward of the bridge.

88. Cruiser HMS *Effingham* off Harstad, 16 May, about to sail for Bodø loaded with vehicles, stores, ammunition and over 1,000 British and French troops.

89. HMS *Effingham* left Harstad early on 17 May; using unfamiliar Norwegian charts, a course was plotted over Faksen shoal, where she grounded heavily at 23 knots, tearing open and flooding the lower hull. Drifted into shallow water and sank on an even keel; troops, ship's company, vehicles and some stores were taken off, the destroyer HMS *Echo* torpedoed and capsized the wreck.

90. Battleship HMS *Rodney*, pre-WW2, her nine 16-inch guns trained to starboard. On 9 April, while flagship of the Home Fleet, she was hit by a 500kg (1,100lb) bomb, which broke up on the 4-inch armour of her middle deck, causing only minor damage.

91. County class heavy cruiser HMS *Suffolk*, 18 April, temporarily beached at Longhope, Scapa Flow, having shipped 2,000 tons of water aft from almost seven hours of accurate bombing, withdrawing from Stavanger after shelling the German airfield. Repairs took 10 months.

92. *Above* HM Trawler *Bradman* of 22nd Anti-Submarine Group; bombed and sunk on 25 April in Romsdalsfjorden, having arrived only on 22 April. Stern rack of depth charges visible with another on a thrower amidships. Norwegian salvage vessel SS *Jason* in background.

93. Escort sloop HMS *Bittern*, stern blown off and burning, after continuous attacks by Ju.87 Stuka dive bombers off Namsos during the morning of 30 April; severely damaged, she was scuttled by the destroyer HMS *Janus*.

94. French destroyer *Bison* before WW2, the first of her four funnels hidden by the bridge structure. Escorting evacuation convoy from Namsos, 3 May, a Ju87 Stuka bomb detonated her forward magazine just after 1000, killing 136. HMS *Afridi* sank the wreck at 1200 and picked up survivors with three other RN destroyers.

95. Tribal class destroyer HMS *Afridi* on trials in 1938 with a flotilla leader's broad black band on first funnel. Escorting evacuation convoy from Namsos, 3 May, hit twice by Ju.87 Stukas just after 1400 and caught fire; sank by the bow with the loss of 52 of her ship's company, 35 survivors from the French destroyer *Bison* and 13 soldiers.

96. HMS *Curlew*, WW1 light cruiser converted into an AA ship 1935-36, 6-inch guns replaced by ten single 4-inch AA guns and an octuple 2-pdr pom-pom; nevertheless, on 26 May bombed by He.111s of K.G. 100 in Lavangsfjord, off Ofot Fjord, capsized and sank with the loss of nine lives.

97. Polish destroyer ORP *Grom* escaped to Britain on the eve of WW2, under a secret agreement, code-named the 'Peking Plan'. One of the fastest destroyers afloat in 1940, was shelling German troops ashore in Rombaks Fjord near Narvik on 4 May when a He.111 of K.G. 100 hit her twice amidships, sinking the ship with heavy loss of life.

98. Heinkel He.111 of K.G. 26 in flight over Norway. An effective anti-ship bomber in the Norwegian campaign, was developed into a capable torpedo bomber used against Arctic convoys later in WW2.

99. Wreck of a Heinkel He.111 in a lake near Stavanger. Despite successes against shipping off Norway and Dunkirk, was vulnerable to modern fighter opposition but stayed in service until 1945.

100. *Above* Junkers Ju.87 'Stuka', a highly accurate and effective dive bomber, especially in the anti-ship role, due to its ability to dive vertically, but vulnerable to opposing fighters when not escorted. U-shaped bomb crutch under fuselage of centre aircraft visible after bomb dropped.

101. Junkers Ju.88; a versatile multi-role aircraft, originally a fast bomber, developed into a dive bomber, torpedo bomber, heavy fighter and night fighter.

102. *Above* Gloster Gladiators were the RAF's final biplane fighter, agile and highly manoeuvrable but not able to meet modern designs on equal terms. K6131, the second production Gladiator, had a short life; delivered to 72 Squadron 22 February 1937 but written off after a forced landing 26 March 1938.

103. Gloster Gladiators of 263 Squadron RAF, burnt out on the frozen surface of Lake Lesjaskogvatnet in April 1940 after Luftwaffe raids. The squadron reformed with replacement Gladiators to fly from Bardufoss near Narvik, joined by Hawker Hurricanes. The surviving aircraft and most personnel were lost when HMS *Glorious* was sunk.

104. Hawker Hurricane MkIIc PZ865, the last of 14,533 Hurricanes built; flies as "The Last of the Many", part of the Battle of Britain Memorial Flight. Photograph taken on 10 September 1944, on a test flight piloted by George Bulman, then Hawker's chief test pilot. The MkIIc Hurricane was armed with four-20mm cannon instead of the eight-.303 Browning machine guns of the Mk1 that fought over Norway and in the Battle of Britain.

105. Fairey Swordfish 1 over aircraft carrier HMS *Glorious* and sister-ship HMS *Courageous* pre-WW2. The *Courageous* was torpedoed and sunk on 17 September 1939 by *U-29* with the loss of 519 lives.

106. HMS *Glorious*, February 1939 in the Mediterranean, heeling as she turns hard to port, Swordfish I on the flight deck, destroyer HMS *Wishart* as planeguard conforming to her turn and Town class cruiser HMS *Glasgow* in the foreground.

107. HMS *Glorious*, late 1930s, pitching into a lively sea, showing the disadvantages of her relatively low forecastle compared with enclosed bows fitted in later RN fleet carriers.

108. A portrait of HMS *Glorious* in the middle 1930s, clearly showing her original WW1 light-battlecruiser hull with amidships anti-torpedo bulge.

109. HMS *Glorious*, 8 June 1940, burning and listing to starboard, fatally damaged by 28cm (11-inch) gunfire from the *Scharnhorst* and *Gneisenau*. Seen from the *Scharnhorst*, she sank shortly after with the loss of 1,207 lives.

110. HMS *Ardent*, one of two destroyers escorting HMS *Glorious*, laid an effective smokescreen protecting the carrier for about 20 minutes but only postponed her inevitable sinking. The *Ardent* came under fire from the *Scharnhorst* and sank after carrying out an unsuccessful torpedo attack.

111. HMS *Acasta* joined her sister-ship protecting HMS *Glorious* with a smokescreen and used it to carry out a successful torpedo attack, hitting the *Scharnhorst* on the starboard side aft, disabling her after turret and causing a five degree list as 2,500 tons of water entered the ship but the *Scharnhorst* sank the *Acasta* with the loss of 161 lives.

112. Battlecruiser or fast battleship KMS *Scharnhorst* after completion of a refit in November 1939, when the forecastle was raised and an 'Atlantic Bow' fitted to improve sea-keeping, a funnel cap was added and the mainmast moved aft, giving her an elegant profile.

113. KMS *Scharnhorst* in a seaway; low freeboard made her a wet ship, even after fitting the 'Atlantic Bow', heavy seas often found their way below, causing damage, particularly to the fore-turret. Catapult-mounted Arado Ar196 floatplane forward of the mainmast.

114. County class heavy cruiser HMS *Devonshire* in the 1930s, exercising her 8-inch main armament. On the evening of 7 June, sailed from Tromsø to Britain with King Haakon VII, Crown Prince Olav, the Norwegian government and Allied diplomatic and military personnel, 461 altogether.

115. Town class cruiser HMS *Southampton*, late 1930s in Plymouth Sound. 9 April, damaged by bombing off Norway. 8 June evacuated Admiral Lord Cork, General Auchinleck, French General Béthouart and the last Allied military personnel, with stores, vehicles and two Walrus aircraft.

116. RMS *Orama*, P&O passenger liner requisitioned as a troopship; sunk off Norway while empty on 8 June by the heavy cruiser KMS *Admiral Hipper* and escorting destroyers during the Allied evacuation.

117. Destroyer KMS *Hans Lody* steams between the *Admiral Hipper* and the *Orama* as she sinks on 8 June. The Germans allowed the accompanying hospital ship *Atlantis* to proceed unhindered.

118. MS *Chrobry*, commissioned 1939 for the Gdynia-America Line, converted to a troopship in Britain. Carrying British troops to Bodø, bombed in Vest Fjord, 14 May, by Ju.87 Stukas suffering serious fires and explosions amongst embarked ammunition. Escorts took off most of the troops but their equipment was left aboard; she burned until sunk by aircraft from HMS *Ark Royal* two days later.

119. Polish liner MS *Batory*, flagship of the Gdynia-America Line in the late 1930s. Converted to a troopship, took part in the Allied evacuation from Norway, sailing in convoy to Britain, 6 June, and served with distinction in worldwide operations throughout WW2.

120. *Above* Blue Star cruise liner SS *Arandora Star*, mid-1930s at Balholm in Norway. Requisitioned as a troopship, evacuated Allied forces from Norway, sailing in convoy, 7 June. Brought British and Polish troops out of French Atlantic ports, June 1940, in Operation Aerial. Torpedoed and sunk by *U-47*, 2 July 1940 on passage to Canada with Italian and German internees and PoWs, with a loss of 805 lives.

121. Cunard liner RMS *Lancastria*; requisitioned as a troopship, evacuated Allied forces from Norway, sailing for Britain in convoy, 6 April. On 17 June, while evacuating British forces and civilians from St Nazaire in Operation Aerial, bombed and sunk with huge loss of life, estimated as at least 4,000, the worst disaster in British maritime history.

122. RMS *Monarch of Bermuda*, in Two Rock Passage, Bermuda, smoke from centre funnel concealing that the aft funnel was a dummy. Requisitioned from Furness Withy Line as a troopship, evacuated Allied forces from Norway, leaving for Britain in convoy on 6 April with the *Batory*, *Lancastria* and four other former liners. Served throughout WW2.

123. Canadian Pacific liner SS *Duchess of York*; requisitioned as a troopship, evacuated Allied forces from Norway, sailing in convoy to Britain on 7 April with the *Arandora Star* and six other former liners. Bombed and set ablaze by Focke-Wulf 200s, 300 miles west of Spanish port of Vigo, July 1943, scuttled by RN escorts.

124. Oiler and supply ship KMS *Jan Wellem*, alongside the ruined Narvik ore terminal about July 1940; scuttled in shallow water but raised. Previously a whale factory ship converted from Hamburg-America lines *Wurttemberg*; an inefficient oiler due to slow rate of fuel transfer.

125. A view eastwards over the salvaged oiler *Jan Wellem* showing details of wrecked ore wagons teetering over the ship in previous photograph.

126. The *Jan Wellem* is in the centre of this view of the eastern end of the largely destroyed Narvik ore terminal looking out towards the harbour.

127. *Below* The scale of the demolitions carried out on the ore terminal and its railway by Allied forces as they withdrew, can be seen in this view from the western end. The *Jan Wellem* is again in the centre.

128. The comprehensive demolitions carried out by the withdrawing Allies included using sufficient explosives to bring down the spans of a railway viaduct and shatter the reinforced concrete supports of another.

129. The complete destruction wreaked on the ore facilities and power station at Narvik ensured that the terminal and its railway could not be used to export iron ore to Germany for eight months.

130. *Above* The rail line from Kiruna to Narvik had been opened in 1903 and entirely electrified in 1922; rail facilities at the ore terminal were destroyed and the line rendered unusable for two miles inland by withdrawing Allied forces. FAA Swordfish also bombed the mouths of tunnels further inland.

131. A view of the wrecked ore terminal from the east about July 1940, with two merchant ships beached in the shallows and the salvaged oiler *Jan Wellem* at the ore quay; she was repaired and finally scrapped at Blyth in 1947.

132. After the two Battles of Narvik were fought, the fjord and harbour were strewn with wrecked and sinking merchant ships.

PART II – Battle Summary No. 17

Battle Summary No.17, 'The Conjunct Expeditions to Norway', was originally written in 1942. It was then, as its title implies, mainly concerned with the landings and inshore operations, with the result that the interesting and instructive Fleet operations of the campaign were not adequately dealt with. Much information about enemy plans and movements, too, has become available from the documents captured at the end of the war.

In the present edition, re-named 'Naval Operations of the Campaign in Norway', emphasis has been laid on the deep sea operations rather than on the amphibious operations on the Norwegian coast. Chapters I and II, dealing with the operations of the Home Fleet from the time of the initial German landings to the arrival in Norway of the Allied expeditionary forces, and Chapter III, dealing with the Allied plans and the general employment of naval forces during the campaign, have been entirely re-written.

In Chapters IV to X, tracing the individual fortunes of the various landings and withdrawals, the original version has been adhered to as closely as possible, but it has been amplified, and where necessary amended in the light of information derived from German and other sources which have now become available; and the subject matter has been re-arranged, in order to conform with chronology.

Chapter XI – Comment and Reflections – is entirely new.

Plans have been produced illustrating initial submarine and U-boat dispositions, and the approximate movements of surface forces during the opening phase of the campaign and the final withdrawal from Narvik.

March, 1950

C.B. 3305 (2)   Restricted

CONFIDENTIAL   Attention is called to the penalties attaching to any infraction of the Official Secrets Acts

NAVAL STAFF HISTORY
SECOND WORLD WAR

BATTLE SUMMARY No. 17

NAVAL OPERATIONS OF THE CAMPAIGN IN NORWAY

APRIL– JUNE 1940

B.R. 1736 (10) dated 1943 and B.R. 1736 (10) (1) dated 1947 are hereby superseded and all copies are to be destroyed in accordance with B.R. 1

This book is based on information available up to and including March, 1950.

Downgraded to B.R. (Restricted) and numbered B.R. 1736(46) – L.C.A.F.O. 73/59 refers.

T.S.D. 57/50
Tactical and Staff Duties Division (Historical Section), Naval Staff, Admiralty, S.W.1

Overview

On 9 April, 1940 Germany invaded Denmark and Norway. Denmark fell in a day and within 48 hours all the airfields and the principal seaports in Norway were in the hands of the invaders. No warning had been given to her victims, though rumours and various pieces of intelligence had pointed to some such development; still less did a *casus belli* exist, especially with Norway, with whom, indeed, there was a traditional friendship of many years standing. The treachery of the proceeding was only equalled by its success.

From the start it was apparent that little could be done by the Allies in the face of German air superiority in the south; but expeditions were hastily organised in an attempt to dislodge them from central and northern Norway. The former speedily failed; but the northern expedition had more success and eventually re-took Narvik. By that time, however, events elsewhere had moved too swiftly; the Low Countries had been overrun, France, beaten to her knees, was about to sue for armistice, and to many invasion seemed to stare the United Kingdom in the face.[1] The decision was taken to abandon Norway.

This battle summary deals with the naval side of the operations of the campaign in Norway. The services of the land and air forces are only touched on in it so far as is necessary to explain the naval movements and operations.

The campaign fell into two well-defined phases, viz.:–

Phase 1

From 7 April, when German invasion forces were first reported at sea, to 14 April, when the Allied counter-offensive in Norway was about to develop. During this period the Allied naval effort was chiefly concentrated on bringing to action the enemy naval forces employed on the operation. These efforts met with varying success, but the German heavy units, with the exception of the 8-in. cruiser *Blücher*, which was sunk by the Norwegian coastal defences, were all back in German ports by 14 April.

Phase 2

The Allied counter-offensive, from 14 April when the first flights of the expeditionary forces were reaching the coasts of Norway, to 14 June, when the last return convoys reached United Kingdom ports. Throughout this phase the Navy's part was chiefly the business of carrying troops and stores to Norway and home again, with some service inshore in support of the advance on Narvik, and the anti-aircraft protection of the temporary bases at Namsos and Åndalsnes.

In studying the story of what Mr. Winston Churchill describes as this 'ramshackle campaign', it must be remembered that the events recorded took place under circumstances very different from those obtaining at the end of the war.

The campaign was the first major clash in history in which all three arms – 'sea, land and air' – were involved. Such knowledge as existed of the potentialities of air attacks on ships and the most effective countermeasures was largely theoretical; radar was still in its infancy; and the experience derived from the remarkable series of amphibious operations which characterised the Allied strategy from the landings at Diego Suarez in 1942 to the end of the war was as yet undreamed of.

The British, too, in those early days, were still paying the penalty of the pre-war policy of 'appeasement' and the consequent unreadiness for war when it came; many months were to elapse before deficiencies both in trained personnel and material of all kinds could be made good. In a word, measures which could, and probably would have been readily undertaken five years later, could not be contemplated at the time the campaign was fought.

The events which led up to the campaign in Norway centred on the great importance, both economic and strategic, of Scandinavia to Germany.

The 1938 statistics showed an annual consumption by Germany of seventeen million tons of pure iron, six and a half million tons of which came from sources which the Allied blockade had already cut off, and six million tons from Sweden. If this latter supply could be denied to her or seriously impaired, it seemed she could not long continue the war. In summer most of it was shipped from the Swedish port of Lulea, in the

Gulf of Bothnia; but in winter this port was ice-bound, and the route then taken was from Narvik and Kirkenes down the coast of Norway. Here, it appeared to the Allies, was a golden opportunity for their superior sea power to strike a serious blow at a vital war commodity;[2] but the whole 1,000-mile passage could be made in Norwegian territorial waters and interference with the traffic would involve the technical infringement of Norwegian neutrality.

It was an intolerable situation that the Allies should be thus shackled by their own scrupulous observance of the letter of that International Law which the Germans notoriously set at nought and outraged whenever it suited them; and as early as 19 September, 1939 the First Lord of the Admiralty[3] had called the attention of the Cabinet to the matter.[4] From then on throughout the winter he strove to obtain approval to force the traffic outside territorial waters, by laying minefields – which would be duly declared – in suitable positions off the Norwegian coast.

The Germans were of course fully aware of the importance of the iron ore to them, but they were confident that arrangements could be made with Sweden, such as a given winter storage at Lulea and, if necessary, transport of the ore by rail to the south, whereby all their needs could be supplied.[5] Meanwhile they were content to rely on Allied respect for international law to protect the traffic on its normal winter route, and decided that at the outset a neutral Norway would be to their advantage. Before many weeks, however, Grand Admiral Raeder, the commander-in-chief of the German Navy and probably the ablest strategist of all the German war leaders, was casting covetous eyes on the Norwegian coast,[6] and on 3 October, 1939 he called the attention of the Führer to the desirability of gaining bases there; this he followed up a week later with definite suggestions for the occupation of that country.

At about the same time, there were indications of increased cordiality between Great Britain and Norway. An Allied footing there[7] would not only menace the iron ore, but might, under certain contingencies, open the 'back door' to the Baltic, with its relatively undefended German seaboard.

The Russian invasion of Finland (30 November) and the proposal of the Allies to send aid to the hard pressed Finns, who could only be reached through such a foothold as the Germans most wished to avoid. This caused serious alarm in Berlin. Contact was established with the

Norwegian traitor Quisling and on 14 December Hitler ordered the Supreme Command to prepare plans for the invasion of Norway and Denmark.

Planning continued throughout the winter, and on 16 March 1940 – through the Russo-Finnish peace treaty just concluded (12 March) had removed the immediate cause of anxiety – Hitler decided that the operation, which was known as 'Weserübung', should take place about a month before his projected invasion of France and the Low Countries, and fixed 9 April as D-Day.[8]

It so happened that towards the end of March Mr. Churchill's representations at last bore fruit and the Allied Governments decided to lay mines off the coast of Norway, in order to 'force traffic outside Norwegian territorial waters'. All possible consideration was to be shown for Norwegian susceptibilities, but it was realised that this step was not unlikely to provoke the Germans to violate Norwegian neutrality and it was therefore decided to hold troops in readiness to land at Stavanger, Bergen, Trondheim and Narvik, should there be clear evidence of their intention to do so. The date chosen for laying the first minefield was 5 April; this was subsequently altered to 8 April.[9]

Thus it came about that each of the belligerents independently was initiating operations scheduled to take place in neutral Norway within the same 24 hours, a sufficiently intriguing situation, though the scope and method of their plans were very different.

Preliminary Events

German Plan of Invasion (Plan 2)

The German plan of invasion hinged on surprise and was characterised by admirable staff work. Seven army divisions under the command of General von Falkenhorst were employed,[10] three in the assault phase, and four in the follow-up. Some eight hundred operational aircraft and between two and three hundred transport planes supplemented the initial seaborne landings, which were planned to take place simultaneously at Oslo, Arendal, Kristiansand (south) and Egersund, Bergen, Trondheim and Narvik.

The whole available German naval strength was to be used in support of this bold operation, undertaken without command of the sea (except as regards the Kattegat and Skagerrak), in the face of very superior Allied naval forces;[11] the latter, it was rightly judged, could be largely neutralised by surprise in the first place and later by air forces operating from captured Norwegian airports. So far as the naval side of the operation was concerned, it was considered that the greatest difficulty and risk would lie in the return of the naval units to Germany after the landings were completed.

On 6 March, 1940 Grand Admiral Raeder issued the directive outlining the naval part in the invasion. The forces allocated to Norway were organised in six groups, Groups 1 and 2 operating in the north and the remaining four groups in the south, as shown in the following table:–

Group	Task

Group 1. Commanded by Vice-Admiral Lütjens[12]

Battlecruisers

Gneisenau (Flag)	To act as covering force for the whole operation, sailing with main landing forces. Having reached the line Shetlands–Bergen, to create a diversion in company with Group 2 in the North Sea; then to patrol in the southern part of the Arctic and after completion of the landings to cover the return of the other naval units to Germany.
Scharnhorst	

Destroyers

Wilhelm Heidkamp (S.O.)	Under Kommodore Bonte, to effect occupation of Narvik, involving the landing of 2,000 men under General Dietl, and then to rejoin the battlecruisers.
Anton Schmitt	
Diether von Roeder	
Hans Lüdemann	
Hermann Künne	
Georg Thiele	
Bernd Von Arnim	
Wolfgang Zenker	
Erich Giese	
Erich Koellner	

Group 2. Commanded by Captain Heye, C.O. *Hipper*

8-in. Cruiser

Hipper	Occupation of Trondheim, involving the landing of about 1,700 men, after which to rejoin the battlecruisers.

Destroyers

Friedrich Eckholdt
Theodor Riedel
Bruno Heinemann
Paul Jacobi

Group 3. Command by F.O. Scouting Forces, Rear-Admiral Schmundt

(a) Light Cruisers

Köln	Occupation of Bergen, involving the landing of 900 men.
Königsberg	
Bremse	
1st E-boat Flotilla (7)	

(b) Commanded by S.O. 6th T.B. Flotilla

Torpedo Boats
   Leopard
   Wolf
Depot Ship *Karl Peters*

The following measures were ordered as protection for the operation:–

(1) The battlecruisers *Scharnhorst* and *Gneisenau*, later to be joined by the *Hipper*, were to patrol the southern part of the Arctic.
(2) Twenty-eight U-boats to be disposed in suitable areas, stretching from Narvik and the Shetlands down to the Skagerrak and Eastern Approaches to the English Channel.
(3) A minefield to be laid in the Skagerrak on the day of the initial landings, and other fields to be declared off the west coast of Norway.[13]
(4) Air reconnaissance and protection during daylight.
(5) Anti-submarine patrols in the Kattegat, Skagerrak and further westward.

The invasion of Denmark, which was to take place simultaneously, was also provided for in the naval plan. A group which included the old battleship *Schleswig-Holstein* was to land a force to occupy Korsör (1,840 men) and Nyborg (150 men) in the Great Belt; and four other groups, consisting of small craft, were charged with the occupation of Copenhagen (1,000 men), the Little Belt bridge, by Middelfart (400 men), and other key points on the Danish coast.

The immediate follow-up for Bergen and the ports to the southward (including Copenhagen) was to be embarked in transports,[14] disguised as ordinary merchant ships, and sailed singly so as to arrive at their destinations shortly after the assault forces. Troops were not to be sent to Narvik and Trondheim by transports owing to the risk of interception on the Shetlands–Stadlandet line; but six steamers camouflaged as ordinary merchant ships and loaded with military stores were to be despatched to these northern ports (three to each) time to arrive before the warships,[15] and arrangements were made for two tankers to arrive at Narvik and one at Trondheim to fuel the naval units.[16]

Further reinforcement and the build-up was to be carried out by the 2nd Sea Transport Division (11 ships totalling 52,500 G.R.T.) and the 3rd Sea Transport Division (12 ships totalling 74,550 G.R.T.) working back and forth between Oslo and German ports.

The British Minefield and Plan 'R.4' (Plan 1)

During the first week of April 1940, while the final German preparations were taking place, the Allies were going forward with their plans for interrupting the ore traffic. The operations, naturally, would be covered by the Home Fleet,[17] based on Scapa Flow and commanded by Admiral Sir Charles Forbes.

It was decided that three areas should be declared dangerous, one off the eastern shore of Vest Fjord, in about 67° 30' N., 14° E.; another off Bud, about 63° N., 7° E., and a third off Stadtlandet, about 62° N., 5° E. Destroyers of the 20th (Minelaying) Flotilla under Captain Bickford were to lay the field in Vest Fjord and the minelayer *Teviot Bank* (Commander King-Harman) that off Stadtlandet, the date for laying being 8 April. No mines were to be actually laid off Bud. All three areas however were to be declared dangerous as soon as the first mines were laid, but not before, in order to reduce the chance of meeting Norwegian ships of war whilst laying; for it was known that Norway would use force to prevent the violation of her neutrality. Indeed, although the Allies considered it essential to lay one minefield, they decided that 'the laying of a second one should be given up rather than have an incident with a Norwegian patrol vessel'.

As already mentioned, the Allies had decided to hold troops ready to occupy the ports of Stavanger, Bergen and Trondheim, and ready to land at Narvik, but they did not intend to land troops in Norway 'until the Germans have violated Norwegian neutrality, or there is clear evidence that they intend to do so'. These measures were known as Plan 'R.4'.

The troops for Stavanger and Bergen, two battalions each, were to sail in cruisers, while a single battalion for Trondheim sailed in a transport, arriving two days later than the others. For Narvik the expedition was planned on a larger scale. There the initial landing was to be carried out by one battalion, which was to sail in a transport accompanied by two cruisers, all under Admiral Sir Edward Evans; these were to be followed by an oiler, by the rest of a British Brigade, and later by some French troops – a total strength of about 18,000 men. The port was then to become a regular base with its local defence forces and fuel supplies.

A striking force consisting of two cruisers and three destroyers under Vice-Admiral Sir George Edward-Collins, 2nd Cruiser Squadron, was to be held in readiness at Rosyth 'to deal with any seaborne expedition the

Germans may send against Norway'; and the Commander-in-Chief, Home Fleet, earmarked three ships of the 18th Cruiser Squadron, under Vice-Admiral Layton, as a striking force from Scapa, though these ships were to continue the service they were employed on in support of the Norwegian convoys until required.

Big ship cover was to be provided by the *Rodney*, *Valiant*, *Renown* and *Repulse*, screened by 10 destroyers. It is to be noted that these operations would have to be undertaken without an aircraft carrier, since the Home Fleet did not possess one, though Germany was at that time the only Power with which we were at war.[18]

Preparations and Movements (Plan 2)

On 3 April the Cabinet took the final decision to proceed with the minelaying and on the following day Admiral Evans hoisted his flag in the cruiser *Aurora* at the Clyde, where the force for Narvik was to start its voyage, with orders to be ready to sail on 8 April. The other cruiser for Narvik, the *Penelope*, left a Norwegian convoy she was protecting and arrived at Scapa on 6 April.

The ships for Stavanger and Bergen assembled in the Forth under Vice-Admiral John Cunningham, 1st Cruiser Squadron, and the troops and stores were embarked in the *Devonshire*, *Berwick*, *York* and *Glasgow* on 7 April.

The *Teviot Bank* escorted by four destroyers[19] of the 3rd Flotilla under Captain Todd (Capt. D.3) left Scapa on 5 April to lay the minefield off Stadtlandet. Since reports indicated that the four heaviest ships of the Norwegian Navy – vessels of some 4000 tons, 40 years old, each mounting two 8-in. guns – might all be in a position to interrupt the laying of mines in Vest Fjord, the Commander-in-Chief decided to send Vice-Admiral Whitworth in the *Renown* with a screen of destroyers[20] to support the northern minelayers; the *Birmingham* and a couple of destroyers,[21] then cruising to the northward against a German fishing fleet, were to join his flag off the coast of Norway. Admiral Whitworth sailed from Scapa in the evening of 5 April, and next morning was joined by Captain Bickford with four minelayers[22] of the 20th Destroyer Flotilla and Captain Warburton-Lee with four[23] of the 2nd Flotilla, which were to escort the minelayers and subsequently to patrol off the minefield. One of the *Renown*'s screen, the *Glowworm*, soon parted company; she stopped to pick up a man fallen overboard. In the thick and blowing weather she lost the squadron, and two days later, meeting a superior force of the enemy she was overwhelmed. Two other destroyers, the *Hyperion* and *Hero*, were sent back for oil, after which they were to pretend to lay the minefield off Bud. With his screen thus depleted, Admiral Whitworth continued his passage intending to meet the *Birmingham* and her destroyers off Vest Fjord in the evening of 7 April.

Meanwhile, the Germans had started embarking troops on 6 April and the first of their groups – those bound for Narvik and Trondheim – left their home waters late that night.

German Fleet Reported at Sea (Plan 2)

At 0848 on 7 April, a reconnaissance aircraft reported a cruiser and two destroyers in 55° 30' N., 6° 37' E. (about 150 miles south of the Naze), steering to the northward. This message reached the Commander-in-Chief, Home Fleet – then at Scapa Flow – at 1120; half an hour later he received a message from the Commander-in-Chief, Rosyth (timed 1120), stating that the cruiser was probably *Nürnberg* Class, with six destroyers,[24] and that 23 Wellingtons and 12 Blenheims were leaving at 1115 and 1150 to bomb the enemy.

A further signal from the Commander-in-Chief, Rosyth (timed 1352) arrived at 1400: aircraft had reported three enemy destroyers in 56° 06' N., 6° 08' E. at 1315. Their course was given as 190°, 12 knots; it looked as though they were homeward bound.

Twenty minutes later (1420) a message from the Admiralty (A.T. 1259/7) came in:–

> 'Recent reports suggest a German expedition is being prepared. Hitler is reported from Copenhagen to have ordered unostentatious movement of one division in ten ships by night to land at Narvik, with simultaneous occupation of Jutland. Sweden to be left alone. Moderates said to be opposing the plan. Date given for arrival at Narvik was 8 April.
>
> All these reports are of doubtful value and may well be only a further move in the war of nerves. Great Belt opened for traffic 5 April.'[25]

Plan 1.
Centre page detail.

C.B.H. 20101 - Wt. 17299 - Dd. PK 4005 - 500 - 6/51

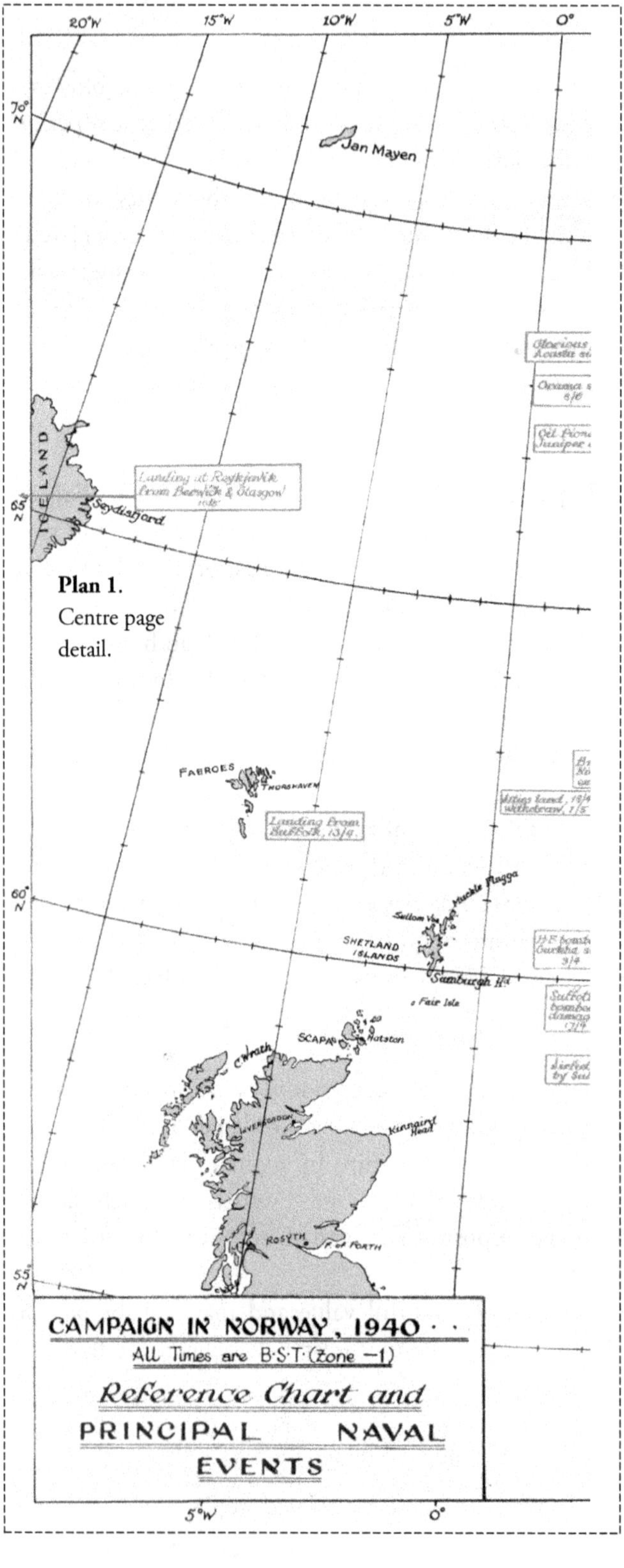

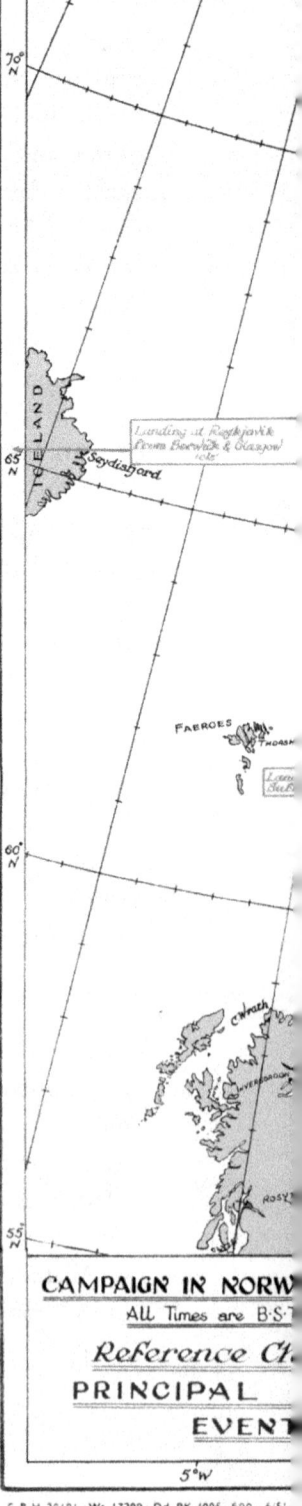

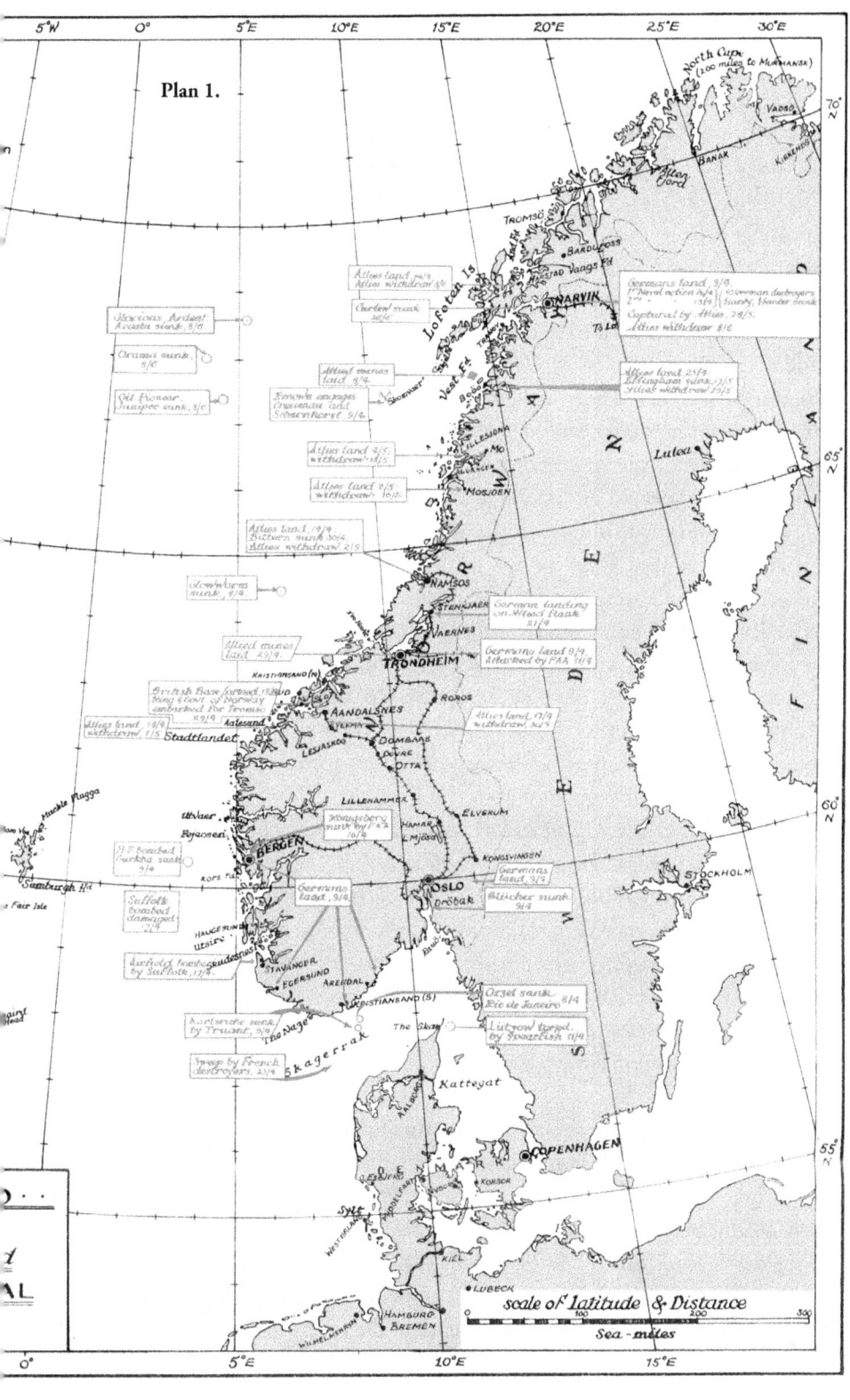

Plan 1.

On receipt of this message, Sir Charles Forbes ordered the fleet to go to one hour's notice for steam. Three hours elapsed.

Then, at 1727, arrived another message from the Admiralty (A.T. 1720): at 1325 an aircraft had sighted two cruisers, one large ship (possibly *Scharnhorst* Class) and 10 destroyers in 56° 48' N., 6° 10' E., steering 320°.[26] This was the first indication of enemy heavy ships being at sea to reach the Commander-in-Chief. He had already ordered certain cruiser and destroyer movements[27] on the strength of the earlier reports, and on receipt of this latter signal[28] he at once ordered all ships at Scapa to raise steam. At 2015, 7 April, the heavy ships of the Home Fleet sailed from Scapa; the Rosyth striking force sailed an hour later.

The report of the enemy fleet being at sea decided the Admiralty to give up the minefield off Stadtlandet, and the *Teviot Bank* was recalled; no change was made in the plan for laying the mines in Vest Fjord.

Having received from Rosyth a more exact account of the enemy, based on photographs, the Commander-in-Chief signalled to the fleet after leaving harbour, 'We are endeavouring to intercept enemy ships reported by aircraft at 1325 in 56° 50' N., 6° 10' E., course 320°, 17 knots; one battlecruiser, one pocket battleship, three cruisers and about 12 destroyers'. With this end in view he steered for a position in 61° 00' N., 1° 00' E. at 19 knots, increasing to 20 knots at midnight, 7/8 April.

He then had in company three capital ships (*Rodney*, *Valiant* and *Repulse*), three cruisers (*Sheffield*, *Penelope* and the French *Emile Bertin*[29] which had arrived at Scapa that afternoon) and 10 destroyers.[30] Vice-Admiral Edward-Collins, with the *Galatea*, *Arethusa* and 11 destroyers[31] was steering from the Forth for the position in 58° 30' N., 3° 30' E., after which he was to sweep to the northward. He was joined next morning by four more destroyers,[32] which had brought a convoy to the Forth.

The *Renown* was already approaching the coast of Norway in support of the Vest Fjord minelayers, and the *Birmingham* was on her way to join her.

Two other cruisers were also at sea, under Vice-Admiral Layton, the *Manchester* (flag) and *Southampton*. They had sailed from Scapa that morning (7 April) to cover two Norwegian convoys; O.N.25 which had left Methil on 5 April escorted by the anti-aircraft cruiser *Calcutta* and four destroyers,[33] and H.N.25 which was about to sail from Bergen.[34] Admiral Layton met O.N.25 some 15 miles north-east of Muckle Flugga during the afternoon, but in consequence of the report of the enemy fleet at sea it was turned back in the evening for British waters, by order of the Commander-in-Chief.[35] Admiral Layton had received a signal from the Commander-in-Chief timed 1934/7, saying that the fleet would be in position 61° N., 1° E. at 0700/8; but the situation at midnight he described as obscure. 'Nothing definite was known of the larger enemy force since 1342', says his diary. 'There was no precise information as to the whereabouts, and no information as to the intentions of the Commander-in-Chief'. He therefore remained with the convoy while it 'continued its slow progress into a north-westerly gale'.

As for destroyers, apart from the ten with his flag, the Commander-in-Chief had nearly 50 under his orders ready for service, with a score refitting, some of which would soon be completed; and six French destroyers had arrived at Scapa that day.[36]

During the night of 7/8 April, the fleet maintained its north-north-easterly course at 20 knots, and at 0530/8 – the time at which the minelaying was completed – was in 60° 28' N., 0° 28' E.

First Enemy Contact: Loss of the *Glowworm* (Plan 2)

Meanwhile Admiral Whitworth had arrived off the mouth of Vest Fjord in the evening of 7 April, expecting to meet the *Birmingham* and her two destroyers; but on reaching the rendezvous he had neither sight nor news of them. The minelayers with their escort were detached and laid their mines between 0430 and 0530/8, while the *Renown* with the *Greyhound* – the only remaining destroyer of her screen – patrolled in roughly 67° 30' N., 10° 30' E., 30 miles to the westward of the entrance to Vest Fjord and 100 miles from the minefield.

At about 0830, Admiral Whitworth received a signal timed 0759/8, from the *Glowworm* (Lieut.-Commander Roope) which had lost the squadron the day before[37] reporting two enemy destroyers in about 65° 04' N., 6° 04' E., 140 miles distant from the *Renown*, which with the *Greyhound* turned to the southward at their best speed and steered to intercept the enemy.[38]

Further signals from the *Glowworm* showed that she was engaging a superior force, the last signal being timed 0855; it was not till the war was over that the details of her fate became known.

The two enemy destroyers reported by the *Glowworm* at 0759 were part of the main German force which had been sighted by British aircraft on the previous day, 7 April; in the bad weather and heavy sea, they had lost contact with their heavier consorts. The first of them to be sighted by the *Glowworm*, soon after 0710, was the *Hans Lüdemann*: the British destroyer fired recognition signals, but on orders from the S.O., 3rd German Destroyer Flotilla, the enemy ship made off to the N.W. at 35 knots, followed by two salvoes from the *Glowworm* which appear to have fallen short.[39] Shortly afterwards the *Glowworm* sighted the second German destroyer, the *Bernd Von Arnim*, on her starboard bow, heading in the other direction. The enemy ship opened fire at 0802 in 64° 05' N., 06° 18' E., and a running fight ensued; in spite of accurate fire on the part of the *Glowworm*, the German destroyer was not hit, though she suffered some damage to her superstructure from the heavy seas, which nearly capsized her. The wireless message sent by the *Bernd Von Arnim* on being attacked was picked up by the main German force which was not far off, and the *Hipper* was at once ordered to the destroyer's assistance. Owing to the bad weather it was not until 0857 that she was able to identify which was the *Hostile* destroyer and to open fire. The *Glowworm* fired a salvo of two or three torpedoes which the *Hipper* avoided; then, considerably damaged by enemy gunfire, the destroyer laid a smoke screen and momentarily disappeared from view. The *Hipper* entered the *Glowworm*'s smoke screen and, failing to answer her helm owing to the high seas, found herself in the path of the British ship. The destroyer rammed her just abaft the starboard anchor wrecking her own bows, then crashing down her side tore away 130 ft. of the *Hipper*'s armoured belt and her starboard torpedo tubes. She herself was fatally damaged: listing heavily with her torpedo tubes under water she lay wrecked and blazing and blew up a few minutes later, sinking in 64° 27' N., 6° 28' E.

The *Hipper* picked up 40 survivors, including one officer, a Sub-Lieutenant; the captain of the *Glowworm* was being hauled aboard and had just reached the cruiser's deck when he let go exhausted and was drowned.[40]

The sinking of SS *Rio de Janeiro* (Plan 2)

Less than three hours after the loss of the *Glowworm*, there occurred some 500 miles to the southward an incident which might well have compromised the German invasion scheme, had the correct inference been drawn. The Polish submarine *Orzeł*, on patrol in the Skagerrak, intercepted the German SS *Rio de Janeiro* (bound for Bergen) just outside territorial waters off Kristiansand. After her crew had been given the opportunity to abandon ship, she was torpedoed, sinking at about noon. A Norwegian destroyer and local fishing folk rescued some hundreds of German soldiers in uniform, who stated that they were on their way to Bergen, to protect it against the Allies. This report reached the Norwegian parliament (the Storting) that evening, but it was not credited and no special steps were taken to warn the Navy and coast defences – the only part of the Norwegian forces mobilised at the time – or to take any other precautionary measures.[41]

The report also reached the British Admiralty, where it seems to have been recognised as evidence that the invasion of Norway was in fact under way; but Admiral Raeder's diversion was having its effect and there the chief interest centred on bringing to action the enemy heavy ships reported at sea the day before. Apart from a hint to the Allied submarines on patrol, which were being re-disposed to intercept the heavy ships, no special action was taken; nor was the report of the *Rio de Janeiro* incident passed to the Commander-in-Chief till 2255 that evening (8 April).[42]

Vice-Admiral Whitworth's Movements (Plan 2)

Meanwhile, Admiral Whitworth had continued to the southward making 20 knots for the first hour, but easing down later, because the flagship showed signs of damage through steaming into the heavy sea. Further signals from the *Glowworm* showed that she was engaging a superior force, the last signal being timed 0855; not long afterwards, it had to be assumed that she was sunk.

At 1045 a signal came from the Admiralty, directing the eight destroyers of the Vest Fjord mining force to join him, and at 1114 a message that the report about a German expedition to Narvik in A.T. 1259/7 might be true and that German ships might be then on their way. 'On the presumption that the enemy would proceed to Narvik,' he writes in his diary, 'and giving their force a maximum speed of 25 knots, I found I could reach the line of advance ahead of them at 1330. I steered for this point. In the visibility, which was now reduced to 2 or 3 miles, there was, however, little chance of intercepting an enemy force with only one destroyer in company; and I decided to turn to the north-eastward, at 1330 and rendezvous with the minelaying force.' The destroyers joined at 1715, some 20 miles west by south from Skomvaer Light; and the

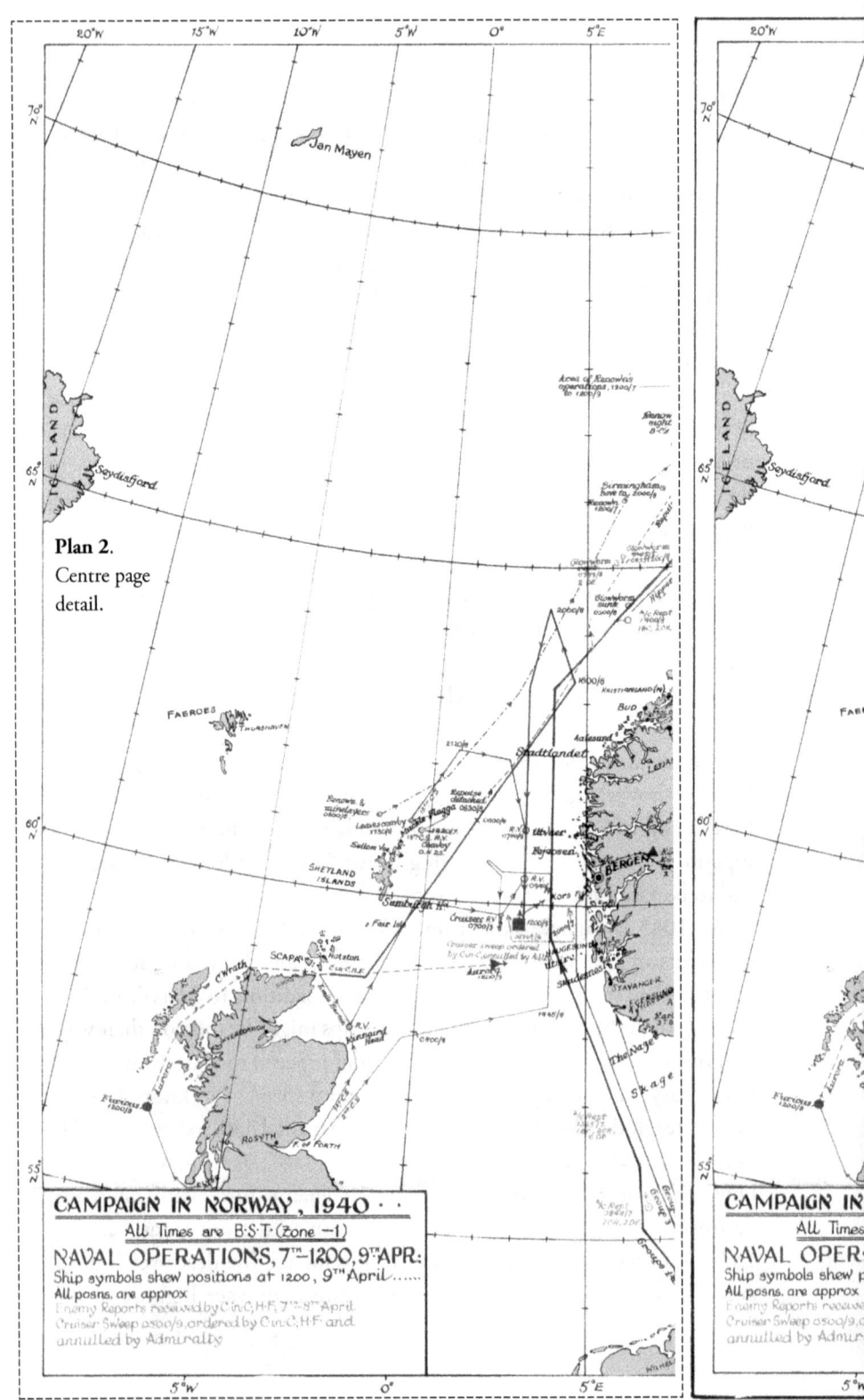

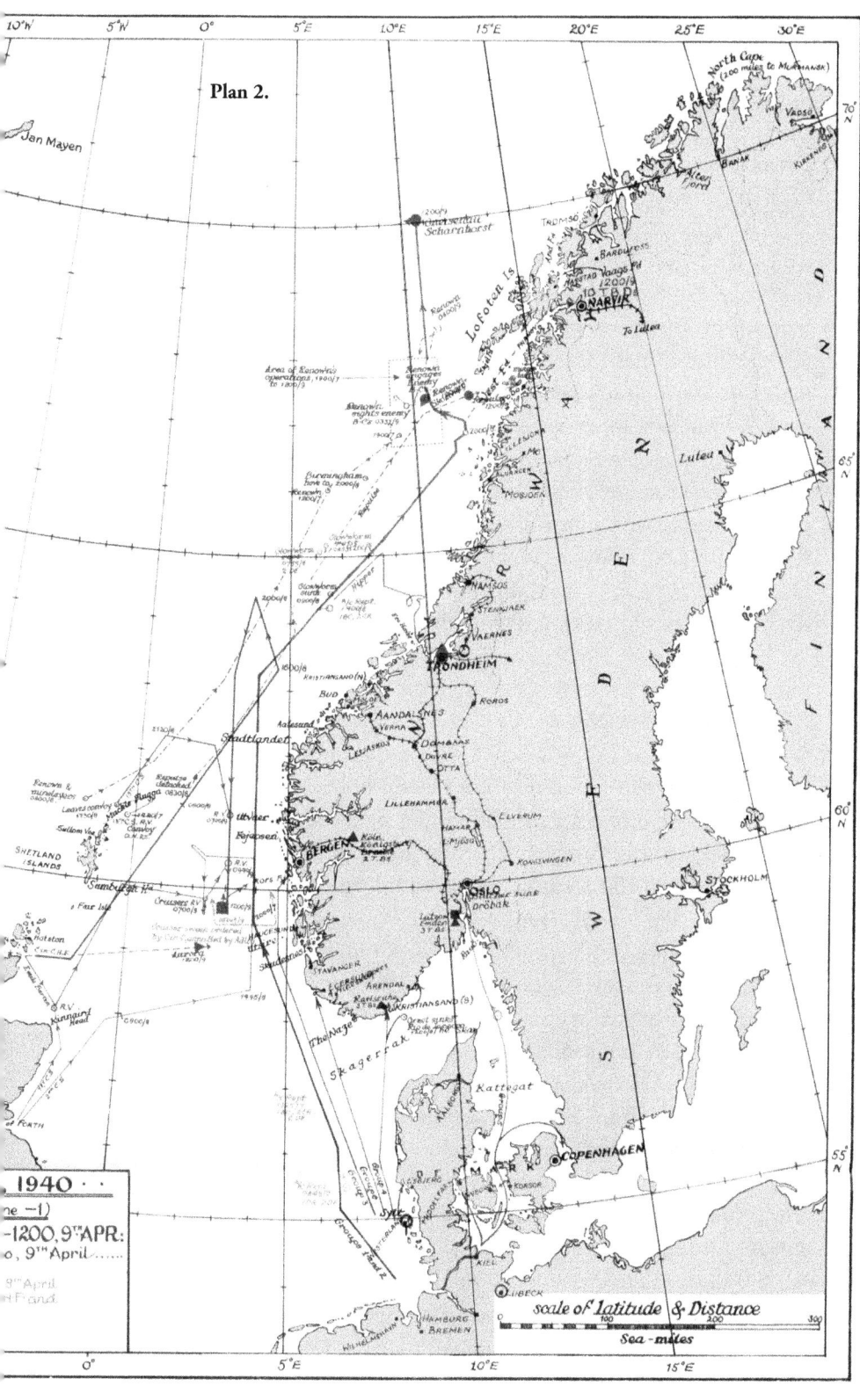

Plan 2.

squadron stood away to the westward to fulfil a plan formed on receiving an aircraft report of the enemy, timed 1400 and received 1516, which put a battlecruiser, two cruisers, and two destroyers in 64° 12' N., 6° 25' E., steering west.

'This force,' says Admiral Whitworth, 'might well have been that which had sunk *Glowworm*, whose last report had given the enemy course as 180°. I appreciated the situation as follows. The German force reported by *Glowworm* might (a) return to their base at once, (b) make for Iceland, (c) make for Murmansk, where it was possible a German tanker was waiting to refuel them, (d) be part of a force proceeding to Narvik. Our own forces were at sea to the southward; and I therefore determined to dispose my force to deal with the situation, if the enemy chose the alternative of proceeding to the northward. Accordingly, I prepared a plan which provided for a line-ahead patrol by destroyers to the westward of Skomvaer Light, with *Renown* in a position some 50 miles to the northward. It was my further intention to form an extended screen at dawn, and sweep to the southward.'

Two hours later (1915) came A.T. 1850/8: 'Most immediate. The force under your orders is to concentrate on preventing any German force proceeding to Narvik.' But, 'the weather was such as to make it advisable to keep my ships concentrated, and I conceived it my first duty to maintain them in a condition of sea-going and fighting efficiency.' The Admiral therefore told his squadron, 'Our object is to prevent German forces reaching Narvik: my present intention is to alter course at 2100 to 280°, and to turn 180° in succession at midnight: enemy heavy ships and light forces have been reported off Norwegian coast; position of *Birmingham* force is not known.' The squadron duly turned to the new course, but the destroyers found themselves unmanageable in the seaway, so the Admiral altered more to the northward. In the meantime he had heard from the Commander-in-Chief that more ships were coming to him, the *Repulse, Penelope, Bedouin, Eskimo, Punjabi* and *Kimberley*, which had parted from Sir Charles Forbes that morning to go to help the *Glowworm*. Accordingly at 2200 Admiral Whitworth signalled his position to the *Birmingham* and *Repulse*: '67° 9' N., 10° 10' E., course 310°, speed 8 knots, to Vest Fjord when weather moderates.' The *Birmingham* never joined him. Soon after making his signal he received her 8 o'clock position: she was 80 miles away in 66° 12' N., 7° 52' E., hove to with one destroyer in company and running short of oil, so

Admiral Whitworth ordered her to Scapa. The *Repulse* and her escorts joined him in the afternoon of 9 April.

Movements of Commander-in-Chief (Plan 2)

As already mentioned the Commander-in-Chief on receipt of the *Glowworm*'s enemy report had detached the *Repulse* with reinforcements to close her position; at the same time, the speed of the fleet was increased to 22 knots.

During the forenoon the Admiralty signal ordering the minelaying destroyers and their screen to join Admiral Whitworth was received (1045). The Commander-in-Chief subsequently remarked that this message, which led to the Vest Fjord being left without any of our forces on patrol in it, had a very far-reaching effect. The situation was not clear to him at the time, but he assumed that the Admiralty would not have withdrawn the destroyers patrolling the minefield without good reason, and he did not wish to break wireless silence as the enemy was between the *Renown* and the battle fleet and the *Repulse*.

In the early afternoon the Admiralty informed the Commander-in-Chief[43] that the cruisers for Plan 'R.4' had been ordered to disembark troops and would leave Rosyth at 1400 to proceed northwards; that the *Aurora*[44] and destroyers in the Clyde were leaving at 1300 for Scapa, and that the *Emile Bertin* and French destroyers were preparing for sea. The *Manchester*, *Southampton*, the four destroyers then with the *Teviot Bank* and the two destroyers off Bud were also put at his disposal.

The abandonment of Plan 'R.4' greatly surprised Sir Charles Forbes, in whose mind the reports of the day before had left no doubt that the operation which Plan 'R.4' had been designed to counter was actually under way.[45] He already had sufficient cruisers at his disposal, and the troops embarked in Vice-Admiral Cunningham's ships might have been very useful. Had they been sailed, for example, as soon as the report of the *Rio de Janeiro* incident reached the Admiralty, they could have got to Stavanger[46] – which with its airfield was to prove the key to the whole campaign on the west coast of Norway – ahead of the Germans.[47] (The *Rodney* and *Valiant* could have been far enough south to provide big ship cover.)

At 1400 a flying boat scouting ahead of the fleet sighted a German squadron of one battlecruiser, two cruisers and two destroyers in 64° 12' N., 6° 25' E. steering west. This was the Trondheim group – *Hipper* and four destroyers – which was cruising in this area till the time arrived to make for the fjord. The westerly course they were reported on thus had no real significance, but was very misleading to the British Commander-in-Chief. The full version of the aircraft's report reached him a little after 1500; and he altered course to north at 1530 to intercept this squadron, altering again to 340° at 1615 because he 'considered on course 000°, allowing enemy speed 18 knots, he might slip past if he steered south of west' – the flagship's position being 63° 21' N., 4° 28' E. at 1600. He also sent off his second flying boat to search at that time and the *Rodney*'s aircraft at 1843, but neither gave him further news of the enemy. By this time it was blowing hard from the N.N.W., and speed had been reduced to 14 knots at about 1800 to ease the destroyers' suffering in the head sea.

In the meanwhile, several messages had been received indicating a large enemy movement in the Kattegat and Skagerrak. At 1512, A.T. 1435 informed the Admiral:– 'Naval Attaché, Copenhagen, reports *Gneisenau* or German warship *Blücher* with two cruisers, three destroyers, passed Langeland Belt, northbound, daylight today, 8 April. Similar force now passing northward of Moen through Sound at 1100. Large concentration of trawlers north Kattegat. Report A.1.' Some hours later a report from the submarine *Triton* stated that the *Gneisenau* and a heavy cruiser, with the *Emden* and some destroyers, passed the Skaw, going westward, at 1800. This force was almost certainly that which had left Kiel at 0200/8, on its way to occupy Oslo. It actually consisted of the *Blücher, Lützow, Emden* and some torpedo boats and light craft. According to the Germans, after passing the Skaw at 1800 it was subjected to constant submarine alarms. Two torpedo tracks were sighted and avoiding action taken, but no damage was suffered.[48] A '*Blücher*' with two other cruisers and a destroyer was also reported by the *Sunfish* at 1815 in 57° 57' N., 11° 07' E. (20 miles north-east of the Skaw) steering north-west.

At about 1930, 8 April, by which time the battle fleet should have intercepted the enemy and the *Repulse* should have been well to the north of him, if the flying boat's estimate of his course was anything like correct, the Commander-in-Chief reviewed the situation. There appeared to be one enemy battlecruiser to the north, but this was by no means certain; if so, whither was she bound? Probably Narvik, as the iron ore trade was the natural objective. There appeared to be a battlecruiser and perhaps two pocket battleships in the Kattegat or Skagerrak. Our own cruiser forces were sweeping up north from the latitude of Rosyth with no big ship covering force in their vicinity. The *Warspite* and *Furious*[49] were proceeding up the west coast of Scotland. The Admiralty had just ordered Admiral Whitworth to concentrate on preventing any German force proceeding to Narvik (A.T. 1850/8).

Under these circumstances the Commander-in-Chief decided to order the *Repulse*, *Penelope* and screen to continue to the northward and to reinforce Admiral Whitworth, while himself would turn to the southward with the *Rodney*, *Valiant*, *Sheffield* and screen, to try to bring the large enemy vessels in the south to action with the help of the cruiser screen.

At 2000 the battle fleet's position was 64° 22' N., 3° 40' E. and ten minutes later course was altered to 195° and speed increased to 18 knots. Just then A.T. 1842/8 arrived, which is digested as follows in the Commander-in-Chief's diary:–

'(a) Two objectives –
   (i) to prevent German northern force returning;
   (ii) to deal with possible German forces reported passing Great Belt at 1400/8, if they are going to Stavanger or Bergen.
(b) The Commander-in-Chief's force to sweep to south with light forces spread to northward, keeping east of 2° 35' E.
(c) Admiral Cunningham's force to sweep to northward, keeping west of 1° 50' E.
(d) Admiral Edward-Collins to act as striking force by night, keeping between 1° 50' E. and 2° 35' E'.

Two further signals from the Admiralty were received that evening: A.T. 2018/8, to the effect that Admiral Layton was to patrol during the night in 62° 10' N. Between 1° 50' E. and 2° 35' E., unless he should receive other orders from Sir Charles Forbes, and A.T. 2102/8, which referring to the *Triton*'s signal and presumably also to the flying boat's report in the North Sea that afternoon, said it was 'possible the two German forces intend to make a junction, which we calculate they could do about 0500 in about 60° N.; not intended to alter instructions in A.T. 1842'.

Accordingly, the Commander-in-Chief ordered the following dispositions (summary of Commander-in-Chief's 2252/8):–

His position at midnight would be 63° 15' N., 3° E., course 180° speed

18 knots. He estimates that the enemy reported by the flying boat in the afternoon 'may have passed south and east of me'.

> 'Admiral Layton to rendezvous at 0700 in 61° 9' N., 3° E. The cruisers with Admirals Edward-Collins and Cunningham to be stationed in pairs along the parallel of 59° 30' N., by 0500, four stations 20 miles apart, stretching westwards from 4° 30' E., and at that hour they should steer 355° at 16 knots until they meet the fleet, when they should turn to 180°'.

The arrangements were annulled by the Admiralty 'because patrol line placed dispersed and weaker forces in position where they might be caught between two enemy forces with our battle fleet 135 miles away'; instead, the cruisers were to rendezvous in 59° 30' N., 2° 30' E. at 0500 on 9 April and thence steer to meet the fleet (A.T. 0210 and 0235/9).

The cruiser admirals could not carry out these instructions exactly. Admiral Edward-Collins, with the *Galatea*, *Arethusa* and 15 destroyers, had reached the position 58° 30' N., 3° 50' E. at 1445/8, and then turned north to sweep.[49] Soon afterwards he received the enemy report from the flying boat, but he considered that the Commander-in-Chief 'knew my position and movements with reasonable accuracy': he therefore kept wireless silence, and decided to steer 000° throughout the night.

He did not long maintain this course, however; first there came the Admiralty orders to act as a striking force between 1° 50' E. and 2° 35' E., then the Commander-in-Chief's order for a cruiser patrol line, and finally the Admiralty order for the cruisers to concentrate and steer to meet the fleet. The first order meant turning to the westward and reducing speed in a head sea, and when the signal to concentrate came it was not possible to reach the new rendezvous without a large increase of speed, so he altered course to meet Admiral Cunningham, who he was aware, 'would steer northward from the position ordered'. Admiral Cunningham had sailed from Rosyth that afternoon (8 April) with the *Devonshire*, *Berwick*, *York* and *Glasgow*, and after meeting Admiral Derrien in the *Emile Bertin* with two French destroyers[50] in 58° N., 2° W. (off Kinnaird Head) stood to the north-eastward to carry out the sweep ordered in A.T. 1842/8.

Events were now moving swiftly, and from 0100, 9 April numerous reports, mostly from the Admiralty, but also from the submarines *Truant* and *Seal* stationed in the Skagerrak, showed that the Germans were invading Norway.

German Invasion of Norway

The German Landings (Plans 1, 3 and 4)

The invasion of Norway was indeed in full swing during the early hours of this eventful day. So far as the Norwegians were concerned, complete surprise was achieved. On the evening of 8 April, the relations between the two countries, between whom a longstanding traditional friendship had hitherto existed, appeared entirely normal; before this night was out, a murderous assault was let loose on all the Norwegian strategic centres. Their Army was not mobilised; no serious opposition could be offered to the landings, once the weak naval forces and coast defences were passed. It is greatly to the credit of the Commanders of these forces that despite the shock of suddenly being confronted by foreign warships arriving out of the darkness, almost without exception they made the instant decision to offer what resistance they could.

But it was of little avail.

At Trondheim and Bergen the landings took place practically unopposed, though at the latter place the *Königsberg*[51] and *Bremse* were damaged by shore batteries; at Kristiansand four separate attempts to enter the fjord were foiled by gunfire from Odderöy Island, and a German steamer ahead of the groups was hit and set on fire; there and at Arendal further delay was caused by mist, but both places were occupied before noon. Only at Oslo was the landing seriously checked.

Oslo lies at the head of Oslo Fjord, some 60 miles from the sea.[52] The German Force (Group 5)[53] reached the entrance to the fjord about midnight, 8/9, and passing the outer defences – a battery at Rauöy, ten miles up the fjord, which opened fire – at high speed, reached the narrows at Dröbak (about 18 miles short of Oslo) at about 0340/9. So far they had only encountered a Norwegian whaleboat armed with one gun, which had opened fire and had been promptly overwhelmed. Just above Dröbak the channel narrows to three cables in width; here were the inner defences, situated on islets, Oscarsborg and Kaholm. At 0420, as Admiral Kummetz leading the force in the *Blücher* approached, the Norwegian batteries on Oscarsborg suddenly opened fire at a range of only 500 yards; the ship was hit repeatedly and the fire control equipment of her main armament was put out of action. Though crippled, she relied on both sides with her heavy and light A/A guns, and increasing to full speed had reached Kaholm, when she was struck by several torpedoes fired by the torpedo battery there. With all her engines out of action, the *Blücher* dropped anchor east of Askholmene, a mile and a half further up the fjord; fierce fires onboard could not be got under control and at 0623 she heeled over to port and sank in deep water. Most of the life-boats and floats had been destroyed by the fires, and the crew and troops were forced to swim ashore, which caused considerable losses.

At 0450, after the *Blücher* had been heavily hit, Admiral Kummetz handed over the command of the group to the Captain of the *Lützow*, Captain Thiele. He, having observed the fate of the *Blücher*, withdrew the force and subsequently landed its troops at Sonsbukten some ten miles to the southward, intending to carry out an attack on the defences guarding the Dröbak Narrows from both land and sea. After heavy attacks by the Luftwaffe, however, the Norwegian resistance gradually gave way; but not before the minelayer *Olav Tryggvason*,[54] stationed at the undefended naval base at Horten, had fought a spirited action with the German torpedo boat *Albatros* and two minesweepers, in which she sank one of the latter (R.17) and forced the *Albatros* to withdraw.

By midday, Oslo was virtually in the hands of the enemy, owing to his overwhelming air superiority; but thanks to the check at Dröbak, the operation had not gone 'according to plan,' and there had been time for the Norwegian Royal Family, Government and Parliament to escape from the capital, taking with them all the gold in the Bank of Norway.

In the north the landing at Narvik had gone exactly as planned. Arriving off the entrance to Vest Fjord in the evening of 8 April, Kommodore Bonte's ten destroyers parted company with the battlecruisers and proceeded up the fjord. Avoiding the British minefield, from which, it will be remembered, the patrolling destroyers had been withdrawn by order of the Admiralty some ten hours previously, they suddenly appeared out of a snow squall off Narvik at early dawn.[55] A gallant, but ineffectual resistance was offered by two Norwegian coast defence vessels, the *Eidsvold* and *Norge*.[56] Outnumbered and taken by surprise[57] there was little they could do. The *Eidsvold*, which was lying outside the harbour, had only time to return a peremptory refusal to a demand for surrender before she was sunk by torpedo and gunfire with the loss of nearly all her crew. The *Norge*, at anchor inside the harbour, opened fire on the *Bernd Von Arnim* as she went alongside to land her troops a few minutes later, but was soon hit by two torpedoes and sunk, with heavy loss of life.[58] The disembarkation of General Dietl's troops then proceeded unopposed.[59]

Admiral Whitworth's Encounter with the *Gneisenau* and *Scharnhorst* (Plan 2)

While this was going on at Narvik, a sharp engagement was taking place to seaward of Vest Fjord between Admiral Whitworth's force and the German battlecruisers. After detaching the destroyers to Narvik (2000, 8 April) the *Gneisenau* and *Scharnhorst* had steered to the north-westward in order to take up their patrolling position in the Arctic. This course brought them into contact with Admiral Whitworth in the *Renown*, who, with his nine destroyers, was then returning to the south-eastward after spending the night to the west of the Lofoten Islands, waiting for the weather to moderate before establishing a patrol off Vest Fjord.

'From midnight onwards,' runs Admiral Whitworth's diary, 'the weather improved; but knowing that the destroyers would be widely strung out on account of the weather I decided to wait until the first sign of dawn and sufficient light to make the turn to the south-eastward without losing touch with them or any part of them.' The squadron turned at 0230/9, snow squalls making 'the visibility variable'; but 'dawn twilight[60] strengthened to the eastward, and conditions improved'. An hour or so later, roughly in 67° 20' N., 9° 40' E., some 50 miles to the westward of Skomvaer Light, they sighted a darkened ship coming out of a snow-squall with apparently a second ship astern of her. The presence of two ships was soon confirmed; they were thought to be a *Scharnhorst* and a *Hipper*, though later evidence has shown that they were the battlecruisers *Scharnhorst* and *Gneisenau*.[61] They joined battle just under half an hour from the first sighting.

When she first sighted the German ships, at 0337, the *Renown* was steering 130°, at 12 knots, with her destroyers stationed astern. The enemy lay broad on the port bow, 10 miles distant or rather more, steering to the north-west, on a course approximately opposite to that of the British force. The *Renown* maintained her course for ten minutes, then altered to 080° increasing speed to 15 knots and soon after to 20 knots; at 0359 she hauled right round to 305°, roughly parallel to the enemy, with her 'A' arcs just open; at 0405, when just abaft the beam of the leading German ship, she opened fire at 18,600 yards. It was not till 0411 that the *Gneisenau* returned the fire; she had sighted the British force at 0350, but in the poor light to the westward had not recognised it as such until 0400, when the alert was sounded for action. The *Scharnhorst* on the other hand did not sight the *Renown* until the latter opened fire at 0405. A fierce engagement ensued during the next ten minutes or so, both the *Gneisenau* and the *Scharnhorst* firing at the *Renown*, which was engaging the *Gneisenau* with her heavy armament, and the *Scharnhorst* with her 4.5-in., all the destroyers joining in with their 4.7-in., though at such range their fire could 'hardly have been effective'. The *Renown* was hit twice, without serious damage; the *Gneisenau* received a hit at 0417 on the foretop at a range of 14,600 yards, destroying the main fire control equipment, and temporarily disabling her main armament. At 0418, with only her secondary armament in action, the *Gneisenau* altered course to 030°, 'with the obvious intention of breaking off the action'. To cover the *Gneisenau*'s retirement, the *Scharnhorst* crossed her stern, making a screen of smoke, whereupon the *Renown*, turning northward, brought all her guns to bear on the *Scharnhorst*.

There followed a chase to windward that lasted an hour and a half, until about 0600. The wind was rising and had shifted from north-north-west to north-north-east, with a heavy swell and a great sea. The destroyers soon fell astern out of the battle. The *Renown* continued to engage the *Scharnhorst* but did not succeed in hitting her; both German ships were firing at the *Renown*, the *Gneisenau* with her after turret, and the *Scharnhorst* yawing occasionally to fire a broadside. At 0434 the *Gneisenau* received a second hit which struck 'A' turret by the left hood of the rangefinder. It wrecked the watertight hood which resulted in the flooding of the turret, putting it out of action. A third hit struck the after A/A gun on the port side of the platform, doing little damage. Just before 0500, the German ships disappeared in a rain-squall. Admiral Whitworth had increased to full speed early in the fight, before the turn to the north, but had soon to ease to 23 knots and afterwards to 20, at

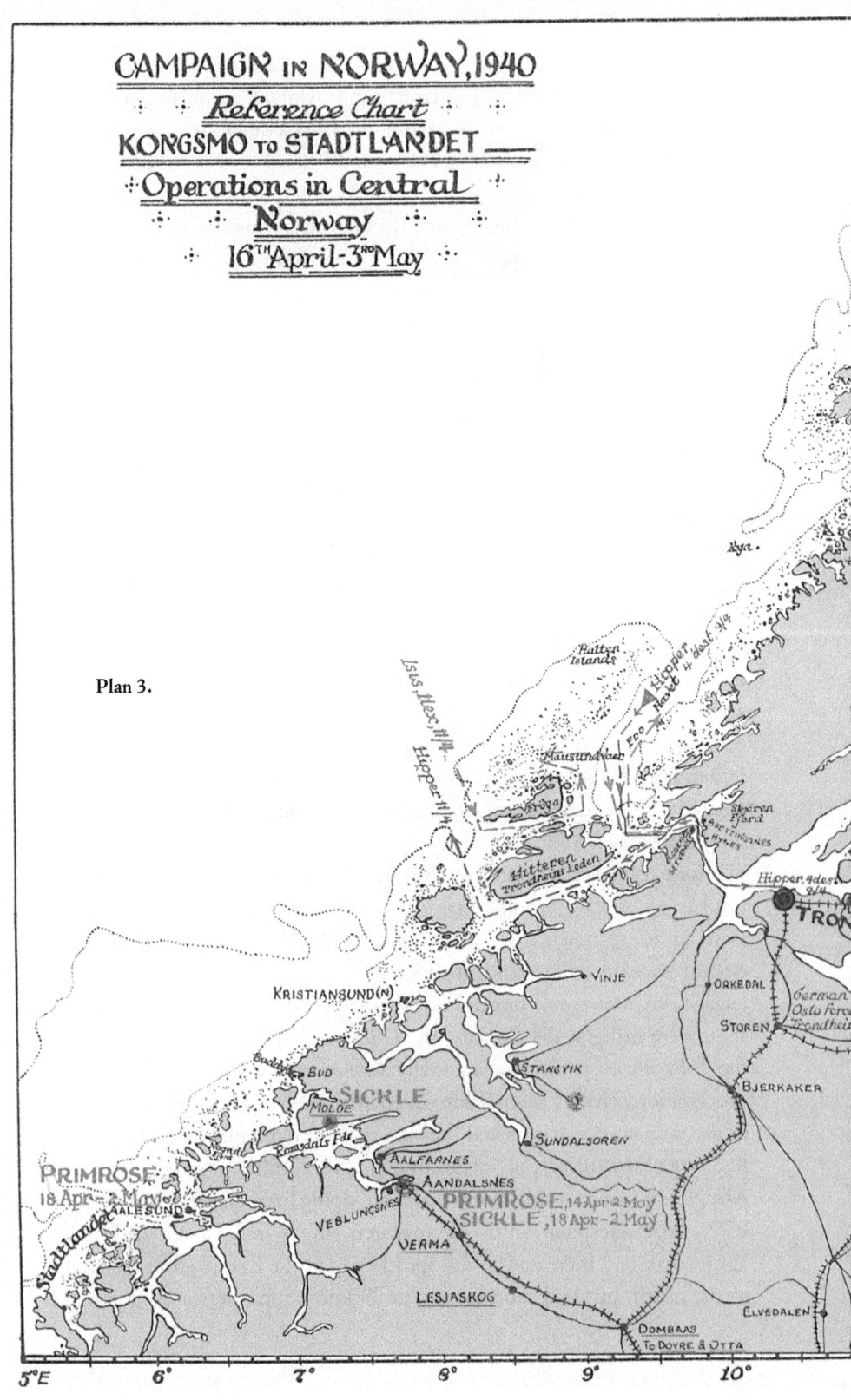

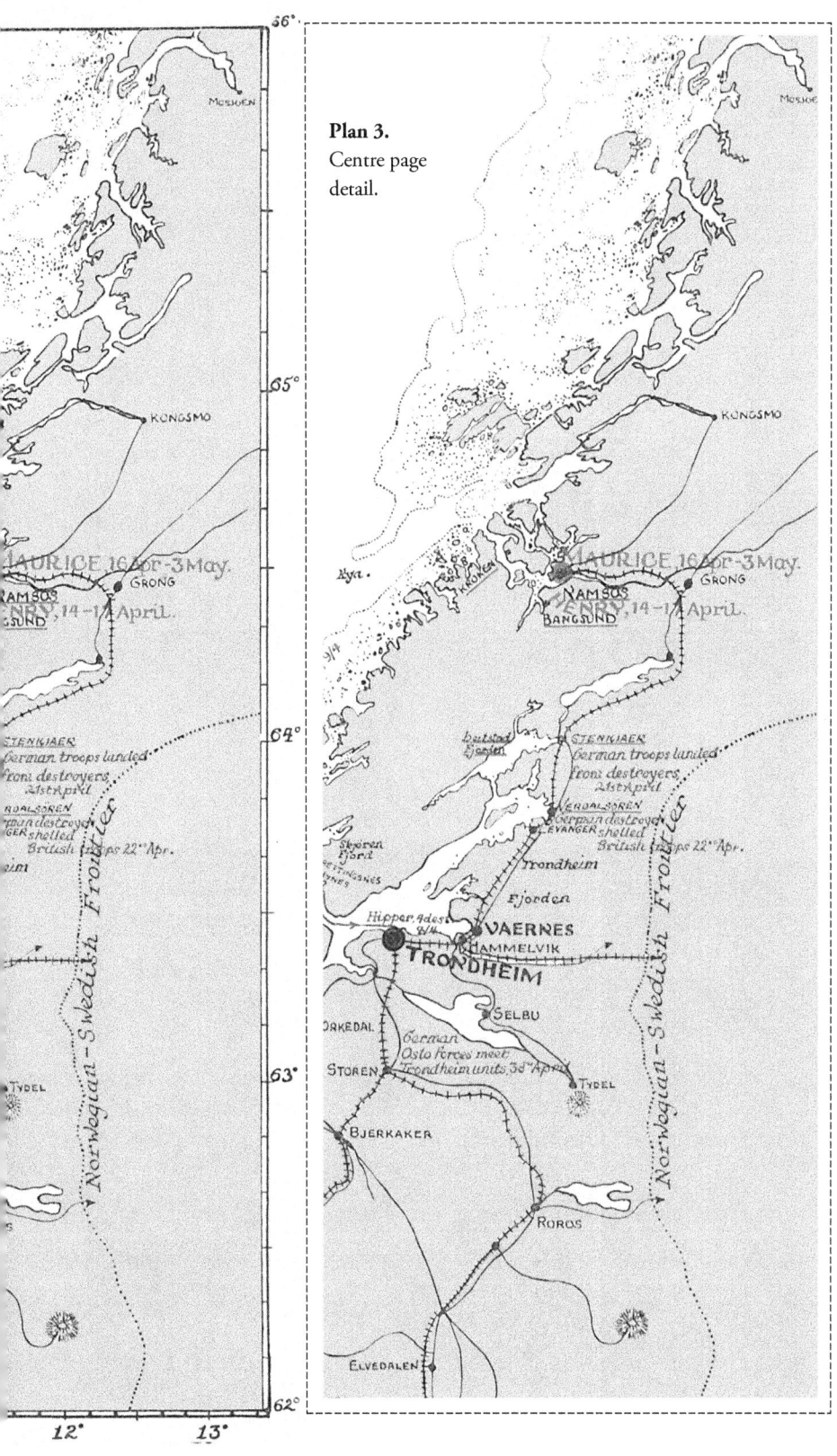

Plan 3. Centre page detail.

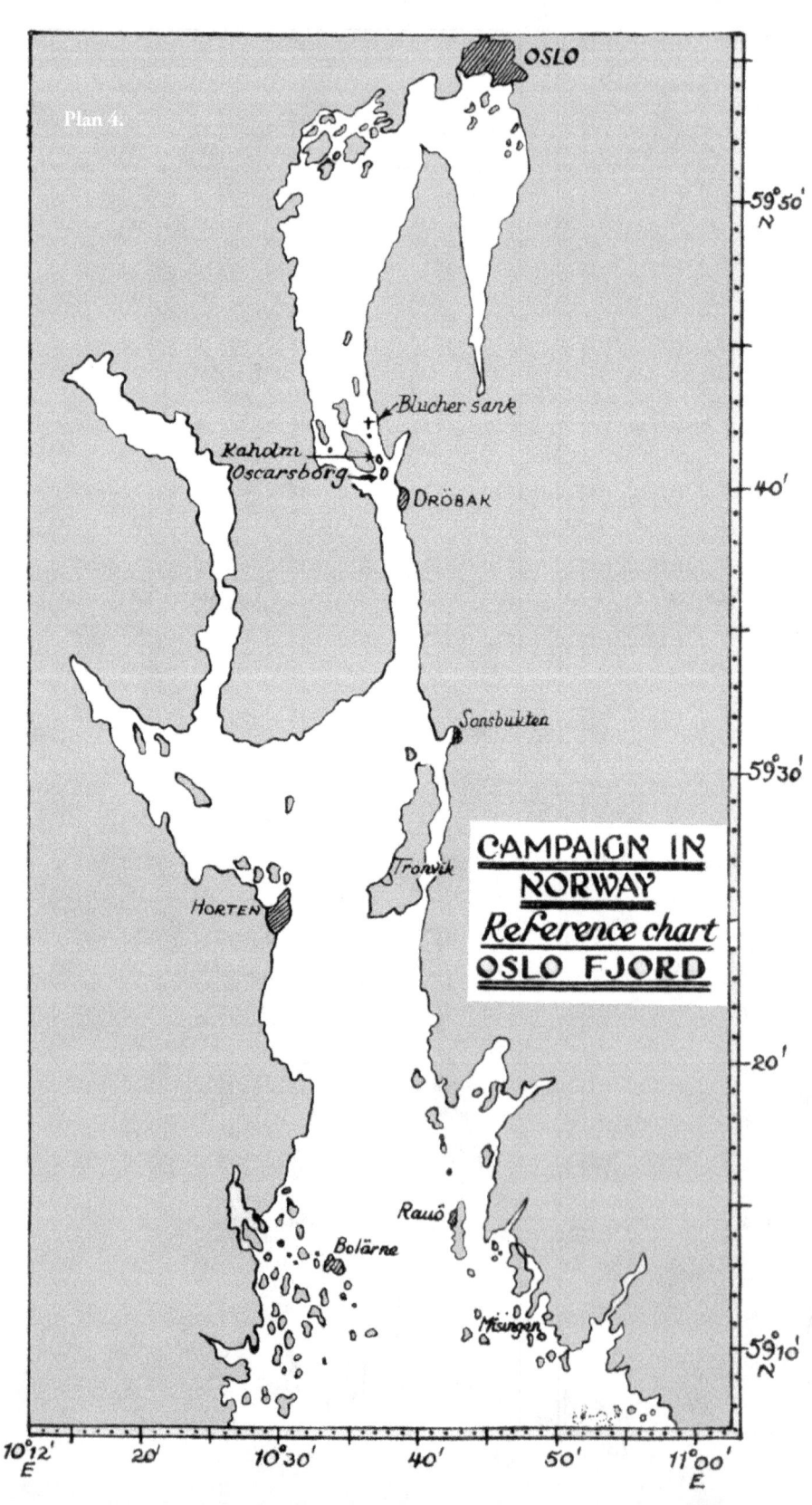

which speed he barely held the range: when the enemy disappeared in the rain, he 'decided to alter course to bring the sea on the other bow and endeavour to make more speed,' and accordingly turned to the eastward and increased to 25 knots. When the weather cleared, however, some 20 minutes later, the German ships were still heading northwards and were farther off than before. The *Renown* turned again to bring the enemy fine on her bow, and opened fire; but the 'fire continued to be ineffective, both sides altering course to avoid the fall of shot'. There were further squalls of rain or sleet hiding the target; the *Renown* strained herself 'to the maximum' in trying to overhaul her opponent (for a few minutes she went 29 knots) but at last the enemy ran out of sight.

The last brief sight of the German ships came at 0615 – 'far ahead and out of range'. Admiral Whitworth stood on to the northward in the *Renown* until a few minutes after 0800; then he turned westward, hoping to cut off the enemy 'should they have broken back to southward', but no further contact occurred.

British Dispositions, Vest Fjord Area (Plan 5)

Vice-Admiral Whitworth had already ordered his destroyers to patrol the mouth of Vest Fjord and the *Repulse* detachment 'to prevent German forces entering Narvik'. Then, soon after 0900, he received A.T. 0820/9, which told the Commander-in-Chief to make plans for attacking the enemy in Bergen and Trondheim, adding 'Narvik must be watched to prevent Germans landing, as we shall probably want to land a force there.' At that, Admiral Whitworth decided to concentrate his force off the fjord: he gave the *Repulse* a rendezvous for 1300 in 67° N., 10° E. – some 60 miles south of his own position when making the signal – and told Captain Warburton-Lee to join at 1800 in 67° N., 10° 30' E.

The Admiralty and the Commander-in-Chief changed these dispositions. In a signal timed 0952/9, Sir Charles Forbes ordered Captain Warburton-Lee to 'send some destroyers up to Narvik to make certain that no enemy troops land'. The Admiralty made A.T. 1200/9, also addressed direct to Captain Warburton-Lee:–[62]

'Press reports state one German ship has arrived Narvik and landed a small force. Proceed Narvik and sink or capture enemy ship. It is at your discretion to land forces, if you think you can recapture Narvik from number of enemy present. Try to get possession of battery, if not already in enemy hands: details of battery follow.'

They had already told Admiral Whitworth that Germans had arrived, and that he must 'ensure that no reinforcements reach them' (A.T. 1138/9), but this signal did not come to him until next day. Captain Warburton-Lee decided to go to Narvik with the four ships of his proper flotilla, the 2nd, leaving Captain Bickford with the rest to patrol the minefield he had laid the day before near the mouth of Vest Fjord. One ship, the *Impulsive*, had gone home in the morning with a damaged paravane boom, which left Captain Bickford the *Esk*, *Icarus* and *Ivanhoe*, minelayers, with no torpedoes and mounting but two guns, and the *Greyhound*, late of the *Renown*'s anti-submarine screen. For Narvik there were the *Hardy*, flotilla leader, the *Hotspur* (Commander Layman), *Havock* (Lieut.-Commander Courage) and *Hunter* (Lieut.-Commander de Villiers); and the *Hostile* (Commander Wright) arrived unexpectedly after the flotilla had started on its mission.[63]

Captain Warburton-Lee meant originally to reach Narvik by 2000 that night, and made his plan as the flotilla steamed up Vest Fjord, passing it by signal to his consorts. But having nothing to go by beyond the press report in the Admiralty's signal he bethought him of the pilots' station at Tranøy, where he arrived about 1600, and sent on shore there for what they could tell him. The pilots had seen six ships 'larger than the *Hardy*' going to Narvik, besides a submarine; the entrance to the harbour was mined; and the Germans held the place very strongly. The English, thought the pilots, would need twice as many ships. Captain Warburton-Lee signalled this intelligence to the Admiralty, the Commander-in-Chief, and Admiral Whitworth, and added: 'Intend attacking at dawn high water'.

This signal, timed 1751, reached Admiral Whitworth a little after 1800. The Admiralty's order to attack had been repeated to him, and he now considered whether he might improve the power of the attack. When the *Repulse* and the ships with her joined, about 1400, he had disposed his force thus: the *Penelope* to patrol a line running south from Skomvaer Light, rather more than 50 miles outside the minefield and about 150 miles from Narvik; the *Renown* and *Repulse* to cruise north and south on a line 30 miles farther west, with the *Bedouin*, *Punjabi*, *Eskimo* and *Kimberley* as a screen. The *Penelope* might go in, and so might the four destroyers, though that would deprive the capital ships of their screen; he had already ordered Captain Bickford to continue the patrol by the minefield, cancelling the signal in the morning that those four destroyers should join his flag at 1800. But the time of high water being 0140/10, Captain Warburton-Lee's signal implied an attack in the morning twilight, for which it was too late to send reinforcements in the thick weather prevailing. Moreover, so Admiral Whitworth reasoned, the plan had been made 'with the forces ordered by the Admiralty'; and 'the addition of other forces, involving delay and revision of the plan, was liable to cause confusion'. He decided, therefore, to leave things as they stood.

Movements of Commander-in-Chief, Home Fleet

(Plans 2 and 6)

While these developments had been taking place in the north, the Commander-in-Chief had been operating in the Bergen-Trondheim area. Throughout the night of 8/9 April, while the various first reports of the invasion were coming in, he held his southerly course, being joined by Vice-Admiral Layton with the *Manchester* and *Southampton* at 0630/9, and by Vice-Admirals Edward-Collins, Cunningham and Derrien with their seven cruisers and 13 destroyers (eight British, three Polish, two French)[64] some three hours later. The *Tartar* and the three Polish destroyers were detached to the northward to join Convoy HN.25[65] – at least 37 ships – then waiting off Hovden (61° 40' N., 4° 45' E.) and escort it to the United Kingdom, the remainder of the fleet continuing to the southward.

By this time it was clear that Germany was carrying out a full scale invasion of Norway, seizing (among other places) all the ports that the Allies had hoped to save from her control by occupying themselves, but the strength of his forces in the various areas was naturally in doubt. At 0630/9, the Commander-in-Chief asked the Admiralty for news of the German strength in Bergen, as he wished to send there Admiral Layton's two cruisers – then just arriving in the fleet. This signal reached the Admiralty about the time A.T. 0820/9 to the Commander-in-Chief was being framed:–

'Prepare plans for attacking German warships and transports in Bergen and for controlling the approaches to the port on the supposition that defences are still in hands of Norwegians.

Similar plans as regards Trondheim should also be prepared, if you have sufficient forces for both.

Narvik must be watched to prevent Germans landing, as we shall probably want to land a force there.

At what time would forces be ready to cross the 3-mile limit in operations against Bergen and Trondheim?'

A first report from reconnoitring aircraft put 'at least one *Köln* class cruiser in Bergen' (A.T. 0935); and at 1015, the Admiralty sanctioned the Commander-in-Chief's proposal to attack there, though warning him later in A.T. 1211, that he must no longer count on the defences being friendly. The attack on the ships in Trondheim was annulled until the German battlecruisers should be found, 'as it would entail dispersion of forces' (A.T. 1132).

Sir Charles Forbes said, in answer to A.T. 0820, that the ships could go in by the fjords north and south of Bergen 'in three hours from the order, Go' (1032/9). By then the Rosyth ships had joined, so he could strengthen the attacking force. Admiral Layton left the fleet accordingly about 1130, an hour after A.T. 1015 came, with the *Manchester* and *Southampton, Glasgow* and *Sheffield* and the seven destroyers of the 4th and 6th Flotillas. He had orders:–

'...to attack enemy forces reported in Bergen: these include one *Köln* class cruiser.

Defences may be in hands of enemy.

Three or four destroyers are to enter by Fejeosen Fjord, 60° 44' N., remainder by Kors Fjord, 60° 8' N. Object, to destroy enemy forces and report situation.

Cruisers are to be in support at both entrances, which U-boats may be patrolling.'

He was south of Bergen, with Fejeosen Fjord nearly 80 miles to the north-east and Kors Fjord, bearing about east-north-east, a dozen miles nearer; it was blowing hard from north-west with a rough sea; the destroyers could keep up only 16 knots. 'Owing to the movement southward of the fleet during the forenoon', writes Admiral Layton, 'it was unfortunately necessary to retrace a lot of ground to windward to get to Bergen. At 1408, aircraft reported that there were two cruisers in

Bergen instead of one. With only seven destroyers available, the prospects of a successful attack now appeared distinctly less, though there was some hope that the enemy could not yet have got the shore guns effectively manned'. However, soon afterwards there came orders from the Admiralty annulling the attack (A.T. 1357/9) and the squadron turned to rejoin the fleet.[66]

The Commander-in-Chief had turned north at noon, being then in 59° 44' N., 2° 57' E. The weather was clear, and German aircraft had been shadowing the fleet since about eight in the morning. In the afternoon their bombers came; between 1430 and 1800 or thereabouts, some part of the fleet was first constantly engaged. The Germans came from the eastward and made their first and apparently their principal attack on Admiral Layton's ships, returning from the coast. Near misses slightly damaged the *Southampton* and *Glasgow*; and the *Gurkha*, which had got separated from the remainder, was so badly damaged that she subsequently sank. Providentially the *Aurora*, in joining the fleet from the Clyde, made contact with her some hours later and in time to save most of her company, a task on which she was still employed at 2130.

As for the main body of the fleet, the business began about 1530, when a diving aircraft hit the flagship *Rodney* with a bomb. After a lull between 1600 and 1700, the attack freshened for about half an hour, both diving and at high level. Several bombs fell near the ships, especially the *Rodney* again, and the *Valiant*, *Devonshire*, *Berwick*, and the destroyers, but there were no more hits. The British fire seems to have brought down one enemy machine, reported by the *York* as falling in flames between the *Devonshire* and the *Berwick*; yet the ships with Admiral Layton spent some 40 per cent of their 4-in. ammunition.

During these attacks from the air, fresh orders came for attempting Bergen. The *Furious* was on her way to the fleet, and the Commander-in-Chief had already suggested in his signal 1032/9 that torpedo attack by her aircraft would give the 'best chance of success', if the Germans had the coast defences in their power: he proposed an attack at dusk on 10 April. The Admiralty agreed, at the same time arranging with the Royal Air Force to send bombers in the evening of 9 April and for the naval air station at Hatston to send some in the morning of 10 April. In the meantime, cruisers and destroyers must patrol the approaches to prevent the enemy from reinforcing Bergen and Stavanger, and to pin down their ships already there: Sir Charles was 'to consider a sweep with light forces

Plan 5.

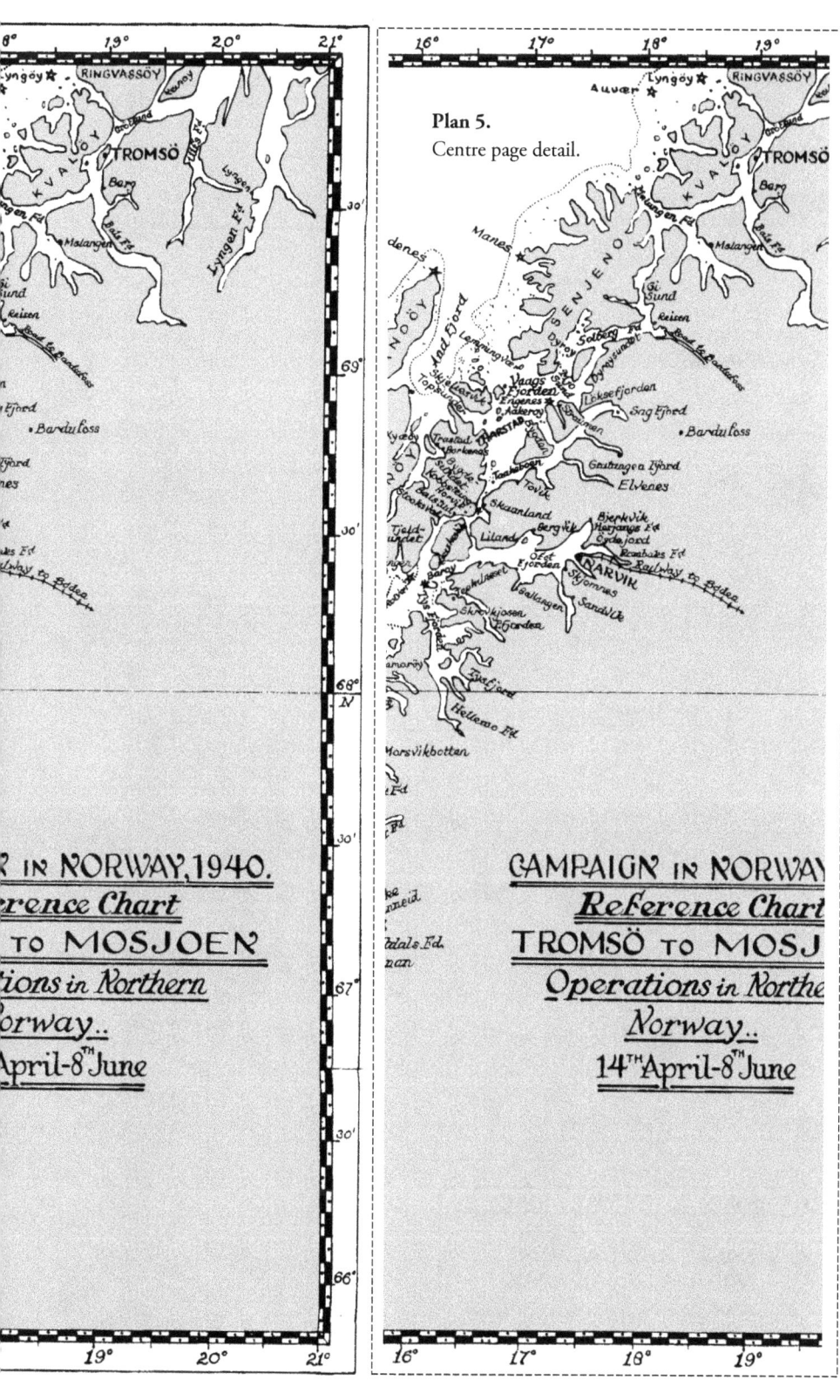

Plan 5. Centre page detail.

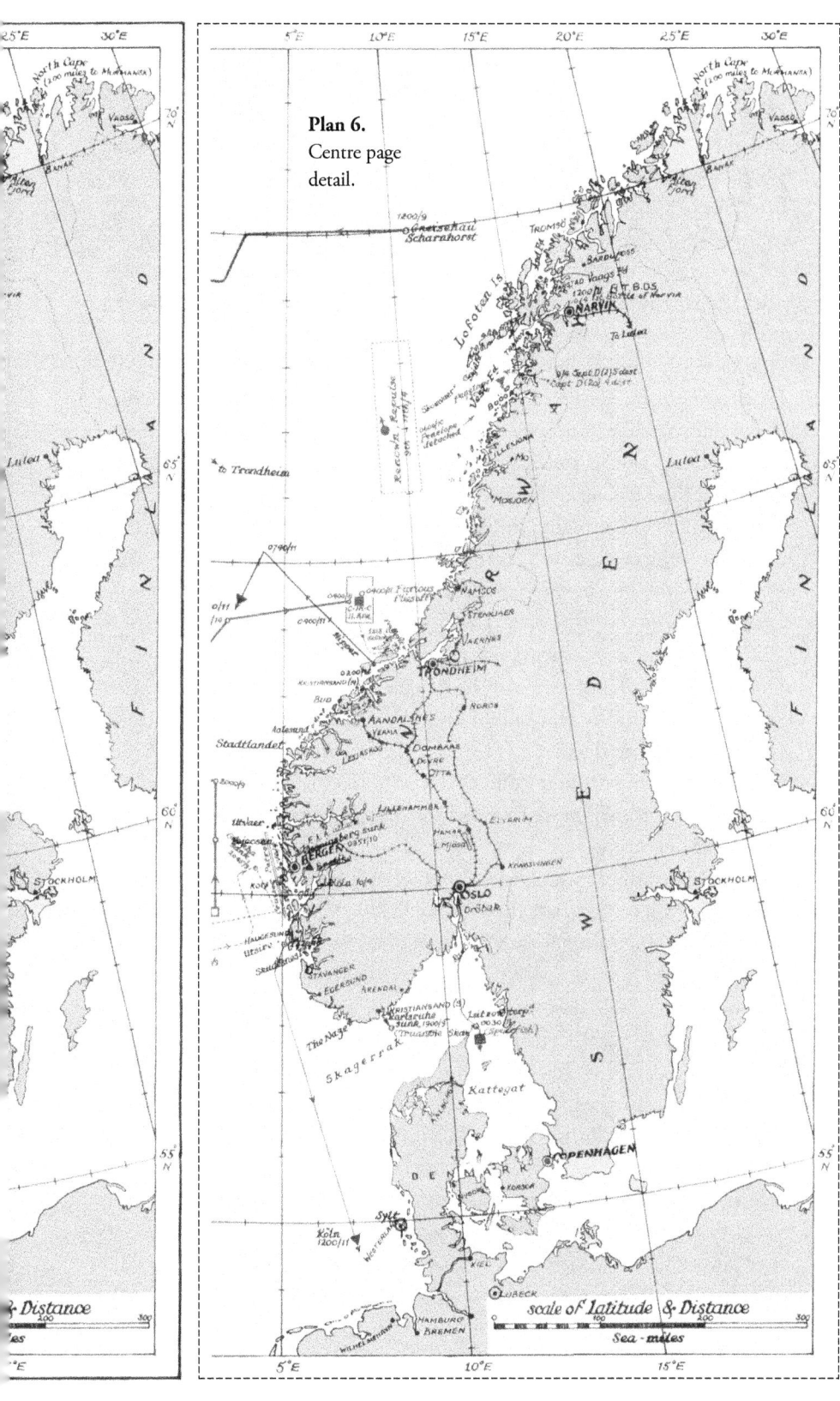

Plan 6. Centre page detail.

off the south-west corner of Norway'. But the afternoon's experience made him change his mind about the *Furious*. She 'could not work in latitude of air attack to-day', so he proposed her attacking the enemy in Trondheim, farther north, 'leaving Bergen to the Royal Air Force': indeed he gave the Admiralty his 'general ideas' in the same signal 2231/9, to 'attack enemy in north with surface forces and military assistance, leaving southern area mostly to submarines, due to German air superiority in south'.

The enemy force which had been sent to occupy Bergen consisted of the cruisers *Köln*, *Königsberg* and *Bremse*, two torpedo boats, and the M.T.B. depot ship *Karl Peters*. At 1800/9, Royal Air Force bombers attacked them, but in spite of near misses, little damage was caused. An hour later, the *Köln*, accompanied by the torpedo boats, put to sea on the return journey to Germany; the *Königsberg* was not considered seaworthy owing to injuries received from the Norwegian batteries, and she remained with the *Bremse* and *Karl Peters* to supplement the harbour defences.

The *Köln* and her consorts did not get far that night. Enemy wireless signals indicated the presence of the British forces which soon afterwards established patrols to seaward of the approaches to Bergen, so Rear-Admiral Schmundt decided to postpone the attempt and anchored at the head of Mauranger Fjord (60° 08' N., 6° 16' E.) till the following evening, 10 April, when he resumed his passage, arriving home without incident on 11 April.

Meanwhile, the Commander-in-Chief, Home Fleet, had sent back Admiral Layton to the coast the evening before, as soon as the Admiralty orders for watching Bergen and Stavanger had been deciphered. Admiral Edward-Collins followed with the *Galatea* and *Arethusa*, the *Emile Bertin*, and the two French destroyers. Sir Charles' 1837/9 thus disposed of them: two of Admiral Layton's cruisers with destroyers 'to sweep down Norwegian coast' from Fejeosen Fjord south of Kors Fjord, and the other half of his force to sweep from Kors Fjord to Obrestad, 20 miles south of Stavanger, while Admiral Edward-Collins patrolled off Fejeosen. The object given was 'to stop reinforcements for Stavanger and Bergen'. They were to cruise until 0400/10, and then to steer for a rendezvous in 61° N., 1° E. It is not clear from his diary how far Admiral Layton acted on these orders, for he says merely that he had instructions (under Sir Charles' 1614/9 and A.T. 1451/9, when he turned back) to 'maintain a patrol off the entrance to Bergen to prevent enemy forces escaping' and that 'this patrol was maintained during the night'; yet he altered course for the rendezvous at four in the morning, as Sir Charles' 1837/9 prescribed. Captain Pegram of the *Glasgow*, commanding the southern patrol, had this latter signal from a consort, the *Sheffield*, but only 0145/10. When approaching the coast the evening before, he had come upon the *Aurora* rescuing the survivors of the *Gurkha*, and she asked to join the *Glasgow*, as she had no other orders. Thereupon, Captain Pegram sent her with one destroyer to stop the gap at Bommel Fjord, 30 miles to the southward, while he patrolled north and south of Kors Fjord, 7 miles off-shore, with the rest of his group. When the *Sheffield* passed on Sir Charles' later signal, it was too late to reach Obrestad in the time, but Captain Pegram stretched south as far at Utsire, 25 miles short of Stavanger, before turning away to seaward for the rendezvous.

No surface contact with the enemy occurred during the night, with the exception of an attempt by the *Manchester* to ram a U-boat. But in the south the submarine *Truant* scored a success, torpedoing the cruiser *Karlsruhe* at 1858/9, an hour after she had left Kristiansand on her homeward passage. She sank at 2150, her end expedited by torpedoes from German torpedo boats, which had taken off her crew.

The various groups of ships off Bergen (with the exception of the *Aurora*, which proceeded direct to Scapa with the *Gurkha*'s survivors) made their way to the rendezvous in the morning and found there the *Codrington* and other destroyers sent by Sir Charles Forbes with orders for them all to proceed to harbour for fuel – the British destroyers to Sullom Voe, the cruisers and the French ships to Scapa – where they arrived that evening, without incident except for an ineffective bombing attack on the 2nd Cruiser Squadron. On arrival, ammunitioning and fuelling was commenced without delay – an operation interrupted by an air raid on Scapa which lasted from 2100 to 2220. About 60 bombers were employed, but warning of their approach had been received by radar; they achieved no damage, but lost six of their number.

The Commander-in-Chief himself, in the meanwhile, had held on to the northward after the air attacks in the afternoon till 2000/9, then steering west at 16 knots from 61° 40' N., 2° 47' E. for the night, and turning to the eastward again at 0500, 10 April. About an hour later, the first news of the destroyer attack on Narvik arrived – an intercepted signal from Captain D (2) to Captain D (20) timed 0551:– 'One cruiser and three destroyers off Narvik, am withdrawing to westward'.

At 0730 in 61° 24' N., 1° W. the *Warspite* and *Furious* joined the fleet, as did several fresh destroyers (at any rate, replenished ones) after which the original destroyer screen went home for oil. The strength of the fleet then stood at the three capital ships, *Rodney*, *Valiant* and *Warspite*; three cruisers, *Devonshire*, *Berwick* and *York*; the *Furious* aircraft carrier and 18 destroyers.

With this force the Commander-in-Chief steered to the north and east, making for a suitable position from which to attack the enemy ships in Trondheim with aircraft at dawn next morning. This course also provided cover for Convoy HN.25, which after its fortunate escape from Bergen[67] was making its way to the United Kingdom escorted by the four destroyers detached from the fleet the day before.

Soon after steadying on the north-easterly course came the pleasing tidings that at 0700 sixteen Skuas led by Lieutenant W. P. Lucy, R.N., and Captain R. T. Partridge, R.M., of the Fleet Air Arm from Hatston had attacked the *Königsberg* at Bergen and sank her with three direct hits with 500 lb. S.A.P.C. bombs;[68] and at 1132 the Commander-in-Chief received news of Captain Warburton-Lee's dawn attack on the enemy in Narvik.

First Battle of Narvik (Plan 7)

To return to the northern area.

As a result of the intelligence received from the pilots at Tranøy in the afternoon of 9 April, Captain Warburton-Lee took his flotilla down the fjord again,[69] turning back half an hour before midnight to arrive off Narvik at dawn. A.T. 2059/9 told them to patrol during the night east of 16° 33' E., in the narrow stretch of Ofot Fjord some 20 miles west of Narvik, lest the enemy should run through Tjeldsundet into Vaagsfjord, thus escaping to the northward; and the signal ended, 'Attack at dawn: all good luck'. Captain Warburton-Lee ignored this signal if he received it: very likely he feared giving away his presence to the enemy, for the Admiralty had warned him before that there might be batteries either side of the narrows, near Ramnes and Hamnes Holm, which the Germans might have seized and manned.[70] If so, they could perhaps report him to friends at Narvik before the time came for his attack, and surprise must have seemed all-important for the little flotilla.

A.T. 0104/10 said the Germans were supposed to have come to Narvik 'in apparently empty ore ships', which might have stores still onboard and must be sunk, if possible; and Captain Warburton-Lee was to try to find out how the enemy did land and in what strength, and whether they had seized the Norwegian batteries. Lastly, A.T. 0136 said: 'Norwegian coast-defence ships *Eidsvold* and *Norge* may be in German hands: you alone can judge whether, in these circumstances, attack should be made. We shall support whatever decision you take'. Perhaps this last message added to Admiral Whitworth's misgivings, though he could now do nothing; it could make no difference to Captain Warburton-Lee, whose mind was made up. The flotilla passed Tranøy again on the way in at 0100/10. They had then 'continuous snowstorms with visibility seldom greater than two cables ... on the one occasion that land was seen the whole flotilla almost ran aground'. Ships lost touch at intervals, twice through merchant vessels crossing the line. But all arrived off Narvik a little after 0400, when the sky cleared and they could see for nearly a mile.

The plan of attack appears in the signals Captain Warburton-Lee made to the flotilla the day before. Apart from the pilots' information and the Admiralty messages described already, A.T. 1307/9 had told him of a three-gun battery, 18- or 12-pounders, on a hill north of the ore quay in the harbour and west of the town, facing north-west; that is to say across the mouths of Herjangs and Rombaks Fjords. It was this signal that gave the warning, too, of possible batteries at the narrows in Ofot Fjord. He proposed the *Hardy*, *Hunter* and *Havock* should attack the shipping inside the harbour. The *Hotspur* and *Hostile* would stay outside to engage the fort if it opened fire; to keep watch for German ships he expected to find patrolling, or coming in from the sea or from the two fjords north of Narvik; to be ready to cover a retreat of the main body with smoke and to take disabled ships in tow. If the business prospered, and 'opposition is silenced' the *Hardy*'s first lieutenant would lead a party to land at ore quay.

The German destroyers had put their troops ashore as planned, during 9 April, and by midnight, three of them, the *Zenker*, *Giese*, *Koellner*, were lying in Herjangs Fjord, off Elvegaard; four more, the *Heidkamp*, *Schmitt*, *Lüdemann* and *Künne*, had made fast alongside the pier in Narvik harbour, and two others, the *Thiele* and *Von Arnim*, were at anchor off Ballangen about 15 miles to the west of Narvik. The *Roeder* had been ordered to patrol the outer reaches of the fjord as a protection against submarines, but at dawn, on 10 April, she entered Narvik

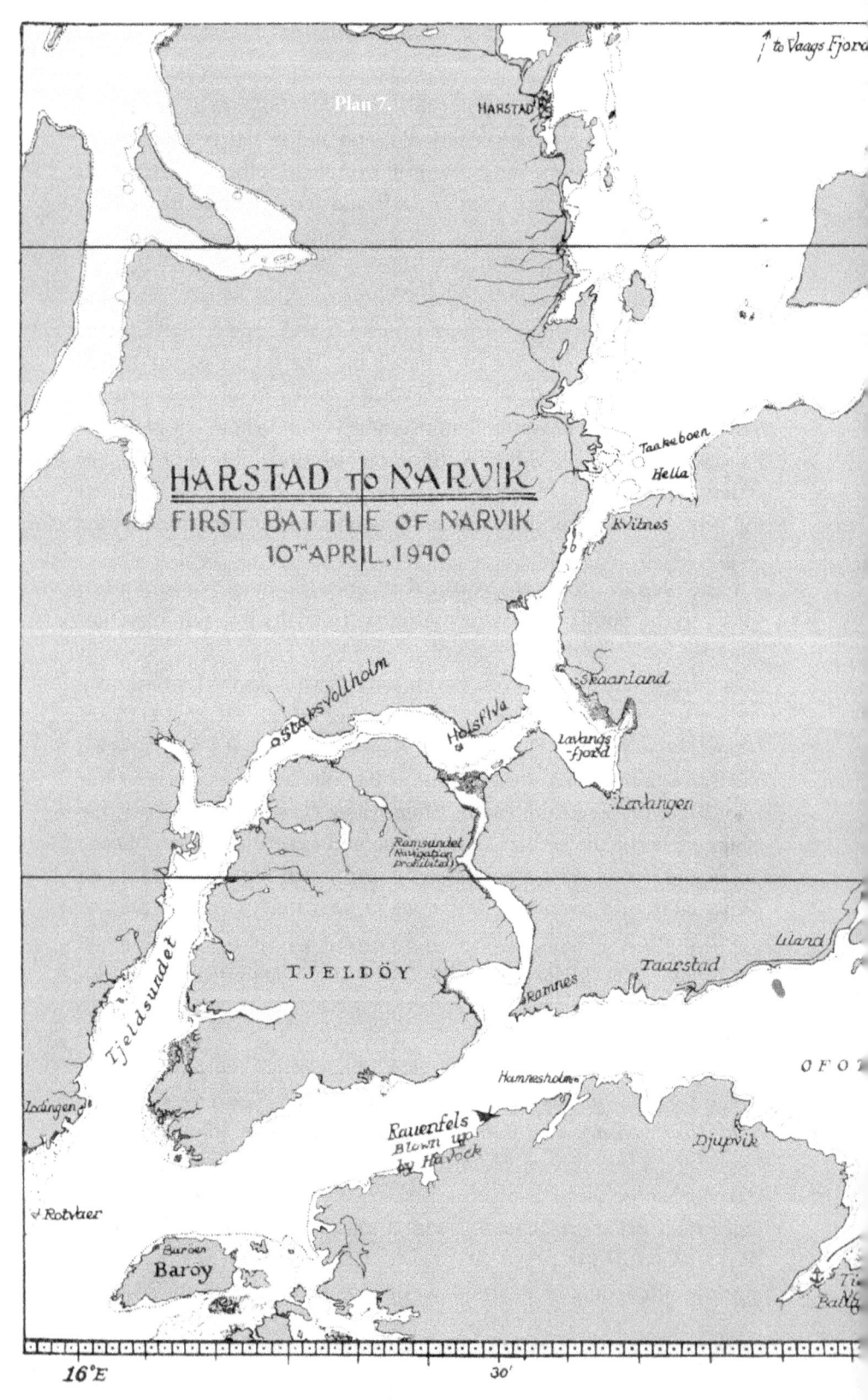

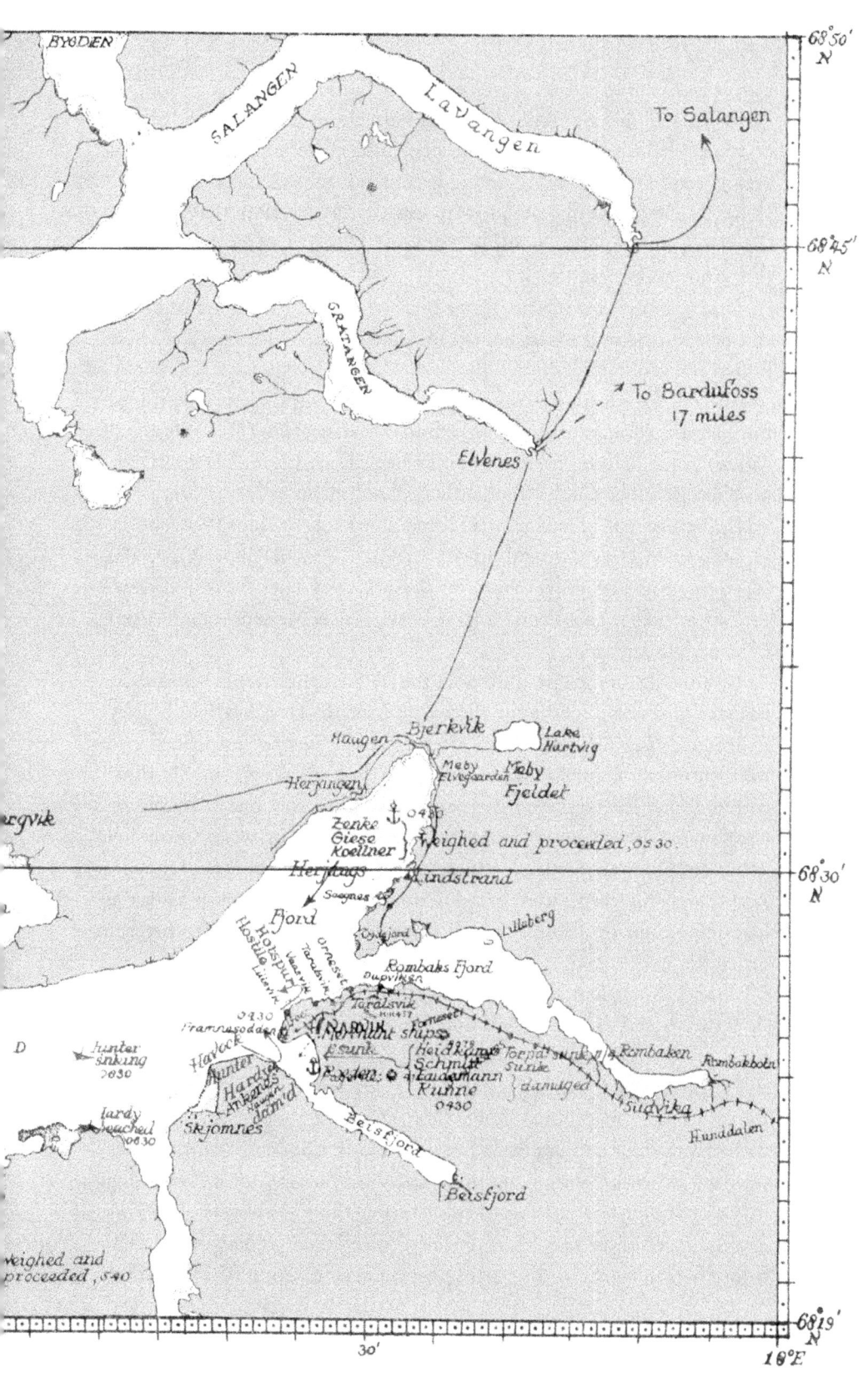

Harbour, anchoring at 0420 off the eastern shore. Ten minutes later, at 0430, the British flotilla made the first of its three attacks. The *Hardy*, *Hunter* and *Havock* went in and engaged the German destroyers alongside the pier with guns and torpedoes; a torpedo from the *Hardy* hit the *Heidkamp* aft, blowing off its stern and killing the German Captain (D), Kommodore Bonte.

The *Anton Schmitt* was hit by one torpedo in the forward engine room, and by a second in the after boiler room, which sealed her fate; she broke in two and sank.

The *Roeder* was hit by two shells which set her on fire and destroyed the fire control equipment. The other two destroyers (*Lüdemann* and *Künne*) in the harbour tried to cast off when the alarm was first given, but both received hits which temporarily disabled them.

In the harbour at anchor were some 23 merchant ships,[71] and heavy explosions marked the end of six of the German ships. One, the *Neuenfels*, had been run ashore on 9 April, and one, the *Jan Wellem*, 11,776 tons (a whale depot ship in service as submarine supply ship) remained undamaged.

Meanwhile, in the mist and snow, the *Hotspur* and *Hostile*, outside the harbour, did not discover the three destroyers in Herjangs Fjord. They joined the *Hardy* in the second attack and the *Hotspur* torpedoed two merchantmen. Captain Warburton-Lee then drew off for a short consultation. The German ships had returned the fire, but had done no harm with either guns or torpedoes and their guns were apparently silenced. After an hour's fighting, no ships had appeared outside. Accordingly the flotilla went in again, this time keeping a mile outside the harbour, except the *Hostile*, which stood in to the entrance to fire her torpedoes.

So far, things had gone well. They had, without loss to themselves, sunk two destroyers, the *Schmitt* and the *Heidkamp*, and put out of action three more inside the harbour, besides sinking half a dozen merchant ships. Their good fortune was now to change; as the flotilla drew off after the last attack, to proceed down Ofot Fjord, they sighted, just before 0600, fresh ships coming from Herjangs Fjord. Captain Warburton-Lee reported them as a cruiser and three destroyers, adding 'am withdrawing to westward'. In actual fact they were the three destroyers, *Wolfgang Zenker*, *Erich Giese* and *Erich Koellner*, which after disembarking their troops had anchored off Elvegaard. It was not until about 0520 that they received the message sent out by the *Lüdemann*: 'Alarm: attack on Narvik'. Weighing anchor immediately, they made at full speed in the direction of Narvik, sighting the British force at 0540. The *Hardy* and her accompanying destroyers increased speed from 15 knots to 30 knots, engaging the new enemy at a range of some 7,000 yards. Then out of the mist ahead appeared two more ships three or four miles off, apparently coming in from the sea. At first it was hoped in the *Hardy* that the newcomers might be British cruisers; they were in fact the German destroyers *Bernd Von Arnim* and *Georg Thiele*, which had been lying at anchor to the west of Narvik in Ballangen Fjord. It was not long before the heavier German guns[72] began to take their toll; they disabled the *Hardy*, which beached herself on the south shore of Ofot Fjord, 7 miles from Narvik.[73] They sank the *Hunter* and disabled the *Hotspur* which drifted on to her sinking consort, exposed to the fire of four enemies, before she managed to get clear. The *Hostile* and *Havock*, 2 miles ahead and practically untouched, turned round to help. The Germans, says Commander Wright of the *Hostile*, were 'zigzagging across the *Hotspur*'s rear, doing target practice at her at a range of about 8,000 yards, surrounding her with splashes'; but the German ships had not escaped damage, and at 0625 the *Thiele* and *Arnim* retired with some of their guns out of action; the remaining destroyers also soon fell back and the three British ships withdrew unhindered. Thus the fight ended at 0630. Half an hour later, as they were on their way out some 25 miles west of Narvik, a large ship appeared out of the snow and mist. This was the German ammunition ship *Rauenfels*. The *Havock* opened fire; she ran herself ashore on the south side of the fjord and blew up when a benzene tank was hit. The loss of her supplies was severely felt by the Germans.

Of the British force, two ships had been sunk, one disabled and its gallant leader killed.[74] German casualties[75] were two destroyers sunk and five damaged; the flotilla had also destroyed half a dozen merchantmen, in addition to the *Rauenfels*, but unfortunately not the large supply ship *Jan Wellem*, which had been lying by the pier and provided stores for many a day.

Operations in Vest Fjord area   (Plans 5 and 7)

Admiral Whitworth received Captain Warburton-Lee's signal, that a cruiser was chasing the flotilla, soon after 0600/10. He sent in the *Penelope* to help, at the same time ordering the four destroyers of his screen to join her, and he told Captain Yates of the *Penelope* 'support retirement of 2nd Destroyer Flotilla, counter-attacking enemy force as necessary. Then establish a patrol off the minefield with the object of preventing further enemy forces reaching Narvik'. Captain Bickford, already by the minefield, sent in his only fully-armed ship, the *Greyhound*, on his own account at 0800, and she met Commander Layman's three ships near Tranøy about an hour and a half later. Commander Layman then decided to go in the *Hotspur* to Skjel Fjord, 50 miles away to the westward in the Lofoten Islands, taking also the *Hostile* to look after the cripple. Captain Yates agreeing when he came up about 1100, the two ships made their way to that haven, which was soon to shelter other cripples.

Admiral Whitworth elaborated his arrangements in the following signal to Captain Yates, timed 1116/10:–

'Present situation. Enemy forces in Narvik consist of one cruiser, five destroyers and one submarine. Troop transports may be expected to arrive through Vest Fjord or through Inner Leads, disregarding minefield.

Your object is to prevent reinforcements reaching Narvik. Establish a destroyer patrol between positions 67° 47' N., 14° 20' E., and 68° 2' N., 13° 40' E., one destroyer also to patrol north-east of minefield during daylight.

Enemy submarine may operate in Vest Fjord. Enemy may debouch in force to attempt to drive you off prior to his reinforcements arriving. Establish warning and A/S patrol 30 miles north-eastward of your patrol line.

Renown and *Repulse*, unescorted, will operate in vicinity of 67° N., 10° E.

Report your dispositions.

Oiler *British Lady*, escorted by *Grenade*, Encounter, are due Skjel Fjord, 68° N., 13° 15' E., p.m. 12 April. This fjord may be used for *Hotspur* if required.'

The destroyer patrol line was 20 miles long, right across Vest Fjord, roughly 10 miles above Skjel Fjord on the north and the minefield on the south side. As it turned out, the *Greyhound* and *Havock* attacked a submarine during the afternoon near the mouth of Vest Fjord, Captain

Yates having sent them down the fjord before receiving the above signal; whereupon Admiral Whitworth ordered them to hunt 'for at least 24 hours – submarine must on no account be allowed to escape'. This left the four big destroyers and the three minelayers at Captain Yates's disposal.

At 1254, however, Admiral Whitworth received a signal (timed 0808/10) from the Commander-in-Chief, ordering him to 'concentrate on allowing no force from Narvik to escape'. As this changed the object, so Admiral Whitworth changed his dispositions (1511/10 to *Penelope*):–

> 'Your object is now to prevent escape of enemy forces from Narvik through Vest Fjord or possibly through Tjeldsundet. Endeavour to maintain a warning destroyer patrol south of Tjeidøy with your main force north-west of Tranøy. If this position is untenable in dark hours, withdraw to south-westward of Tranøy.
>
> You have freedom to alter these dispositions according to weather, local conditions, and enemy counter moves.'

That evening the Admiralty informed the Commander-in-Chief of the policy for the immediate future in A.T. 1904/10, of which the following is an extract:–

> 'As enemy is now established at Narvik, recapture of that place takes priority over operations against Bergen and Trondheim. Expedition is being prepared as quickly as possible, and you will be further informed when plan and time table are completed. In the meantime it is of primary importance to prevent Narvik's being reinforced by sea. Possibility of seizing and holding a temporary base near Narvik with small military force is under urgent examination: in the meantime, you will presumably arrange for a temporary refuelling anchorage in the north. As Narvik must also be of primary importance to the Germans, it seems possible that battlecruisers may turn up there.'

But the Admiralty was anxious to try another naval attack without delay on the enemy ships (believed to consist of two cruisers and half a dozen destroyers) at Narvik, and had already ordered Admiral Layton to send three ships of the 18th Cruiser Squadron – then on their way to Scapa –

with eight destroyers, as soon as they had completed with fuel. These orders were countermanded, as Admiral Layton's ships would be needed to conduct the expedition mentioned in A.T. 1904/10 (above), and the *Penelope* was told off instead (A.T. 2012/10):–

'If, in light of experience this morning, you consider it a justifiable operation, take available destroyers in Narvik area and attack enemy tonight or tomorrow morning.'

And Captain Yates answered (*Penelope* to Admiralty, 2310/10):–

'Consider attack is justifiable, although element of surprise has been lost. Navigation dangerous from wrecks of ships sunk today, eliminating chance of successful night attack. Propose attacking at dawn on Friday (12 April), since operation orders cannot be got out and issued for tomorrow in view of present disposition of destroyers on patrol.'

These signals came to Admiral Whitworth for information only. Still, he felt bound to point out that the ships under his orders had been given three different things to do: to prevent the Germans from escaping from Narvik, to prevent fresh forces from joining them, and to attack them there. 'In my view', he says, 'the situation required clarifying', so he made this signal to the Admiralty, timed 2219:–

'Your 2012/10 April to *Penelope* appears to conflict with the policy outlined in your 1904/10 April, not to *Penelope*, which, in my view, is the correct one under the circumstances.

Further casualties to ships now under my command will jeopardize the prevention of reinforcements reaching Narvik.'

The Admiralty stood by their plan, telling Captain Yates they should 'back whatever decision you make' and approving his attack at dawn on 12 April. But certain occurrences during the night 10/11 April, reported by the *Bedouin*, Senior Officer in Ofot Fjord, raised misgivings, and at 0930/11, Captain Yates signalled to the Admiralty:–

'Senior Officer, Destroyers, reports, while on patrol last night south of Tjeidøy, he approached Baroy Island Light. Several loud explosions took place in his vicinity. The explosions were of a different character and appeared to indicate controlled minefield and shore-fired magnetic torpedoes. Activity was also observed ashore at Baroy Island. The indications were that shore defences were fully prepared. He withdrew his patrol to south-west. He is of opinion that the operation on the lines of yesterday's attack could not be carried out effectively.

In light of this report, I concur, and regret I must reverse decision given in my 2310/10.'

Nevertheless, the Admiralty still hoped to bring off this attack. They told Captain Yates to 'have all preliminary preparations made in case carrying out of attack on enemy forces in Narvik is ordered'. Unhappily, the *Penelope* ran on shore that afternoon on her way to Bodø, and was out of action in consequence for a long time to come. Next day the Admiralty ordered an attack on a different scale.

Rumours of German reinforcements had reached Admiral Whitworth in the meantime through Commander Wright at Skjel Fjord. The Norwegian police there told him that a man-of-war had been seen in the evening of 10 April in Tennholm Fjord, some 50 miles south of the minefield; that a large German tanker was lying there, hoping for a pilot to take her to Narvik; and that several big German merchantmen 'believed to be transports' had arrived at Bodø, at the mouth of Vest Fjord. The Admiral 'considered the first duty of the force under my command remained the prevention of reinforcements reaching Narvik, of which these were apparently some. It also seemed possible that the ships were unloading at Bodø'. Accordingly, he told Captain Yates to 'get a pilot at Tranøy. Take two destroyers and firstly attack enemy transports reported at Bodø ... and secondly, try and capture tanker at Tennholm ...Warship reported at Tennholm must be considered. You should endeavour to be back on your patrol by dark today', 11 April – this last, presumably, that the *Penelope* should be in time to attack Narvik next morning. Then, 'lest there should be doubt as to his first object' Admiral Whitworth added, 'attack on enemy transports must take precedence over attack on Narvik'. The *Penelope* took the *Eskimo* and *Kimberley* with her; but failed to find a pilot at Tranøy, Captain Yates went on to try at Fleinvaer, a few miles from Bodø at the mouth of the outer fjords, meaning to go in without a pilot should he fail again in finding one.

There, however, about 1500/11, the *Penelope* struck a rock. She soon floated off, but had injured herself seriously, and made her way to Skjel Fjord in tow of the *Eskimo* with considerable difficulty. Meanwhile, Captain Yates sent the *Kimberley* up to Bodø, where she learnt that one German merchant ship only had been to the port since the invasion, and that was the *Alster*, which the *Icarus* had captured early that morning while patrolling near the minefield in Vest Fjord with the other minelayers.[76]

The remaining destroyers continued to cruise that day 'to prevent reinforcements reaching Narvik'. Admiral Whitworth gave orders to Captain Bickford 'to control Vest Fjord' north-eastward of the patrol line he had prescribed in his orders to Captain Yates the day before, and to station a warning patrol between Tranøy and Tjeidøy. The Admiral himself continued off the Lofoten Islands with the two capital ships, stretching some 80 miles to the westward of Skomvaer. An Admiralty report of a possible German rendezvous in 67° N. between 4° 30' E. and 6° E. sent him further west to patrol to the northward of this position during the night (11/12); next morning he joined the Commander-in-Chief, who had been moving north from the Trondheim area.[77]

Movements of Commander-in-Chief, Home Fleet

(Plans 6 and 8)

Meanwhile the Commander-in-Chief held his north-easterly course throughout 10 April, altering to the eastward at 2000 that evening for a position some 90 miles north-west of Trondheim, whence the *Furious* was to fly off her aircraft to carry out the attack arranged between the Commander-in-Chief and the Admiralty, on the enemy ships there. These, according to R.A.F. reports consisted of two cruisers, besides destroyers and merchantmen. The last report received before the attack, timed 1645/10, placed a '*Hipper*' class ship at anchor off the town, and a '*Nürnberg*', at the head of the narrows in Trondheim Fjord, 10 miles to the westward.

In fact, when this report was made, the German units in Trondheim consisted of the *Hipper* and four destroyers, the *Paul Jacobi*, *Theodor Riedel*, *Friedrich Eckholdt* and *Bruno Heineman*. They had entered the fjord in the early hours of 9 April and by midnight had put all their troops ashore. At 1500/10 the *Hipper* and three of the destroyers were ordered to leave that night and return to Germany, but shortage of fuel prevented this, and eventually at 2100/10, the *Hipper* got under way, accompanied only by the *Eckholdt*. There was some delay owing to a submarine alarm in the fjord, and it was not till 0200/11, that she passed through Ramsöy Fjord (63° 30' N., 8° 12' E.) – which had been chosen as being less likely to be patrolled by the enemy, owing to its navigational difficulties – and shaped a north-westerly course at high speed to get clear of the land. The *Eckholdt* was ordered back to Trondheim, as she was unable to keep up in the heavy sea. It is interesting to note that had the *Hipper* been a couple of hours earlier her diversionary course would have taken her straight into Admiral Forbes' fleet on its easterly course at about 0200; as it was she passed unseen some 25 to 30 miles to the westward, while the *Furious* was flying off, and, passing through the waters lately traversed by the fleet, turned to the southward for Germany at 0740.

Accordingly when the 18 machines with torpedoes left the *Furious* at about 0400, in 64° 30' N., 8° E., some 90 miles from the town, to attack the German units reported in Trondheim they found the enemy cruiser – or as they believed, the two enemy cruisers – gone. While the fleet cruised north and south of the carrier, with a few destroyers watching the entrance to Fro Havet, the northern approach to Trondheim, the *Furious*'s airmen could see below them in the fjord only two destroyers and a submarine, besides merchantmen. The third destroyer seems to have escaped detection, and the other, the *Eckholdt* which had set out with the *Hipper* on the previous night, did not return until 0530 that morning. The British aircraft attacked both the destroyers they had sighted, but several torpedoes grounded in shallow water, exploding before they reached their targets and the attack was without success.

The 'disappointing result' caused Admiral Forbes to order a 'proper reconnaissance' of Trondheim by two machines, armed with bombs to attack the men-of-war after they had reported what they found in the fjords: they sighted two destroyers, one of which they attacked unsuccessfully, some seaplanes, and a few merchant vessels.

The result was disappointing indeed; yet it was not the airmen's fault, as Captain Troubridge of the *Furious* pointed out in his letter of proceedings. At the end of the month, when the *Furious* went home, he wrote of these young officers and men; 'All were firing their first shot, whether torpedo, bomb, or machine gun, in action; many made their first night landing on 11 April after their first attack at Narvik, and, undeterred by the loss of several of their shipmates, their honour and

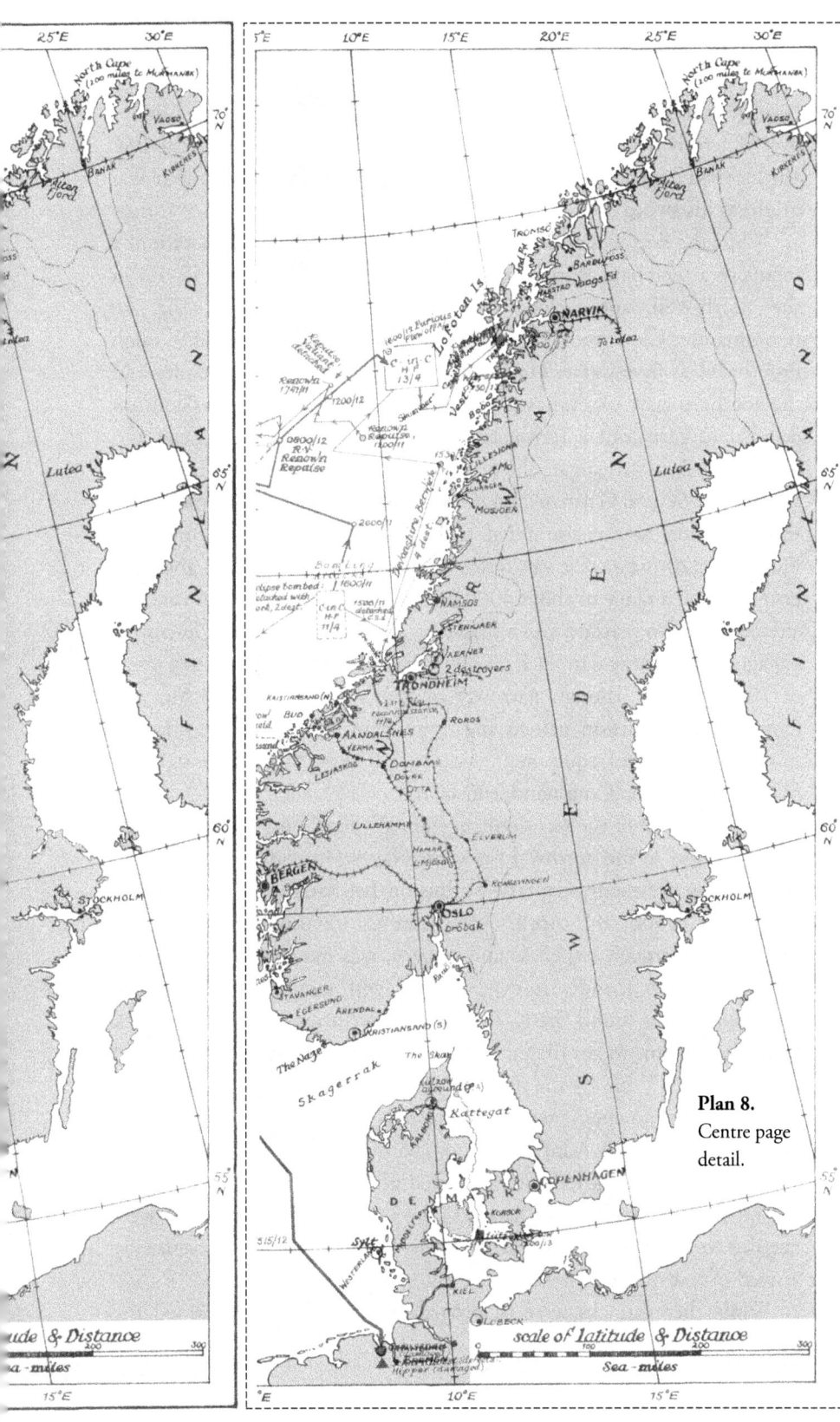

Plan 8. Centre page detail.

courage remained throughout as dazzling as the snow-covered mountains over which they so triumphantly flew' – a tribute reminiscent of Lord St. Vincent's saying of an earlier Thomas Troubridge that 'his honour was bright as his sword'.

While the fleet was cruising in the offing during these air operations a report of a merchant ship near Mausundvaer (63° 51' N., 8° 45' E.) in the north-west approaches to Trondheim was received. The *Isis* (Commander Clouston, S.O.) and *Ilex* were ordered to proceed through Fröy Fjord to investigate. Having searched in the reported vicinity and the southern part of Frohavet without success, Commander Clouston decided to carry out a reconnaissance up Inner Trondheim Lead and Skjorn Fjord, to investigate the outer limit of the defences in Trondheim approach.[78] Several German aircraft were sighted, but no opposition from shore defences was encountered till shortly after entering Trondheim Fjord at 1320, when fire was opened from Brettingsnes, then abaft the port beam, at a range of about 3000 yards. Commander Clouston at once altered course to seaward and a smart engagement ensued, the destroyers engaging the battery with H.E. as they retired under smoke, up to a range of 10,000 yards. Though narrowly missed, neither ship was hit, and Commander Clouston gained the impression that the battery lacked modern fire control equipment. Course was then shaped through Fro Havet to rejoin the Commander-in-Chief.

On the return of the reconnoitring aircraft, the Commander-in-Chief shaped course to the northward towards Narvik, intending to launch an air attack on the enemy Captain Warburton-Lee had fought the morning before. At 1500, 11 April, Vice-Admiral Cunningham with the *Devonshire*, *Berwick*, *Inglefield* and *Imogen*, was detached to search the Inner Lead from Trondheim to Vest Fjord, with instructions to mop up any enemy ships found there. The *Isis* and *Ilex*, then on their way back from Trondheim, were ordered to join this force. The search was carried up to lat. 66° 17' N., by the next day and later on north of Narvik as far as Tromsø, but no enemy was encountered.

Half an hour after Admiral Cunningham parted company, enemy air attacks on the fleet started and continued till 1700. The destroyer *Eclipse* was hit and her engine room flooded. The *York*, *Escort* and *Hyperion* were detailed to stand by her and escort her to Lerwick, where she eventually arrived in tow of the *Escort* on 17 April.

While these attacks were in progress, the Admiralty informed the

Commander-in-Chief (A.T. 1607/11) of a possible enemy rendezvous in the coming twenty-four hours in 67° N., between 4° 30' E., and 6° E. This position was about 150 miles to the north-westward of the Commander-in-Chief, and about half that distance to the south-westward of Vice-Admiral Whitworth, who reported that he was in 67° 50' N., 8° 11' E., at 1741, steering 235° at 24 knots. That night (11/12) the Vice-Admiral patrolled to the northward of the possible rendezvous, while the Commander-in-Chief having reached 65° 43' N., 8° 50' E., at 2000, steered 290° (taking him about 45 miles to the southward of it) till 0445/12, when he altered course to the northward to join the battlecruisers. The junction was effected at 0730 in about 67° N., 6° E. Nothing was seen of any enemy ships; on the contrary, Air Force reports which soon began to come in placed both German battlecruisers and one cruiser in 57° 31' N., 4° 52' E. (off the south-west corner of Norway) at 0857/12, steering 142° at 15 knots. The battlecruisers 'had thus managed to pass all the way from north of the Lofoten Islands to the Skagerrak without being sighted by any of our air or surface vessels',[79] and were then beyond our reach, almost back in their home waters. A brief account of their movements during the invasion period will be found in the following section.

Movements of German Naval Forces (Plans 6 and 8)

After outdistancing the *Renown* in the morning of 9 April, Admiral Lütjens with the *Gneisenau* and *Scharnhorst* had stood to the northward till 1200, when course was altered to west along the parallel 70° N. The general situation as he knew it decided Admiral Lütjens to make the return journey to Germany independently of the Narvik and Trondheim groups, keeping well to the westward and after turning homeward passing close to the Shetlands. Owing to a technical defect in the *Gneisenau* the signal which he sent giving this intention failed to reach the Naval Group Command, West, and at 0800, 10 April, the latter asked him to report his position and intentions. Admiral Lütjens was then in position 69° N., 5° 30' W. (to the north-east of Iceland); he did not wish to give away his position, so at noon sent the *Scharnhorst*'s aircraft to Trondheim with orders to make the report called for three hours after leaving him. This report crossed a signal sent by Group Command, West, at 1500:–

'All available cruisers, destroyers and torpedo boats are to proceed to sea tonight. Narvik destroyers are to concentrate with the Commander-in-Chief. It is left to your discretion whether *Hipper* with three destroyers join you or break through and proceed direct to Home port.'

The Narvik destroyers were unable to put to sea, partly owing to damage inflicted by the 2nd Flotilla, but mainly owing to shortage of fuel; they consequently remained in Narvik, with disastrous results to themselves.

Admiral Lütjens anticipated an alteration to these orders as a result of his signal by the aircraft, but he altered course at 1630 to 105° and steered for the rendezvous between Vest Fjord and Trondheim. When at 2238/10, he received the expected approval of his intentions, he altered course to the south-west, and at 0400/11 – just as the *Hipper* was clearing the Home Fleet 300 miles to the eastward, and the *Furious* was flying off for the abortive attack on Trondheim – he hauled round to the southward. Admiral Lütjens was aware from enemy reports that the main British naval concentration was off the Norwegian coast, in the Trondheim and Lofoten areas; this, combined with the weather – rain and short visibility – facilitated the passage of the battlecruisers, and at 1200/11, being then some 75 miles to the northward of the Faeroes, they altered course for home, and passing 40 miles to the eastward of the Shetlands during the night of 11/12, effected a rendezvous with the *Hipper* 0830/12. It was at this moment that the British reconnaissance aircraft appeared, and shortly afterwards intercepted messages warned the Germans that bombers were on their way to attack them, but the weather seriously deteriorated, visibility fell to under a mile and no contact occurred. That evening the formation reached the Jade without incident.

Mention has been made of how the cruisers at Bergen, Kristiansand and Oslo fared; the only other important unit – the *Lützow* – after the check at Drøbak on 9 April, had anchored off Oslo in the forenoon of 10 April. That afternoon she left for the return journey to Kiel; owing to the danger of enemy submarines, she proceeded southwards at high speed through the western waters of the Skagerrak. On 11 April, at 0029, a torpedo, fired by the British submarine *Spearfish*, struck the *Lützow* aft, seriously damaging and putting out of action her rudder and propellers, tearing a considerable hole in the ship's side and flooding the after part.

The ship drifted before the wind in a south-westerly direction, towards the Skaw, heavily down by the stern. At 0400 she was met by boats of the 17th A/S Flotilla, and the 19th Minesweeper Flotilla, which formed an A/S escort, took her in tow, and kept her head round, for it was feared that the heavy sea then running would break her stern right off. Most of the crew were taken off by patrol boats; the *Lützow* eventually reached Kiel on the evening of 13 April, and was out of action for twelve months.

Furious Aircraft Attack at Narvik (Plans 5 and 8)

After meeting Vice-Admiral Whitworth in the morning of 12 April, the Commander-in-Chief steered to the northward for the Lofoten area. Detachments were again reducing the strength with the flag. The *York* and two destroyers escorting the damaged *Eclipse* had left the fleet the previous afternoon, as had two other destroyers sent in to fuel. Vice-Admiral Cunningham's force was still searching the fjords. And from this time another commitment was influencing the Commander-in-Chief's dispositions – the hastily organised Allied expeditions to Norway. These will be dealt with separately,[80] but the first convoy (N.P.1) consisting of the SS *Empress of Australia*, *Monarch of Bermuda*, and *Reina del Pacifico* had sailed from the Clyde on 11 April, being joined next day off Cape Wrath by the SS *Batory* and *Chrobry* from Scapa, and was steering for Narvik accompanied by Vice-Admiral Layton in the *Manchester*, with the *Birmingham*, *Cairo*, five destroyers and the *Protector*.[81] On the same day (12 April) General Mackesy, commanding the land forces, with an advance party consisting of half a battalion of the Scots Guards, sailed from Scapa in the *Southampton*, and Admiral of the Fleet the Earl of Cork and Orrery hoisted his flag in the *Aurora*[82] and sailed from Rosyth to take charge of the naval side of the combined operations at Narvik,[83] though news of this appointment did not reach the Commander-in-Chief, Home Fleet, till the early hours of 14 April (A.T. 2314/13).

In order to ensure the safe passage of Convoy N.P.1, the Commander-in-Chief detached the *Valiant*, *Repulse*, and three destroyers in the afternoon of 12 April, with orders to meet it, after which the *Valiant* was to provide cover to Vaagsfjord, while the *Repulse* and destroyers proceeded to the base for fuel.

Thus in the afternoon of 12 April, the Commander-in-Chief had with him only the *Rodney*, *Warspite*, *Renown*, *Furious* and six destroyers, while twelve destroyers were working in the southern approaches to Narvik.[84]

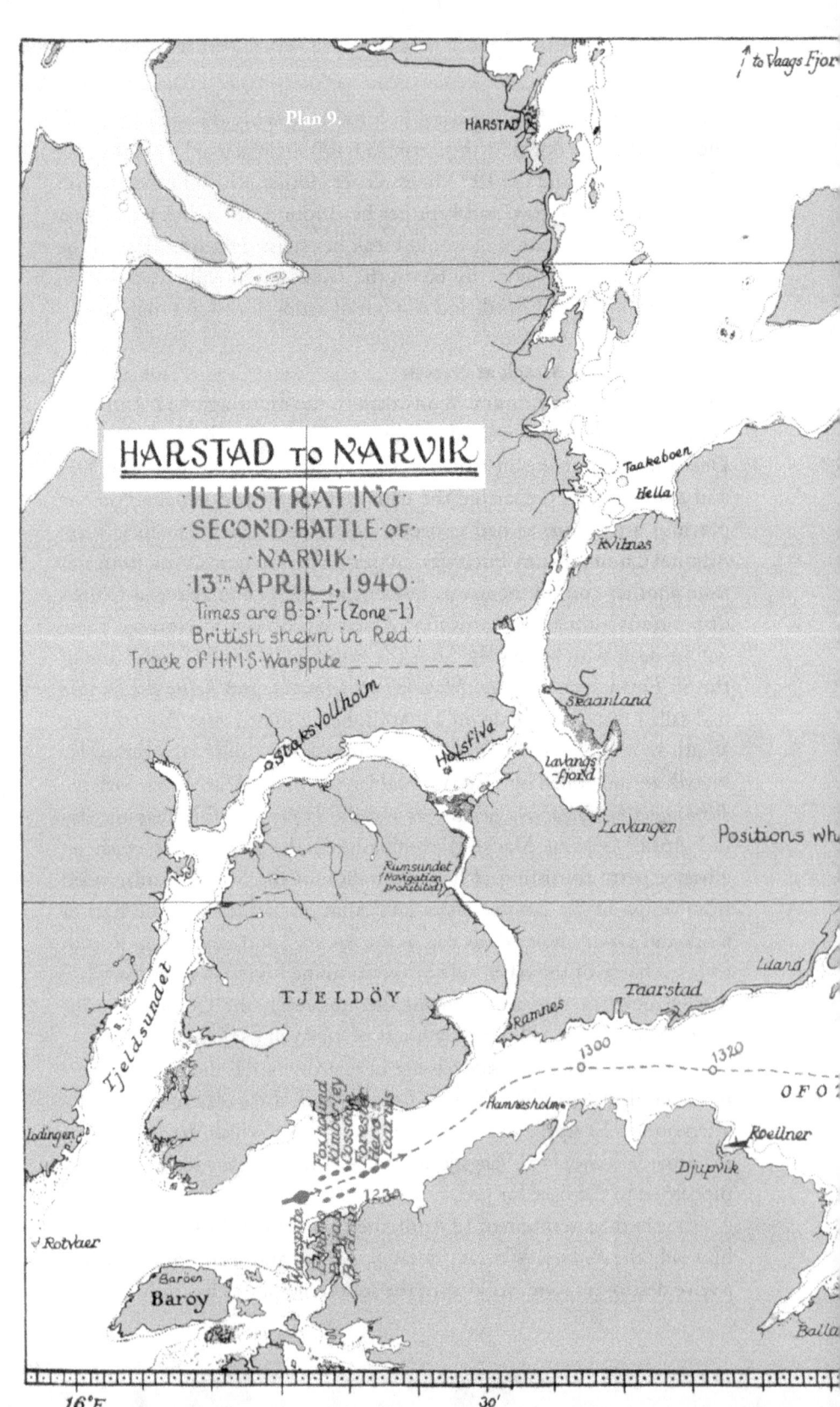

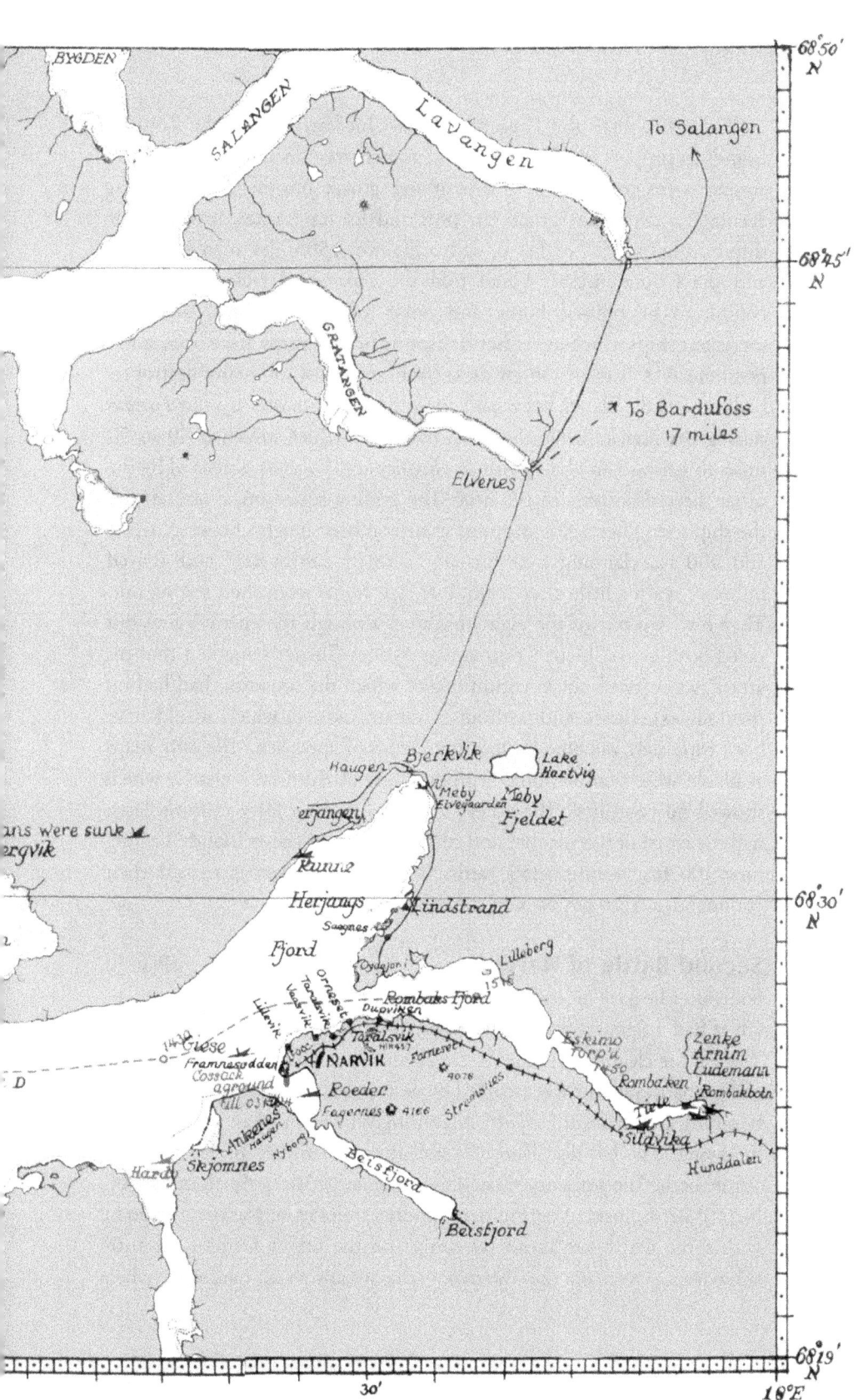

With this force the Commander-in-Chief arrived off the Lofoten Islands to support the *Furious*, whose aircraft were to attack Narvik. The aircraft were to make a dive-bombing attack on the shipping that evening, and to photograph the port and its approaches, leaving their ship in roughly 68° N., 11° E, with a flight of 150 miles or so each way; and the Commander-in-Chief told the *Furious*, 'Attack on ships in Narvik to be pressed home and hope to hear all ships, including merchant ships which are either transports or storeships, have been sunk; no shore A/A batteries so far as known, and most of enemy destroyers badly mauled'. The *Renown* and three destroyers stood by the *Furious* during the attack, while the Commander-in-Chief stretched 40 to 50 miles to seaward and back with the *Rodney* and *Warspite*, screened by the other three destroyers in the fleet. The leading squadron of aircraft left the ship soon after 1600, dropped their bombs at heights between 1,200 and 400 ft., claiming four hits on German destroyers,[85] and arrived onboard again a little after 2000, just four hours from their setting out. They lost two out of the eight machines through the enemy's fire, but saved both crews. Lieut-Commander Sydney-Turner remarked that his attack 'was carried out in conditions of which the squadron had had no previous experience and without a reconnaissance, which would have been extremely valuable in deciding tactics of approach. The only maps available were photographic reproductions of Admiralty charts, which showed no contours'. The other squadron, starting forty minutes later, had the worst of the weather and turned back near Baroy Island. 'Ceiling now 100 ft., visibility 250 yards, very heavy snowstorms', said their commander. They got back in the dark at 2030.

Second Battle of Narvik (Plan 9)

Soon after he gave his instructions for the air attack, the Commander-in-Chief had a signal from the Admiralty to attempt Narvik again by sea:– 'Orders for cleaning up enemy naval forces and batteries in Narvik by using a battleship heavily escorted by destroyers, with synchronized dive-bombing attacks from *Furious*'. Accordingly, he planned an attack for the following day by the *Warspite* and nine destroyers under Admiral Whitworth. The squadron would assemble at 0730 13 April, in 67° 44' N., 13° 22' E. inside Vest Fjord, a hundred miles from Narvik, and go in with some destroyers ahead sweeping and the others forming an anti-submarine screen for the *Warspite* – the sweeps to be hauled in when within 10 miles of Narvik. The *Warspite* would go 'to a position 5 miles from Narvik, depending on circumstances, and from there cover the advance of the destroyers into the harbour and adjacent waters where enemy ships may be located'. The *Furious*, cruising outside with the Commander-in-Chief, had orders to send aircraft to attack shore defences supposed to be on Baroy Island and by Ramnes and the opposite shore in the narrows of Ofot Fjord, and others to attack the ships and batteries in and near Narvik. These attacks would 'synchronize with *Warspite*'s approach' and had stated times in the orders, which Admiral Whitworth was to alter should there be need; but he managed to keep them unchanged. The Commander-in-Chief with the *Rodney*, *Renown*, *Furious* and five destroyers would cruise outside the Lofoten Islands some 30 miles off shore, in the vicinity of 68° N., 11° 30' E. There were also four destroyers at or near Skjel Fjord.[86]

Admiral Whitworth shifted his flag to the *Warspite* in the night, 12/13, after the *Renown* and *Furious* returned to the fleet, and sailed for the rendezvous inside Vest Fjord with the *Cossack*, *Hero*, *Foxhound* and *Forester*. There the *Bedouin* and *Punjabi*, *Kimberley* and *Icarus* joined, while the ninth destroyer, the *Eskimo*, remained patrolling near Tranøy Light, some 60 miles farther in. This was fortunate, for shortly before 1100/13, she sighted a submarine between her and the squadron, then just coming in sight. The submarine dived, and the *Eskimo* and some destroyers of the screen drove it down with depth charges over the area from which it could threaten the *Warspite*. A bomber from the *Furious* duly met the squadron off Baroy soon after 1200, but neither the aircraft nor the *Warspite* could see anything to attack there. Soon afterwards the blackened bow of the *Rauenfels* was passed, a grim reminder of what lay before them. Meanwhile the *Warspite* had sent up her own aircraft to scout, a service it did to perfection. 'I doubt', says the Vice-Admiral, 'if ever a shipborne aircraft has been used to such good purpose'. It first reported a German destroyer off Hamnesholm in the narrows, a dozen miles above the squadron, then another beyond the narrows: these were the *Hermann Künne*, and the *Erich Koellner*. The *Koellner*, although undamaged in the engagement on 10 April, had run aground in Ballangen Fjord shortly before midnight on 11 April; the damage sustained was severe and the ship was no longer seaworthy. Accordingly, it was decided to anchor her off Taarstad where she was to be used as a barrage-battery; she was on the way thither, escorted by the *Künne*, when sighted by the *Warspite*'s aircraft. The *Künne* immediately retired before the British ships, exchanging fire at 12,000 yards, the limit of visibility; the captain of the *Koellner*, realising that he could not accept action, headed for Djupvik Bay, on the south shore of the fjord (68° 24' N., 16° 47' E.), hoping from this position, at a range of 3,000 to 4,000 yards, to be able to use his torpedoes against the approaching squadron, before it could sight him and open fire. The *Warspite*'s aircraft had meanwhile flown to the head of Herjangs Fjord, 20 miles off, where it bombed and sank a submarine, the *U-64*, which fired at and hit the aircraft. On its way back, it sighted the *Koellner* putting into the Djupvik Bay, and its signals enabled the leading British ships to train guns and tubes to starboard, ready to engage the enemy the moment they passed the mouth of the bay. The *Koellner* fired her torpedoes and one salvo from her guns and was then smothered by the British fire; in addition, both the *Bedouin* and the *Eskimo* hit her with torpedoes, while her own torpedoes missed.[87]

It was then nearly 1330. The British ships were a dozen miles from Narvik, looking for the German destroyers in the haze ahead. When the *Künne* first sighted the British at the entrance to Ofot Fjord, she had signalled a warning to the other six destroyers, which were all at anchor in Narvik harbour. The S.O. of the 4th German Destroyer Flotilla, Captain Bey, who had taken over command of the group when Kommodore Bonte was killed on 10 April, immediately ordered them to put out to meet the enemy. The *Hans Lüdemann* was the first to leave, followed by the *Wolfgang Zenker*, and shortly afterwards by the *Bernd Von Arnim*; the *Thiele* and the *Giese* had not got sufficient steam to leave and the *Diether von Roeder* was too badly damaged to move. *U-51*, in harbour at the time, submerged, under the impression that it was an air-raid, but evidently put out into Vest Fjord later on.

As the three German destroyers left the harbour they met the *Künne*, and all four turned so as to fire their torpedoes. Commander Biggs of the *Hero* describes the action outside Narvik harbour in the following words:–

'From 1300 to 1355, *Hero* engaged three separate enemy destroyers with her two foremost guns at ranges between 10,000 and 15,000 yards. During this period it is estimated that only six hits were obtained on enemy ships. This was largely due to the large number of ships firing at a few enemy destroyers from practically the same bearing, which made the picking out of own fall of shot extremely difficult. It was also due to the fact that only the two foremost guns could be brought into action, owing to the restriction imposed by the *Hero*'s being guide of the fleet and also employed on sweeping duties.

Owing to her duties as guide of the fleet, which necessitated long periods on a steady course at a steady speed, *Hero* appeared to be practically continuously under fire, but the ship was not hit except for one small splinter.'

The German destroyers outside the harbour, which were later joined by the *Thiele*, were gradually forced back; German reports claim, however, that up to this point, after an engagement lasting 1½ hours, with the exception of the *Koellner*, sunk in Djupvik Bay, none of their destroyers had been hit. If this was the case, their end came all very suddenly; at 1350 they received the order: 'Retire up Rombaks Fjord'.[88] The *Künne* apparently failed to pick up this message, for she made for Herjangs Fjord; there she beached herself off Troldvik, and her crew were sent to reinforce the 139th German Mountain Regiment, which was defending the area north of Narvik. The *Eskimo*, following hard in her track, came up and torpedoed her, while the other British units were attacking the *Giese*, which had just raised enough steam to leave the harbour: her guns were silenced and she was set on fire in a few minutes, close inshore, north of the harbour, where her captain gave the order to abandon ship at 1330. The *Punjabi* was badly hit at this time and withdrew with main steampipe and guns out of action, but reported herself fit for service an hour later. The *Warspite* was engaging the enemy whenever a target presented itself but, owing to the smoke of the destroyer engagement, fire was intermittent. Speed was adjusted to maintain support of the destroyers, and to keep the flagship clear of the torpedo danger as far as possible.

According to the plan of attack, aircraft from the *Furious* should have joined the battle at this stage. Her aircraft had come punctually over Baroy Island, but the one for Ramnes and Hamnesholm had failed to get beyond Baroy, the weather being very thick when it arrived there. The striking force over Narvik, ten Swordfish under Captain Burch, R.M., 'fought their way', as Captain Troubridge has it, 'through the narrows into Ofot Fjord with a ceiling of 500 ft. and snow squalls that occasionally reduced visibility to a few yards'. As they came to the open fjord, the weather improved, and they arrived at exactly the proper moment. They dived from 2,000 ft. to drop their bombs at 900 ft. – about 100 bombs, of which one in three were 250-pounders, and the rest 20-pounders. They claimed two hits with the large bombs on German destroyers outside Narvik at the cost of two aircraft.[89]

The British destroyers then divided, some going into Narvik harbour, while others chased the enemy up Rombaks Fjord. The *Cossack*, followed later by the *Foxhound* and *Kimberley*, went inside the harbour, where there remained only the crippled *Diether von Roeder*, which they sank after a short but fierce exchange of fire, but not before she had obtained four hits on the *Cossack*, one in No. 2 boiler room cutting the main steam pipe and severing the telemotor leads. Unable to manoeuvre, the *Cossack* went aground 50 yards south of the lighthouse at the entrance; there she remained until 0315 next morning.

The *Foxhound* stopped to rescue survivors from the *Erich Giese*, which lay burning outside the harbour, and the *Kimberley* then joined the other part of the flotilla. The *Eskimo* had seen the Germans make off into Rombaks Fjord, so went after them with the *Forester* and *Hero*, followed by the *Bedouin* and *Icarus*. Five miles in, the fjord narrows to a neck only a quarter of a mile across, opening beyond the neck, but still in places only half a mile wide. The British ships went up the fjord through a smoke cloud laid by the retreating enemy, the *Warspite*'s aircraft keeping them posted about the German destroyers' movements. The leading ships entered the inner fjord, where they sighted and engaged two of the last four German warships afloat in the area; one of them, the *Georg Thiele*, turned to fire her remaining torpedoes, and in doing so ran on shore, disabled, at Sildvika, three miles or so beyond the neck of the fjord; but one of her torpedoes struck the *Eskimo* right forward, blowing off her forecastle as far as abaft 'A' gun. Her 'B' gun's crew, though badly shaken by the explosion, 'magnificently continued firing as if nothing had happened. It looked as if the *Eskimo* would sink immediately'.[90] The *Eskimo* fired her last torpedo, which missed, and then steamed stern first back through the narrows till the wreckage of her bow struck the bottom and brought the ship up. The *Forester* stayed by her, while the *Hero* and *Icarus*, joined by the *Kimberley*, which had come round from Narvik, went on to the head of the fjord.

There, a mile or two beyond Sildvika, they found the last three German destroyers. All seemed deserted, and after a few rounds had been fired to make sure, the survivors of their crews were seen wending their way up the valley. One destroyer, which proved to be the *Hans Lüdemann*, was on an even keel, and the *Hero* and *Icarus* sent armed whalers to examine her. As they approached, another slowly turned over and sank, revealing the third scuttled and aground inshore of her. The whalers took possession of the *Lüdemann* and the white ensign was hoisted above the Nazi flag; she was 'resting on the bottom, upright, with the engine room flooded. There was a fierce fire burning in the tiller flat and it appeared the depth charges might explode any moment.'[91] A swift search for secret matter proved fruitless; all that was found was a mass of charred papers, still burning, on the bridge.

When these last two actions began, the *Warspite* was about 5 miles west of Narvik, slowly following the destroyers, and firing at what seemed at first to be a battery on shore, but proved to be the destroyer alongside in the harbour. The Admiral ceased fire when the *Cossack* and her consorts went inside, and lay off the entrance until that fight was finished. Then he went into the outer part of Rombaks Fjord and ordered all the destroyers available to concentrate in the fjord. This was about the time of the *Eskimo*'s torpedoing and her retreat stern first through the narrows, leaving little room for other ships. The *Hero* and *Icarus* went on through, as we have seen; so did the *Bedouin*, which then reported, at 1520, 'one aground out of action, two more round the corner out of sight (there were actually three). If they have torpedoes, they are in a position of great advantage. *Hero* and *Bedouin*, ammunition almost exhausted. *Bedouin*, 'A' mounting out of action'. On this the Admiral ordered the *Bedouin* out to close him, and when she came in sight he told her to arrange a fresh attack, 'sending most serviceable destroyer first: ram or board if necessary'. Accordingly, the *Bedouin* went in again, stern first this time, as she had four guns aft, but only two fit for action forward. She joined the *Hero*, *Icarus* and *Kimberley* at the head of the fjord about 1630, and ordered the torpedoing of the *Hans Lüdemann* which, although on shore, still remained upright. As soon as the Prize Crew had been taken off and the White Ensign hauled down, a torpedo was fired at her which broke her back and set her on fire forward. 'Had these four enemy destroyers', remarks Commander Biggs of the *Hero*, 'been determined to make one last stand in the farthest end of the inner Rombaks Fjord, and had they been resolutely commanded, it might well have been an expensive business to destroy them, as not more than two

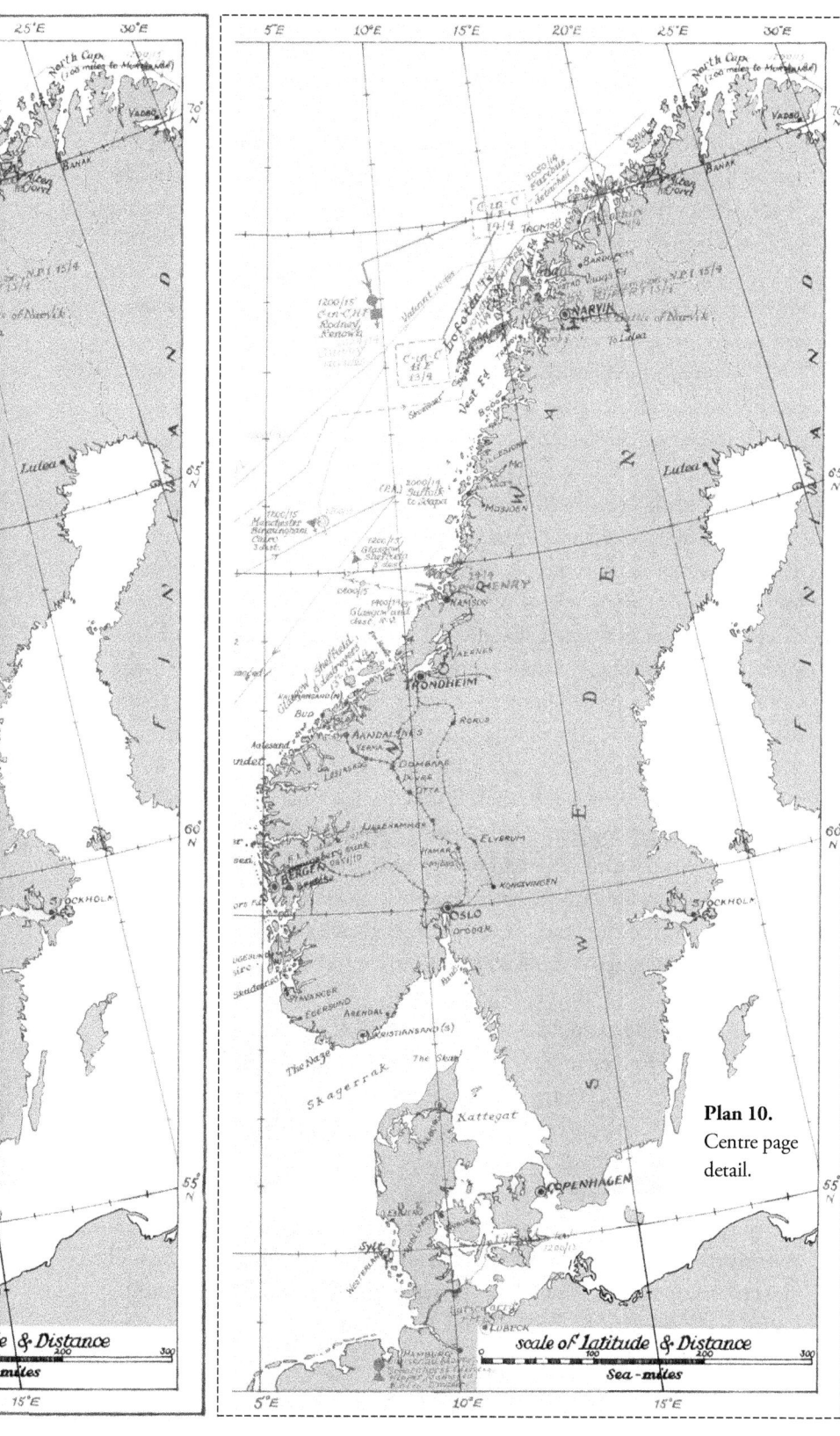

Plan 10. Centre page detail.

of our ships under way could have operated against them at any time.'[92]

Thus ended the second Battle of Narvik. The risks of running the enemy to earth in the confined waters of the fjords had been correctly assessed and boldly accepted, and the result proved an outstanding success. The Germans lost their eight remaining destroyers and the U-boat (*U-64*) sunk by the *Warspite*'s aircraft; their garrison at Narvik was for the time being virtually isolated, and, moreover, the British squadron had found no sign of serious defences established on shore.

The *Warspite* then returned off Narvik. Finding it quiet there at 1730, except for a mild exchange of fire between the grounded *Cossack* and a small gun or two on shore, Admiral Whitworth 'considered the landing of a party to occupy the town, as the opposition had apparently been silenced'. But, his report goes on, 'with the force available only a small party could be landed, and to guard against the inevitable counter-attack, it would be necessary to keep the force concentrated, close to the water front, and to provide strong covering gunfire: in fact, I considered it would be necessary to keep *Warspite* off Narvik'. Then a German officer taken prisoner by the *Foxhound* spoke of submarines in the fjords, and German aircraft appeared, a dozen coming in sight at 1800. 'Apart from the above conditions, I felt that to place, at the end of a long and strenuous day, a party of less than 200 tired seamen and marines in the midst of a force of not less than 2,000 professional German soldiers would be to court disaster, even allowing for the moral effect which the day's engagement must have had on the enemy. The cumulative effect of the roar of *Warspite*'s 15-in. guns reverberating down and around the high mountains of the fjord, the bursts and splashes of those great shells, the sight of their ships sinking and burning around them must have been terrifying...'

That moral effect would not last. To take full advantage of it 'would have required a trained organised military force, ready to land directly the naval engagement had ceased. If such a force had been present, I believe that they would have succeeded in establishing themselves so strongly in Narvik that its eventual capture would only be a matter of time and reinforcements. I thereupon decided against keeping *Warspite* stopped in the fjord off Narvik, subject to submarine and air attack'. Admiral Whitworth started down the fjord accordingly with the *Warspite* and most of his destroyers about 1830, leaving one or two ships to stand by the injured *Eskimo* in Rombaks Fjord and *Cossack* in Narvik; but hearing there were wounded men in the ships left behind, he soon turned back that they might come onboard the *Warspite*, and this took up the rest of the night.[93]

Meanwhile, A.T. 2115/13 had urged on Sir Charles Forbes the 'occupation of town of Narvik to ensure unopposed landing later'. Whether this signal reached Admiral Whitworth does not appear in his report. However, knowing that a regular expedition was on its way to Vaagsfjord, the outer approach to Narvik from the northward, and thinking this expedition might be diverted direct to Narvik, he made this signal to the Commander-in-Chief and the Admiralty (2210/13):–

> 'My impression is that enemy forces in Narvik were thoroughly frightened as a result of today's action, and that the presence of *Warspite* was the chief cause of this. I recommend that the town be occupied without delay by the main landing force.
>
> I intend to visit Narvik again tomorrow, Sunday (14 April), in order to maintain the moral effect of the presence of *Warspite*, and to accept the air and submarine menace involved by this course of action.'

Next day the Admiralty asked for an account of the German strength at Narvik, to which Admiral Whitworth answered (1027/14):–

> 'Your 0913. Information from Norwegian sources estimates 1,500 to 2,000 troops in Narvik. German naval officer prisoner states that there are many more than this, but I think this statement was made with intent to deceive. He also states that guns on shore are being positioned with the main object of opposing a landing, but *Cossack*, aground in Narvik Bay for 12 hours yesterday, was not seriously molested.
>
> My 2210/13. I am convinced that Narvik can be taken by direct assault without fear of meeting serious opposition on landing. I consider that the main landing force need only be small, but it must have the support of Force B (his present squadron) or one of similar composition: a special requirement being ships and destroyers with the best available A/A armaments.'

That morning, the squadron went out into Vest Fjord, leaving the *Ivanhoe* (which had joined from Skjel Fjord the evening before) and the *Kimberley* for the time being at Narvik, with orders to prevent the discharge of cargo, which might include stores and munitions for the German garrison, from several merchantmen, some of them German, which had been left afloat there in the hope of our being able soon to carry them off as prizes. If necessary they were to be sunk; but both destroyers had to leave the port that day, the *Ivanhoe* going to hunt a submarine reported in Vaagsfjord, and there the matter stood.[94]

The *Cossack*, *Eskimo* and *Punjabi* went to Skjel Fjord for repairs before going home; the rest of the squadron stayed in Vest Fjord to meet Lord Cork and to be 'ready to operate against Narvik when required' says Admiral Whitworth. However, the time for that was not yet come, and on 15 April he took the *Warspite* out, and met the Commander-in-Chief in the evening when a redistribution of destroyers was effected; he then cruised to the westward of Skomvaer Light, having orders from Sir Charles Forbes to keep outside Vest Fjord, 'unless required for an operation'. He had three destroyers[95] with the *Warspite* and six working in Vest Fjord, while by this time others had arrived with the expedition.

The Commander-in-Chief himself departed for Scapa the same evening with the *Rodney*, *Renown* and six destroyers,[96] the *Furious* having gone north the day before to oil at Tromsø, carrying out an air reconnaissance of the northern approaches to Narvik on the way.

Cruiser Operations 10/14 April   (Plans 3, 4 and 5)

While the operations off the coast of Norway described in the foregoing sections were taking place, the ships of the 2nd and 18th cruiser squadrons[97] which had returned to Scapa on 10 April had not been idle.

At 0134, 11 April, Vice-Admiral Layton received orders to detail a cruiser to take General Mackesy and an advance party to the Narvik area. He had already been warned by telephone from the Admiralty that his force would probably be required to cover an expedition to Narvik, and at 1032/11 orders arrived from the Commander-in-Chief, Home Fleet, requesting him to organise a force of two cruisers and six destroyers[98] to operate in the south part of the Indreled, sweeping northward along the coast from Aalesund.

Various conferences with General Mackesy, the Commanding Officers and others concerned, were held by Admiral Layton on 11/12 while the ships completed fuelling, ammunitioning and making good defects. The *Glasgow* (Captain Pegram, Senior Officer) and *Sheffield*, with the *Somali, Mashona, Afridi, Sikh, Matabele* and *Mohawk* sailed for the inshore operation at 2000/11; and next day, as already mentioned, Admiral Layton sailed with the *Manchester* and *Birmingham*[99] to meet convoy N.P.I, the *Southampton*, screened by the *Electra* and *Escapade*, with General Mackesy and the advance party having left a few hours previously for Vaagsfjord, where she arrived without incident on 14 April.

Admiral Layton fell in with the troop convoy[100] off Cape Wrath at 1900, 13 April, and shaped course for Vest Fjord at 14 knots, being joined by the *Valiant* sent by the Commander-in-Chief, the *Vindictive* and three destroyers[101] from Scapa and three destroyers[102] from Sollum Voe next afternoon. The passage was uneventful, but at 1907/14 orders were received from the Admiralty diverting the troops in the *Chrobry* and *Empress of Australia* to Namsos. They were then in position 68° 10' N., 10° 20' E., (approximately 130 miles from Vaagsfjord). The convoy therefore divided, Admiral Layton with *Manchester, Birmingham, Cairo, Vanoc, Whirlwind, Highlander*, taking the Namsos detachment, and the remainder, with the *Valiant*, and 10 destroyers continuing for Vaagsfjord. Their further proceedings will be dealt with later.

At just about the time the convoy split, the first British landing on Norwegian soil was taking place. This was by an advance party from the *Glasgow* and *Sheffield* at Namsos (Operation Henry). Captain Pegram's force had arrived off Stadtlandet in the afternoon of 12 April and swept to the northward along the coast of Aalesund. Further north, Vice-Admiral Cunningham's force[103] had reported Namsos and the neighbouring fjords clear on 12 April and then proceeded to rejoin the Commander-in-Chief off the Lofoten Islands. Meanwhile enemy reports from aircraft on 12 April had reported a pocket battleship, a cruiser and many merchant ships on Captain Pegram's station: these he was searching for early on 13 April when he intercepted a signal from the Admiralty to the Commander-in-Chief (A.T. 0216/13) proposing a landing from his two cruisers at Namsos in order to forestall the Germans.[104] Later that day he received orders to carry out this plan. His destroyers, however, which he had sent to Aalesund after the 'many large merchant vessels' (which turned out to be Norwegian) were delayed there, and the parties could not be landed till the evening of 14 April, after which the *Glasgow, Sheffield* and three destroyers cruised in the offing off Kya Light,

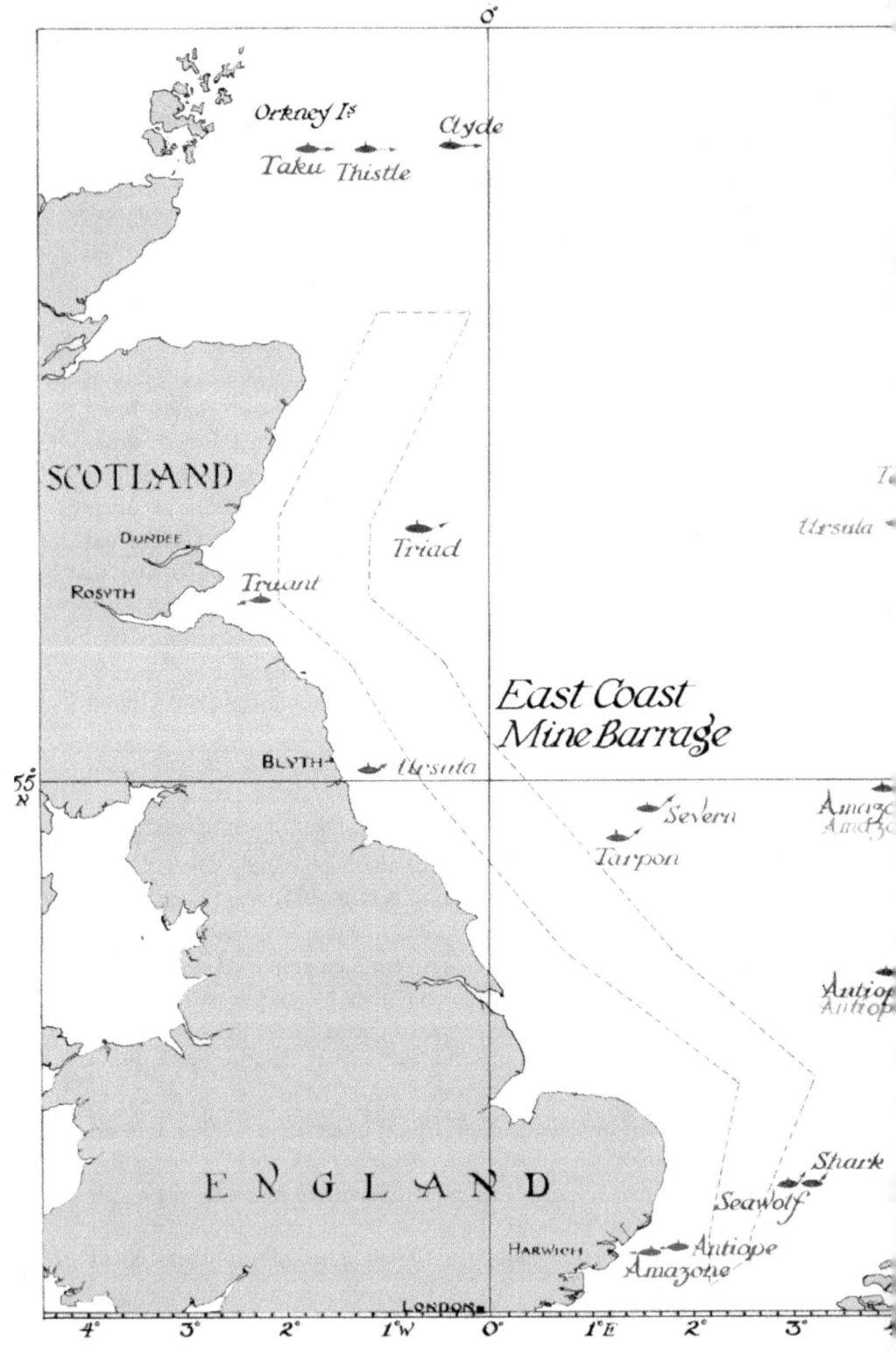

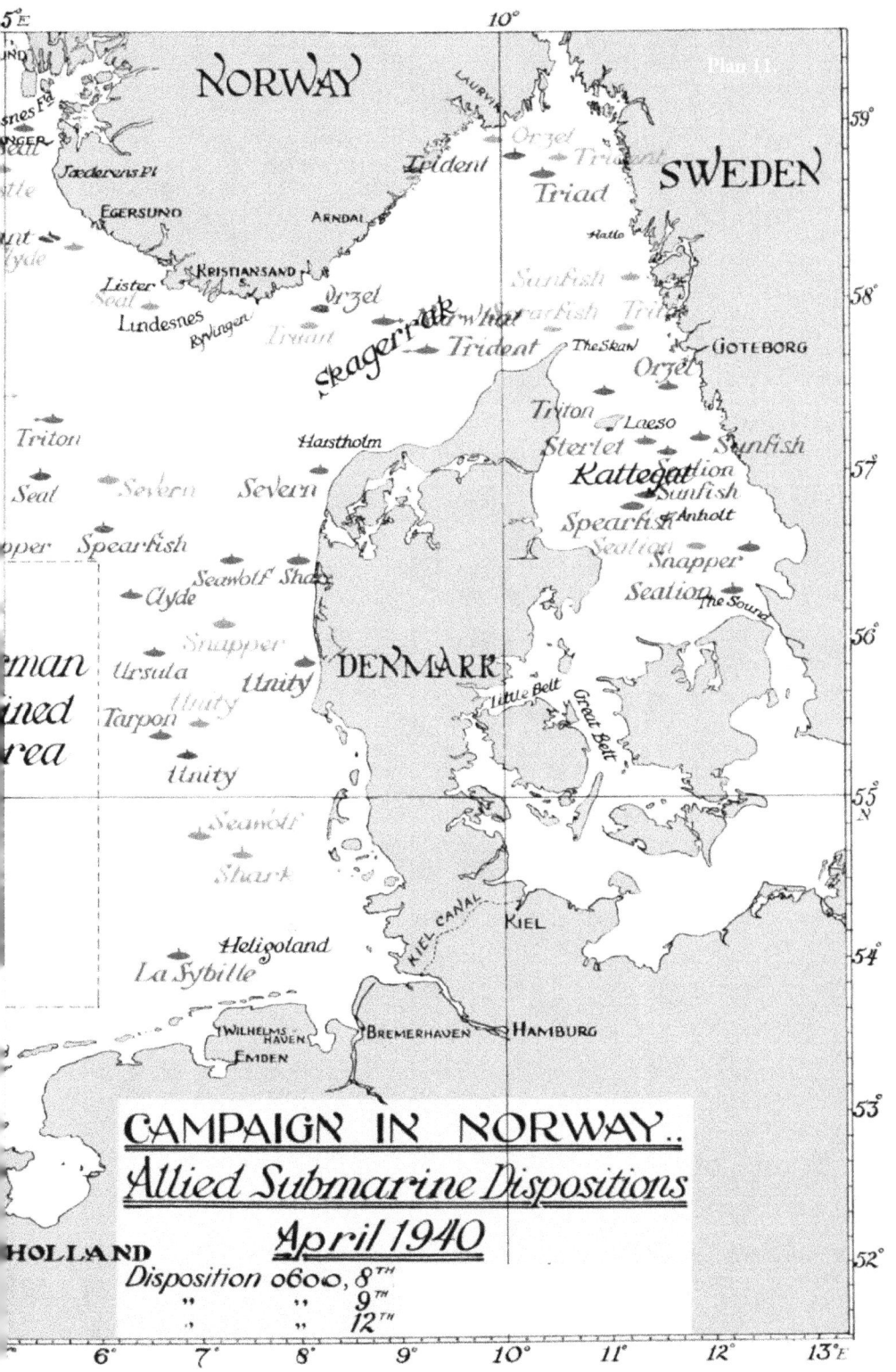

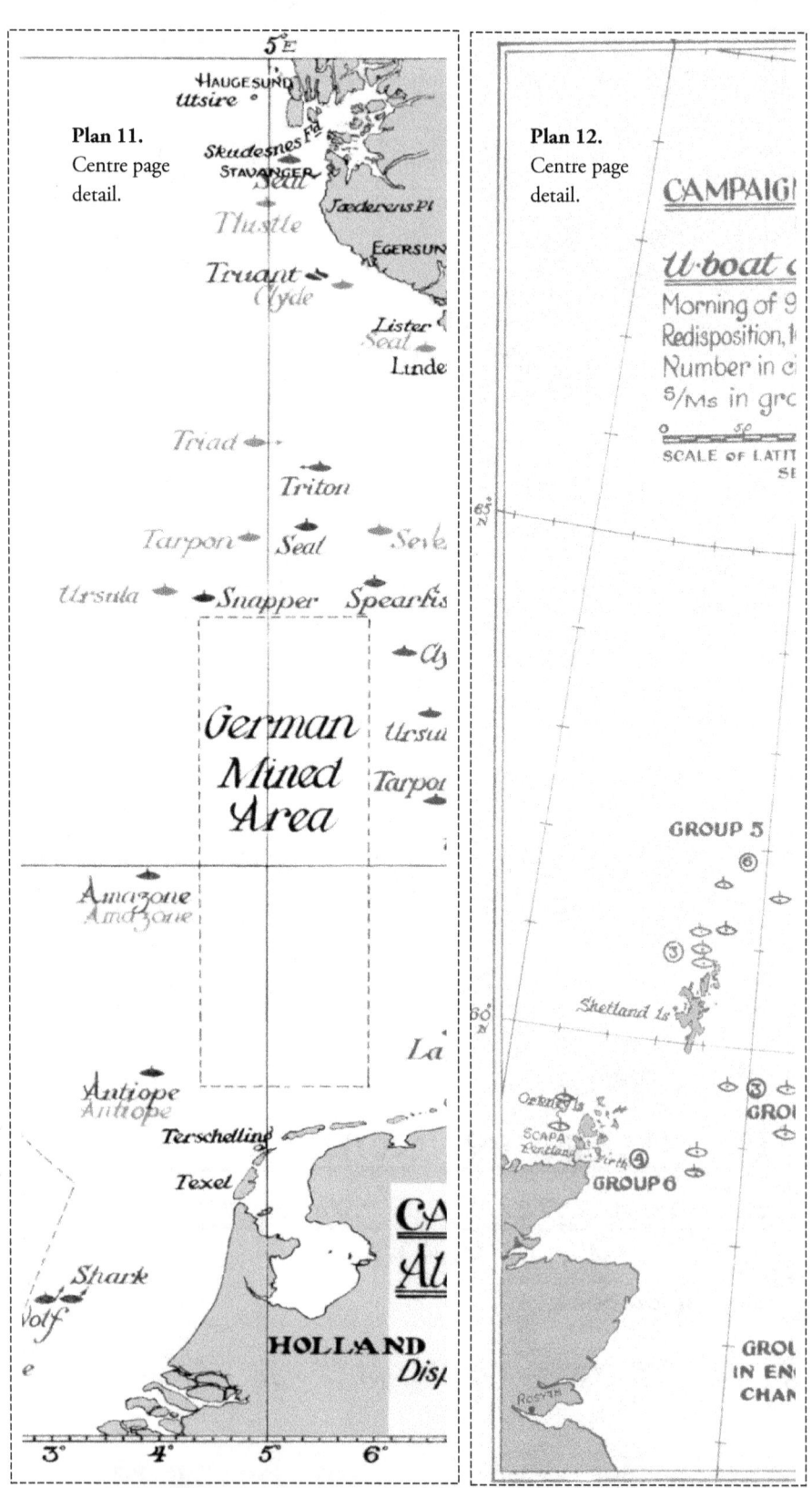

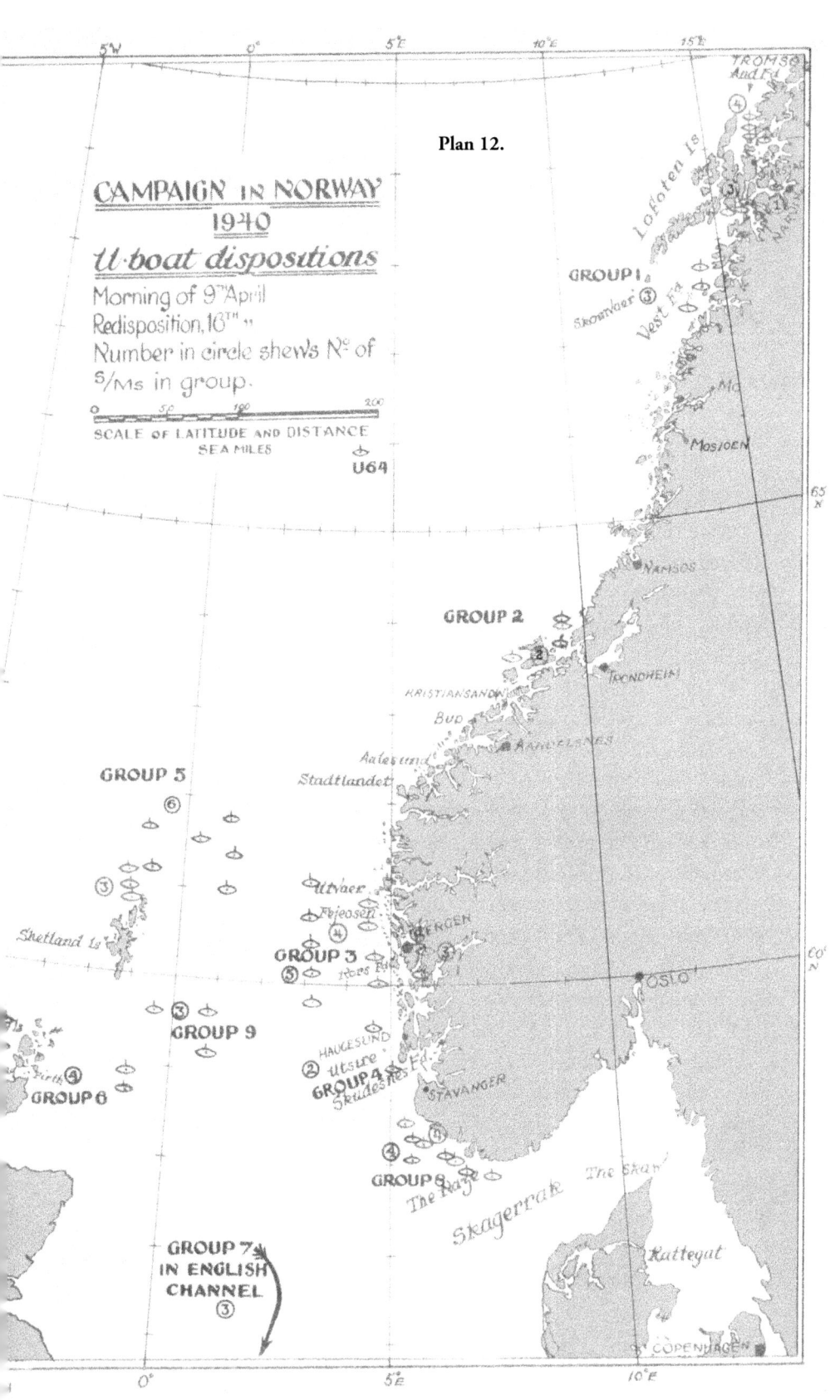

Plan 12.

subsequently joining Admiral Layton. Captain Nicholson (Captain D.6) with three destroyers remained at Namsos to arrange for the landing of the expedition on its way there and to meet General Carton de Wiart, V.C., the Military Commander, who was arriving by air.

Meanwhile Vice-Admiral Edward-Collins had received orders from the Admiralty at 1355, 11 April, to send one ship to Rosyth to hoist the flag of Admiral of the Fleet Lord Cork.[105] He chose the *Aurora*; she left Scapa at 1700 that day, embarked Lord Cork the next forenoon and sailed again at 1300, arriving, after an uneventful passage, at Skjel Fjord on 14 April. Admiral Edward-Collins left Scapa with the *Galatea* and *Arethusa* at 1200, 13 April, for Rosyth, to embark troops for a landing at Namsos (Operation Maurice). Brigadier Morgan and the battalions of the first flights embarked in the two cruisers and the transport *Orion* on 14 April, but delays in embarking a battery of A/A guns in the latter delayed their sailing. That evening the instructions were given to divert part of Admiral Layton's convoy to Namsos, and Admiral Edward-Collins' force remained at Rosyth till 17 April when it sailed for Åndalsnes[106] (Operation Sickle).

While these steps were being taken in the effort to retrieve the situation in Norway, possible repercussions from the occupation of Denmark had to be considered, and it was decided to lose no time in making sure of the Faeroes. HMS *Suffolk* (Captain Durnford) had just completed repairs at Govan when the invasion occurred. She accordingly embarked a force of 250 Royal Marines with two 3.7-in. howitzers at Greenock on 12 April, and sailed that night at high speed for Thorshavn, arriving there next afternoon whither she had been preceded by the destroyers *Hesperus* and *Havant*, which had carried out an anti-submarine search in the vicinity. With the assistance of a couple of trawlers, the *Northern Sky* and *Northern Foam*, all personnel and stores were landed by 2130 on 13 April and the *Suffolk* then sailed for Vest Fjord to join Vice-Admiral Cunningham. Next forenoon, being then in 64° 5' N., 2° E., she fell in with the German tanker off Skagerrak, which was scuttled by her crew to avoid capture. The *Suffolk* then continued on her way to the Lofotens, but that evening she was recalled by the Admiralty (A.T. 1935/14) to Scapa to prepare for a bombarding operation (Operation Duck) in support of the projected landing at Åndalsnes.

Meanwhile Vice-Admiral Cunningham, with the *Devonshire* and *Berwick* had been covering his four destroyers[107] while they searched fjords from Trondheim to the northward during 11 and 12 April. No enemy was encountered, but the *Isis* met the Norwegian gunboat *Nordkapp* in Aluangen (66° 3' N., 12° 55' E.) who informed her that she had sunk a German tanker.[108]

At 1530/12, the destroyers rejoined the cruisers in approximately 66° 30' N., 11° 30' E., and the force then steered for the possible enemy rendezvous between 4° 30' E., and 6° E. in 67° N. as given in A.T. 1607/11,[109] afterwards rejoining the Commander-in-Chief, Home Fleet, at 0930, 13 April off the Lofoten Islands. The destroyers were then sent to Skjel Fjord to fuel, and the cruisers remained with the flag till that afternoon, when they were again detached, this time to investigate conditions at Tromsø (Commander-in-Chief, H. F. 1717/13) being joined by the same four destroyers at 0700/14, in 69° 30' N., 16° 05' E.

Admiral Cunningham sent the *Berwick* with the *Inglefield* and *Imogen* to examine Ands Fjord, Vaagsfjord and various inlets in the neighbourhood of the proposed landing place of the Narvik expedition, while he himself in the *Devonshire* with the other two destroyers proceeded to Tromso, where he arrived at 1500/14. There he made contact with the British Vice-Consul,[110] the Norwegian S.N.O., Captain Bredsdorff, and the G.O.C. of the district, General Fleischer. From them he learned that the situation there was quiet, and that the Norwegian authorities were confident of their ability to repel any German attempt to land from captured fishing boats or small craft; also that considerable quantities of oil fuel were available in the port. After making various arrangements, such as the broadcasting of enemy reports, Admiral Cunningham sailed with the *Isis* and *Ilex*[111] that evening for Kirkenes, in compliance with orders from the Commander-in-Chief (C.-in-C. 1716/14), being joined early next morning (15 April) by the *Berwick* and *Inglefield* off North Cape. The Force arrived at Kirkenes[112] at 1600 that afternoon, sailing for Tromsø the same evening as cover for a Norwegian troop convoy; a second convoy was escorted by the *Imogen* a couple of days later.

Admiral Cunningham remained in these northern waters, based on Tromsø, cooperating with the Norwegian authorities, and working with the *Furious* in operations in connection with the arrival of the Narvik Expeditionary Force (Rupert), until 19 April, when he sailed for Scapa (in response to an urgent signal from the Commander-in-Chief) with the *Berwick* and *Inglefield*.

Submarine Activities[113] 4/14 April   (Plans 7 and 8)

While the focus of the Allied naval effort had thus been moving to the north, the southern area had not been entirely neglected. As already mentioned the weight of the German air attacks on the Home Fleet in the afternoon of 9 April[114] had convinced the Commander-in-Chief of the impossibility of operating surface forces off the southern coasts of Norway without incurring very serious losses. It was therefore left to the Allied submarines to do what they could against the German sea communications with the southern ports. And fine work they did, though it was impossible for them unaided to cut the seaborne pipeline from Germany across the narrow waters of the Skaw and Skagerrak to Norway.

Special submarine dispositions had been ordered on 4 April, with the object of covering the ports involved in the operations under Plan 'R.4', should they be ordered, and on the night of 8 April they were disposed as follows:–

3 in the Kattegat, *Sealion, Sunfish, Triton.*
2 in the Skagerrak, *Trident,* ORP *Orzeł.*
1 entering Skagerrak, *Truant.*
1 south-west of Skagerrak, 56° N., 6° E., *Seal.*
3 off west coast of Denmark, *Spearfish, Snapper, Unity.*
2 East of Dogger Bank, French *Amazone, Antiope.*
6 on passage from the United Kingdom to the eastward, *Severn, Tarpon, Clyde, Thistle, Shark, Seawolf.*

As a result of the reports on 7 and 8 April of the German fleet being at sea the Admiralty in the afternoon of 8 April, after discussion with the Admiral, Submarines (Vice-Admiral Sir Max Horton) had ordered fresh dispositions designed to intercept the enemy heavy ships, with the result that by the morning of 9 April the submarines were moving to cover the approaches to the German ports in the Heligoland Bight, leaving the Norwegian ports somewhat neglected. Admiral Horton, however, had for some time been convinced that the invasion of Norway by the Germans was imminent – an opinion confirmed by the sinking of the *Rio de Janeiro* on 8 April[115], and in his original orders, timed 1931, 4 April, had laid down that if warships and transports were encountered the latter were to be taken as the primary objective. This instruction was allowed to stand; and at 1324 the next day, 9 April, he signalled to the submarines that German merchant ships encountered in the Skagerrak east of 8° E. and in the area to the eastward of the German declared area should be treated as warships and sunk without warning.[116]

Actually, the submarines had already taken a hand in the game as evidenced by the sinking of the *Rio de Janeiro* by the *Orzeł* on 8 April. This was followed up the same afternoon by the sinking of the tanker *Posidonia*[117] (on her maiden voyage) in the mouth of Oslo Fjord by the *Trident*. That night several submarines encountered enemy squadrons and convoys coming out of the Baltic, though no successes were scored; but on 9 April the *Truant* sank the *Karlsruhe* off Kristiansand and on the night of 10/11 the *Spearfish* seriously damaged the *Lützow*[118] with a snap shot on the surface off the Skaw. During the first week of the operations (8-14 April), besides the ships mentioned above, seven other transports and merchant ships were sunk in the Skagerrak or Kattegat – four by the *Sunfish* and one each by the *Triad*, *Sealion* and *Snapper*, while the *Triton* made four hits on a convoy, though severe depth charge attacks prevented her from observing the results.

These successes were not gained without loss. On 10 April the Thistle, which had unsuccessfully attacked a U-boat the day before, was off Stavanger and her Commanding Officer reported his intention of attempting to enter the harbour. Nothing further was heard of her; it is now known that she was sunk by *U-4*. This loss was followed by the sinking by German A/S craft of the *Tarpon* off the west coast of Denmark[119] on 14 April.

The Germans, too, had made special submarine dispositions to cover their landing operations. Practically the whole of their available operational submarines were employed. Indeed, the almost total cessation of U-boat attacks on the Atlantic trade routes was one of the earliest indications that some large-scale operation was brewing elsewhere. They were disposed as follows:–

(A) Off Norwegian Ports
Narvik, 4 in Vest Fjord.
Trondheim, 2 (inner approaches).
Bergen, 4 (2 for each main entrance).
1 to cover Haugesund.

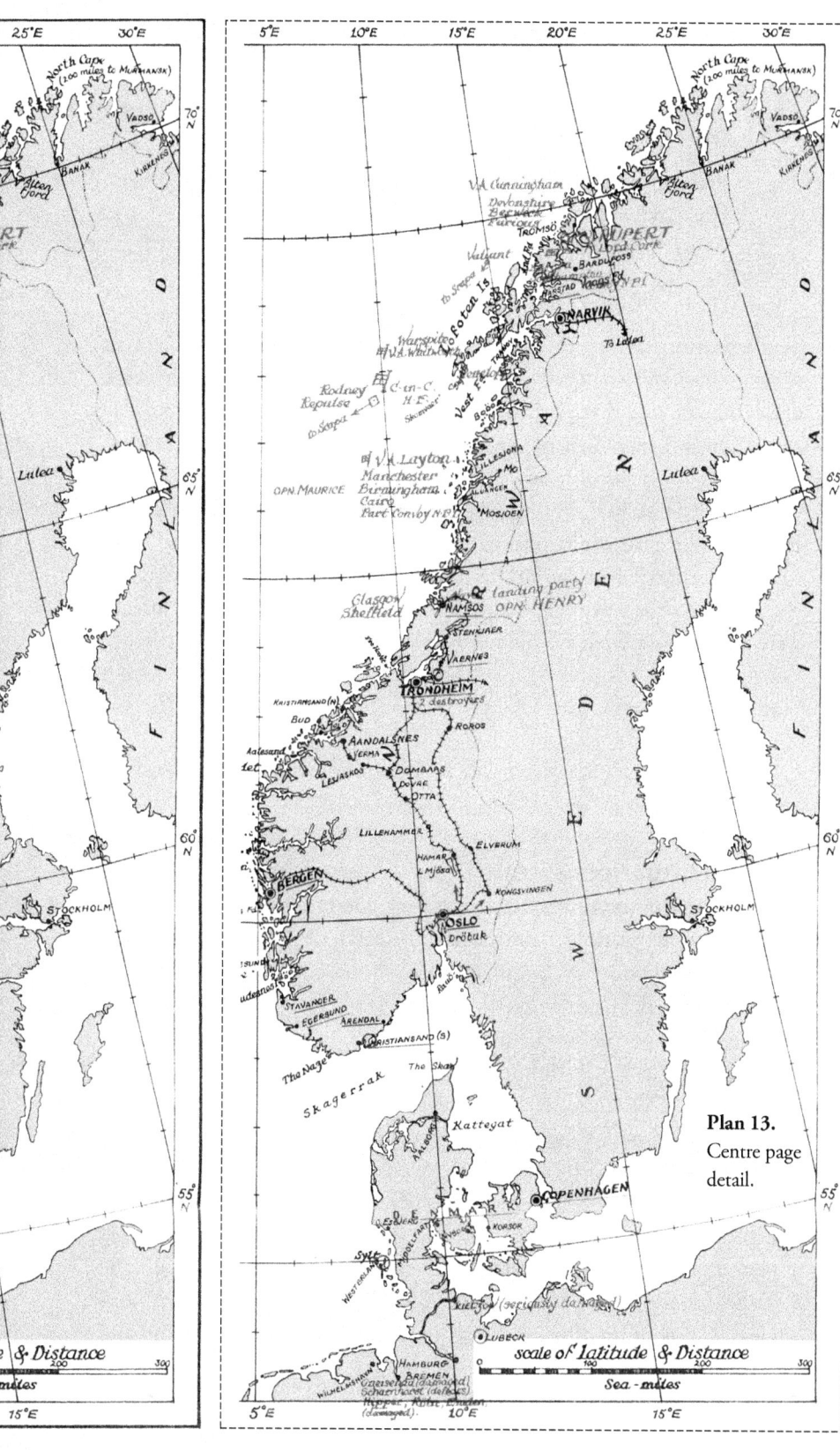

Plan 13. Centre page detail.

(B) Attack Groups
N.E. of Shetlands, 6.
East of Orkneys, 3 (small).
East and west of Pentland Firth, 4 (small).
West of the Naze, 3 (small).
In eastern part of English Channel, 3.

In contradistinction to the success of the British submarines, the German U-boats achieved practically nothing, only succeeding during the whole of April in sinking three British and two neutral merchant ships and one store transport (the *Cedarbank*). When at an early stage in the operations (15 April) their disposition fell into the hands of the British,[120] the Commander-in-Chief, Home Fleet, expressed satisfaction that such an effort should have accomplished so little. It is now known that their torpedoes suffered from serious technical defects.[121] But for this fortunate circumstance, the story might have been different. Actually, many attacks were made by experienced submarine commanders – but without result. On this subject Admiral Dönitz, then Flag Officer, Submarines, waxed bitter. An entry in his War Diary (15 May 1940) reads:–

'I do not believe that ever in the history of war men have been sent against the enemy with such a useless weapon.'

General Situation 15 April (Plan 6)

Vice-Admiral Whitworth's attack at Narvik and the operations described in the foregoing sections marked the conclusion of the first phase of the campaign. Hitherto the chief naval interest had centred on attempts to bring to action the German naval forces and to blockade the detachments in Norwegian ports. From this time onwards it lay in convoying and maintaining the hastily improvised expeditions which the Allies were sending to the succour of the Norwegians, and in inshore operations in support of the troops when landed. Before following the fortunes of these expeditions the first of which were just arriving in Norwegian waters, however, it will be convenient to take stock of the general situation at the conclusion of the first phase as it existed in the evening of 15 April.

In the northern area Vice-Admiral Whitworth was cruising off the Lofoten Islands in the *Warspite*, standing by to support the operations against Narvik of the expedition which had arrived with the *Valiant* and escort at Vaagsfjord that day. The *Valiant* remained in Vaagsfjord on patrol till 1900/15, when she sailed for Scapa, screened by three destroyers.[122] On the same day Admiral of the Fleet Lord Cork, wearing his flag in the *Aurora*, met General Mackesy for the first time in Vaagsfjord, who had arrived there in the *Southampton* the previous day.

Vice-Admiral Cunningham, with the *Devonshire*, *Berwick* and *Furious* was operating in the Tromsø area.

The Commander-in-Chief, Home Fleet, having remained cruising off the Lofoten Islands during 14 April and met Vice-Admiral Whitworth off Skomvaer next day, shaped course to the southward in the evening of 15 April with the *Rodney* and *Renown*, arriving at Scapa on 17 April. Since 14 April, he had been exchanging signals with the Admiralty on the possibility of a frontal attack on Trondheim, to discuss which Rear-Admiral Holland, who had been studying the problem in London, was proceeding to Scapa to meet him. This proposal will be dealt with in the next chapter, but it was already giving the Commander-in-Chief much to consider.

In the central area (Trondheim) Vice-Admiral Layton with the *Manchester*, *Birmingham*, *Cairo*, three destroyers and two transports was nearing Lillesjona, where he had been directed to transfer the troops to destroyers for passage to Namsos, temporarily occupied the day before by parties landed from the *Glasgow* and *Sheffield*, which remained cruising in the offing. Major-General Carton de Wiart, V.C., the military commander in this area, arrived in a flying boat at Namsos on 15 April, where Captain Nicholson in the *Somali* was awaiting him to discuss landing arrangements.

A landing party drawn from the *Hood*, *Nelson* and *Barham*, then in dockyard hands, had sailed from Rosyth in four sloops, the *Black Swan*, *Bittern*, *Flamingo* and *Auckland*, on 14 April and was storm-bound at Invergordon on its way to Åndalsnes (south of Trondheim). The *Suffolk*, on her way to join Admiral Cunningham in the Lofoten Islands, after landing the party in the Faeroes, had been recalled by the Admiralty to prepare for a bombarding operation in support of this landing, and arrived at Scapa in the evening of 15 April.

At Rosyth, Vice-Admiral Edward-Collins was embarking the second flight for Namsos – to be diverted next day to Åndalsnes – in the cruisers *Galatea* and *Arethusa* and the transport *Orion*.

Further afield, Vice-Admiral Wells (V.A.(A)) had been ordered to join the Home Fleet from the Mediterranean in the carrier *Glorious* and had left Gibraltar in the evening of 14 April; his usual flagship, the *Ark Royal* (soon to follow), was ordered to remain at Gibraltar for the time being.

Turning to the enemy, the situation was as follows. Their initial landings had gone almost exactly as planned. Their naval losses had been severe, but not higher than anticipated though the loss of Kommodore Bonte's ten destroyers at Narvik had been a bitter blow[123] – and their surviving main units were by this time all back in German ports.

The initial supply arrangements for the assault forces at the two northern ports,[124] however, had virtually broken down; only one out of the six camouflaged steamers which were to meet the landing parties on arrival reaching her destination. The *Rauenfels* with ammunition for Narvik had been blown up on 10 April, the *Alster* with mechanical transport had been captured, and the *Barenfels*, after being diverted to Bergen, was sunk there while discharging her cargo for Narvik by air attack on 14 April. Of the Trondheim group, the *Sao Paulo* was sunk by mine off Bergen and the *Main* by a Norwegian destroyer; the third ship, the *Levante*, eventually reached Trondheim on 12 April, three days late. Yet another supply ship had been sunk at Stavanger by the Norwegian torpedo boat *Sleipner*[125] on 9 April.

The tankers, too, had been unfortunate, only the *Jan Wellem* from Murmansk reaching Narvik as planned, the other two, the *Kattegat* for Narvik and the *Skagerrak* for Trondheim, having both been scuttled by their crews to avoid capture.

> 'The expectation of the Army and the Air Force to be supplied in time with guns, ammunition, equipment and provisions for the troops that had been landed in the northern harbours was therefore frustrated.'[127]

The German detachments in these two areas (Narvik and Trondheim) thus found themselves in a highly critical position until these deficiencies could be made good. The fate of their destroyers at Narvik, which had been unable to leave for want of fuel, left no doubt as to this. Intercepted Allied signals on 12 April had revealed the probability of an Allied landing at Namsos, and later messages indicated that another landing was impending at Vaagsfjord on 15 April. From the German point of view the fate of Narvik depended on holding the Trondheim area; 'the pivot of all operations was therefore Trondheim'[126] and the following directions were accordingly issued on 14 April.

(a) The Army (Group XXI) was to reinforce the garrison at Trondheim as soon as possible, taking possession of the railway Oslo–Dombaas and Åndalsnes.
(b) The Navy was to concentrate U-boats in the waters round Trondheim and Aalesund, and to arrange for the transport of the most important supplies by U-boats[127] to Trondheim.
(c) The Luftwaffe[128] to destroy enemy troops already landed; to prevent further landings in the Åndalsnes area; to occupy Dombaas with paratroops and to send airborne reinforcements to Trondheim.

Meanwhile, in the south, the follow-up troops and stores had arrived at their destinations between 9 and 12 April in the 1st Transport Division[129] – the ships sailing singly in disguise – more or less as planned. Losses[130] had occurred, from accident and enemy submarine attack, but not on a scale sufficient to cause serious interruption.

The 2nd Transport Division, sailing in convoy, lost two ships and a patrol vessel[131] to British submarines north of Gotenberg, but the remaining nine transports reached Oslo on 12 April; 900 troops, however, had been drowned and in future the passage of troops was restricted to fast warships and small craft using the shortest route between Jutland and the southern Norwegian ports. The 3rd Transport Division, 12 steamers carrying Army supplies, left home ports on 13 April and, sailing in five independent groups, arrived at Oslo 1–16 April after losing two ships.[132] Thereafter the build-up proceeded steadily,[133] the number of troops transported from Frederikshavn and Aalborg to Larvik and Oslo being about 3,000 a day.[134]

On shore the German troops were advancing from Oslo up the railway lines leading to Trondheim through Lillehammer and Dombaas in the west and through Kongsvinger, Elverum and Roros in the east. By 15 April the heads of their columns had reached Strandlokka near the southern end of Lake Mjösa and the western outskirts of Kongsvinger.

The Norwegian Army which numbered no more than six divisions, one of which was stationed in the extreme north, never had a chance to carry out an ordered mobilisation.[135] But by this time detachments were assembled at Storen and Steinkjaer in the Trondheim area. General Ruge had been appointed Commander-in-Chief on 10 April, but in the general confusion and with scanty communications had been unable to establish effective control.

The King of Norway, with the Crown Prince and the Government, closely pursued and ruthlessly bombed whenever their whereabouts became known to the enemy, had retreated north through Hamar, Elverum and Lillehammer, and had found a temporary resting place at Otta (south-east of Dombaas).

Hunted and harried though they were, so long as they remained at liberty, the German invasion was doomed to failure politically, whatever might be effected militarily by brute force. Already Quisling's attempt to form a government had proved abortive; rejected by his fellow countrymen and discarded by the Germans, he had given way to an 'Administrative Council' set up[136] (with the approval of the King) under the Lord Chief Justice of Norway as the Civil Authority in the parts of the country in German occupation, and soon to be replaced in its turn by the Reich Commissioner Terboven on 24 April.

On 26 April the German wireless announced – somewhat belatedly – that a state of war existed between Germany and Norway.

The Allied Counter Offensive and General Employment of Naval Forces

Plans and Policy (Plan 1)

While all this had been going on in Norwegian waters, plans to counter the German invasion were being concerted as rapidly as possible by the Allied Governments. 'Completely outwitted'[137] and forestalled as they were, their plans were necessarily improvisations; events proved that they were undertaken on a totally inadequate scale. The troops and ships earmarked for the discarded plan 'R.4' were at any rate available, but since the organisation and equipment of the troops had been designed for unopposed landings and the Germans were already in possession of the principal ports, new landing places had to be chosen; as already mentioned, the first convoy sailed from the Clyde two days after the German landings, with the Narvik area as its destination.

The first hint of the new plans to reach the Commander-in-Chief, Home Fleet, was contained in A.T. 0820 of 9 April[138] already referred to, which told him to prepare attacks on the German ships of war in Bergen and Trondheim and said 'we shall probably want to land a force' at Narvik. Some sixteen hours later, A.T. 0057/10 went a stage further:–

> 'The policy of the Allies is to give Norway as much assistance as possible. To do this it will be necessary to take Bergen and Trondheim. Narvik will also be taken. The order in which these operations will be undertaken has not been settled, but in the meantime it is important that no reinforcements of any kind should reach these three places.'

This signal crossed the signal 2231/9 which it will be remembered the Commander-in-Chief had sent giving his general ideas after the German air attack on his fleet that afternoon, in which he recommended attacking the enemy in the north with surface forces and military assistance, 'leaving the southern area mostly to submarines, due to German air superiority in the south'. With this view the Admiralty concurred in A.T. 1904/10:–

> 'As enemy is now established at Narvik, recapture of that place takes priority over operations against Bergen and Trondheim. Expedition is being prepared as quickly as possible, and you will be further informed when plan and time-table are completed. In the meantime it is of primary importance to prevent Narvik's being reinforced by sea. Possibility of seizing and holding a temporary base near Narvik with small military force is under urgent examination: in the meantime you will presumably arrange for a temporary refuelling anchorage in the north ...
>
> 'Admiralty consider that interference with communications in southern areas must be left mainly to submarines, air and mining, aided by intermittent sweeps when forces allow.'

As things turned out, no operations (other than air attack) were attempted against Bergen; and the Allied plan finally adopted was confined to landings in two areas – the Vest Fjord area in the north with Narvik as its objective and the Trondheim area some 300 miles further south. This necessarily entailed dispersion of force; indeed at first there seems to have been considerable indecision as to which area should constitute the main effort. The enemy, however, had no such doubts as to their main strategic object and concentrated all their efforts on securing Trondheim, with the result that the Allied forces landed in this area, which never attained a strength of above about 12,000 men, were forced speedily to withdraw.

The Narvik expedition eventually reached a strength of nearly 30,000, counting outlying detachments in the Bodø area – about 100 miles to the southward of Narvik – which, after the withdrawal from the Trondheim area, the Allies attempted to hold, in order to deny the Germans possible sites for airfields for operations against the Narvik expedition. This expedition was known as Rupert; its first units arrived at Harstad in the Lofoten Islands on 14 and 15 April, but it suffered various delays owing to weather and other causes and it was not until 28 May that the actual assault on Narvik took place. By that time Germany had overrun the Netherlands, which led to the decision to withdraw the British and French troops from Norway altogether.

In the central area landings were planned at Namsos, about 150 miles north of Trondheim by rail, and at Åndalsnes about the same distance to the south. It was hoped to initiate a pincer movement against Trondheim from these two areas, and by capturing the railway centre at Dombaas to seal off the town from the German forces advancing from the south. These expeditions were known respectively as Maurice (Namsos) and Sickle (Åndalsnes). Each was preceded by preliminary landings by naval parties in order to forestall the Germans and to ensure unopposed landings for the larger forces – Henry consisting of some 350 seamen and marines from ships then working in the neighbourhood at Namsos, and Primrose, about 700 men drawn from heavy ships in dockyard hands, with field howitzers, high angle pom-poms and two 4-in. guns of position, in the Åndalsnes area.[139]

It is to be noted that none of these expeditions was to land in the face of German opposition on shore. Rupert landed in Vaagsfjord, a long way from the enemy in Narvik. The orders for Henry said 'it is not intended that an opposed landing should be attempted' and the object of that landing was, 'to ensure an unopposed landing for Maurice at Namsos'. Similarly, Primrose and Sickle both had orders not to land if the Germans should be already in Åndalsnes.

The plans for the landings in central Norway were only gradually evolved, the first naval orders – which dealt with Namsos-being contained in A.T. 0216/13. The same day the Government decided to land a small party at Aalesund (approaches to Åndalsnes) to 'create a diversion' and to hinder the passage of the enemy through the Inner Lead in those parts; but as stated above this grew into an advance against Trondheim similar to that from Namsos.

The general intention of these landings was finally conveyed to the Commander-in-Chief, Home Fleet, by the Admiralty in the following signal, timed 2340/13:–

'(i) Government have now decided to land a force in the vicinity of Trondheim, so as to secure a footing from which that place can eventually be taken should it be decided to do so; and the following action is consequently being taken.

(ii) Operation Henry is being carried out.

(iii) A force of about 5000 men will arrive Namsos, probably a.m. 17 April, to hold a place and try and advance to Steinkjaer. This will be known as Operation Maurice.

(iv) A force of marines and seamen from *Nelson*, *Barham* and *Hood*, about 600 strong, will land at Aalesund on about 17 April with object of neutralizing Inner Lead, south of Trondheim and create a diversion. This will be known as Operation Primrose.[140]

(v) Action is being taken to keep down scale of attack from Norwegian aerodromes, but attacks by flying boats and float planes must always remain possible.

(vi) In view of above coming to commitment, it is desirable to have more strength in south than at present.'

Three days later, these intentions were amplified by a message from the C.I.G.S. to General Carton de Wiart, who had been appointed Commander of Maurice (A.T. 0020/16):–

'Capture of Trondheim considered essential. Plan proposed is as follows:–

'Intend landing 600 marines at Åndalsnes (not Aalesund), 17 April, to be reinforced, if possible, at earliest opportunity. Propose you should exploit from Namsos, while force from Åndalsnes will also threaten Trondheim in conjunction with Norwegian forces. Meanwhile, combined operation for direct attack on Trondheim will be developed? to take advantage of your pressure ... only troops available for reinforcing Åndalsnes are Morgan's brigade.'

This leads up to some consideration of the vexed question whether a frontal attack should have been launched on Trondheim, and what were the chances of success, had such an attack been launched.

Question of Direct Attack on Trondheim (Plan 11)

The project of a direct assault on Trondheim was much to the fore during these early days of the campaign. The following series of signals which passed between the Admiralty and the Commander-in-Chief, Home Fleet, gives an outline of what was intended and throws light on the reasons why the plan was given up.

So far as it concerned the Home Fleet, this proposal, named Operation Hammer, first appeared in A.T. 0142 of 14 April, sent a couple of hours after the message describing the expedition to Namsos:–

> 'Intention up to present has been to land at Namsos for the Trondheim area. For many reasons it would be advantageous to land the force inside Trondheim Fjord. Do you consider that the shore batteries could be either destroyed or dominated to such an extent as to permit transports to enter? And, if so, how many ships and of what type would you propose to use?
>
> 'Request early reply, as any plan must depend on the above.'

On this, Sir Charles Forbes, who was then cruising off the Lofoten Islands, asked for details about the defences of Trondheim, both Norwegian batteries that might be in German hands and artillery that the invaders brought with them, and in his 1157/14 he gave his answers to the Admiralty questions:–

> 'Shore batteries could no doubt be either destroyed or dominated by battleship in daylight, swept and screened, if she had high explosive bombardment shells for main armament, but none of Home Fleet have.
>
> 'This, however, is only the minor part of task.
>
> 'The main difficulties are (1), surprise having been lost, to protect troopships from a heavy-scale air attack for over 30 miles in narrow waters, and (2) then to carry out an opposed landing, of which ample warning has been given, under continuous air attack. Nothing, to date, has led me to suppose the necessary freedom from air attack could be assured for length of time operation would take. In fact, reverse would be the case, as within three hours of being sighted Ju. 88 bombers from Germany would be on spot; and if the

information contained in your 0109/13 is correct, bombing would start almost immediately.

'For foregoing reasons, I do not consider operation feasible, unless you are prepared to face very heavy losses in troops and transports.'[141]

The Admiralty answered him in A.T. 0121 of 15 April:–

'We still think that the operation described should be further studied. It could not take place for seven days devoted to careful preparation. Danger from air would not be appreciably less wherever these large troopships are brought into the danger zone; in fact, it might be greater whilst the aerodrome at Trondheim is in action. Our idea would be that, in addition to R.A.F. bombing of Stavanger aerodrome, the *Suffolk* should bombard with high explosive at dawn, hoping thereby to put Stavanger aerodrome out of business. The aerodrome at Trondheim, which is close to the harbour, could be dealt with by F.A/A bombers, and subsequently by bombardment.

(High explosive shell for 15-in. guns has been ordered to Rosyth. The *Furious* and 1st Cruiser Squadron would be required for this operation). Pray, therefore, consider this important project further.'

And instructions from the Chief of the Imperial General Staff to General Carton de Wiart at the same time, mainly about the landing of Maurice, contained this clause: 'Development of operations is dependent on capture of Trondheim; combined plan being developed'.

Meanwhile, Sir Charles Forbes had received particulars of the Trondheim defences, estimates of the German and Norwegian strengths in troops in and about Trondheim, and news that the Germans had seized the coastwise batteries at the entrance of Trondheim Fjord – which is there only a mile and a half wide, leading out of Skjorn Fjorden, two and a half miles wide. He answered the Admiralty message in his 1733/15:–

'(a) What is size of force to be landed?
(b) What is precise position in which it is proposed to land them?
(c) What is precise position of Trondheim aerodrome? I have no shore map.

(d) What is role of 1ˢᵗ Cruiser Squadron? – as they are at present doing very useful work at Kirkenes in accordance with A.T. 0054/14.

(e) If *Furious* is to be used, she will have to proceed to base to re-equip squadron, replenish stores, and embark fighter squadron; and she cannot leave before refuelling at Tromsø 17 April at earliest. This will also deprive Narvik of air co-operation, so suggest *Glorious*.

(f) I think you have misunderstood my 1157/14. I do not anticipate any great difficulty from naval side, except that I cannot provide air defence for transports whilst approaching and carrying out an opposed landing – the chief air menace being from Ju. 88 machines from Germany. And I know, from personal experience, what an opposed landing is like, even without air opposition.

(g) Naval force required would be *Valiant* and *Renown* to give air defence to *Glorious*; *Warspite* to carry out shore bombardments, as she is only 15-in. ship in fleet with 6-in. guns[142]; at least four A/A cruisers; about 20 destroyers; and numerous landing craft.

(h) I request, on my return to Scapa on morning of 18 April, D.C.N.S. or Admiral Holland may be there to discuss whole situation.'

The answer to this came in A.T. 0250 of 17 April, of which this is a digest:–

(a) and (b) 'One brigade of regulars to take aerodrome by assault; 1000 Canadian troops, part to capture forts, part to land near Hommelvik, and part to contact Norwegians near Levanger; 200 Royal Marines to assist in capture of forts.'

(c) The true position of Vaernes aerodrome is 63° 27 N., 10° 56 E.

(d) 1ˢᵗ Cruiser Squadron: 'Not certain, but detailed plan may prove them necessary, and we must be prepared to put everything into this operation.'

(e) and (f) *Ark Royal* and *Glorious* to be used, with total of 45 fighter machines; *Furious* not required.

(g) 'Do you propose to relieve *Warspite* by *Repulse*, or would you like *Resolution* to do so?'

(h) Admiral Holland and the General commanding 'Hammer's'

troops would come to Scapa on 18 April, 'provided agreement on general scope of operation is reached to-day,' otherwise on 19 April.

Rear-Admiral Holland arrived onboard the *Rodney* at Scapa on 18 April, bringing with him the plan of the operation, but the General commanding the assault troops (Major-General Hotblack) had suddenly fallen ill in London, and Major-General Berney-Ficklin – hastily appointed to succeed him – was seriously injured together with two of his staff when his aircraft crashed on landing at Hatston airfield on 19 April. The plan as originally conceived had been altered to meet representations by Sir Charles Forbes so that all the assaulting forces would be carried in men of war instead of transports, and was summarised by him as follows[143]:–

(a) Details of embarkation of assault force
  (i) Rosyth, 21 April: Divisional Headquarters in 'W' Cruiser, Brigade Headquarters and 'C' Battalion, 15th Brigade, in 'X' Cruiser and five destroyers, Canadian Battalion in two destroyers and five sloops.
  (ii) All cruisers to carry approximately 300 men and 30 tons of stores each. Cruisers 'Y' and 'Z' also to carry two armoured landing craft and should therefore be *Southampton* class. Cruiser 'X' should be *Southampton* or *York* class.
  (iii) In addition, a Royal Marine battery of 7 3.7-in. howitzers to be embarked. Three guns stores and crews and half Battery Headquarters in each 'Y' and 'Z' cruiser. One gun and crew in 'X' Cruiser.
  (iv) Destroyers carrying Canadians to carry 100 men with blankets, tents and 7 days' rations. Remaining destroyers to carry 100 men, blankets and 48 hours' rations.
  (v) Sloops to carry 150 men each, with blankets, tents and 7 days' rations.
  (vi) Ships concerned to embark H.E. ammunition before sailing, as arranged by Commander-in-Chief, Rosyth, and Flag Officer-in-Charge, Greenock.
  (vii) Time of arrival of Troops and gear to be signalled in due course.

(b) Details of embarkation of reserve, 147th Brigade
   (viii) Naval base staff and stores embark on 19 April in *Sobieski* and *Duchess of Athol* at Clyde and in steamship *Orion* at Rosyth. These troops with blankets, tents and 7 days' rations to be transferred at Scapa on 21 April to cruiser detailed.
   (ix) *Sobieski* to embark one new type motor landing craft and *Oronsay* one old armoured motor landing craft, both ex SS *Empire* after daylight.

The details of the naval side of this plan were worked out on 18/19 April, but late on 19 April the operation was cancelled.

Up to 17 April, the Chiefs of Staff had been in favour of the attempt; but, during 18 April, a vehement and decisive change in the opinion of the Chiefs of Staff and of the Admiralty occurred. This change was brought about first by increasing realisation of the magnitude of the naval stake in hazarding so many of our finest capital ships, and also by War Office arguments that even if the fleet got in and got out again, the opposed landing of the troops in the face of the German Air Power would be perilous'.[144] On 20 April, A.T. 1140/20 to the Commander-in-Chief, Home Fleet, confirmed that 'Hammer is cancelled' and some six hours later A.T. 1731/20[145] forecast the employment of the Hammer forces in the Åndalsnes area.

But before this Sir Charles Forbes, who from the first had regarded the project with misgivings, had evidently come to the conclusion that it was over-hazardous. A signal sent by him on 18 April, outlining his proposals for the future employment of naval forces, provided for supporting the army at Narvik, Namsos and Åndalsnes, but said of Trondheim only 'operate in inner routes against supplies for enemy military and air forces in Trondheim and Bergen area'.[146] As usual, there was difficulty in collecting enough destroyers to cope with the many calls upon them. His 'destroyers requirements' were given in a signal sent at 0201, 19 April (before A.T. 0117/19, summarised above, reached him), and amounted to 68, of which he earmarked 45 for Hammer; he then only had 63 at his command and a margin above the 68 to allow for loss or damage was essential. As regards the situation at Trondheim, reports made the German strength to be some 2000 men on 16/17, chiefly at Vaernes and in the forts that guard the entrance to the fjord, where there were said to be 6-in. and 8-in. guns. The troops were Austrian and Bavarian Highlanders, young men, active and well-equipped. Whether they had mobile artillery was doubtful; but they were strong in the air – at Vaernes and on a frozen lake 5 miles south-east of Trondheim – and they were well off for anti-aircraft guns. Later reports said that more troops were arriving by air, land and sea.

The question whether this assault should have been attempted or not became the subject of considerable public controversy. For this reason, the Commander-in-Chief, Home Fleet, deemed it advisable to put on record his opinion

> '...that it was a gamble that might have succeeded, but probably would not. It appeared to him that it was only in the fleet, which had had practical experience in the matter, that the scale of air attack that the enemy could develop on the Norwegian coast was properly appreciated. The experience of the attacks on the fleet on 9 and 11 April, and on the *Suffolk*[147] on 17 April, left no doubt in his mind that 45 F.A/A fighters operating from carriers could not have afforded adequate protection in the circumstances of this assault, which, as he had pointed out, necessitated a long approach in narrow waters.
>
> An opposed landing with very slightly superior forces had to be undertaken which, from previous experience and in view of what happened at Narvik, was bound to be a hazardous operation, and withal the combined operation had to be hastily planned and then performed without any practice at all, in fact ad hoc.'[148]

With this view the German Naval Staff was in substantial agreement:–

> 'A direct assault on Trondheim would only have been possible in the first days of the German operations, while coastal batteries were still unprepared and before the German Air Force was able to operate effectively against the attacker. Even then the invader could only hope to consolidate his position if, by using extensive air transportation, he could establish air superiority in the Norwegian area and could land a powerfully equipped and modernly trained expeditionary force. In addition the British would have had to prevent any further reinforcements of German troops on the

Skagerrak route to southern Norway. Thus it cannot be held against the British if, with their uncertainty as to the actual situation in southern Norway and with ignorance of the results of their submarine attacks in the Kattegat and Skagerrak, they did not decide on a direct attack against the harbours already in German occupation.'[149]

The French view, on the other hand, emerges from the following extracts from the minutes of conversations held in Paris on 22 and 23 April. At the first meeting the First Sea Lord (Admiral of the Fleet Sir Dudley Pound) and Vice-Admiral Sir Geoffrey Blake saw Admiral Darlan and Captain Auphan, when the French, runs the minute, 'were emphatic' that the Norwegian theatre of operations 'is vital, and that nothing short of the actual outbreak of war in the Mediterranean should be allowed to deflect forces from the Allied effort there. They offered further naval help if required …' 'They regarded the capture of Trondheim as vital.'

Next day, Sir Geoffrey Blake saw Admiral le Luc and Captain Auphan. 'The French did not disguise their profound regret that Hammer had been cancelled, and urged that, although the operation would now be a more difficult one, the question of undertaking it should be re-examined.'[150]

There was, too, a considerable body of opinion in the United Kingdom in favour of the attempt, typified by the debates which took place in Parliament.[151]

The question may well provide food for academic debate for many years to come; but it may be noted that the view of the responsible Naval Commander on the spot, Admiral Sir Charles Forbes, and the considered opinion of the German Naval Staff, were in close agreement that at this stage of the operations – over a week after the original landings, by which time the German defence was a going concern – the attempt was unlikely to have succeeded; and subsequent events of the Norwegian Campaign tend to confirm this opinion.

General Employment of Home Fleet April/June (Plan 1)
With the abandonment of operation Hammer the Home Fleet settled down to the business of convoying the various expeditions to and from Norway, and rendering such assistance as possible to the troops on shore.

Cruisers, destroyers and sloops, as well as merchant ships, served as troopships; and when troops sailed in unarmed ships one or two cruisers generally accompanied them, besides an anti-submarine screen of destroyers. Thus the convoys had no great strength (especially those for Åndalsnes), for every cruiser troopship carried several hundred men and sometimes a couple of hundred tons of stores, including guns and wagons. But seemingly the Germans did not intend to hazard their surface craft in attempts on the expeditions while on passage, though they sometimes brought off air attacks. A.T. 1701/19 informed the Commander-in-Chief, Home Fleet, that the Admiralty had 'no reliable reports of main German units later than 12 April, but that it was probable that all their large ships were in their home waters'.[152]

The Commander-in-Chief, Home Fleet, arrived back at Scapa from the Lofoten Islands on 17 April, and the next day he signalled to the Admiralty his 'outline proposals for the future employment' of the fleet as follows:–

'(a) Maintain close blockade of Narvik and support military forces there.
(b) Support military forces in Namsos and Åndalsnes area.
(c) Operate in inner routes against supplies for enemy military and air forces in Trondheim and Bergen area.
(d) Submarines to operate in Skagerrak and off south-western coast of Norway against enemy lines of communication.
(e) Sweep by surface forces into Skagerrak to be undertaken to relieve pressure of enemy anti-submarine measures when weather conditions are suitable – vide my 2009/17 April. (Such a sweep 'not an operation of war except in fog, due to air attacks enemy can bring to bear'.)
(f) Kattegat to be intensively mined up to limit of Swedish territorial waters, both by magnetic and contact mines, starting from southward and working north.
(g) Continuous harassing of all enemy aerodromes in Norway, except in Narvik area, to be a special task of Royal Air Force.'

In pursuance of this policy the *Warspite* flying Vice-Admiral Whitworth's flag remained in support of Lord Cork till 24 April, when she proceeded to Scapa and the Clyde en route for the Mediterranean, her place in the Narvik area being taken on 26 April by the *Resolution*, detached from the Halifax escort force. The *Repulse* sailed from Scapa on 17 April to protect the first French convoy to Namsos, but she was diverted to the assistance of the *Suffolk*, which had been disabled by air attack, and did not join the convoy till the last day of its passage (19 April). She then took a single transport to Vaagsfjord afterwards returning to Scapa, where she stayed till June. As to the remainder of the capital ships of the Home Fleet, the *Rodney* remained at Scapa till the German raid on homecoming convoys from Narvik in June; the *Renown* went to Rosyth for repairs, rejoining the fleet towards the end of May; and the *Valiant* went out again at the end of April for service in the central Norwegian area.

The Home Fleet destroyers (apart from a dozen or so with Lord Cork in the Narvik Squadron) were required for convoy duty almost continuously throughout the campaign. Some had other service on the coast, and together with cruisers, A/A cruisers, sloops and small craft did fine work in support of the military forces on shore, which will be described in succeeding chapters on the various landings.

Under clause (c) of the Commander-in-Chief's proposals four destroyers cruised in the Inner Lead about Trondheim in pairs between 21 and 28 April, with occasional breaks when ships had to go home for oil or were required for convoys. The *Ashanti* and *Mohawk*, *Somali* and *Tartar*, *Sikh* and *Nubian* all took part in this patrol; they found no enemy at sea, but the *Nubian* and *Ashanti* suffered slightly from near misses in an air attack on 28 April. Vice-Admiral Layton supported the patrol during the nights of 26/27 with the *Manchester* and *Birmingham* after landing troops at Molde and Åndalsnes; and two nights later (29 April) mines were laid in Trondheim Lead by the *Ivanhoe*, *Icarus* and *Impulsive* (Operation Z.M.A.).

The month of May saw a considerable reduction in the Home Fleet effectives. The German threat to the Low Countries was becoming plainer every day and on 7 May Vice-Admiral Edward-Collins in the *Galatea*, with the *Arethusa*, was sent to Sheerness, and eight destroyers[153] to Harwich to work under the Commander-in-Chief, The Nore.

On the same day, the *Berwick* and *Glasgow* embarked the 2nd Battalion, R. M. Brigade, under Colonel R. G. Sturges, at Greenock, and sailed next morning for Iceland, escorted by the *Fearless* and *Fortune*. Reykjavik was occupied without incident on 10 May,[154] and the two cruisers then proceeded to Liverpool for long refits, the destroyers returning to Scapa.

On 14 April, increased tension with Italy caused the transfer of the eight destroyers detached to Harwich and in addition nine more,[155] with the A/A cruiser *Carlisle* and three sloops, to the Mediterranean. Taking into account the numbers under repair from war damage, those working in the Narvik area under Lord Cork and those required for Narvik convoys, this latter detachment left the Commander-in-Chief, Home Fleet, with no destroyers for screening heavy ships for the rest of the month. Three more destroyers[156] were ordered to the Humber on 18 May, and on 26 May Vice-Admiral Layton, with the *Manchester*, *Birmingham* and *Sheffield* was also sent there and placed under the command of the Commander-in-Chief, The Nore.

Carrier and FA/A Operations

The carriers and Fleet Air Arm played a conspicuous part throughout the campaign. The vital need was to neutralise the strong German Air Force, firstly by providing fighter cover over ports of disembarkation and ships engaged in it; secondly by giving air reconnaissance, air spotting and ground attack; and thirdly by air attack on enemy airfields, depots and transport, both ashore and afloat. For the first two requirements the home bases were too far distant for the employment of R.A.F. fighters; for the third, the limited numbers of R.A.F. bombers available and the distances to be flown rendered help by naval aircraft essential.

At the beginning of the campaign, the only carrier in home waters was the *Furious*. As already mentioned, she arrived in Norwegian waters on 11 April and when the Commander-in-Chief shaped course for Scapa on 15 April, she remained working under Lord Cork in the Narvik area until 26 April. She had no fighters embarked and by that time her two T.S.R. Squadrons had lost 50 per cent of their numbers;[157] she herself had sustained damage to her turbines by a near miss, and she then proceeded to Greenock for repairs.

The *Glorious* and the *Ark Royal* from the Mediterranean joined the Home Fleet at Scapa on 23 April, and sailed for central Norway the same day under Vice-Admiral Wells, flying his flag in the *Ark Royal*, with the

Berwick, Curlew and six destroyers[158] (Operation DX). Their object was to provide fighter protection for the southern expedition; to attack the enemy in Trondheim; and to land some Royal Air Force machines to work from the frozen Lake Lesjaskog (between Åndalsnes and Dombaas), known to the squadron as 'Gladiator Lake'.

The R.A.F. Squadron of Gladiators was flown off the *Glorious* between 1730 and 1800 on 24 April, and reached their landing ground without opposition, but the lake was shortly afterwards heavily bombed and all the R.A.F. aircraft were put out of action. All fighter support then devolved on the carriers' naval aircraft.

The carriers sent up fighters to patrol over Åndalsnes as soon as snow allowed in the evening of 24 April and each day afterwards up to 28 April a few aircraft patrolled over Åndalsnes or Namsos. In the course of these patrols, fighters engaged enemy aircraft attacking the railways, the airfield on 'Gladiator Lake' and two convoys approaching Åndalsnes; they also helped to defend the *Flamingo* lying at that port. Apart from this work, the carriers kept anti-submarine and fighter patrols in the air 'whenever submarine or enemy aircraft attack was likely'.[159]

On 27 April the *Glorious* was detached to fuel, rejoining on 1 May; the *Sheffield* relieved the *Curlew* as radar guardship on 28 April, being relieved in her turn by the *Valiant* on 30 April, and oiling requirements occasioned changes in the destroyer screen; otherwise the squadron operated till the night of 1 May.

Admiral Wells worked from positions about 120 miles from the targets or patrol areas, going to seaward between operations – except the first day, when the aircraft had 400 miles to fly on passage alone, which the Admiral described as 'a very hazardous flight, most gallantly carried out'. Bombing attacks on Trondheim were made by 34 aircraft on 25 April and by 18 (the *Glorious* having by then parted company) on 28 April. No German warships were seen there, but merchant shipping was attacked; and heavy damage was inflicted on the airfield and naval aircraft at Vaernes, especially by the raid on 25 April.

In the evening of 28 April the squadron drew off to seaward to rest the airmen, who had been in action for five successive days and 'were showing definite signs of strain'. The carriers, too, had not been without excitement; enemy aircraft attacked them on 28 April, when the *Ark Royal* shot down an enemy machine, and there were encounters with submarines on 27-29.

Admiral Wells moved in again on 30 April in order to provide cover for the troops retreating from Åndalsnes next day. The *Glorious* rejoined his flag on 1 May, bringing fresh aircraft to replace casualties and to cover the retreat from Namsos, scheduled for 2/3 May, the Royal Air Force then taking over the protection of the Åndalsnes expedition. But throughout 1 May the squadron was subjected to air attacks, which occupied the attention of the fighters intended to augment the patrols over Namsos, and the German bombs fell sometimes 'unpleasantly close'. These attacks convinced the Vice-Admiral that he could no longer 'maintain a position from which aircraft could give support to our forces' and, with the approval of the Commander-in-Chief, he accordingly withdrew that evening, and crossing the North Sea in 65° N., came west of the Shetlands to Scapa, arriving on 3 May.

During these operations, the squadron estimated that they had destroyed 21 enemy aircraft (not counting the seaplanes in Trondheim Fjord), besides damaging a further 20; their own losses amounted to 13 aircraft destroyed and two rendered unserviceable.

With the failure of the campaign in central Norway the focus of naval interest once more shifted to Lord Cork's command. Vice-Admiral Wells only remained at Scapa long enough to make good aircraft losses, and sailed on 4 May in the *Ark Royal* for the Narvik area. There she remained till 24 May, providing fighters for the Narvik and Bodø areas, until R.A.F. landing grounds had been prepared, and launching almost daily attacks by Skuas and Swordfish on enemy railway lines, military stores, etc. During this period the *Furious* transported R.A.F. fighters and landed them at Bardufoss (21 May) and the *Glorious*' six Walruses to Harstad (18 May), and Hurricanes to Bardufoss (26 May), as the newly prepared airfields became ready. After a brief interval between 25 and 30 May in Home Waters, the *Ark Royal* and *Glorious* once more proceeded to the Narvik area in connection with the final evacuation – a service from which the *Glorious* never returned.

The contribution of the Fleet Air Arm to the campaign was not limited to the work of the carrier-borne aircraft. Mention has already been made of the eminently successful attack by Skuas from Hatston on the *Königsberg* in Bergen. A number of attacks were carried out from this base during April and May against enemy shipping, small war vessels and oil tanks. During three attacks in May the Squadron (806) was escorted by R.A.F. Blenheims. Surprise was attained on every occasion and British losses were small; the success of the dive bombing method of attack seemed to be confirmed. Three attacks against oil tanks were particularly successful, resulting in the almost complete destruction of three separate oil depots.

Between 18 May and 6 June, a squadron of six Walruses was based on Harstad, whence they were employed on anti-submarine patrols, convoying, occasional ferrying and especially communication duties – a difficult problem in that mountainous country, broken by waterways and with few roads. Out of some 250 flights during the period, more than three-quarters were devoted to transporting British and French officers on such missions. The base was closed down on 6 June and the squadron re-embarked in the *Ark Royal*; on the last day, however, the five remaining Walruses carried out a spirited bombing attack on German troops and installations at Solfolla.

In addition to these duties directly in connection with the Allied expeditions, minelaying operations were carried out by Swordfish (specially equipped with long distance tanks) from Hatston; the first of these took place in the narrow Inner Lead channel south of Haugesund (between Bergen and Stavanger) on the night of 17/18 May. And throughout the operations, land based F.A/A fighters from Hatston and Wick maintained the air defence of Scapa, while Swordfish carried out anti-submarine operations as required. If any had previously doubted the necessity of a naval air arm or the scope of the operations it might legitimately be called upon to perform, surely the events in Norway from April to June 1940 gave the answer in no uncertain terms.

Employment of A/A Cruisers and Sloops

The individual efforts of A/A cruisers and sloops will appear in the succeeding chapters on the landing operations; but some general indication of their services will not be out of place at this stage. In the words of the Commander-in-Chief, Home Fleet, 'the scale of air attack that would be developed against our military forces on shore and our naval forces off the Norwegian coast was grievously under-estimated when the operations were undertaken. In the result, when the situation on shore became desperate, we were committed and desperate measures had to be taken'.[160] In the absence of Allied fighters and adequate A/A defences, any expedient which might mitigate the severity of the attacks on the Allied bases had to be resorted to. A/A cruisers and sloops seemed the readiest means at hand, though they would be severely handicapped by operating in confined waters, surrounded by high cliffs.

Accordingly on 21 April the Commander-in-Chief, Home Fleet, received orders from the Admiralty that an A/A ship or sloop was to be kept at Namsos and Åndalsnes, the *Black Swan, Auckland, Pelican* and *Fleetwood* being placed under his orders for this purpose (A.T. 1929/21). The next day further orders from the Admiralty (A.T. 1037/22) directed that two of these ships should be kept at both Namsos and Åndalsnes, and added the *Bittern* and *Flamingo* to the Force.

Meanwhile, HMS *Carlisle*, flying the flag of Rear-Admiral Vivian, had arrived at Åndalsnes on 20 April, where she remained till 22 April, later moving to Namsos; there she stayed – except for a trip to Skjel Fjord for fuel – till the evacuation on the night of 2/3 May. The *Calcutta* was at Namsos from 22–27 April, when she proceeded to Åndalsnes and was there during the final evacuation on the night of 1/2 May. The *Curacoa* arrived at Åndalsnes on the night of 21/22 April, but was seriously damaged by a bomb on 24 April and returned to the United Kingdom escorted by the *Flamingo*, which had arrived there that afternoon. The *Flamingo* returned to Åndalsnes early on 26 April, sailing the same night after expending all her ammunition.

The *Black Swan* and *Auckland* were already in Norwegian waters when the Admiralty orders reached the Commander-in-Chief. The *Black Swan* was hit at Åndalsnes on 28 April by a bomb which went right through the ship, doing surprisingly little damage, but enough to force her to return to the United Kingdom. The *Auckland* arrived at Namsos on 22 April and sailed in the evening of 24 April, having fired practically all her ammunition. She returned to Åndalsnes on 30 April, and remained there till the final evacuation. The *Pelican* was hit by a bomb and had her stern blown off on 22 April, while still some 50 miles from the shore on her way to Åndalsnes; she eventually reached Lerwick on 24 April in tow of the *Fleetwood* which had just parted company from her for Namsos when she was hit. The *Fleetwood* was employed subsequently at Åndalsnes from 29-30; then, having expended most of her ammunition, she returned to Scapa with some evacuated personnel. The *Bittern* was at Namsos from 24 to 30 April, when she was hit and set on fire by dive bombers; after survivors had been taken off she was sunk by torpedo in 100 fathoms by order of Rear-Admiral Vivian.

Commenting on this employment of these ships, the Commander-in-Chief, Home Fleet, remarked that it became evident at an early stage that the slight degree of protection that they could afford to the bases, being due mainly to the fact that they were primarily chosen as targets by the bombers, was out of all proportion to their expenditure of ammunition and the damage they were sustaining. Although he realised that the moral effect of their presence was considerable he was of the opinion that the use of the ships for this purpose was wasteful and that considerable reinforcements would be required owing to the number of ships that had been damaged. This view he represented to the Admiralty on 26 April[161] and on the next day, owing to the heavy attacks on them, he ordered the A/A guardships to withdraw during daylight hours.

A/S Trawlers on the Norwegian Coast

Some mention should be made here of the work of the A/S trawlers. On 13 April, the Admiralty ordered the 21st A/S Group Striking Force and the 23rd A/S to sail from Scotland for Namsos, and on 17/12/22 April A/S Groups to sail for Åndalsnes. These were followed later by the 15th and 16th A/S Striking Forces, which went to Namsos.[162]

These trawlers were sent to Norway primarily to give A/S protection to HM ships and transports in the fjords, but no sooner had they arrived than they were subjected to frequent heavy air attacks, high level and dive bombing and machine gunning, which made it suicidal for them to carry out A/S patrols except during the few hours of darkness. They suffered severe casualties, eleven out of a total of 29 being sunk or driven ashore. During daylight hours, after the first day or two, they were forced to take shelter under high cliffs, partly to evade bombing and partly to rest their crews. While so placed, some of the crews endeavoured to camouflage their vessels with evergreen and small trees and themselves took refuge on shore, in some instances leaving their guns' crews onboard to engage the enemy aircraft; but even when on shore, the crews were machine-gunned on the hillside.

As most of the work of disembarking troops and stores and the evacuation were done at night, some of the trawlers did useful work ferrying between the transports and the shore, while others were employed on A/S patrols. 'Despite these arduous and hazardous conditions', wrote the Commander-in-Chief, Home Fleet, 'the morale and gallantry of officers and men remained magnificent'.[163]

As an example of what could be done by these little ships with scratch crews, if well led, the Commander-in-Chief went on to give some details from a report written by Lieutenant R. B. Stannard,[164] who was in command of the *Arab*:–

'In the early afternoon of 28 April, after a heavy bombing attack which had started fires among the stores and ammunition on the pier at Namsos, the *Arab* and *Angle* were ordered to tow off the transport *Saumur*, which was aground with a wire round her propeller. The *Angle* managed to get her off alone, so the *Arab* returned to the burning pier and her Commanding Officer, keeping her bows in by going slow ahead, ran two hoses over the forecastle and tried to put out the burning ammunition dump. While thus engaged, another air attack by sixteen planes developed, and as there was no hope of putting out the fire he left and went down the fjord.

On 30 April, after helping HMS *Bittern* to drive off air attacks and helping other trawlers in various ways, he decided to put his crew ashore. He landed Lewis guns, food and blankets, and had them taken to a large cave, and then established a number of machine-gun posts at the top of the cliff. There the crew slept with look-outs on duty.

Next day, the *Aston Villa* made fast about 100 yards south of the *Arab*. There was continuous bombing and machine-gunning by high and dive bombers which came over in flights of six, nine and twelve planes. The positions ashore were also machine-gunned. The *Gaul* was hit and sank. The crews of the three trawlers then manned the positions ashore. The *Aston Villa* was set on fire by a direct hit from a dive bomber. Luckily only a few of her crew were still onboard. The wounded were rescued and transferred in extemporised stretchers to the top of the cliff. As the *Aston Villa* was still on fire and in danger of blowing up, Lieutenant Stannard, with two others boarded the *Arab*, cut her lines and succeeded in moving her another 100 yards away before the explosion occurred.

Finally, when leaving the fjord in his damaged vessel to return to Scapa after five days at Namsos, he was attacked by a single German bomber which ordered him to steer east or be sunk. Instead, he continued his course, held his fire until the aircraft was about 800 yards away, and then opened fire with every gun onboard and brought the aircraft down'.[165]

The Southern Area: Surface Operations (Plan 1)

Operations by surface craft off the southern coasts of Norway had been virtually ruled out – except on special occasions – by the Commander-in-Chief, Home Fleet, with the concurrence of the Admiralty, and this area was mainly left to submarines. Three operations by surface craft were, however, carried out; the first – a bombardment of Stavanger airfield by the *Suffolk* on 17 April – certainly confirmed the Commander-in-Chief's appreciation of the power of the German Air Force. The bombardment (Operation Duck) was ordered by the Admiralty in support of the Naval landing at Åndalsnes (Operation Primrose) and its object was defined as 'to inflict the greatest possible damage to the aerodrome so as to restrict the operation of aircraft therefrom'.

The *Suffolk* (Captain J. W. Durnford)[166] screened by the *Kipling, Juno, Janus* and *Hereward* towing T.S.D.S. sailed from Scapa in the afternoon of 16 April and crossed the North Sea at 26 knots; at 0414, 17 April, the submarine *Seal* which had been ordered to mark position 'A' (58° 57' N., 5° 10' E.) was sighted and five minutes later a spotting Walrus was catapulted from the *Suffolk*. At 0432, the *Seal* was passed on a course of 110°, and at about this time rockets and A/A gunfire were sighted, presumably coming from the defences of the airfield. This prevented the identification of a flare which a R.A.F. Hudson was to drop to indicate the position of the target. It was then getting fairly light; the land could be seen, but with no detail; the sea was calm, sky clear, with a light easterly wind. At 0445 speed was reduced to 15 knots and two minutes later the force turned to the bombarding course of 181°, a second Walrus being catapulted at about this time. Unfortunately wireless communication with the aircraft could not be established and in consequence the bombardment did not start till 0513, the range being about 20,000 yards. Three runs were carried out, in the course of which 202 rounds were fired. The failure of wireless communication with the aircraft was 'most disappointing and inevitably had an adverse effect on the bombardment'[168]; nevertheless, casualties were caused to the German naval air contingent there, two petrol dumps were destroyed and other damage inflicted.

After an hour in the air in the vicinity of the airfield, the two Walruses and the Hudson returned to Scotland, and at 0604 the force commenced its withdrawal at 30 knots, steering 270°. Orders had been received from the Admiralty the previous evening (A.T. 2300/16) for the force to sweep to the northward on completion of Operation Duck, in order to intercept enemy destroyers; Captain Durnford accordingly stood to the westward till 0704 and then altered course to the northward, reducing speed to 25 knots (to conserve fuel) and informing the Admiralty of his position, course and speed at 0720. Fighter escort had been arranged with Coastal Command, but this failed to make contact – it subsequently transpired, because the fighters had apparently expected the force to sweep north close inshore. Thus it came about that the squadron was entirely dependent on its own resources in event of air attack.

This was not long in coming. The first attack took place at 0825, when an emergency air attack report was made. From then on, the *Suffolk* was under continuous attack – both high level and dive bombing – for six hours and 47 minutes.[167] After about an hour and a quarter, Captain Durnford decided to withdraw to the westward, as offering the best chance of obtaining air support as early as possible. At 1037 the ship was hit by a heavy bomb, which caused very severe damage, put 'X' and 'Y' turrets out of action, reduced her speed to 18 knots and caused flooding to the extent of some 1,500 tons of water in 20 minutes. Repeated requests for fighter support, giving the position, failed to have any apparent effect.

Meanwhile, the attacks continued. By 1305 both steering motors were out of action but temporary repairs were effected 20 minutes later; near misses, which blew in lower deck scuttles and punctured the ship's side, caused further extensive flooding. Help was, however, on its way. At 1119, the Commander-in-Chief, Home Fleet, then nearing Scapa from the Lofoten Islands, ordered all Skuas at Hatston to be sent to the *Suffolk*'s assistance; he also sent the *Renown* and the *Repulse*, the latter of which was screening the first French convoy to the northward.[168] The Commander-in-Chief, Rosyth, informed the *Suffolk* at 1140 that three Blenheims and three Hudsons should reach him by 1230.

It was not, however, till 1415 that friendly aircraft were observed arriving; by 1430, nine were in company, but despite this there were four attacks between then and 1512 – with the exception of the one which hit 'the most dangerous and accurate experienced.'[169] At 1620 the two battlecruisers were sighted ahead, and eventually the *Suffolk* managed to struggle into Scapa on 18 April with her quarterdeck awash.[170] She was beached at Longhope for temporary repairs and sailed for the Clyde on 5 May for permanent repairs.

Within a week of the *Suffolk*'s return to Scapa, a sweep into the Skagerrak by the French contre-torpilleurs *L'Indomptable*, *Le Malin* and *Le Triomphant* was arranged by the Admiralty. By this time the enemy anti-submarine measures were making themselves felt and the operation was aimed at the destruction of their patrols. The force left Rosyth in the afternoon of 23 April, intending to cross the meridian of 6° 13' E. at 2100 and that of Kristiansand south before 0500/24. The force entered the Skagerrak unobserved, and during the night sank two motor torpedo boats and a trawler and damaged a second trawler.[171] When retiring across the North Sea at high speed, the destroyers were heavily attacked by aircraft, despite a battle flight escort, but escaped without damage. Two aircraft of the escort, however, were shot down by enemy fighters.

On only one other occasion during the campaign did surface forces operate in the waters to the south-west of Norway. This was a sweep directed against enemy minelaying forces on 9/10 May. By this time the withdrawal from central Norway had been completed and the centre of naval interest was shifting to the southward.

At 0900/9 the Commander-in-Chief, Home Fleet, received information from the Admiralty (A.T. 0827) of the probable positions of two enemy forces near the Little Fisher bank that evening. As it happened, the *Birmingham*, with the *Janus*, *Hyperion*, *Hereward* and *Havock* had left Rosyth bound to the southward at 0645/9. These ships were ordered by the Admiralty to steer 080°, 20 knots, after passing May Island; and at the same time, Captain (D) 5 (Captain Lord Louis Mountbatten), in the *Kelly* with the *Kimberley* and the *Kandahar* with the *Hostile*, which were then just to the southward of St. Abbs Head, were ordered to turn to the northward and join the *Birmingham*. The Commander-in-Chief, Home Fleet, sailed a further unit of five destroyers, the *Fury*, *Foresight*, *Mohawk*, *Bulldog* and *Gallant* from Scapa at 1150.

Instructions to these forces were signalled by the Commander-in-

Chief at 1024. The *Birmingham* and her destroyers were directed to pass through 56° 39' N., 3° 37' E. at 1930/9, and then to steer 097° to meet an enemy force of three destroyers, one torpedo boat and four minelayers which were expected to approach that position from 56° 28' N., 6° 10' E. The *Fury* and her group were to be in 57° 21' N., 2° 22' E. at 1850, where six enemy motor torpedo boats were expected to be encountered. After sinking them, this group was to join the *Birmingham* at high speed. If nothing was sighted by 2230, all forces were to search back to the westward. Air escort by fighters was arranged for the *Birmingham*.

Lord Louis Mountbatten's destroyers joined the *Birmingham* in the afternoon, but the *Kimberley* soon afterwards had to return to Rosyth owing to shortage of fuel. The remainder of the forces continued to the eastward. The prospects seemed promising, but they were doomed to disappointment.

At 1940, an enemy report from a reconnaissance aircraft was received; it placed the force expected – four minelayers, three destroyers and a transport barge [sic] – in 57° 12' N., 5° 30' E., steering 080°. Unfortunately, no amplifying report giving the speed was made. This position was about 70 miles east-north-east of the expected position (which the *Birmingham* had reached) and on the assumption that the enemy was retiring at speed, there was little chance of overtaking him before he reached the Skaw; our forces therefore continued in accordance with their instructions. It was not till nearly seven hours later (0232/10 May) that an amplifying report[172] giving the speed of the enemy as 6 knots was received, and it was then realised that contact would have been possible about 2300 the previous evening.

Meanwhile the *Kelly* and *Kandahar*, which had been detached to hunt a submarine at 1935, had not received the original enemy report till 2018, when the *Birmingham* was nearly out of sight ahead. Both destroyers immediately proceeded at high speed to join her, but visibility was falling and they did not in fact do so during the operation. They were, however, joined at 2050 by the *Bulldog*, which had become detached from the *Fury*'s force at 1730 when sinking a floating mine and had afterwards (at 1958) ineffectively engaged what appeared to be a motor yacht, which escaped to the eastward at high speed making smoke. Unfortunately, the *Bulldog* made no enemy report.

At 2235 the *Kelly* and *Kandahar*, being then in 56° 48' N., 5° 9' E.

sighted enemy motor torpedo boats. One,[173] which was lying almost stopped in the track of our destroyers, fired torpedoes at the visibility distance of about four cables and hit the *Kelly* under the bridge. During the next hour and a half there were several contacts with motor torpedo boats; the *Kandahar* reported two at 2240, the *Birmingham* one at 2256 and the *Hostile* one at 2353. Attempts to sink these were unsuccessful, and they retired under their own smoke.

Meanwhile the *Kelly* had been badly damaged – a fact which was not known till 0013 on 10 May, when a signal timed 2300/9, from the *Bulldog* was received. The *Bulldog* took the *Kelly* in tow, and subsequently reported that no other ships were in company and she was steering 262° at 7 knots. Visibility was very bad, and at 0010/10, an enemy motor torpedo boat rammed both destroyers, further damaging the *Kelly*. The *Bulldog* sustained minor damage only, and the motor torpedo boat was thought to have sunk.

As a result of these reports, the *Birmingham* and all destroyers taking part in the operation were ordered to cover the withdrawal of the *Kelly*, and Vice-Admiral Layton in the *Manchester*, with the *Sheffield*, was sailed from Scapa to assist. Air protection for the whole force was arranged. But that night big events were taking place to the south; Holland and Belgium were invaded, and at 0616/10, the *Birmingham* and all the destroyers except two as escort for the *Kelly* in tow were ordered to proceed towards Terschelling at maximum speed.

Admiral Layton made contact with the tow at 1507/10, and covered the withdrawal till the next afternoon, when he was ordered to Rosyth by the Commander-in-Chief, owing to the suspected presence of U-boats. The whole force was bombed by enemy aircraft off and on the whole time. Tugs reached the *Kelly* and had her in tow by 0430 on 12 May, and she eventually reached the Tyne at 1600/13, 'very largely due' in the words of the Commander-in-Chief, Home Fleet, 'to the fine determined spirit shown by Captain the Lord Louis Mountbatten, G.C.V.O.' [174]

The Southern Area: Submarine Activities

For the first three weeks of the campaign, Allied submarines continued to harass the German supply lines in the Skagerrak and Kattegat. As time went on, however, two factors were increasingly against them, viz. shorter hours of darkness and increased German anti-submarine measures, and added to these was the need to conserve and re-dispose them for the impending invasion of the Low Countries. For these reasons, the patrols in the Skagerrak and Kattegat with the exception of the minelayers *Narwhal* and *Seal* were mainly withdrawn on 28 April,[175] many of the smaller submarines being employed in the southern part of the North Sea during the invasion of the Low Countries and subsequent events, while the larger submarines continued the attack on enemy communications further north along the Norwegian coast.

But before they were withdrawn from the Eastern Skagerrak and Kattegat attacks on the German convoys were of almost daily occurrence and many successes were scored. Thus on 15 April the *Sterlet* sank the *Brummer* which was escorting a convoy, and the *Snapper* two A/S trawlers; on 18 April, the *Seawolf* seriously damaged two ships in convoy, setting one on fire and sinking her; the *Triad* attacked a convoy on 20 April, and the *Tetrarch* a large transport on 24 April – both, however, without success. On 1 May the *Narwhal*, while on a minelaying operation, sank the SS *Buenos Aires* and damaged the *Bahia Castillo*. All these attacks took place within 30 miles of the Skaw or to the northward. Further west, the French *Orphée* attacked two U-boats about 90 miles south-west of the Naze and claimed one sunk on 21 April.[176]

Three British submarines came to grief in the latter part of April, however – the *Sterlet*, sunk by enemy A/S craft in the East Skagerrak on 18 April; the *Truant*, damaged by an explosion, possibly a magnetic torpedo, on 25 April, while on passage[177] to Sogne Fjord with Liaison Officers and S.A. ammunition; and the *Unity*, which accidentally met an Allied convoy in a fog and was rammed and sunk by the Norwegian SS *Atlejarl*, in 55° 13' N., 1° 20' E.

Off the west coast of Norway, the *Trident* drove aground and badly damaged a 4000-ton merchant vessel[178] on 2 May in Kors Fjord (Bergen area) after a 10-mile chase in broad daylight, and two days later the *Severn* chased and sank a German prize, the Swedish SS *Monark*, on passage from Stavanger to Germany.

A sad incident occurred on 5 May, when the *Seal*, which had been laying mines in the Kattegat, was seriously damaged by a mine or depth charge. Attempts to reach Swedish territorial waters off Goteborg failed, and she was captured and towed ignominiously into a German port.

Next day the *Sealion* attacked two large transports to the southward of Oslo Fjord, and on 8 May the *Taku*, two 3,000-ton merchant vessels escorted by torpedo boats west of the Skagerrak; she was severely hunted, but survived undamaged. Neither of these attacks achieved success, but on 20 May the *Spearfish*, after capturing their crews, sank two Danish fishing vessels to the east of the Dogger Bank, and on 23 May the *Tetrarch* sank one Danish fishing vessel some 70 miles south of the Naze, and sent another in prize to Leith – a distance of 340 miles.

Minefields were laid by the French *Rubis* on 10 and 25 May; by the *Narwhal* on 1 and 11 May, and by the *Porpoise* on 15 May.

The Conjunct Expeditions (Plan 1)

The foregoing sections give a brief summary of the principal naval activities during the period of the Allied operations in Norway. It is now proposed to turn to the amphibious expeditions which they were designed to support.

From a naval point of view, four main localities were involved in these operations, viz.:–

Central Norway: Objective Trondheim[179]

Namsos (Operations Henry and Maurice). First landing 14 April: evacuation 2 May.

Åndalsnes (Operations Primrose and Sickle). First landing 17 April: evacuation 1 May.

Northern Norway: Objective Narvik[180]

Harstad (Operation Rupert). First landing 14 April: evacuation 8 June. Bodø area (between the Central and Northern areas). First landing 29 April in an attempt to check German interference at Narvik after the evacuation of the Trondheim area. Evacuated 29 May.

The ensuing chapters follow the fortunes of each of these expeditions in some detail. Both the central and northern campaigns opened with the landings of parties on Norwegian soil on the same day – 14 April; but whereas the former venture was over in under three weeks, the latter dragged on until the capture of Narvik on 28 May and the final evacuation some ten days later. For this reason the campaign in Central Norway will be dealt with first; but it must be remembered that operations in the Narvik area were being conducted concurrently.

The Landings at Namsos

Operation Henry (Plan 11)

It will be remembered that none of the projected Allied landings was to take place if the Germans were in a position to oppose it (otherwise than from the air) and consequently it was of the utmost importance to forestall the arrival of enemy troops at the chosen places by whatever means were available. This was the reason for Operation Henry – a purely temporary measure designed to ensure that on the arrival of the first flight of troops at Namsos, they would not find it already occupied by Germans.

Vice-Admiral Cunningham had reported Namsos and the adjacent fjords clear of the enemy on 12 April, then proceeding north to rejoin the Commander-in-Chief off the Lofoten Islands, but the troops destined for Narnsos could not arrive for some days. Further south, Captain Pegram with the *Glasgow*, *Sheffield* and six destroyers[181] was operating in the Aalesund area; early on 13 April[182] he was searching for a pocket battleship, a cruiser and many large merchant ships reported by aircraft the previous day, when he intercepted A.T. 0216/13 addressed to the Commander-in-Chief:–

> 'In order to forestall the Germans at Namsos and to ensure an unopposed landing for a larger force, which will arrive at Namsos (about 16 April) propose, if you see no objection, that *Sheffield* and *Glasgow* should each prepare a landing party of about 150 men. A decision as to whether these parties will be required to land should be received by *Glasgow* and *Sheffield* about 1500 today (Saturday). Party should have provisions for seven days. Time of landing will be at the discretion of the Commanding Officer, HMS *Glasgow*. Operation will be called 'Henry'.'

The Commander-in-Chief had 'no objection, as a very temporary measure; but, as both ships' main armaments will be practically out of action for this period, consider it essential R.A.F. bombers should clear up pocket-battleships, cruisers, destroyers, and 15,000-ton storeship in Molde area'. The Admiralty therefore told Captain Pegram to carry on, and A.T. 1627/13 gave him particular instructions (extract):–

'Your object is to secure Namsen Fjord. so that a force of two battalions can be landed, a.m., 17 April. Landing parties should secure quays at Namsos and Bangsund and bridge across River Namsen; road south from Bangsund to be secured, if possible. Norwegians should be given every encouragement and assistance with rifles and ammunition.

    About 4000 German troops in Trondheim area; outposts reported at Steinkjaer.

    Norwegian units reported at Snass (64° 25' N., 12° 18' E.) and Verdalsoren area (63° 47' N., 11° 30' E.).

    Cruisers are to withdraw to the westward when fjord has been secured. Daily contact is to be made with landing party by destroyer'.

Captain Pegram prepared to land his party at dawn on 14 April, shifting the men into two destroyers off Kroken, on the east shore in the widest part of Namsen Fjord, a dozen miles short of Namsos, where the cruisers would wait. Captain Nicholson with the 6th Flotilla would then conduct the landing at Namsos, while the three ships of the 4th Flotilla covered the mouth of the fjord. But Captain Pegram had sent all six destroyers to Aalesund 'to mop up the many large merchant vessels' (which turned out to be Norwegian); once there they stayed all 13 April, the Senior Officer, Captain Nicholson, being impressed with the importance of that neighbourhood, on which the local authorities insisted, and expecting that the landing might be diverted there from Namsos. 'Admiral Tank-Nielson', he reported, 'considers Romsdals Fjord the most strategic point on the west coast; main importance lies in position of railway and road and the existence of ammunition stocks at Molde'. Captain Pegram therefore decided to land in the evening, despite the greater risk from the air; but for a time this danger made him hesitate, presumably on hearing of the destroyers' experiences on 13 April, when a score of German aircraft bombed them during their visit to Aalesund and Molde. Although the destroyers drove off the enemy with the loss of three machines, and without injury to themselves, the strength of the attack showed that ships would run considerable danger in the fjords.

The party landed from the destroyers 'without difficulty' at dusk on 14 April, 'although,' said Captain Pegram, 'I am certain our presence was known to the enemy' through reconnaissance aircraft. About 350 seamen and marines landed under Captain Edds, R.M., of the *Sheffield*. They took with them demolition gear to destroy the wharves and bridges in case of need, and extra rifles and cartridges to supply the wants of their Norwegian allies. A staff officer of the main expedition had arrived in the afternoon, flying to Norway ahead of his general; and, in consultation with him, it was decided to send the *Glasgow*'s party to Bangsund, and to take post south of it, while the *Sheffield*'s landed at Namsos and took post to the eastward. The British staff officer and the Norwegian officers saw no difficulty in 'Henry's holding its own for a time', but they did not feel sanguine about future movements: snow covered the district; Namsos and Bangsund were small, they gave little concealment, and they were short of fresh water; 'the southward move of any force much larger than one battalion must be both slow and conspicuous from the air'.

After landing 'Henry', Captain Nicholson stayed at Namsos in the *Somali* to arrange for the landing of 'Maurice' and to meet its commander, General Carton de Wiart, who arrived in a flying boat on 15 April. The other two ships of the 6th Flotilla went out to meet and assist the troopship convoy on its arrival. Captain Pegram, with the *Glasgow*, *Sheffield* and the three destroyers of the 4th Flotilla (two of which had oiled from the cruisers under way in Namsen Fjord) went out also to cruise in the offing near Kya Light, and afterwards to join Admiral Layton, who was bringing over the British troops of 'Maurice' and expected to reach Namsen Fjord by dusk on 15 April. The discouraging report from the army officers, quoted above, decided the Government to hold up the landing, however, and the first troops did not land until the following night. 'Henry's task then ending, the *Sikh* and *Matabele*, after landing some troops of 'Maurice', brought off the naval parties from Namsos and Bangsund, and carried them to their proper ships early on 17 April.

Operation Maurice: First Landings (Plan 11)

Under the original plan, as mentioned previously,[183] Vice-Admiral Edward-Collins was to have conducted the naval side of this expedition, the first flight of which then consisted of two battalions under Brigadier Morgan, embarked in the cruisers *Galatea* and *Arethusa* and the transport *Orion*. These were to have arrived at Namsos on 17 April, followed a few days later by a full brigade, with wagons, stores, ammunition and petrol embarked in transports. Admiral Whitworth's victory at Narvik on 13 April, however, produced a wave of optimism as to the task of the northern expedition and in the evening of 14 April the Government diverted to Namsos one of the two brigades then on passage to Narvik under Admiral Layton 'because expected opposition at the latter place had been considerably reduced by naval action'.

That evening Admiral Layton's convoy divided, he himself in the *Manchester*, with the *Birmingham*, *Cairo* and three destroyers, and two transports, the *Empress of Australia* and *Chrobry*, carrying the 146th Brigade (battalions of the Lincolnshire, the King's Own Yorkshire Light Infantry and the York and Lancaster regiments) steering for Namsos, while the remainder of the convoy escorted by the *Valiant* and nine destroyers continued for Narvik.[184] This detachment then became the first flight for Central Norway.

On 15 April, however, the account of conditions in and about Namsos led the Government to put off the landing and to order the convoy to go to Lillesjona, more than 100 miles farther north. They gave the last order probably on receiving a signal from Captain Nicholson, who reported 'facilities for landing and accommodation of large numbers of troops at Namsos very inadequate ... impossible to deal with more than one transport at anchor at a time ... very grave risk to town and transports unless command of air is certain'. On the other hand, he said, 'If transports could be sent elsewhere, destroyers could embark troops and land them at Namsos and Bangsund ... This would enable troops to be dispersed by rail from Namsos and by road from Bangsund. All disembarkation of troops should take place at dusk, and might be continued well into the night, provided weather is clear'. The following signal gave the new arrangements – A.T. 1722/15, addressed to Admiral Layton:–

'General Carton de Wiart will probably join you Lillesjona. Subject to what Carton de Wiart may report after visiting Namsos, it is probable that a decision will be given that troops should be transferred to destroyers at Lillesjona and proceed in destroyers to Namsos, taking as much stores with them as possible. It is hoped that, after discussion with General, you will be able to land first flight at Namsos tomorrow, Tuesday, at dusk. Early arrival is of first importance from political point of view'.

Admiral Layton welcomed the change of plan. To begin with, the size of the transports caused embarrassment, especially the *Empress of Australia*, which had in-turning screws; he had already arranged to send the troops onboard destroyers in Namsen Fjord, but Lillesjona was clearly to be preferred. Then the *Cairo* and the old destroyers with him were running short of oil, which the Admiralty provided for by diverting to Lillesjona the oiler *War Pindari*, on her way to Tromsø. Lastly, like everybody else, Admiral Layton felt anxious about the danger from the air. Under the original plan for the landing, there had been two anti-aircraft ships told off to protect the troopships. Now there was only the *Cairo*; the Admiralty had ordered the *Curlew* to join the convoy, but bad weather delayed her, which was unlucky, said Admiral Layton, 'as it appeared that every possible anti-aircraft protection would be needed'. The convoy kept out at sea until dark on 15 April to avoid being shadowed from the air, and anchored in Lillesjona early on 16 April. Four of Captain Pegram's destroyers joined on the way to the anchorage. The *War Pindari* arrived in the forenoon and oiled the destroyers before they took the troops from the transports. Later still, General Carton de Wiart arrived in the *Somali* from Namsos, which place he had reached by air the day before. In the evening the *Curlew* arrived; and the *War Pindari* sailed for Tromsø, having finished her task for Admiral Layton, but left behind one of her escorting destroyers, the *Nubian*, that the *Somali* might go home for ammunition, which she had run out of the day before in encounters with German aircraft.[185]

The influence of the air appears also in messages the General sent the War Office during the night (15/16). In the first, after giving his first thoughts about landing the troops, he emphasized 'the difficulties presented by enemy air activity, whereas we have no planes at all'. In the second, 0126/16, he says:–

'Concealment of troops by day is very difficult. There is little cover and still a great deal of snow. However, if it is essential to advance, the sooner it is done the better.

I cannot at present judge situation at Trondheim; but it will be essential that strong action should be taken as regards enemy air activity when I attack. If there is to be naval attack at Trondheim, and it is successful, General Audet should attack as soon as possible after it. If you could inform me of date of this attack, it would help decide definite date of my attack. My orders to General Audet would be to attack if naval operations succeeded. If you could ensure his having close liaison with Navy, this would be possible.'[186]

He had already sent the commander of the 146th Brigade his first thoughts about a landing. While held up by weather on his way across the North Sea, thinking the troops would land at Namsos on 15 April, he said they should take their stand covering Henry, the naval party, and make ready to advance at short notice towards Trondheim. While going from Namsos to join the brigade, he said he proposed landing two battalions from destroyers during the night 16/17: two companies to land at Bangsund, the rest at Namsos, and the destroyers should be ready to leave Lillesjona at noon. This plan was carried out, though a couple of hours late, during an attack from the air. The *Afridi, Nubian, Sikh, Matabele* and *Mashona* went alongside the transports as they finished oiling and took onboard the two battalions, while the Germans dropped bombs in the anchorage, narrowly missing the two transports and the *War Pindari*, each of which had destroyers alongside during the attack. They sailed in the afternoon, the Lincolnshire and half the York and Lancaster going to Namsos, the other two companies of the York and Lancaster to Bangsund. The General went in with his men, making his headquarters onboard the *Afridi*, and from her he reported thus to the War Office a little before midnight:

'Have brought 1000 men to Namsos today, and hope to bring remainder of Phillips's brigade tomorrow ... Am occupying Grong, Bangsund and probably positions astride Beitstad Fjord, 25 miles south of Namsos. No fresh information of the enemy. Enemy aircraft still bombing at leisure'.

The King's Own Yorkshire Light Infantry should have landed from destroyers next day, the transport *Chrobry* going in at the same time with all the stores of the brigade. But, said Admiral Layton,

> 'when it became clear the air attacks were persisting, I had to review the plans made with the General. It was true that air attacks were not so far on a very large scale, though practically continuous; but I could see no reason why they should not increase, and continue at short intervals; and it was impossible to ignore the risk of a disastrous hit on a liner full of troops. I was confirmed in my opinion by a visit I paid to the troopships in the course of the afternoon, when it became clear to me that the morale of the young and untried soldiers was likely to suffer if they were subjected to prolonged attacks of this kind while still embarked.
>
> I therefore decided that it would be necessary to leave the anchorage before daylight the next morning. This made it impossible to use the destroyers as arranged. Accordingly, I decided to move the third battalion from the *Empress of Australia* to the *Chrobry*, and send the latter in alone to Namsos'.

The soldiers and all but 170 tons of the stores having been shifted into the *Chrobry*, the convoy sailed about 0330 on 17 April, and stood out to sea for the day. The *Highlander* had run on shore in the night, while patrolling outside Lillesjona, and she had to go home, leaving only the *Vanoc* and *Whirlwind* for a screen, but before she actually parted company she forced a German submarine to dive, some distance ahead, and thus enabled the convoy to avoid attack. About 1000 the screen gained strength by the return of the ships that had landed the first battalions, General Carton de Wiart returning with them in the *Afridi*. Later still in the forenoon, with the General agreeing, Admiral Layton sent home the *Empress of Australia*, escorted by the *Birmingham* and two old destroyers. 'There seemed no alternative', says the Admiral, 'to letting the 170 tons of stores still in her go back to the United Kingdom and be shipped back in a smaller vessel, and the sooner this was done the better'. The rest of the convoy turned back in time to reach Namsen Fjord at sunset, about 1945. There the *Chrobry* parted company for Namsos, with the *Curlew* and the five '*Tribals*' for escort, while the Admiral, in the

Manchester, went out to sea again for the night, and the *Cairo* went north to Skjel Fjord for oil. The soldiers landed during the night without interruption from the enemy; but at 0200/18, 'the military working parties were withdrawn, presumably in order to take cover before daylight: this cessation left 130 tons of stores still onboard the *Chrobry*, and the G.O.C. agreed to these remaining'. All the ships returned to the Admiral in 65° N., 7° 50' E., at noon.

Naval Movements and Landing of French (Plan 11)

Ever since landing their parties for 'Henry', the *Glasgow* and *Sheffield* had been cruising off the coast. Captain Pegram had sent his destroyers to join Admiral Layton at Lillesjona, when the signals showed him that they would be needed to land 'Maurice', but he kept his cruisers away from the land, lest their presence near Namsos should arouse suspicion in the enemy. He went back to Namsen Fjord early on 17 April to take onboard his landing parties; and, having no further orders, he then stretched away to the southward to help the *York*, which, with the *Effingham*, *Calcutta* and *Ashanti*, was searching for five German destroyers, reported by aircraft off Stavanger the evening before and perhaps trying to land a force at Åndalsnes. The *York* and her consorts finding nothing, Captain Pegram turned north again in the afternoon, and later received a signal from the Admiralty telling him to go to Namsen Fjord to give anti-aircraft protection for the *Chrobry*'s landing, and to oil the *Mashona* and *Nubian*, after which the *Glasgow* and *Sheffield* were to go to Scapa. The two cruisers gave some 200 tons of oil each to the *Mashona* and *Nubian* in Namsen Fjord during the night, joined the Admiral outside next day, and then went to Scapa to get oil themselves, arriving there on 19 April.

Admiral Layton's service on that part of the coast was ending, too. The next troops for 'Maurice' were French. General Audet was bringing the first three battalions of his Chasseurs-Alpins in four troopships, escorted by the French Admiral with the *Emile Bertin* and some French destroyers. They should have arrived on 18 April, but were a day late, so Admiral Layton took the opportunity to send in the *Chrobry* again to land the last of her stores in the evening of 18 April, and she went home next day with a cargo of timber from Namsos. Meanwhile, Sir Charles Forbes ordered home nearly all the British ships to prepare for the intended landing at Trondheim (Operation Hammer). Accordingly Admiral Layton steered towards Rosyth on 19 April, and made ready for the *Manchester* for taking troops and stores onboard. The *Matabele* had gone home for oil on 18 April, the *Sikh* and *Mashona* took the *Chrobry* home, the *Afridi* and *Nubian* started for home after landing General Carton de Wiart and some Norwegian pilots they had collected to meet the French. This left the *Cairo* only, for the *Curlew* had to go home, too, for oil; and Admiral Layton 'viewed this position with some anxiety, especially as the next convoy was to be the first French one and in view of the growing probability of submarines operating off the entrance to Namsen Fjord'. Evidently Sir Charles Forbes saw things in the same light, for he ordered the *Manchester* to go back, but she had run 400 miles to the southward on her way home and could not get back in time 'for the first and critical French landings', so Admiral Layton 'adjusted course and speed with a view to meeting the convoy on its return journey'.

Fortunately the *Cairo* was still on the spot and she led the French convoy in to Namsos. German aircraft attacked it during its passage through the fjords in the evening of 19 April, as they had attacked the British part of 'Maurice' at Lillesjona. They hit the *Emile Bertin*, flagship of Admiral Derrien, early in the attack, about 1800, and she went home.[187] The *Cairo* and the French destroyers took the troopships to Namsos: *El d'Jezair* (Admiral Cadart), *El Mansour*, *El Kantara*, each of 5,000-6,000 tons, and the *Ville d'Oran*, above 10,000 tons. They had no further casualty, though the last-named transport was slightly damaged. The troops landed in the night with all but a few tons of ammunition and stores, and the convoy went home, escorted by the *Cairo*, being joined by the *Manchester* in the evening of 20 April, which remained in company till off the Shetlands next day and then proceeded to Scapa.

German Air Attacks on Namsos

A few hours after the ships had gone on 20 April, German aircraft attacked Namsos itself, there being no defence. The *Nubian* came back that night, and Commander Ravenhill says: 'The whole place was a mass of flames from end to end, and the glare on the snows of the surrounding mountains produced an unforgettable spectacle'. General Carton de Wiart came onboard to say that 'the storehouses on the jetties had been destroyed and that, owing to the evacuation of the Norwegians, all his transport had disappeared; in consequence, any stores landed would be exposed to almost certain destruction before there was any hope of removing them, even troops might not be got to safety in time ... unless the Germans could be drastically restricted in their air activities within a very short time, the expedition was doomed'. And early on 21 April the General thus reported the state of affairs to the War Office:–

> 'Enemy aircraft have almost completely destroyed Namsos, beginning on railhead target, diving indiscriminately. At present impossible to land more men or material. If I am to continue operations, it seems that I must largely depend on road-borne supplies, either through Mosjoen (150 miles away by road) or from Sweden ... Acute shortage of cars and petrol here. I see little chance of carrying out decisive or, indeed, any operations unless enemy air activity is considerably restricted. Audet wishes Gamelin informed of situation. Phillips's brigade at present Verdal, Steinkjaer, Foldafoss. French take over around Namsos.'

There were more attacks from the air on 21 April, though less harmful than the day before. The *Auckland* sloop, coming in the afternoon to relieve the *Nubian*, was attacked with bombs and machine-gun fire throughout her passage up Namsen Fjord. The following remarks in Commander Ravenhill's letter of proceedings, written as the *Nubian* went back to Scapa, describe an experience common to all small ships employed at the expeditionary bases:–

> Just before my departure (on 22 April), a French naval officer came onboard and expressed the gratification of the French General at the effect the presence of the ships had had in curtailing enemy air activity. He asked me to press very strongly for the continued presence of the ships. Personally, I doubt whether the presence of so small a force of ships does stop the enemy making raids: the gunfire certainly makes the bombing wilder, and has the effect of easing pressure tremendously on the land forces, as the enemy appear to go exclusively for the ships when there are any present. I was not surprised when I heard a severe raid had taken place in the evening after my departure, and I don't suppose my presence would have averted it.

A very great strain is imposed on the personnel of these A/A ships when employed on this type of duty. Owing to the high mountains, no warning can be obtained of the approach of hostile aircraft; and in ships whose entire armament is manned for A/A fire it is essential to be in at least the second degree of readiness during daylight hours from about 0300 to 2100. Reversion to third degree of readiness during the six hours of darkness does not provide much relaxation. The ships are continually underway, day and night, and when the attacks come there is little room to manoeuvre. There is continued tension, and the knowledge that before the day is over there is almost certain to be at least one severe attack and that nothing can come to your assistance is trying to the nerves.

I am not trying to pretend that *Nubian* has performed any arduous duty, as we had a very short period under these conditions, but enough to realise what it might be like for any length of time.

If ships have to be used for A/A defence of a port which lies so close to an enemy air base as does Namsos, I submit that at least three ships are necessary to be effective, and they will have to be carefully disposed, so as to obtain freedom of manoeuvre in the restricted waters without getting in each other's way.'

Final Reinforcements, Namsos (Plan 11)

In the meantime, the next body of French troops had sailed from Scapa in the 10,000-ton transport *Ville d'Alger*, escorted by the *Calcutta* and a couple of French destroyers, to which Admiral Layton added the *Birmingham* for the latter part of the passage across the North Sea. They were to arrive on 21 April, but as things stood the General would not let them land, so the transport, arriving before they could stop her, was ordered to sea again. The *Calcutta* brought her in next day and a storeship came the same evening. The storeship went alongside to unload; but the big Frenchman could not manage it, so she had to anchor, the troops going on shore in the *Auckland* and a destroyer, and she sailed again without landing her heavy stores, among them some anti-tank guns and an anti-aircraft battery.

No more infantry landed at Namsos. General Carton de Wiart had mentioned the possibility of having to withdraw as early as 21 April, as follows (*Nubian*'s 2335/21):–

'Phillips's brigade attacked by enemy landed from cruiser and torpedo boat early this morning, 21 April: our troops being pressed, but situation not yet clear. Am endeavouring to push up French troops; but lorries promised by Norway staff have not yet materialized. Enemy aircraft again very active and dominating situation.

'Fear our position becomes untenable, for although jetties not destroyed, approaches very difficult, owing to debris and craters. Only three small storehouses standing, so no room to hide stores. Railhead damaged. No labour available. All civilians left Namsos. No cars left.

'Should you decide on evacuating, send ships larger than 5,000 tons maximum and fear it requires two nights to embark'.[188]

The German troops mentioned had artillery, and landed at Steinkjaer, which ships could reach through narrow fjords from Trondheim. Next day a German destroyer shelled the troops at Verdalsoren, some 15 miles farther south. And on 23 April the General signalled again that he feared 'there is no alternative to evacuation' unless he could have superiority in the air. In these circumstances, the next convoy of Chasseurs-Alpins joined the Narvik expedition instead. On the other hand, guns and stores were landed at Namsos on 27 and 28 April, including those the *Ville d'Alger* had carried home again and another battery of anti-aircraft guns and a battery of howitzers manned by the Royal Marines.

The Landings at Åndalsnes, Aalesund and Molde

Operation Primrose (Plans 1 and 3)

While the expedition to Namsos was fizzling out to its inevitable conclusion the Åndalsnes venture was having little better fortune.

The original intention was to occupy Aalesund, half-way between Bud and the peninsula of Stadtlandet, 'with the object of neutralizing' the Indreled on that part of the coast and to 'create a diversion' south of Trondheim, while troops were landing at Namsos, north of that place. This operation received the code name of 'Primrose', and was to be carried out by marines and seamen drawn from certain ships of the Home Fleet then in dockyard hands. Meanwhile, however, the Norwegians made known their anxiety for Romsdals Fjord, where they feared a German attack, and which Admiral Tank-Nielsen called 'the most strategic point on the west coast'. This fjord is some 40 miles north and east of Aalesund and farther inland. Near its mouth, actually outside the fjord proper, lies Molde, which has a little harbour like Aalesund; at the inland end of the fjord is Åndalsnes, from which the railway runs south through Dombaas, 60 miles away, and through Lillehammer to Oslo, a branch line from Dombaas running back northward to Trondheim, distant about 100 miles from Dombaas. The Norwegian Army had its general headquarters at Lillehammer, while a column of troops some 2,000 strong lay between Åndalsnes and Dombaas, and there were stocks of munitions at Molde. For these reasons, presumably, and to make ready for the enveloping attack on Trondheim from north and south, the British Government changed the destination of 'Primrose' to Åndalsnes.

The parties had begun to make ready two days before the expedition was decided on, in compliance with A.T. 1209/11, addressed to the *Hood*, *Nelson* and *Barham*, which ran as follows: 'Marine detachments of 100 men from each ship and seamen field gun's crews may be required for a special operation to occupy small islands for limited period shortly; parties would be required to be self-supporting for one month, and to land and mount 12-pdr. gun or 3.7-in. howitzer; necessary preliminary preparations to be made'. Orders next day increased each party by 70 men; and on 13 April came orders for the 21st Light Anti-aircraft Battery, Royal Marines, and two detachments of the 11th Searchlight Regiment, Royal Marines, to join the expedition. On the same day Lieutenant-Colonel Simpson, R. M., was appointed in command of the force, which was to be transported to Norway in the sloops *Black Swan*, *Flamingo*, *Auckland* and *Bittern*. Some 45 officers and 680 men actually sailed, with three 3.7-in. howitzers and eight anti-aircraft pom-poms for the field force, and two 4-in. guns for Aalesund; but the searchlights stayed behind.

Colonel Simpson came to Rosyth in the morning of 14 April, and the rest of the expedition arrived during the day. The *Barham*'s party arrived first from Liverpool, then the *Hood*'s from Plymouth, the anti-aircraft battery from Tynemouth, the *Nelson*'s from Portsmouth, and last, a little before midnight, the searchlight detachments from Yeovil. Men and gear went onboard the sloops as they arrived, for the expedition had orders to sail the same day, so had not time for 'any pre-arranged and useful order' of stowage. For instance, the seamen and marines from the *Nelson* sailed in different ships, to make room for the anti-aircraft guns to sail in two ships also and avoid the risk of having all in one basket, but the *Nelson*'s had not expected nor prepared for this when loading their train. Although Captain Poland of the *Black Swan* spared the greater part of one month's supply of victuals for the expedition from the three months' outfit in his flotilla, that the force might use the spare thus saved for essential equipment instead of the victuals they had brought with them, they had still to go without some of their stores; among other things there was no room for the searchlights. As it was, the ships drew a foot more water than their normal draught, and had to stow much heavy gear on their upper decks, besides carrying an extra number of men equal to their own crews, 'most unfavourable' weather forecasts notwithstanding. 'It is for consideration', wrote Colonel Simpson afterwards, 'whether, in similar circumstances, a delay of some hours in sailing is not justifiable in order to allow a reasonable loading plan'.

The *Auckland* did sail that evening, with the *Barham*'s party and one of the 4-in. guns, that she might gain a footing at Aalesund betimes and keep pace with the Namsos expedition, whose first troops were also embarking at Rosyth that day. Owing to the late arrival of the rest of the force, the other three ships could not sail until 0330/15. But they soon overtook the *Auckland*. She had met with a gale of wind in the night, and finding he could not keep the speed required to arrive by dawn on 16 April, Commander Hewitt decided to wait for his consorts. They joined him off Buchan Ness, and steered away for Invergordon soon afterwards to shelter. The sea was rising, the ships could barely steam 10 knots, their crowded passengers were sea-sick. 'It would not have been possible to arrive at our destination at or near dawn on the desired day', said Captain Poland in his subsequent report, 'and 'Primrose' would also have been a very wilted flower by the time it arrived'. At Invergordon they received A.T. 1926/15, which changed their destination to Åndalsnes:–

'Inform Lieut.-Colonel Simpson that ... force is now to proceed to Åndalsnes, which is understood to be in Norwegian hands. If Germans are in Åndalsnes, no landing is to be made, and situation reported. It is possible that other military forces will be landed later at Åndalsnes ... '

The gale which forced them in to Invergordon gave Colonel Simpson time and opportunity at last to meet his officers and to explain his plans for the landing and for future service, though there was not much he could do before the expedition arrived, as he lacked maps and knew little of the country he was bound for, the Norway Pilot being his only source of knowledge.

The wind and sea abating, the expedition set out again on 16 April. During the passage, two further signals affecting the operation were sent. A.T. 1633/16 ordered 1,000 soldiers, under Brigadier Morgan, to follow as soon as possible; and A.T. 1507/17 told Colonel Simpson to mount his 4-in. guns at Aalesund and to land men to hold that place as well as Åndalsnes.

The force arrived at Åndalsnes at 2200/17; and the *Black Swan* went alongside the quay to unload, with the *Bittern* outside her, while the other two ships patrolled in the fjord. When the *Black Swan* finished the *Bittern* took her place, the *Flamingo* going alongside her in turn, and so they proceeded. All had finished by 0700/18, much helped by the use of a 5-ton travelling crane on the quay – an unexpected resource – and unmolested by the enemy, though they had sighted and fired on a German aircraft a few hours before they arrived. Then the *Auckland* and *Bittern* put to sea again to take the *Barham*'s party and the 4-in. guns to Aalesund, and another party went to Molde, to form a base there, with Captain Denny as Naval Officer-in-Charge. Thus the expedition had an easy passage, apart from the weather, and it landed without hindrance. Yet there had been reason for anxiety in reports on 16 April that Germans from seaplanes might forestall 'Primrose' and that German destroyers had been seen off Stavanger. On receiving the first report, Captain Poland made up his mind to disregard his routeing orders and to go direct from Fair Island to his destination, chancing discovery from the air as he steered along the Norwegian coast, instead of standing farther north before crossing the North Sea.

German aircraft bombed Åndalsnes nearly every day from 20 April onwards. The attacks grew worse, so all the work of the base was done at night, the men taking shelter in the woods and on the hillsides during the raids. In the end the Germans destroyed the town, most of which was built of wood, but the marines' anti-aircraft gunners claim to have protected the railway and the quay successfully. The *Hood*'s field howitzer went into action against some German parachute troops between Dombaas and Dovre the day after landing, and helped the Norwegians in rounding them up. Otherwise, 'Primrose' encountered enemy land forces only on the last day of the expedition, when a few marines at an outpost beyond Verma covered the retreat from that place. For the rest, 'Primrose' became part of 'Sickle' when the latter expedition arrived. Brigadier Morgan sent his first battalions forward to Dombaas and beyond, as soon as he could learn the state of affairs, leaving only light anti-aircraft guns at Åndalsnes. 'He relied upon me', said Colonel Simpson, 'to hold the Åndalsnes area with its vital railhead and landing place', and this remained the principal object of the naval party. Colonel Simpson had made his own arrangements with this in view at his landing. The marines established 'six platoon posts, with one in reserve, covering important tactical positions such as road bridges, the electrical power station at Verma, about 28 miles inland, and possible lines of enemy approach, as well as the aerodrome at Lesjaswick (Lake Lesjaskog

– 'Gladiator Lake'), about 40 miles inland. Some positions were changed as the situation altered, but the functions of the detachments remained the same'. The anti-aircraft pom-poms were posted at various points about the town. The seamen served mainly as a working party at the base. Captain Denny wrote from Molde; 'It is fortunate that the first party to be landed was a seaman and Royal Marines' force and that this party largely remained in the vicinity of Åndalsnes; the unavoidable absence of any proper base personnel and equipment in the earlier stages of the expedition produced a local situation which, in my opinion, was only mastered through the adaptability to be expected of naval units'.[189]

As for Aalesund, its party arrived there in the afternoon of 18 April. The Norwegians received the party with enthusiasm, all but its 4-in. guns, which they held would invite attack from the air, and against that they had no defence. The local Norwegian commander thought the guns unnecessary for controlling the Indreled, since dangerous areas had been declared off Bud and Stadtlandet on 8 April, nor did he expect attack by sea now that Åndalsnes was occupied. On his behalf Commander Hewitt of the *Auckland* asked for two 3-in. high-angle guns, and 'strongly recommended' taking away the coast defence weapons, unless some sort of anti-aircraft guns could be provided for the port. In the meantime, Major Lumley, of the *Hood*, whom Colonel Simpson had placed in command at Aalesund, set about digging the gun-pits, though he had leave to put off mounting the guns, which in fact were never mounted. Apart from the objection to having the guns at all, Major Lumley found they lacked several essential articles of equipment. It was the same with the 3-in. high-angle guns, when they came on 23 April; 'many essential items had been omitted'. One or two transports coaled at Aalesund before going home after landing men or gear at Åndalsnes, but little else happened there during the stay of the British party except the almost daily attacks from the air.

Operation Sickle (Plan 11)

Meanwhile, before the 'Primrose' force had even reached Åndalsnes, the decision had been taken to increase the scale of operations in this area, and preliminary orders issued for Operation Sickle. The first hint of this operation came on 16 April and was contained in a message from the C.I.G.S. to General Carton de Wiart (A.T. 0020/16)[190] which stated that the naval party would be reinforced, if possible, but that the only troops immediately available were those under Brigadier Morgan's command. These consisted of two weak territorial battalions, the 5th Leicestershire and the 8th Sherwood Foresters, with four Bofors anti-aircraft guns, hitherto destined for Namsos.

Later that day orders were sent to Vice-Admiral Edward-Collins, who conducted the first flight of the expedition, and to Brigadier Morgan. Those to the Admiral (A.T. 1633/16) ran as follows:–

'It has been decided to land a military force at Åndalsnes as soon as possible, in addition to 'Primrose' force. *Galatea, Arethusa, Carlisle, Curacoa* and two destroyers are placed under your command, and a total of approximately 1000 troops under Brigadier Morgan are to be embarked in these ships. Forces to sail as soon as ready. Cruisers can go alongside at Molde, and it is recommended that troops from cruisers should be disembarked at that place, being subsequently ferried to Åndalsnes ... It is of great importance to get troops out of ships as soon as possible on account of air attack ... Your action on arrival must depend on situation; unless immediate action is essential, a landing at dusk is considered advisable on account of air attack.'

Brigadier Morgan's instructions followed in A.T. 2014/16:–

'Your role to land Åndalsnes area, secure Dombaas, then operate northwards and take offensive action against Germans in Trondheim area. Not intended that you should land in face of opposition. Second echelon your force will follow you two days later. As you are without transport, you should rely on Norwegian rolling stock and locally impressed transport. You will be kept informed of progress and timings of other British forces operating Trondheim area.

Your force independent command under War Office until receipt further orders. Intention later place you under commander general operations Trondheim area.

During the voyage and during landing operations, senior naval officer will be in command. He will decide, in co-operation with you, where and when to land.'

And in A.T. 2217/17:–

'Denial to Germans of use of railway through Dombaas northward becomes vital. Indications point to improbability of your encountering serious German opposition between Åndalsnes and Dombaas, if you move quickly. Consider full possibility of pushing even small detachments on to Dombaas really rapidly, and act as you judge best. When you have secured Dombaas, you are to prevent Germans using railway to reinforce Trondheim. Am sending small demolition party ... You should make touch with Norwegian G.H.Q., believed to be in area Lillehammer, and avoid isolating Norwegian forces operating towards Oslo.'

Most of the troops and stores had to shift from the transport *Orion*, onboard of which they had been under the earlier arrangements for Namsos; and the work, says Admiral Edward-Collins, was 'much hampered by the impossibility of berthing a cruiser directly under the derricks of the *Orion* and the fact that the stores had been loaded as received, and those required were generally at the bottom of the holds'. However, the expedition sailed from Rosyth early on 17 April in the cruisers and anti-aircraft ships named in the orders and in the *Arrow* and *Acheron*. In the evening of 18 April they found the *York* outside Buddybet, the northern approach to Molde and Åndalsnes, where she was cruising to protect the expeditions' arrival; the Admiral released her from her watch, likewise the *Effingham*, which was covering the southern approach. Inside the fjords were the *Black Swan*, *Flamingo* and *Bittern* sloops: German aircraft had attacked these ships in the afternoon, but 'Sickle' arrived and landed without interference. The Admiral had learnt from the *Black Swan* that cruisers could go alongside at Åndalsnes, so he left the *Curacoa* and *Arethusa* to land at Molde, and took the rest of the expedition to Åndalsnes, arriving between 2000 and 2100/18. The *Galatea* went alongside at once, the two destroyers taking turns to go alongside her to land their troops and to receive fuel from her; then the *Carlisle* took the *Galatea*'s place, and at 0300/19 the ships sailed. At Molde, of course, the work was finished earlier; local craft collected by Captain Denny (Naval Officer-in-Charge) ferried the troops and stores thence to Åndalsnes, some arriving before the Admiral left. The *Galatea* and *Arethusa* arrived back at Rosyth without incident on 20 April.

The landing at Åndalsnes, said the Admiral 'was completed more rapidly than I had expected ... a 5-ton travelling crane on the quay was of great assistance in expediting the unloading of stores'. He went on:–

> 'It is my belief that operation 'Sickle' was carried out without the knowledge of the enemy, and that this was probably due to the absence of any troop transport with the force, from which aircraft could deduce its object.[191]
>
> In spite of sea-sickness and the general discomfort of the voyage, all the troops landed in good order; and by 0100 an advance party had entrained and left for Dombaas Junction, which there appeared to be every prospect they would reach without opposition. I consider this a very creditable performance on the part of the ships and troops concerned. I consider the facilities at Åndalsnes excellent for the landing of a small force; but it is most desirable that adequate shore air defence be provided at the earliest possible moment to prevent damage to the quay and railway station, which are the great assets of the place. The quay, though good, is very short, and there is only one crane; one large well-aimed bomb would wreck both.'

In the evening of 19 April, the *Carlisle* (Flag, Rear-Admiral Vivian) turned back on her way home, and relieved the *Black Swan* as Senior Naval Officer at Åndalsnes, taking the place of the 'Primrose' sloops as anti-aircraft guardship. Admiral Vivian's experience and that of his successor, Captain Aylmer in the *Curacoa*, proved the wisdom of landing the troops at night. German aircraft that appeared on 19 April after the troopships had sailed did not drop bombs, perhaps owing to the good shooting of the *Black Swan*; but bombing attacks greeted the *Carlisle* within three hours of her coming on 20 April, and continued all day. The *Curacoa* arrived on 22 April to find full employment up to the evening of 24 April, when she was hit and had to go home. Here is Captain Aylmer's account of affairs in a signal made a few hours before his ship was disabled:–

> 'Åndalsnes and *Curacoa* have been repeatedly bombed each day: high, low, and dive bombing attacks, and machine-gunned in the

fjord. During daylight hours hostile aircraft are never absent from the sky. Attacks usually well pressed home. Some damage to town; many near misses on *Curacoa*. In dive bombing, bombs appear set delay approximately 12 seconds and burst deep; this undoubtedly saved *Curacoa*'s stern from serious damage. Hits on ship must be expected while doing anti-aircraft guardship. Personnel continuously closed up at action stations and getting no rest. Services of friendly aircraft in this area urgently required and will be most welcome. Reliable sources give seven hostile aircraft brought down by anti-aircraft fire and others damaged. *Curacoa* running short 4-in. ammunition: am drawing from small stock ashore, when fused.'

Enemy aircraft constantly attacked Aalesund, too, particularly when ships lay there, but Molde came off lightly until the last few days of the expedition. The letters of proceedings discuss various methods of coping with the attacks. All commanding officers agreed that ships must keep underway during daylight, with good speed at command. The high ground bordering the narrow fjords made gunfire difficult – generally a case of 'snap shoots' as Captain Poland of the *Black Swan* had it – and radio direction finding was no help in these conditions. All paid tribute to the steadiness and spirit of the men in long periods of constant duty. One officer mentioned the 'tremendously heartening effect' of having another anti-aircraft ship in company. Sir Charles Forbes, however, had come to the conclusion that the employment of ships for this purpose was wasteful.[192] On 26 April he 'recommended Admiralty to send A/A batteries and Royal Air Force fighters to counter enemy air action at bases on Norwegian coast in preference to using ships' and next day he said he should not 'keep a sloop or A/A cruiser at Åndalsnes during daylight hours. Does not effectively protect base and they shoot away all their ammunition in one day'.[193]

Sickle Reinforcements (Plans 1 and 11)

Unlike the principal flights, the first reinforcement for 'Sickle' came in transports: 600 men in the little *St. Magnus* and *St. Sunniva*, escorted by the destroyers *Jackal* and *Javelin*. The storeship *Cedarbank* in the same convoy was torpedoed and sunk on passage by a U-boat – a serious loss, since she carried A/A guns and equipment, and transport – but the remainder arrived in daylight[194] on 21 April, a day of snowstorms and low clouds, however, which screened the port from enemy aircraft – one of the few days at Åndalsnes free from attack. Such immunity was exceptional, and the next day aircraft disabled the *Pelican* sloop some 50 miles from the coast on her way there to give anti-aircraft protection. That evening the *Arethusa*[195] arrived, laden chiefly with stores. She brought among other things some much-wanted 4-in. ammunition for the sloops, machine-guns for the Norwegians, a battery of Oerlikon anti-aircraft guns and the advance party and some stores for the Royal Air Force station on Lesjaskog Lake. She landed everything in a little over four hours that night, which was thought a good evolution; but her captain remarked that 'a great saving of labour for the ship's company and a reduction of the chaos which occurs when embarking stores for these expeditions could be made if there was a sea transport officer at the place of embarkation who knew what had to be embarked and who could inform the ship's officers what they had to take and whom it was for'. Admiral Edward-Collins, in forwarding the report, concurred: 'I fully agree ... the recent operations have been in the nature of rush evolutions; but the old proverb of more haste, less speed, has been very much in evidence.'[196]

As soon as Hammer (the direct attack on Trondheim) was given up, further reinforcements for Sickle were decided on. Major-General Paget went out to take command, two brigades of regular infantry were earmarked, and possibly some field artillery might have followed. As it turned out, only one brigade reached Åndalsnes before the Government decided to withdraw. The following signal shows, however, a distinct advance in the importance of the expedition (A.T. 1731/20 April):–

'(i) It is intended to land a considerable force in the Åndalsnes area with the ultimate object of capturing Trondheim in conjunction with General de Wiart's force at Namsos. Two brigades originally allocated to 'Hammer' will be landed in Åndalsnes area, so as to gain control of the Dombaas area and isolate Trondheim from the south. Further troops will follow.
(ii) This operation will still be referred to as 'Sickle'.
(iii) 'Maurice' is being reinforced by French troops.
(iv) The first of the brigades referred to in paragraph 1 will probably land p.m. 23 and p.m. 25 April.

(v) Immediate steps are being taken to obtain small transports suitable for entering the fjords; in the meantime it will be necessary for HM ships to be used for transporting troops.'

The 15th Brigade actually went, three battalions of Yorkshire regiments, about 2700 all told, with nine anti-tank guns and a battery of Bofors anti-aircraft guns. They sailed in two parties: Admiral Edward-Collins taking the 1st York and Lancaster Regiment and the 1st King's Own Yorkshire Light Infantry, the anti-tank guns and half the Bofors guns; and Admiral Layton taking a battalion of the Green Howards, the rest of the Bofors guns and their crews, General Paget and his staff, and the headquarters troops. There seem to have been ideas of withdrawing already, owing to the threatened destruction of the base by air attack, for the Admiralty made this signal to Captain Denny at Molde (A.T. 2013/21):–

'It must be accepted that piers at Åndalsnes may be destroyed by aircraft at any time: termination of operation on this account cannot be accepted, and you should accordingly be prepared to unload ships into small craft and land stores anywhere you can. Report what could be done about motor transport and guns in these circumstances.'

This one brigade landed successfully at Molde and Åndalsnes.

Admiral Edward-Collins left Rosyth on 22 April with the *Galatea*, *Sheffield*, *Glasgow*, and the *Vansittart* and *Campbell*, *Ivanhoe* and *Icarus*, *Impulsive* and *Witch*. The flagship carried about 400 men, the two larger ships 700 each, the destroyers 60 each. Besides the land forces they took one of the belated searchlights with its crew and two 3-in. high-angle guns for the naval party at Aalesund, officers and men for the naval base, and a quantity of stores. They arrived in the evening of 23 April without incident, the *Sheffield* and two destroyers going to Molde, while the rest went on to Åndalsnes. The *Sheffield* went alongside to unload, as did the *Galatea* at Åndalsnes, but the *Glasgow* anchored and sent men and gear on shore in destroyers and local small craft. Having finished their task the cruisers sailed separately for home, each with a couple of destroyers in company, but the *Glasgow* rejoined the flag in the evening, 24 April, a few miles north and east of the Shetlands. Soon afterwards, a couple of aircraft attacked them without result. Apart from that, as Admiral Edward-Collins pointed out: 'It is remarkable that my ships have now carried out this operation three times without molestation.'[197]

Admiral Layton left Rosyth on 24 April. He had the *Manchester* and *Birmingham* just home from serving with 'Maurice' at Namsos, the *York* and the destroyers *Arrow*, *Acheron* and *Griffin*, each ship taking her quota of troops and stores, a little under 1600 men and some 300 tons of stores altogether. The *Manchester* went alongside at Molde in the evening of 25 April, and her 'unloading ... was carried out with unexpected rapidity'. The *Birmingham* and *York* anchored at Åndalsnes, the destroyers and local craft ferrying troops and stores to the quay. Early in the morning (26 April) the *York* and the destroyers sailed for the United Kingdom, but the *Manchester* and *Birmingham* stayed on the coast to support the destroyers cruising in the Trondheim approaches.

On the way north towards Trondheim, before the *York* and destroyers were out of sight, Admiral Layton's ships fell in with German armed trawlers disguised as Dutchmen.

The *Birmingham* sank one, a minelayer, which on falling in with the destroyers had hoisted German colours and managed to ram the *Arrow*, necessitating her return home escorted by the *Acheron*. A little later the *Griffin* captured another trawler fitted for supplying submarines and armed with torpedoes.

These encounters led the Commander-in-Chief to suspect the presence of enemy transports astern of the trawlers, and he accordingly ordered Admiral Layton to sweep to the southward, who altered course accordingly at 1045. Shortly afterwards six destroyers hove in sight, steering to the south-westward. These proved to be the aircraft carriers' relieved screen proceeding to Sullom Voe for fuel. Admiral Layton thereupon ordered them to spread on a line of bearing on their way south and to keep a lookout for enemy supply ships, while he himself with the *Birmingham* covered the area to the eastward of them till 1600/26, when he turned to the northward to take up a covering position for the night off the entrance to Trondheim Fjord.

The *Manchester* and *Birmingham* remained in this vicinity till the forenoon of 28 April and then they returned to Scapa, for by this time the retreat from Åndalsnes had been decided on and it was necessary for them to fill up with oil before playing their part in withdrawal.

During this service they had not been free from air attack. German aircraft had dropped a few bombs, some of which nearly hit the *Birmingham*, in the afternoon of 25 April, three hours before the convoy entered Buddybet; another machine attacked the *Manchester* early on 26 April, after she had cleared the fjords again. Yet another attacked the *Manchester* and *Birmingham* in the evening of 27 April, a hundred miles or so from the coast, as they were going in for the night patrol. But the main weight of the air attacks was falling on the inshore operations. That afternoon (27 April), a supply convoy had been seriously harassed – four ships escorted by the *Afridi*, *Witherington* and *Amazon*. So fierce was the attack that only two ships unloaded, one at Molde, the other at Åndalsnes, and the latter did not land all her cargo. The convoy sailed again at 0200 next morning, the escort strengthened by the *Sikh* and *Mohawk*, withdrawn from their patrol in Trondheim Leden; aircraft attacked the convoy again from 1000 to 1400/28. This convoy should have arrived in the evening of 26 April, but was late; and a warning had been sent from Åndalsnes in the morning of 27 April saying, 'Ships must not berth alongside until 2100, and leave by 0200, proceeding to sea for day with escort, otherwise ships will be lost by air attack'; but this warning may not have reached the *Afridi*.

The Situation on Shore 27/28 April (Plans 1 and 11)

To return to Åndalsnes. General Paget arrived on 25 April to hear from Captain Denny that his base and line of communication must soon fail unless protected from the enemy in the air. Forty-eight hours later came a definite proposal to give up the expedition. On 27 April, the General having gone to the front, the commander of the army base staff told the War Office he was 'planning to evacuate Åndalsnes between 1 and 10 May'. The work of the base was restricted to the dark hours, between 2000 and 0600, both afloat and on shore; the wooden piers were all burnt, and only the concrete quay remained; the roads were pitted with craters and badly scarred by heavy traffic in melting snow. They were also losing small craft: by the end of the month, for instance, they had lost by air attack seven anti-submarine trawlers out of 12 – the first to go being the four cricketers, *Larwood* and *Jardine*, *Bradman* and *Hammond*. Patrols of fighter aircraft from Admiral Wells's carriers did something to protect the base and the troops, yet the General felt bound to put these words in a memorandum he sent home on 27 April: 'Our own air:

conspicuous by its absence'. The squadron of Gladiators, flown from the *Glorious* to Lesjaskog Lake on 24 April, had been virtually destroyed next day, and the ice melting, the lake could no longer serve as a landing ground.

As for the troops at the front, Brigadier Morgan's two battalions had 'had a dusting', and were now to come out of the fighting zone. The first two battalions of the 15th Brigade took post at Otta, 30 miles beyond Dombaas on the way to Lillehammer, while its last battalion lay farther back near Dombaas itself. The Norwegians had 'probably about the remains of two brigades' in the district; they had worked on skis on the flanks of Morgan's men, but were 'liable to disappear without warning'. The enemy 'may have up to two or three divisions', with probably Bavarians and Austrians accustomed to skis, and served by 6-in. howitzers working very effectively with aircraft, whereas the British had neither guns nor planes. General Paget asked for help in the air, for field artillery (25-pounders), for anti-aircraft guns both long- and short-range, for more infantry. 'Unless immediate help is forthcoming on above lines at once', said the memorandum of 27 April, 'the whole force may be jeopardized within a period of from four to five days'.

This was no exaggeration. Three days later, on 30 April, the advance troops of the German Army Group XXI made contact with elements of the Trondheim occupation force at Storen (the railway junction some 30 miles to the southward of Trondheim) and in the words of the German Naval Staff appreciation, 'the situation of the Allied troops south of Trondheim can be regarded as desperate'.

But the position had already been recognised by the Allied High Command as hopeless and that night the re-embarkation from the Molde and Åndalsnes area began.

The Withdrawal from Central Norway

The Decision to Withdraw 28 April

As previously mentioned, General Carton de Wiart had begun to consider withdrawing from Namsos as early as 21 April, within five days of his arrival there. General Paget, when he reached Åndalsnes on 25 April – a bare week after the first British troops had moved out to meet the enemy – likewise saw that he might soon find that area untenable; and this opinion he had reiterated in his memorandum of 27 April.

Early next day came the order for a general withdrawal from Central Norway (A.T. 0339):– 'It has been decided to re-embark the force landed at Namsos and Åndalsnes areas as soon as possible ...' The principal cause of the giving up of these southern expeditions was the German strength in the air. This allowed them to send an army to Norway by sea, unhindered except within the limited capacity of submarines and mining. Once established in Norway, their working with an adequate air force gave German soldiers further advantages. Aircraft transported small parties of troops and quantities of supplies, they directed the fire of artillery, and especially they destroyed the Allies' bases almost at leisure, interrupted only by a few machines working from carriers or flying occasionally the long distance from the British Isles, and by a few short-range guns on shore backed by the long-range fire of one or two sloops, destroyers, or anti-aircraft ships. The immediate occasion of the retreat seems to have been this gradual destruction of the bases, on which the troops depended for almost every need, whether of victuals, fuel or ammunition; but so long as the Germans retained command of the sea in the Skagerrak and were thus able to reinforce their troops in Southern Norway at will, the final decision in Central Norway could scarcely be in doubt. 'It is impossible' said the First Lord of the Admiralty, when explaining to Sir Charles Forbes the decision to withdraw from Åndalsnes, 'for 3,000 or 4,000 men without artillery or air superiority to withstand advance of 70,000 or 80,000 thoroughly equipped Germans'. At the same time he said, 'Feel sure you must be very proud of the way your A/A craft and, above all, the Fleet Air Arm are comporting themselves'.[198]

Plan of the Evacuation (Plan 11)

The first plan was to bring off the troops of both expeditions at the same time. Each would need two nights, 1/2 and 2/3 May; but most of 'Primrose' and 'Sickle' would come from Molde, using Åndalsnes on one night only, and that might have to be a day sooner than the others. The Admiralty put several transports at Sir Charles Forbes's disposal, some of them large ships. The War Office directed that the men should be withdrawn 'regardless of loss of equipment'; they calculated there were 6200 men to come from Namsos and 5500 from the Åndalsnes district. Aircraft from Admiral Wells's carriers were to cover the retreat, protecting landing places and troopships and attacking the enemy's troops. There was also a plan to attack the forts near Trondheim in order to divert attention: 'It has been agreed a bombardment of the forts, at Trondheim, should be undertaken by battleships or 8-in. cruisers, when desired by G.O.C., during periods of evacuation'. Ships of war 'escorting one or two liners', said a later signal, should arrive off the approaches at dusk on the first night of embarking, and 'after dark, liners and escorts turn and steer westwards, remainder of force carrying out bombardment of fort at entrance'. Sir Charles Forbes replied to this that the *Valiant* might leave Admiral Wells, with whose carriers she was cruising, in time to attack the forts at dawn on 2 May, but he had no liners nor destroyers for screening them, 'every destroyer fit to fight and available is being used'.

For the evacuations, he ordered Vice-Admiral Edward-Collins to take charge of the Aandaslnes operations on the first night, and Vice-Admiral Layton to take charge on the second night, while Vice-Admiral Cunningham was to be in command at Namsos on both nights. In order to provide the necessary cruisers and destroyers, he requested that the *Southampton* and *Aurora* should be released from Narvik, and that the *Sheffield*, then giving cover to the *Ark Royal* should be detached to rendezvous with Admiral Edward-Collins. He also asked for the loan of three French contre-torpilleurs.[199]

The actual arrangements differed from the original plan, which could be a point of departure to work from only. 'Primrose' and 'Sickle' embarked in two nights, 30 April/1 May and 1/2 May, but nearly all came from Åndalsnes, not counting the party from Aalesund. Only some 50 people embarked at Molde; no troops could go there, owing to the damage to the roads about the town and to the lack of small craft for ferries. 'Maurice' embarked in one night at Namsos, 2/3 May. Furthermore, air attacks on the carriers on 1 May hampered their work and caused Admiral Wells to give it up that evening; nor did the bombardment of the Trondheim forts take place.

No German surface ships interfered with the withdrawal. There were one or two Asdic contacts with submarines, but the enemy attacked the convoys from the air only, and chiefly the ships from Namsos. Yet between 1 and 4 May there were always convoys of troops at sea, with generally the cruisers and sometimes the destroyers full of passengers. As a rule each convoy came home divided into small groups of ships, which crossed the North Sea between roughly 63° and 66° N., until they reached the longitude of the Shetlands, when they turned to pass west of those islands and the Orkneys. Admiral Wells, who reached Scapa with the carriers on 3 May, had the *Valiant* in his squadron from 30 April onwards. Besides her, there were three capital ships in the Home Fleet: the *Resolution*, working under Lord Cork in the Narvik-Tromsø area far to the northward; the *Rodney* and *Repulse* at Scapa with Admiral Forbes, the last-named ship ready 'to meet possibility of attack on ships engaging in evacuation', and her screen of destroyers earmarked.

Before the evacuation of troops took place, the *Glasgow* was sent to Molde to take away the King of Norway. She arrived there with two destroyers, the *Jackal* and *Javelin*, late on 29 April and sailed again the same night, attacked from the air as she cast off from the burning quay – she had come alongside, says Captain Denny, 'with fire hoses playing, the whole scene being brilliantly lit by the flames of the flaming town'. She took onboard the King, the Crown Prince, members of the Government and of the Allies' legations, and part of the base staff and so on, anticipating the general withdrawal – about 280 people all told, besides a quantity of gold bullion. They went to Malangen Fjord, near Tromsø, where the Norwegian passengers shifted into a Norwegian man-of-war to go to Tromsø, and the British ships went home.

The Retreat from Åndalsnes, Molde and Aalesund
(Plan 11)

Captain Pegram of the *Glasgow* found at Molde that Captain Denny had not received the signals about withdrawing. Captain Denny and Brigadier Hogg, commander of the army base staff, expected ships on 29 April, the day before that actually arranged;[200] they had planned to send away 1,000 men from Åndalsnes that night and supposed the *Glasgow* had come for that purpose. The growing scale of attack from the air added to the difficulties. The *Black Swan* had been hit on 28 April, after a couple of strenuous days in which she had fired 2,000 rounds of 4-in. and 4,000 of pom-pom ammunition; and she had sailed for Scapa next day, making 12 knots in a heavy sea despite a three-foot hole in her bottom.[201] On 29/30 April, for the first time, the enemy attacked throughout the night. The *Fleetwood*, which had relieved the *Black Swan*, speedily expended her ammunition, and went home early on 30 April, taking 340 troops – part of those collected against the arrival of ships from home on 29 April – a prodigious number of passengers for a vessel of her size. 'A/A fire from ships subject to continuous attacks themselves all day', said Captain Poland, 'will never meet situation; strong A/A backed up by full aircraft support essential'. Still the departure of the sloops meant taking away the only long-range weapons there were, apart from those in the ships that came to carry troops away on 30 April, until the arrival on 1 May of the *Auckland* and *Calcutta*, sent in haste by Sir Charles Forbes from Scapa.

Owing to the air attacks, nobody could tell whether ships would still be able to go alongside, when the time came, or whether men and gear must come off in boats. Apart from that, General Paget could give little notice of the moment for withdrawing from the battle. Moreover, communication was precarious between the base and the fighting zone and between the two ports themselves, and after the *Fleetwood* sailed the expedition had no communication with the ships coming to its relief. In these circumstances there was little scope for preparing beforehand. 'The comparative success achieved', remarked Captain Denny, 'was due more to good fortune than to thorough organisation such as displayed at Gallipoli'. And the good fortune, he added, lay in the absence of attack from the air each night the expedition embarked. Admiral Layton considered, from the way the Germans bombed possible troop-billets right up to the end, that they did not expect an immediate retreat.[202]

Admiral Edward-Collins arrived for the first night's work at Åndalsnes at 2230/30 with the *Galatea* and *Arethusa*, the *Sheffield*, wearing the flag of Rear-Admiral Clarke,[203] and *Southampton*, six destroyers[204] and the small transport *Ulster Monarch*, having sent the *Tartar* and the *Ulster Prince* to Molde the same night. All had come from Scapa except the *Sheffield* and *Southampton*, which joined at sea, the former from cruising with Admiral Wells and the latter from the Narvik squadron. There had been neither time nor information enough to give written orders, and the Admiral made his final arrangements during the passage. Brigadier Hogg signalled during the afternoon, as the ships approached the coast: 'Probably unsafe to berth transports, but worth while trying with destroyers; if this fails, propose using destroyers' boats along south shore eastwards of Åndalsnes'. But the Admiral determined to go alongside if he could, 'as most fortunately proved to be the case. We should never have embarked the numbers concerned in the time available in ships' boats from the beach in the dark'. Accordingly, he went in the *Galatea* straight alongside the concrete quay, the one proper landing place that survived. The *Walker*, outside the flagship, carried troops to the *Sheffield*, which had anchored off the town. The *Arethusa* went alongside after the *Galatea* had finished, and took onboard the last party that night from Åndalsnes itself. Some 1800 men embarked in the three cruisers. 'Although dead beat and ravenously hungry' they went onboard 'in a well-disciplined and orderly manner' but many 'were without arms or equipment'.

There were two outlying parties near Åndalsnes to gather in, besides Captain Denny's people at Molde: about 300 men had been sent to Alfarnes 6 miles north of Åndalsnes at the mouth of another fjord, and about 100 marines were at Veblungsnes, a mile or so from Åndalsnes on the west point of the river's mouth. Admiral Edward-Collins had sent the *Wanderer* and *Sikh* to Alfarnes as the squadron came in, and the *Southampton* when he found he did not need her for the main body. The *Wanderer* took the ground with 150 troops onboard, and the *Sikh* had to tow her off; eventually the *Sikh* and *Southampton* brought the whole party away. The *Westcott* and *Walker* brought off the marines in their boats; Colonel Simpson, who was wounded, and two or three people with him at Veblungsnes had gone onboard the *Mashona* already.

Meanwhile, the *Tartar* and *Ulster Prince* had embarked Captain Denny and the remainder of his staff, Admiral Diesen and other Norwegian officers, and a few soldiers and others – all there were to come from Molde, in fact, but General Ruge and his staff, the General refusing to leave unless he could be sure of going direct to another port in Norway. Thus each ship had her work to do, except the transport *Ulster Monarch*, which went away empty. The Admiral had told off destroyers to support the main embarkation with their guns and others to carry out an anti-submarine patrol in the fjord, but the business of embarking troops left little opportunity for other services; it was as well there was no enemy about. The only opposition came from the air later, as the ships were leaving the outer fjords between 0300 and 0400 on 1 May, when German aircraft dropped a few bombs near some ships without effect. 'Once again', says Admiral Edward-Collins, 'and contrary to all expectations, Romsdals Fjord was entered, the operation completed, and forces withdrawn without loss or damage through enemy action'.

The ships had sailed as they finished their tasks, and they crossed the North Sea again in ones and twos. They had onboard some 2200 men, but no guns. The number still to come was unknown. In a signal to Admiral Layton, then on his way to Åndalsnes with two cruisers and three destroyers for the second night's work, Admiral Edward-Collins put the number of British troops at 1500 with possibly Norwegian troops and refugees as well, but he warned his successor that 'as a result of continual bombing night and day, all ... at Åndalsnes are shaken, and it appeared no one there really knew the position at the front'. The *Ulster Monarch* joined Admiral Layton 'in view of the indefinite numbers'; unluckily she had to turn back with a cracked piston, but the *Somali* and *Mashona* did a second night's service. Later in the day, Sir Charles Forbes ordered the *Southampton* and some more destroyers to go once again to Åndalsnes in case a third night should prove necessary, the War Office having worked out that there might be 2900 British troops still to come away, some of whom might not be able to reach Åndalsnes from the fighting zone in time to embark in Admiral Layton's ships. However, two nights sufficed.

Åndalsnes suffered the usual attacks from the air on 1 May. A Royal Air Force patrol flew above the town for its protection in the morning, and first the *Auckland* and then the *Calcutta* arrived from home, the

Auckland having seen the attack on Admiral Edward-Collins as she came through another fjord south of him. The Germans dropped bombs occasionally throughout the day, but made a determined attack on the two ships late in the afternoon for above an hour and a half. During this attack there came peremptory orders from Sir Charles Forbes to withdraw: he had already told the two ships to go out, 'if bombing is severe', until required for the night's work. They went out accordingly, Commander Hewitt of the *Auckland* remarking: 'It was most heartening to observe that *Calcutta* adjusted her speed so as to remain in company – this in spite of the fact that she was the more heavily attacked'; and the two ships cheered one another when the attack was over. They reached open water outside Buddybet in time to meet and to turn back with Admiral Layton. Aircraft had made several attacks on Admiral Layton's ships during the afternoon. No sooner did he enter Buddybet in the evening than more appeared, perhaps the same machines that had lately harassed the *Calcutta* and *Auckland*, and the squadron was attacked intermittently for an hour or so as it steamed through the fjords. The fire of the two large cruisers and the *Calcutta* and *Auckland* brought down one machine, but bombs from another very nearly hit the flagship.

Admiral Layton now had the *Manchester* and *Birmingham* and five destroyers[205] besides the two A/A ships. Sir Charles Forbes had offered him two small transports as well, but their speed was only 16 knots and 'a quick get away would be essential' so he refused them, though he accepted the *Ulster Monarch* from Admiral Edward-Collins on learning how uncertain was the number of troops he had to deal with. Like his predecessor, he had given no written orders, 'the situation being so doubtful', but contented himself with giving general instructions by word of mouth before leaving Scapa. As the squadron approached the coast of Norway, he had sent the *Somali* to Aalesund to collect the Primrose detachment there. Off Molde, which was covered with a pall of smoke, the *Diana* parted company to carry General Ruge and his staff from Molde to Tromsø. The other ships came to Åndalsnes a little before 2300/1. The cruisers anchored, being too long to go alongside, while two of the three destroyers went to the quay, which was still undamaged, and in an hour or so nearly 1300 men were ferried to the two cruisers. General Paget then said there remained but a rearguard of some 200 men. The Admiral wanted to sail betimes, that the ships might reach open water before dawn, when he expected fog; he did not want to be held up in the fjords with the ships full of troops. The *Birmingham* therefore sailed as soon as she had her quota, and the *Manchester* followed shortly afterwards with the destroyers. This left the *Calcutta* and *Auckland* for the rearguard. The *Calcutta* found some 700 men, whom she got onboard in 15 minutes, and the *Auckland* took the true rearguard, about 240 men, who 'embarked with such commendable promptitude that the ship was alongside for only 7 minutes'. They all reached home with no more than patches of fog to contend with in the fjords, the ships carrying much the same numbers from Åndalsnes as the night before, about 2200, to which the 250 from Aalesund in the *Somali* must be added. The five remaining anti-submarine trawlers attached to the expedition went home also.

The Retreat from Namsos (Plan 11)

When the order came on 28 April to withdraw, there were at Namsos the *Carlisle* anti-aircraft ship, flying Rear-Admiral Vivian's flag, the *Bittern* sloop, and some trawlers. There were also two French storeships with their escort of two destroyers, whose presence enabled General Carton de Wiart to take the first step towards withdrawing by sending back a French battalion of 850 men then in Namsos itself; they sailed for Scapa on 29 April. A small party (about 100 Chasseurs-Alpins and a section of British light A/A guns) left in the *Janus* next day for Mosjoen – the first of a series of landings in this area designed to impede the advance of the enemy on Narvik after the withdrawal from Central Norway.[206]

The *Carlisle* which had gone north Skjel Fjord to oil on 29 April returning on 30 April found the *Bittern* disabled by a bomb, and Admiral Vivian had to order her to be sunk. Attacks from the air had also disabled three trawlers, which had to be sunk, too, leaving five fit for service. Having consulted with the General, who said 'the presence of a cruiser was of great moral value, but of little value for direct defence', Admiral Vivian then proposed to the Commander-in-Chief that the *Carlisle* and three trawlers should go to sea during daylight hours to preserve them for their coming duties; for the *Carlisle* would be wanted to protect the troopships from air attack, while the trawlers were to serve as ferries. This signal crossing one from Sir Charles that gave orders in the same sense, the *Carlisle* sailed at daylight. Fog prevented her return at night, and early on 2 May, when about 130 miles from the coast, she joined Vice-Admiral Cunningham, who was coming to fetch away the expedition.

Admiral Cunningham had the *Devonshire* and *York*, the *Montcalm* (Admiral Derrien), five destroyers[207] and the transports *El d' Jezair* (Admiral Cadart), *El Kantara* and *El Mansour*, while four destroyers[208] had gone ahead in circumstances to be described later. He had sailed from Scapa on 29 April meaning to bring off half the expedition in the transports in the night of 1–2 May and the other half in the cruisers the night following; and Sir Charles Forbes warning him that the work might have to be done all in one night, he had an alternative plan for that contingency. 'I was fortunate', he writes, 'in that time admitted of my interviewing Admirals Derrien and Cadart, and of my being able to explain my intentions in detail to the majority of the commanding officers of cruisers and destroyers in my force, to issue certain written instructions, and to acquaint French warships and transports of what cruising dispositions I proposed to use'.

In outline the first plan was as follows. The three transports and six destroyers would leave the flag at 2000 on 1 May off Kya Light, some 20 miles south-west of the mouth of Namsen Fjord and 40 short of Namsos. They were to fetch the first half of the troops, about 3,000 men; and as soon as each transport had her load she would sail independently with one destroyer. The Admiral would cruise off Kya Light during the night, with the cruisers and three destroyers, ready to meet the loaded transports in the morning and to escort them to the westward until the time came for the cruisers to go in with six destroyers for the rest of the troops. He would make Kya Light again at 2000 on 2 May on his way in. On arrival off Namsos, the cruisers were to keep underway, while destroyers and trawlers brought off the troops as before, and this time the destroyers, too, were to carry troops, as were the *Carlisle* and *Bittern*.

Admiral Cunningham gave out his alternative plan by signal on 30 April, by which time he knew that one battalion had left Namsos already, so that the number still to come was but 5,400 men. He proposed to reach the mouth of Namsen Fjord at 2100 on the appointed day, when the three transports were to go in with four destroyers, followed in half an hour by the *York* and a destroyer, while the *Devonshire*, *Montcalm* and the other destroyers stayed outside. Each transport was to embark 1700 men at the stone pier and sail again with one destroyer when ready; the

York and her destroyer were to stop a couple of miles short of Namsos to receive troops from trawlers, and would sail with the *Carlisle* after the last transport; the fifth destroyer would stay for stragglers. The convoy would go home in two, perhaps three, groups of ships. In the main, this second plan was actually followed.

In the evening of 30 April, when the signal describing the above arrangements had been made, Admiral Cunningham passed the carrier squadron then on the way to cover the retreat from Åndalsnes with its fighter aircraft, and Admiral Wells signalled that he should send up fighters over Namsos on 2 May; but this unhappily fell through, owing to the German air attack on 1 May. German aircraft molested Admiral Cunningham also on 1 May, and two machines, attacking in the afternoon, nearly hit the *Devonshire* and a transport with their bombs. Then the squadron ran into thick and widespread fog in the evening, some 40 miles short of Kya Light, which forced the Admiral to turn out to sea and prevented him from sending the transports to Namsos that night. The *Maori* went on, however, having missed the signal to turn to seaward, and reported herself near Kya Light about 2200 with a visibility of 2 cables. On this, Captain Lord Louis Mountbatten suggested his joining the *Maori* with his own three ships, *Kelly, Grenade, Griffin*, 'with a view to the four of us taking off most of the troops due to be evacuated from Namsos on this, the first night'. Admiral Cunningham approved, so the little flotilla groped its way in by sounding and Asdic, the fog growing thicker than ever, only to find it quite clear in Namsen Fjord at 0500 on 2 May. Namsos thus exposed 'once more to bombing attacks', Lord Louis decided to go out again hide in fog banks until he might join the squadron on its way to Namsos in the evening. He met the Admiral again about 2000 with the *Maori* slightly damaged by a near miss (she had 23 casualties), a German aircraft having sighted the destroyers on the edge of a fog bank too low to cover their masts.

The delay caused by the fog made Admiral Cunningham specially anxious to do his business in one night. He had signalled the gist of his plan for this to Namsos, suggesting 1/2 May as the date. General Carton de Wiart had received the signal through Admiral Vivian, but had to answer that it would not do; he could not disengage all his troops in time for that night; moreover he must have two nights for the whole task. When the squadron turned back out of the fog in the evening of 1 May,

Admiral Cunningham had once more proposed to Admiral Vivian that they should embark the whole expedition the following night; again Admiral Vivian, who was then at sea in the *Carlisle*, answered that two nights were needed, which agrees with a signal the General made to the War Office, that it was 'not a question of shipping, but of hours of dark'. But next morning, Admiral Cunningham decided to send ships enough to Namsos to bring off all the troops that night, if the weather allowed, and made known his intention to the Admiralty by signal. His reasoning appears in his report as follows:–

> '840 of the 6,200 troops which I had originally been informed would be evacuated from Namsos had already been removed ... on the night of 28/29 April, leaving about 5,400 to be embarked. I had sufficient transport for this number, but, as far as time required to embark was concerned, I appeared to be limited by (a) the number of large ships that could be safely operated at Namsos at one time; (b) the facilities, piers, ferrying craft, etc., available, which were reported as sadly lacking; (c) the reiterated statements of C.S.20, and military authorities through him, that evacuation could not be carried out on one night only, because of the above.'[209]
>
> I was uncertain of the state of affairs ashore and how long evacuation could be delayed with safety from the military point of view; and I could not lose sight of the fact that should the fog persist or recur after to-night I might be faced with the necessity of attempting to carry out the remainder of the evacuation in daylight, a project which all the evidence tended to show would be extremely hazardous, if not impossible ... I was convinced that to attempt to spread evacuation over two nights would be courting disaster. I therefore decided in any case to throw enough shipping into Namsos on first night to permit of complete evacuation and, if the General was unable to disengage his troops in time to take advantage of the opportunity thus afforded, to endeavour to evacuate the remnant in the remaining cruisers and destroyers the following night.
>
> In coming to this decision, I was much influenced, firstly by the gallant bearing of Admiral Cadart and by his confidence in his ability to place two of his transports simultaneously, and subsequently the third, alongside the stone pier; and secondly by my own conviction, formed from discussions on 29 April with Captain

Lees of HMS *Calcutta* and Commander Ravenhill of HMS *Nubian*, both lately returned from Namsos, that the present reports upon the damage to the wooden pier were somewhat overdrawn.'

Admiral Vivian had joined Admiral Cunningham in the morning of 2 May, fog preventing the *Carlisle*'s return to Namsos the night before. Early in the afternoon came a signal from the Admiralty to say the General reported things 'getting serious' and he wished to see a naval officer who knew the plan for withdrawing the expedition. Admiral Cunningham then gave Admiral Vivian the detailed plan of 30 April for embarking all in one night, and sent him ahead to Namsos. As soon as he arrived, about 2000 that evening, Admiral Vivian consulted with Generals Carton de Wiart and Audet. He told them it was essential that the last troopship should be loaded by 0200 next morning, so that all might be clear of the fjord by 0330, and that guns and stores should be embarked only if it could be done at the same time as the men. The Generals agreed.

In the meantime Admiral Cunningham had approached the coast, seeking shelter in banks of fog from shadowing aircraft. The French transports had fuel enough for one night more only, so the Admiral prepared to do the work with the ships of war alone, should the fog persist. However, Admiral Vivian reported clear weather inshore, and soon after 1830 the squadron ran out of the fog some 40 miles from the mouth of Namsen Fjord. Then the transports and their escorts parted company, while the Admiral cruised off Kya Light with the *Devonshire*, *Montcalm* and four destroyers.

Captain Vivian in the *Afridi* led the transports in, followed by the *York* and *Nubian*, and joined in the fjord by the *Kelly*, *Grenade* and *Griffin*. Admiral Cadart went straight alongside the stone pier in the *El d'Jezair* about 2230, and the *El Kantara* secured outside him. The *El Mansour*, underway off the town, and the *York*, further out, as had been arranged, both got their loads from trawlers and destroyers, which fetched the troops from the wooden pier. The transports sailed as soon as they had their loads, followed by the *York* and *Carlisle*, all accompanied by destroyers. The *El Mansour* cleared the fjord at 0230, about the time the last transport was leaving the pier that morning of 3 May. Admiral Cunningham joined a second destroyer to her escort and sent the *York* and *Nubian* to overtake her. SQ, too, the *Montcalm* and *Bison* joined the

El Kantara and her destroyer, while the *Devonshire*, *Carlisle* and four destroyers joined the *El d'Jezair*.

The first group of ships crossed the North Sea independently, and reached Scapa without adventure. But German aircraft harassed the rest of the squadron that day for nearly seven hours. Admiral Cunningham had hoped to find shelter in fog until well away from the coast, but the fog cleared as the sun rose, so they had 'perfect bombing weather'. The enemy attacked five times between 0845 and 1530, at distances of from 140 to 220 miles from their airfield at Vaernes near Trondheim; they succeeded in destroying two ships, the *Bison* and *Afridi*, at a cost of two or three machines shot down out of some 50 that attacked.[210] For the first three attacks – 0845–1030 – the aircraft came in waves of a dozen, and singled out the *Devonshire* and *Montcalm*, dropping bombs very near those ships, and disabling the *Bison* in the last attack of the three. Her survivors were rescued by the *Grenade*, *Afridi* and *Imperial*; 'Commander R. C. Boyle, R.N., of the *Grenade* very gallantly secured the stern of his ship to the sinking *Bison*, despite burning oil and exploding ammunition and was responsible for saving the lives of many of the *Bison*'s ship's company by this act'.[211] At 1400, whilst rejoining the squadron after sinking the wreck of the *Bison*, the *Afridi* was hit by two bombs, and she eventually capsized, losing about 100 killed, including some of the *Bison*'s people and some men of the *York* and *Lancaster* regiment – the only army casualties incurred in the evacuation – that she had onboard. In the last attack, at 1530, the enemy bombed the *Griffin* and *Imperial*, but without effect, as these ships were rejoining the flag with survivors from the *Afridi*.

After the attacks in the forenoon, Admiral Cunningham concentrated his ships and Admiral Derrien's, forming cruisers and transports in single line ahead 'for mutual support' with the *Carlisle* astern. They arrived at Scapa on 5 April, a day later than the *York*'s group. The Admiral writes of this passage from Norway:–

> 'The manner in which the transports *El d'Jezair* and *El Kantara*, under the command of Contre-amiral Cadart, were manoeuvred at high speed to conform to the movements of the escorting vessels during the air attacks is worthy of the highest praise; they also hotly engaged all aircraft sighted, and thereby contributed their quota to

the general defence of the convoy. The loyal and understanding co-operation afforded to me by Contre-amiral Derrien and his squadron greatly lightened my task and contributed materially to the success of the operation ... and the bearing of officers and men in all ships of my force, under extremely trying conditions, was fully in accordance with the highest tradition.'

The arrival at Scapa of Vice-Admiral Cunningham's force from Namsos brought to a close the sorry story of the campaign in Central Norway. Though it was impossible not to regret the turn events had taken, declared the Commander-in-Chief, Home Fleet, he could not but admire the way in which all units under his command had done their duty and overcome every difficulty with which they had been confronted; and he accordingly sent the following message to all concerned:–

'To Home Fleet, British, Polish, French and Norwegian Warships and merchant vessels attached to the Home Fleet:–

During the last three weeks you have been engaged upon two of the most difficult operations of war that naval forces are required to undertake. You may be proud that you have carried out these operations with the loss at sea of only about twelve officers and men of the Army in the face of heavy air attacks. I am proud to command a fleet that has shown itself capable of meeting the heavy demands made upon it with such determination and success.'

Herjangs Fjord opposite Narvik | under bombardment

The Expedition to Narvik: Phase I

Inception of Operation Rupert

In the meantime, while the brief campaign in Central Norway was reaching its inevitable conclusion, the expedition to Narvik, though not as yet seriously threatened by the enemy, had also received a check. The rosy hopes of a speedy recapture of the port, before the enemy recovered from the effects of Admiral Whitworth's blow on 13 April, speedily vanished, for reasons which will be apparent later. Once missed, the opportunity did not recur. Moreover, an unusually protracted spell of bad weather and deep snow compelled the postponement of a serious attempt till the latter part of May.

To recapitulate, the Government decided on 10 April to send this expedition, which was, in fact, the child of 'Avonmouth' in Plan 'R4'; its first troops left British waters on 12 April; but half these troops went to Namsos instead, the Government then expecting 'reduced opposition' at Narvik, and desiring to recover Trondheim as soon as possible. So early as 11 April, at a meeting of the naval staff that night, Admiral Phillips (Deputy Chief of the Staff) had questioned the wisdom of sending 'all our readily available' troops to Narvik. He argued that it had been decided at a time when Norway seemed at the point of coming to terms with Germany, when 'it would be essential to secure our important interests in the Narvik area;' now he 'considered that the taking of Narvik would not help the Norwegians directly, nor would it improve our position in the eyes of the world to any great extent' whereas 'Namsos was the key to retaking Trondheim, and ... a footing in that area was important from a military point of view'. However, the Admiralty and the War Office decided to go on with 'Rupert' as arranged, and to give 'further consideration' to a landing at Namsos. The change of plan on 14 April and the diversion to Namsos of other troops later meant that 'Rupert' had but one brigade of infantry until 27 April, when three battalions of Chasseurs-Alpins joined. Yet this does not seem to have affected the fortunes of the expedition greatly; for, apart from other things, without troops trained and equipped to fight in deep snow, very little could be done before the 'long awaited' thaw, which came only at the end of the month.

Opening Moves: Conflicting Instructions (Plan 14)

The *Southampton*, screened by the *Escapade* and *Electra*, arrived in Vaagsfjord early on 14 April, having onboard General Mackesy, commanding the land forces; Captain Maund, the naval chief of staff; and two companies of the 1st Scots Guards. In the first place they went to Harstad on the west shore of the fjord, where the army base was to be. The General having consulted with the authorities at the place, and learning that the 6th Norwegian Division under General Fleischer lay in the Bardu district north-east of Narvik, they crossed then to the mainland, and the Scots Guards landed near Salangen in Sag Fjord to work with the Norwegian troops.

Lord Cork had sailed in the *Aurora* from Rosyth to take command of the expedition by sea at the same time as General Mackesy left Scapa. He, too, meant to go first to Harstad to join the General; for he had not met him before. On 14 April, however, as the *Aurora* approached the coast, a signal from Admiral Whitworth, then in Vest Fjord with the *Warspite* and some destroyers, put the German strength in Narvik at some 2000 men, probably with little artillery, and emphasized his 'impressions' of the night before, that the Germans were 'thoroughly frightened' by saying:–

> 'I am convinced that Narvik can be taken by direct assault without fear of meeting serious opposition on landing. I consider that the main landing force need only be small, but it must have the support of (his squadron) or one of similar composition.' [212]

Thereupon Lord Cork, whose 'impression on leaving London was quite clear that it was desired by HM Government to turn the enemy out of Narvik at the earliest possible moment, and that I was to act with all promptitude in order to attain this result', ordered the *Southampton* to meet him that night in Skjel Fjord. He thought of attempting Narvik next morning with the 350 Scots Guards from the *Southampton* and a

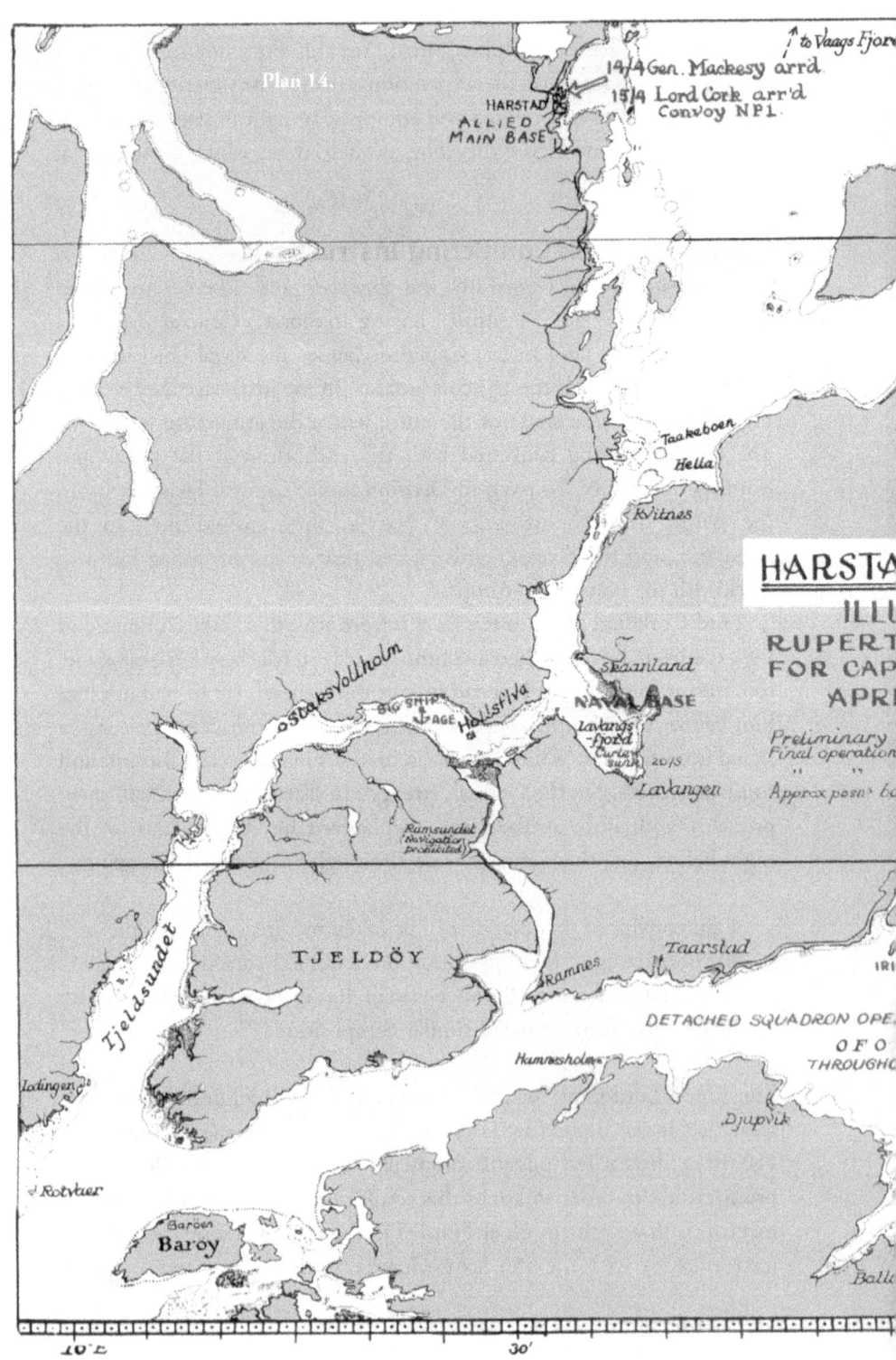

Norwegian Venture: Battles for the Fjords 1940

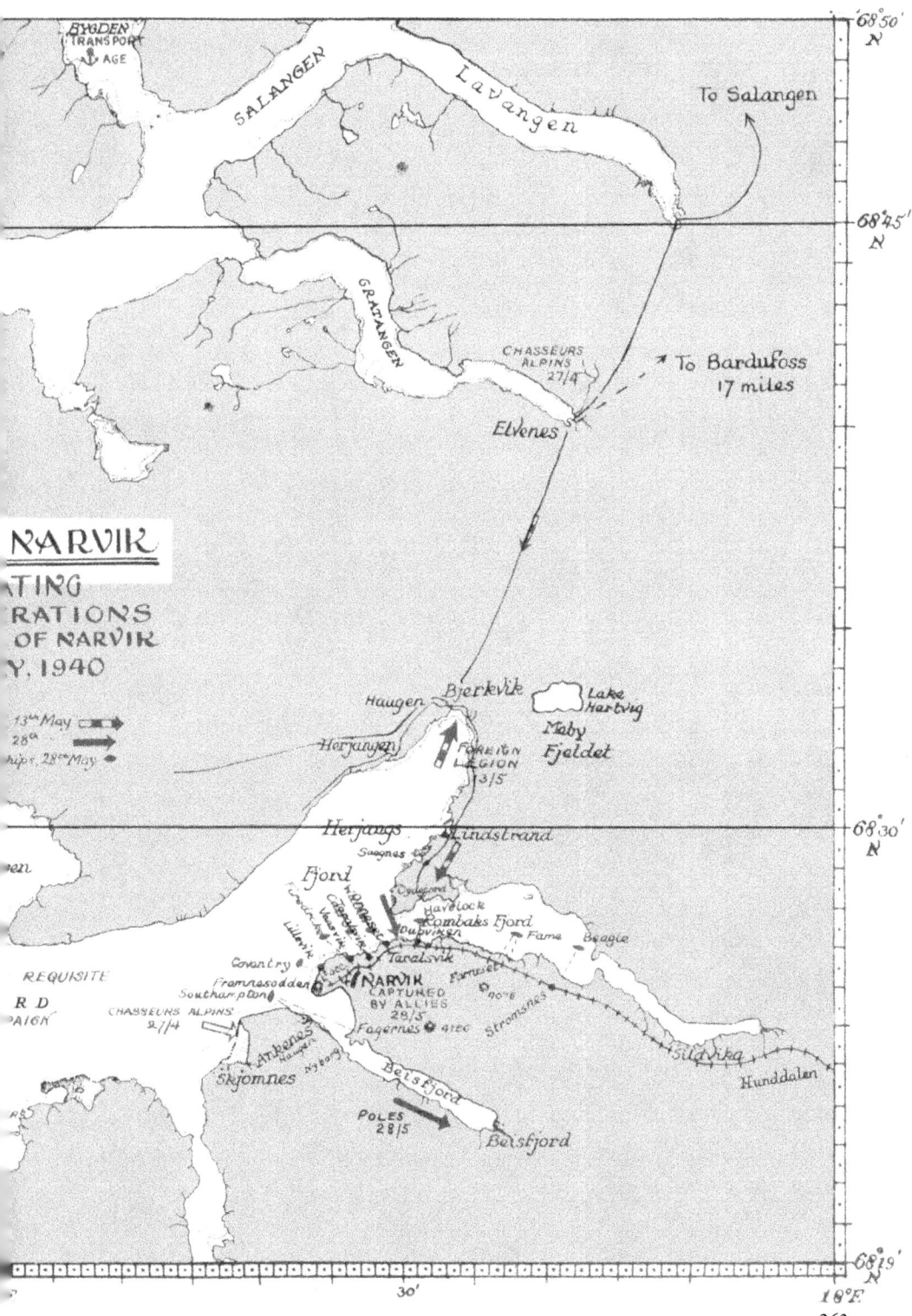

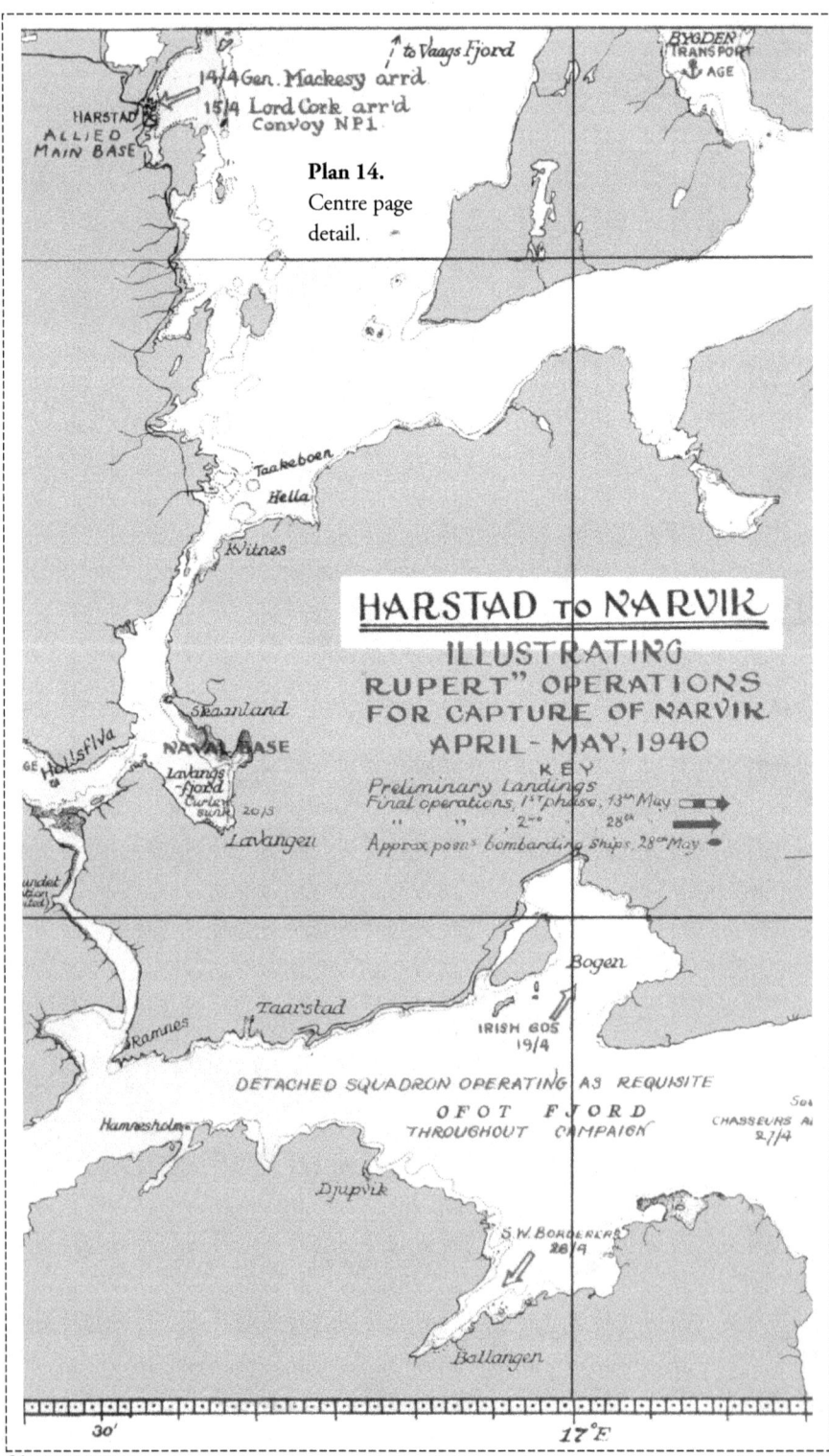

Plan 14. Centre page detail.

party of seamen and marines from all the larger ships and from the *Penelope* and destroyers repairing at Skjel Fjord. He made this signal to the General:–

'In view of successful naval action at Narvik yesterday, 13 April, and as enemy appear thoroughly frightened, suggest we take every advantage of this before enemy has recovered. If you concur and subject to information we shall receive tonight 14 April, from *Warspite*, I should be most willing to land military force now in *Southampton* at Narvik at daylight tomorrow, Monday, from *Aurora* and destroyers. Supporting fire could be provided by cruisers and destroyers, and I could assist with a naval and marine landing party of 200 if you wish.'

But nothing came of this plan. Owing to the peculiar wireless-telegraphy conditions in Norway, the *Southampton* did not receive Lord Cork's first signal until the afternoon, by which time her troops had landed in Sag Fjord to join the Norwegians – 'one of the first objects laid down for the army by the War Office'. And, says Lord Cork, 'any idea of making an attempt with naval forces would have, in any case, been rendered difficult by receipt of A.T. 2341/14, in which appears: "We think it imperative that you and General should be together and act together and that no attack should be made except in concert".' During the night, therefore, the *Aurora* went round towards Vaagsfjord.

The main body of the troops arrived next day, meeting the *Aurora* outside by the mouth of And Fjord in the morning. They were the 24th Brigade: the 1st Irish Guards, 2nd South Wales Borderers, and the rest of the 1st Scots Guards. They came in three large transports, with the *Protector* netlayer and *Vindictive* repair ship, convoyed by the *Valiant* and nine destroyers. The little harbour of Harstad having but a narrow entrance, the transports were to anchor in Bygden, a channel between two islands 10 miles across the fjord, whence destroyers and local shipping would ferry soldiers and stores to the base. But as they were steaming through And Fjord, a 'military outpost' reported a submarine in Vaagsfjord. The *Fearless* and *Brazen*, screening ahead, proceeded through Topsundet and carried out an attack with five depth charges, 'which literally blew the U-boat to the surface in the middle of the pattern. The crew abandoned their vessel, U.49, and started screaming in the most dreadful fashion;'[213] nearly all were saved, and while engaged on this rescue work, the *Brazen* picked up papers which gave the whole of the U-boat disposition for the invasion of Norway.[214]

The convoy arrived at Vaagsfjord in due course, landing troops and stores that afternoon and the day following. German aircraft harassed them at the anchorage and during the passage to Harstad, as they did the troops for Namsos at Lillesjona. They did no material damage; but the General remarks that his force had no defence against these attacks, which complicated the operation of landing.

While this was going on, Captain de Salis was reconnoitring Narvik harbour and Rombaks Fjord with the *Faulknor* and *Zulu*, two of the destroyers Admiral Whitworth had working in Vest Fjord; and that night Captain de Salis signalled his opinion that a landing on Rombaks Fjord, to advance on Narvik from the north-east, would not be opposed by fixed defences, and might be covered by destroyers' guns. Lord Cork had intended to assault the place on 16 April, when disappointed of his plan for the day before. The chances of success would depend largely on how much Admiral Whitworth's action had affected the spirit of the enemy and how far ships' guns could support the infantry; for the Germans had probably as many men as the British, and they seem to have had a few Norwegian guns as well, whereas the British had no artillery.

But at this stage an unexpected difficulty confronted him; for at his first meeting with General Mackesy on 15 April he 'was astonished to hear' that the General's orders, given him just prior to sailing, 'ruled out any idea of attempting an opposed landing. Thus the General and myself left the United Kingdom with diametrically opposite views as to what was required'.

General Mackesy gives his views in his final report:–

'During 14 April and the following days, all available information pointed to Narvik itself being strongly held, and to the fact that the naval action of 13 April had by no means demoralized the garrison as a whole. The probability was that the garrison had, in fact, been increased by nearly 1000 good fighting men from the sunken German ships; this was fully confirmed by subsequent intelligence reports. My troops had been embarked for a peaceful landing at a friendly and organised port and could not be ready for active operations for some days ...

The country was covered by snow up to four feet and more in depth; even at sea level there were several feet of snow. Blizzards, heavy snowstorms, bitter winds, and very low night temperature were normal. Indeed, until the middle of May, even those magnificent mountain soldiers the French Chasseurs-Alpins suffered severely from frostbite and snow blindness. Troops who were not equipped with and skilled in the use of skis or snow-shoes were absolutely incapable of operating tactically at all. I had no such troops at my disposal when I first landed. Shelter from the weather was of vital importance.

It soon became certain that the enemy held Narvik in considerable strength. All the existing defences had been handed over intact by the Norwegian garrison. A personal reconnaissance convinced me that topography favoured the defence, and that an opposed landing was quite out of the question so long as the deep snow and existing weather conditions persisted, and so long as my force lacked landing craft, tanks, adequate artillery support, adequate anti-aircraft defence and air co-operation. The problem was, of course, not merely one of landing, but one of carrying out a subsequent advance of several miles; yet, owing to the configuration of the ground, not even during the first mile could support be given by ships' guns.

I decided, therefore, that my first objective must be to secure the Oijord and Ankenes peninsulas, north and south of Narvik, from which in due course observed fire could be brought to bear on the enemy defences. Both these peninsulas were held by the enemy.'

Lord Cork gave up his thoughts of immediate attack, and he reported so on 16 April. On this the Admiralty urged the importance of an 'early capture', warning him at the same time that certain battalions of chasseurs-alpins would not be coming, though apparently earmarked for Narvik hitherto, that the *Warspite* and some of his destroyers would be soon wanted elsewhere, that the Germans would reinforce and supply their garrison by air. But Lord Cork himself, now that 'the chance of a coup de main had passed' had to own defeat by the snow. 'I personally tested this', he says, 'and also landed a section of marines to do the same, and found it easy to sink to one's waist, and to make any progress was exhausting'. Instead of a direct assault, he proposed to bombard Narvik from the sea, 'in the hope that the result might cause the enemy to evacuate or surrender the town'. If that failed – as it did – they must wait upon the weather; and as a step towards the General's plan of securing a foothold either side of the port, the Irish Guards landed on 19 April in Bogen Inlet, on the north shore of Ofot Fjord, and the South Wales Borderers went to Ballangen, on the south shore, a week later. As for the Chasseurs, General Mackesy protested that without them he was 'definitely inferior' to the enemy, so he asked for other troops in their room, but the War Office said they had none to send.[215]

On 20 April the Government appointed Lord Cork supreme commander of the expedition.

Operations in Ofot Fjord 16/26 April (Plan 14)

Throughout the operation of 'Rupert' force a detached squadron in Ofot Fjord harassed the enemy continuously in a smaller way. The service seems to have started from a request of General Mackesy's on 16 April to destroy shipping in Rombaks and Herjangs Fjords, through which the Germans supplied their outlying posts, especially about Gratangen, 15 miles north of Narvik. This request Lord Cork had passed on to Admiral Whitworth, who suggested cruisers and destroyers should be used to attack shipping, piers, and bridges in and near the fjords, including the merchantmen in Narvik, which 'were left afloat on 13 April because it was believed that Narvik harbour could be occupied almost immediately'. Captain de Salis commanded at first with a couple of destroyers. Then Captain Hamilton came in the *Aurora* with more destroyers – it was in the *Aurora* on 20 April that General Mackesy made the reconnaissance he mentions in his report quoted above. The *Enterprise*, which had arrived from home on 17 April, joined Captain Hamilton after that reconnaissance; they destroyed a railway bridge on 21 April and fired on Narvik next day 'to harass the enemy' on the promontory. Captain Hamilton reports that, out of two cruisers and five destroyers at his command, 'one cruiser and at least two destroyers were continuously on patrol night and day, and on frequent occasions all ships available were employed simultaneously'.

On 24 April, the bombardment took place.[216] Lord Cork, wearing his flag in the *Effingham*, which had arrived from Southern Norway on 20 April, personally directed the operation; with him were General Mackesy and Brigadier Fraser, Commander of the 24th Brigade. The other ships to attack were the *Warspite*, *Aurora*, *Enterprise* and *Zulu*, while the *Vindictive*[217] embarked the Irish Guards from Bogen ready to land them should the cannonading give an opportunity.

The thick weather, with heavy snowstorms, forbade support by aircraft from the *Furious*; nor could German machines interrupt the attack. The *Aurora* and *Zulu* first attacked from Rombaks Fjord for some 40 minutes, going thence to engage enemy positions in Herjangs Fjord. Then, about 0700, the other three ships attacked 'the fixed defence areas' about Narvik, as Admiral Whitworth describes it. The main bombardment lasted about three hours, but Lord Cork's hopes were disappointed. 'The climatic conditions were … entirely against' a landing; 'the low visibility entirely prevented any estimate of the effect achieved by the bombardment'; and it appeared later that 'nothing indicated any intention to surrender', though the attack 'had considerable effect'.

The next day there was a further heavy fall of snow, and as weather conditions compelled postponement of any direct attack on Narvik, attention was given to movements of troops designed to bring pressure on the enemy to the north and south of the Narvik peninsula on 26 April. Ballangen (as already mentioned) was occupied by the South Wales Borderers, and further dispositions were made as the arrival of reinforcements permitted.

Changes in Squadron: Army Reinforcements (Plan 14)

Directly after this affair, Vice-Admiral Whitworth sailed for the United Kingdom in the *Warspite*, her place being taken by the *Resolution*,[218] which arrived next day. As already mentioned, the *Furious*, after suffering damage from an air attack near Tromsø and with only eight aircraft remaining serviceable, and the *Southampton*, required for duty at the withdrawal from Åndalsnes, also left Lord Cork's command; Vice-Admiral Cunningham, with the *Devonshire* and *Berwick*, had already left the Tromsø area on 19 April. The Narvik destroyers varied continually, reliefs being supplied by exchanging with convoy escorts. By arrangement with the Commander-in-Chief, Home Fleet, there was to be a standing flotilla of ten destroyers, half for Vest Fjord and half for Vaagsfjord, besides a screen for the capital ship; but in actual practice, no standing flotilla ever materialised. However, there were generally some fifteen all told until the Germans invaded the Low Countries, when the Admiralty recalled destroyers from Norway for employment in the southern part of the North Sea, and the total then came down to eight. The destroyers led a busy life. For instance, the *Electra* records on 8 May that for the first time since 3 April she lay with steam at longer notice than half an hour, while the *Fame*'s report says she had steam on her main engines continuously from 10 May to 8 June.

Against this reduction in the ships of war, there was an increase in the strength of the land forces. Three battalions of Chasseurs-Alpins arrived on 27 April: two battalions went to Gratangen to work with the Norwegians north of Narvik, the third went to the Ankenes peninsula, joining the South Wales Borderers, who came there from Ballangen. A week later two battalions of the Foreign Legion and four of Poles arrived: the Foreign Legion went to the Ballangen neighbourhood, while the Polish battalions took up stations in reserve. Besides infantry, the French brought twelve field guns and ten small tanks. Moreover, a few 'much needed' motor landing craft arrived at the end of April, and with them came a battery of 25-pounders, the only British field artillery other than naval guns to land in Norway. The army received a few light anti-aircraft guns to land in Norway. The army received a few light anti-aircraft guns in April, too, both British and French; but no heavy pieces came until 6 May, just three weeks after the arrival of the first infantry.

With the coming of fresh troops – and of the thaw – Lord Cork turned again to plans for attacking Narvik. The stout-hearted General Bethouart had arrived from Namsos on 28 April to command the French contingent, and the Admiral took him to spy out the land in the *Codrington* the same day. 'I imagine', remarks Captain Creasy of the *Codrington*, 'the only occasion on which a destroyer with the Union flag ... has ever engaged an enemy', for she fired on German gun positions and the railway near Narvik during the reconnaissance. On 1 May, Lord Cork went once more into Ofot Fjord 'to keep in touch with events'; this time his flagship, the *Effingham*, with the *Resolution* and *Aurora*, bombarded German positions in Beisfjord and about Ankenes to help

Fjord | Dong Zhang

the Borderers in their attempts to make headway on the peninsula.[219] The fruits of these two days, apparently, was an order to prepare for a direct assault on Narvik by British troops on 8 May. This plan fell through, but it was followed by a plan to land the Foreign Legion in Herjangs Fjord to seize Bjerkvik and clear the Germans out of all that country, while Chasseurs-Alpins and Norwegians from Gratangen way attacked southward from Elvenes and through the valley Graesdalen, further eastward, and then to march on Oydejord.

Meanwhile, since the retreat from Central Norway, the British Government had been sending small parties of troops to Bodø, Mo and Mosjoen, south of Narvik, to hinder the enemy's advance northward. A company of Scots Guards had already been sent from the Narvik force to Bodø before the end of April; and from then onwards this imposed an increasing strain on the 'Rupert' forces, both naval and military. On 7 May this area was added to Lord Cork's command.

It will be convenient, therefore, at this stage to follow the fortunes of these operations before dealing with the final events of the campaign against Narvik.

Operations at Bodø, Mo and Mosjoen

Object of Operations (Plan 12)

The object of the supplementary landings which took place in the Bodø-Mosjoen area on the collapse of the campaign in Central Norway was to delay the German advance northward towards Narvik, and especially the increasing reach of their air power.

The Government had considered sending small bodies of troops to intermediate positions between the main areas of hostilities while the British and French troops were still fighting in Central Norway. Thus as early as 21 April a trawler was sent to report on the facilities of Mosjoen, at the head of Vefsen Fjord, some 90 miles north eastward from Namsos; and on 25 April there came a suggestion from Sir Charles Forbes to use Mosjoen or Kongsmoen 'if suitable landing ground could be found in their vicinity', apparently to relieve Namsos, where they were feeling the strain of continual attacks from the air on an overcrowded base. Two days later he again 'urged on the Admiralty ... necessity of landing in Mosjoen or Mo area, properly organised', the *Penelope* having reported several spots suitable for landing grounds on the island of Heroy in that neighbourhood.[220] In view of the decision that day to withdraw from Central Norway, the Commander-in-Chief added: 'Landing will now only be with object of denying area to enemy air force to start with. If he establishes air force in Mosjoen or Bodø area, same state of affairs will shortly take place at Narvik as at Åndalsnes and Molde'.

The First Landings (Plan 12)

Positive orders came on 29 April, when Lord Cork was told he must occupy the head of Salt Fjord, near the mouth of which lies Bodø, to prevent the enemy from arriving by parachute. Accordingly, he sent first a destroyer, which reported there were no Germans nor shipping of any sort in the neighbourhood, and then a company of the Scots Guards, which landed at Bodø and worked eastward. General Carton de Wiart had orders the same day to send a party from Namsos to Mosjoen, so the *Janus* (Commander Tothill) sailed the following night with 100 Chasseurs-Alpins and a section of British light anti-aircraft guns; she landed her party late on 2 May unopposed and unobserved. Commander Tothill remarked on this point:–

> 'The success of the operation depended entirely on not being observed by reconnaissance planes. Mosjoen is within range of enemy dive bombing planes; the fjords are in places narrow, with no room to manoeuvre and, owing to the shortness of darkness, the fjords have to be navigated during daylight hours. Now that the enemy air force are no longer occupied with forces operating further to the southward, sea communication with Mosjoen is not considered to fall within the limits of a justifiable risk.'

By this, presumably, he meant that troops must rely on the country to replenish supplies.

On 1 May, the Admiralty ordered Lord Cork to send a destroyer to Mo to prevent an enemy landing, and made the 'excellent proposal'[221] to the Commander-in-Chief, Home Fleet, that a Destroyer Division should be established to patrol the coast from Namsos to the northward, to prevent the movement of enemy troopships by sea. Unfortunately, owing to shortage of destroyers, this suggestion could not be carried out. Two flying boats were sent from the United Kingdom to reconnoitre airfields in the Bodø area, but they were caught in the water and put out of action by enemy aircraft on 4 May.

The next military landing took place at Mo, situated at the head of North Ranen Fjord, some 45 miles to the northward of Mosjoen. The troops consisted of the 1st Independent Company – 300 men or double the strength of an ordinary battalion company – which arrived from the United Kingdom in the transport *Royal Ulsterman*, escorted by the *Mohawk*, on 4 May and accomplished their landing 'apparently unobserved'.

Three more independent companies went out a few days after the party for Mo, two companies to Mosjoen, in the *Ulster Prince* with Colonel Gubbins, the Senior Officer of all these out-lying forces, and one to Bodø, in the *Royal Scotsman*. They sailed from home together, escorted by four destroyers, parting company off the coast of Norway to go to their respective destinations; both landed on 9 May, and the *Ulster Prince* brought away the Chasseurs-Alpins from Mosjoen. Altogether, five independent companies went to Norway, the last arriving at Bodø on 13 or 14 May in the *Royal Ulsterman*, escorted by the *Matabele*.

Area Placed under Narvik Command

Before this, however, various changes had taken place in Norway. On 4 May, Lord Cork had asked the Admiralty to explain 'the general policy regarding Bodø, Mo and Mosjoen', saying also: 'It seems most important to hold in force the Mo road leading north', but 'it appears the forces being sent are hardly adequate for this purpose, and with such weak detachments in the air another naval commitment comes into being'. The Admiralty answered on 5 May, as Lord Cork records, 'that it was not possible to maintain large forces in face of enemy air superiority well in advance of established fighter aerodrome, that Bodø was the only place south of Narvik where such could be established, that small parties only would be maintained at Mo and Mosjoen with the object of obstructing enemy advance and to prevent landings by sea and air;' and on 7 May the Government put the independent companies directly under the Narvik command. The Germans were then pressing northward, the Norwegians in those parts were tiring, and as soon as he arrived at Mosjoen, on 9 May, Colonel Gubbins seems to have decided he must begin to withdraw, agreeably to his instructions to harass and delay the enemy, but to go back gradually to Mo and Bodø. Thereupon, Lord Cork arranged to send reinforcements, apparently anticipating a signal from home (A.T. 0053/10), which ran thus: 'Essential Bodø should be held pending full examination of problem involved, which is now in progress; if necessary, garrison must be reinforced from resources at your disposal'.

German Landing at Hemnes (Plan 11)

But the Germans moved first. In the evening of 10 May they landed some 300 troops at Hemnes, in Ranen Fjord, 15 miles west of Mo, part from aircraft and part from a captured coasting steamer, while another captured steamer probably landed troops at or near Mosjoen the same evening. Lord Cork had news of their coming up the coast, the first message reaching him at 1100 and reporting two steamers in the Inner Lead a little north of Namsos; and he ordered the *Calcutta* and *Zulu* to intercept them.[222] The steamer for Hemnes arrived there about 1900, and her troops landed after the town had been bombed and set on fire, other troops coming by air at the same time. The British ships arrived two hours afterwards, too late to stop the landing of troops, but in time to sink the transport with nearly all the stores still onboard. They went on to Mo, which they found unmolested, and the *Zulu* picked up some soldiers who had escaped from Hemnes, where part of the independent company at Mo had been stationed; then they went to join the *Penelope*, which was to sail in tow from Skjel Fjord that night to go home under their escort.

Colonel Gubbins heard of the German movement by sea at some time in the afternoon or early evening of 10 May, and he believed they would land at Elsfjorden, south of the Hemnes peninsula. Had he doubts before about withdrawing, the enemy's landing behind him must have made plain the need to do so. He left Mosjoen that night, and retired by land and by water up Vefsen Fjord, and went to Sandnessjøen on the western shore of Alsten Island in the Inner Lead, some 20 miles from Mosjoen and 45 miles from Mo. The Germans occupied Mosjoen soon after he had gone. The army headquarters passed on this news to Lord Cork and suggested that a 'little warship should try to keep in touch with Gubbins'. As we have seen, Lord Cork had now but few ships at his command. The *Calcutta* and *Zulu* had sailed already for Hemnes, and must return to escort the *Penelope* as soon as they had finished their work there; other ships were about to sail for Mo with the Scots Guards; the French attack on Bjerkvik was making ready; and, apart from these things, the usual services in Vaagsfjord and Ofot Fjord had to go on. However, in the afternoon of the next day, he recalled the *Jackal* and *Javelin*, which had arrived that morning with a convoy from home, and sailed again when they had oiled, having Admiralty orders to go home immediately. He told them to go on to Mo and 'report fully on situation ... from naval point of view'; to gain touch with Colonel Gubbins, who was last reported at Sandnessjøen, and help him to 'establish himself'.

Commander Napier, of the *Jackal*, knew no more than this signal told him, but he met the *Penelope*'s convoy and gained 'a little information' from the *Calcutta*. He went on at 25 knots to Mo, where he landed an officer, who learned, among other things, that Colonel Gubbins was still at Sandnessjøen, and wished Commander Napier to go to him, but first to bombard Sund near the town of Hemnes. This he did, each ship firing 30 rounds with no opposition, and he remarked in a signal to Lord Cork that 'this position is particularly open to naval attack'. On the way back down Ranen Fjord he met the *Enterprise*, with other ships, bringing the Scots Guards to Mo, so he went onboard her to give what news he had. He arrived at Sandnessjøen at 0300/12, to find Colonel Gubbins with 450 men ready and waiting to go to Bodø. 'I was deeply impressed with the personality and leadership of the commanding officer', he writes, 'and the quality of his officers and men. They had lost all their gear, were short of food and sleep, and had been hard at it fighting a delaying action against superior forces, unsupported, in a strange country, and subjected to the complete German air superiority. They were of a very fine type, and their cheerfulness and enthusiasm beyond praise'. The *Jackal* took the Colonel and 100 men accordingly; the rest were already onboard a local steamer which the *Javelin* escorted by another route; both parties reached Bodø by midday. The *Jackal*, arriving first, spared the little column several thousands of small-arms cartridges and two months' allowance of provisions, and went out to meet the *Javelin*; together they distracted the attention of some German aircraft, while the transport went safely in. Then they set course for Scapa, still dodging bombs for another hour or so. 'It appeared to me', remarks Commander Napier, 'that an air position is rapidly developing in Northern Norway similar to that complete ascendancy established with such unfortunate results in Åndalsnes and Namsos areas'.[223]

Mo and Bodø Reinforced (Plan 11)

In the meantime, three companies of the Scots Guards with four field and four light anti-aircraft guns had sailed on 11 May for Mo, if it should prove to be still in friendly hands, or for Bodø otherwise. The *Enterprise*, *Hesperus* and *Fleetwood* carried the troops between them, the stores going in the transport *Margot*; and the *Cairo* was joined to the convoy at the request of Captain Annesley of the *Enterprise*, who asked also for protection by fighters from the *Ark Royal*. The ships reached Mo in the morning of 12 May, having fired on the wharf at Hemnes on their way. The troops were all on shore before 0800, but the Germans attacked from the air and hindered the unloading of the *Margot*, which took nine hours even with the help of a working party from the *Hesperus*. Two or three fighters patrolled overhead for some hours, as they had for a time during the convoy's passage the day before, but no more aircraft could be spared, for the *Ark Royal* had to provide patrols over the *Penelope* at the same time. The *Cairo* and *Fleetwood*, said Captain Annesley, were of the greatest value on the occasion, armed as they were entirely with high-angle guns, though the *Fleetwood* spent all her ammunition. Apparently the *Enterprise* sailed alone for Bodø in the afternoon, firing on Hemnes again as she went out, and 'was bombed continuously from Hemnes to open sea'. The *Cairo* brought away the rest of the convoy later; they escaped further attention from the German bombers, being 'favoured by bad visibility and low clouds'.

Both the *Enterprise* and *Cairo* signalled to Lord Cork afterwards suggesting the use of small craft for supplying the troops in future, the *Cairo* adding: 'Passage through Ranen Fjord could not be made in clear weather by slow convoy without extreme probability of loss and damage due to large scale of attacks by dive and level bombers'. And Captain Annesley remarked on these points again after consulting with Colonel Gubbins and a Norwegian naval captain at Bodø: 'All emphatic that no large ships, with possible exception A/A cruisers, should enter Ranen Fjord ... Supplies should be conveyed in puffers or small coasters, and troops in destroyers'. They also suggested destroyer patrols in the approaches to Ranen and Vefsen Fjords and motor boats for service inshore. The army asked that the *Cairo* should stay at Mo until they could mount heavy anti-aircraft guns there, as ships had been stationed off Namsos and Åndalsnes in April, and that other ships should cruise near Hemnes to hamper the German advance and stop reinforcements from coming down Els Fjorden. Unluckily there were not ships for every service required or desirable.

On 13 May came the Foreign Legion's landing at Bjerkvik. Directly afterwards General Auchinleck took over from General Mackesy, and deciding to use all the British troops in the force to the southward, he put Brigadier Fraser in command of the whole, with orders 'to hold Bodø permanently and Mo for as long as he could'. The Norwegian Generals Ruge and Fleischer also stressed the importance of these places; indeed, they longed 'to pass from the defensive to the offensive and recapture Mosjoen'. Brigadier Fraser embarked in the *Somali* in the evening of 13 May, when she had finished her part in the Bjerkvik landing, and she sailed from Tjeldsundet with the French destroyer *Foudroyant* next morning. They were to visit Mo, that the Brigadier might see how the land lay before he set up his headquarters at Bodø; and whilst he was on shore at Mo, the ships were to harass the German communications on the Hemnes peninsula and in Els Fjorden. This they did in the evening of 14 May, the *Foudroyant* shelling Hemnes and sinking boats and seaplanes in the fjord, while the *Somali* fired on a party of the enemy near Finneid, where there was a British outpost. Early next morning, on the way back to Bodø with the Brigadier, news came that the Polish transport, *Chrobry*, which was taking the Irish Guards and other troops to Bodø, had been bombed in Vest Fjord some 30 miles short of her destination. The *Somali* and *Foudroyant* steered towards her, but aircraft attacked them in their turn as they steamed through Traen Fjorden, south of Bodø, and a near miss damaged the *Somali* so much that Captain Nicholson decided to go straight home, escorted by the *Foudroyant*. As Brigadier Fraser had thus to go home, too, he signalled his impressions to General Auchinleck; he thought that 'to continue holding Mo is militarily unsound so long as German air superiority continues'.[224] On the other hand, Lord Cork told the Admiralty the same day, 'I feel we must hold on and fight at Mo; if that goes the whole Narvik situation becomes precarious'.

Loss of the *Chrobry* and *Effingham* (Plan 11)

The *Chrobry* had sailed from Tjeldsundet in the evening of 14 May, escorted by the *Wolverine* and *Stork*. She had onboard her the 24th Brigade Headquarters, the Irish Guards, some anti-aircraft guns, and a troop of the 3rd Hussars, besides some sappers and a field ambulance. German aircraft attacked the ships before they left the anchorage without effect, but they saw no more of the enemy till a little before midnight, when dive bombers attacked the *Chrobry* three times in five minutes in the middle of Vest Fjord, setting her on fire, exploding ammunition, and killing several army officers and men. The *Wolverine* went alongside the blazing troopship and took onboard nearly 700 men, while the *Stork* lay off to guard against further attack. Then the *Wolverine* made the best of her way to Harstad. Meanwhile, the *Stork* had driven off three more aircraft that threatened attack, and when her consort left her she turned to rescuing the rest of the troopship's passengers and crew, going afterwards to Harstad also; she did not wait to sink the troopship, for she had 300 passengers to think of, and aircraft were still about. In the end, aircraft from the *Ark Royal* sank the *Chrobry* on 16 May, the guns, the tanks, and the rest of the equipment going to the bottom in her.[225]

Early on 17 May the South Wales Borderers sailed for Bodø, a battalion of Poles having relieved them on the Ankenes peninsula. They sailed in the *Effingham* from Harstad, escorted by the *Coventry* (flag, Rear-Admiral Vivian), *Cairo* and two destroyers.[226] Instead of taking the short way through Tjeldsundet, they went outside the islands to lessen the risk of attack from the air. When approaching Bodø in the evening, however, they tried a short cut, this time to lessen the danger from submarines, and the *Effingham* and the *Matabele* ran on shore between Briksvaer and the Terra Islands. The destroyer escaped with slight damage, but the *Effingham* was lost. The other ships and some local vessels sent for from Bodø took off the troops and ship's company and part of the large consignment of stores the cruiser was carrying, including some of the machine-gun carriers; attempts to tow off the ship into deep water failed, so she was torpedoed where she lay.

In the end the Borderers and the Irish Guards went to Bodø by detachments in destroyers and local small craft ('puffers'), landing between 20 and 25 May. On 21 May Colonel Gubbins had been made a brigadier and appointed to command all the outlying troops – some 4000 men with four field pieces. He had small chance indeed against the growing strength of the German advance from the south. By 23 May, they, too, were believed to have 4000 men, but with ample artillery and tanks, in the Mo-Mosjoen area and, according to General Auchinleck, 'the operations ... were marked throughout by an unrelenting pressure on the enemy's part, both on the ground and in the air, and by a steady resistance by our troops, handicapped as they were by an almost complete absence of any support in the air or any means of hitting back at their enemy'.

The whole business, whether of maintaining the force in action or of bringing it away, naturally depended very largely on the shipping available. Lord Cork's destroyers now numbered eight, besides which he had two sloops and some 30 trawlers. Most of the latter were anti-submarine craft or minesweepers; but a small trawler force under Acting-Commander W. R. Fell arrived from England at Skjel Fjord on 18 May for work in the Bodø area. These vessels proved quite unsuitable but Commander Fell organised a force of 10 puffers and took them south a few days later, where they became known as the Gubbins Flotilla. They performed remarkable work and were almost continuously in action for seven days'.[227]

By then the efforts in the Bodø area were nearing their conclusion, for on 25 May the Government decided to order the complete withdrawal of all forces from Norway. The evacuation of the Bodø force will be dealt with in – The Retreat from Northern Norway (Page 280).

The Expedition to Narvik: Phase II

Development of Base: Harstad Area   (Plan 14)

While the operations described in the previous chapter were in progress to the southward and preparations were maturing for the direct assault on the port of Narvik, much attention was being paid to the development and defence of the base in the Harstad area.

The facilities at Harstad left much to be desired, and the unloading of transports was a continual difficulty. There were only two wharves and the average rate of discharge was two ships in five days. Disembarkation of personnel was usually done while the ships were in Bygden anchorage; destroyers and HMS *Protector* did good service in connection with this work. Large numbers of local craft were hired for the various water transport services; but they were not very reliable, being prone to disappear into neighbouring fjords at the sound of an air raid warning and to remain there for a considerable time afterwards.[228] As there were over 140 raids on Harstad during the eight weeks of the operations, a good deal of time was lost by this practice.

The use of Harstad – itself on an island – as Military Headquarters and main point of disembarkation meant that the Navy had a very large area to protect against submarines and aircraft; at the same time offensive patrols to harass the enemy in the Narvik region had to be maintained. In addition Skjel Fjord (some 90 miles distant) required protection so long as the *Penelope* and other damaged ships were there (till 10 May).

A preliminary request for guns for fixed defences and for harbour defence Asdics was sent on 22 April and on 28 April the Admiralty informed Lord Cork that the M.N.B.D.O. would be sent to mount the guns and asked for site prospecting to be carried out. The next day Rear-Admiral Lyster was appointed to command the defences and their development; he arrived by air on 5 May, and assumed the responsibility.

Meanwhile, the following proposals had been signalled to the

Admiralty on 1 May:–

The main Naval Base to be in Tjeldsundet with a large ship anchorage to the west of Holsflva, other ships in Lavangsfjord and west of Skaanland: advanced anchorages at Bogen and Ballangen. A minefield extending 1½ miles 310° from Baroen on Baroy Island. 6-in. battery south of Lodingen Church, 4.7-in. battery north of Kvitnes. 12-pdr. battery on west side of Tjelsundet 1 mile south of Staksvollholm. Further batteries considered desirable for south and north ends of Tjelsundet. Minefields N.E. and south of Steinvaer. Harbour defence Asdics off S.W. corner of Baroy Island and Botvaer Island, with control station off Lodingen. Port war signal station on Rotvaer Island. B.1 indicator net and gate west of Staksvollholm. Indicator net or mines at northern entrance to Tjelsundet from Taakeboen beacon to Hella.[229]

These proposals never actually came to fruition. The *Mashobra* arrived with the Royal Marine Fortress unit under Lieutenant-Colonel H. R. Lambert, on 10 May; their work, both in mounting A/A guns and preparing the surface defences, 'merited the highest praise'.[230] But by the time the evacuation was ordered, none of the coast defence guns had been mounted, though the sites had been prepared; mining had not got beyond the planning stage; and though progress had been made in laying the nets and booms they had not been completed.[231] The defence of the bases throughout the operations, therefore, really depended on surface patrols, which were established early and worked regularly, supplemented by A/S air patrols when the necessary Walrus aircraft were available.

Actually, after the sinking of *U-49* on 15 April, no contacts with enemy submarines occurred, though there were many reports of their being sighted. An Irish Guardsman fishing at Bogen landed a used escape apparatus belonging to *U-64*.

The possibility of enemy minelaying by aircraft always had to be envisaged, but this most awkward form of attack does not seem to have been resorted to until 29 May, when five enemy aircraft were seen laying mines in Tjeldsundet South Channel; subsequent sweeping operations exploded four mines, two by non-magnetic sweep and two by magnetic.

But defence against the enemy bomber attack was the prime necessity. This started on the day the first convoy arrived and continued throughout the campaign, greatly increasing in frequency and intensity after the Allied withdrawal from the Trondheim area.

'Fighter aircraft of the Fleet Air Arm[232] and Royal Air Force, in those periods when they were available, wrought great havoc among the enemy and afforded a very welcome relief'; but from the earliest days the establishment of airfields was a major preoccupation. The problem presented unusual difficulties, the land being covered by snow, three or more feet deep, but the work of clearing the Norwegian airfield at Bardufoss was put in hand, and a suitable ground was found at Skaanland in Lavangs Fjord, between Harstad and Tjelsundet. It was hoped to have these landing grounds in operation by 15 May, but the lateness of the thaw caused a 'depressing delay' and it was not till 21 May that the first Gladiator Squadron landed at Bardufoss.

So for the greater part of the campaign, reliance had to be placed on A/A artillery and HM ships with good A/A armament. This need was emphasised in a telegram to the Admiralty on 25 April; the reply came on 30 April, that 48 3.7-in. H.A. guns and 48 Bofors (in addition to 12 already in the area) would be sent; two A/A cruisers were to join Lord Cork's forces on completion of certain other operations. The next day, as if to emphasise the matter, the enemy obtained a direct hit on the building used for Naval accommodation in Harstad, fortunately killing only two ratings. At the same time they bombed the Hospital Ship *Atlantis*, anchored wide away from all other ships, and a Norwegian Hospital ship, causing many casualties in the latter'.

The first 3.7-in. A/A guns arrived on 6 May, and four of them were in action at Harstad on 9 May, four more being on their way to Bardufoss, which had already received Bofors guns on 7 May. 'Men bombed on shore could now begin to feel that they had some chance of hitting back; a psychological factor of considerable importance'.

The allotment of the limited guns available was made on the principle that it was only possible to give a minimum degree of protection to really vital areas and that smaller and less important areas must go without.[232]

The final distribution of anti-aircraft artillery at the end of May was:–

Situation	Heavy Guns	Light Guns
Bardufoss	12	12
Sorreisa		2
Elvenes		4
Tromsø	4	4
Harstad	12	5
Skaanland	15	10
Ballangen		4
Ankenes		4
Bjerkvik		4
Bodø		2
Loaded for Bodø	4	4
In a 'Q' ship		1

The Landing at Bjerkvik 12/13 May   (Plan 14)

To return to the operations against Narvik itself, which had made little direct progress since the bombardment on 24 April.

The detached squadron, strengthened for a few days early in May by the *Resolution*, continued its activities in Ofot Fjord. It stopped traffic by water; it worked with the South Wales Borderers along the shore near Ankenes; it fired on parties of German troops and on piers and bridges, ammunition stores and gun positions; it tried, but unsuccessfully, to stop the enemy from moving men and stores by air; and in the intervals the destroyers searched outlying fjords for submarines and carried out regular anti-submarine patrols. The Germans retaliated chiefly from the air. They failed in an attempt upon the *Aurora* with the General onboard her; but later on, when attacking 'on an average once daily', they sank the *Grom* (4 May), disabled a turret in the *Aurora* (7 May), and damaged one or two other ships.[234] Later on, in the middle of May, Rear-Admiral Vivian relieved Captain Hamilton with the *Coventry*, and for a while the *Cairo*, but having other duties as well these ships spent less time in the fjord than had Captain Hamilton's cruisers.

The plan finally adopted for the assault on Narvik was to be carried out in two stages, firstly a landing at Bjerkvik at the head of Herjangs Fjord, with the object of securing Oydejord and obtaining control of

Rombaks Fjord; and secondly, after these positions had been consolidated, a direct attack on Narvik from Oydejord across Rombaks Fjord.

The landing in Herjangs Fjord was planned to take place in the early hours of 13 May, served by the following ships: *Effingham*, *Resolution* and *Aurora*; *Somali*, *Havelock*, *Fame*, *Wren* and *Basilisk*; *Vindictive* and *Protector* – with two trawlers, four assault landing craft, and three motor landing craft. They were to assemble near Ballangen the day before to embark the Legion, and sail about 2100 to reach their destination 20 miles away by midnight. An advance guard of 120 men of the first battalion were to make the whole passage in the four assault landing craft under their own power; the rest of the 1500 infantry in the *Vindictive* and *Protector* and the two cruisers, from which they were to land in ships' boats and assault landing craft in turns; there were also five tanks, which took passage in the *Resolution*, and were to land in the motor landing craft.[235] The trawlers' task was to tow the motor landing craft to the fjord, and then to patrol against submarines outside. This left the destroyers, unhampered by other duties, to support the soldiers with their fire from positions within a few cables' lengths of the shore, while the big ships lay further out. Lastly, fighter protection for ships and troops, reconnaissance of the enemy's positions, and bombing attacks were to be supplied by aircraft from the *Ark Royal* which had been working off the coast since 6 May.

Three tanks were to land first, followed by the advance guard already in its landing craft, then the rest of the first battalion – 'when ordered by the flagship' – in flights of 350 in men-of-war's boats or 120 in the assault landing craft; all to land on the beach, near Bjerkvik, at the top of the fjord. The second battalion was to go on shore in the same way later, headed by the other two tanks, but landing at Meby about a mile to the right of the first battalion. Lord Cork's original orders laid down that there should be no 'preliminary bombardment unless the enemy open fire on the force during the approach or is sighted by ships or aircraft'. For this, the *Resolution*, the cruisers, and all five destroyers had target areas allotted to them along the foreshore, the targets being chiefly machine-gun posts in houses, along the beach, and on the wooded hillsides beyond the villages; and the orders ran: 'Every effort should be made to locate targets in these areas, but fire is not to be withheld because targets have not been located, as the object is to produce the maximum volume of fire on possible enemy positions'. Lord Cork revised this plan later by ordering the leading destroyers, as soon as they should reach their stations off the pier, 'to open fire without further orders and destroy all houses in Bjerkvik, particularly those near the landing beach; if troops are seen leaving houses they are to be engaged in preference to the houses'. A naval officer was to go on shore with the second flight of infantry to control the fire of the ships in support of the troops as they moved inland.

The ships arrived punctually in their stations at midnight 12/13 May. General Béthouart was in the *Effingham* with the Admiral, as was General Auchinleck, who had arrived from the United Kingdom the day before to succeed General Mackesy. The *Somali*, *Havelock* and *Fame* immediately opened fire on the village of Bjerkvik, while the *Resolution* hoisted out the tanks, and the *Effingham* and *Aurora* hauled up the boats they had already in tow. This preliminary bombardment lasted a quarter of an hour, setting houses ablaze and exploding stores of ammunition, but the Germans continued to reply with machine-guns, so the Admiral ordered a general bombardment that went on till 0100/13. Then, in the growing light, the tanks went on shore, and the advance guard, and the second flight in its open boats, followed by the rest of the first battalion in due course. Most of the battalion had to edge away to the left and land near Haugen, a mile or so west of Bjerkvik; helped by the tanks, however, the legionaries soon fought their way back to the village and began their northward advance up the Elvenes road to join hands with the Chasseurs-Alpins.

The ships had shifted their fire inland, 'a creeping barrage', the *Wren* called it, but at 0200 they left off, their work over until the time came to prepare the way for the second battalion. The enemy's fire obliged these latter troops, too, to seek a better landing place. With the ships firing overhead, they began to land about 0300, rather south of Meby; they worked north-eastward to seize Elvegaarden, at the foot of the mountain Mebyfjeldet, and secured the coastwise road to Oydejord – their two tanks, says an officer of the Legion, 'frisking about like young puppies, firing all the time, in the midst of fields which were here free from snow'.

About 0600 General Bethouart reported to Lord Cork that he no longer required the support of HM Ships, beyond those normally on patrol in that area, and went on shore. Soon afterwards Lord Cork and General Auchinleck returned to Harstad in the *Effingham*, the other big ships departing as the last troops left them, while some of the destroyers stayed to support the attack. Later in the day the Polish battalion from Bogen arrived by land to join the Legion.

That afternoon (13 May), on arrival at Harstad, General Auckinleck assumed command of the military and air forces in accordance with his instructions from the War Office.[236]

Thus the attack succeeded, and with very little loss to the legionaries. It is hard to judge from the scanty reports how much the ships' guns contributed to this result. Captain Stevens of the *Havelock* remarked that 'enemy machine-gun posts were immediately, but only temporarily, silenced by a few rounds of 4.7-in. shell. These posts were well concealed and probably equipped with light automatic guns, which could be lowered and raised as easily as a rifle'. General Auchinleck called the bombardment heavy and the landing completely successful in spite of 'appreciable opposition' from the German machine-guns. 'Although I was present in the capacity of a spectator only,' he went on, 'I am constrained to express my admiration for the way in which the whole operation was conceived and effected by all concerned. I was particularly struck by the businesslike efficiency of the French Foreign Legion ... That the landing was not interfered with by enemy aircraft was almost certainly due to the fortunate weather conditions prevailing at the time. At this period there were no land-based aircraft available in Norway with which to counter enemy air attacks, and a bombing raid might well have turned the operation from a success into a failure'.

The weather also affected the *Ark Royal's* aircraft. Patrols of three fighters at a time flew above the embarking troops near Ballangen in the evening of 12 May, but by 2200 the clouds were as low as 500 ft., so they had to give up. Nor could flying start again before 0200/13, which meant that the first fighter patrol for the landing arrived only when the second battalion was going on shore, and the bombers had not time to reach the positions near Lake Hartvig, 3 miles east of Bjerkvik, that Lord Cork wished them to attack during the landing – instead, rather later in the morning, they attacked the railway near Sildvik and Hunddalen, about 9 and 12 miles beyond Narvik respectively. Low clouds and fog made effective reconnaissance impossible. Several aircraft had to land in Vaagsfjord, prevented by thick fog from returning to their ship, after carrying out their various tasks. On the other hand, no German aircraft appeared at all on either day; and after the landing Lord Cork made the following signal to Admiral Wells in the *Ark Royal*: 'Many thanks for your close support this morning. It was most comforting to see them'.[237]

The French soon occupied Oydejord, and went on to master the north shore of Rombaks Fjord, General Dietl withdrawing his troops to the mountains to the north and east. General Auchinleck points out that possession of this shore would give a larger choice of landing places, avoiding 'difficult beaches which were believed to be strongly defended by machine-guns'. It would allow of using the French field guns to support the landing, and it would make possible some degree of surprise, for the landing craft could assemble secretly under a mile from their destination instead of being 'marshalled in Ofot Fjord in daylight in full view of the enemy'. The ships stationed in Vest Fjord worked with the French troops to gain possession; and Commander Walter of the *Fame* took 150 Chasseurs-Alpins to Lilleberg, half-way to the narrows, and landed them in 'puffers' in the little harbour on 21 May, the *Cairo* and the big French destroyer *Milan* coming inside the fjord in support; there the Chasseurs joined forces with other French soldiers and pushed further eastward. On the other side of Narvik a Polish battalion relieved the South Wales Borderers on the Ankenes peninsula, that the Borderers might reinforce Bodø, while the Poles made ready to attack towards the head of Beisfjord.

Preparations for Assault on Narvik

So far as the army was concerned, the assault on Narvik might have taken place a day or two after the little expedition to Lilleberg. But the danger from the air seemed to grow worse. In contrast with the lucky day of the landing at Bjerkvik, despite the gallant efforts of the *Ark Royal*'s few machines up to her leaving for home on 21 May, in the fortnight after Bjerkvik, the German aircraft destroyed or damaged above a dozen ships of war, transports and storeships, beginning with the troopship *Chrobry*, on 14 May, and ending with the *Curlew*, which they sank in Tjeldsundet on 26 May. Lord Cork and the generals therefore resolved they must have adequate protection for the assault: in the Admiral's words, 'either such weather conditions as were likely to largely reduce or abolish any danger of air attack or the ability to provide efficient fighter protection overhead'. The need of shore-based aircraft to counter enemy attacks appeared more urgent with each German raid, but the airfields at Bardufoss, and at Skaanland, for the Royal Air Force fighters that the *Glorious* and *Furious* were to bring from home, were not yet ready. The squadron from the latter ship landed at Bardufoss on 21 May, but Skaanland could not receive aircraft until 26 May. This determined the date of the assault; for besides the wish to have as many aircraft as possible for that occasion, the two remaining motor landing craft were busy up to the last moment transporting guns and stores of all kinds for the airfields.[238] The view of the commanders appears in the following signal, which Lord Cork made on 20 May in answer to messages from home that 'expressed … increased disappointment at stagnation round Narvik and at delay in occupying town' and urged its immediate capture:–

> 'I fully understand that the occupation of the town of Narvik is desired, and am anxious to report its capture. The most important work at the moment, however, is the completion and protection of the aerodromes, and for these all motor landing craft are required. If we are to maintain our position here, it is of paramount importance that we can operate aircraft as quickly as possible and be able to counter German bombers; indeed, it might be described as a necessary preliminary to a combined operation on whatever scale …
>
> It would be folly under existing conditions, to switch off from the essential preparation of aerodromes to that of attacking Narvik, a place which does not affect the main issue and can be got on with at the end of this week. A delay there does not matter. A delay with aerodromes has become dangerous.'

Only a few days after this – 24 May – the Government decided to retreat from Norway altogether. They wished, however, to have the port of Narvik and the railway destroyed, and they thought the defeat of the German troops in the district would make easier the task of withdrawing. The commanders agreed, General Auchinleck remarking that, 'apart from the desirability of making sure whether the facilities for shipping ore from Narvik had, in fact, been destroyed as thoroughly as had been reported, the chances that a successful attack would do much to conceal our intention to evacuate … would outweigh the possible disadvantages involved in extending our commitments by establishing troops in close contact with the enemy on the Narvik peninsula, where his main force was thought to be located'.

Accordingly, they resolved to attack in the night of 27/28 May, by which time the second squadron of fighters should be ready for service.

Plan of Operations (Plan 14)

'The plan is open to criticism in details – its great merit, however, was in that it was the plan of those who had to carry it out. The weak point in the plan was that owing to the paucity of transport available – a less bold man than General Béthouart might well have made this an excuse for inaction – it was necessary to leave the First Flight… unsupported for an unduly long time…'[239]

The two battalions of the Foreign Legion, the Narvik battalion of the Norwegian Army, and four tanks were to attack across Rombaks Fjord. They would land on the beach east of Orneset, at the mouth of the fjord, supported by the fire of the ships and of two batteries of French field pieces and one of Norwegian mountain guns posted on Hill 145 about a thousand yards inland from Oydejord. The first flight would come round from Lindstrand or Saegnes in Herjangs Fjord, in the three assault and two motor landing craft (the only vessels of these types remaining) and keep the shore close onboard as long as possible to hide themselves, whereas later flights were to embark at Oydejord and thence cross direct. The first flight would thus number 290 men, which the generals thought dangerously weak, especially as these troops must fight alone for three-quarters of an hour before the next flight could join them; moreover, as the motor landing craft would then be wanted for the tanks, the next few flights of infantry would muster only 90, with perhaps a few more in fishing smacks. As it happened, all went well in that respect, but General Auchinleck wrote of 'the barest margin of safety' and commented on the landing as follows:–

> 'Had the enemy been able to launch an immediate counter-attack the result might have been disastrous. It must always, in my opinion, be unwise to embark on operations of this character unless landing craft are available to land a first flight of adequate strength and, in addition, provide an adequate floating reserve to meet unforeseen contingencies. Moreover, the absence of bomber aircraft deprived the attack of one of the most effective means of repulsing an enemy

counter-attack... The broken and intricate nature of the ground prevented accurate observation by the supporting ships and artillery. The risk, however, was in my opinion worth taking, and as things turned out it was justified.'

Besides this main attack, the Chasseurs from Lilleberg and farther east were to feint towards the head of Rombaken, the inner part of Rombacks Fjord; and the Poles, with two field guns and two tanks, were to attack Ankenes and march towards the head of Beisfjord to threaten the German line of retreat south-east of Narvik.

The soldiers had much less support from the sea than they might have had in April or for the attack projected early in May. Lord Cork had now no capital ship; and he had only one ship with 6-in. guns, the *Southampton* (Flag, Rear-Admiral Clarke), the *Enterprise* and *Aurora* having gone home. The table below gives the arrangements for the preliminary bombardment: each ship lay about 1,000 yards off shore with a firing range of roughly 2000 yards, except that the *Southampton* was over 4000 yards from Fagernes.

In Rombaks Fjord

Ship *Beagle* **Target** Stromnes railway station.

Ship *Fame* **Target** The mouths of two railway tunnels behind Forsneset.

Ship *Havelock* **Target** The mouth of a tunnel behind Djupviken.

Ship *Walker* **Target** The mouth of a tunnel behind the landing beach near Orneset.

In Ofot Fjord

Ship *Cairo* **Target** The hill east of Vaasvik 'to destroy enemy positions there'.

Ship *Firedrake* **Target** Ditto. The hill east of Lillevik.

Ship *Coventry* **Target** The ridge north of Framnesodden

Ship *Southampton* **Target** (1) Fagernes promontory 'to destroy enemy positions there and to prevent reinforcements proceeding from there to the Ankenes Peninsula'.

(2) The village of Ankenes, east of the church – actually, she fired on the second target first.

The orders said 'there has been considerable enemy activity in the railway tunnels east of Narvik, but with what object is not known;' apparently the Germans were believed to use the tunnels as shelters for troops and guns. The bombardment was to start twenty minutes before the first flight of legionaries reached the shore. The ships inside Rombaks Fjord were to leave off as the first landing craft passed them. Signals from the flagship would govern the firing of the ships outside. After the landing, naval officers attached to the troops would signal the targets to be attacked by reference to a gridded map. Besides the eight bombarding ships, there was the *Stork* sloop to protect the landing craft from air attack.

The Capture of Narvik 28 May (Plan 14)

The ships arrived in their stations independently just after 2330/27, with Generals Auchinleck and Béthouart onboard the *Cairo* in which Lord Cork was wearing his flag. They immediately began engaging, as did the field guns above Oydejord. The bombardment, said General Auchinleck, 'was heavy and accurate, but close support of the attacking troops was hampered throughout by the broken nature of the terrain and the difficulty of accurate observation in the birch scrub which covered the lower slopes of the hills'; and Captain Stevens of the *Havelock* remarked – as he did after Bjerkvik – that 'while 4.7-in. fire immediately silenced enemy machine-guns, it did not apparently succeed in destroying them,' though he quickly destroyed a German machine-gun and its crew with his own half-inch machine-gun at 1800 yards range. The first flight of legionaries landed punctually at midnight without loss, the opposition 'weaker than expected' according to Lieutenant Francklin, who commanded the landing flotilla. The next party, however, was not ready at Oydejord when the landing craft came there; German field guns and mortars opened a galling fire on the pier, while the party was embarking; and the French sent round their later flights to embark at Saegnes in Herjangs Fjord, which 'slowed up the operation very considerably' and prevented the use of fishing smacks to supplement the landing craft, owing to the shallow water. None the less, the first battalion of the Legion and the Narvik battalion were both on shore by 0400/28, or sooner, which was well within the time table. On the other hand, the first couple of tanks – apparently the only tanks put on shore that side – stuck in the soft mud and sand of their landing beach at Taraldsvik, and did no service.

It was as well that the landing so far had gone punctually, for German bombers appeared about 0500, apparently 30 or more, with the air to themselves. The Royal Air Force fighter patrols which had been arranged to protect the ships and troops became fog-bound at Bardufoss some twenty minutes before the Germans appeared over Narvik. For two hours the German aircraft attacked. They seem to have helped their comrades on the ground in a counterstroke that gave the Allies a hard fight to hold what they had won, and to have hindered the landing of the second battalion of legionaries. Although the aircraft actually hit the *Cairo* only[240] each ship had to manoeuvre to avoid bombs in a way that made it impossible to support the troops with gunfire. Luckily the ships had virtually finished their task, and General Béthouart wanted now but two destroyers, and was ready to go on shore himself. Lord Cork withdrew accordingly about 0630, leaving Admiral Vivian to attend on the soldiers with the *Coventry*, *Firedrake* and *Beagle*, to which were added the *Delight* and *Echo* in the afternoon.

According to one report the German counter-stroke came when they saw the ships retire. The Allies were then attacking Hill 457, a plateau south-east of the landing beach, and the Germans drove them back across the railway and up the hill by Orneset. They also brought machine-guns to bear on the beach, where part of the second battalion of the Legion was still coming on shore, so another landing place was found further to the westward. The first battalion renewed its attack, with the *Beagle* and the field guns at Oydejord supporting, and before long the legionaries and the Norwegians gained the plateau. Later on the second battalion seized the high ground north and west of Narvik.

German aircraft attacked the troops again in the evening, and nearly hit the *Coventry*; this time some British fighters came to the rescue, though with what effect the reports do not say.

By 2200 that night, the whole of Narvik peninsula west of a line from Fagernes to Forsneset had fallen to the Allies. To the south, the Poles had stiff fighting round Ankenes. They eventually established themselves on the side of a hill above that village, overlooking Narvik harbour. The *Southampton* had supported them in the morning, firing on Ankenes and Nyborg and across the harbour on Fagernes; for a time, too, the *Firedrake* engaged German machine-guns near the Ore Quay. Admiral Clarke remarked that 'in general, the shore signal station was not helpful in communicating clearly what was wanted, in fact, it did not appear always to know', and that none of the *Southampton*'s targets 'was really identified, although the result of the bombardment appeared to be what was wanted' – certainly the Poles seem to have been entirely satisfied.

In the two days following the capture of Narvik, the French continued their advance along both sides of Rombaks Fjord as far as the narrows by Stromsnes (where the *Eskimo* had been torpedoed on 13 April). General Fleischer's division lay north and east of the fjord in touch with the Chasseurs-Alpins, except that his Narvik battalion lay as garrison in its name town. The Poles reached the head of Beisfjord, and had three battalions in the district between Ankenes and the head of the fjord by the end of the month. All these troops were in touch with the enemy.

The German General Dietl was in fact in a critical situation, and had it been possible for the Allies to carry the operations to their logical conclusion, must soon have been faced with the alternatives of surrender or withdrawal across the Swedish frontier. Actually, provisional arrangements were made for the latter.

'Thus ended an operation', wrote General Auchinleck, 'which, in my opinion, reflects great credit on the judgment and pertinacity of General Béthouart and on the fighting qualities of his troops. Reconnaissance after the capture of the town revealed the full difficulties of landing on the beaches close to the town and the wisdom of the plan finally adopted. Though he knew of the decision to evacuate Norway before the operation started, General Béthouart persevered with his plan; and the vigour with which the advance eastwards was pressed after the capture of the town drove the enemy back on to his main position covering Sildvik and Hunddalen, thus making it difficult for him to attempt a counter-attack against Narvik at short notice; this enabled the subsequent evacuation to be carried out under more favourable conditions than at one time seemed likely'. But he said too:–

'The plans for the landing on the peninsula north of Narvik had continually to be changed and postponed, owing to the lack of proper landing craft, particularly of motor landing craft, which were required to land tanks. These motor landing craft were also in constant demand for the vital task of landing heavy anti-aircraft guns for the protection of the base area. The landing at Narvik was also successful thanks to the most effective co-operation of the Royal Navy, the excellent support given by the guns of HM ships, and the skill and determination of General Béthouart's troops; but with the facilities available the transfer of three battalions across a narrow fjord some 1500 yards wide took over seven hours, and the strength of the first fight had to be limited to 300 men. The landing of such a small advanced party on a hostile shore entailed considerable risk; and in view of the likelihood of such operations having to be repeated in other theatres of war, it is urgently necessary that an ample supply of modern landing craft should be provided without further delay. It is unfair to expect any troops to undertake such hazardous operations with such inadequate means.'

The Retreat from Northern Norway

The Decision to Withdraw

The British and French Governments' decision to leave Norway altogether reached Lord Cork during the night of 24/25 May in the following signal from the Chiefs of Staff (A.T. 2004/24):–

> 'His Majesty's Government has decided your forces are to evacuate Northern Norway at earliest moment.
> Reason for this is that the troops, ships, guns and certain equipment are urgently required for defence of United Kingdom.
> We understand, from military point of view, operations evacuations will be facilitated if enemy forces are largely destroyed or captured. Moreover, destruction of railways and Narvik port facilities make its capture highly desirable. Nevertheless, speed of evacuation, once begun, should be of primary consideration in order to limit duration maximum naval efforts. Two officers will be sent at once from United Kingdom to concert evacuation plans with you and General Auchinleck. Evacuation of all equipment, vehicles and stores will clearly take too long: following are required to be evacuated in order of importance from point of view of defence of United Kingdom, (a) personnel, (b) light anti-aircraft guns and ammunition, (c) 25-pounders, (d) heavy anti-aircraft guns and ammunition. Tactical conditions must rule; but, so far as they permit, plan should be framed accordingly.
> Norwegian Government have not yet been informed and greatest secrecy should be observed.'

The following morning Lord Cork discussed the matter with General Auchinleck; both were agreed that the safety of the force made secrecy vital and that the information should only be imparted to those Senior

Officers it was imperative should know it. Next day General Béthouart was informed. He received the news with 'characteristic calm, though one point upon which he was insistent was that for reasons of national honour he could not abandon the Norwegian Army he had been working with, in the lurch on the field of battle. The whole question was discussed and it was agreed that pressure on the enemy must be kept up until the last, that the attack on Narvik ... must go on, and that this operation would of itself be the best possible way of concealing our intentions from the enemy'.[241]

There remained the difficult question of breaking the news to the Norwegians. Clearly, it was only fair that this should be done as soon as possible. After communication with the Foreign Office, the decision was taken on 1 June that Sir Cecil Dormer (HBM Minister to Norway) should inform the King of Norway in the morning of 2 June and that the Norwegian Cabinet and the Commander-in-Chief, General Ruge, should be informed later that day. Vice-Admiral Cunningham, who had been operating in the Tromsø area since 10 May, was also told and directed to arrange for the passage of the King and Government.

Naturally, at first, there was a feeling of soreness and disillusionment among the Norwegians on learning of the evacuation, but on the whole the decision was received as being inevitable under the circumstances and every help was given to facilitate the withdrawal. Cordial letters were exchanged between Lord Cork and the Norwegian Admiral Diesen, who undertook to send all effective Norwegian ships, including submarines, to the Shetlands and to destroy the rest.

As a first step, it was decided to evacuate the troops from the Bodø area. Brigadier Gubbins had already reported that he must not retire later than 1 June unless reinforcements could be sent to him and this was under consideration, but the idea was necessarily abandoned in view of the new policy, and orders for withdrawal were accordingly issued.

Withdrawal from Mo and Bodø (Plan 11)

The situation in the Bodø area when the decision was taken to withdraw was as follows.

The Scots Guards had been falling back from Mo since 18 May; a week later they reached Rognan, at the head of Saltdals Fjord, some 40 miles by water to the eastward of Bodø and 12 miles south of the main position near Fauske, where the Irish Guards and the five independent companies lay. The Brigadier's plan was to bring back the Scots Guards from Rognan to Hopen, about 10 miles east of Bodø, when the troops near Fauske were to retreat through them and embark; the Scots Guards were to retreat in turn through the South Wales Borderers, posted nearer in, and the whole force was to leave Bodø in destroyers in three flights between 29 May and 1 June.

Commander Fell's flotilla of puffers had reached the area on 24 May, and it was on these craft that the programme principally fell in the first place. His first task was to ferry troops to Bodø on 25 May. Thenceforward the flotilla worked unceasingly in the service of the troops between Rognan and Bodø until the last straggler had embarked on 1 June. The ships and their native crews might change – they were not fighting units and 'most of the Norwegian crews took flight or sabotaged their engines, if left for a moment unguarded' under fire – but the work went on with new puffers and new crews.

On 29 May, the day the retreat from Bodø began, the Admiralty had signalled to Lord Cork that 'aircraft carriers and four fast liners will arrive Bodø area on 2 June for evacuation of garrison' and 'it appears undesirable to attempt embarking Bodø garrison without fighter protection from carriers'. It was, however, decided not to wait and to carry on with the evacuation by destroyers as planned, though less than half a dozen aircraft at Bodø only become operational on 26 May. Nor were there any anti-aircraft guns worth mentioning.

During the last few days before the embarkation German bombers raided Bodø and attacked the troops several times, but the enemy's main concern was with attacks on the base at Harstad and the shipping in the fjords to the northward. On 26 and 27 May the few Royal Air Force fighters shot down three or four Germans, a number almost equal to their own strength. On 28 May the enemy arrived in force and destroyed the town and damaged the airfield. Fortunately they missed the quay from which the embarkation was to take place and they did not appear while the troops were actually going onboard; the evacuation was successfully completed on 29, 30 and 31 May, 1000 men being taken directly to the United Kingdom in the *Vindictive* and the remainder to Harstad in destroyers[242] and small craft. A considerable amount of equipment was brought away, but four 25-pdr. guns, four Bofors, and three Bren carriers which had been salved from the *Effingham*, together with such material as could not be moved by the men had to be abandoned.

Mention should be made of the useful work of SS *Ranen*, a small Norwegian passenger steamer which had been taken up and armed with one Bofors, one Oerlikon and numerous machine guns as a decoy ship. Commanded by Commander Sir Geoffrey Congreve and manned by a mixed party of naval ratings, Irish Guardsmen and Borderers, she harried the enemy in their advance up the coast from Bodø. She also added to General Dietl's perplexities by cutting the telephone cables by which the Germans communicated their progress northwards.

Plan of General Withdrawal

Meanwhile, plans had been got out for the general withdrawal.

By this time Germany had all Holland and nearly all Belgium in her power; her advancing armies, well inside France, seriously threatened the Channel ports. The evacuation of the British Army from Dunkirk was in full swing[243] and the Admiralty had warned Sir Charles Forbes that the risk of invasion by airborne and seaborne troops, perhaps assisted by 'the Fifth Column', was thought to be 'very real'. In these circumstances, plans for retreat – which followed hard upon the heels of the final plans for taking Narvik – must rely as little as possible on outside help, whether for ferrying the troops and stores to the transports or for protection during the passage home. As Admiral Forbes put it: 'The naval effort during evacuation will of necessity be large and prolonged, unless a disaster is courted, and will take place at a time when our naval effort might well be required in the North Sea, 1,000 miles away'.

Lord Cork's plan had three phases. Under the first he sent home certain stores, including some French tanks and guns, before the end of May in ships he had already in Norway, escorted by some of his own trawlers. For the main embarkation, to be carried out in the two later phases, he needed ships to take the rest of the stores and some 24,500 troops – all the expeditionary force except the 1,000 men that went direct from Bodø. These transports were to arrive in two groups during the first week in June.

As for ships of war, the Admiral expected to have one large cruiser, three anti-aircraft cruisers and about 10 destroyers of his own; he asked for five more destroyers to maintain his patrols, whilst the bulk of the flotilla ferried troops to the transports at rendezvous in the outer fjords or at sea, but the Admiralty could spare him only three. As things turned out, the *Curlew* was sunk before the end of May, and the *Cairo* and a destroyer had to go home disabled, all the result of attacks from the air; thus the actual strength was considerably less than Lord Cork had counted on.[244]

On the other hand, the expedition was to have invaluable protection in the air up to the last moment of embarking, and indeed during the passage home, for Vice-Admiral Wells arrived off the coast with the *Ark Royal* and *Glorious* in the evening of 2 June. The *Ark Royal* had fighters to patrol above the embarking troops and bombers to attack the German troops and communications – for instance, the airfield at Bodø and troops at Fauske, both places so lately in British hands, besides their old targets of a few weeks before, the railway at Hunddalen and Sildvik. When the last troops sailed she went most of the way home with them, and her aircraft patrolled round the convoy. The *Glorious* had come to carry home the Royal Air Force fighters from Bardufoss. That the cloudy weather of their last few days in Norway favoured the departing troops does not lessen the credit due to the Royal Air Force, who in General Auchinleck's words had inspired their opponents with a 'genuine fear' of their prowess, and who shared in the work of protecting the troops until a few hours before the rearguard left the shore.

The following arrangements were made to protect the expedition during its passage home. All the ships of the Narvik squadron were needed for embarking troops or giving local protection to the end, so Lord Cork originally intended to keep the first group at one of his distant rendezvous until the last soldiers had embarked, when four destroyers would go ahead to join it, while the rest of the squadron escorted the other troopships and the main storeship convoy. But the Commander-in-Chief, Home Fleet, asked the Admiralty on 30 May to keep him posted with the situation, 'particularly as regards' the sailing of the two groups of troopships, 'and also whether battlecruiser may be required to provide cover'. Although Lord Cork does not seem to have intercepted this signal, he answered it in effect next day, when he told Admiral Forbes his arrangements, and said 'much appreciate if some covering protection could be given'. Then, the Admiralty having desired that the troops should return as soon as possible to fit in with other movements they had to provide for, Lord Cork further informed him that the first group would leave the rendezvous on 7 June in charge of the *Vindictive*, but without other escort; and he asked, 'Could covering force be provided, and convoy met, where you consider necessary – all destroyers in area required for rapid embarkation last flight'. Sir Charles replied that 'cover and anti-submarine escort will be sent to meet Group One', adding later that the *Valiant* (Captain Rawlings) would sail from Scapa on 6 June to accompany this first group as far south as 61° N., and then go north again to meet the second group in its turn, also that destroyers would join the first group and stay with it to the Clyde.

Admiral Forbes had meant originally to send the *Renown* and *Repulse*, but on 5 June 'two unknown vessels', possibly raiders, were sighted about 200 miles north-east of the Faeroes steering towards the Iceland–Faeroes passage, and Vice-Admiral Whitworth with the two battlecruisers, the *Newcastle*, *Sussex* and five destroyers[245] was sent to intercept them. Two days later, Admiral Whitworth's force proceeded to the coast of Iceland, on a report of an enemy landing there; but on 8 June the Admiralty ordered the *Renown* and two destroyers back to Scapa, as it was considered 'there should not be less than two capital ships available to proceed south in case of invasion'.

Thus it came about in the event that during the evacuation the Home Fleet heavy forces were considerably dispersed.

The Withdrawal (Plan 15)

The transports for the two later phases of the withdrawal went out singly or in small groups, some with escorts for the whole or part of the way, some with none. Most of the storeships went to Harstad to load, and sailed again in the evening of 7 June as an independent group – the slow convoy – with an escort of its own that joined it next day when the last troops had sailed; but a few storeships loaded at Tromsø, whence they sailed also on 7 June, meeting an escort of trawlers later. The fifteen troopships, two of which were not used, went first to one or other of two distant rendezvous appointed by Lord Cork about 180 miles from the coast,[246] where the two main groups were to assemble before closing the coast to receive troops, and where individual ships were to wait after loading or between partial loadings until their group was ready to go home. Rear-Admiral Vivian in the *Coventry*, in general charge of the embarking, met the main groups at sea as they approached the coast to give them their instructions and to protect them from air attack while near the shore, and three or four of the hard-worked destroyers gave them anti-submarine protection in the intervals between turns of ferrying. Three of the troopships were small cross-channel steamers, two of which shipped men and stores at Harstad; the others got their passengers from destroyers in outlying fjords or at rendezvous some 40 miles out at sea. The soldiers left the shore at night, when experience taught that German aircraft gave least trouble, though it was daylight all round the clock. They embarked from places in Ofot Fjord and Tjeldsundet, from Harstad and the little fjords or sounds north of it, sometimes from puffers into destroyers, sometimes direct into destroyers, which carried them to the troopships, and all the time the airmen of both Services watched over them, and destroyers and the *Stork* and trawlers patrolled against possible submarines. The first main group of troopships, six large merchantmen and the *Vindictive*, took nearly 15,000 men in three early morning loadings between 4 and 6 June. The second group, four large and three small merchantmen, took a little under 10,000 men on 7 and 8 June.

Moreover, 'a great deal more stores and equipment was loaded' than the General had hoped, though most of the anti-aircraft guns and many wagons were abandoned.

All the troops had left the shore by the early morning of 8 June without hindrance from the enemy. General Auchinleck had been anxious lest German troops advancing from the Bodø district should embarrass the departure of the troops round Narvik, who were in touch with the enemy to the last. But General Béthouart skilfully withdrew his rearguard, a battalion each of Poles and the Foreign Legion; and the nearest the Germans got to interfering was the landing of a few men by parachute near Ballangen in the afternoon of 7 June, as reported by the *Stork*. When in due course they re-occupied Narvik, they found it in a sorry state. Ore quays and electric power had been totally destroyed and the railway line for 2 miles east of Narvik partially destroyed. It was estimated that the ore quays and electrical supply would take nine months to repair; and this, combined with clearing the harbour, in which some 20 ships had been sunk, would preclude the export of ore in appreciable quantities for about a year.[247]

During the last few days before the retirement, steps were taken to deny to the enemy anything of value that could not be taken away in the area held by the Allies. The M.N.B. ship *Mashobra* which had been bombed on 25 May and beached was blown up; the 7,000-ton oiler, *Oleander*, severely damaged by a near miss on 26 May, was sunk; disabled trawlers were destroyed; harbour defence booms and nets were sunk and all traces removed. An attempt was made to tow away the A.L.C.s, but finally they and the M.L.C.s were scuttled.

Nor was the destruction confined to what the Allies had brought with them. For example, Sir Geoffrey Congreve in the *Ranen*, with the trawler *Northern Gem*, destroyed the oil tanks at Solfolla[248] (on the north shore of Vest Fjord) in the night of 7 June. 'This successful exploit ended with a most spirited engagement, on his part, with the enemy'.[249] The bombing attack by the Walrus aircraft on the installations at Solfolla has already been mentioned.

The last men to be embarked in the transports were the ground staff of Bardufoss airfield. The Gladiators had been flown onboard the *Glorious*, but it was feared that the eight Hurricanes that remained efficient would have to be abandoned. The Royal Air Force had orders to keep in action to the last, and then destroy their aircraft, should the enemy air activity necessitate it; but the cloudy weather and their own quality enabled them to take their aircraft away in the *Glorious*. 'The courageous action of the pilots in volunteering to fly their machines on to the flying deck of *Glorious* and of Group Captain Moore in allowing it to be done resulted in all eight being got safely away – an achievement which deserved a better fate than that which befell the gallant men who had carried it out successfully.'[250]

The organisation of the convoys carrying the expedition to the United Kingdom was as follows:–

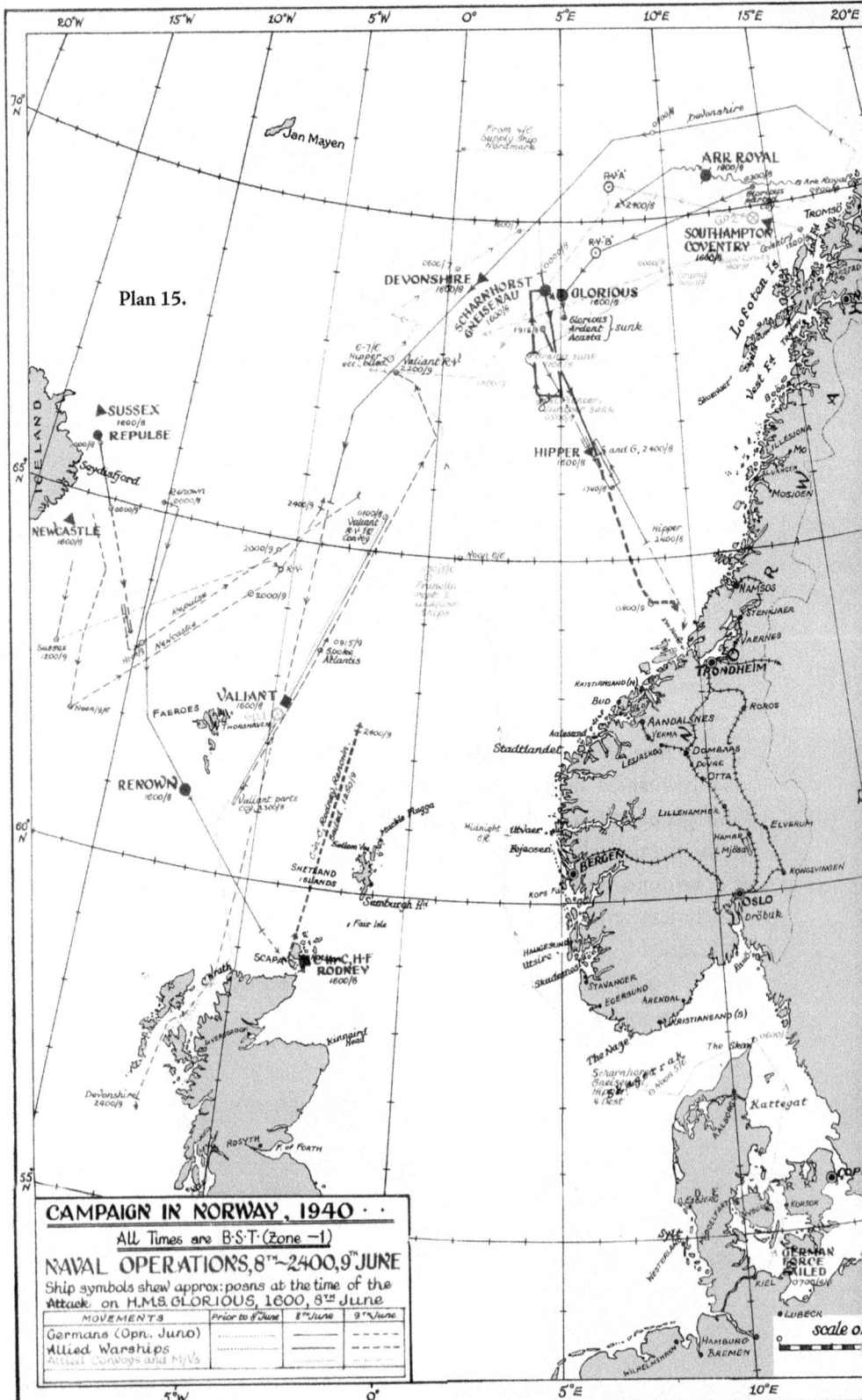

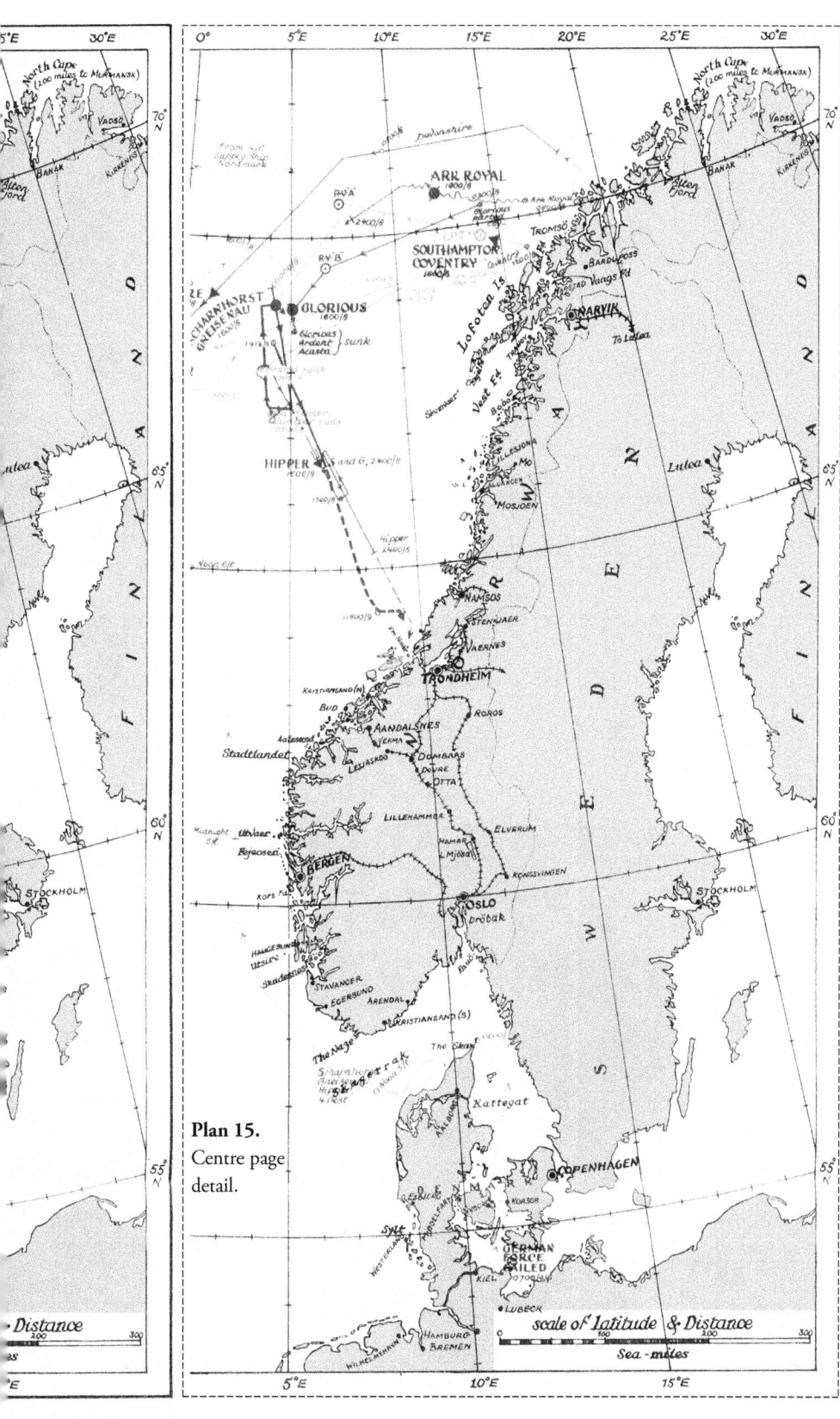

Plan 15. Centre page detail.

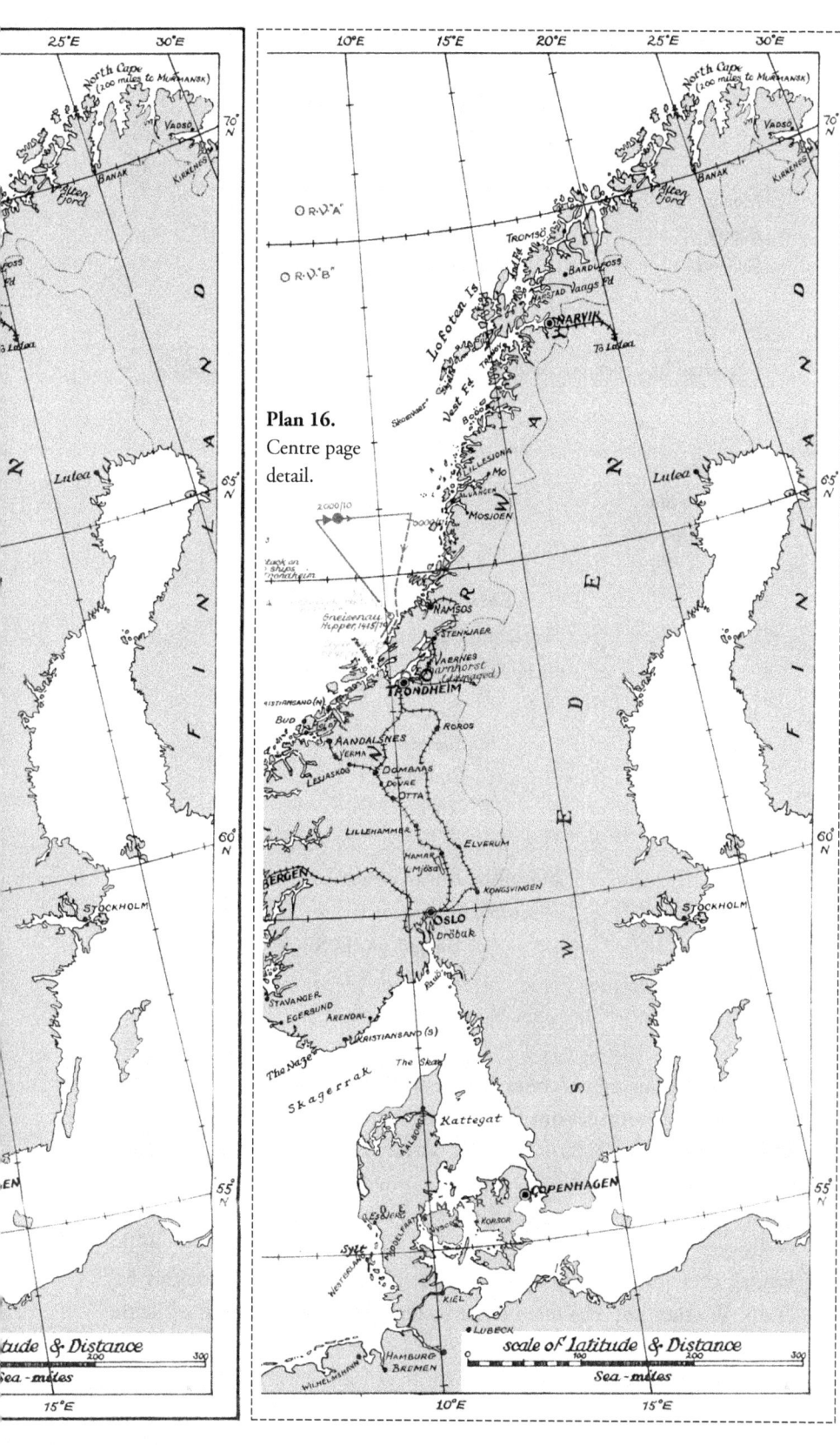

Plan 16. Centre page detail.

Group 1
escorted by the *Vindictive*

Monarch of Bermuda	*Franconia*
Batory	*Lancastria*
Sobieski	*Georgic*

Group 2
escorted by *Coventry, Southampton, Havelock, Fame, Firedrake, Beagle, Delight*

Oronsay	*Ulster Prince*
Ormonde	*Ulster Monarch*
Arandora Star	*Duchess of York*
Royal Ulsterman	*Vandyck*[251]

Slow Convoy
Storeships from Harstad
escorted by *Stork, Arrow*, 10 trawlers

Blackheath	*Theseus*
Oligarch	*Alacrity*
Harmattan	*Coxwold*
Cromarty Firth	*Couch*

Storeships from Tromsø
escorted by 4 trawlers

Oil Pioneer	*Arbroath* (A.S.I.S.)
Yermont	*Nyakoa* (A.S.I.S.)

some Norwegian vessels.

Under the arrangements come to with the Commander-in-Chief, Home Fleet, the first group set out from the distant rendezvous early on 7 June and duly met the *Valiant* and her screen of four destroyers[252] about 0100/8, in 65° 30' N., 1° 50' W., roughly half-way between the rendezvous and 61° N., where the *Valiant* was to part company. The five destroyers[253] for the troopships were late, but in spite of thick fog off the Faeroes they joined the convoy at about 2300 that night in roughly 61° N., 6° W.; then the *Valiant* and her screen turned north again, while the convoy stood on for the Clyde. The troopships' passage was uneventful except for an attack on 8 June by a single aircraft, which the *Vindictive* drove away by her fire.

The store convoys sailed from Harstad and Tromsø on 7 June, and that evening Vice-Admiral Cunningham embarked HM the King of Norway, the Crown Prince and various notables[254] in the *Devonshire* at Tromsø, sailing at 2030 independently for the Clyde.

The last group of transports had cleared And Fjord by 2300/8 June, and left its distant rendezvous in the morning of 9 June, escorted by the *Southampton, Coventry* and five destroyers. Rear-Admiral Vivian was placed in charge of the convoy and Lord Cork, who was accompanied by Generals Auchinleck and Béthouart, wore his flag in the *Southampton*. The *Glorious* had been detached at 0300/8, owing to shortage of fuel, and ordered to proceed home independently with the *Acasta* and *Ardent* as screen; but the *Ark Royal*, with her screen of three destroyers,[255] accompanied the convoy, some of her aircraft searching for enemy surface craft in the most probable direction of their approach and others providing overhead cover against air attack.

At midnight, 9/10 June, being clear of Norwegian waters, the operations came under the command of the Commander-in-Chief, Home Fleet, and Lord Cork accordingly hauled down his flag, having directed that the *Southampton* was to remain with the convoy for the passage.

But before this, misfortune had overtaken the expedition. Since the middle of April, both men-of-war and transports had crossed and recrossed the North Sea, in ones or twos or in weakly protected convoys, with never a sign that German surface craft might interrupt their passage. On 8 June, however, they suddenly appeared in force off Northern Norway, where they caught and sank six ships going home independently of the convoys.

The German Naval Sortie ('Operation Juno')   (Plan 15)

The presence of the German ships off Northern Norway was entirely fortuitous so far as the British evacuation was concerned. Of this, the secret had been well kept; the Allied Commanders had disguised the movements of troops and shipping with 'conflicting rumours and bogus instructions' and the Germans were quite unaware of what was in hand.

The object of their operation, known as Operation 'Juno', was to relieve, the German land forces in Narvik by attacking enemy transports and warships in the Narvik–Harstad area, and for this purpose a force consisting of the *Scharnhorst* and *Gneisenau*, the *Hipper* and four destroyers, the *Galster, Lody, Steinbrink* and *Schoemann* under Admiral Marschall, had left Kiel at 0700, 6 June, with orders to carry out a surprise attack on And and Vaagsfjords, the destruction of enemy warships, transports and installations found there being the object: if, however, later reports showed that an attack on Ofot Fjord and Narvik itself would be profitable, this would then become the principal task.

At 2000, 6 June, the force was in 68° N., 2° 30' W., and during the night the *Hipper* and destroyers completed with oil from the store ship *Dithmarschen*, which had previously been ordered to a waiting position in this neighbourhood.

It was not until 7 June that the first report of an Allied convoy being at sea off the coast of Norway reached the German ships. This placed four large and three small ships in 67° 57' N., 3° 50' E., steering southerly at 0700/7, that is some 150 miles south east of the Germans.

Admiral Marschall took no notice of this report, as he supposed them to be empty transports returning to the United Kingdom; but later that day, at 1955, came a report of an Allied convoy on a westerly course just off the entrance to And Fjord at 1325 and two aircraft carriers about 45 miles north of Andenes at 1400; and then, suspecting that a general withdrawal from Norway was in progress,[256] he decided to postpone the attack on Harstad, which he had planned for the night of 8/9,[257] and steered to intercept these ships instead, informing the Admiral, Group West, at 0300, 8 June, of his intention. This change of plan was not approved by Group Command, West, and a signal in reply was sent at 0430 pointing out that the main objective remained the 'destruction of enemy naval forces in the area Harstad–Narvik'.

An hour later Admiral Marschall fell in with his first victims. These were the 5,000-ton tanker *Oil Pioneer* from Tromsø, with her escorting trawler, the *Juniper*, which the German ships sighted at 0531/8, and sank an hour and a half later in 67° 26.5' N., 4° 23' E., picking up 25 survivors from the tanker, and four from her escort.

The *Scharnhorst* and *Hipper* then each flew off an aircraft to search for further prey. These soon reported a 12,000-ton merchant ship and a hospital ship to the north, and a cruiser and a merchant ship to the south. The *Hipper* was ordered to deal with the former, which proved to be the 20,000-ton troopship *Orama* and the hospital ship *Atlantis*, which had left the Norwegian coast the day before, the troopship being sent home alone and empty[258] because she had arrived without sufficient oil or water to wait for the rest of her group. The *Hipper* sank the *Orama* at 1106 in 68° 2' N., 3° 36' E., picking up a total of 275 survivors. The Germans were successful in jamming the S.O.S. signals of all these three ships; as the *Atlantis* observed strictly the provisions of the Geneva Convention and did not use her wireless, they respected her privilege of immunity from attack and let her go unmolested.

The *Scharnhorst* and *Gneisenau* meanwhile, after vainly searching for the ships reported to the south, had turned to a northerly course and the whole force proceeded in company till 1400, when the *Hipper* with the destroyers was detached and ordered to Trondheim[259] while Admiral Marschall, who still had no reconnaissance reports of Harstad and was convinced that Vaagsfjord no longer offered a worth while objective, continued to the north with the battlecruisers, in the somewhat vague hope of falling in with the aircraft carriers which had been located in the Andenes area several times during the last few days. His luck was in and he had not long to wait. At 1545 a masthead was sighted to the eastward; course was altered to close and in a few minutes it was identified as a large aircraft carrier, with destroyer escort.

The Sinking of the *Glorious, Ardent* and *Acasta* (Plan 15)

This proved to be the *Glorious*, which, after being detached at 0300 that morning, had proceeded on a course 250° at 17 knots. The wind was N.W., 2–3, and a north westerly swell was running; visibility was extreme. No reconnaissance aircraft were up, and none had been since parting from the *Ark Royal*, for the whole previous day and night had been spent piloting the R.A.F. Hurricanes onboard.[260] It was shortly after 1600 that the Germans were sighted to the northwestward; the *Ardent* was ordered to investigate, while the *Glorious* turned to the southward, bringing the enemy on to her starboard quarter steering south-east, and orders were given to range the Swordfish; but it was too late, and none of them got away.

At 1631 the *Scharnhorst* opened fire at a range of 27,800 yards, soon followed by the *Gneisenau*; the *Ardent* made for the enemy at high speed, and both destroyers started laying a smoke screen, which was very effective and caused the guns of both battlecruisers to cease fire for some time. Shortly after the action commenced, however, the *Glorious* had received a hit in the forward upper hangar which started a fire; this was got under control, but it destroyed the Hurricanes, and prevented any torpedoes being got out. The fire curtains had to be lowered. A salvo hit the bridge about 1700, and a heavy shell struck her aft about 1715. The Commander was then apparently in charge of the ship. The *Glorious* was of course completely outranged and her 4.7-in. guns could do little against the enemy. One main wireless aerial was shot away at an early stage of the action.

The order to abandon ship was given about 1720, and some 20 minutes later, listing heavily to starboard, she sank. The *Ardent* after firing two four-tube salvoes at the enemy, had been sunk about 1728, leaving the *Acasta*, faced by overwhelming odds, to fight gallantly to the last. With her guns still firing she steered to the south-east, temporarily concealed by smoke. There seemed a chance of escape, but this was not Commander Glasfurd's idea. He passed a message to all positions 'you may think we are running away from the enemy; we are not, our chummy ship (*Ardent*) has sunk, the *Glorious* is sinking, the least we can do is to make a show' – and altering course through the smoke screen towards the enemy, he fired a four-tube salvo, of which one torpedo hit the *Scharnhorst* abreast the after 11-in. turret. A final salvo hit the *Acasta* at 1808, and the order was given to abandon ship; her heroic Commander was last seen taking a cigarette from his case and lighting it, as he leant over the bridge waving encouragement to his men.[261] Then she sank. But her single torpedo had a big result; the *Scharnhorst* was severely damaged and her speed reduced; Admiral Marschall abandoned his cruise and with both battlecruisers steered for Trondheim, where they arrived at 1430, 9 June. To this alone the Earl of Cork's troop convoy to the northward owed its safety.

The sinking of the *Glorious* and the two destroyers was attended by heavy loss of life, the naval losses amounting to 1474,[262] and the R.A.F. to 41 – a total of 1515. A large number of men got on to Carley floats, but it had not been possible to provide provisions and water in all of them, owing to fire damage. It was very cold (temperature 46°); there was a sea running, which capsized the *Acasta*'s boats, and within a few hours men were collapsing from exhaustion. On one float, which started with 22 officers and men, the number was reduced to four by next morning. Poignancy is added to the story by the fact that survivors sighted a British cruiser some 5 miles to the north-west on 9 June and later in the day two aircraft from the *Ark Royal*, in the course of a search for the enemy, passed close over the rafts but did not see them; had they done so, many might even then have been saved.

It was not until 0030 on 11 June – some 54 hours after the ships sank, that 38 (three officers, 35 ratings) from the *Glorious*, and one rating from the *Acasta* were picked up by the small Norwegian vessel *Borgund* and landed in the Faeroes. Another Norwegian fishing vessel, the *Svalbard II*, rescued five men from the *Glorious*, who, with two survivors from the *Ardent*, picked up by a German seaplane, were made prisoners-of-war. Among the hundreds lost were nearly all those airmen who had performed the supremely difficult task of flying their land machines onboard the *Glorious*. And in addition was the loss of one of our few aircraft carriers, whose services in this Norwegian campaign had enhanced their value – a most serious blow.

British Reactions   (Plans 15 and 16)

The first news to reach the British that German ships were at sea came from the *Atlantis*, which met the *Valiant* about 0900/9, just 24 hours after the *Orama* was sunk. Once again[263] the German battlecruisers had traversed the North Sea undetected by British air reconnaissance.[263]

The *Valiant* was on her way back to join Admiral Vivian's convoy. She broadcast the hospital ship's account of a battleship and two destroyers attacking a two-funnelled transport (the *Orama*), and increased speed towards the troopships, then some 400 miles to the northward, and about 100 miles from where the Atlantis had seen the enemy. The *Valiant*'s signal brought one from Admiral Cunningham, in the *Devonshire* with the King of Norway onboard. The *Devonshire* must have been 100 miles or so westward of the *Glorious*, when that ship sighted the enemy and turned away to the southeastward. She, and she only, had received an enemy report the *Glorious* made to Admiral Wells. It was 'a barely readable signal;' for technical reasons it was 'probably corrupt and referred to some other matter;' and Admiral Cunningham decided not to break wireless silence, for 'to do so would have involved serious risk of revealing *Devonshire*'s position at a time when air attack was likely, which in the circumstances was in the highest degree undesirable'. Next day, however, when German shadowing aircraft had sighted the *Devonshire*, and the *Valiant*'s signal 'indicated the possible vital importance of this message', the Admiral made his 1031/9, which ran: '*Valiant*'s 0901/9, following was read, reception very doubtful on 3700 kc/s, at 1720/8. Begins – Vice-Admiral (A) from *Glorious*: my 1615, two P.B. Time of origin, 1640–ends. *Glorious*'s 1615 not received'. Not until the afternoon of 9 June when the Germans claimed in a wireless news bulletin to have had two squadrons of ships at sea, including the *Scharnhorst* and *Gneisenau*, and to have sunk the *Glorious* and a destroyer, the *Orama*, the *Oil Pioneer*, and a 'U-boat chaser' (*Juniper*), was there serious anxiety about the carrier.

The Commander-in-Chief, Home Fleet, however, had taken steps to support the returning expedition as soon as the *Valiant*'s signal reached him on 9 June. He ordered that ship to make the best of her way to Admiral Vivian's convoy, which in fact she was doing already, having begun to work up to full speed on hearing of the enemy from the *Atlantis*; and he made a signal to the *Glorious* to join the *Valiant*, if she had oil enough. The *Repulse*, *Newcastle*, *Sussex* and three destroyers, then at sea between Iceland and the Faeroes he ordered also to join Admiral Vivian. He raised steam in the *Rodney* and *Renown* at Scapa, and sailed with them and six destroyers in the afternoon to protect the convoys.

These ships – four capital ships, two cruisers and 13 destroyers, counting the *Valiant* and her screen – were all Sir Charles Forbes had now under his command (except for one or two more destroyers oiling or cleaning boilers) after the detachment of Home Fleet cruisers and destroyers to the Humber, Sheerness and Mediterranean. As always, there was an overall shortage of destroyers, and at this time many had been engaged in bringing away the Army from France, with heavy damage and loss; indeed, the want of destroyers had led Sir Charles to tell the Admiralty on 3 June that 'in event of heavy ships being required to proceed to sea, battlecruisers only will be sailed unless occasion is vital'.

To go back to the convoys. Admiral Vivian also received the signals from the *Valiant* and *Devonshire*, and the Admiralty's reproduction of the

German broadcast on 9 June. These signals explained wreckage reported by the *Ark Royal*'s patrolling aircraft and bodies seen by the *Southampton* that day, for the route the troopships followed lay not far from the Germans' track of the day before; indeed, survivors of the *Glorious* said they saw the convoy and friendly aircraft pass them by. In the afternoon, German aircraft shadowed and attacked the *Valiant* on her way to join the troopships. 'I reported the attack', said Captain Rawlings, 'as I was leading aircraft straight to the convoy and considered they would probably steer further to the westward'. When this report came, Admiral Wells recommended that the convoy should keep further westward, away from the enemy's air station at Trondheim, and that his aircraft should inform the *Valiant* of the new course and deal with the convoy shadower. Lord Cork agreed, so the convoy turned in the evening, anticipating an Admiralty order to do so. The aircraft duly informed the *Valiant* and drove off the shadowing enemy, and she and her destroyers joined about 2200 near 67° 30' N., 1° W. The same night, however, several aircraft tried to attack the *Ark Royal*; her fire and the *Valiant*'s kept them at arm's length, whilst her fighters shot down one and damaged others. Next morning, 10 June, the *Newcastle*, *Sussex* and *Repulse* arrived, the first two departing to join the Harstad store convoy on the battlecruiser's approach, and at midday the *Ark Royal* left to join Sir Charles Forbes, then some 70 miles off to the eastward. The *Repulse* and *Valiant* parted company from the convoy on 11 June, and went to Scapa. On 12 June, the convoy came safe to the Clyde. The storeships also arrived safely. The *Newcastle* and *Sussex* took the Harstad convoy to Scapa, and the Tromsø ships came home later, escorted by a couple of trawlers.

Apart from the ships sunk by Admiral Marschall's squadron, only one other ship came to grief – the *Vandyck*, armed boarding vessel. She was a spare troopship in the second group, but instead of going back alone, like the *Orama*, she had orders to cruise on a station 130 miles to seaward, while the other ships loaded, and to join them at the distant rendezvous in time to go home on 9 June. By some mistake she seems to have gone to one of the inner rendezvous, from which she reported herself by signal some hours after the convoy had proceeded, though she was afterwards reported as having spoken a trawler more than 100 miles away within two hours of making her original signal. Aircraft and a destroyer sent to find her failed to do so, and the Naval Attaché at Stockholm informed the Admiralty on 11 June that she had been sunk off Andenes the day before by German aircraft.

Movements of the Commander-in-Chief, Home Fleet
(Plans 15 and 16)

The Commander-in-Chief, having left Scapa at 1250, 9 June, in the *Rodney*, wearing the Union at the main for the first time at sea,[264] with the *Renown* and destroyer screen, steered to the northward at best possible speed until the evening of 10 June to cover the returning troop convoy.

At 1625/9 he received a message from the Admiralty (A.T. 1330/9) informing him that he was in command of all forces in the northern area of the North Sea, i.e. including those hitherto commanded by Lord Cork, who hauled down his flag that night. Aircraft of Coastal Command, reconnoitring Trondheim at 0846, reported four enemy cruisers there, subsequently modified to a battlecruiser, two cruisers and about seven destroyers; this was in fact Admiral Marschall's force. The *Hipper* and the four destroyers had reached Trondheim on the morning of 9 June, and the *Gneisenau* and damaged *Scharnhorst* a few hours later in the afternoon. Despite Admiral Marschall's important success in sinking the *Glorious*, the German Naval Staff was not pleased with his action in withdrawing his force to Trondheim, and ordered him to resume operations forthwith against the British convoys, about which numerous reports were coming in. Accordingly, he sent the *Gneisenau* and *Hipper* to sea on 10 June; they were reported – as 'a *Scheer* and a *Hipper*' – in 64° 35' N., 9° 45' E., steering 300°, at 1400 that day by the submarine *Clyde*. But it was clear to Admiral Marschall that by this time the convoys were beyond their reach, and they were recalled to Trondheim that night.[265]

After receiving the aircraft report of the force in Trondheim, Admiral Forbes at 1000/10, ordered the *Ark Royal* to leave the troopships and join him, the Admiralty having asked him to arrange a torpedo attack by aircraft, should the Royal Air Force find the enemy in port; but on receipt of the *Clyde*'s report, the Admiralty cancelled the operation against Trondheim and ordered the Commander-in-Chief to concentrate on the ships reported. Sir Charles Forbes accordingly at 1600 stood to the eastward and south-eastward towards them, with aircraft scouting ahead; at the same time he asked Vice-Admiral Wells if he could send an air striking force as the 'only hope of getting the ships'. An extensive reconnaissance failed to find the enemy and at midnight, having no further report of them, he turned back to 320°, to provide cover for the slow convoy and storeships from Narvik, which were still at sea. By the morning of 11 June the last convoy was well to the westward, though the fleet kept meeting trawlers and merchantmen, chiefly Norwegian, 'all over the ocean'.

The same afternoon, 11 June, the Royal Air Force machines attacked the ships at Trondheim, reporting there a capital ship and two cruisers, and claiming a hit with a 250 lb. bomb on each cruiser. The *Gneisenau* and *Hipper* had returned by that time from their short sortie, having realised that the convoys were beyond their reach, and there were consequently in Trondheim, when the aircraft attacked, two capital ships (*Scharnhorst*, *Gneisenau*), one cruiser (*Hipper*), and four destroyers. None of the ships was hit or damaged in the attack.

The Commander-in-Chief with the fleet was then somewhere beyond 67° N., and the Admiralty suggested that naval aircraft should attack; the fleet accordingly moved south that evening, in thick weather. Passing the last Tromsø store convoy next morning, the Admiral turned eastward, having decided to attack with 15 Skuas, from 65° N., 4° 40' E., early next morning, provided he could reach the flying-off position undiscovered. German aircraft shadowed the fleet in the afternoon. 'It does not look hopeful for tomorrow, his reconnaissance is too efficient', signalled the Commander-in-Chief to Admiral Wells. However, 15 Skuas left the carrier in the appointed position in time to attack at 0200/13. They believed that they hit the *Scharnhorst* with at least one bomb; this was true, but the bomb failed to explode, a tragic turn of fate as eight of the aircraft were lost in the attack. Some Royal Air Force machines bombed the neighbouring airfield of Vaernes at the same time to distract attention from the Skuas, while others gave the naval machines fighter protection. The fleet returned to Scapa as soon as the surviving Skuas returned, the *Ark Royal* and her screen entering harbour on 14 June, the two capital ships (*Rodney* and *Renown*) with their screen on 1700/15.

The campaign for Norway was at an end.

Comment and Reflections

The Commander-in-Chief, Home Fleet's Remarks

The various reports on the campaign in Norway naturally teem with lessons suggestions and recommendations.

Most of these are of a topical or technical nature, and have been either confirmed or rendered obsolete by the experiences of the later years of the war – for example, suggestions as to the best ways of dealing with air attack on surface craft, and remarks on the value and limitations of the handful of A.L.C.s and M.L.C.s in the Narvik operations, the forerunners of the vast fleets of landing craft which reached their climax on the Normandy beaches in 1944. Such lessons, though possibly of archaeological interest, would serve no useful purpose now, and therefore no attempt is made to enumerate them.

Nevertheless, much of permanent value may be culled from this campaign. As already pointed out, it was the first large-scale operation in history involving the employment of all three arms – sea, air and land. The Commander-in-Chief, Home Fleet, in his general remarks on the operations, stressed the necessity of correctly balancing these components in any operation of war.

There was little doubt in his mind that the general basis of the (German) plan was the conviction that our sea power in the north could be broken by means of air power and submarines ...

It had, the Commander-in-Chief considered, been proved again, *but was apt to be forgotten*,[267] that a preponderance in power of each form of fighting force was required, each in its own element, to control that element. For instance, naval forces were required to control sea communications; air forces or military forces could not do so, but could help the naval force, each in its own element. Air forces were required to control the air; naval and military forces could not do so, but could help. Military forces were required to control the land; the two other forces by themselves could not do so, but could help ... [268]

On our part, the scale of air attack that would be developed against our military forces on shore and our naval forces off the Norwegian coast was grievously under-estimated when the operations were undertaken ...²⁶⁹

It was this latter factor – the scale of air attack – that went a long way to ensuring the German success in Norway. After the air attack on the Home Fleet in the first afternoon of the campaign, it was speedily recognised – at least in the Fleet – that ships could not operate with a reasonable chance of success in proximity to shore bases operating air forces virtually unopposed in the air. On the other hand, as the campaign progressed, the counter to this new menace, which when properly developed would largely neutralise it, became apparent, viz., the presence of friendly fighters.

System of Command

From the British naval point of view, perhaps the most important aspect of the campaign was the system of high command, especially as regards the relations between the Admiralty and the Commander-in-Chief, Home Fleet.

The right and duty of the Admiralty to exercise general control of all naval forces has always been recognised; but just how detailed this control should be, in order to produce the best results, is a difficult and delicate problem. The Admiralty keeps the Commanders-in-Chief informed of the general policy and strategy (including, naturally, enemy intelligence), and allocates the forces deemed necessary to implement them. In the eighteenth century an attempt was made to pass on the experience of the Senior Officers at the Admiralty by means of the 'Fighting Instructions'. More than that, in those days of slow and uncertain communications, could not be done.

A great change was brought about at the beginning of the twentieth century by the invention of Wireless Telegraphy. This enables the Admiralty to exercise constant direct control over the doings of the Commanders-in-Chief afloat, and, if so desired, to communicate direct with subordinate Commanders. It is now recognised that the eighteenth century fighting instructions, though admirable in their inception, succeeded in paralysing the initiative of the Commanders afloat for nearly a century; and there seems a possibility that too rigid distant control by wireless might well produce similar results. At some stage the

Commander afloat must assume unfettered control; the difficulty is to determine precisely when.

The importance of having a clearly defined working arrangement had been recognised both ashore and afloat before the war, and correspondence on the subject had taken place between the First Sea Lord and the Commander-in-Chief, Home Fleet; but the question had not been definitely settled and there was some doubt as to precisely how things would work out in practice. The Norwegian campaign presented the first full scale opportunity for testing the arrangements.

In the event the Admiralty controlled the operations in considerable detail. It would almost appear that this on occasions introduced an element of uncertainty into the situation.[270]

The importance of the Commander-in-Chief afloat not revealing his position by the use of wireless enters the problem nowadays and may be advanced as an argument in favour of the Admiralty making operational signals direct to various units of the fleet. But there are other methods of communication, for example, the despatch of the *Codrington* by Admiral Forbes on 10 April to a rendezvous with directions to the cruisers, or the aircraft sent by the German Admiral Lütjens to Trondheim, with orders to make an important signal three hours after leaving him.[271]

The whole matter of course bristles with difficulties, but it is of such importance as to merit the most serious consideration and discussion in time of peace, if it is to work smoothly in the early days of any war. The difficulties are not lessened by the fact that personalities are bound to enter into it. An understanding which might work well between one Admiralty Administration or C.N.S. and one Commander-in-Chief, might produce confusion or friction between others.

On the whole, the events of the Norwegian Campaign seem to indicate that as a general rule, subject to the ultimate responsibility and consequent duty of the Admiralty to take what measures they think fit in an emergency (as, for example, the sudden arrival of unexpected enemy intelligence) the aim should be for them normally to limit themselves (a) to giving the Commander-in-Chief directions as to broad policy and strategy on a high level, including early warning of projected operations; and (b) to keeping him well posted in intelligence, both enemy (especially, of course, new operational intelligence) and information of other friendly forces, etc., which may be operating within the area of his command.

It is interesting to note that the Germans also found difficulties in adjusting the relationship between the Naval High Command ashore, and the Commander-in-Chief afloat, as a result of which Admiral Marschall after his not unsuccessful handling of Operation Juno was relieved of his command because he exercised his judgment to modify the plan to meet a new situation that had arisen since he put to sea, and which could not have been known to the Naval Staff when the operation was planned. Apart from the fact now known, that on 8 June the attack on Harstad would have been too late and that Admiral Marschall's initiative led to the destruction of the *Glorious*, surely the exercise of his discretion under such circumstances should have been well within the competence of the Commander-in-Chief afloat.

The appointment of Lord Cork – an Admiral of the Fleet, senior to the Commander-in-Chief, Home Fleet – to a command within the operational area of the latter was an unusual feature in the Command set up of the Norwegian campaign, which, despite the careful definition of the geographical limits of Lord Cork's command, might well have introduced complications. Lord Cork had been in close contact with the First Lord of the Admiralty for several months, examining the question of Baltic strategy, and the latter and the First Sea Lord 'were both agreed ... that Lord Cork should command the Naval forces in this amphibious adventure in the north'.[272] There were no doubt strong reasons for the appointment in this particular case, though Lord Cork's seniority was likely to produce a delicate situation alike in his relations with the Commander-in-Chief, Home Fleet, and even more so with the Military Commander of the Narvik expedition, Major-General Mackesy.

The divergence between the instructions given to Lord Cork and those given to General Mackesy requires no comment; but the episode well illustrates the difficulty of gearing the normal administrative machinery to the necessities of war, after a comparatively long period of peace.

The Importance of Wireless Silence

The importance of ships so far as possible keeping wireless silence in order to avoid giving away their positions has already been touched on in connection with the exercise of command afloat. But there is another and even more important reason, applying equally to shore stations as well as ships, for limiting the use of wireless: the danger that the enemy may have succeeded in breaking the codes and ciphers in use.²⁷³ This happened in the Norwegian campaign. As early as 12 April the Germans intercepted and deciphered a signal from Vice-Admiral Cunningham indicating Namsos and Mosjoen as suitable for landing and three days later they similarly learned that the *Chrobry* and *Batory* were earmarked for landings at Namsos and that General Carton de Wiart was the Commander in this area.

The problem of whether and when to break wireless silence must usually be a difficult one, and the decision must be made by the officer concerned after a most careful appreciation of the situation as known to him at the time.

Vice-Admiral Cunningham's decisions on 8 and 9 of June are of interest in this respect. At 1740, 8 June, the *Devonshire* intercepted a 'barely readable' signal (timed 1640) from the *Glorious* to the Vice-Admiral, Aircraft Carriers, which subsequent events proved probably an amplifying report identifying two pocket battleships. The *Devonshire* at the time was proceeding alone to the United Kingdom; she had onboard the King of Norway and most of the Norwegian Cabinet, and was then some 300 miles to the westward of Harstad. Clearly it was no time to draw attention to herself and the Vice-Admiral decided to maintain wireless silence. Next forenoon, at 0938, the *Devonshire* intercepted the *Valiant*'s report from the *Atlantis* of the attack on the *Orama*. The *Devonshire* was then to the eastward of the Faeroes; wireless silence had already been broken to request air and destroyer escort, and the *Valiant*'s signal gave an ominous significance to the *Glorious*'s message intercepted the day before; Admiral Cunningham immediately passed it to the Commander-in-Chief, to whom it brought the first hint that there might be cause for anxiety about the carrier.

No hard and fast rule can be laid down, except that wireless should be used as sparingly as possible, having due regard for the efficient performance of the operations in hand.²⁷⁴ A common doctrine, thoroughly permeating the fleet, will tend to reduce the necessity for many of such signals. A good example of this occurred a year after the Norwegian campaign during the chase of the *Bismarck*. Captain Vian, with a division of destroyers, was steering to the east-north-east under orders to join the Commander-in-Chief, when he intercepted a signal placing the *Bismarck* some 75 miles to the southward of him. He immediately altered course without orders to the south-east to intercept; making contact most opportunely just as the sun set, he then shadowed and harassed her throughout the night. 'I *knew*[275] you would wish me to steer to intercept the enemy ...', he subsequently wrote to the Commander-in-Chief.[276]

Tactical Loading of Expeditionary Forces

A lesson of importance which emerges from the campaign is the necessity for loading an expeditionary force tactically, even though it may not be anticipated that its landing will be opposed. Plan 'R.4' was abandoned by orders from the Admiralty at the very outset; but had the troops been kept embarked and had they been tactically stowed, it is easy to see in retrospect what a very important role they might have played. For example, the cruisers at Rosyth could have reached Stavanger before the Germans;[277] or, alternatively, had they been sent to the north, and been able to land their troops immediately after Admiral Whitworth's action on 13 April, there seems little doubt that Narvik could have been occupied at once.

But it is doubtful whether the loading arrangements were sufficiently flexible for the troops to have landed for active operations, even if they had been kept embarked. The fact that on the splitting of convoy N.P.1, when the 146th Brigade was diverted to Namsos, its Brigadier was onboard one of the ships which continued to Harstad, is an indication of the sort of contretemps which might have been experienced.

Risks and Chances

The campaign well illustrates what might be termed the 'lost principle of war', viz., that nothing decisive can be achieved without taking risks.[278] This does not mean, of course, that risks should be blindly courted; but it does mean that having been recognised and carefully assessed, and every possible provision made to minimise them, they must be accepted for an adequate object.

Thus the very audacity of the German plan for the original landings – a great risk, recognised and accepted by Admiral Raeder – largely contributed to its triumphant conclusion; and in a lesser degree, the decision of the Admiralty to accept the risk to the *Warspite* in penetrating Ofot Fjord at the second Battle of Narvik produced the one resounding Allied success in the whole campaign.

The campaign is also interesting as emphasising the narrow chances[279] on which important events so often turn. On the whole, the chances favoured the Germans; perhaps they deserved it. The sighting of the *Hipper* at the moment she chanced to be on a westerly course for no reason except to fill in time had the effect of causing the Commander-in-Chief, Home Fleet, to steer away from the Norwegian coast in the afternoon before the invasion; similarly, the U-boat report of Captain Warburton-Lee's destroyers steering away from Narvik (also filling in time) must have misled Kommodore Bonte. Had the U-boat sighted and reported them steering towards Narvik before they turned south-westerly, there can be little doubt the German destroyers would have been more on the alert and the result of the ensuing action would have been very different.

Other examples which will occur to the reader are the escape of the *Hipper* from Trondheim on 10 April, when a fortuitous delay in sailing saved her from her diversionary course taking her straight into Sir Charles Forbes' battle fleet; the sinking of the *Rio de Janeiro*, which might have compromised the whole German plan of invasion, had the correct inference been drawn and acted upon; and the colour given to Admiral Raeder's planned diversion in the north by the chance encounter with the *Glowworm*, while she was seeking Admiral Whitworth's force the day before the invasion.

The Principles of War as Applied in the Campaign

That the occupation of Norway was a great military success for Germany cannot be denied. But it must never be forgotten that it was a treacherous and unprovoked attack – ruthlessly carried out – on a small friendly nation against whom she had no shadow of complaint. There had been no diplomatic hint,[280] let alone *pour-parlers*, ultimatum, or declaration of war when the blow fell; and it was on this refusal to be bound by the hitherto accepted usage of civilised nations, or any moral principles whatever,[281] that their whole plan of invasion hinged. In the year 1940 the implications of 'total war' were not generally understood outside Germany; despite what had happened to Belgium in 1914, and quite recently to Austria, Czechoslovakia and Poland, civilised nations did not expect even Germany suddenly to fall upon a neighbour for no better reason than that it suited her.

It is important to realise the immense initial advantage conferred on the Germans by this attitude when considering other factors that contributed to their success.

From the naval point of view, they accurately appreciated the risks from the first; serious losses were anticipated, and in fact occurred, but no capital ship was lost. There was, however, one very serious weakness in their plan, which directly led to the loss of Kommodore Bonte's ten destroyers at Narvik. If the destroyers could not make the passage to Narvik and back at the required speed without re-fuelling, they should have used cruisers for this purpose and the destroyers to convey the troops to Bergen and Trondheim,[282] rather than trust to the arrival of independently routed, unescorted oilers to get them home.

Turning to the Allied effort, the Higher Command had not the same freedom of action as the enemy, whose gangster methods, already referred to, had secured them the initiative, and the scope of whose operations came as an unpleasant surprise;[283] pre-war policy, moreover, had tended to retard rearmament, and there was a serious shortage both of material and trained personnel. Nevertheless, it is questionable whether the best use was made of such resources as did exist.[284]

In this connection, it is worth while to consider briefly the Principles of War (agreed between the three fighting Services)[285] as applied to the operations in Norway, both as a test of their validity, and as possibly providing an explanation of some of the events that occurred.

In the early days the Allied aim[286] did not seem to have been clearly thought out, much less maintained. The abandonment of Plan 'R.4' will occur to the reader; and later, was the main effort to be at Trondheim, or elsewhere in Central Norway? Or in the north at Narvik? This appearance of vacillation at the very top,[287] percolating through, was likely to affect morale adversely sooner or later; the fact that the morale of all forces so finely stood the strain can be accounted for partly by the British character and partly because the final withdrawals were not delayed too long. The Germans, on the other hand, carefully defined and adhered to their aim. For the first phase, it was to capture the capital and to secure a foothold in the principal ports; as soon as this was accomplished, their next aim was to consolidate the position at Trondheim, and to this end all their efforts were directed, until the collapse of the Allied campaign in that region. Their morale, already high, was naturally enhanced by their steady advance. Offensive action was the keynote of their whole campaign. The Allies, too, took offensive action locally, and were eventually successful at Narvik; but the advisability of offensive action under such handicaps as obtained in Central Norway – almost complete lack of air power and, in addition, feeble anti-aircraft protection against a powerful air force well within range – may be open to doubt.

The fourth principle, security, with its somewhat pointed reference to the 'adequate defence of vulnerable bases'[288] could not be attained so long as the enemy held unfettered control of the air. Other instances where neglect of this principle brought its consequences will occur to the reader – notably the omission in the German plan to ensure oil for the Narvik destroyers and Kommodore Bonte's inadequate arrangements, which cost him his life and enabled Captain Warburton-Lee, with a force only half his own, to inflict a signal defeat on him. This action, of course, also illustrated the value of surprise, as did Admiral Whitworth's (to a lesser degree) three days later; unfortunately there were no balanced forces readily available to exploit the advantage. But the outstanding example of surprise was the whole German campaign.

As to concentration of force, the modest forces available at first to the Allies were immediately dispersed between Narvik and Central Norway; while the eventual employment of some 35,000 troops and considerable naval forces – with inadequate air support – to evict some 3000 Germans from Narvik may be held to have infringed the principle of economy of effort. *Per contra*, the successful initial German occupation of five of the principal Norwegian ports by no more than 7700 troops (suitably supported by sea and air) could scarcely have been effected more economically.

Lack of flexibility in the Allied arrangements was instanced by the difficulty of switching troops, already nearing Vest Fjord, from Harstad to Narvik, when Admiral Whitworth's victory on 13 April offered a fleeting chance of immediate success.

Regarding cooperation, there was ample good will; but the diverse instructions given to Lord Cork and General Mackesy show what a long path had to be travelled before the true cooperation reached in the latter stages of the war was achieved. As was only to be expected at this early period of the war, various weaknesses in the administrative arrangements revealed themselves as the campaign progressed.

Conclusion

Though it must be admitted that the Allied 'ramshackle campaign' in Norway was a failure from the military point of view, it provided sufficient breathing space for the Norwegians to steady themselves after the first shock, and enabled the King and Government, by transferring their activities to the United Kingdom and remaining 'in being', to defeat the German political aim.

The bright spot in an otherwise dismal story is the fine style in which the Allied morale, of all services and all nations – despite conflicting orders, lack of equipment, prolonged and almost unopposed air attack and constant reverses – stood the strain. The Royal Navy in particular can be proud of its share in the venture, and apart from its assistance in air defence and other activities inshore in support of the landings, the fact that it succeeded in transporting, maintaining and finally evacuating the other Services with a loss of only 13 troops killed and nine wounded[289] and 41 airmen[290] while afloat under its care, may justly be regarded as a source of pride and satisfaction.

Appendix A

Allied Warships Employed in Connection with Operations in Norway, April – June 1940, with Main Armament and Commanding Officers

I. Home Fleet.
II. Minelayers.
III. HM ships other than Home Fleet.
IV. French ships.

I – Home Fleet
(From 'Pink' List, 9 April 1940)
Rodney (9 16-in., 12 6-in., 6 4.7-in. H.A.) Flag, Admiral Sir Charles Forbes, G.C.B.,
  D.S.O., Commander-in-Chief, Home Fleet. Captain F. H. G. Dalrymple-Hamilton.
Warspite (8 15-in., 8 6-in, 8 4-in. H.A.) Captain V. A. C. Crutchley, V.C., D.S.C.
Valiant (8 15-in., 20 4.5-in.) Captain H. B. Rawlings, O.B.E.
Nelson[291] (9 16-in., 12 6-in., 6 4.7-in. H.A.) Captain G. J. A. Miles.
Barham[292] (8 15-in., 12 6-in., 8 4-in. H.A.) Captain C. G. Cooke.

Battlecruiser Squadron
Renown (6 15-in., 20 4.5-in. H.A.) Flag, Vice-Admiral W. J. Whitworth (V.A.C.B.C.S.).
  Captain C. E. B. Simeon.
Repulse (6 15-in., 12 4-in., 8 4-in. H.A.) Captain E. J. Spooner, D.S.O.
Hood[293] (8 15-in., 12 5.5-in., 8 4-in. H.A.) Captain I. G. Glennie.

Aircraft Carrier
Furious (12 4-in. H.A./L.A.) Captain T. H. Troubridge.

A/A Cruisers
Devonshire[294] (8 8-in., 8 4-in. H.A.) Flag, Vice-Admiral J. H. D. Cunningham, C.B.,
  M.V.O.
Captain J. M. Mansfield, D.S.C.
Berwick (8 8-in., 8 4-in. H.A.) Captain I. M. Palmer, D.S.C.
York (6 8-in., 4 4-in. H.A.) Captain R. H. Portal, D.S.C.
Sussex[295] (8 8-in., 8 4-in H.A.) Captain A. R. Hammick.
Norfolk[296] (8 8-in., 8 4-in. H.A.) Captain A. J. L. Phillips.
Suffolk[297] (8 8-in., 8 4-in. H.A.) Captain J. W. Durnford.

Second Cruiser Squadron
Galatea (6 6-in., 4 4-in. H.A.) Flag, Vice-Admiral Sir G. F. Edward-Collins K.C.V.O., C.B. Captain B. B. Schofield.
Arethusa (6 6-in., 4 4-in H.A.) Captain G. D. Graham.
Penelope (6 6-in., 8 4-in. H.A.) Captain G. D. Yates.
Aurora (6 6-in., 8 4-in. H.A) Captain L. H. K. Hamilton, D.S.O.

Eighteenth Cruiser Squadron
Manchester (12 6-in., 8 4-in. H.A.) Flag, Vice-Admiral G. Layton, C.B., D.S.O., Commanding 18th C.S. Captain H.A. Packer.
Sheffield (12 6-in., 8 4-in. H.A.) Flag, Rear-Admiral M. L. Clarke, D.S.C, 2nd in Command, 18th C.S. (21 April – 6 May). Captain C. A. A. Larcom.
Southampton (12 6-in., 8 4-in H.A.) Flag, Rear-Admiral M. L. Clarke, D.S.C. (6 May). Captain F. W. H. Jeans, C.V.O.
Glasgow (12 6-in., 8 4-in. H.A.) Captain F. H. Pegram.
Birmingham (12 6-in., 8 4-in. H.A.) Captain A. C. G. Madden.
Edinburgh[298] (12 6-in., 12 4-in. H.A.) Captain C. M. Blackman, D.S.O.
Newcastle[299] (12 6-in., 8 4-in. H.A.) Captain J. Figgins.

Destroyer Flotillas
Woolwich (Depot Ship) Flag, Rear-Admiral R. H. C. Hallifax (R.A. (D)).

Second Destroyer Flotilla
Hardy (5 4.7-in., 8 21-in. tubes) Captain (D)2 B. A. W. Warburton-Lee.
Hotspur (4 4.7-in., 8 21-in. tubes) Com. H. F. H. Layman.
Havock (4 4.7-in., 8 21-in. tubes) Lt.-Com. R. E. Courage.
Hero (4 4.7-in., 8 21-in. tubes) Com. H. W. Biggs.
Hereward[300] (4 4.7-in., 8 21-in. tubes) Lt.-Com. C. W. Greening.
Hyperion (4 4.7-in., 8 21-in. tubes) Com. H. St. L. Nicholson.
Hunter (4 4.7-in., 8 21-in. tubes) Lt.-Com. L. de Villiers.
Hostile (4 4.7-in., 8 21-in. tubes) Com. J. P. Wright.
Hasty[301] (4 4.7-in., 8 21-in. tubes) Lt.-Com. L. R. K. Tyrwhitt.

Third Destroyer Flotilla
Inglefield (5 4.7-in., 10 21-in. tubes) Captain (D)3 P. Todd.
Isis (4 4.7-in., 10 21-in. tubes) Com. J. C. Clouston.
Ilex (4 4.7-in., 10 21-in. tubes) Lt.-Com. P. L. Saumarez, D.S.C.
Imperial[302] (4 4.7-in., 10 21-in. tubes) Lt.-Com C. A. de W. Kitcat.
Delight (4 4.7-in., 10 21-in. tubes) Com. M. Fogg-Elliott.
Imogen (4 4.7-in., 10 21-in. tubes) Com. C. L. Firth, M.V.O.
Diana[303] (4 4.7-in., 10 21-in. tubes) Lt.-Com. E. G. Le Geyt.

Fourth Destroyer Flotilla
Afridi (8 4.7-in., 4 21-in. tubes) Captain (D)4 P. L. Vian, D.S.O.
Gurkha (8 4.7-in., 4 21-in. tubes) Com. A. W. Buzzard.
Sikh (8 4.7-in., 4 21-in. tubes) Com. J. A. Gifford.
Mohawk (8 4.7-in., 4 21-in. tubes) Com. J. W. M. Eaton.
Zulu (8 4.7-in., 4 21-in. tubes) Com. J. S. Crawford.

Cossack (8 4.7-in., 4 21-in. tubes) Com. R. St. V. Sherbrooke.
Maori (8 4.7-in., 4 21-in. tubes) Com. G. N. Brewer.
Nubian[304] (8 4.7-in., 4 21-in. tubes) Com. R. W. Ravenhill.

Fifth Destroyer Flotilla
Kelly[305] (6 4.7-in., 10 21-in. tubes) Captain (D)5 Lord Louis Mountbatten, G.C.V.O.
Kashmir (6 4.7-in., 10 21-in. tubes) Com. H. A. King.
Kelvin (6 4.7-in., 10 21-in. tubes) Lt.-Com. J. L. Machin.
Kipling[306] (6 4.7-in., 10 21-in. tubes) Com. A. St. Clair Ford.
Kimberley (6 4.7-in., 10 21-in. tubes) Lt.-Com. R. G. K. Knowling.
Kandahar[307] (6 4.7-in., 10 21-in. tubes) Com. W. G. A. Robson.
Khartoum[308] (6 4.7-in., 10 21-in. tubes) Com. D. T. Dowler.
Kingston[309] (6 4.7-in., 10 21-in. tubes) Lt.-Com. P. Somerville, D.S.O.

Sixth Destroyer Flotilla
Somali (8 4.7-in., 4 21-in tubes) Captain (D)6 R. S. G. Nicholson, D.S.O., D.S.C.
Ashanti (8 4.7-in., 4 21-in. tubes) Com. W. G. Davis.
Matabele (8 4.7-in., 4 21-in tubes) Com. G. K. Whiting-Smith.
Mashona (8 4.7-in., 4 21-in. tubes) Com. W. H. Selby.
Bedouin (8 4.7-in., 4 21-in. tubes) Com. J. A. McCoy.
Punjabi (8 4.7-in., 4 21-in tubes) Com. J. T. Lean.
Eskimo (8 4.7-in., 4 21-in tubes) Com. St. J. A. Micklethwaite, D.S.O.
Tartar (8 4.7-in., 4 21-in tubes) Com. L. P. Skipwith.

Seventh Destroyer Flotilla
Jervis[310] (6 4.7-in., 10 21-in. tubes) Captain (D)7 P. J. Mack.
Janus (6 4.7-in., 10 21-in. tubes) Com. J. A. W. Tothill.
Javelin (6 4.7-in., 10 21-in. tubes) Com. A. F. Pugsley.
Jersey[311] (6 4.7-in., 10 21-in. tubes) Lt. W. R. Patterson, O.B.E.
Juno (6 4.7-in., 10 21-in. tubes) Lt.-Com. A. M. McKillop.
Jupiter (6 4.7-in., 10 21-in. tubes) Com. D. B. Wyburd.
Jackal[312] (6 4.7-in., 10 21-in. tubes) Com. T. M. Napier.
Jaguar[313] (6 4.7-in., 10 21-in. tubes) Lt.-Com. J. F. W. Hine.

Eighth Destroyer Flotilla
Faulknor (5 4.7-in., 8 21-in. tubes) Captain (D)8 A. F. de Salis.
Fearless (4 4.7-in., 8 21-in. tubes) Com. K. L. Harkness.
Foxhound (4 4.7-in., 8 21-in. tubes) Lt.-Com. G. H. Peters.
Fury (4 4.7-in., 8 21-in. tubes) Com. G. F. Burghard.
Forester (4 4.7-in., 8 21-in. tubes) Lt.-Com. E. B. Tancock, D.S.C.
Fortune (4 4.7-in., 8 21-in. tubes) Com. E. A. Gibbs, D.S.O.
Fame[314] (4 4.7-in., 8 21-in. tubes) Lt.-Com. W. S. Clouston.
Foresight[315] (4 4.7-in., 8 21-in. tubes) Lt.-Com. G. T. Lambert.
Firedrake[316] (4 4.7-in., 8 21-in. tubes) Lt.-Com. S. H. Norris, D.S.C.

First Destroyer Flotilla[315]
Codington (5 4.7-in., 8 21-in. tubes) Captain (D)1 G. E. Creasy, M.V.O.
Grenade (4 4.7-in., 8 21-in. tubes) Com. R. C. Boyle.
ORP *Blyscawica* (7 4.7-in, 6 21-in. tubes) Com. Stanislaus Nahorski.
ORP *Grom* (7 4.7-in., 6 21-in. tubes) Com. Alexander Hulewicz.
ORP *Burza* (4 5.1-in., 6 21.7-in. tubes)
Greyhound (4 4.7-in., 8 21-in. tubes) Com. W. R. Marshall-A'Deane.
Glowworm (4 4.7-in., 8 21-in. tubes) Lt.-Com. G. B. Roope.
Griffin (4 4.7-in., 8 21-in. tubes) Lt.-Com. J. Lee-Barber.
Gallant[317] (4 4.7-in., 8 21-in. tubes) Lt.-Com. C. P. F. Brown.
Grafton[318] (4 4.7-in., 8 21-in. tubes) Com. C. E. C. Robinson.

Twelfth Destroyer Flotilla[319]
Electra (4 4.7-in., 8 21-in. tubes) Lt.-Com. S. A. Buss.
Echo[320] (4 4.7-in., 8 21-in. tubes) Com. S. H. K. Spurgeon, D.S.O., R.A.N.
Escort[321] (4 4.7-in., 8 21-in. tubes) Lt.-Com. J. Bostock.
Escapade (4 4.7-in., 8 21-in. tubes) Com. H. R. Graham.
Encounter (4 4.7-in., 8 21-in. tubes) Lt.-Com. E. V. St. J. Morgan.
Eclipse (4 4.7-in., 8 21-in. tubes) Lt.-Com. I. T. Clark.

Miscellaneous
Protector (Netlayer) Captain W. Y. La R. Beverley.
Vindictive (Repair Ship) Captain A. R. Halfhide, C.B.E.

Submarine Command
Vice Admiral Sir Max K. Horton, K.C.B., D.S.O. (V.A. S/M), H.Q., London

Second Submarine Flotilla
Depot Ship, *Forth* (Rosyth) Captain G. C. P. Menzies, Capt. (S)2.
Thistle (6 21-in. tubes, bow, 4 external) Com. W. F. Haselfoot.
Triad (6 21-in. tubes, bow, 4 external) Lt.-Com. E. R. J. Oddie.
Trident (6 21-in. tubes, bow, 4 external) Com. A. J. L. Seale.
Triton (6 21-in. tubes, bow, 4 external) Lt.-Com. E. F. Pizey.
Truant (6 21-in. tubes, bow, 4 external) Lt.-Com. C. H. Hutchinson.
Seal[322] (6 21-in. tubes, bow, minelayer) Lt.-Com. R. P. Lonsdale.
Porpoise[323] (6 21-in. tubes, bow, minelayer) Com. P. Q. Roberts.
ORP *Orzeł* (12 21.7-in. tubes) Lt.-Com. J. Grudzinski.
Tribune[324] (6 21-in. tubes, bow, 4 external) Lt.-Com. H. J. Caldwell.
Triumph[325] (6 21-in. tubes, bow, 2 external) Lt.-Com. J. S. Stevens.
ORP *Wilk*[326] (6 21.7-in tubes) Lt.-Com. B. Krawezyk.

Third Submarine Flotilla
Depot Ship, *Cyclops* (Harwich) Captain P. Ruck-Keene, Capt. (S) 3.
Sealion (6 21-in. tubes, bow) Lt.-Com. B. Bryant.
Seawolf (6 21-in. tubes, bow) Lt.-Com. J. W. Studholme.
Shark (6 21-in. tubes, bow) Lieut. P. M. Buckley.
Snapper (6 21-in. tubes, bow) Lieut. W. D. A. King.
Sterlet (6 21-in. tubes, bow) Lieut. G. H. S. Haward.

Sunfish (6 21-in. tubes, bow) Lt.-Com. J. E. Slaughter.
Salmon[325] (6 21-in. tubes, bow) Com. E. O. B. Bickford, D.S.O.

Sixth Submarine Flotilla
Depot Ship, *Titania*[327] Captain J. S. Bethell, Capt. (S)6.
Unity (4 21-in. tubes, bow, 2 external) Lieut. J. F. B. Brown.
Spearfish (6 21-in. tubes, bow) Lt.-Com. J. H. Forbes.
Swordfish (6 21-in. tubes, bow) Lieut. P. J. Cowell.
Clyde[328] (6 21-in. tubes, bow) Lt.-Com. R. L. S. Gaisford.
Severn[329] (6 21-in. tubes, bow) Lt.-Com. B. W. Taylor.
Sturgeon[328] (6 21-in. tubes, bow) Lieut. G. D. A. Gregory, D.S.O.
Narwhal (6 21-in. tubes, bow, minelayer) Lieut. C. S. Green.
Ursula[330] (6 21-in. tubes, bow, 2 external) Com. G. C. Phillips, D.S.O.

Tenth Submarine Flotilla
16th French Submarine Division
Depot Ship *Jules Verne* (Harwich)
Amazone (6 21.7-in., 2 15.7-in. tubes)
Antiope (6 21.7-in., 2 15.7-in. tubes)
La Sibylle (6 21.7-in., 2 15.7-in. tubes)

II – Minelayers
Teviot Bank Com. R. D. King-Harman (ret.).

Twentieth Destroyer Flotilla
Esk (2 4.7-in. guns, 60 mines) Captain (D)20 J. G. Bickford, D.S.C.
Impulsive (2 4.7-in. guns, 60 mines) Lt.-Com. R. J. H. Couch.
Ivanhoe (2 4.7-in. guns, 60 mines) Lt.-Com. W. S. Thomas.
Icarus (2 4.7-in. guns, 60 mines) Com. P. H. Hadow.
Intrepid[331] (2 4.7-in. guns, 60 mines) Lt.-Com. C. D. Maud.
Express[332] (2 4.7-in. guns, 60 mines) Com. R. C. Gordon.

III – HM Ships Other than Home Fleet
Battleship
3rd B.S. (America and W.I.)
Resolution (8 15-in., 12 6-in., 8 4-in. H.A.) Captain O. Bevir.

Aircraft Carriers
Mediterranean
Ark Royal (16 4.5-in.) Flag, Vice-Admiral L. V. Wells, C.B., D.S.O. Captain C. S. Holland.
Glorious (16 4.7-in. H.A./L.A.) Captain G. D'Oyley-Hughes, D.S.O., D.S.C.

Cruisers
America and W.I. Command
Enterprise (7 6-in., 3 4-in. H.A.) Captain J. C. Annesley, D.S.O. Captain J. M. Howson.
Effingham (9 6-in., 8 4-in. H.A.)

A/A Cruisers
20th C.S.
Coventry (8 4-in. H.A./L.A.) Flag, Rear-Admiral J. G. P. Vivian. Captain D. Gilmour.
Curlew (8 4-in. H.A./L.A. Captain B. C. B. Brooke.
Curacoa (8 4-in. H.A./L.A.) Captain E. A. Aylmer, D.S.C.
Carlisle (8 4-in. H.A./L.A.) Captain G. M. B. Langley, O.B.E.

Destroyers
18th D.F., Western Approaches
Acasta (4 4.7-in., 8 21-in. tubes) Com. C. E. Glasfurd.
Ardent (4 4.7-in., 8 21-in. tubes) Lt.-Com. J. F. Barker.

16th D.F., Portsmouth.
Arrow (4 4.7-in., 8 21-in. tubes) Com. H. W. Williams.

19th D.F., Dover.
Basilisk (4 4.7-in., 8 21-in. tubes) Com. M. Richmond, O.B.E.
Brazen (4 4.7-in., 8 21-in. tubes) Lt.-Com. Sir Michael Culme-Seymour, Bt.
Havelock (3 4.7-in., 8 21-in. tubes) Captain (D.9) E. B. K. Stevens, D.S.C.

9th D.F., Western Approaches
Hesperus (3 4.7-in., 8 21-in. tubes) Lt.-Com. D. G. F. W. MacIntyre.
Highlander (3 4.7-in., 8 21-in. tubes) Com. W. A. Dallmeyer.
Vanoc (4 4-in., 6 21-in. tubes) Lt.-Com. J. G. W. Deneys.

11th D.F., Western Approaches
Veteran (4 4-in., 6 21-in. tubes) Com. J. E. Broome.
Walker (4 4-in., 6 21-in. tubes) Lt.-Com. A. A. Tait.
Whirlwind (4 4-in., 6 21-in. tubes) Lt.-Com. J. M. Rogers.

15th D.F., Western Approaches
Wolverine (4 4-in., 6 21-in. tubes) Com. R. H. Craske.

18th D.F., Western Approaches
Wren (4 4-in., 6 21-in. tubes) Com. H. T. Armstrong.

Sloops
Rosyth
Auckland (8 4-in. H.A.) Com. J. G. Hewitt.
Bittern (6 4-in. H.A./L.A) Lieut. T. Johnston.
Black Swan (6 4-in. H.A.) Captain A. L. Poland, D.S.C.
Flamingo (6 4-in. H.A.) Com. J. H. Huntley.
Fleetwood (4 4-in. H.A./L.A.) Com. A. N. Grey.
Pelican (8 4-in. H.A.) Com. L. A. K. Boswell, D.S.O.
Stork (6 4-in. H.A./L.A.) Com. A. C. Behague.

IV – French Warships
Cruisers
Emile Bertin (9 6-in., 4 3.5-in. H.A./L.A.) Flag, Rear-Admiral Derrien.
Montcalm (9 6-in., 8 3.5-in. H.A./L.A.)

Destroyers
Bison (5 5.4-in., 6 21.7-in tubes)
Milan (5 5.4-in., 7 21.7-in. tubes)
Maillé Brézé (5 5.4-in., 7 21.7-in. tubes)
Foudroyant (4 5.1-in., 6 21.7-in. tubes)
L'Indomptable (5 5.4-in., 9 21.7-in. tubes)
Le Malin (5 5.4-in., 9 21.7-in. tubes)
Le Triomphant (5 5.4-in., 9 21.7-in. best)

A/S Trawlers Employed on Norwegian Coast
21st Striking Force
Arrived Namsos area 16 April. Ordered by C.-in-C., H.F., to proceed to Skjel Fjord on 20 April after a heavy air attack in which the Rutlandshire was sunk. The surviving trawlers remained in the Narvik area.
Danemon
Lady Elsa
Man of War
Wellard

23rd A/S Group
Arrived Namsos area 16 April. Ordered by C.-in-C., H.F., to proceed to Skjel Fjord on 20 April after a heavy air attack in which the Rutlandshire was sunk. The surviving trawlers remained in the Narvik area.
Indian Star
Melbourne
Berkshire
Rutlandshire[333]

22nd A/S Group
Arrived Åndalsnes area 21 April.
Warwickshire[332]
Hammond[332]
Larwood[332]
Bradman[332]
Jardine[332]

12th A/S Group
Escorted petrol carrier to Namsos, arriving 23 April. Then to Skjel Fjord and to Molde, 27 April. Remained in Molde area till evacuation 30 April/1 May.
Stella Capella
Cape Argona
Cape Cheluyskin[332]
Blackfly[334]

11th A/S Striking Force
Arrived Molde–Åndalsnes area on 27 April and left after final evacuation 30 April/1 May.
Cape Siretoko[335]
Argyleshire
Northern Pride[336]
Wisteria[337]

15th A/S Striking Force
Arrived Namsos area 27 April. Left Namsos after final evacuation of 2/3 May for Narvik area.
Cape Pessaro[338]
St. Gotan[339]
St. Kenan
St. Lomas

16th A/S Striking Force
Arrived Namsos area 27 April. Left Namsos after final evacuation of 2/3 May for Narvik area.
Aston Villa[340]
Gaul[341]
Angle
Arab

Naval Commands in Norway
I. Narvik Area
Flag Officer, Narvik, and C.-in-C., Northern Expeditionary Force. Admiral of the Fleet, the Earl of Cork and Orrery, G.C.B., G.C.V.O.
Chief of Staff Captain L. E. H. Maund, R.N.
Flag Officer, Harstad Rear-Admiral A. L. St. G. Lyster, C.V.O., D.S.O.
O.I.C., M.N.B.D.O., Harstad Lt.-Colonel H. R. Lambert, D.S.C., R.M.
C.O.F.A/A Narvik Area Capt. R. S. Armour, R.N.

II. Central Area
N.O.I.C., Molde (Åndalsnes area) Captain M. M. Denny, R.N.
S.O.R.M., Åndalsnes Lt.-Colonel H. W. Simpson, R.M.
S.O.R.M., Aalesund Major H. Lumley, R.M.

Appendix B

German Warships Mentioned in Narrative with Main Armament: Norway, April – June 1940

Battlecruisers
Gneisenau (9 11-in., 12 5.9-in. H.A./L.A., 14 4.1-in. H.A.) Flag Admiral Lütjens (C.-in-C.). Damaged by *Renown*, 9 April.
Scharnhorst (9 11-in., 12 5.9-in. H.A./L.A., 14 4.1-in. H.A.) Captain Hoffman. Damaged by *Acasta* (torpedo), 8 June.

Armoured Ships336
Lützow (6 11-in., 8 5.9-in., 6 4.1-in H.A.) Captain Thiele. Damaged Oslo coastal batteries, 9 April; and by *Spearfish* (torpedo), 11 April. Refitting during Norwegian operations.
Admiral Sheer (6 11-in., 8 5.9-in., 6 4.1-in H.A.)

Cruisers
Blücher (8 8-in., 12 4.1-in. H.A.) Flag, Rear-Admiral Kummetz. Sunk, Oslo coast defences, 9 April.
Admiral Hipper (8 8-in., 12 4.1-in. H.A.) Captain Heye. Rammed and damaged by *Glowworm*, 8 April.
Leipzig (9 5.9-in., 6 3.5-in. H.A.) Under repair (Kiel) during Norwegian operations.
Köln (9 5.9-in., 6 3.5-in. H.A.)
Königsberg (9 5.9-in., 6 3.5-in. H.A.) Captain Ruhfus. Sunk. Bombed by F.A/A, Bergen, 10 April.
Karlsruhe (9 5.9-in., 6 3.5-in. H.A.) Captain Rieve. Sunk. Torpedoed by *Truant*, 9 April.
Emden (8 5.9-in., 3 3.5-in. H.A.)
Nürnberg (9 5.9-in., 8 3.5-in. H.A.) Under repair (Kiel) till 10 May 1940.

Old Battleship (1905)
Schleswig Holstein (4 11-in., 10 5.9-in.)

Gunnery Training Ships
Bremse Damaged, Bergen coastal batteries, 9 April.
Brummer Sunk. Torpedoed by submarine, 15 April.

Destroyers
Wilhelm Heidkamp (5 5-in., H.A./L.A., 8 21-in. tubes) Broad pendant, Kommodore Bonte, S.O., Narvik. Torpedoed and sunk, 10 April.
Georg Thiele (5 5-in., H.A./L.A., 8 21-in. tubes) Damaged, 10 April; destroyed 13 April, Narvik.
Hans Lüdemann (5 5-in., H.A./L.A., 8 21-in. tubes) Damaged, 10 April; destroyed 13 April, Narvik.
Anton Schmidt (5 5-in., H.A./L.A., 8 21-in. tubes) Torpedoed and sunk, 10 April, Narvik.
Hermann Künne (5 5-in., H.A./L.A., 8 21-in. tubes) Damaged, 10 April; destroyed 13 April, Narvik.
Dieher von Roeder (5 5-in., H.A./L.A., 8 21-in. tubes) Damaged, 10 April; destroyed 13 April, Narvik.
Wolfgang Zenker (5 5-in. H.A./L.A., 8 21-in. tubes) Destroyed, Narvik, 13 April.
Erich Giese (5 5-in. H.A./L.A., 8 21-in. tubes) Destroyed, Narvik, 13 April.
Erich Koellner (5 5-in. H.A./L.A., 8 21-in. tubes) Destroyed, Narvik, 13 April.
Bernd Von Arnim (5 5-in. H.A./L.A., 8 21-in. tubes) Damaged, 10 April; destroyed 13 April, Narvik.
Freidrich Eckholdt (5 5-in. H.A./L.A., 8 21-in. tubes)
Theodor Riedel (5 5-in. H.A./L.A., 8 21-in. tubes)
Bruno Heinemann (5 5-in. H.A./L.A., 8 21-in. tubes)
Paul Jacobi (5 5-in. H.A./L.A., 8 21-in. tubes)

Torpedo Boats
Kondor (3 4.1-in. H.A./L.A., 6 21-in. tubes)
Möwe (3 4.1-in. H.A./L.A., 6 21-in. tubes)
Falke (3 4.1-in. H.A./L.A., 6 21-in. tubes)
Wolf (3 4.1-in. H.A./L.A., 6 21-in. tubes)
Seeadler (3 4.1-in. H.A./L.A., 6 21-in. tubes)
Greif (3 4.1-in. H.A./L.A., 6 21-in. tubes)
Albatros (3 4.1-in. H.A./L.A., 6 21-in. tubes) Wrecked, Oslo, 9 April.
Luchs (3 5-in., 6 21-in. tubes)
Leopard (3 5-in., 6 21-in. tubes)

Appendix C

Disposition of the Home Fleet, Noon, 9 April

I – Off the Coast of Norway
(a) Detached under Vice-Admiral Whitworth: Renown – near 67° N., 10° E. *Repulse, Penelope, Bedouin, Punjabi, Eskimo, Kimberley* – about to join the flag in 67° N., 10° E.
Esk, Icarus, Ivanhoe, Greyhound – patrolling the Vest Fjord minefield.
Hardy, Havock, Hotspur, Hunter, Hostile (joined p.m.) – going up Vest Fjord to Narvik.
(b) With C.-in-C., Home Fleet – near 60° N., 3° E.: *Rodney, Valiant, Galatea, Arethusa, Devonshire, Berwick, York, Emile Bertin, Codrington, Griffin, Jupiter, Electra, Escapade, Brazen, Tartu, Maille Breze.*
(c) Detached under Vice-Admiral Layton – making towards Bergen: *Manchester, Southampton, Glasgow, Sheffield, Afridi, Gurkha, Sikh, Mohawk, Somali, Matabele, Mashona.*
(d) On passage to join Vice-Admiral Layton from United Kingdom: *Aurora.*
(e) Going to fetch Convoy H.N.25 from Bergen rendezvous: *Tartar, Blyskawica, Grom, Burza.*

II – Other Ships at Sea
(a) On passage to join Admiral Forbes: *Warspite, Furious, Ashanti, Maori, Fortune.*
(b) On passage to base short of fuel, disabled, etc.: *Birmingham, Fearless, Hyperion, Hero, Zulu, Cossack, Kashmir, Kelvin, Impulsive, Delight.*
(**Note**.– The *Delight* had been screening the *Furious* from the Clyde; the others were in the North Sea.)
(c) Escorting Convoy O.N.25: *Javelin, Janus, Juno, Eclipse, Grenade.*

III – In Harbour: Sullum Voe or Scapa
Cairo, Calcutta, Inglefield, Isis, Ilex, Imogen, Escort, Encounter, Faulknor, Foxhound, Forester, Brestois, Boulonnais, Foudroyant, Le Chevalier Paul.

Total :–
5 capital ships
13 cruisers
1 aircraft carrier
2 anti-aircraft ships
62 destroyers

Dispositions During the Retreat from Central Norway 30 April – 3 May

I – The Convoys
(**Note**. – The figures against a ship's name show the approximate number of passengers she brought away; numbers under 20 not shown.)

(a) From Åndalsnes, etc., 30 April – 1 May – Vice-Admiral Edward-Collins: *Galatea* (660), *Arethusa* (520), *Sheffield* (590), *Southampton* (200), *Wanderer, Walker,* (70), *Westcott* (50), *Sikh* (120), *Tartar, Somali, Mashona, Ulster Prince* (50), *Ulster Monarch.*
(b) From Åndalsnes, etc., 1–2 May – Vice-Admiral Layton: *Manchester* (860), *Birmingham* (390), *Calcutta* (720), *Inglefield, Delight, Mashona, Somali* (250), *Auckland* (240).
The Diana took General Ruge and 30 Norwegian staff officers from Molde to Tromsø.
(c) From Namsos, 2–3 May – Vice-Admiral Cunningham: *Devonshire, York* (1170), *Montcalm, Carlisle, Afridi* (40), *Nubian, Maori, Kelly, Hasty, Imperial, Grenade, Griffin, Bison, El d'Jezair* (1300), *El Kantara* (1100), *El Mansour* (1750).

II – Other Ships off the Coast of Norway
(a) With Lord Cork about Narvik: Resolution, Effingham (flag), *Aurora, Enterprise,* and about a dozen destroyers.
(b) Taking the King of Norway, etc., from Molde to Tromsø: *Glasgow, Jackal, Javelin.*

(c) The Carrier Squadron – Vice-Admiral Wells: *Valiant, Berwick, Ark Royal* (flag), *Glorious*, and a destroyer screen (varied between three and ten).

III – At Scapa with C.-in-C., Home Fleet

Rodney (flag), *Repulse, Curlew,* and half a dozen destroyers.

Note.– There were some 30 destroyers besides those mentioned above. A few had special duties (e.g., three were screening the *Warspite* on her way to the Mediterranean), the rest were engaged with convoys, chiefly between the Narvik command and British ports.

Dispositions, 8 June

I – On Passage from Northern Norway

(a) With first group of troopships near Faeroe Islands: *Valiant, Tartar, Mashona, Bedouin, Ashanti.*
(b) Proceeding independently:–
(i) *Devonshire* (Flag, Admiral Cunningham).
(ii) *Glorious, Ardent, Acasta.*
(c) On passage to assembly rendezvous for second group of troopships:–
(i) *Southampton* (Flag, Admiral of the Fleet Lord Cork), *Coventry* (Flag, Rear-Admiral Vivian), *Havelock, Fame, Firedrake, Beagle, Echo, Delight.*
(ii) *Ark Royal* (Flag, Vice-Admiral Wells), *Diana, Acheron, Highlander.*
(d) Others:–
(i) *Arrow, Walker* and *Stork* – with Harstad store convoy.
(ii) *Campbell* – to join Tromsø store convoy.
(iii) *Veteran, Vanoc* – to join Vice-Admiral Cunningham, after ferry duties. Actually, owing to shortage of fuel, these destroyers did not join him.

II – Other Ships at Sea

(a) On passage from Scapa to meet first group of troopships: *Atherstone, Wolverine, Witherington, Antelope, Viscount.*
(b) Returning to Scapa from coast of Iceland: *Renown* (Flag, Vice-Admiral Whitworth), *Zulu, Kelvin.*
(c) Off the coast of Iceland: *Repulse, Newcastle, Sussex, Maori, Forester, Foxhound.*

III – At Scapa
Rodney (Flag, Admiral of the Fleet Sit Charles Forbes, C.-in-C., Home Fleet), *Inglefield, Amazon, Electra, Escort, Escapade, Fearless, Whirlwind*.
Note.– Some of these destroyers may have been at sea or at Sullom Voe.

Dispositions of Allied Submarines During British Minelaying and German Invasion of Norway, 8–9 April

8 April Kattegat:
Sealion, Sunfish and *Triton*
9 April Kattegat:
Sealion, Sunfish and *Triton*

8 April Skagerrak:–
Trident and *Orzeł* (Polish).
9 April Skagerrak:–
Trident, Orzeł, Truant and *Spearfish*

8 April Entering Skagerrak:–
Truant
9 April South-west Coast, Norway:–
Seal, Clyde and *Thistle*

8 April Outside Skagerrak:–
Seal 57° N., 6° E.
9 April Outside Skagerrak:–
Severn 57° N., 7° E., *Tarpon* 57° N., 5° E. and *Ursula* 57° N., 4° E.

8 April West Coast, Denmark:–
Spearfish, Snapper and *Unity*
9 April West Coast, Denmark:–
Snapper and *Unity*

8 April East of Dogger Bank:–
Amazone (French) and *Antiope* (French)
9 April East of Dogger Bank:–
Amazone 55° N., 4° E. and *Antiope* 53° N., 3° E.

9 April Heglioland Bight:–
Shark and *Seawolf*

8 April On passage out:–
Severn, Tarpon, Clyde, Thistle, Shark and *Seawolf*
9 April On passage out:–
Triad and *Sterlet*

8 April On passage home:–
Swordfish

8 April Under sailing orders:–
Ursula and *Triad*
9 April Under sailing orders:–
La Sybille (French)

Notes.–
(1) These dispositions are for 0600 each day, according to the daily position signal made by Vice-Admiral, Submarines. The number of submarines in the Kattegat, Skagerrak or off the Norwegian coast rose from 10 on 9 April to 14 on 12 April. The strength decreased from 14 April, however, and by 18 April there was only half that number in those waters.
(2) The object of the patrol is stated in a signal made by Vice-Admiral, submarines, dated 1931/4 April: 'To attack and then report enemy transports and warships; when transports escorted by warships are encountered it is more important to attack the transports.'
(3) The first result of these measures was the sinking of a German troopship near Kristiansand by the *Orzel* at midday, 8 April, and of a laden tanker in the mouth of Oslo Fjord by the *Trident* early that afternoon. On 9 April the *Truant* sank the cruiser *Karlsruhe* off Kristiansand, and in the night, 10/11, the *Spearfish* damaged the *Lützow* near the Skaw.
(4) Four submarines were lost during the Norwegian operations: the *Thistle, Tarpon* and *Sterlet* in April, and the *Seal* early in May.

Appendix D

Similarity of German Silhouettes

The similarity of the silhouettes of the German ships of various classes frequently caused confusion and uncertainty to their opponents. The reports of submarines and aircraft on 8 April, and Admiral Whitworth's engagement on 9 April are examples of this; and it is almost certain that on 24 May 1941 the *Hood* at first mistook the *Prinz Eugen* for the *Bismarck*.

Vice-Admiral Whitworth in his report of the action of 9 April 1940 against the *Gneisenau* and *Scharnhorst* remarked: 'Both were known to be either of the *Scharnhorst* or *Hipper* class, but throughout the action observation of the details of the enemy was so difficult that even direct comparison with the silhouette cards failed to establish the identity.'

Evidence from control personnel after the action and fragments of an 11-in. shell found onboard the *Renown* seemed to confirm that the leading ship was a battlecruiser and the second ship a cruiser of the *Hipper* class, and they were so referred to throughout in the original reports. Could it have been established that both German battlecruisers were in the Lofoten Islands area at this stage of the operations, it would have been of great value to the Commander-in-Chief, Home Fleet, and the Admiralty.

The Commander-in-Chief subsequently remarked that this difficulty in identification must always be borne in mind when enemy reports were received.

The similarity of the German silhouettes was not a deliberate policy adopted for purposes of deception, but arose from the fact that all their later ships were designed under the same Chief Constructor, who applied so far as possible the same arrangement and features to all classes, which resulted in their remarkably similar appearance.

It is worth noting that if – all other things being equal – such similarity in appearance can be produced, it is almost certain to cause confusion and might well entail serious consequences for the enemy, while it is difficult to see that it could have any disadvantage for friends.

Appendix E

Summary of Air Attacks on HMS *Suffolk* 17 April 1940

Attack 1 Time 0825 Distance of Nearest Splash (in yards) 1000 Type of Attack H.L.B.
Attack 2 Time 0831 Distance of Nearest Splash (in yards) 70 Type of Attack H.L.B.
Attack 3 Time 0842 Distance of Nearest Splash (in yards) 100 Type of Attack H.L.B.
Attack 4 Time 0901 Distance of Nearest Splash (in yards) 40 Type of Attack H.L.B.
Attack 5 Time 0903 Distance of Nearest Splash (in yards) 25 Type of Attack H.L.B.
Attack 6 Time 0914 Distance of Nearest Splash (in yards) 80 Type of Attack H.L.B.
Attack 7 Time 0919 Distance of Nearest Splash (in yards) 40 Type of Attack H.L.B.
Attack 8 Time 0922 Distance of Nearest Splash (in yards) 75 Type of Attack H.L.B.
Attack 9 Time 1030 Distance of Nearest Splash (in yards) 20 Type of Attack D.B.
Attack 10 Time 1037 HIT Type of Attack D.B.
Attack 11 Time 1046 Distance of Nearest Splash (in yards) 150 Type of Attack D.B.
Attack 12 Time 1048 Distance of Nearest Splash (in yards) 120 Type of Attack D.B.[337]
Attack 13 Time 1100 Distance of Nearest Splash (in yards) 70 Type of Attack D.B.
Attack 14 Time 1120 Distance of Nearest Splash (in yards) 120 Type of Attack H.L.B.
Attack 15 Time 1134 Distance of Nearest Splash (in yards) 120 Type of Attack H.L.B.[338]
Attack 16 Time 1141 Distance of Nearest Splash (in yards) 100 Type of Attack D.B.
Attack 17 Time 1149 Distance of Nearest Splash (in yards) 150 Type of Attack H.L.B.
Attack 18 Time 1207 Distance of Nearest Splash (in yards) 120 Type of Attack H.L.B.
Attack 19 Time 1208 Distance of Nearest Splash (in yards) 20 Type of Attack H.L.B.
Attack 20 Time 1226 Distance of Nearest Splash (in yards) 130 Type of Attack H.L.B.
Attack 21 Time 1231 Distance of Nearest Splash (in yards) 160 Type of Attack H.L.B.
Attack 22 Time 1236 Distance of Nearest Splash (in yards) 80 Type of Attack D.B.
At 1305 – Steering motor out of action
Attack 23 Time 1315 Distance of Nearest Splash (in yards) 20 Type of Attack H.L.B.
Attack 24 Time 1323 Distance of Nearest Splash (in yards) 40 Type of Attack D.B.
Attack 25 Time 1325 Distance of Nearest Splash (in yards) 5 Type of Attack D.B.[339]
At 1328 – Steering motor in action again
Attack 26 Time 1332 Distance of Nearest Splash (in yards) 60 Type of Attack D.B.
Attack 27 Time 1333 Distance of Nearest Splash (in yards) 140 Type of Attack H.L.B.
Attack 28 Time 1345 Distance of Nearest Splash (in yards) 75 Type of Attack H.L.B.
Attack 29 Time 1347 Distance of Nearest Splash (in yards) 30 Type of Attack D.B.340
Attack 30 Time 1430 Distance of Nearest Splash (in yards) 5 Type of Attack H.L.B.
Attack 31 Time 1445 Distance of Nearest Splash (in yards) 10 Type of Attack H.L.B.
Attack 32 Time 1503 Distance of Nearest Splash (in yards) 20 Type of Attack D.B.
Attack 33 Time 1512 Distance of Nearest Splash (in yards) 10 Type of Attack H.L.B.

Total number of bomb splashes seen 88
Total number of attacks 33
H.L.B. High level bombing attacks 21
D.B. Dive bombing attacks 12

Appendix F

HMS *Furious*
Statistics of Operations in Norway During the Period 11 April 1940 to 24 April 1940

1. Distance flown by aircraft 23,870 miles.
2. Bombs dropped – 250 lb. S.A.P. 116 in number. 20 lb. H.E. 293 in number.

Total weight 15¼ tons.

3. Torpedoes dropped 18
4. Aircraft totally lost 9
5. Aircraft hit by enemy 17
6. Aircraft damaged beyond facilities for repair onboard Nil.
7. Photographs taken 295
8. Casualties – Officers 2 killed, 3 wounded, 1 missing, 1 injured.
Air Gunners 1 killed, 2 wounded, 1 missing, 1 injured.

Appendix G

Extracts of General Auchinleck's Despatch, 19 June 1940 (M.017624/40)

In the Narvik as in the other expeditions to Norway, the German mastery in the air gained the day for them, the taking of the port after a six weeks' campaign notwithstanding. Indeed, the delay before the attack was largely the effect of the German strength in the air. The following extracts of General Auchinleck's despatch deal with this subject:–

> Paragraph 38:– 'On 13 May the Germans had a powerful air force in southern Norway and several excellent air bases from which to operate it. We, on the other hand, had not a single aerodrome or landing ground fit for use. The enemy thus had complete mastery in the air, except on the somewhat rare occasions when the Fleet Air Arm were able to intervene with carrier-borne aircraft. The vigour and daring of the pilots of the Fleet Air Arm, when they were able to engage the enemy, earned the admiration of the whole force; but even their strenuous efforts could not compensate for the absence of land-based aircraft ... '
>
> Paragraph 40, when it was decided to send Royal Air Force machines to work from Bardufoss:– 'The need for some support in the air for both the sea and land forces was urgent, particularly for HM ships, which were suffering heavily from the daily and almost continuous attacks made on them in the narrow waters round Narvik by the thoroughly efficient enemy bomber aircraft. Nevertheless, Group-Captain Moore, rightly, in my opinion, resisted all pressure to induce him to call for the aircraft to be sent before he was quite satisfied that the landing grounds could be said to be reasonably ready to receive them.'

Paragraphs 114–116:– 'Surprise landings from aircraft had far-reaching effects, owing to the ability they conferred on the enemy to outflank positions or take them in the rear. The action on the Hemnes Peninsula, south of Mo, provides an outstanding example of these tactics. The sequence of this action was, first, bombing and low-flying attacks on our troops holding the position. These attacks were followed almost immediately by landings from seaplanes in two places on each flank of the peninsula. Once these landings had been secured, they were promptly reinforced by small coastal steamers; and further reinforcements were brought up to the outflanking detachments by seaplanes on succeeding days ...

The outstanding example of the supply by air is the maintenance of the German detachments in the Narvik area ... His troops, to the number of 3000 or 4000, have been successfully supplied by air for many weeks ...

As regards the control of sea communications, the enemy's supremacy in the air made the use inshore of naval vessels of the type co-operating with this force highly dangerous and uneconomical. Though it might have been possible to use high-speed coastal motor-boats, armed with small guns, to prevent movement of enemy craft in these waters, the use of trawlers, owing to their extreme vulnerability to air attack, was not considered practicable. On the other hand, the inshore waterways were used at will by the Germans, who constantly employed local boats and steamers to ferry their troops about, thus entailing more dispersion of the defending forces on land. In an attempt to send considerable reinforcements and wheeled vehicles to Bodø, the Polish steamer *Chrobry* was sunk before she reached port. The unloading of large supply ships, which, owing to the limited facilities available, would have taken many hours, had to be ruled out as impracticable; and reinforcements to Bodø could therefore be sent only by destroyers or by small local craft. Thus, the provision of adequate reinforcements in guns and vehicles was made extremely difficult.'

As for anti-aircraft artillery, General Auchinleck states that he had only half the strength he asked for; yet he only asked for two-thirds of the War Office calculation of what would be required.

The General also has remarks about water transport.

Paragraph 17:– 'The force was maintained through the base area which had been established from the outset at Harstad, the forward delivery to units and formations in contact being made by locally procured water transport to Fjord Head, where approximately 10 days' reserve supplies, etc., were held. Inland water transport was thus the main agency for forward maintenance. Yet, although a study of the map would have shown that this was so, no provision had been made to send with the force at the outset the necessary personnel to organise and operate inland water transport in the way that railway units are sent to operate railways in the theatre where the railway is the main transport agency.'

Paragraph 48:– '... the weak link in the administrative system was the locally procured inland water transport which the navy had endeavoured to organise. It was weak because the craft were owner-driven diesel-engined fishing craft of 10 to 50 tons, and also because of the lack of adequate control or organisation. In consequence, though willing workers, the personnel could not be relied upon, whilst the distances to be covered were great. All immediately procurable craft ('puffers') and seven small coastal steamers, two of which were used as hospital carriers, were located at Harstad and in the vicinity of the forward field supply depots.'

Paragraph 50:– 'Great difficulties were experienced in the handling of heavy equipment and stores at places other than Harstad, as there was no means of putting them ashore except by motor landing craft. These were few in number, and were also required for tactical operations. In consequence, the establishment of anti-aircraft guns in position and the creation and stocking of aerodromes at Bardufoss and Skaanland were seriously delayed ... '

Appendix H

Naval Losses and Damage (Allied and German)

Note.– Total losses are shown in *ITALIC CAPITALS*. For damage to A/S Trawlers, *see* Appendix A.

Allied Capital Ships 2 damaged
HMS *Renown* Slight damage, gunfire, 9 April.
HMS *Rodney* Slight damage, bomb, 9 April.

German Capital Ships 3 damaged
Gneisenau Damage, gunfire, Renown, 9 April.
Lützow Severe damage, torpedo, Spearfish, 11 April.
Scharnhorst Severe damage, torpedo, Acasta, 8 June.

Allied Aircraft Carriers 1 sunk, 1 damaged
HMS *Furious* Damage to turbines, near miss, bombs, 18 April.
HMS *GLORIOUS* Sunk, gunfire, German battlecruisers, 8 June.

Allied Cruisers 2 sunk, 8 damaged
HMS *Aurora* (6-in.) Damaged, bomb, Ofot Fjord, 7 May.
HMS *Cairo* (A/A) Damage, bombs, Narvik, 28 May.
HMS *Curacoa* (A/A) Severe damage, bomb, 24 April.
HMS *CURLEW* (A/A) Sunk, bombs, Skjel Fjord, 26 May.
HMS *EFFINGHAM* (6-in.) Grounded, total loss, 17 May.
French *Emile Bertin* Damage, bombs off Namsos, 19 April.
HMS *Enterprise* (6-in.) Damage, near misses, bombs, Narvik area.
HMS *Glasgow* (6-in.) Slight damage, near miss, bombs, 9 April.
HMS *Penelope* (6-in.) Damaged, grounding, 11 April.
HMS *Southampton* (6-in.) Slight damage, near miss, bombs, 9 April; ditto, 26 May, Narvik area.
HMS *Suffolk* (6-in.) Severe damage, bombs, 17 April (see Appendix E).

German Cruisers 4 sunk, 2 damaged
BLÜCHER (8-in.) Sunk, coast defences, Oslo Fjord, 9 April.
Bremse (Training) Damage, coast defences, Bergen, 9 April.
BRUMMER (Training) Sunk, torpedo, Sterlet, 15 April.
KARLSRUHE (6-in.) Sunk, torpedo, Truant, 9 April.
KÖNIGSBERG (6-in.) Damage, coast defences, Bergen, 9 April.

Allied Coast Defence Vessels 2 sunk
H Nor. MS *EIDSVOLD* and H Nor. MS *NORGE* Sunk, gunfire and torpedoes, Narvik, 9 April.

Allied Destroyers 9 sunk, 12 damaged
HMS *ACASTA* and HMS *ARDENT* Sunk, gunfire, German battlecruisers, 8 June.
HMS *AFRIDI* Sunk, bombs, evacuation from 3 May.
HMS *Arrow* Damaged, rammed, German trawler, 26 April.
French *BISON* Sunk, bombs, evacuation from Namsos, 3 May.
ORP *Blyskawica* Damaged, gunfire, Narvik area, 2 May.
HMS *Cossack* Damaged, gunfire, 2nd Battle of Narvik.
HMS *Eclipse* Damaged, bombs, 11 April.
HMS *Eskimo* Damaged, torpedo, 2nd Battle of Narvik.
HMS *Fame* Damaged, gunfire, Narvik area, 23 May.
HMS *GLOWWORM* Sunk, gunfire and ramming, Hipper, 8 April.
ORP *GROM* Sunk, bombs, Ofot Fjord, 4 May.
HMS *GURKHA* Sunk, bombs, off Bergen, 9 April.
HMS *HARDY* Damaged, gunfire, and beached; total loss: 1st Battle of Narvik.
HMS *Hesperus* Slight damage, near misses, Narvik area.
HMS *Hotspur* Damaged, gunfire, 1st Battle of Narvik.
HMS *HUNTER* Sunk, gunfire, 1st Battle of Narvk, 10 April.
HMS *Kashmir* Severe damage, collision, 9 April.
HMS *Kelly* Severe damage, torpedo, M.T.B., 9 May.
HMS *Kelvin* Severe damage, collision, 9 April.
HMS *Matabele* Slight damage, grounding, 17 May.
French *Milan* Damaged, bomb, 23 May, Narvik area.
HMS *Punjabi* Damaged, gunfire, 2nd Battle of Narvik.
HMS *Somali* Damaged, near miss, bomb, off Bodø, 15 May.
HMS *Vansittart* Damaged, bomb, off Narvik, 10 May.
HMS *Wanderer* Damage, grounded, Alfarnes, 30 April.
HMS *Walker* Damaged, near miss, bomb, 27 May, Narvik area.

German Destroyers 10 sunk
Destroyed, 1st and 2nd Battles of Narvik.
ANTON SCHMITT
BERND VON ARNIM
DIETHER VON ROEDER
ERICH GIESE
ERICH KOELLNER
GEORG THIELE
HANS LÜDEMAN
HERMANN KÜNNE
WILHELM HEIDKAMP
WOLFGANG ZENKER

Allied Submarines 4 sunk, 2 damaged
HMS *Seal* Damaged, mine or depth charge, Kattegat; captured by Germans, 5 May.
HMS *STERLET* Sunk by A/S Craft, Skagerrak, 18 April.
HMS *TARPON* Sunk by A/S Craft off Denmark, 14 April.
HMS *THISTLE* Sunk by U.4 off Stavanger, 10 April.
HMS *TRUANT* Damaged, explosion, possibly magnetic torpedo, 25 April.
HMS *UNITY* Sunk, rammed by SS *Atlejarl*.

German Submarines sunk
U-22 Lost in North Sea, possibly by French *Orphée*, 21 April.
U-46 Sunk, *Warspite*'s aircraft, Herjangs Fjord.
U-49 Sunk by *Brazen* and *Fearless*. Vaagsfjord.

Allied Sloops 1 sunk, 2 damaged
HMS *Black Swan* Damaged, bomb, 28 April.
HMS *BITTERN* Severe damage, bomb; sunk, 30 April.
HMS *Pelican* Severe damage, bomb, 22 April.

Endnotes

1. The Commander-in-Chief, Home Fleet, never considered invasion possible under the conditions existing at any time in 1940.
2. Actually, this view under-estimated the importance of scrap iron to the German war economy, and it exaggerated the difference which the stoppage of the Narvik route alone would make to the overall importation from Sweden.
3. The Right Hon. Winston S. Churchill, C.H., M.P.
4. Churchill, *The Second World War*, Vol. I, p. 421 (English Edition).
5. In January 1940 the Swedish Foreign Minister informed the Norwegians privately that it was 'technically possible' to export 90 per cent of the iron via the Baltic.
6. The German Admiral Wegener, in his book published in 1929, *Sea Strategy of the World War*, had stressed the strategic advantages that would accrue to the German Navy from the possession of the coast of Norway. No doubt Admiral Raeder was familiar with this work.
7. This was precisely what the Allies were most desirous of obtaining by diplomatic methods, which, however, received scant encouragement from the Scandinavian Governments.
8. It is probable that the *Altmark* incident, when on 16 February Captain Vian in the *Cossack* demonstrated that there was a limit to Great Britain's patience and that under certain circumstances she was prepared to violate Norwegian neutrality, played its part in producing this decision.
9. Had the original date been adhered to, it is probable that the Norwegians would have been more on the *qui vive* on 9 April.
10. One for Denmark, six for Norway.
11. The risks were soberly assessed and accepted by Grand Admiral Raeder. '... The operation in itself is contrary to all principles in the theory of naval warfare. According to this theory it could be carried out by us only if we had naval supremacy. We do not have this; on the contrary we are carrying out the operation in face of the vastly superior British Fleet. In spite of this, the Commander-in-Chief, Navy, believes that, provided surprise is complete, our troops can and will successfully be transported to Norway.

    On many occasions in the history of war those very operations have been successful which went against all the principles of warfare, provided they were carried out by surprise ...' – Report of Commander-in-Chief, Navy, to Führer dated 9 March 1940.

Actually, no principle was contravened, since the plan involved no invasion by sea, except across the Skagerrak, where they exercised local command. North of Bergen the operation was of the nature of synchronised raids. No seaborne follow-up was contemplated, reliance for this being placed on the air, of which they had full control, and the advance of the army overland from Oslo.

12. Deputy Commander-in-Chief. The Commander-in-Chief, Admiral Marshall, was sick.
13. It had been intended that aircraft should lay mines in Scapa Flow, to hamper the movements of the Home Fleet, and this operation had been arranged to start on 28 March, when it was cancelled on 27 March by Reichs Marshal Goering without reference to the Naval Authorities, much to Admiral Raeder's annoyance.
14. The 1st Sea Transport Division consisting of 15 ships with a total of 72,000 G.R.T., carrying 3761 troops, 672 horses, 1377 vehicles and 5935 tons of Army stores.
15. For Narvik, the *Rauenfels*, *Alster* and *Barenfels*; for Trondheim, the *Sao Paulo*, *Main* and *Levante*. As things turned out, of these ships the *Levante* alone reached her destination and she was three days late.
16. The *Jan Wellem* and *Kattegat* for Narvik and the *Skagerrak* for Trondheim. Only the *Jan Wellem* (from Murmansk) reached her destination.
17. See Appendix A.
18. The *Ark Royal* and *Glorious* were in the Mediterranean in order to carry out essential training. The *Furious*, though belonging to the Home Fleet, had been refitting at Devonport, and was then at the Clyde, but was not yet fully operationally fit.
19. The *Inglefield, Ilex, Isis, Imogen.*
20. The *Greyhound, Glowworm, Hyperion, Hero.*
21. The *Hostile, Fearless.*
22. The *Esk, Impulsive, Icarus, Ivanhoe.*
23. The *Hardy, Hotspur, Havock, Hunter.*
24. They were escorted by eight aircraft which drove away the British shadower.
25. The Commander-in-Chief subsequently remarked that in the light of later events 'it was unfortunate that the last paragraph was included'.

There had been various indications that some large scale naval operation was afoot; after the second week in March, all U-boat activities against the trade routes had abruptly ceased, pointing to their employment elsewhere; U-boat and destroyer minelaying was also suspended; Germany's two capital ships, the *Scharnhorst* and *Gneisenau*, had been seen in Wilhelmshavn roads on 4 April, and German wireless from that port had been unusually active since the evening of 6 April. Several aircraft reported intense activity during the night 6/7 April in Kiel and Eckenforde, Hamburg and Lubeck, with wharves brilliantly lighted by arc lamps, and much motor traffic with unshaded headlights. Cumulatively, this intelligence pointed in one direction, as can be clearly seen now; but unfortunately at the time it was wrongly assessed.

26. The two German forces reported at 0848 and 1325 were almost certainly the same force, consisting of the *Gneisenau, Scharnhorst, Hipper* and 12 destroyers. They had left port in two groups shortly before midnight 6 April and joined up at 0300/7. The positions in which the British aircraft reported them correspond closely to their own reckoning at the time, though the German ships sighted no hostile aircraft till 1330.

27. At 1546, four destroyers nearing Rosyth with Convoy H.N.24 were ordered to complete with fuel on arrival and to keep steam. At 1558, the *Sheffield* and four destroyers were ordered to raise steam; and at 1607, Vice-Admiral Edward-Collins was ordered to proceed, as soon as the four destroyers with H.N.24 had fuelled, in the *Galatea*, with the *Arethusa* and eight destroyers to arrive in position 58° 30' N., 3° 30' E. at 1700 (if possible) 8 April, and then sweep to the northward.

28. The important enemy report contained in this signal was brought back by the R.A.F. bombers after their attack on the enemy ships, which had taken place west of Jutland in approximately 57° N., 6° E. between 1322 and 1327. The projected force of 35 bombers had been reduced to 18 Blenheims; of these, 12 succeeded in attacking, but they could claim no hits. They did not get back till between 1612 and 1652, which accounts for the delay between time of sighting (1325) and the receipt of the report by the Commander-in-Chief (1727). An attack report made on the way home was not received.

29. The *Emile Bertin* lost contact soon after putting to sea and returned to Scapa.

30. Codrington (D.1), *Griffin, Jupiter, Electra, Escapade, Brazen, Bedouin, Punjabi, Eskimo, Kimberley*.

31. The *Afridi* (D.4), *Gurkha, Sikh, Mohawk, Zulu, Cossack, Kashmir, Kelvin*; ORP *Grom, Blyskawica, Burza*.

32. The *Somali* (D.6), *Matabele, Mashona, Tartar*.

33. The *Javelin, Janus, Juno, Grenade*.

34. The Commander-in-Chief, Rosyth, asked the Admiralty to stop the convoy at Bergen; but it 'fortunately weighed anchor contrary to instructions', says the Rosyth diary, and proceeded to a rendezvous outside on 8 April, thus escaping from the invading Germans. About noon on 9 April, Captain J. S. Pinkney, Master of SS *Flyingdale*, who had been appointed 'guide of the convoy', fell in with the German tanker *Skagerrak*, then on her way to Trondheim. Her conduct aroused his suspicions, and hearing soon afterwards from a Swedish ship that the Germans had landed at Bergen, he took charge of the convoy and put to sea, falling in with a destroyer escort sent by the Commander-in-Chief, Home Fleet, a couple of hours later. Captain Pinkney was subsequently awarded the O.B.E. for his initiative on this occasion.

35. Twenty-four ships, however, lost touch and continued their voyage. Of these, 13 sunk or captured by the enemy.
36. See Appendix A. Appendix C gives the disposition at noon, 9 April.
37. The *Glowworm* after losing touch had proceeded back towards Scapa, as she had no rendezvous, until ordered by the Commander-in-Chief to proceed north once more to a position 67° 00' N., 10° 00' E. to meet the V.A., B.C.S.
38. At about the same time the Commander-in-Chief, then some 300 miles to the south-west of the *Glowworm*'s position, detached the *Repulse*, *Penelope* and four destroyers to proceed at their best speed to her assistance. The Commander-in-Chief remarked that if this was the same German force as that reported by aircraft on 7 April, it would have had to have made good 27 knots, which, though possible, he deemed improbable. The explanation seems to be that the *Glowworm*'s signalled position was in error nearly 60 miles to the northward. The Germans placed the encounter at 64° 05' N., 6° 18' E.
39. The German ships had orders to avoid action until their missions in Norway had been completed.
40. When the details of the *Glowworm*'s gallant action became known, HM The King approved the posthumous award of the Victoria Cross to her Commanding Officer Lieut.-Commander G. B. Roope.
41. Carl J. Hambro, President of the Storting, I SAW IT HAPPEN IN NORWAY.
42. The episode considerably perturbed the German Naval War Staff, who noted in the War Diary that it 'must result in disclosing the German operation and alarming the Norwegians so that surprise is no longer possible. Reuter reported at 2030 from Oslo 'that the ship had been torpedoed near Kristiansand with 300 men onboard.' Thus the enemy has been warned and action by him must be expected at any moment.'
43. A.T.1216/8 received 1300 and A.T.1317/8 received 1400.
44. Admiral Sir Edward Evans was ordered to haul down his flag, but to remain in the *Aurora* if he so desired. This the Admiral decided to do, and he accompanied her to sea.
45. It is not known why Plan 'R.4' was thus easily given up at this particular juncture. It must have been envisaged from the first that any German expedition would be covered by their fleet, and the Commander-in-Chief Home Fleet had at his disposal forces superior to the whole German naval strength, without counting the cruisers used as troop carriers in Plan 'R.4'.
46. Rosyth to Stavanger, 350 miles, i.e. 18 hours at 20 knots or 14 hours at 25 knots. The Germans landed only 150 men at Egersund and 1100 men at Kristiansand (south). Rail communication from Stavanger ran through Egersund only as far as Lister Fjord, i.e. about half-way between Stavanger and Kristiansand.
47. The Commander-in-Chief was by this time so certain that the Germans were about to invade Norway that he personally told the pilot of this Walrus that he

was to allow himself enough fuel to land in Norwegian waters and then give himself up; that he would be free next day, since Germany was going to war with Norway, when he was to get hold of enough fuel to take him back to the Shetlands. All of this he did.

48. The *Triton* had unsuccessfully attacked the *Gneisenau* before making her enemy report. The *Furious* had been ordered north from the Clyde on 8 April. Her two T.S.R. Squadrons were embarked, but unfortunately her Fighter Squadron (801) was at Evanton and therefore too far off to comply with what was obviously an urgent order. She was therefore unable to provide any fighter protection in the ensuing days.

49. The *Glowworm*'s signals were received in the forenoon, but the Admiral thought her too far north 'to warrant my departing from the Commander-in-Chief's ordered plan'.

50. The *Tartu, Maillé Brézé*.

51. The *Königsberg* received three hits by 8-in. shells fired by the Kvarven battery, which inflicted such damage that her Captain decided he could not take her to sea that evening to return to Germany, as had been intended. She was consequently still at Bergen next morning, when the F.A/A carried out an attack which sank her.

52. See Plan 13.

53. See pages 106-118.

54. The *Olav Tryggvason*, built 1934, 1747 tons, 4 4.7-in., 1 3-in H.A. guns, 2 17.7-in torpedo tubes.

55. Sunrise at Narvik, 9 April, 0425; Civil twilight (sun 6° below horizon) commenced 0323.

56. The *Norge* and *Eidsvold*, 2 8.2-in.; 6 5.9-in., 2 3-pdr. H.A.

57. Actually, the surprise was not complete. The Naval Authorities at Oslo had warned the '3rd District' (which included Narvik) at 1925, 8 April, that a German attack was imminent. Two lookout boats sighted and reported the Germans at 0310/9, by wireless, as British. The receipt of this signal just before the arrival of the Germans raised doubts as to their identity in the coast defence vessels.

58. About half the crew of the *Norge* was lost. Among the survivors was the Norwegian Senior Naval Officer, Kommodore Askim, who, having gone down with his ship, was rescued in an unconscious state. When the final Allied evacuation took place (June, 1940) Kommodore Askim succeeded in escaping from Norway and was subsequently Naval Attaché in the U.S.A. On the night of 8/9 May, 1945, as Naval member of the Allied Supreme Commission representing General Eisenhower, he had the pleasure of handing to the German General Böhme at Lillehammer the written order for the surrender of the German Naval units then in Norway.

59. Major Sundlo, the Norwegian officer commanding in Narvik, was one of the few Norwegian traitors working in touch with Quisling. His action was speedily

disavowed by the Norwegian officers in the area, but not in time for any resistance to be made in Narvik.

60. Sunrise at Narvik, 9 April, 0425; civil twilight (sun 6° below horizon) commenced 0323.

61. The strong similarity of the silhouettes of the modern German ships of various classes frequently rendered their identification very difficult. This difficulty was emphasised in the conditions of light and storm under which this action was fought. The Germans, too, were in doubt as to what they were fighting, the identification in the *Scharnhorst* being a *Renown* class and in the *Gneisenau* the *Nelson*. In the latter the opinion was held that two enemy heavy ships were present, though only one was seen at a time.

62. Repeated to Admiral Whitworth.

63. The *Hostile* had been with the *Birmingham*, cruising against the German fishing fleet. Being detached with a prize, and intercepting signals about the enemy and the British concentration off Vest Fjord on 8 April, she went north to find Admiral Whitworth, and eventually joined Captain Warburton-Lee instead, p.m. 9 April.

64. Admiral Edward-Collins originally had 15 destroyers with him. But an accident robbed him of four in the early morning of 9 April, when the *Kelvin* ran onboard the *Kashmir*, both ships being so severely damaged that they had to return to harbour escorted by the *Zulu* and *Cossack*.

65. See pages 248-257.

66. Looking back on this affair, I consider that the Admiralty kept too close a control upon the Commander-in-Chief, and after learning his original intention to force the passage into Bergen, we should have confined ourselves to sending him information.' Churchill, *The Second World War,* Vol. I, p. 470.

67. See pages 248-259.

68. Of this fine attack, the Vice-Admiral, Orkneys and Shetlands (Vice-Admiral Sir Hugh Binney) remarked: 'This was, I think, the first occasion on which Skuas had been used in action for the real purpose for which they were designed, viz., a dive-bombing attack on an enemy warship. The ship was sunk, the attack was a complete success and I consider it was brilliantly executed ... the distance to Bergen and back is 560 miles, not greatly inside the maximum endurance of the Skua'.

69. The flotilla was reported on a south-westerly course in Vest Fjord by U-51 at 2100, 9 April. (Admiral Dönitz, War Diary.)

70. Actually these batteries (according to the Germans) were non-existent.

71. British 5, Swedish 5, Norwegian 4, Dutch 1, German 8. (B.R. 1337, Merchant Ship Losses, 1946). The German ships were apparently the *Aachen, Altona, Bockenheim, Frielinghaus, Hein Hoyer, Jan Wellem* (undamaged), *Martha Hendrik Fisser, Neuenfels* (beached). (War Diary, April 1940, p. 288.)

72. The German destroyers all had five 5-in. guns. The British destroyers had four 4.7-in. guns except the *Hardy*, which had five 4.7-in.

73. The *Hardy* floated off next high water, and drifted ashore 2½ miles to the eastward, near Skjomnes, where she remained a wreck.

74. HM The King approved the posthumous award of the Victoria Cross to Captain Warburton-Lee.

75. Losses and damage inflicted by the 2ⁿᵈ Destroyer Flotilla at Narvik on 10 April 1940.

    Wilhelm Heidkamp out of action, Captain (D), Kommodore Bonte, killed: sunk on the morning of 11 April, 81 dead.

    Anton Schmitt sunk, 50 dead.

    Diether Von Roeder, hit five times by gunfire; boiler room 2 out of action; severe damage to the ship's side; no longer seaworthy, 13 dead.

    Hans Lüdeman, hits on No. 1 Gun and Compartment II. No. 1 Gun out of action; fire in Compartment III, magazine flooded, 2 dead.

    Hermann Künne, damaged by splinters; so badly shaken by the torpedo explosion on *Anton Schmitt*, which lay alongside her, that the main and auxiliary engines and electrical equipment were rendered useless until after the battle, 9 dead.

    Georg Thiele, seven hits by gunfire; fire control apparatus and No. 1 gun disabled; magazine flooded, fires in both the forward and after parts of the ship, 13 dead.

    Bernd Von Arnim, five hits by gunfire; boilers, 3, 2 out of action; seaworthiness reduced by hits on the ship's side and forecastle, 2 dead.

    Wolfgang Zenker, *Eric Giese* and *Erich Koellner* – No damage or losses. Roughly 50 per cent of their ammunition used.

76. The *Alster* had sailed from Brunsbüttel with the motor transport for Narvik on 3 April. She left Bodø p.m. 10 April, and the *Icarus* turned her over to a guard from the *Penelope* at Skjel Fjord before that ship sailed for Bodø on 11 April. The mechanical transport was turned over to the Norwegians; the *Alster* was used to hoist out the *Eskimo*'s mountings after the second Battle of Narvik, and subsequently to load and bring down a cargo of iron ore from Kirkenes. The Norwegians sank the tanker (the *Kattegat*) reported in Tennholm Fjord.

77. See pages 69-72.

78. See Plan 11.

79. Commander-in-Chief, Home Fleet's report. The Commander-in-Chief was of course working on the identification of the two German battlecruisers by Admiral Whitworth's force on 9 April as one battlecruiser and one cruiser.

80. See pages 191-196.

81. The convoy was joined by the repair ship *Vindictive* with six destroyers on 13 April.

82. Admiral Sir Edward Evans had left the *Aurora* on her arrival at Scapa in the evening of 10 April and proceeded by air to Stockholm with an Allied Anglo-French Mission to establish contact with the Norwegian Authorities. On the conclusion of the work of the Mission he was again sent to Scandinavia on a special mission from the British Government to the King of Norway.

83. The following force came under Lord Cork's command when within 100 miles of Vaagsfjord: *Effingham, Enterprise, Cairo, Vindictive, Protector* and auxiliary craft, and the convoy destroyers; also the *Aurora* and *Southampton* until the troops in Convoy N.P.1 had landed, when these two ships rejoined the Commander-in-Chief, Home Fleet. The *Protector* was to return to Rosyth after net laying.

84. The number of Narvik destroyers includes the *Grenade* and *Encounter*, which arrived at Skjel Fjord with the oiler *British Lady* p.m. 12 April.

85. According to the Germans, no hits were obtained on the destroyers; some casualties, mostly on land, were caused by splinters.

86. Admiral Whiteworth's force was as follows: *Warspite* (Captain Crutchley), *Bedouin* (Commander McCoy), *Cossack* (Commander Sherbrooke), *Eskimo* (Commander Micklethwait), *Punjabi* (Commander Lean), *Hero* (Commander Biggs), *Icarus* (Lieut.-Commander Maud), *Kimberley* (Lieut.-Commander Knowling), *Forester* (Lieut.-Commander Tancock), *Foxhound* (Lieut.-Commander Peters).

87. The *Warspite*'s aircraft thus played its part in carrying out the following clause in the orders: 'It is specially important that destroyers sighted should be engaged before they can fire torpedoes at *Warspite*'. The *Penelope*, lying disabled at Skjel Fjord, also signalled reports she received of the enemy's leaving Narvik (*Penelope* to *Eskimo*, 1155/13).

88. By this time the German destroyers were practically out of ammunition, having expended a good deal in the action of 10 April.

89. The German narrative suggests that none of the destroyers received a direct hit; bombs fell very near the *Hermann Künne*, and the *Bernd Von Arnim*, but did very little damage.

90. Vice-Admiral Whitworth's report stated that the *Cossack* drifted on to a submerged wreck, but there is no mention of this in the *Cossack*'s detailed report of the incident.

91. Report of Commanding Officer, HMS *Forester*.

92. Report of Commanding Officer, HMS *Hero*.

93. According to German sources their destroyers had by that time expended all their ammunition.

94. German aircraft attacked the *Ivanhoe*, which was patrolling near Baroy Island after a search by the Skjel Fjord destroyers for the submarine sighted in the morning by the *Eskimo*, but they did not molest the *Warspite* and ships in her company. The *Foxhound* encountered a submarine off Hamnesholm as the squadron steered westward down the fjord in the evening.

95. The *Ivanhoe* and *Kimberley* went home with the Commander-in-Chief the following day.
96. The *Hostile, Havock, Foxhound*.
97. The *Esk, Ivanhoe, Forester, Icarus, Kimberley*.
98. The *Galatea* (Flag, Vice-Admiral Edward-Collins), *Arethusa, Aurora*; *Manchester* (Flag, Vice-Admiral Layton), *Birmingham, Southampton, Glasgow, Sheffield*.
99. This latter order caused considerable embarrassment to Rear-Admiral (D), who found it quite impossible to provide another force of six destroyers in addition to those already earmarked for Admiral Layton's force and a relief screen for the battleships which would be required shortly. Verbal approval was obtained by telephone from the Admiralty to use some of the former, as extra destroyers from the Western Approaches Command were accompanying the troop convoy.
100. SS *Empress of Australia, Monarch of Bermuda, Reina del Pacifico, Batory, Chrobry, Protector*, escorted by the *Cairo, Witherington, Volunteer, Vanoc, Whirlwind, Highlander*.
101. Codrington (Captain D.1), S.O., *Escort, Acasta, Ardent*.
102. *Fearless, Griffin, Brazen*.
103. See pages 153-157.
104. See pages 219-220.
105. The *Effingham* and *Enterprise* were to be sailed from Portsmouth to Narvik as soon as possible when Lord Cork was to transfer his flag to the *Effingham*, and the *Aurora* was to rejoin the 2nd C.S. Actually the *Aurora* remained with Lord Cork for some time longer.
106. See pages 198-201.
107. The *Inglefield, Imogen, Isis, Ilex*. See pages 153-157.
108. The *Kattegat*.
109. See pages 201-205.
110. Lieut.-Commander Cumming, D.S.C., R.N. (ret.).
111. The *Isis* and were detached at 0100, 15 April, to rendezvous with the *Furious* which was on her way to Tromsø.
112. The situation at Kirkenes was complicated by uncertainty as to the Russian intentions: this made the Norwegians reluctant to denude their north-eastern frontier of troops.
113. These are fully dealt with in Naval Staff History, Submarines.
114. It has been remarked that had the German aircraft which then attacked been armed with torpedoes and pressed home their attacks the fate of the *Prince of Wales* and *Repulse* might have been anticipated by some 18 months by the *Rodney* and *Valiant*.
115. The report of this bad been received before Admiral Horton's visit to the Admiralty that afternoon.

116. Hitherto submarines had been forbidden to sink merchant ships without ensuring the safety of their crews in accordance with international law. The decision to remove this ban in the area referred to was reached by the Cabinet on 9 April. The 'German declared area' was bounded by lines passing through positions (a) 53° 36 N. 4° 25' E., (b) 53° 36' N. 6° 2' E., (c) 56° 30' N. 6° 2' E., (d) 56° 30' N. 4° 25' E. On 11 April the ban was further relaxed to include any ships, merchant or otherwise, under way within 10 miles of the Norwegian coast south of 61° N. and anywhere east of 6° E. as far south as 54° N. to be attacked on sight. Ships at anchor may be attacked if identified as enemy. (V.A.S. 1956/11.)

117. The *Posidonia* (8100 gr. tons) was taken over by O.K.M. and renamed *Stedingen*. She was to have acted as a supply ship for Kristiansand (south) and for U-boats.

118. The *Lützow* was so seriously damaged by the torpedo, and later grounding in the *Kattegat* on her way home, that she was out of action for 12 months.

119. 56° 45.5' N. 8° 15' E.

120. See pages 261-263.

121. The torpedoes suffered in two respects:—
    (a) The depth-keeping gear was defective and caused many misses.
    (b) The magnetic pistols were adversely affected by the proximity of the magnetic pole in the high latitudes and frequently failed to detonate.

122. The *Fearless, Griffin, Brazen*.

123. 'Ten of our modern destroyers, half of our destroyer fleet, are lying shot to bits, damaged or sunk in Ofot and Rombakenfjord.' – German Naval Staff War Diary.

124. See pages 106-108.

125. The *Sleipner*, 3 3.9-in.; 1 1.5-in. A/A guns; 2 2.1-in. torpedo tubes.

126. B.R. 1840 (1) The German Campaign in Norway.

127. B.R. 1840 (1) The German Campaign in Norway.

128. Several U-boats had been earmarked for this duty since 10 April. Within a week three sailed, each carrying 40 to 50 tons of small arms and A/A ammunition.

129. Luftflotte 5 for the conduct of all operations in Norway had been formed under the command of Colonel-General Milch on 12 April, and was operating from airfields near Trondheim, Stavanger and Kristiansand (south) in Norway, Aalborg in Denmark, Westerland in Sylt (Frisian Islands) and Lubeck and Luneberg in Northern Germany.

130. See pages 106-108.

131. The *Curityba* ran aground north of Helsingborg, 7 April; arrived Oslo, 10 April. *Rio de Janeiro, Antares* and *Jonia* sunk by submarines.

132. The *Friedenau, Wigbert*, Patrol Vessel 1507.

133. The *Florida* sunk by submarine in Kattegat; *Urundi* ran aground in Leads west of Faerdor.

134. B.R. 1840(1) gives the following statistics of transportation (other than by warships) for the Norwegian campaign. 270 ships and 100 trawlers, totalling 1,192,000 g.r.t., carried up to 15 June:–
    107,581 officers and men.
    16,102 horses.
    20,339 vehicles.
    109,400 tons of supplies.
Of the above, 21 ships totalling 111,700 g.r.t. were lost, and of the 4344 officers and men in these ships, about 1000 were lost: a large part of their cargoes was salved.

135. General Erichsen commanding the 1st Division succeeded in mobilising to the south-east of Oslo but he was isolated from Norwegian Headquarters and entirely without A/A guns or aircraft. After a week of fighting he was faced with the alternative of surrender or internment in Sweden. He chose the latter.

136. 16 April.

137. Churchill, The Second World War, Vol. I, p. 474

138. See pages 135-140.

139. Each of these operations will be treated in detail in succeeding chapters.

140. A.T. 1347/14 explained: 'This operation is designed to synchronise with Operation Maurice.'

141. A.T. 0109/13 reported a dive-bomber group at Vaernes, 15 miles east of Trondheim, and possibly a group of Ju. 88's at Narvik.

142. The *Warspite* had 8 15-in., 8 6-in., 8 4-in. H.A. *Valiant* had 8 15-in., 20 4.5-in. *Renown* had 6 15-in., 20 4.5-in. As it turned out, the *Valiant* actually prepared for bombarding, sailing from Scapa for Rosyth on 19 April to ship the special projectiles. The *Renown* sailed with her, but to dock and repair the damage received in the bad weather and her fight on 9 April. The *Resolution* (from the Halifax escort force) relieved the *Warspite* at Narvik, and the latter went to the Mediterranean.

143. Home Fleet Narrative. These proposals were confirmed in A.T. 0117/19.

144. Churchill, The Second World War, Vol. I, p.494.
    These reasons savour of the opinion expressed by the Commander-in-Chief, Home Fleet, in his signal 1157/14. At the Admiralty, moreover, there was anxiety about the reserves of H/A ammunition, which were running low; and the experience of the *Suffolk*, which was seriously damaged by air attack on 17 May, may have influenced the decision. In any case, in view of the commitments at Narvik, Namsos and Åndalsnes, it is difficult to see how the cruisers, destroyers and sloops required for Hammer could have been provided.

145. See Chapter V, Operation Sickle (pages 235-239).

146. Commander-in-Chief, H.F., 1203/18: See pages 201-202.

147. See pages 211-214.
148. Home Fleet, Narrative, para 230.
149. B.R. 1840(1), page 60.
150. It is probably that the French view was influenced by the desire to support any operations in distant Norway which might divert German forces from the attack on France in the near future, which was foreseen and which took place a month later.
151. H. of C. Deb., Vol. 360, 1126.
152. Actually, apart from destroyers, submarines and small craft the *Köln* and *Emden* were the only undamaged ships at the disposal of the Germans at this date.
153. The *Janus, Hyperion, Hereward, Havock, Kelly, Kimberley, Kandahar, Hostile*. The *Kelly* was damaged in an operation on 9 May (See pages 118-121) and never got to Harwich.
154. The Royal Marines arrived back in the Clyde on 24 May in the transports *Franconia* and *Lancastria*, which had brought an infantry brigade to relieve them on 17 May.
155. The *Hero, Hasty, Ilex, Imperial, Juno, Mohawk, Nubian, Khartoum, Kingston*.
156. The *Fury, Fortune, Foresight*.
157. See Appendix F.
158. The *Hyperion, Hereward, Hasty, Fearless, Fury, Juno*.
159. Report of V.A. (A). Operation DX.
160. Home Fleet Narrative, para. 269.
161. Commander-in-Chief 1030/26. In the same signal he recommended that immediate steps should be taken to establish A/A ground defences and adequate R.A.F. fighter protection, both at Åndalsnes and Namsos; and that endeavour should be made to ascertain whether any suitable localities for landing grounds existed north of Namsos, as he had by this time become convinced that the use of Mosjen or Kongsmoen was essential as a landing place for army stores, if we were to maintain our forces in this area.
162. See Appendix A. Composition of forces and brief statement of their movements.
163. Home Fleet Narrative.
164. HM The King approved the award of the Victoria Cross to Lieutenant Stannard for his gallantry during these operations.
165. Home Fleet Narrative.
166. Commanding Officer, *Suffolk*, report.
167. Thirty-three attacks took place (21 high level, 12 dive bombing), in the course of which 88 splashes were observed. (See Appendix E.)
168. 'The Commander-in-Chief, Home Fleet, was at sea when this operation was

ordered and carried out. He took it for granted that a very strong air escort would be provided since the *Suffolk* would be within range of enemy air bases, including those in Germany; and he also took it for granted, in view of the *Norfolk*'s experience at Scapa on 16 March, that the vulnerability of these ships to even a 250-kg. bomb was fully appreciated.' Home Fleet Narrative.

169. Commanding officer, HMS *Suffolk*, report. Captain Durnford, remarked that the fighters in pursuit of the enemy appeared to have left the overhead area unguarded.

170. For the last 164 miles she was steered by her screws, the steering gear having finally broken down at 1604/17.

171. This report seems to have been exaggerated. According to German information only two A/S trawlers were engaged of which one was damaged.

172. Made at 2335/9 from Area Headquarters, Donibristle, after the sighting aircraft had landed.

173. It was thought this M.T.B. might have been co-operating with a Dornier aircraft which had been engaged by the *Kelly* at 2052.

174. Home Fleet Narrative.

175. This decision was taken on 23 April.

176. U.22 was lost in the North Sea in April 1940, due to a cause unknown.

177. 58° 03' N., 11° 19' E.

178. She was, however, subsequently salved.

179. The military forces in the Namsos area were under the command of Maj.-Gen. Carton de Wiart, V.C.; those in the Åndalsnes area under Maj.-Gen Paget. Lt.-Gen. Massy was appointed Commander-in-Chief, Forces operating in Central Norway, on 19 April, but he exercised his command from the United Kingdom, as the course of events did not permit of opening a H.Q. in Norway.

180. The military forces in Northern Norway were commanded by Maj.-Gen. Mackesy till 13 May, when he was superseded by Lt.-Gen. Auchinleck. On 20 April Admiral of the Fleet Lord Cork was appointed in supreme command of all expeditionary forces in this area.

181. The *Somali*, *Mashona*, *Matabele* (of 6th Flotilla), *Afridi*, *Sikh*, *Mohawk* (of 4th Flotilla).

182. See pages 215-216.

183. See pages 215-216.

184. See pages 174-178 and 186-190.

185. The *Somali* was attacked three times at Namsos on 15 April and had 60 bombs aimed at her without effect, but she spent all her ammunition and at the end fired practice ammunition 'for moral effect'.

186. The first troops of General Audet's command reached Namsos in the night, 19/20.

187. The *Montcalm* took the place of the *Emile Bertin* in the Home Fleet.

188. It is interesting to notice that the Germans, who were not fully aware of the effect of their air attacks or of the weakness in numbers and equipment of the Allied troops in Central Norway, regarded the situation in the Trondheim area as much more serious from their point of view than it actually was. Thus it came about that on 21 April, just when General Carton de Wiart was describing his position as 'untenable,' Hitler was informing the Naval Staff that he had decided to use fast liners, including the *Bremen* and *Europa*, to carry reinforcements to Trondheim. This plan was dropped, as the result of representations by the Naval Staff that it could not guarantee safe passage; but that it should have been put forward is a measure of the anxiety the Germans were feeling at the time.

189. Captain Denny added: 'This force, it must be remembered, was ashore throughout the period of the operation, and consequently were exposed for the longest period to the effects of air bombardment: in general, they behaved like seasoned veterans.'

190. See pages 191-193.

191. This has been confirmed from German sources.

192. See pages 207-209.

193. An ominous note had been struck by A.T. 0003/20 from the First Sea Lord to the Commander-in-Chief, which ran:–
'Recent expenditure of destroyer long range anti-aircraft ammunition has been heavy if the total size of the reserve held is appreciated. This is now reduced to 13,000 rounds of which 6,000 are abroad. Deliveries in the next three weeks should reach 6,000 rounds after which further supplies are not immediately in sight. Although am unwilling to suggest restriction in the use of any anti-aircraft gun, it is obvious that expenditure of this nature at the recent high rates must be curtailed. Action has been taken to accelerate supply to the maximum and you will be informed when the margin is ample.'
Clearly it was of great importance to keep this information from the fleet, but the Commander-in-Chief had to bear it constantly in mind.

194. The other reinforcements arrived after dark except a convoy which arrived the afternoon of 27 April; indeed, they had specific orders to arrive at dusk and 'to sail at daylight even if disembarkation is incomplete'.

195. The *Arethusa* left Rosyth alone on 22 April, the day after her return from landing troops of the first flight. (See pages 141-144.)

196. Much confusion and delay occurred in landing stores, ammunition, etc., because no working parties were organised by the Army to clear them from the jetties, as they were put ashore.

197. The *Arethusa* belonged to Admiral Edward-Collins's squadron.

198. A.T. 1939/29 April. A.T. 1904/10 had given the Admiralty ruling that 'interference with communications in southern areas must be left mainly to submarines, air and mining, aided by intermittent sweeps when forces allow'.

199. These could not be spared, as they were required for service in the Mediterranean. It was later decided, too, that the *Aurora* should not take part in the operation.

200. A.T. 2127/29, announcing the decision to commence the evacuation on the night of 30 April/1 May, was made in Flag Officer's cypher and as it did not include instructions to pass the message to the military authorities, the Commander-in-Chief, H.F., presumed that the War Office would inform the G.O.C., Aandassnes.

201. The Commander-in-Chief, concurring with R.A., Destroyers, considered the *Black Swan*'s conduct on the occasion 'outstanding and in accordance with the very highest traditions'.

202. The German Naval Appreciation, from air reports, was that the enemy intended 'to re-embark troops landed at Åndalsnes as quickly as possible during the night, and to use them at another place, that is at Namsos'.

203. Rear-Admiral M. L. Clarke, D.S.C., had hoisted his flag as R.A. 2nd in command 18th C.S. on 21 April.

204. The *Somali, Mashoma, Sikh, Wanderer, Walker, Westcott*.

205. The *Inglefield, Delight, Diana, Somali, Mashona*.

206. See pages 272-279.

207. The *Afridi, Nubian, Hasty, Imperial*: French *Bison*.

208. The *Kelly, Grenade, Griffin, Maori*.

209. C.S.20 was Admiral Vivian. Presumably the General's signal, that it was not a question of shipping, had not yet reached Admiral Cunningham.

210. Admiral Cunningham says 'the *Carlisle* gave ample warning of every attack, and her assistance in this respect and by reason of the accuracy of her anti-aircraft fire proved invaluable'; but she had only an hour and a half's allowance of ammunition left after the third attack.

211. Commander-in-Chief, Home Fleet (H.F. Narrative, par. 254.)

212. See pages 164-173.

213. Home Fleet Narrative, para. 219.

214. See pages 182-184.
    The Admiralty promulgated these dispositions on 16 and 17 April, and at 0210/17, directed Rear-Admiral (D) to arrange for an anti-submarine striking force of nine destroyers to operate against the U-boats in the Orkney and Shetland areas; but it was found impossible, owing to other commitments, to provide this number.

215. General Mackesy's protest is in his signal, 2105/17, to the War Office. Presumably the French troops that did not then join 'Rupert' were those General Audet took to Namsos.

216. General Mackesy was opposed to this bombardment on humanitarian grounds, out of consideration for the Norwegian inhabitants of Narvik; but his views were not supported by the Defence Committee, which considered the protest he made to Lord Cork.

217. The *Hostile, Havock, Hero* and *Foxhound* screened the *Warspite* on the occasion. The *Electra* attended the *Vindictive*.

218. The *Resolution* remained with Lord Cork until 18 May, when he sent her home 'to avoid exposing her to constant bombing' (by which she had already been slightly damaged) with the request, however, that she should be earmarked for his service for ten days longer.

219. Further successful bombardment of this area was carried out by the *Resolution* and *Aurora* on 3 May; in the course of their operations the Polish destroyers *Grom* and *Blyskawica* suffered damage from gunfire.

220. Kongsmoen is the same as Kongsmo in 64° 55' N., 12° 35' E., at the head of Indre Folden Fjord and half-way between Namsos and Mosjoen. Captain Yates of the *Penelope* received and passed on much general intelligence during his ship's stay at Skjel Fjord, repairing to go home after her grounding near Bodø.

221. Lord Cork's despatch.

222. The *Calcutta* had proceeded to sea the day before to reinforce the *Jackal* and *Javelin* which were escorting an east-bound convoy, and was some 50 miles W.N.W. of Skomvaer, when Lord Cork's signal (timed 1150/10) reached her at 1301. The *Zulu* was at Skjel Fjord. They effected a rendezvous off Myken Light about 1700 (the earliest the *Zulu* could get there), and shaped course for Mo, which had been indicated in a further signal from Lord Cork as the possible destination of the enemy.

223. A signal from the army headquarters to the War Office says 500 to 1000 Germans with four guns and several tanks were reported advancing north of Mosjoen on 13 May.

224. Brigadier Fraser later succeeded in transferring to the *Curlew* and returned to Harstad; but he was suffering from a wound previously received at Ankenes, and was invalided home by a Medical Board.

225. The signal 'Rupert' force to War Office, 1915/14 May, details the troops that were to have sailed in the *Chrobry*, but the field guns referred to in this signal were countermanded.

226. The *Matabele, Echo*.

227. Lord Cork's despatch.

228. Discontinuance of the warning system led to a strike among the Norwegian labourers and small craft crews.

229. The finalised details of these proposals are given in Lord Cork's despatch.

230. Lord Cook's despatch.

231. At the evacuation, all nets were sunk and all traces were removed.

232. See pages 204-206.

233. On 20 May it was decided that the best disposition would be as follows, but for various reasons, this could not be adhered to:–

Bardufoss Heavy Guns 8 (16) Light Guns 12 (24)
Harstand and Skaanland Heavy Guns 24 (48) Light Guns 18 (36)
Bodø Heavy Guns 8 (16) Light Guns 12 (12)
Tromsø Heavy Guns 8 (24) Light Guns 6 (24)
The figures in brackets show the number of guns considered necessary to give really accurate protection in each area. (General Auchinleck's despatch).

234. See Appendix H.

235. This was the first occasion on which tanks were landed in a combined operation.

236. General Auchinleck was appointed G.O.C.-in-C. designate of the Anglo-French land forces and of the British Air Component in the theatre of operations. It was the intention of the C.I.G.S. that he should take over when the Government decided to end the system of unified command under Lord Cork, but that if, on arrival, local conditions appeared to necessitate the step, he was to assume the command, placing himself under Lord Cork.

237. The *Ark Royal* could not spare fighters before the evening of 12 May, though Lord Cork asked to have them in the forenoon, because they had been protecting the *Penelope*, which was going home in tow after her temporary repair in Skjel Fjord, and the *Enterprise* and her convoy of troops, who landed that day at Mo.

238. The delay at Skaanland meant that the *Glorious* had to go home again to oil before landing her squadron of aircraft; and in the end Skaanland would not do, so all the machines worked from Bardufoss.

The *Cairo* records that she engaged enemy aircraft every day but two between 11 and 27 May, and in that period she expended 5,700 rounds of 4-in.

239. Lord Cork's despatch.

240. The *Cairo* was hit by two small bombs and lost 30 men, killed and wounded. The casualties to the landing forces from the bombing amounted to only one small landing craft loaded with ammunition.

241. Lord Cork's despatch.

242. The *Firedrake, Vanoc, Arrow, Havelock, Echo*.
General Auchinleck in his despatch remarked:–

'The swiftness and efficiency with which the evacuation was carried out reflects great credit on Brigadier Gubbins and his staff. The destroyers of the Royal Navy were very well handled and carried out the programme laid down to the minute.'

243. The evacuation from Dunkirk started on 26 May and ended on 4 June.

244. See Appendix C.

245. The *Zulu, Kelvin, Maori, Forester, Foxhound*.

246. Rendezvous A. Lat. 70° 30' N., Long. 7° 20' E.
Rendezvous B. Lat. 69° 30' N., Long. 6° 40' E.

247. Actually the first iron ore steamer sailed from Narvik on 8 January, 1941.

248. Lat. 68° 40' N., Long. 14° 34' E.

249. Lord Cork's despatch.

250. Lord Cork's despatch.
All these pilots were lost in the *Glorious* on the way home.

251. The *Vandyck* failed to make the rendezvous and was subsequently sunk off Andenes by German aircraft.

252. The *Tartar, Mashona, Bedouin, Ashanti*.

253. The *Atherstone, Wolverine, Witherington, Antelope, Viscount*.

254. The party included HM the King of Norway, the Crown Prince and their attendants; H.B.M. Minister, the French and Polish Ministers, and members of the *Corps diplomatique*; the Norwegian Prime Minister, 10 ministers, staffs and families; certain members of the Norwegian Air Force; political refugees; 33 British officers and 306 other ranks – a total of 435 men and 26 women.

255. The *Diana, Acheron, Highlander*.

256. Admiral Marschall's War Diary.

257. Log of *Scharnhorst*, 6 June, 1940.

258. About 100 German prisoners were embarked in her.

259. Admiral Marschall considered that these ships would have no further opportunity of oiling at sea, once the British heard of the sinkings. They were therefore to complete with fuel at Trondheim and then give protection to the German convoys between there and Bodø.

260. One T.S.R. aircraft and one section of Gladiators were being kept at 10 minutes' notice.

261. The details of the *Acasta*'s flight are taken from an account written by her sole survivor, Able Seaman C. Carter.

262. *Glorious* Officers 76 Ratings 1086 Total 1162
Acasta Officers 8 Ratings 152 Total 160
Ardent Officers 10 Ratings 142 Total 152

263. See pages 154-157.

264. The inadequacy of British air reconnaissance caused grave concern to the Commander-in-Chief, Home Fleet, who on 15 June called the attention of the Admiralty to it, and made various suggestions for its improvement. (Commander-in-Chief, Home Fleet, 1541 on 15 June.) He also pressed for the reintroduction of a daily intelligence signal, giving disposition of enemy main units, which since 21 May 1940 had been discontinued.

265. Sir Charles Forbes had been promoted to Admiral of the Fleet on 8 May, 1940. This was the first occasion in history – as was pointed out to Sir Charles Forbes by HM The King – that an Admiral of the Fleet had flown the Union at the main as Commander-in-Chief of a fleet in time of war. (Lord St. Vincent, on taking

command of the Channel Fleet in 1806, was authorised to wear the Union at the main as a special mark of distinction, because he had formerly been First Lord of the Admiralty; but he was not promoted to Admiral of the Fleet till 15 years later.)

266. The German Naval War Staff was dissatisfied with Admiral Marschall's whole conduct of the operation. In its view, his decision to attack the convoys was 'operationally false'; it involved a risk of revealing the position of the battlecruisers before their main task of attacking Harstad had been carried out, and it could produce no relieving effect on the land situation at Narvik. The Naval Staff also considered that the torpedo hit on the *Scharnhorst* might have been avoided by better tactical conduct of the action, and that the ships should not have withdrawn to Trondheim immediately afterwards. That he did eventually intercept and sink the *Glorious*, the Staff ascribed to 'an extraordinary stroke of luck'.

This seems less than just to Admiral Marschall, as had he persisted in going to Harstad on the night of the 8/9, he would have found nothing there to attack: and whether by luck or skill, he did score an important success in sinking of the *Glorious*. The net result so far as he was concerned was that he was relieved of his command as Commander-in-Chief, Afloat, and replaced by Vice-Admiral Lütjens, who perished a year later in the *Bismarck*.

267. Author's italics.

268. In special circumstances there are, of course, exceptions to this rule, e.g. a powerful fort can control the sea within range of its guns, or a really strong air force can control the sea or land within a reasonable distance of its airfields, if – as happened in Norway – the other side has virtually no air force present.

269. Home Fleet Narrative, para. 269 (extract).

270. See pages 120-125, 133-142, 149-153 and 211-214.

271. The Commander-in-Chief will almost always be in a position to request Admiralty to issue instructions to his forces, if from difficulties in communications or other causes, he is unable to control them himself. This was done by Admiral Sir John Tovey a couple of years later in the course of operations against the *Tirpitz* in support of a convoy to North Russia.

272. Churchill, *The Second World War*, Vol. I, p. 483.

273. These, of course, were lessons of the War of 1914–18. Since then the advance of science, enabling more accurate bearings to be taken, and new technique have enhanced their importance, and will no doubt continue to do so.

274. Several instances occurred during the war where security in this respect was overdone e.g. a decision in the *Cumberland* in October 1939 to maintain wireless silence, which resulted in information not reaching the Commander-in-Chief, South Atlantic, that in his opinion might have led to the early destruction of the *Graf Spee*; and in connection with the *Cornwall*'s encounter with Raider No.33 (which she sank) in May 1941, the Admiralty remarked '... rigid adherence to wireless silence resulted in essential reports not being made ...

275. Author's italics.

276. Incidentally, it is pertinent to remark that had the *Bismarck* kept wireless silence, she might well have escaped.

277. See pages 121-126.

278. 'The boldest methods are the safest; nothing great can be achieved without risk.' – Nelson.
'It seems to be a law inflexible and inexorable that he who will not risk cannot win.' – *John Paul Jones*.
'All naval expeditions ... have always failed, because the Admirals ... have learned - where I do not know – that war can be made without running risks.' – Napoleon.

279. 'Something must be left to chance: nothing is sure in a sea fight beyond all others.' – Nelson.
'There is no human affair which stands so constantly and so generally in close connection with chance, as war.' – Clausewitz.

280. Unless the exhibition by the German Minister in Oslo – at a party to which Members of the Norwegian Government were invited shortly before the invasion started – of a film depicting the 'terror' bombing of Warsaw can be considered as such.

281. Some German apologists are already (1950) attempting to depict the invasion as a 'race for Norway' between the Allies and themselves (which they won), with the implication that there was not much to choose between the two. This, of course, is a travesty of the facts. While the Allies were formally approaching the Norwegians by recognised diplomatic channels and genuinely seeking some solution of their legitimate grievance over the unhampered iron ore traffic, the Germans were conspiring with such traitors as Quisling to seize the whole country. The Allied precautionary measure, Plan 'R.4', was only to be put into execution after Germany had invaded Norway, or when there was clear evidence she was about to do so; and then it was to be carried out with every consideration for Norwegian susceptibilities. The German plan, on the other hand, relied on treachery and terror bombing from the outset for its fulfilment. Contrast this with the Admiralty instructions with regard to laying the minefields (admittedly a technical breach of neutrality) in which the sentence occurs '... should force have to be used we must refrain from replying to Norwegian fire until the situation becomes intolerable.' (A.T. 1925 May.)

282. The Germans were aware that they would not meet a British submarine north of Trondheim, so the destroyers were not needed to screen the battlecruisers.

283. A report of the German landing at Narvik was at first not credited, and the Prime Minister (the Rt. Hon. Neville Chamberlain) expressed the opinion that this actually referred to Larvik (at the entrance to Oslo Fjord).

284. Mr. Winston Churchill has made it plain that the system of higher direction in force at this time suffered from inherent weaknesses, which rendered the efficient

conduct of the war impossible. (*The Second World War*, Vol. I, pp. 528-530, English Edn.) This subject is outside the scope of a Naval Staff History, but if the narrative of the campaign indicates that the principles of war, on which much thought had been expended by the Service Staffs in the inter-war years, were discarded at the first serious clash of arms, and that unfortunate results ensued, surely all other lessons pale into insignificance.

It is from this angle that the following points are raised, and in no spirit of criticism of Service Ministries or Staffs – still less individuals, all of whom were doing their best under circumstances of extraordinary stress and complexity.

285. Naval War Manual, 1947, pp. 6–8.
286. Apart from the overall aim of keeping the Norwegians in the fight and beating the Germans somehow, sometime.
287. This was of course known to only a few very Senior Officers, but its effects (constant changes of orders, etc.) would be bound to be noticed generally before long.
288. Naval War Manual, 1947, p. 7.
289. Embarked in the *Afridi* when bombed 3 May 1940.
This does not include casualties in the *Chrobry*, which was in the nature of an inshore operation: 6 officers were killed on this occasion, but nearly all the troops were saved.
290. Embarked in the *Glorious*, 8 June 1940.
291. Refit Portsmouth till mid-June.
292. Refit Liverpool till early July.
293. Refit Plymouth.
294. Detached from 20th C.S.
295. On passage from East Indies: then refit till 25 May.
296. Repairs Clyde till 6 July.
297. Refit and repairs, Govan, till 10 April.
298. Refit, Tyne, till end of June.
299. Defects, Tyne.
300. Repairs, Portsmouth, till 17 April.
301. Repairs, Dundee.
302. Repairs, Tyne, till 13 April.
303. Docked, Hull.
304. Repairs, Tyne, till 12 April.
305. Repairs, Blackwall, till 27 April.
306. Repairs, Tyne, till 16 April.
307. Refit and repairs, Hull, till 11 May.

308. Repairs, Falmouth, till 15 May.
309. Repairs, Tyne, till 3 July.
310. Repairs, Hull, till July.
311. Repairs, Blyth.
312. Repairs, Dundee.
313. Repairs, Grimsby, till 10 April.
314. Repairs, Grimsby, till 1 May.
315. Defects, Cardiff, till 1 May (?).
316. Nore Command (Harwich) temporarily attached to Home Fleet.
317. Refit, Southampton.
318. Refit, Hull, till 15 April.
319. Rosyth Command, temporarily attached to Home Fleet.
320. Refit, Leith.
321. Repairs, Rosyth.
322. Temporarily attached.
323. Repairs, Greenock.
324. Repairs, Chatham, till end September.
325. Refit, Dundee, till 5 May.
326. Refit, Chatham, till 10 May.
327. Tyne, refit till early June. Com. (S) ashore at Blyth.
328. Temporarily attached.
329. Refit, Tyne, till 20 April.
330. Docked, Blyth.
331. Repairs, Middlesbrough.
332. Repairs, Hartlepool.
333. Sunk or driven ashore.
334. Damaged in collision; remained Skjel Fjord.
335. Attached from 12th A/S Striking Force.
336. Attached from 19th A/S Striking Force.
337. 'Pocket Battleships.'
338. This attack was reported as being an aerial torpedo, but no track was seen coming towards the ship. The aircraft came very low – to about 150 feet.
339. This was definitely an incendiary bomb, being silver in colour and entering the water with a 'sizzle.'
340. The machine dived at a 70° angle of sight and sprayed the hangar with machine gun fire. It flew astern of the ship from starboard to port after dropping the bomb and

turned E.S.E. emitting smoke and losing height. The machine was not seen to come down.

341. After this dive bombing attack, the machine appeared to be on fire, lost height, dropped her load of bombs, and later came down in the sea about four miles away on the starboard quarter.

PART III

Narvik | 1940s

B.R. 1840 (1) Restricted

CONFIDENTIAL Attention is called to the penalties attaching to any infraction of the Official Secrets Acts

GERMAN NAVAL HISTORY SERIES

THE GERMAN CAMPAIGN IN NORWAY

APRIL– JUNE 1940

Origin of the plan, execution of the operation, and measures against Allied counter-attack.

This book is for the use of persons in His Majesty's Service only and must not be shown or made available to the Press or to any member of the public.

T.S.D. 57/50
Tactical and Staff Duties Division (Foreign Documents Section), Naval Staff, Admiralty S.W.1

Admiralty, S.W.1
27 November, 1948

B.R.1840 (1) Restricted – *German Naval History Series* – (*The German Campaign in Norway*) – having been approved by My Lords Commissioners of the Admiralty, is hereby promulgated for information.

By Command of their Lordships

This work has been written by the German Naval Historian, ex-Vice-Admiral Kurt Assmann and is based mainly on the captured German Naval records in the custody of the Admiralty. It constitutes the first consecutive account of events and factors governing German policy in regard to Norway during April, May and June, 1940, with particular reference to the German Navy's part in the occupation.

Some of the references to Allied operations have been obtained from certain British sources which, however, cannot be considered as entirely reliable until a full British History is written. The work can therefore be regarded as authoritative from the German point of view, but not necessarily so as regards Allied operations.

Contents

Part III

Overview 382

Chapter I
Operational Preparations
The Strategic Significance of Norway 383
The Origin of the Plan of Campaign 385
The Operational Preparations 392
The Organisation of the Assault Groups 396
The Organisation of the Transport Groups 398
The Organisation of Command 400

Chapter II
The Advance and the Landing
The Enemy Situation Upon Commencement 409
Norway 412
The Advance of Groups I and II 413
The Occupation of Narvik 423
The Occupation of Trondheim 426
The Occupation of Bergen 428
The Landings on the South-West Coast 431
The Occupation of Oslo 432
The Occupation of the Danish Ports 436

Chapter III
Events in the Landing Ports and the Return of Naval Forces
10 April in Narvik 438
The Last Fight of the German Destroyers at Narvik 443
The Return of the Battleships and Trondheim and Bergen Groups 448
The Return Journey of the Kristiansand and Oslo Groups 451
The Transport of Supplies 453

Chapter IV
Measures Against Allied Counter-Attacks
The Allied Plan of Invasion 459
The Battle for Trondheim 461
The Final Battle for Narvik 470
Operation Juno 481
Concluding Remarks 492

Endnotes 495

Overview

The German campaign in Norway will always have a particular place in history as being the first large-scale combined operation, in which all three components – Army, Navy and Air – of a modern defence organisation were thrown in with equal weight. Another feature of particular interest is that the two principal antagonists, Britain and Germany, almost simultaneously launched an attack with the same strategic objective, namely the occupation of the Norwegian zone, and it was only by a hair's breadth that one of them preceded the other in reaching the objective.

This work deals with the preparation and operational planning of the German campaign in Norway, the execution of the landing, and the defence against the ensuing Anglo-French counter-attack up to the Allied evacuation of Narvik. The account is based on the war diaries and battle reports of the German Naval Staff, and of the German Naval commanders who took part.

Originally the intention was to base this story exclusively on these German documents, but it soon became apparent that this would have made a one-sided and unclear picture, as the German reports were often based on observations and assumptions unrelated to reality. In such cases it has been necessary to complete the story with supplementary information from the British account. This applies especially to Chapter IV in which the principal German operations are described which took place on land and in the air, details of which are not to be found to any extent in the German naval archives.

Operational Preparations

The Strategic Significance of Norway in the War Between Britain and Germany

The strategic significance of Norway in the war between England and Germany was first referred to by Raeder in his conversation with Hitler on 10 October, 1939.

The German Naval Staff took the following view of the questions involved:–

It was absolutely essential to prevent England from occupying Norway, since this would have brought Sweden also under English influence, and would have seriously endangered German sea communications in the Baltic. It would have interrupted the supply of Swedish ore to Germany, and would have allowed England to intensify her air war on Germany. The maintenance of German naval supremacy in the Baltic and the continued supply of Swedish ore were both vital to Germany's conduct of the war. The Naval Staff considered that the loss of Norway to England would be synonymous with losing the war.

It might also happen that England, without actually occupying Norway, would, through military action, disregarding Norwegian neutrality, interrupt the ore traffic from Narvik to the German ports. This could not be permitted, since in the winter and up to the late spring the alternative Baltic route was blocked by ice.

The radical solution to this danger consisted in bringing Norway within the sphere of German power, and this involved action by the German armed forces; England would never have occupied Norway without using force, and Norway was in no position, with her own small resources, to counter the attack. The occupation of Norway could occur either on a peaceful basis, the Norwegians requesting German forces to occupy the country, or through military action, if necessary by using force.

Apart from countering the threat from England, the occupation of Norwegian bases would extend the operational base for German naval and air force activity against England. The Naval Staff was nevertheless aware that the strategic value of this extension must not be over-rated. The centre of gravity of German naval warfare on England was the Atlantic; Norway was far from the Atlantic and separated from it by the patrol lines Scotland–Iceland and Greenland, which were easily watched by the English. At that time the strategic significance of the Arctic was still small, as Germany and Russia were at peace.

A German occupation of Norway also involved considerable disadvantages. The transport of Swedish ore from Narvik to Germany took place safely and without difficulty within the protection afforded by Norwegian territorial waters, and this would hold good so long as Norway's neutrality was respected by the English; but if the lengthy Norwegian coastline became a battleground this would be a heavy commitment for the German forces. Furthermore, any offensive action in Norway would, in view of British sea power, involve the use of the whole of the German Navy. This was a serious consideration, since the occupation of Norway was not really a principal factor in attacking England. This consideration applied also to the other parts of the German armed forces which would be diverted from more vital tasks.

From the point of view of international law, the occupation of Norway would only be justified if British action against that country were imminent.

Weighing up all these factors, the German Naval Staff concluded that it would be best to let the Norwegian question lie until there was acute danger of British occupation, or until England no longer respected Norwegian territorial waters. Every preparation had to be made, however, so as to be ready to act at once should either of these circumstances arise. There was no question of any effective resistance by Norway to a British attack. It was hoped that any German action would occur with the peaceful co-operation of Norway, but should this prove impossible force would have to be used.

This was the unvarying view of Raeder during the winter of 1939-1940. As the possession of Norway was much more important to the British in their conduct of the war than to Germany, it was most necessary to keep a close watch on the British attitude so that any action by Germany would not occur too late.

The Origin of the Plan of Campaign

As early as the beginning of October, 1939, intelligence reached the Naval Staff that plans were being considered in England to operate against Norway, and it was later confirmed that concealed preparations were being made. The Russo-Finnish war accentuated the situation, as it might afford a pretext for Britain to provide assistance to Finland by landing in Norway. On the other hand, the contact that was made with the Norwegian Councillor Quisling at the beginning of December appeared to offer the possibility of solving the problem with Norway's agreement. Quisling believed that England was about to attack. On 12 December Hitler approved the launching of preparations for the occupation of Norway, either peacefully by making use of Quisling or, if necessary, by force. Thereupon the Supreme Command of the Armed Forces began a study on an inter-service basis of this operation, which was given the cover name 'Weserübung'.

In his conversation with Hitler on 30 December, 1939, Raeder mentioned that:–

> 'volunteers from England might carry out a disguised occupation of Norway without fighting. Serious opposition cannot be expected either from the Norwegians or the Swedes.'[1]

At the beginning of January, 1940, the entire foreign press confirmed imminent active British help for Finland, stating that the defeat of Finland would be perilous for the Western Powers, and that Northern Norway must on no account be allowed to fall into Russian or German hands.

The Norwegian question was one of the few cases in which Raeder's own views did not fully accord with those of his Operational Staff. The study of the question by the Supreme Command prompted the Naval Operational Staff to the following comments on 13 January:–

> The Chief of the Naval Staff (Raeder) is still firmly convinced that England intends before long to occupy Norway for the purpose of stopping supplies from that country to Germany, and to prevent the latter from making use of the Norwegian bases. He also believes that there will be no Norwegian resistance.

The Operations Division of the Naval Staff, however, does not believe that the occupation of Norway by England is imminent. Apart from the lack of resources, it is doubtful whether this operation would be undertaken now in view of the great risk involved, and because of the difficult situation that would arise between England and Russia. The presence of British forces in Norwegian bases would provoke an imminent extension of German operations to Denmark and, if necessary, to Sweden, and would expose the British forces in Southern Norway to grave threats by German naval and air forces.

Any British pressure from Norway on Sweden would provoke immediate and effective German counter-action in that country, and this could be stronger and quicker than any British action from Norway.

It is doubtful whether Britain has sufficient forces available for the occupation of Norway, and for countering the ensuing German threat.'

The report goes on to state the view of the Operations Division that the occupation of Norway would be dangerous for Germany as well, since the whole of the coastline as far north as the base at Polarnoye, on the Murmansk coast, would have to be protected, and this could not be guaranteed. Raeder agreed that the best solution, at the moment, was to maintain the present position of strict neutrality while making every preparation for a sudden forceful occupation.

The German Foreign Office at this time did not believe that Britain was about to embark on active operations against Norway, but considered that the course of the Russo-Finnish war was favourable to any eventual British intention. Events in Finland had lost Germany any sympathy in Scandinavian countries. It was believed that the Norwegian Government would offer considerable resistance to British action, but this would not be reflected among the Norwegian people.[2]

On 16 February the Naval Staff was alarmed through the British attack on the German tanker *Altmark* in Joessing Fjord. The tanker had served as a supply ship to the pocket battleship *Graf Spee*, and was on her way home with 300 prisoners from the *Graf Spee*. Although the *Altmark* was under the protection of Norwegian torpedo boats, the British destroyer *Cossack* proceeded alongside and forced the handing over of the prisoners. This incident was a clear warning that in future Norwegian territorial waters would no longer afford protection for German shipping. A military occupation of Norway by England was, however, 'not considered at all probable at this juncture.'[3]

At the talk between Raeder and Hitler on 20 February no decision was reached as to the date of carrying out the operation. When questioned by Hitler on the safety of iron ore transport after the eventual occupation of Norway by Germany, Raeder replied that 'he still considered the maintenance of Norwegian neutrality as the best solution'.[4] According to a report from the German Embassy in Oslo any action by the Western Powers for the support of Finland in Norway was regarded as highly dangerous for the Scandinavian States. The latter would, however, be obliged to conform to the will of the Western Powers. It seemed probable that the British intended completely to interrupt German supplies from the Northern Scandinavian countries.[5]

At the end of February the impression existed in Sweden that the British intended to land troops at Kirkenes, thereby infringing Norwegian neutrality. The danger of large-scale action by the Western Powers in Scandinavia had become imminent. Again the German Naval Staff maintained that the preservation of Norwegian neutrality would be best, but that any attempt by Britain to land in Norway must be resisted with all available forces.[6]

In the first days of March there were increasing indications of immediate British action against Norway. Reports from that country showed that its Government was prepared to defend its neutrality by every means, but that effective resistance to British military action would not be feasible. The Norwegian armed forces were issued with instructions not to fire on any opponent without express permission. Under certain conditions it might be a question, under Article XVI of the Covenant of the League of Nations, of allowing the right of transit through a country. It was also reported that the Finnish Government had appealed to the people to continue resistance, in view of the probable arrival of considerable help from foreign powers.

Under the threat of this immediate danger the Naval Staff now felt anxiety over the Norwegian question and this applied also to the Supreme Command, who on 4 March issued instructions, approved by

Hitler, that preparations for 'Weserübung' were to be pushed on quickly in order that by 10 March only four days' notice would be needed for launching the attack.

Raeder reported his views to Hitler on 9 March as follows:–

'I have always held and still hold the view that a British occupation of Norway would be fatal to Germany, as Sweden would then probably also be drawn in against us, and the whole of the Swedish ore would be cut off. Under the pretext of help for Finland the British now have the desired opportunity of sending troops through Norway and Sweden and, if necessary, to occupy these countries. Operation 'Weserübung' is, therefore, urgently necessary. It is, however, my duty to explain to you the nature of the naval operation involved. This operation runs counter to all the lessons of naval warfare, which indicate that it would only be justified if we possessed the necessary sea power, and this is not the case. On the contrary the operation will have to be carried out in the face of the greatly superior British Fleet. I believe, however, that given complete surprise the despatch of the troops can and will succeed. History shows many cases of success in operations, which violated the principles of war, always provided there is the element of surprise. The critical moment occurs at the penetration past the coastal defences into the enemy's harbours. I believe that with surprise this will succeed and that the Norwegians will not decide on action with sufficient speed, if indeed they will ever decide to open fire.

The most difficult part of the operation is the return journey in the face of British naval forces. The main British Fleet has recently returned to Scapa, where at the moment there are two battlecruisers, three battleships, and at least three to four heavy cruisers. The enemy's light naval forces will keep contact with our forces, and will endeavour to lead their battle fleet towards us. Thus we shall have to use the whole of our available forces ... We cannot leave any destroyers, let alone cruisers, behind in Narvik or Trondheim. Since this operation involves the fate of the whole German Fleet an operation on the largest scale by the German Air Force will be necessary.'[7]

In the following days numbers of reports were received pointing to supporting action for Finland by the Western Powers, who would claim the right of passage through Norway, in accordance with Article XVI. The B.B.C. announced that the Western Powers were resolved to render aid to Finland on a big scale should the latter ask for it. The German Naval Staff associated the concentration of the British Fleet at Scapa with the above.

In the meantime, peace negotiations had commenced between Finland and Russia. The Finnish Foreign Minister announced that should the Russian demands be too exorbitant the Finnish Government would invoke immediate official support from the Western Powers. This support had been promised regardless of the inevitable extension of the theatre of war to the northern area. This was confirmed on 10 March by an official statement by the British Prime Minister, Chamberlain.

On this date occurs the following entry in the War Diary of the Naval Staff:–

> 'The enemy sees no possibility of achieving victory in the European theatre. The extension' of the theatre of war to the north, for the purpose of cutting off German iron ore supplies, is regarded by him as an urgent strategic necessity. In view of the threat to Finland this operation must be carried out very soon, and Finland will be his excuse for action in face of the expected and feared German offensive in the west. Ice conditions in the Baltic preclude German operations there at present.'

The Naval Staff considered that the following counter-measures were necessary:–

'On receipt of the first intelligence of any British landing in Northern or Western Norway:–

(a) Transportation of powerful Army and Air Forces to Southern Norway for the occupation of Oslo, Kristiansand and other ports, according to the situation.
(b) Immediate occupation of Denmark.
(c) Laying of the Skagerrak mine barrage.

(d) Air attacks on British bases in Norway, on ships disembarking troops, and on naval forces.
(e) The strongest political pressure on Sweden.'

On 12 March the French Prime Minister, Daladier, stated in the Chamber that it had already been decided on 5 February to take action, and that French transports and troops had been in readiness since 26 February. But no request for help had yet arrived from Finland, and this was essential in order to justify any action to the Swedish and Norwegian Governments, who had so far shown strong opposition to the granting of passage through their countries.

On this day the conclusion of peace between Russia and Finland eased the situation somewhat. Should England now still undertake action in Norway, this could no longer be regarded as help to Finland. Under these circumstances, the Naval Staff considered that the British would not immediately resort to action but would await a favourable opportunity.

The détente was of short duration. All intelligence received recently by the Naval Staff from various sources indicated the desire of the Western Powers to occupy Norway under any circumstances, and possibly also Sweden. This was confirmed by other reliable reports indicating that the Western Powers had made every effort to prevent the conclusion of the Finnish peace, in order that the pretext for help to that country should not disappear. There was, however, little doubt that England would act in any case when the time was ripe. This view was held also at Hitler's Headquarters. He himself regarded the carrying out of 'Weserübung' as essential, but ordered that preparations should not be hurried, but should be brought to a stage where the operation could be launched at short notice.

The Naval Staff also took note of the appreciable strengthening of destroyer forces in the British Home Fleet, and of the appearance in the eastern part of the North Sea of considerable numbers of British submarines, the number at sea being about three times the normal.

The following passage occurs in the War Dairy for 15 March:–

'Radio interception has produced two very important items of intelligence showing British preparations for sending troops to Norway:–

(1) Several of the British submarines off Skagerrak and in the German Bight are returning to their home ports on 15 March. From this it may be concluded that the unexpected Finnish peace has caused a postponement of the operation.
(2) Partial deciphering of a British signal intercepted on 14 March, at 1437, from Admiralty to Commander-in-Chief, Home Fleet and others gives the following results:–
  (a) An extensive embarkation of troops has been completed. The transports are ready and troops are either embarked in them or ready to embark. The transports were apparently to proceed from the Channel ports northward along the west coast.
  (b) Transports are to be put at varying notice, from 48 hours to 80 hours, according to the political situation. The movements of the cruiser *Galatea* and the Flag Officer Commanding 2nd Cruiser Squadron are associated with movements of transports.
  Both the above indicate a postponement of the operation. There is no question of the British having cancelled the Norwegian operation, and from 'Y' reports it is evident that the operation has been thoroughly planned. German action must take account of this fact.'

In the period that followed, the Naval Staff was concerned at the frequent interference with German merchant ships inside Norwegian territorial waters by British warships and aircraft. On 23 March the Norwegian Government sent a sharp protest to London, and ordered its naval forces to open fire on any warship or aircraft if found to be acting against International Law.

Germany could not leave things in their present state. If action were to be taken in Norway it would have to occur very soon. The general war situation did not permit holding all the Navy's forces for an indefinite period while waiting for the Norwegian operation, and the element of surprise would also be endangered.

Raeder spoke to Hitler on 26 March in this sense and added that, in his opinion, the British landing was not imminent; but as Germany would have to make up her mind sooner or later, he suggested that

'Weserübung' should take place in the next new moon period (new moon 7 April).

Thereupon Hitler ordered the operation to be carried out, the commencing date being still undecided. Quisling had wanted to postpone German action until by means of political action he could prepare the ground for a peaceful occupation. But he could not guarantee any date for this.

In the following days there was further anxiety over the British measures against German shipping in Norwegian territorial waters. Information from a particularly reliable source pointed to impending British action to take over officially the protection of Norwegian territorial waters. The Norwegian Government had not yet decided how it should act in this eventuality.

Semi-official press announcements in London showed that England intended to intercept German shipping in Norwegian waters, not by using force but by political pressure on Norway. All this confirmed the Naval Staff in its view that British action in Scandinavia was imminent. 'Weserübung' is developing into a race between England and Germany as to who shall get to Scandinavia first.[8]

On 2 April Hitler ordered that 9 April should be D-Day for the operation.

The following entry occurs in the War Diary of the Naval Staff for 6 April:–

> The measures taken by the enemy show that he is on the point of taking action in the Norwegian area ... It is not clear how far he has committed himself or whether he has actually started operations, but it is necessary for 'Weserübung' to take place as soon as possible.'

The Operational Preparations

Following upon Hitler's orders to prepare the operation, the principal front-line commanders of the German armed forces were summoned to the Admiralty in Berlin on 5 March and informed verbally of the intended measures, which until now had been known only to very few people.

Secrecy was of the utmost importance, but would be difficult in view of the extensive preparation of shipping involved. The general operation comprised two separate and independent phases:–

(a) Sudden occupation.
(b) Reinforcements in troops and equipment for enlarging the initial positions.

The sudden occupation must occur simultaneously with surprise at the various selected points. It was decided that the necessary troops were to be embarked in warships, and also, as far as capacity allowed, in aircraft. In view of British naval superiority the landing forces must be transported by the quickest and safest route. In the event of Norwegian opposition either when entering the fjords or when actually landing, the warships were to use their guns. As the carrying capacity of the warships was low it would be necessary to put weapons, equipment and ammunition in transports which must arrive at the same time; but being slower than the warships, they would have to start earlier. The transports were to be camouflaged to appear as ordinary cargo ships.

The following landing places were chosen:–

Oslo, Bergen, Kristiansand, Trondheim, Arandel, Narvik and Egersund (Cable Station)

Stavanger was to be occupied from the air, and airborne troops were to co-operate in the occupation of Oslo. It was expected that Norway would not offer any organised or determined resistance, but would confine herself to diplomatic protests and attempts to delay the landings. To achieve complete surprise, transports were to enter the fjords during darkness and landings were to take place at dawn. The landings at Trondheim and Narvik were regarded as the more difficult, not because of any Norwegian opposition but because of possible British interference during the long journey. The shorter routes to the landing ports in Southern Norway would be largely covered by the German Air Force. At the commencement of the operation the western entrance to the Skagerrak was to be mined with several fields, which would provide flank protection for the routes to Kristiansand and Oslo. It was anticipated that British submarines would be active in the confined waters of the Skagerrak and Kattegat where there would be a considerable concentration of German shipping.

There was much discussion on the question as to how long the warships were to remain at the landing ports after disembarking their troops. This applied particularly to Narvik and Trondheim, which, owing to their distance from German air bases, could not count on adequate air cover. The Army wanted the warships to remain as long as possible to provide cover for the landing units, and Hitler was inclined to agree with this. But the Naval Staff, which saw the return journey of the warships as the most dangerous part, demanded their immediate return. Eventually Hitler decided that no warships were to remain at Narvik after the landing, but that two destroyers were to remain at Trondheim.

Hitler had decided that to ensure safe arrival of reinforcements Denmark must be occupied simultaneously with Norway. The Army was to move into Jutland while Copenhagen was to be occupied from the sea, and forces were to be landed for defence of the bridge across the Little Belt and of the ferry between Korsoer and Nyborg. The German Air Force was to occupy Danish aerodromes. No opposition was anticipated in Denmark.

For safeguarding the whole operation the battleships *Scharnhorst* and *Gneisenau* were to proceed to the southern part of the Arctic, and about 28 U-Boats were to be disposed off the Norwegian coast, and in the Shetland-Orkney areas as follows:–

5 off Narvik	4 Pentland Firth
2 off Trondheim	3 eastern part of English Channel
3 off Bergen	4 west of Skagerrak
2 off Stavanger	4 south-east of the Shetlands.
3 north-east of the Shetlands	

After the landings some of these U-Boats were to take up positions at the entrance to the fjords. The minefields in the Skagerrak were to be laid on the day of the operation. From 7 April air reconnaissances would be provided over the operational area by F.d.L. West and Fliegerkorps X, as well as close fighter escort protection in daylight for the ships proceeding northward.

U-Boats, anti-submarine vessels and patrol vessels were to be stationed in the area of the Kattegat and Skagerrak and westwards, also for watching the minefields and the Baltic entrances.

Operational orders contained the following features:–

(1) Assembly of troops to take place outside the ports of embarkation. Troops to be embarked at night and ships to proceed immediately to waiting positions.
(2) No troops to be visible on deck until the moment of landing.
(3) While on passage avoid meeting the enemy at all costs.
(4) The advance to be disguised as far as possible by misleading courses, screened recognition signals, use of British recognition signals.
(5) The operation must be carried out under all circumstances, even if spotted by enemy or neutral aircraft, submarines, or ships, or under navigational difficulties or bad weather.
(6) Alternative landing places to be selected in case the original ones were found to be obstructed.
(7) As far as possible the operation should take the form of a peaceful occupation, and guns and other arms are not to be used unless first used by the Norwegians.
(8) On the return journey ships are to avoid the enemy if possible.
(9) The German naval forces must be kept intact, as far as possible, for future operations.
(10) The German Air Force to avoid attacks on submarines in the Kattegat, Skagerrak and Northern North Sea from D-4 Day until further orders. From D-Day no attacks on any ship East of 2 degrees East and North of 55 degrees North.

The warships were to fly the British White Ensign until the beginning of the landing; but on 8 April this instruction was cancelled.

It was expected that there would be heavy losses. The Naval Group Commander, East, Admiral Carls, stated on 7 April:–

> 'The risk is great and losses will occur. But in view of the importance of the whole operation it would not be too high a price to lose the greater part of the surface warships. The loss of about half the naval forces must be expected if there is Norwegian or British resistance.'

The Organisation of the Assault Groups
Almost all the surface forces of the German Navy were allocated for the operation and divided into nine groups as follows:–

Group I for Narvik: *Gneisenau, Scharnhorst* and ten destroyers; the destroyers carrying altogether 2,000 landing troops.

Group II for Trondheim: *Hipper* and four destroyers, carrying together 1,700 landing troops.

These two groups were under the command of the Commander-in-Chief of the Fleet, Vice-Admiral Lütjens; the Senior Officer of Destroyers, Kommodore Bonte, was in charge of the Narvik operation, and the Commanding Officer of *Hipper*, Captain Heye, was in charge of the Trondheim operation.

These two groups were to sail in company and disperse at an agreed point for their respective tasks. The battleships were then to proceed into the Arctic area for diversionary purposes, and were to be joined by *Hipper* after Trondheim had been occupied. On completion of the Narvik and Trondheim operations both groups were to return in company to Germany.

Group III for Bergen: *Köln, Königsberg, Bremse*, two torpedo boats, one M.T.B. flotilla (seven boats), and several smaller vessels, carrying a total of 1,900 landing troops.

This group was under Admiral Commanding Scouting Forces, Rear-Admiral Schmundt.

Group IV for Kristiansand and Arendal: *Karlsruhe*, three torpedo boats, 2nd M.T.B. Flotilla (seven boats) with their parent ship *Tsingtau*, carrying 1,100 landing troops.

This group was under the Commanding Officer of *Karlsruhe*, Captain Rieve.

Group V for Oslo: *Blücher, Lützow, Emden*, three torpedo boats and several smaller vessels, carrying together 2,000 landing troops, all under the command of Rear-Admiral Kummetz.

Group VI for Egersund: four minesweepers under the Commanding Officer of the 2nd M/S Flotilla, carrying 150 men for occupying the Cable Station.

Denmark:–

> Group VII for Korsoer-Nyborg: battleship *Schleswig-Holstein* with some training and experimental vessels, and 2,000 landing troops under the Commanding Officer of the battleship Captain Kleikamp.
> Group VIII for Copenhagen: steamer *Hansestadt Danzig* with two patrol vessels, and 1,000 landing troops, under Captain (Reserve) Schroeder.
> Group IX for Middelfart: Minelayer *Rugard* and a number of smaller vessels, with 400 landing troops, under the Senior Officer of Patrol Forces in the Baltic, Captain Leissner.

There were also two small groups for establishing naval bases on the coast of Jutland, and transportation of one battalion by the normal *Gjedser* ferry for use in protecting the ferry installations.

All groups contained guns crews and communications personnel for manning the coastal batteries and signal stations, so as to liberate Army troops for immediate operations in the interior of the country.

The composition of these battle groups did not fulfil the requirements of speed, armament and striking power for such an operation, and the forces were not sufficiently integrated. Moreover, regardless of speed or fighting power, every available vessel of the small German Navy was enlisted for the operation. Hence the impression among operational units that the High Command did not expect serious Norwegian resistance. The most comprehensive battle groups were those for Narvik and Trondheim, but even they were weak in relation to their tasks.

The battle group for Oslo was not finally formed until 6 April. The pocket battleship *Lützow*, originally allocated to this group, was withdrawn on 26 March and replaced by the heavy cruiser *Blücher*. It was decided that *Lützow*, after disembarking 2,400 men at Trondheim, was to be available at once for operations in the Atlantic. Just before she was due to sail engine room defects developed, causing cancellation of the Atlantic operation, and after partial repairs *Lützow* was again allocated to the Oslo Group. *Blücher* also remained in this group, although she had only just finished her trials and her crew were still untrained. It was known that the Droebak Narrows in Oslo Fjord were strongly fortified, but none of the ships of this group were in a condition to go into action against heavy coastal artillery. In retrospect it therefore seems that the Naval War Staff did not expect resistance from these forts; and yet should there be no resistance the strength of this group was excessive.

At first it was intended to use the old battleships *Schleswig-Holstein* and *Schlesien* for the Oslo task, owing to the suitability of their guns and side armour, but their antiquated underwater protection and lack of horizontal armour caused this idea to be dropped. A single torpedo or bomb hit during the approach would have proved fatal. Under these circumstances the Naval Staff ran a great risk in planning the forcing of the Droebak Narrows. The landing troops could be put ashore (as actually happened) to capture the coastal forts from landward.

The Organisation of the Transport Groups

The formation of these Assault Groups did not take so long, and was not as difficult to conceal, as the organisation of the Transport Groups, the embarkation of the Army troops, and equipment or the provision of reinforcements. It was essential that on the day of the occupation the following should reach the landing ports:–

(a) Weapons, equipment, munitions, and provisions for troops embarked in warships.
(b) Formations of troops and equipment considered essential as reinforcements for the initial landing troops.
(c) Supply of fuel for the return journey of the naval forces, and for the immediate requirements of the Army and the Air Force.

As regards (a), a so-called 'Export Group' consisting of seven steamers, of 48,700 tons in all, was to leave Hamburg for Narvik, Trondheim and Stavanger. These ships were to appear as normal traffic to Murmansk, and were to arrive at their real destination ahead of the warships.

As regards (b), the '1st Sea Transport Division', consisting of fifteen ships with a total of 72,000 G.R.T., was to proceed from Stettin to Copenhagen, Oslo, Kristiansand, Stavanger and Bergen carrying in all 3,761 troops, 672 horses, 1,377 vehicles and 5,935 tons of Army stores.

Regarding (c), there were three tankers carrying 21,000 tons of fuel oil: *Kattegat* and *Skagerrak* from Wilhelmshaven to Narvik and Trondheim, and *Jan Wellem* from the 'Northern Base' (Murmansk) to Narvik.

In addition five smaller ships carrying oil were to proceed from Hamburg to Oslo, Stavanger, Bergen and Trondheim.

The ships mentioned in (b) and (c) were to proceed singly and inconspicuously outside territorial waters so as to arrive at their destination on the day of occupation. No noticeable measures were to be taken for their protection. Thus these ships were indirectly safeguarded only through existing air reconnaissance, and by the anti-submarine escorts of warships in the vicinity.

For reinforcements of troops and equipment the following further shipping was made available:–

(d) 2nd Sea Transport Division' consisting of eleven ships (52,500 G.R.T.) from Gotenhafen/Königsberg to Oslo carrying 8,450 men, 969 horses, 1,283 vehicles and 2,170 tons of Army stores.

(e) 3rd Sea Transport Division' consisting of twelve ships (74,550 G.R.T.) from Hamburg to Oslo carrying 6,065 men, 893 horses, 1,347 vehicles and 6,050 tons of Army Stores.

The 2nd Division was to arrive at Oslo two days after occupation, and the 3rd Division four days later. Further reinforcements totalling 40,000 men, 4,000 horses, 10,000 vehicles and 40,000 tons of Army stores were to be shipped in these two Divisions by later journeys back and forth between Oslo and German ports. These reinforcements were destined for the Army, for Coastal Defence, and for the Air Force.

All this embarkation was centrally controlled by the Supreme Command, not only up to the moment of disembarkation but also beyond that date. None of the ships were allowed to sail earlier than six days before the landing date, as will be seen later. This order from the Supreme Command caused serious difficulties, for the time allowed was insufficient for the ships to reach their destination.

In accordance with Hitler's decision of 26 March, the surface naval forces were ordered to be ready to proceed from 4 April. The date of launching the operation was largely dependent on the ice situation. Owing to a severe and long winter the Baltic and its approaches were blocked with ice up to the beginning of April. The Great Belt was not navigable in daytime until 4 April, or at night-time until 7 April. These were the latest permissible dates if landings were to occur on 8 April.

Unfortunately ice conditions in the approaches to the Baltic prevented operations in time against enemy submarines in the Kattegat and Skagerrak.

The Organisation of Command

Since the Norwegian undertaking was the first instance in this war of a combined operation by the three Services it is understandable that the Supreme Command did not merely confine itself to directives, but assumed actual control of the operations so as to ensure smooth co-operation.

At the end of February General von Falkenhorst had been detailed by the Supreme Command as Head of the Planning and Operational Staff for 'Weserübung', and also as Commander-in-Chief Designate of the Army Command, Norway. The Army units under his orders were formed into Army Group XXI.

These consisted of Infantry Divisions 69, 163, 181, 196 and 214, and the 3rd Mountain Division, as well as several Territorial and tank formations, and railway and communications troops. The battle headquarters of Army Group XXI was at Hamburg, later at Oslo.

For the occupation of Denmark Army Command XXI was formed under Air General Kaupisch, under whom were the reinforced Infantry Divisions 170 and 198, and the 11th (Motorised) Rifle Brigade.

Operational command of the Luftwaffe was given to Air General Geisler, with Fliegerkorps X and battle headquarters at Hamburg; various German Air Force units of different kinds were added to this command. It included K.G. 4, 26, 30 and one group of K.G. 100. [Note: K.G. means Bomber Group.]

K.G. 30 was allocated one heavy fighter squadron, one fighter and one dive bomber squadron, two reconnaissance flights (Ju. 88), and a Coastal Flying Squadron (No. 506) consisting of three flights of sea planes. Three flak companies, four paratroop companies, several airborne troop units and the necessary ground formations were allocated to Fliegerkorps X for the operation.

The air units of the Navy were not subordinated to Fliegerkorps X but came under the Naval Group Commanders, East and West.

For the period of the operation the command of all units at sea was vested in the Navy. Admiral Carls (Naval Group Commander, East) was in charge of operations in the Baltic area, including the Kattegat, and as far as the Skagerrak minefield; General-Admiral Saalwächter, (Naval Group Commander, West) was in charge of operations in the North Sea area. The central control exercised by the Supreme Command involved the Naval War Staff in closer conduct of the operations than was normally the case. The operational orders for individual battle groups were issued mostly by the Naval Staff, and this produced in the Naval Group Commanders a feeling of constraint in their operational freedom.

The conduct of the landing and command ashore were to be vested in the senior Army officer at each place. In the event of resistance to landing, it was the task of the Naval forces in conjunction with Army troops to break the resistance.

Transportation by air was to be in the hands of the Luftwaffe up to the moment of landing. Immediately after the landing individual centres were to establish a local commander of the armed forces, either an Army or a Naval officer.

The further conduct of the Norwegian campaign was to be vested in the Commander-in-Chief of the Armed Forces, Norway, General von Falkenhorst. Overall command of the Navy was vested in the Admiral Commanding Norway, Admiral Boehm, with headquarters at Oslo. He had authority to represent Raeder in all questions affecting Norway as a base of naval operations. The coastal artillery defences of the whole Norwegian coast were also under him, and the requirements of the Naval Staff in coastal defence were to have priority over requirements of land operations. As numerous Army coastal batteries were involved in this organisation, this ruling was to become a constant source of friction between the Army and the Navy.

In the coastal area to be occupied the following were appointed as senior naval officers, under the Admiral, Norway:–

(a) The Admiral, Norwegian South Coast, Rear-Admiral Schenk, at Kristiansand.
(b) The Admiral, Norwegian West Coast, Vice-Admiral von Schrader, at Bergen.

The Commander of the Armed Forces in Denmark was Air General Kaupisch, and the Coastal Commander was Vice-Admiral Mewis, both with headquarters at Copenhagen.

On 7 April, shortly before midnight, Groups I and II (Narvik and Trondheim) left their home ports, assembling at 0300 off the river mouths for the advance into the North Sea. They were under the command of the Deputy Commander-in-Chief, Vice-Admiral Lütjens, as the Commander-in-Chief, Admiral Marschall was sick. The seven steamers of the 'Export Group' and part of the 1st Sea Transport Division had already left Hamburg and Stettin on 3 and 5 April respectively. The remainder of this Transport Division followed on 7 April.

The operation for the capture of Norway had started.

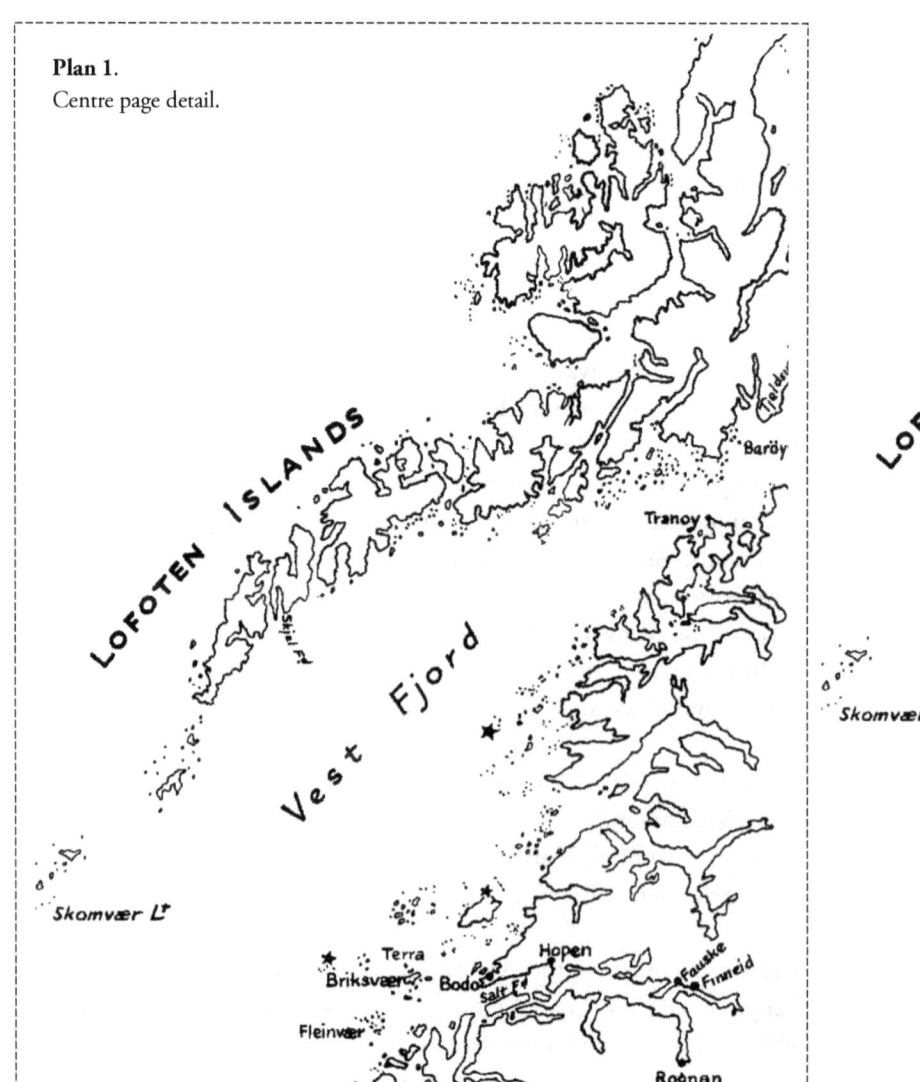

Plan 1.
Centre page detail.

Plan 1.

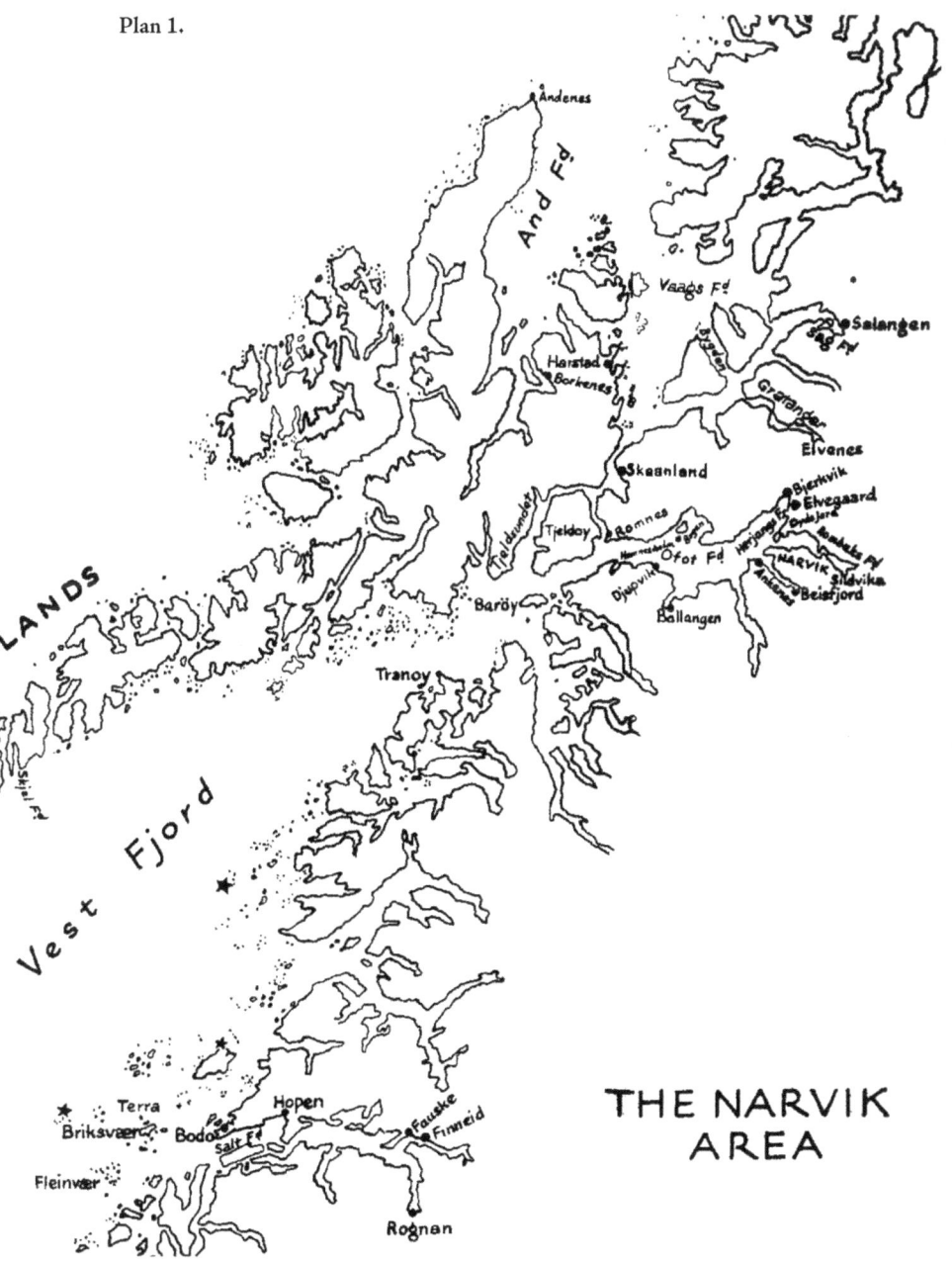

THE NARVIK AREA

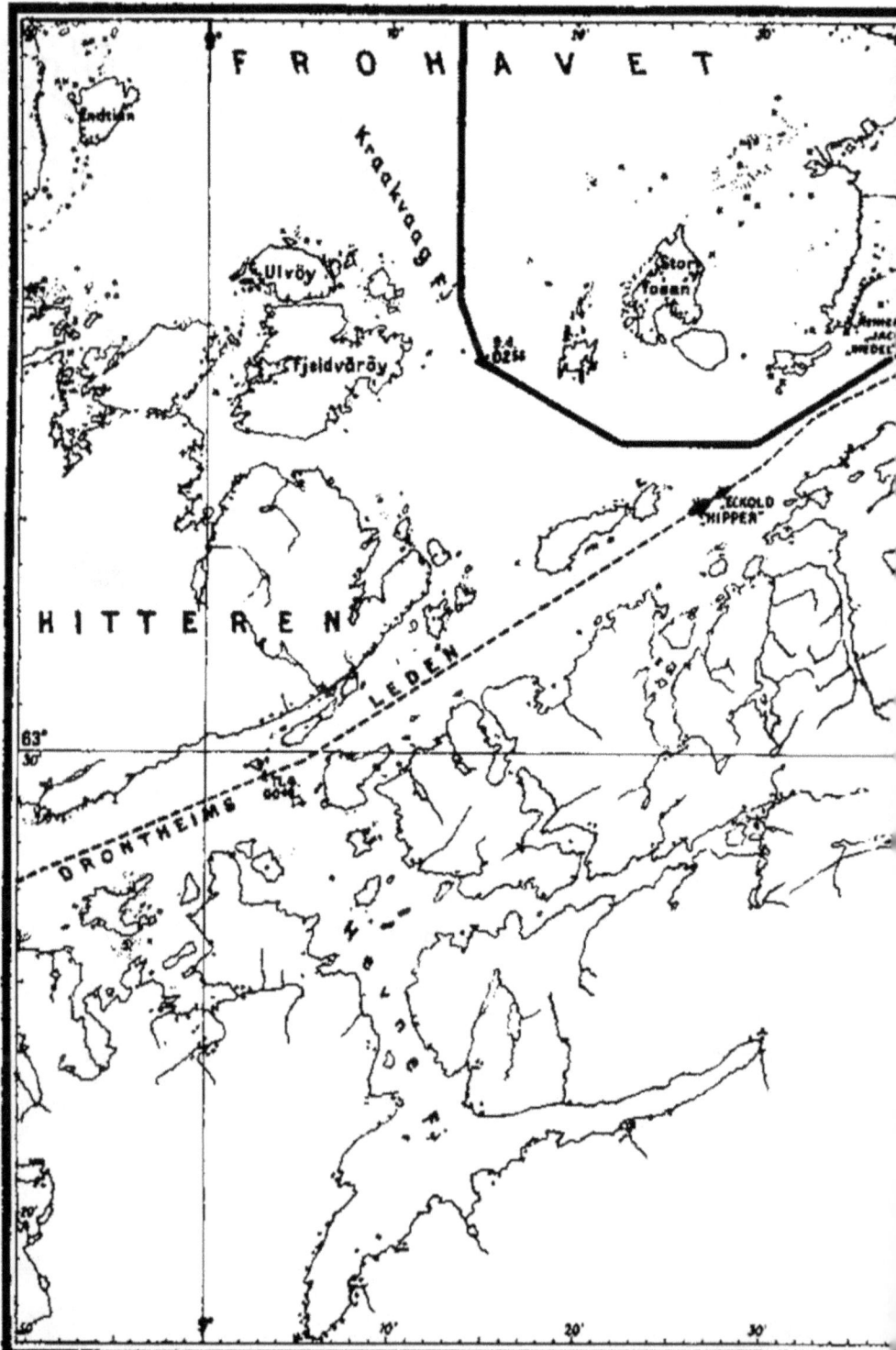

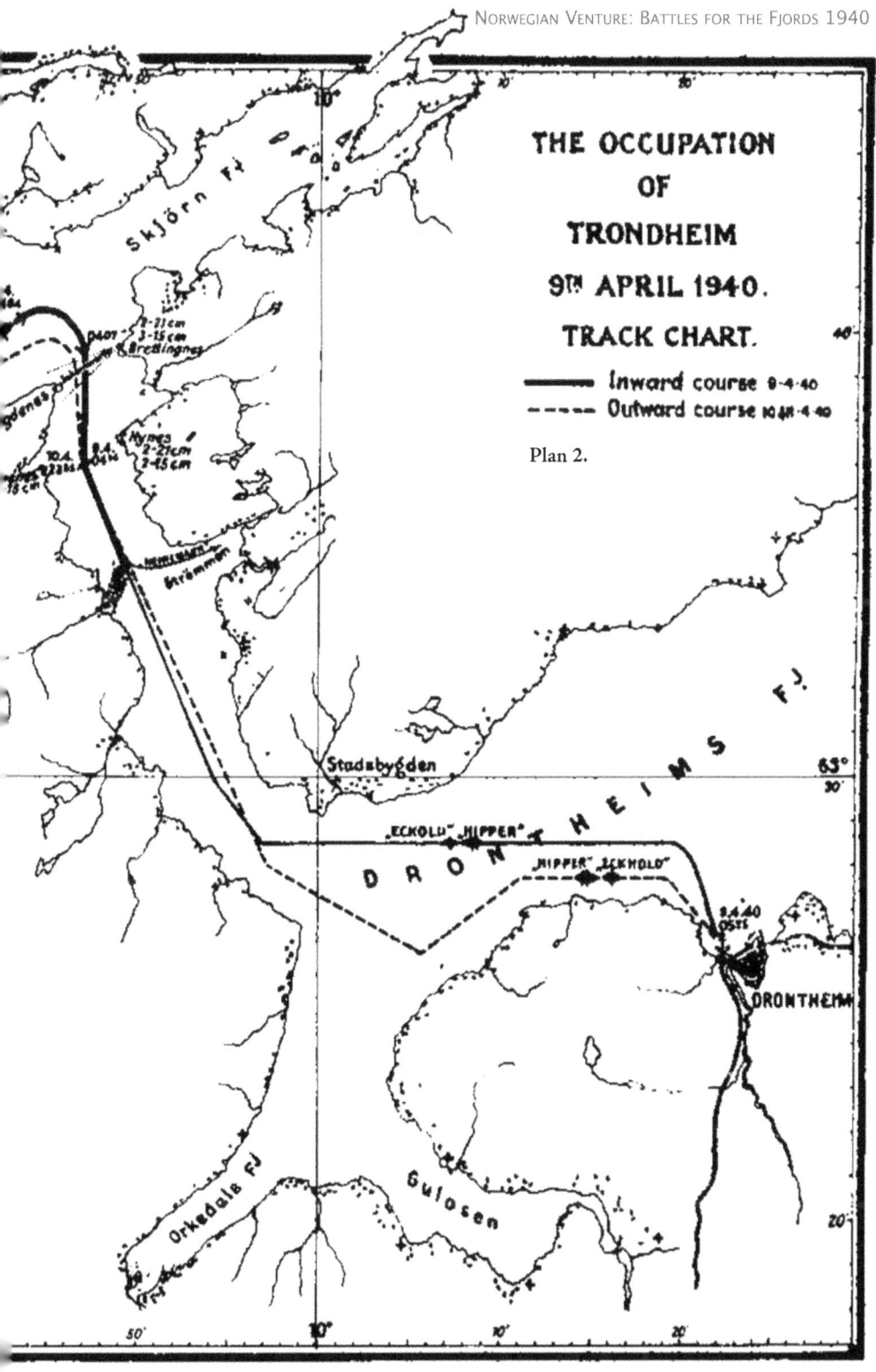

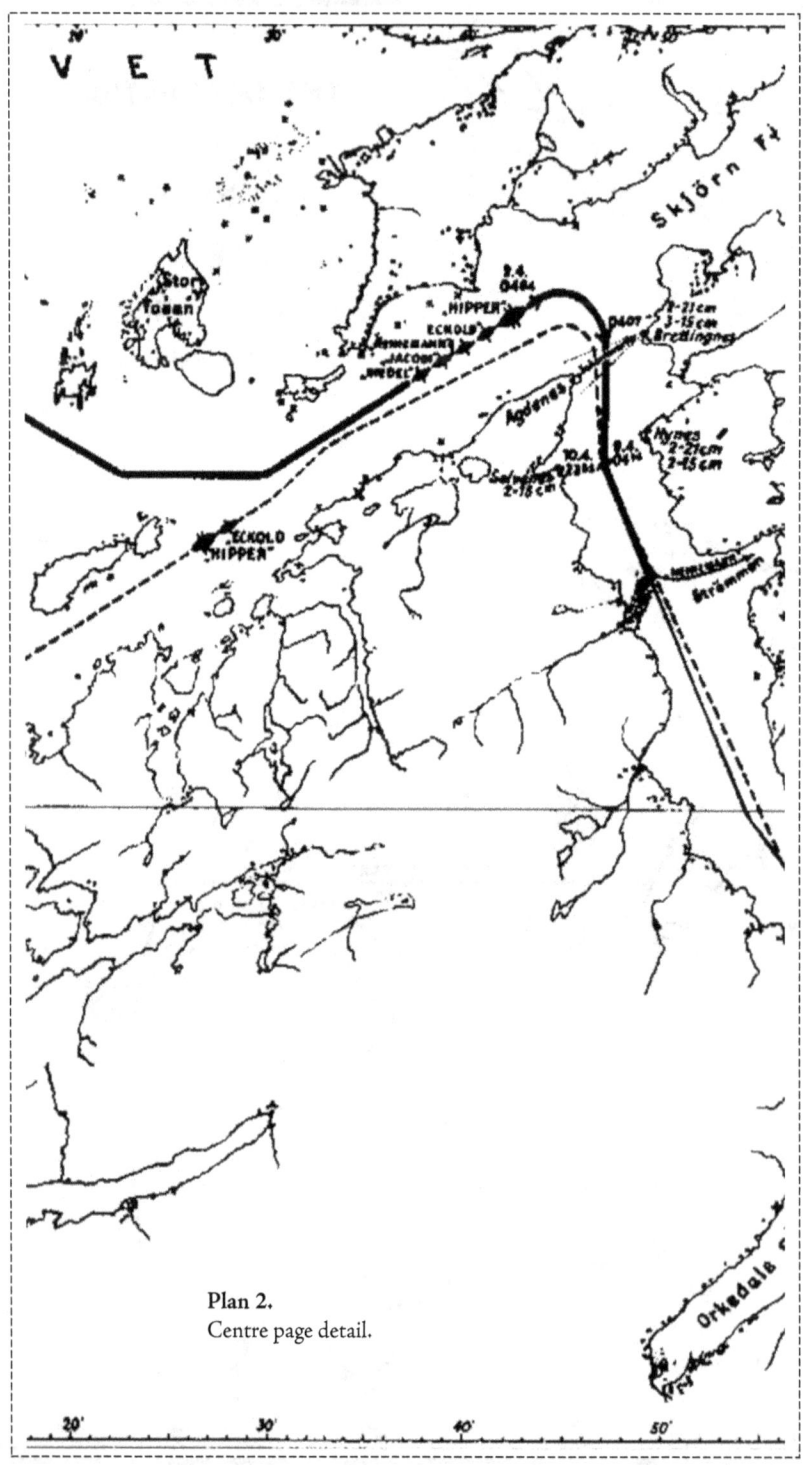

Plan 2.
Centre page detail.

NORWEGIAN VENTURE: BATTLES FOR THE FJORDS 1940

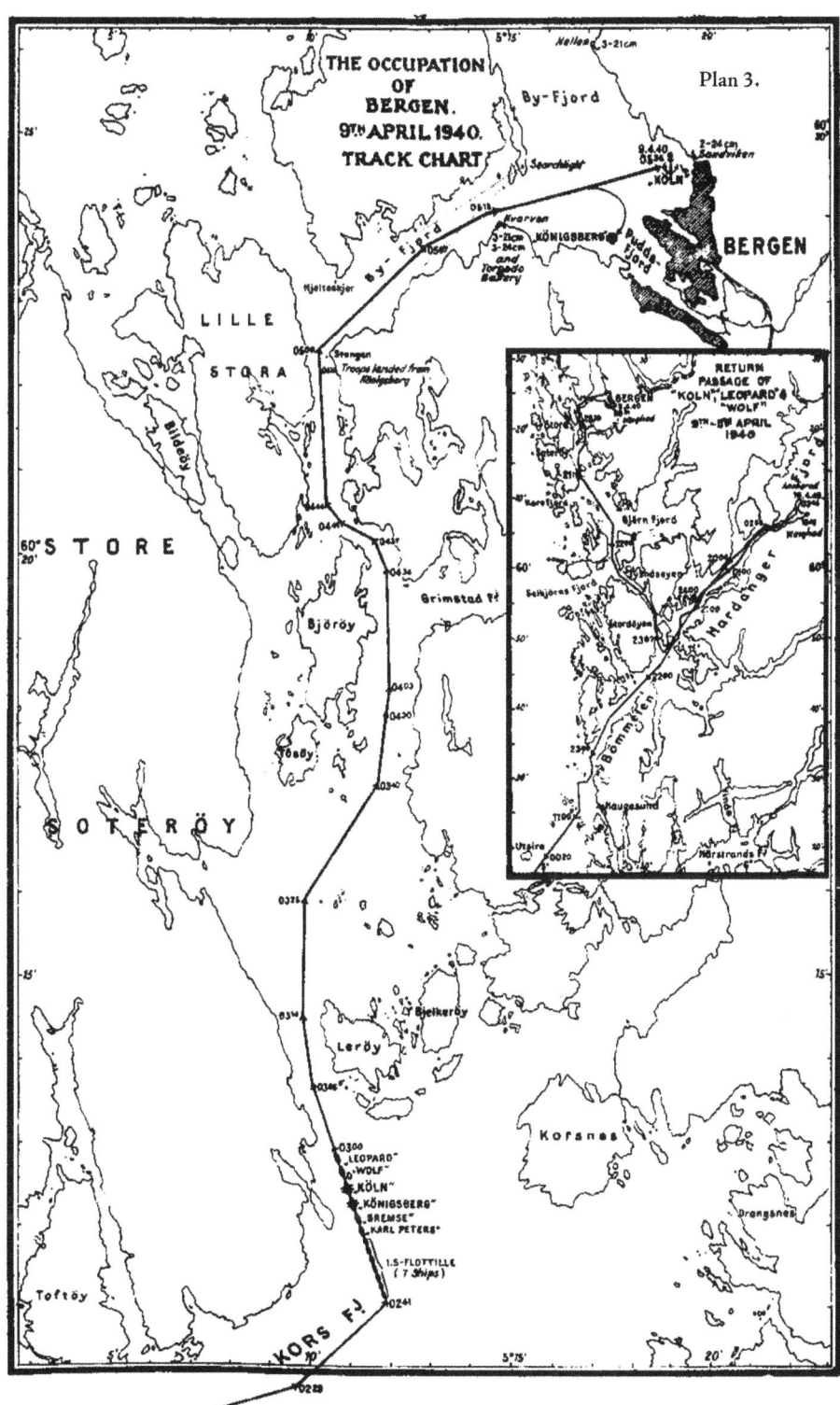

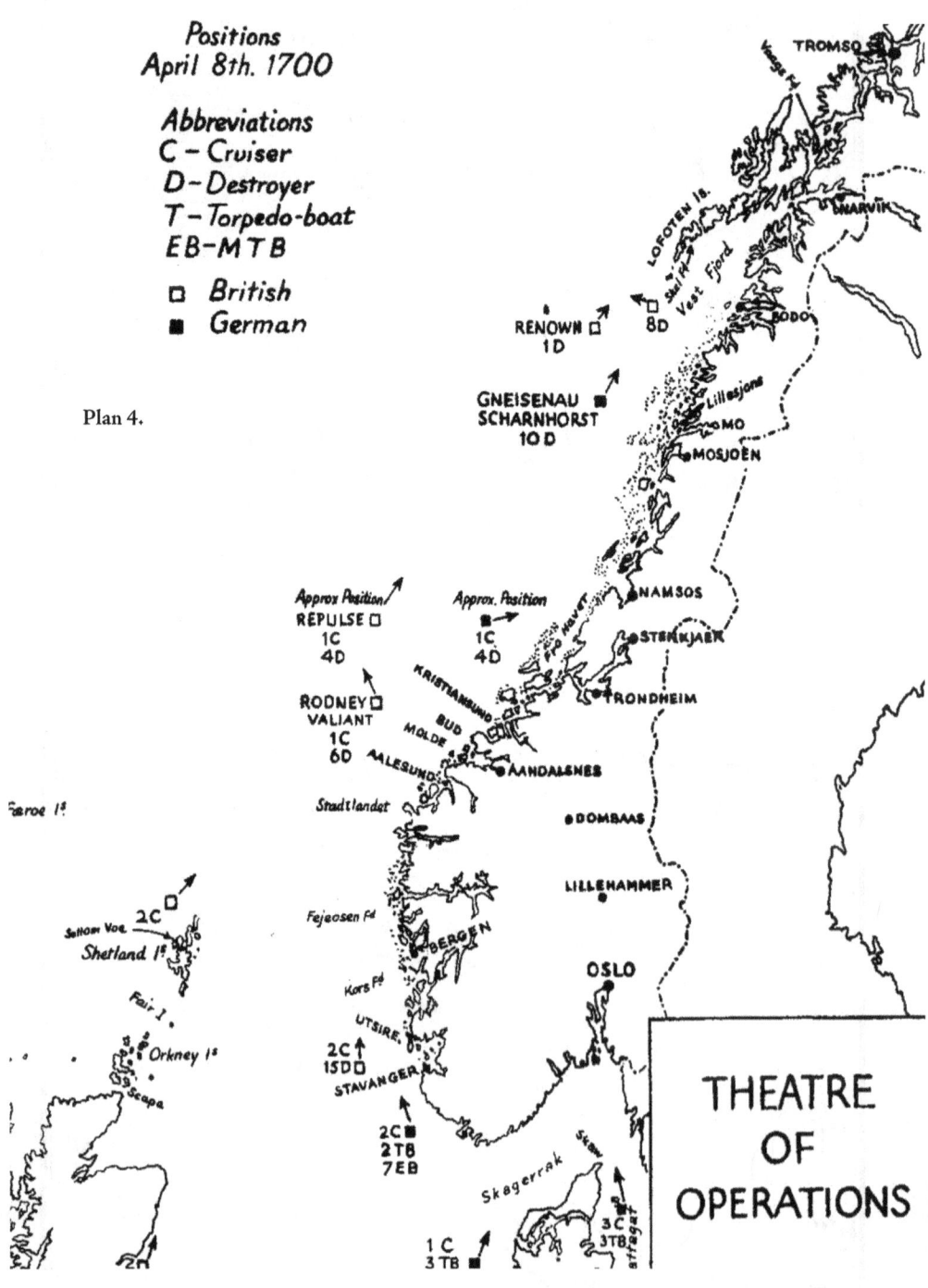

Plan 4.

The Advance and the Landing

The Enemy Situation at the Commencement of the Operation England

At the end of March the German authorities decided to occupy Norway because they considered Allied action imminent, either for landing in Norway or for the interruption of German shipping in Norwegian Territorial Waters. How far did this estimate by the German authorities correspond to the facts?

As a result of plans made on 31 January and 1 February, 1940, by the Allied Military authorities the meeting of the Supreme War Council decided on 5 February to prepare Franco-British forces for transport to Norway. On 6 February Lord Halifax informed the Norwegian Minister in London that England wished to establish certain bases on the Norwegian coast, 'in order to stop the German transport of ore from Narvik.' But the British intentions actually went beyond this purpose. At the meeting of the Supreme Council already referred to the majority of the members, acting under British influence, had wished to extend the Scandinavian operation to include the Swedish ore mines at Gaellivare. At this meeting the view was expressed that action should not be dependent on a Finnish request for help, but should take the form of an independent surprise operation, 'in order to save Finland or at least to seize the Swedish ore and the northern harbours.'[9] The operation was to be conducted by the British authorities. In the middle of February British and French Staff officers inspected possible landing places, with Norwegian concurrence. By the beginning of March the Franco-British Expeditionary Force was ready.

A decision to carry out a modified landing operation and form bases in Norway was made on 28 March, and the departure of the first transports was fixed for 5 April.

The course of events in Norway was decisively affected by the last-minute postponement of this date. On 5 April the British High Command informed the Commander-in-Chief of the French Navy that the first British convoy would not be able to sail before 8 April. It was only this postponement that allowed Germany to win the race for Norway and to 'seize (among other places) all the ports that the Allies had hoped to save from their control by occupying themselves.'[10]

The postponement was due to the fact that by 5 April the British Admiralty had not the necessary transport available. According to the British account the Allied plan envisaged 'the laying of mines off the coast of Norway to force traffic outside Norwegian Territorial Waters, and to make ready for a landing of British and French troops in Norway, because the laying of mines may lead to German reaction in Scandinavia.'[10]

Mine-laying was to take place, independently of the landings, on 8 April at Westfjord (Narvik) in about 67° 30' N., 14° E., and off Stadtlandet in about 62° N., 5° E. A third area at Bud in 63° N., 7° E., was also to be declared a mined area, but mines were not actually to be laid there.

The landing intentions were contained in Plan 'R.4' wherein the Allies 'had decided to hold troops ready to occupy the ports of Stavanger, Bergen and Trondheim, and ready to land at Narvik; but they did not intend to land troops in Norway until the Germans had violated Norwegian territory, or there was clear evidence that they intend to do so.' The similarity to the German attitude is noteworthy.

When at 0300 on 7 April the German Groups I and II commenced their sortie from the North Sea ports towards Norway, the position in the North Sea and in the Arctic was characterised by the following distribution and intentions of the British naval forces:–

(a) Waters around Norway:

Four destroyers of the 20th Destroyer Flotilla, under Captain Bickford, were proceeding towards Westfjord for the purpose of laying mines. On the morning of 6 April this force was joined by Vice-Admiral Whitworth in Battlecruiser *Renown*, accompanied by four escorting destroyers and four further destroyers of the 2nd Destroyer Flotilla, under Captain Warburton-Lee. The latter had orders to cover Captain Bickford's destroyers during the minelaying operation, and later to keep watch on the minefields. But in the course of 6 April *Renown*'s destroyer escort was reduced to one ship (*Greyhound*). *Glowworm* had dropped behind to pick up a man overboard, and had been unable to resume contact because of bad visibility. Two further destroyers had been detached to feign the laying of mines at Bud. It was intended that on the evening of 7 April, *Birmingham* and two destroyers coming from the Arctic should join *Renown* off Westfjord.

A further destroyer division, under Captain Todd, and the minelayer *Teviot Bank* were proceeding towards Stadtlandet for the purpose of laying mines.

The number of submarines at sea had been considerably increased to cope with possible German counter-measures.

(b) At British Bases:–

In the Firth of Forth the Cruisers *Devonshire*, *Berwick*, *York* and *Glasgow*, under Vice-Admiral Cunningham, embarked two battalions of British troops on 7 April which were destined for Stavanger and Bergen. A further battalion, intended for Trondheim, was to follow two days later in transports.

In the Clyde a squadron destined for Narvik was assembling under the command of Admiral Evans. The first battalion for Narvik was to be embarked in transports and escorted by *Aurora* and *Penelope*. This force was to be ready to sail on 8 April. Further troops, including French units, were to follow later. A total of 18,000 men were earmarked for Narvik, which was to be established as a regular base with local coastal defences and supply depots.

Each group was allocated a number of destroyers as escort.

At Rosyth a striking force of cruisers and three destroyers was assembled under Vice-Admiral Edward-Collins, 'to deal with any seaborne expedition the Germans may send against Norway'. A further striking force, three cruisers under Vice-Admiral Layton, was to operate from Scapa to protect Norwegian convoys in case of need.

The Commander-in-Chief of the Fleet, Sir Charles Forbes, was at Scapa on 7 April with the main forces of the Home Fleet, the battleships *Rodney*, *Valiant*, *Repulse*, and the cruisers *Sheffield* and *Penelope* and ten destroyers.

These details were not known to the German authorities at the beginning of the Norwegian operation. The German Naval Staff's estimate, based on observations, gave the British naval forces in the North Sea and in Northern waters as follows:–

Five battleships, and possibly two French battleships.
About fourteen cruisers, one French cruiser.
One or two aircraft carriers.
About six destroyer flotillas.
Fifteen to twenty-seven submarines.

The preliminaries of the German operation against Norway had envisaged frequent air attacks on Scapa, with the object of driving the Home Fleet to the harbours on the west coast of Scotland. And it was understood that, following an air attack on 16 March, the British battleships had left Scapa. Because of weather conditions and insufficient air reconnaissance these German attacks could not be repeated, and German interception had established that the ships had returned to Scapa on 29 March.

The German Staff knew that the regular convoys between the Norwegian coast and the Orkneys-Shetlands were escorted by naval forces. In addition it was believed that several cruisers and destroyers were in the vicinity of the Norwegian coast, and it was assumed that certain positions between Heligoland, Skagerrak and Utsire were constantly occupied by British submarines.

Norway

Information was available that the total strength of the Norwegian Army was about 90,000 men, which could be increased to 110,000 – 120,000 by calling up reserves. In addition about 100,000 trained men, mostly Territorials, were available, but only a small number of these could be equipped and armed. The task of the Norwegian armed forces was

(a) defence against a Russian attack on Narvik, possibly in conjunction with Swedish troops;
(b) defence against enemy attempts to land in the principal Norwegian harbours.

All forces had been instructed, through a statement by the Norwegian Government, to open fire immediately on any foreign warship or aircraft which infringed the neutrality of the country. However, according to reliable reports this order was not to apply to British ships or aircraft.

There was information available up to the end of March as to the location of Norwegian naval forces, but their exact position on 9 April could not be anticipated. The German Naval Staff had the following information concerning defences:–

(a) Oslo Fjord, strongly fortified, including a large number of heavy guns up to 28 c.m.
(b) Kristiansand, Bergen and Trondheim had medium defences with guns up to 24 c.m.

Further light defences were reported to be at Narvik and Vardoe, but no details were available. In general, it was considered that coastal defences were inadequate and not particularly efficient. It was reported that mine barrages existed in Oslo Fjord and were under permanent observation.

The Advance of Groups I and II

On 7 April, at 0948 (German time), part of the formation was sighted for the first time by British air reconnaissance in 55° 53' N., 6° 37' E. The British aircraft reported one cruiser, six destroyers and eight aircraft, and this report was intercepted by the Germans. At 1425, British reconnaissance reported one big ship, possibly *Scharnhorst* Class, two cruisers and ten destroyers in 56° 48' N., 6° 10' E. About this time the German formation was attacked by Wellington bombers, without success. Twelve aircraft were counted. A total of thirty-five bombers had been started by the Royal Air Force for attacks on ships, and most of these had apparently not located the German forces. From noon onwards visibility had deteriorated, and this was welcomed by the Germans. On the other hand the change in the weather resulted in restricting German air reconnaissance to the line Stavanger/Peterhead.

The British were thus aware of the launching of an operation towards the north by German naval forces, and it was observed that German radio traffic from Wilhelmshaven was exceptionally active since the evening of 6 April. The purpose and direction of the operation were not then apparent from the reconnaissance reports. The British Admiralty had received a report from Copenhagen and passed it on to the Commander-in-Chief of the Home Fleet on 7 April, which stated that a German expedition, consisting of troops embarked in ten ships, was reported to be proceeding to Narvik with the object of landing there on 8 April. In passing on this information to the Commander-in-Chief of the Home Fleet, the Admiralty added: 'reports are of doubtful value and may be part of war of nerves'. The report from Copenhagen was probably occasioned by the intense northward traffic that had been observed in the Baltic Approaches during the previous few days.

The information that the German Fleet was at sea led the British authorities to make some vital decisions. The British intention to land – Plan "R.4" – was abandoned, the troops onboard the four cruisers in the Firth of Forth were disembarked, the ships proceeding towards Stadtlandet for minelaying were recalled, and all operations were directed towards intercepting the German squadron, which was shown by photographic reconnaissance on the evening of 7 April to consist of one battlecruiser, one pocket battleship, three cruisers and twelve destroyers. At 2115 on 7 April, the Commander-in-Chief, Home Fleet, left Scapa with his main forces, and an hour later the Rosyth Group put to sea. On the following day, after disembarking troops, the cruiser squadron left the Firth of Forth.

It is noteworthy that the British gave up the landing plan at this moment. According to Plan 'R.4', the landing was to be carried out 'as soon as the Germans have violated Norwegian territory or there is clear evidence that they intend to do so.' There were clear indications (such as the German advances and the report from Copenhagen) that the latter condition had been realised. Under these circumstances it might be assumed that the British authorities would make every effort to forestall the Germans at the last moment. Presumably the British decision was governed by a desire first to defeat the enemy with superior forces, and then to carry out the original intention to land in their own time. The fact that the departure date of the first British transport was postponed from 5 to 8 April may indicate that the British were not ready on 7 April to proceed to sea to forestall the German occupation.

After the attack by Wellington bombers no further incident marked the progress of the German forces. There were several contacts between

British and German air units. At 2200, Group West reported to the German Naval Commander-in-Chief as follows:– 'The enemy has discovered our operational intentions, and is employing light naval forces. So far there is no indication of large scale British action.' During the night of 8 April, the German formation crossed the line Shetlands/Norway without contacting the enemy. During this period the south-westerly wind increased considerably, which caused the troop-carrying destroyers some difficulty. Nine destroyers could not maintain speed and dropped astern, although speed had been reduced from 26 to 22 knots.

At 0800 on 8 April the formation was in 64° 7' N., 5° 55' E., opposite Trondheim. At 0820 one of our escorting destroyers sighted a British destroyer; the latter, *Glowworm*, could not keep up her speed and came into action with the German destroyer *Bernd Von Arnim*, which was further astern. *Glowworm* had lost contact with *Renown* on the 6 April and had failed to find her again. In the ensuing destroyer action in heavy weather the seaworthiness of *Glowworm* proved superior. She proceeded on varying courses at high speed, and rode the sea well, while the German destroyer plunged heavily, which caused considerable damage and severely affected her gunnery. Under these conditions, the superior armament of the German destroyer (5 12.7 c.m. guns against 4 12 c.m.) did not make itself felt. Although *Glowworm* received three hits her fighting power did not appear to suffer, and it was not until *Hipper*, having been ordered to join the action, arrived, that *Glowworm* was sunk, at short range through gunfire and finally by ramming. In spite of heavy seas *Hipper* was able to pick up 38 survivors. At noon Group II – *Hipper* and four destroyers – were detached to carry out the Trondheim task.

Group I, while proceeding northward at 24 knots, learned of the British declaration of three mined areas off the Norwegian coast and mostly inside territorial waters. Actually only Westfjord had been mined, as planned, on the morning of 8 April.

The political effect of the British action in laying mines was regarded as favourable by the Germans, since their own operations could now appear justified in the eyes of the neutrals; but militarily the position became more difficult. It was now to be anticipated that there would be contact with enemy naval forces in the vicinity of the mined areas, and the German transports and supply ships on passage were regarded as particularly endangered. There could however be no question of breaking off the operation because of the British action; the transports could not be recalled, since the success of the operation depended on their punctual arrival at the ports of destination. They were therefore ordered to pass round the dangerous areas outside territorial waters, and to proceed to their destinations.

On the afternoon of 8 April the first news was received of the torpedoing of steamers in the Skagerrak. At 1420 the transport *Rio de Janeiro*, belonging to the 1st Sea Transport Division, was torpedoed and sunk near Lillesand, East of Kristiansand, by the Polish submarine *Orzel*. At 1815, near Stavanger, the tanker *Stedingen* was sunk by the British submarine *Trident*.

The result of the torpedoing of the *Rio de Janeiro* was serious, and the Naval Staff commented as follows in the War Diary:—

'Our objections to the premature appearance of the transports in Norwegian waters have been justified. The torpedoing of this ship, and the landing of German survivors in German uniform, must result in disclosing the German operation and alarming the Norwegians, so that surprise is no longer possible. Reuter reported at 2030 from Oslo 'that the ship had been torpedoed near Kristiansand with 300 men onboard.' Thus the enemy has been warned, and action by him must be expected at any moment.' [11]

The Naval Staff realised too late that it would have been best to disguise the steamers of the 1st Sea Transport Division as neutrals, and to dress the troops onboard them as civilians.

At 2100 on 8 April the Commander-in-Chief with Group I was off the entrance to Westfjord, and ordered the ten destroyers to proceed to Narvik for their task. In the course of the afternoon he had received from Group West several enemy reports, obtained from air reconnaissance, which showed that one force – consisting of one *Malaya*, one *Nelson*, one *Sheffield* and six destroyers – was proceeding north-westwards in position 71° N., 1° E., that is about 340 miles to the north of his own position; also that several groups of light cruisers and destroyers were believed to be in the area between the Orkneys/Shetlands and the Norwegian coast. This information did not influence the course of the operation. In one case German radar had picked up a target at a distance of 18,000 metres, and further contact was avoided by altering course.

After detaching the Narvik destroyers, the German Commander-in-Chief with *Scharnhorst* and *Gneisenau* proceeded on a course of 290°, with the object of penetrating to Northern Waters. Owing to heavy seas speed had soon to be reduced to seven knots. At 2233, Group West informed him that two *Renown*s were believed to be at sea, and that during the day one British cruiser and one destroyer had been seen at Westfjord. During the night further reports of the enemy were received including one fairly near, in position 65° 50' N., 9° E. At 0400 on 9 April the Commander-in-Chief's position was 67° 40' N., 10° E., course 310°, wind Nor'-Nor'-West 6-7, heavy swell, sea 6, good visibility. Speed was increased to 12 knots. At 0449 there was a radar contact, bearing 280°, distant 18,500 metres, and almost at once a large warship was sighted. The two battleships altered course to 350°. At 0508, HMS *Renown* opened fire.

What were the enemy's movements that led to this contact? During the minelaying on the morning of 8 April Admiral Whitworth with *Renown* and the destroyer *Greyhound* was patrolling off the entrance to Westfjord when at 0930 he received a report from *Glowworm* that she was in action with a superior enemy. He proceeded southward to the scene of action at the greatest speed that weather would permit, but he realised that he would be too late. About noon he received orders from the Admiralty to concentrate with the eight destroyers of the Westfjord mining force, and he was told 'that the previous report about a German expedition to Narvik might be true, and that German ships might be on their way to Narvik.' Having regard to the relative positions of British and German ships, Admiral Whitworth considered it possible to place himself on the line of advance of the enemy. But first it would be necessary to pick up the eight destroyers, since visibility had dropped to two to three miles, which would not allow him with *Greyhound* alone to find the enemy. At 1815 the rendezvous occurred with the destroyers twenty miles west of Skonvaer, near the entrance to Westfjord, and this was just two and three-quarter hours before the German formation arrived in the same area.

The situation, which so far was clear to the British, became confused through an aircraft report, received at 1616, according to which one battlecruiser, two cruisers and two destroyers were sighted on a westerly course at 1500 in position 64° 12' N., 6° 25' E., that is, at the latitude of Trondheim.[12] After weighing the various possibilities of action by this

German force near Trondheim, Admiral Whitworth decided to operate so as to block the enemy's advance, should he decide to proceed into Northern Waters. He knew that the German main forces were in the south, and possibly thought that their approach to Narvik was sufficiently covered. He ordered his forces to form an arc of search for the night from Skonvaer to the northward, and thus he freed the approach to Narvik. One and a half hours later, at about 1915, he received urgent orders from the Admiralty 'to concentrate on preventing any German force proceeding to Narvik.' In the meantime the weather had so deteriorated that the Admiral considered it necessary to keep his forces together during the night, and to steer courses which would not harm his destroyers. He received information from his Commander-in-Chief that *Repulse, Penelope, Birmingham* and four destroyers were proceeding to his support. He gave the latter his position at 2300 as 67° 9' N., 10° 10' E., course 310°, that is, about sixty miles West of Skonvaer. *Birmingham* had to be detached to Scapa because of fuel shortage. Before the remainder joined him he contacted the enemy.

There had been a slow improvement in the weather, and at break of day Admiral Whitworth had turned towards the Norwegian coast. At 0437, at the time when the German destroyer flotilla, unhampered by British naval forces, was approaching Narvik, the British force, which was then about fifty miles west of Skonvaer, sighted to the eastward two German warships on a north-westerly course which were thought to be one *Scharnhorst* and one *Hipper,* and in the ensuing action the British still failed to identify the second ship as also a *Scharnhorst*. Visibility was variable with frequent snowstorms. Conditions of light were favourable to the British, as the Germans were on the eastern, lightening horizon. Admiral Whitworth continued his course of 130° until at 1459 he turned on to an action course of 305°. At 0509 *Renown* was able to open fire, followed three minutes later by fire from the German battleships. The commencing range for the British was 17,000 metres, and for the Germans 14,800 metres. The fire from *Renown* was supported by the 4.7-in. guns of the destroyers astern of her, but at this long range the fire from the destroyers was considered by the British Admiral to be ineffective. The Germans, seeing the extended gun flashes of their opponents, estimated that they were opposed by several ships. Observation of fall of shot by the Germans was very difficult under the conditions of visibility.

As the German Commander-in-Chief's object was to avoid action if possible, he decided to turn away and continue the action on a north-easterly course, using his after guns only. A possible contributory factor to this manoeuvre was his ignorance as to the strength of the opponent. The Germans thought that the enemy consisted of two or three big ships, of which one was believed to be either *Nelson* or *Rodney*. During the next quarter of an hour a lively action ensued. At 0518 Admiral Whitworth turned also on to a north-easterly course, which brought the Germans on to his starboard bow. At this time *Gneisenau* received a hit in the foretop, which put her main fire control out of action. A splinter struck the rangefinder hood of the forward turret and this caused serious ingress of water due to the seas that were breaking over the ship. *Renown* received two hits which caused no serious damage. The German battleships had temporarily increased speed to 28 knots at 0528, and *Renown* gradually dropped astern and was intermittently obscured by snow squalls. Contact was maintained until about 0700, with occasional exchange of salvoes, according to visibility, but on both sides the gunfire was ineffective. The German ships suffered severely from the breaking seas. At 0640 the forward turrets of both ships were put out of action from this cause, and speed had to be reduced to 20 knots; *Renown* finally disappeared from sight at 0654. The British last sighted their opponents momentarily at 0715 'far ahead and out of range'.

After the action Admiral Whitworth detached his destroyers to Westfjord to guard the entrance. He also ordered the *Repulse* Group to prevent German penetration into Narvik, but in the meantime the Germans had landed there. He himself, with *Renown*, pursued the German battleships until 1000, when the Admiralty again directed him to watch Narvik. He then concentrated all his forces on this task.

After the action the German battleships proceeded towards Northern Waters at best speed, and concentrated on repair of the damage. *Scharnhorst*'s speed had been reduced through engine defects. From noon the ships proceeded on a westerly course in latitude 70° N., until at 2000 they reached longitude 1° 20' E. During the day the German Commander-in-Chief was kept informed as to the enemy's movements by Group West, and by intercepted aircraft and submarine reports.

The scope of this work does not call for a detailed description of the movements of units of the Home Fleet between Scotland and the

Norwegian coast on 8/9 April. It has already been explained how the German destroyers managed to reach Narvik without interference. In the occupation of the other Norwegian ports there was no contact between the German naval units and the ships of the Home Fleet, and the movements of the latter did not affect the German operations.

The activities of the air and submarine forces on both sides will now be mentioned.

The operational decisions by the British Naval Commander-in-Chief were adversely affected by the misleading air reconnaissance report at 1500 on 8 April. At this time he was on a north-easterly course at the latitude of Trondheim and in longitude 4° 30' East. The aircraft report caused him to change to 000° and later to 340°, which led him away from the scene of action. At noon on 9 April Admiral Forbes disposed in all of five battleships or battlecruisers, thirteen cruisers, one aircraft carrier, two flak cruisers and sixty-two destroyers.

For several hours on the afternoon of 9 April there were running attacks by German air units, firstly on Vice-Admiral Layton's squadron and then on the main forces. These were made by the German Bomber Groups K.G. 26 and K.G. 30, using Ju. 88's and He.111's. They claimed to have obtained a large number of hits on the British ships and also on a troop transport, but the results were actually as follows: Destroyer *Gurkha* sunk. One hit on *Rodney*, and slight damage through near misses on the cruisers *Southampton* and *Glasgow*. Numerous further near misses were observed by the British, but they caused no damage.

At 1824 on 9 April the German Naval Group Command West reported the situation as follows to the Commander-in-Chief:–

'Occupation of Narvik, Trondheim, Bergen, Stavanger, Kristiansand, Arandel completed. Occupation of Oslo by airborne troops proceeding. South of Oslo, resistance by coast and island fortifications. Norwegian Government has evacuated Oslo, events in Denmark according to plan'.

The German Naval Commander-in-Chief was now faced with the second part of his task, namely, the safeguarding of the return journey. From numerous reports received on 9 April, he realized that the tankers necessary for refuelling the German destroyers at Narvik and Trondheim had not arrived. *Hipper* reported at 1907:–

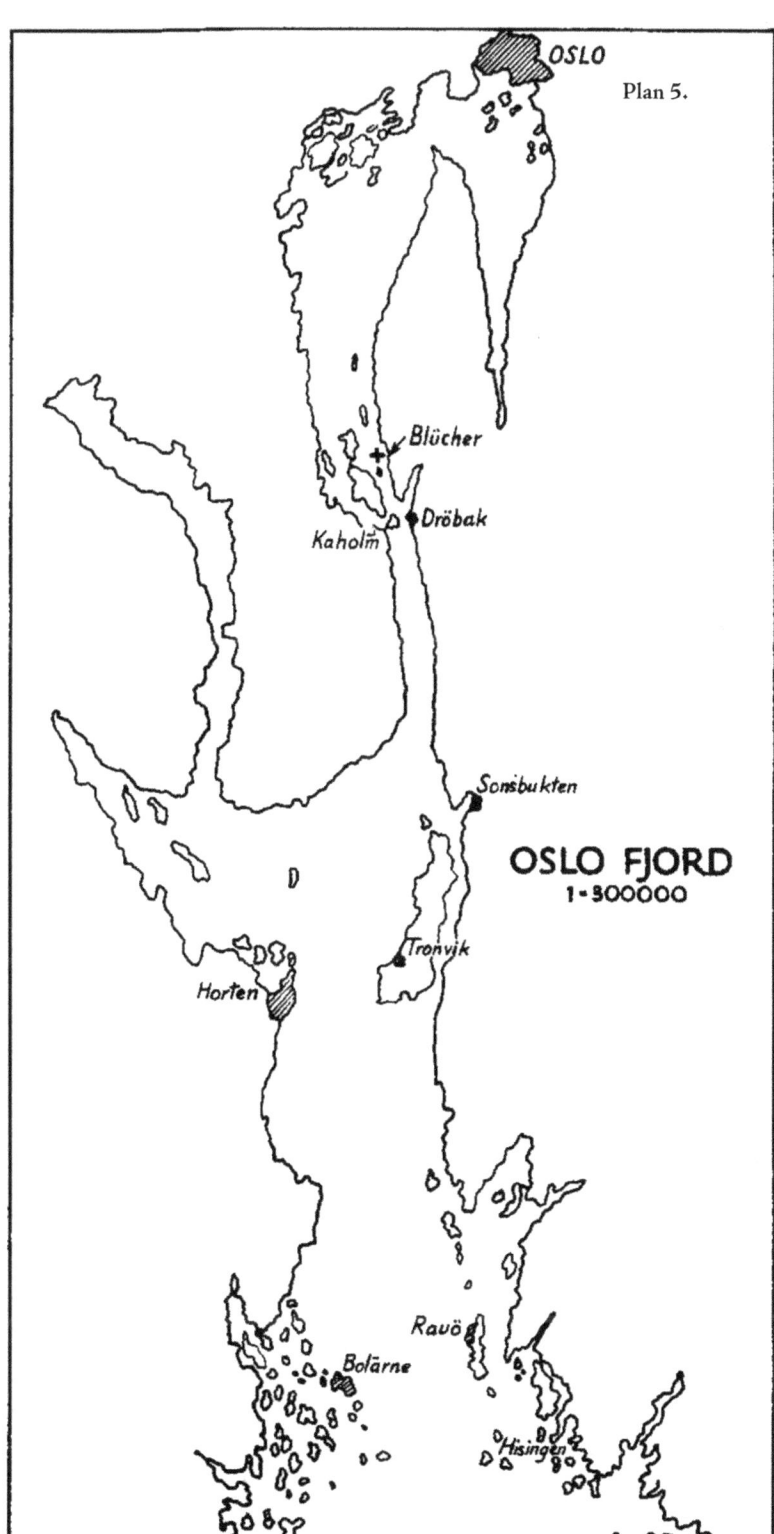

Plan 5.

'Am ready to proceed today on direct homeward journey with no reserve of fuel, two destroyers will be ready tomorrow. *Hipper* was sighted by British aircraft while leaving harbour'.[13]

At 2032, Naval Group West reported:–

'It is expected that the destroyers will leave Narvik in the evening of 10 April. Earlier departure of Group II from Trondheim at your discretion'.

Group West passed the following information about the enemy at 2043:–

'Southern Enemy Group consisting of four heavy ships (possibly including *Dunkerque*) three heavy and light cruisers, several flotillas in position 60° 30' N., 2° E., steering North. Five light cruisers with the 4th and 6th Destroyer Flotillas have received orders to attack an unidentified target. No indication of position of Northern Group consisting presumably of two British battlecruisers'.

Based on the available intelligence, the German Commander-in-Chief gave his intentions as follows:–

'Either the German battleships must join up with Groups I and II for the southward journey, or each group must return independently, in which case the battleships, by keeping well to the westward, will cause a diversion and so relieve the other groups.

'As *Hipper* is short of fuel, and the earliest time of departure of destroyers of both groups is not yet known, there seems no advantage in concentrating the battleships with Groups I and II and there would, in fact, be considerable loss of time, which would almost certainly provoke attacks by at least one of the enemy groups. Hence I have decided that the battleships shall return alone and, in view of the repairs still being made to *Scharnhorst*'s machinery, and the extreme visibility, both ships will proceed westward so as to break through from the north-west on the night of 11/12 April, passing close to the Shetlands'.

The Commander-in-Chief's decision corresponded to the requirements of the situation. It could be anticipated that the diversionary effect of this move would be greater than the advantage of a concentration of forces for the homeward journey, and the latter alternative could not be planned, as it was not known when the groups would be ready to proceed.

The Occupation Of Narvik (Plan 1)

The ten destroyers, under Kommodore Bonte, which had been detailed for Narvik were detached and arrived at Westfjord on the evening of 8 April. The Kommodore received a report at 2310 from Naval Group West, stating that one British cruiser and destroyer had been seen in Westfjord on that day. Consequently he warned his ships to expect contact with the enemy, and to have their torpedoes ready for immediate action. Early on the morning of 9 April he was informed that the Norwegian Government had ordered all coastal navigation lights to be extinguished, but this had obviously not been carried out everywhere, for most of the lights were on, and facilitated the approach in the prevailing frequent snowstorms. Tranøy was passed at 0300 and Baroe at 0410, without sighting the enemy. Shortly afterwards the formation passed two Norwegian patrol vessels, of which one reported by signal that eight warships were in Ofot Fjord. The destroyers passed the Narrows at Ramnes–Hamnes at 0440, land being in sight on both sides, but no fortifications were identifiable. Three destroyers were left there, under the Commanding Officer of the 3rd Destroyer Flotilla, to guard the Narrows and to occupy the fortifications that were presumed to be there. One destroyer was placed on patrol at Baroe, and the other two landed their troops without opposition, but no batteries were located. A Norwegian patrol vessel, enquiring as to the intentions of the destroyers, was informed that resistance would be useless. Shortly before arrival at Narvik three further destroyers under the Commanding Officer of the 4th Destroyer Flotilla were detached at Elvegaard and in Herjangs Fjord; there was no opposition. The two other destroyers landed their troops at Elvegaard some hours later.

In the meantime Kommodore Bonte took his three destroyers into Narvik and the Norwegian coastal defence ship *Eidsvold* came into view between snowstorms in the entrance at 0510. This vessel signalled to the

Germans to stop, and fired a shot near the stern of the Flotilla Leader. The Kommodore stopped his ships and sent a staff officer to negotiate with the Norwegian. After telephonic communication with the coastal defence vessel *Norge*, which was lying in the harbour, the Commanding Officer of the *Eidsvold* refused to agree to the German demands and trained his guns on the Flotilla Leader. As soon as the German staff officer had left the Norwegian ship he fired the agreed danger signal, a red Very light. The Norwegian ship was then hit by two torpedoes from *Wilhelm Heidkamp* (the German Flotilla Leader) and she broke in half and sank almost immediately. Only a few survivors could be picked up.

In the meantime the other two destroyers, *Arnim* and *Thiele*, had entered Narvik. While she was proceeding alongside *Arnim* was called on the morse lamp by the *Norge*, but as no answer was received the Norwegian ship opened fire at a range of 5,000 to 6,000 metres, using her 21 c.m. and 15 c.m. guns. The first salvo fell short, and the remainder went over the *Arnim* into the town. The German destroyer replied with all her port guns, while the assault company was already landing from her starboard side. The *Norge* shared the fate of the *Eidsvold*. After receiving two torpedo hits she capsized and sank. Fifty to sixty survivors were picked up.

The landing of the troops in Narvik occurred without further incident. Major-General Dietl, who was in command, took over the town from the Norwegian Commander, Colonel Sundlo without fighting, and at 0810 Kommodore Bonte reported to Group West that Narvik had been handed over to the German Army Commander. The task of the German destroyers was now completed, and they could have returned home the same evening if the tankers detailed for refuelling had arrived according to plan.

The harbour at Narvik was full of German and other shipping, but of the supply ships detailed for the operation only one had arrived in time; this was the tanker *Jan Wellem* from Murmansk. Thus the Mountain troops that were landed lacked guns and anti-aircraft weapons; the mountain guns embarked in the destroyers had been swept overboard by the sea, and these troops were supplied by the destroyers with all available machine guns, small arms and ammunition. No Norwegian guns were found ashore. The coastal defences that were believed to exist at Ramnes-Hamnes were not there. It had been intended to occupy them and use them as protection for the harbour entrance, and the troops that had been landed for this purpose were withdrawn, but the two destroyers required by Group XXI for support of the landing were to be retained at Narvik for local defence, and this was agreed to by the Kommodore. The further course of events rendered this decision void.

As only one tanker had arrived the departure of the ten destroyers, planned for the evening of 9 April, was impossible. Each destroyer required 500 to 600 tons of fuel and this was beyond the tanker's capacity. Only two destroyers could refuel at a time, and this took seven to eight hours so that the whole would not have been ready to leave until midnight on 10 April, *Arnim* and *Thiele* were refuelled first. At 1145 the Kommodore was informed that the second tanker could not be expected; when it became clear to Group West that the tankers for Narvik and Trondheim would not arrive in time, they were ordered to take up positions for refuelling the ships at sea. At 1457 Kommodore Bonte informed the Commander-in-Chief and Group West that he had decided not to sail until the evening of 10 April, after completing with fuel. Group West approved this decision and informed the Commander-in-Chief and Groups I and II of the positions of the tankers. He also informed all concerned that the U-Boats had taken up their inner positions for guarding the entrance to the fjords.

The position remained quiet at Narvik throughout 9 April. The Kommodore anticipated enemy counter-action by air or from British naval forces in Ofot Fjord. The absence of batteries at Ramnes-Hamnes was a disadvantage, but the Kommodore believed that the U-Boats would provide excellent protection. He expected that they would not only give early reports of the approach of enemy forces but would be able to inflict damage on them, and he asked Group West to instruct the U-Boats accordingly. He did not like keeping his ten destroyers in the narrow bay of Narvik longer than was absolutely necessary, and ordered the following disposition for the night of 10 April:– Five destroyers in Narvik for refuelling. Three destroyers at Herjangs Fjord and two destroyers in Ballangenfjord. The Senior Officer of the 3rd Destroyer Flotilla at Narvik was ordered to place one ship on patrol in the entrance to Narvik Bay and to have her relieved according to the refuelling situation. Further reference will be made later to the organisation of this patrol service, which was important in the light of subsequent events.

At 2122 a signal was received from *U-51* that five enemy destroyers were in sight in Westfjord steering south-west at medium speed. Since this course indicated that the ships were apparently leaving Westfjord, where their presence had already been reported, the signal from *U-51* caused no undue alarm.

The Occupation of Trondheim (Plan 2)

Group II, *Hipper* and four destroyers, under the Commanding Officer of *Hipper*, Captain Heye, approached Frohavet after dark on 8 April. Penetration into the fjord occurred without incident. When *Hipper* was in the Narrows at Kraagsvaag Fjord at 0400 on 9 April, she was told about the extinction of Norwegian coastal lights, and about an action in Oslo Fjord from which the Commanding Officer assumed that he would shortly be in action too. A Norwegian patrol vessel was sighted off Belan, and was approached, while showing navigation lights. To gain time *Hipper* sent a long morse signal to the vessel. The patrol vessel, after receiving this, demanded that *Hipper* should stop, and gave the alarm. The formation proceeded at 25 knots, and at 0430 passed a searchlight barrage. Shortly afterwards the Hysnes battery opened fire, which was returned by *Hipper* with her big guns, and before long the battery ceased fire without having obtained any hits. Three destroyers then began to disembark the Army troops in Strommen Bay for occupying the batteries, but disembarkation on the western side of the fjord had to be stopped as Norwegian batteries reopened fire. Meanwhile, *Hipper* with the four destroyers approached the town of Trondheim and troops were landed there without incident and without resistance. The troops landed at Strommen Bay did not succeed in taking the outer batteries, and for this reason disembarkation at Trondheim was stopped and the assault troops against the batteries were reinforced. *Hipper* weighed anchor in the afternoon, and proceeded towards the batteries to provide support with her guns. At this time a British reconnaissance machine flew over her.[14] All troops were landed during the night of 10 April, but it was not until the following evening that all the outer batteries were in German hands.

Captain Heye had requested air support to break down the resistance, and one flight from Fliegerkorps X was detailed for this purpose, but it had to be used instead at Oslo. No other air formations were available, and snow precluded the use of the landing ground at Trondheim.

Norwegian Venture: Battles for the Fjords 1940

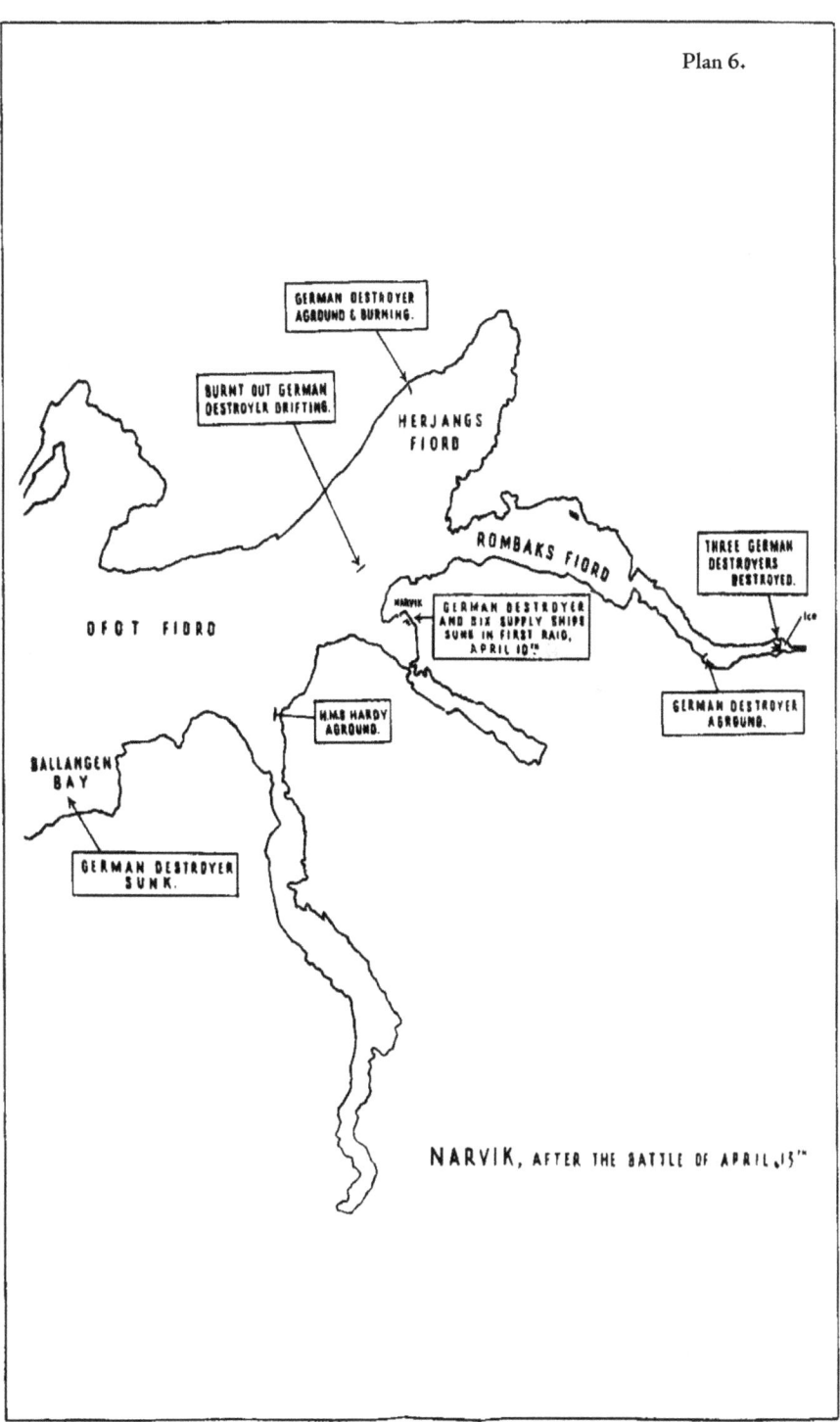

Plan 6.

Neither the tanker *Skagerrak* nor the other steamers had arrived in time at Trondheim. Group II needed 2,300 tons of fuel and only 800 tons were available in the town. When at 2042 Group West reported that the Narvik destroyers were expected to leave on the evening of 10 April and suggested that the Trondheim group should leave earlier, Captain Heye decided that in the unsettled situation *Hipper* should remain longer at Trondheim. All destroyers needed fuel, and *Hipper* had only enough remaining to proceed on the direct route home, which restricted her freedom of action. But as the ship had been sighted by British aircraft, it was probable that she would be attacked on the homeward journey. Captain Heye therefore decided to remain at Trondheim, although Group West had suggested that he should proceed with at least two destroyers on the night of 10 April to rendezvous with the tanker at sea. This was not an order from Group West, who rightly expected the local commander to decide for himself.

The Occupation of Bergen (Plan 3)

Group II, detailed for Bergen, was under Rear-Admiral Schmundt, Commander of the Scouting Forces. *Köln*, *Königsberg* and *Bremse* left Wilhelmshaven, at 0040, on 8 April and were to join up with torpedo boats and M.T.B.s from Cuxhaven and Heligoland at 1115, in 56° 20' N., 6° 20' E. The following are extracts from the situation report by the Rear-Admiral:–

> 'Particularly exposed to enemy action are the groups at Trondheim and Bergen. The first two are a long distance from the British bases, while Bergen is much nearer and can be reached from Scapa in eight to nine hours. Thus the British will probably go for Bergen first, although they may co-ordinate the operation with attacks further north.
>
> 'For the Bergen operation two older cruisers and two slow vessels (*Bremse* and *Karl Peters*) are available but maximum speed of advance will be 18 knots, which means that much of the approach will have to take place in daylight.
>
> 'Since the Narvik and Trondheim groups are a day ahead of Group II, it is likely that the latter will encounter British naval forces off the Norwegian coast. For this reason passage along the Norwegian coast in daylight is not possible if visibility is good,

neither can a roundabout route be used because of the slow speed. Thus, if there is contact with the enemy, escape to the eastward to Skagerrak is the only course. In this event the break-through of the fast ships (cruisers, torpedo boats and M.T.B.s) to Bergen may be possible, but this depends on the situation.'

In the forenoon there were several attacks by submarines on the cruisers, but torpedo tracks were spotted and avoiding action could be taken in all cases. The weather conditions were favourable to the advance. Visibility at 0850 was five to seven miles, with occasional rain and complete cloud cover, but two hours later visibility was 500 metres with very low clouds. Later and up to 1700 there was thick fog. Air escort had to be broken off and the rendezvous with the other units had to be postponed because of the fog, but this was not important in relation to the fact that, in spite of contact with enemy submarines, the further movements of our force were hidden from the British. Plan 4 shows that at 1700 on 8 April a British force of two cruisers and fifteen destroyers was only sixty miles from Group II, and between it and its objective at Bergen. It can only be ascribed to failure of air reconnaissance that these two forces did not come into action; the result would have been fatal to us in view of the British superiority in destroyers.

At 0000 on 9 April the formation was twelve miles west of Selbjoerne Fjord, and at 0044 turned eastward for the approach to Korsfjord. The night was clear, and Norwegian coastal lights were extinguished. At 0200, when passing the entrance to the fjord, the cruisers were picked up by searchlights, and a patrol vessel fired red lights. *Köln* made a recognition signal 'HMS *Cairo*', and during the further approach the ships were several times picked up and were hailed by morse signals. A reply was made in English to a shore signal station which fired several warning shots across the bows, but the formation continued its course. At 0430 a Norwegian torpedo boat was passed at short range. *Köln* signalled to her in English: 'I am proceeding to Bergen for a short visit,' and the Norwegian took no further action.

The ships then stopped at Stangen at the entrance to By Fjord and disembarked troops for occupying the batteries of Kvarven, which command the entrance to the fjord. To keep to the time-table for arrival at Bergen at 0515, it was not possible to await the capture of the batteries and the ships proceeded to force an entrance. As they turned into the fjord search lights appeared and the batteries, consisting of three 21 c.m. and three 10 c.m. guns, opened fire. *Köln* and the torpedo boats broke through without damage, but *Königsberg* received three hits and *Bremse* one hit. The effect on the former was a reduction in speed, while the latter's seaworthiness was affected.

Disembarkation of the troops at the pier occurred without interference, but there was slight resistance at one or two places when occupying the town. At 0700 four German aircraft – He.111's – appeared over the town. Shortly afterwards the Sandviken battery (two 24 c.m. guns) opened fire on *Köln*, and the flak battery opened fire on the aircraft. When *Köln* and *Königsberg* replied to the fire and the aircraft dropped bombs the batteries ceased fire. Disembarkation was completed at 0820, and shortly afterwards the Sandviken and Kvarven batteries were captured. The Norwegian Captain of the port then arranged details of the surrender with the German Admiral of the West Coast of Norway, who was embarked in *Karl Peters*. A Norwegian minesweeper was taken in charge and numerous merchant ships in the harbour were forbidden to leave or to use their radio. The ships of the 1st Sea Transport Division, having by now reached the outer fjord, were escorted into the harbour by the motor torpedo boats.

The task of Group III was completed and the Commander summed up the situation at 1100 as follows:–

(i) The landing has been completed, but the situation ashore is not secure, as the batteries are not yet ready for action.
(ii) *Königsberg* is not fit to go to sea.
(iii) Strong enemy forces are reported at sea and they will presumably be close to Bergen by the afternoon, so that an attack from seaward is probable.

However, Admiral Schmundt decided to commence the return journey in the evening with *Köln* and the torpedo boats, and to leave the damaged *Königsberg* behind to serve as harbour protection. The *Königsberg*'s aircraft was launched at 1330 for reconnaissance at sea and returned at 1800 with a report that no enemy was visible between Kors Fjord and Skudesnes. At 1900 the formation was attacked by six Vickers-Wellington bombers. The attack was pressed home vigorously and the bombs fell close, but there were no hits. One aircraft dived towards *Köln* firing machine guns, which resulted in three dead and five wounded, and one enemy aircraft was shot down.

At 2000 Admiral Schmundt proceeded to sea for the return journey with *Köln* and two torpedo boats. The *Königsberg*'s aircraft had been flown off again and reported at 2005 that the coast was clear. Between 2100 and 2130 three enemy aircraft made several attacks on the ships, without result. The departure of the ships had now been discovered, and the Admiral concluded from interception of enemy radio traffic that British light cruisers and several destroyer flotillas were proceeding towards the exits from Bergen.[15] In these circumstances he decided to give up the breakthrough for this night. To gain space to the south and to avoid detection he decided to proceed in the darkness inside the Leads to Mauranger Fjord, a secondary fjord of Hardanger, which is only 800 metres wide and protected against reconnaissance by high cliffs.

The Landings on the South-West Coast

Group IV (Kristiansand and Arandel) left Wesermunde, where it had been got ready, at 0500 on 8 April, and was under the command of the Captain of *Karlsruhe*, Captain Rieve. Visibility was good but in the afternoon fell to 30 metres, and fog remained during the night, having spread from the west into the Skagerrak. This prevented approach to the Norwegian coast according to time-table, and hence the schedule could not be maintained.

On 9 April, at 0345, the 200 metre line off the entrance to Kristiansand was reached in thick fog, and the fog did not improve until 0600 when the ships could make each other out. At 0630 the formation, led by *Karlsruhe*, entered the fjord. The ships had only just passed the lighthouses at Oksoe and Groenningen when the Norwegian batteries on the elevated island of Oddery, commanding the approach to the town, opened fire with two 21 c.m., six 15 c.m. and four 24 c.m. Howitzers. The range was about 5,000 metres and the fire was heavy, so that the tactical situation was most unfavourable to the ships, which were full of troops. Since the ships were in single line ahead and the batteries were dead ahead, *Karlsruhe* could only use her forward turret. Captain Rieve therefore ordered a 180° turn, and covered the retreat of the ships by dropping smoke floats. Shortly after 0700 a second attempt to enter was made after five aircraft had dropped bombs on the batteries, but this attempt also failed. The Norwegian batteries again fired some accurate salvoes, and again the ships had to withdraw under cover of artificial fog and smoke.

Captain Rieve then decided to reform outside the entrance to the fjord, and to approach on courses which would allow all guns to bear on the batteries. The torpedo boats were to be sent in to land their troops under the protection of *Karlsruhe*'s guns. The ships began to fire at 0750 and continued for half an hour at ranges of 13,000 to 14,000 metres, but before the torpedo boats could enter thick fog set in and prevented the landing operation. In this difficult situation Captain Rieve decided, at 0925, to force an entrance alone with *Karlsruhe*, but this attempt also failed. The cruiser missed the entrance and very nearly went on the rocks.

The weather cleared sufficiently by 1100 to continue the operation. In the meantime assault troops had been embarked in three motor torpedo boats. When the ships, with torpedo boats and M.T.B.s, again entered the fjord the Norwegian batteries did not fire, and troops were landed without opposition. Shortly afterwards the batteries on Oddery were captured by assault troops. *Karlsruhe* anchored in the harbour at 1145, and disembarkation of troops in Kristiansand was completed by 1500. There was only slight resistance in the town.

By 1700 the town and defences were occupied by Army troops, and Rear-Admiral Schenk took over command of the Norwegian south coast. Three ships of the 1st Sea Transport Division, with troops and equipment, entered the harbour during the afternoon.

In the forenoon the torpedo boat *Greif* landed troops at Arandel without resistance, and the same occurred at the Cable Station in Egersund where Group VI, with four minesweepers, landed 150 men. The torpedo boats and minesweepers then proceeded to Kristiansand. *Karlsruhe* and three torpedo boats left at 1900 for the Baltic. The incidents during this journey will be referred to later.

Stavanger was occupied by airborne troops according to plan early on 9 April. During the operation the steamer *Roda* of the 1st Sea Transport Division, was sunk in the harbour by the Norwegian torpedo boat *Sleitner*, who was herself sunk almost immediately by German bombs.

The Occupation of Oslo (Plan 5)

The assault group for Oslo was collected in Kiel Bay under Rear-Admiral Kummetz, flying his flag in the new heavy cruiser *Blücher*, and commenced the journey to Oslo Fjord at 0300 on 8 April. The main body of the troops was embarked in the cruisers *Blücher*, *Lützow* and *Emden* and similar parties, embarked in minesweepers and torpedo boats, were to be landed before passing the Droebak Narrows to occupy the fortified islands of Bolaerne and Ranoey, and the naval harbour at Horten. In case the Droebak Narrows should prove unpassable, alternative landing places for the Oslo troops were to be at Moss and Sonsbukten. After Skagen was passed, at 1900, there were attacks by submarines, and it was possible to take avoiding action when torpedo tracks were sighted. The entrance to Oslo Fjord was reached at midnight; the outer coastal lights were extinguished. A Norwegian torpedo boat illuminated the formation and fired a shot across the bows of the torpedo boat *Albatros,* who attempted to go alongside the Norwegian but was rammed by the latter. A few shots sufficed to sink the Norwegian vessel; fourteen of whose crew were saved. Shortly afterwards a patrol boat off Ranoey signalled to the formation, and the coastal batteries at Ranoey and Bolaerne put a searchlight barrier on to the ships and fired warning shots at 0050. The ships continued their course, visibility becoming poor, but the trans-shipment of the assault troops for landing at the entrance could be carried out without interference, and was completed by 0330. The weather became clearer and at 0440, with the commencement of dawn, the main formation was at the entrance to the Droebak Narrows. *Blücher* was illuminated, but as nothing further occurred Rear-Admiral Kummetz assumed that there would be no further resistance and that a rapid entrance would possible.

When *Blücher* was about 500 metres from the entrance in growing daylight the coastal batteries opened fire; to port the 28 c.m. battery at Oskarsburg, and to starboard the 15 c.m. at Droebak. Subsequent events occurred so rapidly that it was impossible to cancel the plan to force entrance, and for *Blücher* it was a question of passing the danger zone as quickly as possible. Unfortunately the formation's speed of advance was only 12 knots. The action report does not explain why maximum speed was not used. It would have allowed the ships to pass the batteries quickly, and would have lessened the effectiveness of their fire. *Blücher* increased to full speed when fire was opened, but there was no time for this to have any effect.

Blücher very soon received two hits from 28 c.m. guns and at least twenty from 15 c.m. guns which caused severe damage[16]. The second 28 c.m. shell set the aircraft hangar and both aircraft on fire, and this caused a major petrol fire. The second hit damaged the steering gear. As the ship at that moment was under port helm, she turned towards Kaholm, and only by going astern on her starboard engine could she avoid the rocks. At this juncture there were two heavy explosions in the ship. She had been struck by two torpedoes from the battery at Kaholm. In spite of this *Blücher* still proceeded slow ahead, and after only three or four minutes of action the enemy guns became silent as the ship got out of their arc of fire. A reply to the enemy fire was hardly possible, since the shore targets could not be identified. As the torpedo hits had put the engines out of action, the Captain decided to anchor. In spite of the heavy damage she had received there was no apparent danger of the ship becoming lost, and the Chief Engineer believed that the outer engines could be made serviceable. The ship at this time was listing 12°, which later increased to 18°. The raging fires constituted the chief danger, and when at 0630 a 10.5 c.m. magazine, situated in the centre of the ship, which could not be flooded, blew up, the ship's fate was sealed. At 0700 the Commanding Officer ordered her to be abandoned. Half an hour later she capsized and sank. The survivors, crew and Army troops were able to swim ashore, and were taken prisoner by the Norwegians.

In conclusion it may be said that it would certainly have been better to use the torpedo boat *Möwe* to lead the formation through the Narrows in order to test the reaction of the Norwegian batteries. If she had been attacked she could easily have used smoke and alterations of course to withdraw from the danger zone.

After the disappearance of *Blücher*, the command of the Oslo Group fell to the Commanding Officer of *Lützow*, Captain Thiele. *Lützow* had entered into the action as far as her position astern of *Blücher* permitted, and had received three hits, one of which temporarily silenced her forward 28 c.m. turret. Captain Thiele rightly withdrew the rest of the formation from the danger zone, since he considered the conditions impossible for forcing the Narrows. He decided to land the troops at Sonsbukten and to attack the defences of the Droebak Narrows from land and from the sea. The disembarkation was completed without resistance by 0910.

Meanwhile it had been reported that the landing of troops at Ranoey and Bolaerne had not so far succeeded. At Horten only small Army and Naval units had been landed, and the entry of the torpedo boats and minesweepers into the harbour had been impeded by vigorous fire from the Norwegian warships lying there, minesweeper R.17 being sunk. Hence the Captain of *Lützow* ordered the troops that were embarked in these vessels to be landed at Sonsbukten and Tronvik, where there were naval installations. At 1530 Horten hoisted the white flag. The assault troops that had been landed in the morning had obtained its surrender without fighting. At the same time Ranoey was reported occupied, but it was not until the evening of 10 April that the defences at Bolaerne ceased resistance and capitulated. During the fighting for Bolaerne, the torpedo boat *Albatros* ran ashore and could not be hauled off with available resources.

Army Group XXI issued the following directive for the commencement of the attack on the Droebak Narrows:–

'The main point of the operation consists in the taking of Droebak. It is unimportant whether taken from the sea or the land.'

Naval Group East then ordered the Commanding Officer of *Lützow* to support the Army troops, with the proviso that the ships were not to be jeopardised. Captain Thiele prepared an attack for the afternoon of 9 April, using all available ships and boats. *Lützow* and *Emden* were to provide protective fire, while the torpedo boats and minesweepers were to penetrate and set their troops ashore for the capture of the batteries. Several preliminary air attacks took place, in order to weaken the resistance of the batteries. The operation was completely successful. At 1900 the troops were able to report the occupation of Droebak without a fight, while the negotiations for the surrender at Kahlom were protracted until the following morning. The torpedo boat *Kondor* and the minesweepers proceeded through the Narrows on the night of 10 April to collect the crew of the *Blücher*. At 0900 on 10 April the German flag was hoisted on Kaholm. The cruiser formation then passed the Narrows to Oslo, where they arrived at 1145.

At Oslo the situation had developed as follows:– On 9 April at 0800 the first German aircraft appeared over the town and the Norwegian flak opened fire, but was unable to prevent the aerodrome at Oslo-Fornebo from falling into German hands. At noon six companies of airborne troops landed there and occupied important points in the town. The political situation was obscure. Quisling was trying to form a new Government with German support, but there was no response among the population. The old Government did not resign, but withdrew to the interior. Discussions between the King and the German Ambassador were fruitless. The former absolutely refused to hand over the Government to Quisling, or to consider the matter at all. The German Naval Attaché in Oslo reported that 'in Oslo no German action had been expected until news arrived that the steamer *Rio de Janeiro* had been torpedoed'. It was not until the night of 9 April that the serious decision was made which led to Norwegian resistance. If the German warships had entered Oslo early on 9 April without fighting, then he believed that agreement with the King and the Government would have been possible.[17] Even after the fighting at Oslo the Germans considered a rapid termination of the war to be politically feasible.

The Occupation of the Danish Ports

The occupation of Denmark took place according to plan on 9 April. Apart from a few small incidents there was no opposition by the Danes. A brief summary of the operation follows:–

The leading ship of Group VII, the battleship *Schleswig-Holstein* under Captain Kleikamp, ran aground temporarily on the Vengeance Bank in the Great Belt, owing to compass failure. Her troops were trans-shipped to other units to continue the journey and landed unopposed at 0600 on 9 April at Korsoer and Nyborg. In co-operation with Danish officials they took charge of the ferry there. Hansestadt-Danzig of Group VIII landed troops at the same time in Copenhagen, returned on the same day to Warnemuende, and embarked troops, taking them to Roenne for the occupation of Bornholm. Group IX occupied the bridge over the Little Belt at Middelfahrt and the ferry at Gjedser. Minesweeping units entered Esbjezg and Thyboroen while Army troops entered Jutland and met with very slight local opposition. A motorised rifle regiment arrived on the evening of 9 April at the Little Belt bridge for anti-aircraft protection, and some of the naval vessels then proceeded from there to occupy Aarhus.

Vice-Admiral Mevis, Commanding Coast of Denmark, arrived at Copenhagen on 9 April and reached agreement with the Danish authorities, whereby Germany took over the defence of territorial waters from the Danish Police, and also supervised the Danish minefields in the Belts.

On the evening of 9 April the Naval War Staff remarked as follows:–

To sum up, the advance of the naval forces and the landing operations in Norwegian and Danish harbours were favoured by luck, and were successful. Surprise could not be guaranteed and there had been signs of stiffening resistance among the Norwegians. The losses incurred, particularly the latest heavy cruiser *Blücher*, are painful, but in view of the risk cannot be considered as excessive.

The situation has been made more difficult for the return journey of the naval forces in that the enemy's minelaying in Norwegian Territorial Waters, and his planned occupation of Norwegian bases, coincides with our operation. Since enemy troop transports were in company with his battleships when they were attacked by the German Air Force, it can be assumed that he was about to land and still intends to do so. In the northern part of the North Sea, as far as the Lofoten, numerous and powerful British and French naval forces are present. The danger of air attacks on the German occupied bases is serious, having regard to the weakness of flak protection and the likelihood of attacks by carrier borne aircraft. The danger of S/M attacks in the Kattegat and Skagerrak is realized, and the protection of transports and reinforcements on the route to Oslo is a heavy burden.

The Naval Staff considers the following tasks most urgent:–

(i) Return to home ports, as soon as possible, of the battleships and of all naval forces at present in Norway.
(ii) Strengthening of the Skagerrak mine barrage against enemy surface forces.
(iii) Concentration of German U-Boats off Narvik and Trondheim.
(iv) German anti-submarine operation by all available forces in the Kattegat and Skagerrak.
(v) Escort for the Sea Transport Divisions.
(vi) Request to the political authorities to arrange for reinforcements using Swedish and Norwegian railways, as reinforcements through the western ports of Norway are not feasible, and continuous control of the waters in the Kattegat and Skagerrak cannot be guaranteed because of enemy submarines.'

Events in the Landing Ports and the Homeward Journey of the Naval Forces

10 April in Narvik

When dawn broke on 10 April in Narvik Bay a snowstorm limited visibility to between 100 and 1,000 metres. Two destroyers were refuelling in the harbour from the tanker *Jan Wellem*. Three others were lying at anchor, two in the inner harbour and one nearer the entrance.

About 0530 a number of heavy explosions occurred in the harbour, and great columns of water rose near the destroyers and steamers and at the quays. The surprise was so complete that an air attack was surmised. A few seconds later *Heidkamp*, at anchor in the inner harbour, was hit aft by a torpedo which caused the after magazine to blow up, and the after part of the ship broke off; Kommodore Bonte was killed. A shell struck the port side of the bridge. The ship remained afloat and was secured alongside a steamer. At the same time the destroyer *Schmitt* in the inner harbour was struck by a shell, followed shortly by a torpedo in the forward engine room, and a second torpedo in the after boiler room, causing the ship to break in half, each part sinking almost at once. Further torpedoes sank or damaged merchant ships in the harbour or exploded on the banks.

The destroyer *Roeder* then observed gun flashes coming from the harbour entrance, and later identified and opened fire on a destroyer. Eight torpedoes were also fired in the direction of the harbour entrance without result. *Roeder* very soon received many hits, causing fires and other damage. The Commanding Officer attempted to get under way, but the anchor gear being out of action through shellfire, he could not slip his cable; so he went astern, dragging the anchor, and brought the stern alongside the pier. In view of the heavy damage he considered the ship to be lost, and ordered her to be abandoned.

As soon as the action commenced the two German destroyers lying alongside slipped their wires. *Lüdemann* received two hits which put one gun out of action, and caused a fire which necessitated the flooding of the after magazine. The other destroyer, *Künne*, was not hit, but her engines were temporarily out of action owing to the concussion from the torpedo hit on the destroyer *Schmitt*, which was only 40 metres away. Both destroyers fired on the enemy's gun flashes at the harbour entrance but could not identify their targets.

Who was the attacker and how had it been possible for him to achieve a complete surprise attack on the German destroyers? Captain Warburton-Lee who, with the 2nd Destroyer Flotilla, was patrolling the entrance to Westfjord on the morning of 9 April, after the action with *Scharnhorst* and *Gneisenau,* received Admiralty instructions in the early afternoon to proceed to Narvik where, according to a Press report, one German ship had entered and had landed a small number of troops. When Captain Warburton-Lee in *Hardy* with *Hotspur, Havoc, Hunter* and *Hostile* arrived off the Pilot Station at Tranøy, he asked for information about the situation in Narvik and was told that six ships 'larger than *Hardy*' had been seen proceeding to Narvik; that the harbour entrance was heavily mined, and that the port was occupied in force. The pilots estimated that the British would need double the number of ships. Captain Warburton-Lee reported this to the Admiralty, the Commander-in-Chief, Home Fleet, and to Admiral Whitworth, and added 'intend attacking at dawn high water'. The Admiralty left the decision to him whether, under the circumstances, he was to attack or not, and stated 'we shall support whatever decision you take'. Captain Warburton-Lee kept to his purpose. As it was still too early to proceed to Narvik he took the flotilla down the fjord, and turned back again at midnight for the approach. It was during his run to seaward that 'V-51' sighted and reported the formation.[18]

Both the British and German Admiralty were mistaken in believing that the entrance to the Narvik Fjord was fortified; Captain Warburton-Lee had been warned of the batteries which, in fact, did not exist, and the approach of the destroyers to Narvik took place without incident, though the snowstorm rendered navigation difficult. However, the British flotilla was at the harbour entrance on time at break of dawn on 10 April. Three successive approaches were made by his ships with the results already described. For the first approach he left *Hotspur* and

Hostile behind to watch the side fjords outside the harbour entrance. Since no enemy showed up there, he ordered the two destroyers to take part in the further attacks. The return fire by the German destroyers was ineffective, except for a hit which *Hostile* received during the third run.

While *Hardy* was turning to the west during the third approach, one supposed cruiser and three destroyers appeared to the northward coming out of Herjangs Fjord, at a distance of 10,000 metres. Captain Warburton-Lee increased to 30 knots and proceeded down the fjord with his ships. Shortly afterwards two further warships were sighted right ahead, coming from seaward, and it was hoped that these were coming to support the British.

These two formations were the German destroyers that had spent the night in Herjangs Fjord and Ballangen Fjord. At 0615 the 4th Destroyer Flotilla at Herjangs Fjord had received a radio warning of the attack on Narvik, and had proceeded towards the town at 0630. Ten minutes later they opened fire on the enemy as he was proceeding seawards. The action developed into a chase on a westerly course. The British fall of shot was short at first, and remained ineffective.[19] The German 1st Destroyer Flotilla from Ballangen, delayed by local fog, proceeded at 0640 on a northerly course into Ofot Fjord, and, when the enemy came in sight to the eastward, turned towards him. The British were now attacked from both sides; on their starboard quarter they were pursued by the Herjangs Group, and ahead were the destroyers from Ballangen. The action with the latter, who turned on to a westerly course, developed at close range and caused losses to the British. *Hardy* was so heavily hit that she hauled out of line, and had to be beached. Captain Warburton-Lee shared the fate of his German opponent; he was mortally wounded by a hit on the bridge. *Hunter* and *Hotspur* were heavily hit, and the Germans observed their torpedoes to hit. According to the British several explosions occurred in *Hunter* and fire broke out; she lost speed and came into collision with *Hotspur*, who had been following her. At this moment *Hotspur's* steering gear was damaged, but after a short interval she succeeded in getting clear of *Hunter* and, in spite of heavy damage, joined up with *Havoc* and *Hostile*. The latter were almost undamaged. The damage to *Hunter* necessitated her being sunk in deep water. After the action, *Hostile*, *Havoc* and *Hotspur* withdrew to the westward, and in the entrance to the fjord they met the German supply ship *Rauenfels*, which was sunk.

From the German action reports it appears that the heavy losses suffered by the British destroyers in this sector were entirely due to the German destroyers from Ballangen, namely *Thiele* and *Arnim*, who themselves had received hits affecting their gunfire. During the action, at 0715, the two German groups passed each other to starboard on opposite courses and *Thiele* and *Arnim* turned into line astern of the Herjangs Group for a running fight; but owing to the damage they had suffered they soon broke off to enter Narvik, leaving the Herjangs Group to pursue the enemy. The three destroyers of the Herjangs Group, *Zenker*, *Koellner* and *Giese*, were undamaged, and had scored few, if any, hits on their opponent. They had not refuelled and at the end of the action their tanks were empty, so they had to abandon the pursuit. They fired on *Hardy*, who was aground, in order to make her unserviceable, and then picked up fifty survivors from *Hunter*. Ten of these died later. The German destroyers then proceeded into Narvik.

The losses and damage suffered by the Germans in this action were as follows:–

Schmitt – sunk, fifty dead.
Heidkamp – sinking, eighty-one dead.
Roeder – five hits, unseaworthy, thirteen dead.
Lüdemann – two hits, magazines partly flooded, two dead.
Künne – splinter damage, engines usable.
Thiele – several hits, two guns out of action, fire, magazine flooded, thirteen dead.
Arnim – five hits, boiler out of action, barely seaworthy.
Zenker, Koellner and *Giese* – undamaged, half the ammunition expended.

In spite of the heavy losses sustained by the British the tactical success was theirs, and the strategical effect was to prevent the return home of the German destroyers, which had been planned for the night of 11 April. The course of the action had shown the perilous situation of the British flotilla attacking Narvik, because of the flanking positions of the Germans at Herjangs Fjord. No plan existed on 9 April for co-ordinating the movements of the three German destroyer groups at Narvik, Herjangs and Ballangen in the event of a British attack, and yet this distribution of ships afforded a most favourable opportunity for dealing with an enemy attack. If the alarm had been raised in sufficient time, the British destroyer flotilla could have been attacked from three sides and annihilated.

There was an immediate and detailed investigation in Narvik of the circumstances which led to the German destroyers being taken completely by surprise. But it could not be established what orders Kommodore Bonte had given for the patrol, since he was no longer available. It is certain that he ordered a destroyer to patrol the entrance, but it was not known whether this patrol had been ordered for the harbour entrance only, or for the outer position to the westward in Ofot Fjord, in the Ramnes-Hamnes Narrows. Only the latter position would have provided sufficient warning. The first patrol destroyer – *Künne* – was in Ofot Fjord, and the *Schmitt* and *Roeder* were on guard in the immediate vicinity of the harbour entrance. There were doubts about the period of time covered by the patrol. The Commanding Officer of the 3rd Destroyer Flotilla stated that *Roeder* had been told by him to remain on patrol until relieved by *Lüdemann*, but the entry in *Roeders*' diary reads: 'am relieving *Schmitt* from 0400 as anti-submarine patrol in the harbour entrance until dawn', and this ship entered the harbour shortly after 0500. Thus at the critical moment the patrol position was unoccupied.

Kommodore Bonte had relied for protection chiefly on the U-boats stationed in the outer fjords. On 11 April the Commanding Officer of U-46 stated that conditions in the fjords did not allow U-boats to perform an efficient patrol. According to *U-46* British destroyers constantly kept U-boats under water through dropping depth charges, and the nights were too short and light to allow regular charging of the batteries. In addition visibility had become so poor on the night of the attack that observation was ineffective. In spite of good opportunities for torpedo hits there were instances of torpedo failures in the area of Westfjord, and no hits were scored. The fault was mainly due to the magnetic pistols which, in the latitude of Northern Norway, were subjected to quite different magnetic influences from those existing in the North Sea and the Baltic. The depth keeping of the torpedoes was also unsatisfactory, so that torpedoes with the normal contact pistol often passed under the target.

The Last Fight of the German Destroyers at Narvik

After the death of Kommodore Bonte the command of the Narvik destroyers passed to the Senior Officer of the 4th Destroyer Flotilla, Captain Bey. After reporting the situation to Naval Group West he received instructions to refuel those destroyers which were fit for sea, and to use personnel and equipment from the damaged destroyers to support the Army ashore. The survivors of the *Heidkamp* and *Schmitt* were formed into the naval battalion 'Erdmenger', and equipment and ammunition was salved from *Heidkamp* and *Roeder* (Plan 6).

At 1544 on 10 April, Group West ordered the seaworthy destroyers at Narvik to be ready to sail that night to join the Commander-in-Chief. At this time only *Giese* and *Zenker* were ready for sea, and refuelling of *Koellner* could not be completed before 0100. At 2044 Captain Bey with *Giese* and *Zenker* sailed. At Tranøy he contacted a British patrol. The night was clear and light, and one cruiser and two destroyers could be distinguished at a great distance. Captain Bey decided that it would be useless to break through and, in view of the good visibility, he did not wish to break out to the northward through Tjeld Sound and Vaagsfjord, since he estimated that the enemy were watching this also. He took his two destroyers back to Narvik and at noon reported to Group West that a break out that evening was impossible.

Group West was anxious to get all seaworthy destroyers out of Narvik as soon as possible, and kept the Commanding Officer of the 4th Destroyer Flotilla currently informed of the enemy position. At 1540/12 Captain Bey was told to seize any opportunity of bad visibility at night to break out, but in view of the short nights he expected to have to wait some time for the requisite conditions. On the afternoon of 12 April he reported that *Lüdemann* and *Künne* were ready for sea in all respects, that *Giese*, *Arnim* and *Thiele* would shortly be ready with 28 knots, and *Zenker* with 20 knots, because of propeller damage. *Koellner* was seriously damaged and fit only for local defence. During the night *Koellner* and *Zenker* had been aground and as a result the former was unfit for sea, and the latter had damaged propellers. *Koellner* was to be used as a defence battery near the bridge at Taarstad in the eastern entrance of Ramnes-Hamnes, *Roeder* was to be used for local defence in the harbour. A standing patrol had been established in Ofot Fjord.

At 1845, nine enemy biplanes attacked the harbour without hitting the destroyers. Bomb splinters caused some casualties, mostly on land, and two British aircraft were lost. The attack delayed the work on *Koellner*, whose movement to Taarstad had to be postponed until the following night. When *U-64* entered Narvik late on 12 April she reported having seen searchlights from darkened ships in the entrance to Westfjord, which was heavily patrolled by enemy destroyers.

On the same day the Germans received the first indication of a major enemy attack on Narvik. Radio interception showed that this was planned for the afternoon of 13 April. At 0144/13, Group West sent the following signal to Narvik:–

'German aircraft reported the following warships to be in Westfjord at the Narrows at Tranøy on the afternoon of 12 April: one big ship with two funnels, one smaller ship with one funnel, four torpedo boats and three destroyers further out'.

At 1010 a further signal received at Narvik stated that enemy action was expected that afternoon, and that *Repulse*, *Warspite*, five Tribals, four other destroyers and an aircraft carrier would take part. The Senior Officer of Destroyers at Narvik then ordered the following:–

(i) Disposition of all seaworthy destroyers in the side fjords, so as to effect the encirclement of British light forces, as occurred on 10 April.
(ii) Destroyers unfit for sea are to be ready for action by 1300.
(iii) Immediate move of *Koellner* to Taarstad for use as local defence.

At noon *Koellner* escorted by *Künne* was in Ofot Fjord on the way to the anchorage at Taarstad, with three miles to go, when a British aircraft was seen to the west. Ten minutes later *Künne* in prevailing clear weather sighted nine British destroyers off Baroe, and reported that they were breaking through. This was the first enemy contact on 13 April – a day fatal to the German destroyers.

The British attackers were 'Force B' under Vice-Admiral Whitworth, consisting of *Warspite* and nine destroyers – *Bedouin*, *Punjabi*, *Eskimo*, *Cossack*, *Kimberley*, *Forester*, *Icarus*, *Hero* and *Foxhound*. The British

Admiralty regarded the recapture of Narvik as having priority over all other Norwegian operations. Admiral Forbes, whose main forces had concentrated with Admiral Whitworth's battlecruisers in the Lofoten area on 12 April, received orders that afternoon 'for cleaning up enemy naval forces and batteries in Narvik by using a battleship, heavily escorted by destroyers, with synchronized dive-bombing attacks from *Furious*'. He ordered Admiral Whitworth to carry out the attack with this force on 13 April. *Furious* was to co-ordinate attacks by bombers on the coastal defences that were assumed to be in the fjord, and on sea and land targets in Narvik.

On the forenoon of 13 April 'Force B' with destroyers as anti-submarine and anti-mine escort proceeded up the fjord, and by 1252 (German time)[20] had reached a position five miles west of Baroe, while *Warspite*'s aircraft was launched on a reconnaissance flight which was to prove of the greatest value. Shortly afterwards a Swordfish aircraft from *Furious* was sighted and it was concluded that the air attacks which had been ordered were already in progress. The fortifications at Baroe and in the Ramnes Narrows could not be bombed, as they did not exist.

On first sighting the enemy the German destroyer *Künne* was about 22,000 metres away. The range was closed to about 20,000 metres when the destroyer turned to an opposite course, and while turning the enemy opened fire, his shots falling very short. As *Koellner* could not reach the position in Taarstad in time, she turned to the south and entered Djupvik Bay where she was concealed from seaward by a cliff promontory, which provided an excellent flank position, but this could not be exploited as had been hoped. When the first British destroyers appeared beyond the point, *Koellner* opened fire with all guns at about 3,500 metres. This attack did not altogether surprise the British, for the *Warspite*'s aircraft had spotted the German destroyer in her hideout in good time, and had reported her. The torpedoes fired by *Koellner* missed. Three or four British destroyers concentrated their fire on her, and *Warspite* also joined in. *Koellner* was very soon shot up, and her bows were blown off by a torpedo; at 1315 she sank, with 31 killed and 34 wounded.

Meanwhile *Künne*, who had given the alarm, had withdrawn from the British towards Narvik. She laid a smokescreen across the fjord to conceal the departure of the remaining Narvik destroyers, but the screen was soon scattered by the wind.

When the alarm was received in Narvik the proposed disposition of destroyers in the side fjords had not yet materialized. Some of the destroyers had not yet raised steam, as the departure had been ordered for 1300. *Lüdemann* was the first to leave at 1215, followed by *Zenker* and *Arnim*, but *Thiele* and *Giese* were not ready.

When the departing destroyers had reached Ballangen Fjord the enemy was within range. At 1245 *Lüdemann* opened fire at 17,000 metres. The ensuing action was fought on the German side by *Künne*, *Lüdemann*, *Zenker*, later *Arnim*, and at 1340 *Thiele*, and lasted nearly one and a half hours. It is remarkable that in spite of the length of the action the result on either side was almost nothing, although both sides claimed to have secured many hits on their opponent. In this action the German destroyers received no hits whatever. On the British side *Punjabi* was temporarily out of action owing to a break in the main steam pipe, and all her guns were temporarily unserviceable. There was no result either from the attack by carrier-borne aircraft from *Furious*, which had been planned as part of the operation. The German destroyers, which had been gradually driven towards the entrance of Herjangs Fjord, found themselves at 1315 with practically no ammunition left, since they had expended quite a lot on 10 April. Captain Bey therefore ordered a withdrawal to Rombaks Fjord. The Commanding Officer of *Künne* did not receive this order and, after expending all his ammunition, beached his ship on the north bank of the fjord and blew her up. The explosion broke off the after part of the ship which floated for several days. The remaining four destroyers escaped into Rombaks Fjord.

At this time *Giese* came into view at the entrance to the harbour and was immediately engaged by six British destroyers, from whose concentrated fire she received many hits. At 1430 her Captain, having expended all his ammunition, ordered the sinking ship to be abandoned. Eighty-three officers and men lost their lives. While *Giese* was sinking in the Bay of Narvik *Warspite* with a group of destroyers advanced towards the harbour, from which the remaining destroyer *Roeder*, who was no longer capable of moving, was firing. Her fire was at first believed to be coming from a coastal battery. *Cossack*, *Foxhound* and *Kimberley* penetrated into the harbour. At ranges varying between 8,000 and 2,000 metres, *Roeder* received a number of hits which did not put her out of action. She sank herself by using depth charges, the sinking occurring two minutes after the explosion. *Roeder* claimed to have set an enemy destroyer on fire, and observed that *Cossack* ran ashore after receiving several hits. Actually *Cossack* struck a rock and was refloated the following morning.

The four destroyers that had entered Rombaks Fjord were pursued by the British. *Zenker* and *Arnim* made for the eastern end of the fjord and prepared to scuttle. *Thiele* and *Lüdemann*, who still had some ammunition and torpedoes, remained stopped to the eastward of Stroemmen, a favourable position for attacking the enemy during his entry. *Lüdemann*, who had received several hits, having expended her ammunition, was also compelled to proceed to the eastern end of the fjord.

The torpedoes that she had fired missed. *Thiele* received many hits, but the last torpedo fired by her hit the British destroyer *Eskimo*, whose bows were blown off. When *Thiele*'s ammunition had been expended the wounded Captain himself moved the telegraphs to full speed ahead, as the bridge personnel had all been killed, and his ship, on fire fore and aft, was put on the rocks at Sildvik, where she capsized and sank. This last action of the *Thiele* lasting until 1500 permitted the rescue, without interference, of the crews of *Zenker*, *Arnim* and *Lüdemann*. The two former could be sunk before British destroyers approached. *Lüdemann* remained afloat after the detonation; she was examined by the British and then torpedoed, but did not sink until the following day.

The last fight of the destroyers in Rombaks Fjord concluded the events of 13 April in Narvik. Admiral Whitworth considered whether he should immediately attempt to occupy Narvik with a landing party from his ships. He believed that the psychological effect of the day's events would favour such an undertaking, but he held the view that the task could only be undertaken with properly equipped military troops, and as none were available he did not proceed with the plan, but ordered his ships to withdraw.

All ten destroyers that had entered Narvik on 9 April were destroyed by the afternoon of 13 April. In addition, U-64 had been sunk in Herjangs Fjord at noon on 13 April by *Warspite*'s aircraft, the officers and thirty-six of the crew being saved. No losses had occurred among the British ships. The severely damaged destroyers *Eskimo* and *Cossack* could be brought into Skelfjord, and the damage to the *Punjabi* could be made good the same day, with the exception of one boiler out of action.

The loss of the Narvik destroyers was a heavy blow to the small German Fleet, as it halved the destroyer strength of the Navy. This sacrifice was not in vain, for their crews, amounting to 2,500 men, were incorporated into the shore defence force, more than doubling its operational strength. If Major General Dietl had not received this reinforcement, or had the destroyers carried out the original plan of returning home on 9 April, it would probably have been impossible to hold this important position in Northern Norway against the British assault which followed.

The Return of the Battleships and of the Trondheim and Bergen Groups

The general position had decided the German Naval Commander-in-Chief to undertake the return journey independently of the Narvik and Trondheim groups, by proceeding to the westward, and then turning homeward, passing close to the Shetlands. The short signal in which he gave this intention failed to reach the Naval Group Commander West owing to a technical defect in *Gneisenau*, and thus the Shore Commander remained ignorant of his position and intentions.

On 10 April at 0800 Vice-Admiral Lütjens, with *Gneisenau* and *Scharnhorst*, was north-east of Iceland in position 69° N., 5° 30' W., and was asked to report his position and intentions to Naval Group West. To avoid giving away his position, he sent *Scharnhorst*'s aircraft to Trondheim at noon, the range being just within the capacity of the aircraft.

The aircraft had orders to make the report three hours after leaving *Scharnhorst*. This radio report crossed an order from Group West at 1500 stating: 'All available cruisers, destroyers and torpedo boats are to proceed to sea tonight. Narvik destroyers are to concentrate with Commander-in-Chief. It is left to your discretion whether *Hipper* with three destroyers join you or break through and proceed direct to home port.' Although the German Commander-in-Chief, who meanwhile had received information of the destroyer action on 10 April at Narvik, expected an alteration to this directive, as a result of the signal which he had transmitted, he nevertheless steered a course of 105° from 1630, making for the rendezvous between Westfjord and Trondheim. As anticipated, at 2238 he received a further message from Naval Group West approving his intentions and cancelling the rendezvous.

Vice-Admiral Lütjens then altered course to the south-west and later to south, and from noon on 11 April shaped course to cross the Shetlands–Norway line. From enemy reports he concluded that the main British naval concentration was off the Norwegian coast at Trondheim and in the Lofoten area; this was particularly favourable to the return journey of the battleships. The weather was also in his favour, for after a temporary improvement, there was rain and poor visibility.

After an uneventful night the battleships met *Hipper* at 0830/12, north-west of the Great Fisher Bank. At this moment two British aircraft were sighted and their urgent enemy reports were intercepted by Naval Group West. The deteriorating visibility was thus very favourable to the Germans. The Germans also intercepted the British shadowing aircraft's report at 0900 of reduced visibility and low clouds. From radio interception the Germans also gathered that further British reconnaissance flights and four bomber flights were sent against the battleships at 1000. Further British bomber flights were in readiness in case the weather improved. German fighters were launched to attack the British air formations, but no contact was made. At 1035 the last British shadowing plane reported having lost contact, and the German aircraft had to break off the escort at noon, as visibility was only one mile and there was danger of icing. At 1100 the destroyers *Beitzen* and *Schoemann*, who had been sent by Group West towards the battleships, took over anti-submarine escort. That evening the formation entered the Jade without further incident. The bad weather front and the icing danger had provided the ships with the best possible protection against enemy air attacks, and had once again shown the dependability of the Air Force on weather conditions.

The cruiser *Hipper* with the destroyer *Eckhold* had left Trondheim at 2200/10. Of the three remaining destroyers of the Trondheim group two had engine room defects, and the third had to remain there for lack of fuel, since the supply ship had not arrived. Captain Heye, assuming that Frohavet was being watched by the British, chose to leave by the navigationally difficult Ramso Fjord and, after reaching the open sea during the night he proceeded on a north-westerly course at full speed to get clear of the coast. Because of the sea, the accompanying destroyer *Eckhold* could not maintain her position and was sent back to Trondheim. At 0700 the following morning *Hipper* altered course to the south. As visibility was bad and fuel was short, she made directly for the

Shetlands-Bergen line, passing it at 29 knots, and joined the battleships early on 12 April. On reaching the Jade she had only eighty tons of fuel remaining.

The destroyer *Eckhold* was attacked early on 11 April near Trondheim by nine British torpedo bombers, who fired nine torpedoes in a fan without scoring a hit. As it was expected that British submarines would penetrate the fjord, the German destroyers equipped their ships' boats with depth charges. The destroyers were at instant readiness during the following day, anticipating British landing attempts. On 12 April some fuel was discovered in Trondheim, and at 1900/14 *Eckhold* and *Heinemann* started their return journey, which was without incident except for an unsuccessful attack by two British aircraft on the afternoon of 15 April. The destroyers *Jacobi* and *Riedel* did not return to Wilhelmshaven until May and June respectively, after German dockyard personnel had repaired their machinery.

The British aircraft that had attacked *Eckhold* on 11 April had been launched by *Furious*. When the British formation that included *Furious* was approaching Narvik on the afternoon of 11 April it was attacked by German bombers belonging to K.G.26. In this attack the destroyer *Eclipse* was damaged, and had to return to England.

Rear-Admiral Schmundt, with *Köln* and the torpedo boat *Leopard*, had lain in Mauranger Fjord, south of Bergen, on the night of 9/10.[21] *Königsberg*, not entirely seaworthy, and the slower ships of the group had remained at Bergen. At 1520 a German reconnaissance report stated that only two enemy destroyers had been sighted, in good visibility, in the area up to 62° N. The *Köln* group continued its homeward journey at 1845, leaving by Boemmelen and reaching the open sea at 2310.

Two destroyers allocated to this group as anti-submarine escort joined *Köln* at the Great Fisher Bank early on 11 April. From 0810 close escort was provided by two He.111's. From noon three Me.110's were provided as fighter escort, and the formation reached the Jade at 1700 without incident.

In the meantime Vice-Admiral von Schrader had taken over in Bergen as Admiral of the Norwegian West Coast. At 0800 on 10 April twelve British dive bombers made further attacks, *Königsberg* receiving two hits and three close misses. The ship was burned out, and capsized at 1100. Only some small arms and ammunition were salvaged. The crew was incorporated into the defences of the town, which were properly organised in the following days. The batteries at Kvarven (3 21 c.m., 3 24 c.m. Howitzers) and of Hellen and Sandviken (3 21 c.m., 2 24 c.m. Howitzers) were ready for action on 13 April. Minefields were laid in By Fjord and in Soer Fjord. The minelayer 'Ship 111' ran on to rocks in a snowstorm and had to be beached. The Norwegian torpedo boat *Brand* was put into service under the German flag. After the German supply ship *Sao Paolo* had been sunk by a mine in the entrance to Bergen, an auxiliary minesweeping flotilla was formed to safeguard the entrance. Unfortunately three of the four vessels ran on to German mines through faulty navigation, and on 11 April a request had to be sent to Group West to stop the further transports that were due at Bergen, and to send personnel and vessels for the minesweeping service. Enemy counter-action during these days was confined to more air attacks. At 1700/12 British dive bombers again attacked the harbour without result, but one motor torpedo boat was damaged with one killed and eight wounded. On 14 April at 0700 a bomb hit caused a fire in the transport *Barenfels* while discharging cargo, and she sank. Harbour vessels and equipment in her vicinity were damaged. Two British aircraft were shot down in this attack.

The Return of the Kristiansand and Oslo Groups

The German Naval Staff was aware that a large number of enemy submarines were in the Skagerrak and Kattegat and there was concern over the safety of the naval forces returning from Kristiansand and Oslo. One anti-submarine flotilla and one patrol flotilla were detailed to watch the entrance to Kristiansand and the area off Oslo Fjord.

Karlsruhe, with three torpedo boats as A/S escort, left the harbour of Kristiansand at 1900 on 9 April. The speed of advance was 21 knots zig-zagging. At 1958, when about ten miles south of the fjord, a submarine fired four torpedoes at the cruiser who took avoiding action but received one hit, which put both engines and the steering gear out of action. Five compartments were flooded and pumps were unusable. The ship was slowly sinking and the Commanding Officer, thinking that she would be lost, transferred the crew to the torpedo boats, and ordered *Karlsruhe* to be sunk with two torpedoes. The torpedo boats reached Kiel without incident.

On 10 April most of the guns in Kristiansand were ready for use, and the Norwegian warships in the harbour – three destroyers, four torpedo boats and two submarines – were immobilised, small German parties being put onboard. They could not be used because of lack of personnel. On 12 April there was an unsuccessful attack by British aircraft, five of which were shot down by our fighters.

The military situation in Oslo on 10 April did not permit the return of all the German warships that had arrived on that day. Only *Lützow* was to return at once as she was required for an operation, and (after the experience with the *Königsberg* in Bergen) it was considered unwise to expose her to the air menace in Oslo Fjord.

Lützow left Oslo at 1540/10. There had been anti-submarine and aircraft patrols on that day in the area between Laeso, Skagen and Paternoster off Oslo Fjord, but without result. After *Lützow* had got under way, three steamers of the 2nd Sea Transport Division were torpedoed the Swedish coast, near Paternoster, and Captain Thiele therefore chose the westward route by Skagen. When the Group Commander, East, Admiral Carls, heard of the torpedoing he considered whether to order *Lützow* to return to Oslo, but decided that this would not improve the position of the ship and that her high speed and the dark hours would offer the best protection against submarines. No vessels with sufficient speed were available as anti-submarine escort for *Lützow*.

At 0129/11 *Lützow*, while ten miles north-east of Skagen, received a torpedo hit aft from HMS *Spearfish* which put the propellers and rudder out of action and caused heavy flooding. Unable to move, she drifted in a south-westerly direction towards Skagen. The only protection against further submarine attacks on this clear night consisted in the ship's picket boat, which was lowered and circled round the ship; strangely, however, there were no further attacks. Naval Group East immediately despatched the 17th Anti-Submarine Flotilla, the 19th Minesweeper Flotilla, and six tugs to the scene. At 0500 *Lützow* was taken in tow towards Kiel, with a strong anti-submarine escort. For some time there was danger that the stern would break off, and the Captain considered putting the ship aground in shallow water to prevent her sinking. He decided to continue, as salvage tugs with pumps were to meet the ship in the afternoon. The tugs took the ships through the navigationally difficult Lasoe channel, as the shallow water was the best protection against submarine attack.

Lützow, with her increased draught, went aground in the channel but was towed off. The ship was saved under great difficulty. At very slow speed, she was towed through the Belt to Kiel where she arrived on the evening of 13 April.

The Transport of Supplies

Of the seven steamers, camouflaged as normal merchant ships, which were destined, three for Narvik, three for Trondheim and one for Stavanger, and due to arrive at these ports before the warships, not one reached its destination on time. Some were considerably delayed at the Kabbervig, at the entrance to the Norwegian Leads, because the Norwegian pilot station had apparently no pilots available. On the further journey the *Rauenfels* of the Narvik group was sunk by the British in Westfjord,[22] *Alster* was captured, and the third ship of the Narvik group, *Barenfels*, which had been diverted to Bergen, arrived there on 11 April. On 14 April, while discharging the cargo destined for Narvik, she was sunk by British dive bombers.

Of the Trondheim group *Sao Paolo* hit a Norwegian mine while entering Bergen and sank; *Main* was sunk by a Norwegian destroyer, and only the third ship *Levante* arrived at Trondheim on 12 April, three days late. The only ship due at Stavanger was attacked, while entering on 9 April, by the Norwegian torpedo boat *Sleitner*, and sank.[23] The supply of arms and equipment for Narvik and Stavanger thus failed, and of the three ships destined for Trondheim only the smallest arrived, while one of the Narvik steamers had to use Bergen as an emergency port and, as already mentioned, was sunk by aircraft.

The expectation of the Army and the Air Force to be supplied in time with guns, ammunition, equipment and provisions for the troops that had been landed in the northern harbours was therefore frustrated.

Of the tankers, *Jan Wellem* from Murmansk arrived on the morning of 9 April at Narvik as planned. The second tanker for Narvik, the *Kattegat*, was fired on shortly before her arrival on the evening of 9 April at Glom Fjord by the Norwegian auxiliary vessel *Nordkapp*, and was sunk by her own crew. Later she was refloated and towed to Bodø. The tanker *Skagerrak*, destined for Trondheim, which had been diverted by Group West to a waiting position at sea, was stopped on 14 April by a British cruiser in 64° 5' N., 2° E. Her Captain sank her to prevent her falling into British hands. It has already been shown how serious the consequences of these losses were to the further conduct of the Norwegian operations. The five smaller tankers that belonged to this group, which were due to arrive at Oslo, Stavanger, Bergen, and Trondheim a few days after the occupation, reached their destinations according to plan, except for the *Moonsund* which was sunk by a British submarine off Narvik on 12 April, while proceeding to Trondheim.

The trans-shipment of troops to the southern harbours, including Bergen, by the 1st Sea Transport Division took place as planned. These ships were to arrive soon after their original occupation. Reinforcements to the harbours of Trondheim and Narvik were not sent by the precious troop transports, in view of the danger of interception by British and French naval forces on the line Shetlands-Norway. The ships of the 1st Sea Transport Division proceeded singly so as to appear as normal merchant ships, and it was hoped their passage through the Danish Narrows would not arouse suspicion. They were to remain inside territorial waters, and troops were to be kept below decks while within sight of land. The heaviest transport casualties occurred on the way to Bergen, which was the most distant port. Of the three steamers due there, only *Marie Leonhardt* arrived on 11 April. The *Curityba* ran aground on 7 April north of Helsingborg, and had to enter Oslo on 10 April. The *Rio de Janeiro* was sunk by a British submarine at Lillesand.[24] Three of the Kristiansand group of steamers arrived on 9 April as planned, and the fourth, which was pursued by a submarine and driven back, eventually arrived on 12 April so that the troops disembarked there received all their supplies. The three steamers due at Stavanger arrived there safely on the evening of 9 April.

There was delay in the arrival of the five steamers of the Oslo group, as the individual forts in the Droebak Narrows could not be captured until 10 April. The steamer *Antares* was sunk by a British submarine at 2100/10 April, west of Uddevalla Fjord. The *Jania* was also torpedoed by a submarine on 11 April off Oslo Fjord. She remained afloat for a little while, but capsized when an attempt was made to tow her into Larvik Fjord. The crews of both ships were saved except for seventeen men. They carried mainly Army supplies. The remaining three steamers of the group arrived at Oslo on 11 April, together with the 2nd Sea Transport Division.

The eleven steamers of this division were not disguised, as Denmark was already in German hands when they passed through those waters in convoy with air and anti-submarine escort.

On the evening of 10 April, north of Gotenburg, the convoy was attacked by British submarines who sank the steamers *Friedenau* and *Wigbert*, and scattered the convoy. Patrol vessel 1507 was also sunk. The remaining ships of the division arrived in Oslo on 12 April, except for *Scharnhorst* which went into Frederikshaven. The submarine attacks on the 2nd Transport Division resulted in the loss of 900 troops. This caused the Naval Staff to order that in future troops were not to proceed in convoys but only in fast warships, and other small and fast vessels, and on the shortest route between Jutland and the South Norwegian ports. This restriction did not apply to the transport of supplies. Attempts were to be made to send over from Skagen ammunition, material and provisions by using fishing boats and cutters, so as to relieve pressure on the transports.

The 3rd Sea Transport Division left home ports on 13 April for Oslo. It consisted of twelve steamers in convoy, carrying Army supplies, but was divided into five independent groups according to the speed of the ships. This was effective, for in spite of the activity of British submarines and the bad weather, which necessitated the return of the escorting minesweepers, the losses were relatively small. The steamer *Florida*, with ammunition and equipment, was lost through a submarine attack in the Kattegat on 14 April; part of the crew were saved and brought to Skagen. On 15 April, as a result of an explosion, probably due to mines, the minesweepers *M.1701* and *M.1072* sank. On the same day, in bad visibility, the steamer *Urundi* ran aground in the Leads, west of Faerder, and *M.1101* also sank in the same place after running aground. The remainder of the ships arrived safely in Oslo on 15/16 April.

The transportation of troops in fast ships between North Jutland and Southern Norway was entirely satisfactory. After overcoming the initial difficulties due to improvisation, the number of troops trans-shipped from Frederikshaven and Aalborg to Larvik and Oslo during the main period of reinforcement could be stepped up to 3,000 men per day. From the middle of April to the middle of June it was possible by this means to transport 42,000 men to Southern Norway, without losses. The supplementary transportation by fishing boats from Skagen also suffered

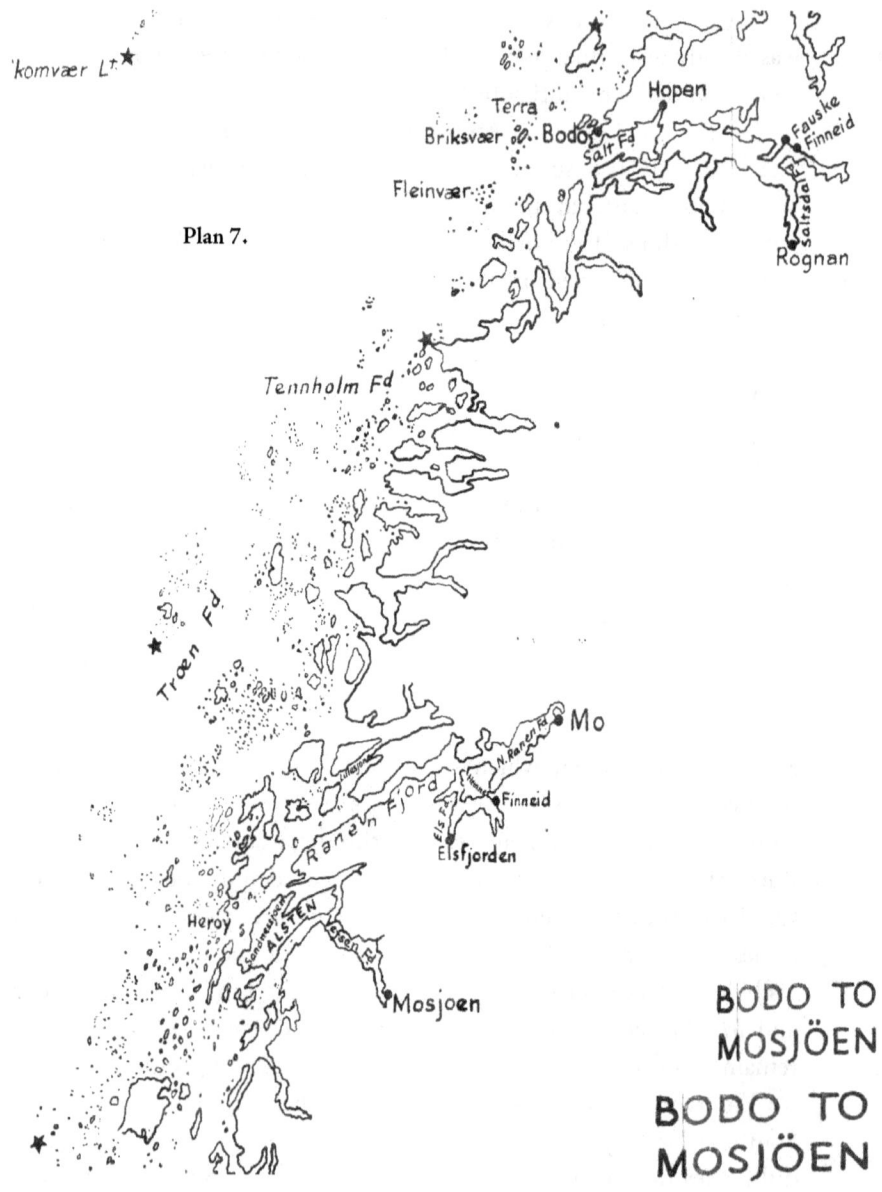

Plan 7.

BODO TO MOSJÖEN

no losses. About 8,000 tons of Army equipment were carried by them to Southern Norway between 14 April and 22 May.

The menace from British submarines reached its climax in the middle of April, and by the end of the month decreased considerably through German anti-submarine measures, and through the effect of the mine barrage. Nevertheless, the convoys still suffered some serious losses. On 15 April the gunnery training ship *Brummer*, which was being used to escort convoys, was sunk by a torpedo; on 18 April the steamship *Hamm*, returning from Oslo, was seriously damaged north of Skagen. On 1 May the steamers *Bahia Castillo* and *Buenos Aires*, bound for Norway, were hit simultaneously while under escort of the 2nd Minesweeping Flotilla. The first ship could be towed into Frederikshaven but the second sank with the loss of the cargo; most of the crew were saved.

The enemy made only one attempt with surface ships to interfere with the transports in the Skagerrak. Early on the morning of 24 April French Flotilla Leaders broke into the Skagerrak and came into action south of Kristiansand with 7th Patrol Flotilla, who suffered only slight damage. The French ships, while steaming away to the south-west at high speed after the action, were pursued by the 2nd Motor Torpedo Boat Flotilla, who could not catch up with them. The Naval Staff had expected such attacks by surface ships in the Skagerrak, but there were only small forces available for use against such raids, and the chief defence lay in the mine barrages and, especially, in the German air superiority in this area.

A more difficult problem than supplies for Southern Norway was that of further reinforcements to the German bases at Bergen, Trondheim and Narvik. The Naval Staff had prepared for the transport of a Mountain Division to Bergen using fast transport ships, which were to be protected by the Fleet, including battleships. This plan did not materialise, since in the meantime the operations of the German Army had resulted in establishing land communication between Oslo and Bergen, so the Mountain Division was landed at Oslo.

Statistics of transportation (other than by warships) during the capture of Norway, including losses, are given in the following summary:

270 ships and 100 trawlers, totalling 1,192,000 G.R.T., carried up to 15 June:–

107,581 officers and men;
16,102 horses;
20,339 vehicles;
109,400 tons of war supplies.

Of the above, twenty-one ships totalling 111,700 G.R.T. were lost, and of the 4,344 officers and men in these ships about 1,000 were lost, while a large part of the cargo of the ships could be salved.

Measures Against Allied Counter – Attacks

The Allied Plan of Invasion
The first indication of an impending Allied counter-landing in Norway came to the Germans through radio interception on 12 April. It showed that the Flag Officer Commanding the British 1st Cruiser Squadron had indicated Namsos and Mosjoen as suitable for landing. It was not clear to the Germans from this intercept whether a landing had actually occurred. Further observation of enemy radio traffic told the German Naval Staff that preparations were being made for landing troops in Vaagsfjord, commencing on 15 April. On 13 April Trondheim reported that British troops were believed to have landed at Åndalsnes. The German Naval Staff interpreted the situation as follows:–

> 'The enemy has ignored the harbours that we have occupied and is concentrating on landing in other places, which however involve him in military disadvantages. The enemy's apparent intention is to use his almost unmolested landing places as bases for flanking attacks on the vital strategic positions at Narvik and Trondheim, to be preceded by attacks with carrier-borne aircraft. He intends first to destroy the German naval forces in these harbours. At the same time he proposes to block the supply routes and the approaches for German naval forces, by extensive use of the Franco-British naval forces.'[25]

Actually, as soon as the Allied Supreme Command realized that Plan R.4 had been nullified by the German landings in Norway, it decided to take steps to reconquer Norway; and this had to occur as quickly as possible before the Germans could succeed in establishing their position in the country. Previous preparations for the concentration and transportation of troops under Plan R.4 allowed the Allies to act quickly. The equipment of the troops had been designed for landing at undefended places along the coast, and under the new situation it was therefore decided not to attack the ports that had already been occupied by the enemy. The Germans were already in occupation of the important places that had been intended as Allied landing points, namely, Stavanger, Bergen, Trondheim and Narvik. The Allied troops had therefore to be landed at places where no material resistance could be expected. They were chosen with a view to recapturing these harbours with Norwegian support, before the main German forces could arrive from Southern Norway.

For the recapture of Trondheim the Allies regarded Folden Fjord–Namsos – north of Trondheim, and Molde Fjord–Aalesund and Åndalsnes – to the southward, as the most suitable landing points and operational bases. It was intended to use these two areas for a pincer movement against Trondheim, and by capturing the railway centre at Dombaas to seal off Trondheim from the south. At one time a direct attack on Trondheim was also considered, but the two Army brigades intended for this were eventually sent to reinforce the troops that had been landed at Åndalsnes.

The first objective of the Allies, however, was to recapture Narvik, the terminal port for Swedish ore. If the Germans could be prevented from using this place the success of their Norwegian operation would be in doubt. From a military point of view also the recapture of Narvik was much easier for the Allies than the expulsion of the Germans from Trondheim, since the great distance and difficulty of topography made the bringing up of German reinforcements from the south a matter of extreme difficulty.

Vaagsfjord–Harstad–Salangen were selected by the Allies as the starting point for the reconquest of Narvik. It was also important to the Allies to put small forces ashore between Trondheim and Narvik so as to prevent the Germans establishing bases along the coast for the Luftwaffe and for use in sending reinforcements by land or sea from Trondheim to Narvik. With this object the following places were selected by the Allies: – Versenfjord, Mosjoen, Raanenfjord, Mo, Saltenfjord, Bodø. All these fjords extended deeply into the land, and at their extremities, in this narrow part of Norway, they were not far from the Swedish frontier, so that any German troops advancing by land could be impeded without much difficulty. The Allied landings in these places did not occur until the operation against Narvik had been launched.

The Battle for Trondheim (Plan 2)

For the Allies the reconquest of Narvik had priority over operations in Central Norway, but the opposite applied to the Germans, who in the event of losing the Trondheim area could not expect to hold Narvik. For the Germans the pivot of all operations was therefore Trondheim and this was explained in an O.K.W. directive, dated 14 April, which gave details for its defence by the various Armed forces as follows:–

(a) Group XXI is to reinforce the garrison of Trondheim as soon as possible, and take possession of the railway Oslo–Dombaas and Åndalsnes.
(b) The Navy is to concentrate U-boats in the waters round Trondheim and Aalesund, and to arrange for the transport of the most important supplies by means of U-boats to Trondheim.
(c) The Luftwaffe is to destroy enemy troops already landed; to prevent further landings in the Åndalsnes area; to occupy Dombaas with paratroops and to send airborne reinforcements to Trondheim.

On 12 April Luftflotte 5 was formed for the conduct of all air operations in Norway, under the command of Colonel General Milch. The German Supreme Command attached the greatest importance to securing the area south of Trondheim, which would enable them to establish land communications between Oslo and Trondheim.

An air reconnaissance report on 15 April showed Molde Fjord and Åndalsnes to be clear of the enemy; 'Y' reports gave the transports *Chrobry* and *Batory* as earmarked for landings at Namsos. On the following day *Glasgow*, the British 4th Destroyer Flotilla and one of these transports were reported off Namsos, and three cruisers and four destroyers off Åndalsnes. The extent of the landing fleet was not known, but General Carton de Wiart was known to be the Commander in the Namsos area.

In the meantime enemy landings had commenced. At Namsos and in Molde Fjord Royal Marines and landing parties from the warships had been put ashore. On the evening of 14 April 350 men landed at Namsos Fjord, partly at Bangsund and partly in Namsos, and on 15 April the General took over command. At Molde Fjord the advance party consisted of 700 men. The main landing under Lieutenant-Colonel Simpson occurred two days later. It was intended to land at Aalesund, but the Norwegians having stressed the great strategic importance of Åndalsnes, Colonel Simpson was ordered to land only four 4 in. guns at the former place, and to put his main forces ashore at the latter. This occurred on 17/18 April without opposition. Simultaneously the landing ground at Stavanger was bombarded from the sea to help the southern landings and this caused some casualties in the German naval air contingent there. The German bombers of K.G. 22 and K.G. 30 made contact with the bombarding ships west of Haugesund, and a bomb hit damaged the cruiser *Suffolk* sufficiently to necessitate her return to Scapa 'with the sea lapping over her quarterdeck.'

The Germans also expected a direct attack on Trondheim from the sea, but on 16 April it was considered that the situation there was fairly secure. Naval air and Air Force units were operationally available, and two torpedo batteries at Selven and Hysnes were ready for action. In addition coastal batteries were ready at Bettinges – 2 21 c.m., 3 15 c.m., and at Hysnes – 2 21 c.m. and 2 15 c.m. The Flag Officer Commanding U-Boats was ordered to provide three medium and three small U-boats for the protection of the Trondheim area. The Naval Staff received orders to ensure the transport of heavy arms and ammunition for the troops by the sea route. Six large U-boats were detailed as transports for essential supplies and the first of these, *U-26* and *U-43*, arrived at Trondheim on 18 April. An attempt to use camouflaged trawlers to bring guns to Trondheim failed. The first two trawlers on this task were lost through enemy action. On the land front of Trondheim there was a successful advance on 16 April along the railway up to the Swedish frontier.

On 19 April the German Naval Staff believed that major enemy landings had not yet taken place at Åndalsnes, and that the enemy's main operational area was north of Trondheim. This was true up to the evening of 18 April, but German reconnaissance had not observed that further landings had taken place on the night of 18/19 April at Molde and Åndalsnes; these were 1,000 men under General Morgan, who had originally been detailed for Namsos. The British Command having originally looked on the landing south of Trondheim as a diversion, decided on 16 April to build up this area also as an operational base, and diverted the Morgan group to Åndalsnes. Their place at Namsos was taken by one of the two brigades en route for Narvik. After the destruction of the German destroyers at Narvik on 13 April, it was considered unnecessary to send it there. The troops were transported in warships only. General Morgan was ordered to secure Dombaas to prevent the Germans from using the railway there, and then to co-operate with the other forces for an offensive against Trondheim. Speed was essential, and he was told to expect reinforcement. But he was also instructed only to land if this could be undertaken without resistance, since his troops were not equipped for fighting on the beaches. The landing took place without opposition, and small reinforcements followed on 21-22 April, including a company for securing a landing ground on Lake Lesjaskog, situated between Åndalsnes and Dombaas. The main body of troops under General Paget landed on the nights of 22 April and 24 April. Originally they were intended for a direct attack on Trondheim, but were diverted to Åndalsnes.[26] These reinforcements brought the total strength of the troops in the Åndalsnes area to 6,000 men.

It is remarkable that none of these landings were interrupted by the German Air Force, although numerous attacks took place in Molde Fjord during these days. The reason probably lies in the fact that the troops were disembarked only during the night hours, and that only one small transport was used, which landed its troops on 21 April under cover of snowstorms and low clouds; all the remaining troops were landed from warships.

Nor was the Luftwaffe able to prevent reinforcements for the Northern Arm of the Trondheim pincers. The first wave of transports consisted of the 146 Brigade, originally intended for Narvik, which was diverted to Namsos on 14 April. The troops were embarked in transports which, owing to the difficulty and danger of landing at Namsos, were sent to Lillesjona, about 100 miles to the northward, where they were trans-shipped to destroyers for the further journey. While the destroyers were lying alongside the transports on the morning of 16 April, they were attacked by German aircraft and bombs fell very near them. In the afternoon the destroyers proceeded to Namsos where on the night of 16/17 April they landed about 1,000 troops at Bangsund. The landing parties that had been put ashore from the cruisers on the evening of 14 April were then withdrawn. The rest of the brigade was landed at Namsos on the night of 17/18 April by the transport *Chrobry*.

The next wave consisted of French troops under General Audet. It consisted of four medium sized transports which, while approaching the landing place inside the fjord in the evening of 19 April, were attacked by German aircraft. *Emile Bertin* was severely damaged and had to return home, and the transport *Ville d'Oran* (10,000 tons) was slightly damaged. The troops were landed without incident on the night of 19/20 April, and shortly afterwards heavy air attacks caused devastation in the town and harbour of Namsos, as there was no local anti-aircraft defence.

The last transport, *Ville D'Algers*, was due to land its troops (French) on the night 20/21 April, but was held back in view of the situation in Namsos; the troops were landed on 22 April but without their heavy equipment or anti-tank guns and flak battery, which were particularly required there, but could not be put ashore owing to lack of facilities. The total strength of the troops landed at Namsos was then 6,000 men.

As long as German forces on their way from Oslo to Central Norway had not achieved contact with Trondheim, the defence against Allied landings rested almost exclusively with the Luftwaffe, whose available operational forces on 19 April were as follows:–

Trondheim: Two flights of Squadron 506.
Stavanger: One coastal reconnaissance flight 1/106.
    One reconnaissance flight of Ju.88's.
    One dive bomber flight.
    One heavy fighter squadron.
Kristiansand: One fighter squadron.
Aalborg: One heavy fighter squadron.
    One long distance flight.
    One bomber flight of K.G. 30.
    Two bomber squadrons of K.G. 26.
Westerland: K.G. 30.
    One long distance reconnaissance flight of Ju.88's.
Lubeck: One reconnaissance flight.
Lueneburg: One bomber squadron of K.G. 4.
    One fighter bomber squadron K.G. 100.

The Luftwaffe could not prevent the landings, but when the enemy began the second and more difficult part of his task, namely, the preparation of the troops for operations, he was exposed to continuous and energetic German air operations which were only temporarily interrupted by bad weather. At both Åndalsnes and Molde and at Namsos the harbour installations and sheds were extensively destroyed and disembarkation of supplies was much retarded, having to take place in the dark. Many stores and much equipment that had been landed were lost through bombing attacks, and many small craft used for landing were sunk. The flak cruiser *Curacoa* was heavily damaged in Molde Fjord and had to be sent home. German radio interception of a British signal revealed the British situation at Namsos, after a heavy German air attack, as desperate, and it was reported that the town was in flames. The Luftwaffe could drive its attacks home, since anti-aircraft weapons were almost non-existent among the troops that had been landed, and A/A defence was available only in the warships and among the carrier-borne aircraft.

The general effect of Luftwaffe operations during this period was decisive, but the results on the enemy's warships and transports were below expectation, and certainly far less than claimed by the air crews. These claims were examined sceptically by the Naval Staff. From the beginning of operations to the end of April actual results against the landing fleet in Central Norway were:–

- 17 April: cruiser *Suffolk*, heavily damaged at Haugesund.
- 19 April: French cruiser *Emile Bertin*, damaged while entering Namsos.
- 22 April: sloop *Pelican*, damaged while proceeding to Åndalsnes.
- 24 April: flak cruiser *Curacoa*, damaged at Åndalsnes.
- 28 April: sloop *Black Swan*, damaged at Åndalsnes, and seven trawlers sunk.
- 30 April: sloop *Bittern* and three trawlers sunk at Namsos.

It is due to the continuous activity of the German Air Force that, within a few days of landing at both places, the local Allied commanders came to the conclusion that the position was untenable, and began to think of the problem of evacuation. But the evacuation was not seriously contemplated until the first German counter-attacks from the land threatened the Allied positions on shore.

The German Command was not fully aware of the total effect on the enemy of German air attacks, or of the weakness in the numbers and equipment of the Allied troops that had been landed in Central Norway. Consequently right up to the time that the enemy was considering evacuation, the Germans believed the situation at Trondheim to be much more serious than it ever was.

The German Army met with great difficulties of terrain on its advance from Oslo to the north and, since no date for establishing contact with Trondheim could be given, Hitler on 21 April informed the German Naval Staff that he intended to reinforce the garrison of Trondheim by using the fast liners, including *Bremen* and *Europa*. The Naval Staff advised strongly against this, as it could not guarantee safe passage, and the plan was dropped. The only safe sea communication with Trondheim was by transport U-boats, which were used to carry important stores, aviation petrol, anti-aircraft guns and bombs. Enemy air attacks on Trondheim were limited to operations from his carriers, which resulted on 25 April in heavy damage to the aerodrome and naval aircraft at Vaernes; a second attack on 28 April caused less damage.

The first action between German troops and enemy forces occurred on 21 April, north-east of Trondheim, at Steinkjaer at the end of Beistad Fjord. Here, 40 k.m. south of Namsos, the country between the ends of the fjord and the long inland lake of Snaasen formed a tongue of land only 10 k.m. wide, whose strategic importance was recognized by both sides. The British troops that had been sent from Namsos to Steinkjaer to occupy the territory were engaged there early on 21 April by German troops with superior artillery, who had been transported by naval forces from Trondheim.

General Carton de Wiart considered that British reinforcements from Namsos would be very difficult, as ships were not available. On 22 April the British troops who had occupied positions at Verdalsoeren, about thirty miles south of Steinkjaer, were fired upon by a German destroyer from Trondheim. As a result of this attack, which in itself was not important, the British General decided that the position was untenable and therefore recommended its evacuation.

To the south of Trondheim fighting did not occur until some days later. As already mentioned, the key position here was in the Dombaas area which General Morgan, coming from Åndalsnes, had occupied in accordance with previous instructions. Two battalions of his brigade were in an advanced position about 40 k.m. along the Gudbrand valley near Otta, and the third battalion was at Dombaas. General Morgan anticipated the approach of Group XXI against his front, while in his rear parts of the German garrison from Trondheim advanced 50 k.m. southwards to Storen. By 26 April the forward units of Group XXI, advancing in two columns eastward in the Oester valley and westward in the Gudbrand valley, had moved so far north that the German Command expected the relief of Trondheim to take place very shortly. The eastern group met with some Norwegian resistance at Roeros in the Oester valley. In the Gudbrand valley the British troops at Dombaas were driven back by superior German forces, who possessed 15 c.m. Howitzers and enjoyed good air support, 'whereas the British had neither guns nor planes.'[27] Aircraft from *Glorious*, which on 24 April had landed on Lesjaskog lake for support of land operations, were destroyed by German air attacks on the following day, and the lake became unusable owing to the thaw. On 27 April General Paget reported that unless immediate support by air, and field and anti-aircraft artillery could be provided, and infantry reinforcements sent, the whole force was in danger of collapse.

Thereupon on 28 April the Allied Command ordered a withdrawal from the whole of Central Norway. The main reason given was German air superiority which allowed reinforcements to be sent uninterrupted to Norway, thus permitting the rapid advance of the troops. On the same day the British radio announced, presumably in order to conceal the intention to evacuate, that further successful landings had taken place in Åndalsnes. In fact the German Naval Staff concluded on 28 April that the enemy's landing operations had now been completed, and that the pincer movement on Trondheim would follow.

On the following day, however, German air reconnaissance obtained the impression that the enemy was beginning to evacuate Namsos. On 30 April the advance troops of Group XXI met parts of the German Trondheim force at Storen, thus establishing the link between Oslo and Trondheim, and the Naval Staff commented as follows:–

> 'The South Norwegian area as far as north of Trondheim is now securely in German hands. The situation of the Allied troops south of Trondheim can be regarded as desperate.'

The embarkation of the British troops from Molde Fjord took place on the night of 1/2 May. The Luftwaffe made daylight attacks on 30 April and 1 May on the harbour and the numerous naval forces and ships. On 1 May several air attacks on the *Glorious* had no result. The embarkation of troops at night was unhindered, and the British concluded that the Germans had not discovered the evacuation. Actually the numerous movements of British ships in Molde Fjord, reported on the evening of 30 April and on the morning of 1 May by German aircraft, had not yet produced a clear picture as to the enemy's intentions. But the German Naval Staff concluded from these reports that the enemy intended 'to re-embark troops landed at Åndalsnes as quickly as possible during the night, and to use them at another place, that is at Namsos.' It was believed that the enemy had come to the conclusion that developments on land demanded the withdrawal of the force landed south of Trondheim. The withdrawal of the Allied forces from the area south of Trondheim was officially announced in the British Army Bulletin on 2 May.

The embarkation of the troops from Namsos was completed without interference on the night of 2/3 May, a French battalion of 850 men already having been sent to Scapa three days earlier. On 29 April the German Air Force had reported:– 'The attack on the town of Namsos was cancelled because the town and railway station had already been severely damaged by air attacks, and there were no signs of life. The Fliegerfuehrer, Trondheim, has reported that the enemy is evacuating Namsos, and this is being checked.' On 2 May the German Air Force attacked some destroyers entering Namsos in foggy weather, and the *Maori* was damaged by bombs. On the following day the returning transports, while from 140 to 220 miles off the coast, were subjected during nearly seven hours to powerful German air attacks. These were the result of the earlier reconnaissance which established the evacuation of Namsos. The result of the air attacks was the loss of the French destroyer *Bison* and of the British destroyer *Afridi*, who lost 100 men. The remaining ships reached Scapa undamaged on 5 May.

It was during this air attack on 2 May that German aircraft claimed to have sunk an enemy battleship. One 250 k.g. bomb was alleged to have hit the ship between two forward turrets, causing a flame to shoot 500 metres into the air, and when the smoke cloud cleared the ship was no longer visible. The German Naval Staff, sceptical of these eye-witness accounts, believed that the case referred to a much smaller ship. Later, however, when further reports from various authorities, including Naval observers, poured in, describing in detail that the sunken ship had two funnels and two quadruple turrets forward, even the Naval Staff believed the loss of a battleship to be possible. Actually this story must have related to one of the destroyers *Afridi* or *Bison*, and it illustrates how difficult the identification of warships from the air can be. Doubtless the observers honestly reported their belief, though the desire to report a great success must necessarily influence the reliability of such reports.

After the enemy's attack on Central Norway had been successfully overcome the German Command ordered Group XXI as its next operational objective to occupy the coastal sector from Namsos to Bodø and to use the aerodrome at Bodø as a base for the eventual support of Narvik, thus safeguarding the Swedish ore area.

On 8 May the Prime Minister, Mr. Neville Chamberlain, gave the following reasons for the failure of the operations at Trondheim:–

(i) the impossibility of obtaining or securing air bases;
(ii) the unexpectedly rapid arrival of German reinforcements.

Admiral of the Fleet Sir Roger Keyes rejected this explanation and stated that a direct attack on Trondheim, which in his opinion was both feasible and promising, had not been attempted. The attitude of the German Naval Staff towards this question was as follows:–

> 'A direct assault on Trondheim would only have been possible in the first days of the German operations, while coastal batteries were still unprepared and before the German Air Force was able to operate effectively against the attacker. Even then the invader could only hope to consolidate his position if, by using extensive air transportation he could establish air superiority in the Norwegian area and could land a powerfully equipped and modernly trained expeditionary force. In addition, the British would have had to prevent any further reinforcements of German troops on the Skagerrak route to Southern Norway. Thus it cannot be held against the British if, with their uncertainty as to the actual situation in

Southern Norway and with ignorance of the results of their submarine attacks in the Kattegat and Skagerrak, they did not decide on a direct attack against the harbours already in German occupation. The British operations in the Trondheim area, and their landing of limited numbers of troops at Åndalsnes and Namsos, were operational mistakes attributable to the following factors:–

(i) Overestimation of British sea power in a coastal area dominated by the German Air Force;
(ii) Failure to realize the rapid conquest of Norwegian territory by Germany;
(iii) Anxiety over further loss of prestige to Great Britain;
(iv) Lack of planning and decision in the British Command after the upsetting of their original plan;
(v) The hope of still holding on to the North Norwegian area with consequent effective action against the ore supplies for Germany'.

The German Naval Staff, summing up the vital role of the German Air Force in repelling the attack, stated:–

'It has been firmly established that the operation of heavy forces in the coastal area in which Germany has no equivalent fleet involves the greatest risk to the units taking part, particularly if within operational range of the German dive bombers, and incurs a risk that Britain will not be able to afford in the future'.

The Final Battle for Narvik (Plans 1 and 7)

After the destruction of the ten German destroyers at Narvik the local German Commander ashore, General Dietl, regarded the addition of the crews of these ships to his local troops as an extremely valuable reinforcement; for he now disposed of more than 4,000 men. The Naval crews were formed into a regiment under Commander Berger, and the technical personnel were used to repair and maintain the ore railway.

However, the position of this distant German base was bound to be threatened as soon as the expected British attack for its recapture was launched. The whole of the ship-borne supplies for the German troops having been lost, they had neither guns nor means of defence against air attacks. The destroyers' crews could only be equipped with small arms and were untrained for fighting in the difficult mountainous country. Further supplies from sea could not be expected, neither could the date be foreseen when Army Group XXI, which was preparing at Oslo for an advance to the northward, could establish contact with the distant base at Narvik. The mountainous character of the territory, the lack of roads, and the prevalent snow were bound to make the Army's advance extremely difficult. No immediate support by the German Air Force could be counted on in view of the great distance from air bases. The only available landing ground in the Narvik area was the frozen Lake Hartwig, to the east of Elvegaardsmoen. Supplies of ammunition were first dropped from the air on 11 April.

Immediate measures were taken by the German Command on 12 April, when it was known that the stores for the troops had been lost, by supplying Narvik by using U-boats and naval seaplanes of type D.26. Negotiations were entered into with Sweden to allow her railway to be used for transporting material to Narvik, particularly artillery and air equipment for bombers and reconnaissance machines. Radio interception on 12 April had shown the German Naval Staff that the British blockade position off Narvik was being strengthened, and that they were preparing to land at Vaagsfjord on the 15 April. The transports *Batory* and *Chrobry* were reported to have left Scapa on 12 April, and it was also known that the British intended to land in Central Norway.[28] The German Naval Staff therefore ordered five U-boats to be stationed in Central Norway at threatened points off the coast, and four U-boats at Vaagsfjord, with another four at Westfjord. As Hitler had ordered the defence of Trondheim to take priority, the Naval Staff ordered the first transport U-boats to proceed there instead of to Narvik.

As mentioned earlier, the use of U-boats in Vaagsfjord and Westfjord proved a failure, and the blocking of Rombaks Fjord by a mine-laying U-boat, which had been requested by the Narvik group, had to be refused because of the difficult tactical situation. Indeed, after *U-78* had tried in vain to break through to Narvik the Naval Staff on 15 April decided to withdraw U-boats from the narrow fjords and station them in positions where the danger was less, while possibilities of attack still existed.

In connection with Narvik, Hitler was anxious to avoid unnecessary expenditure of forces, particularly of the Air Force, and wanted a concentration for the defence of Trondheim. The Naval Staff was against this and counted on the capacity for prolonged resistance of the Narvik division. It was also considered that the continuous pinning down of the enemy in the Narvik area would afford considerable relief to the position in Central Norway. The position in Narvik, based on reports from General Dietl and on reconnaissance, was summed up as follows:–

'British destroyers were in Gratangsbottem, West of Elvenes, on the evening of 14 April. The destroyers in Rombaks Fjord prevent contact with the German troops at Elvegaardsmoen. Deep snow hinders the movement of troops and identification of landing ground for aircraft. Air reconnaissance at Harstad has identified sixteen merchant ships, five transports and one cruiser, and extensive disembarkation of troops. The German Mountain Division anticipates an Anglo-Norwegian attack on Narvik and Elvegaardsmoen. There is nothing to prevent the enemy operating against the ore railway. The British destroyers sailed at noon and returned in the evening to renew the bombardment. About 2,100 poorly equipped men from the German destroyers have been incorporated in the land defences. Carrier-borne aircraft and Norwegian aircraft from Bardufoss are making bombing attacks on Narvik and Lake Hartwig, with no result so far.'

On the evening of 14 April the Narvik Group received the following directive from the Supreme Command:–

'Should the situation force you to give up your present positions, you are to establish a base in the mountains, if possible on the railway, and defend it with reinforcements to be dropped from the air. The ore railway forward of your base is to be thoroughly destroyed.'

The support by the Luftwaffe of night operations that had been planned could not take place on account of the weather, but there was a successful landing of Army supplies, ammunition and clothing.

Reports of heavy concentration of ships in Harstad showed that the enemy had already landed there. The first two British companies under Major General Mackesy were landed on 14 April from *Southampton* at Salangen in Sag Fjord, where they contacted Norwegian troops, The main body of the British troops, constituting the 24th Brigade, was landed on 15 and 16 April. When entering the fjord the escorting destroyers sank a U-boat. During the disembarkation of troops there was a German air attack, which scored no hits but caused difficulties because the British had no anti-aircraft defences.

Admiral Lord Cork had arrived in the area on 14 April with the intention of proceeding immediately to the capture of Narvik, as he believed that the events of 13 April had shaken the Germans in their power of resistance. A landing party from the ships, including 350 men from *Southampton*, was to be formed for this purpose, but *Southampton* had meanwhile disembarked her troops at Sag Fjord, and General Mackesy considered that, far from being shaken, the German defences had been strengthened through the naval reinforcements from the destroyers. He stated that his troops were only fit for an unopposed landing, and that the conditions of snow and weather would restrict their mobility ashore.

The direct assault on Narvik was therefore abandoned, and instead sections of the troops landed in Sag Fjord were moved to Bogen Fjord, and later to Ballangen Fjord, in order to form bases on both sides of the harbour for the coming operations against Narvik. Admiral Lord Cork, who on 20 April assumed overall command of the operations, hoped that the Germans would be forced to give up Narvik after a prolonged bombardment of the town; but should this not succeed, it would be necessary to await improvement in the weather and the start of the thaw before landing. This plan characterised the course of events up to the beginning of May. Although General Dietl realised that he could not count on reinforcements, he did not yet regard the situation in Narvik as threatening. Even after he realised the British had established themselves in Bogen Fjord, he reported to the German Command that he would hold Narvik in any circumstances; but nothing could be done to prevent the British naval forces from moving freely in the fjords round Narvik and bombarding the German positions, since the German troops had no weapons to deal with such a situation, and only the Luftwaffe could bring relief. Hence the German General urgently and repeatedly demanded increased air effort against the enemy; he requested that the fjord entrances should be blocked with A/C mines to prevent the British naval forces from using Rombaken and Beis Fjords for flank and rear bombardment of the Germans. This request could not at the time be granted because of the distance of the objective from the German air bases. Under the circumstances the Luftwaffe did everything possible to support the Germans at Narvik, by dropping weapons, ammunition and supplies, and by attacking the naval forces. During an air attack on Harstad and Tromsø on 18 April a near miss on *Furious* damaged her machinery. This carrier, whose strength in aircraft had been considerably reduced through frequent operations, soon left the operational area.

On 24 April there was a very heavy bombardment of the town and the ore railway by a force estimated by Narvik to consist of two battleships, two cruisers and seven destroyers, but no serious damage was done. German land positions at Elvenes, Gratangen Fjord and Oalge Pass were attacked from the north by Norwegian troops. Anticipating the possible necessity for evacuating Narvik, the non-combatant troops and prisoners were moved to the interior by rail, and the equipment for loading the ore was destroyed. The enemy's bombardment on 27 April had a more serious effect, causing severe damage and the destruction of the railway at Rombaks Fjord, and this interrupted supplies to Narvik and Elvegaardsmoen.

Although he considered the bombardment on 24 April to have been effective Admiral Lord Cork received the impression that the enemy's resistance was still intact and that in the prevailing weather conditions an attempt to land in Narvik, even under the protection of the ships' guns, would be unsuccessful. In the ensuing period a large part of the British naval forces were sent home, while the expeditionary force was considerably increased. Three battalions of Chasseurs-Alpins were landed on 27 April. Two were sent to Gratangen to join the Norwegian troops there, and one battalion, together with some British troops from Ballangen, occupied the Ankenes Peninsula, which formed the west bank of Beis Fjord. The preparations for the intended siege of Narvik were thus considerably advanced. One week later two battalions of the Foreign Legion and four Polish battalions arrived. The former reinforced the garrison at Ballangen, and the latter were held in reserve. The troops were equipped with small tanks and guns.

Both sides had so far suffered from the unfavourable weather, but the advantage was with the defender. At the end of April the snow melted, and the enemy prepared to attack. Not until 29 April did the Narvik Group regard the position as serious. The German patrols had to be withdrawn in face of superior forces, and General Dietl believed that only increased use of the Luftwaffe could relieve the situation.

On 1 May the siege was strengthened by the landing of enemy troops at Ankenes, and the situation became from day to day more difficult, as the German forces were inadequate to cope with the increasing threat to their flank. The troops were short of snow shoes, and the enemy was helped by experienced Norwegian guides. On 4 May the Narvik Group urgently demanded reinforcements by air of one company of Alpine troops with snow shoes. Difficulty was caused by the interruption of supplies along the ore railway, through British destroyers operating in Rombaks Fjord. General Dietl decided to hold on to Narvik and the area of Elvegaardsmoen as long as possible. A survey of the mountainous country east of Rombaken, and experience so far had shown 'that the defence of a mountain pass could not guaranteed for any length of time against a superior enemy'. General Dietl first considered the evacuation of Narvik on 6 May, when the enemy's pressure on General Windisch's troops on the east wing of the German positions became more severe.

After the clearing up of the situation in Central Norway the German High Command had placed the Narvik Group under the command of Group XXI, and had instructed General von Falkenhorst to give priority to supplies for Narvik by using all the available forces of Luftflotte 5. The Supreme Command directive to the Narvik Group stated: 'hold on as long as possible, otherwise withdraw to Bodø'. The German Air Force now switched its main activities to Narvik. On 7 May one of the turrets of the *Aurora* was put out of action by a bomb hit, and one or two other ships were damaged. On 14 May the former Polish destroyer *Grom* was sunk. Narvik had also requested support from U-boats, but this was refused by the Naval Staff on the grounds that opportunities were lacking for U-boats. The German troops who, after capturing Namsos, had turned in the direction of Mosjoen, advanced very slowly. The Norwegians had destroyed many bridges, and exceptional difficulties were encountered in the trackless mountain country. It was therefore decided to support the advance of the Army by transporting troops along the coast, and a coastal steamer was sent from Oslo with mountain troops to be landed at Ranan Fjord (Mo). Here, on the evening of 10 April, contact was made with the enemy.

In the meantime the Allies, following their operational plan, had landed, without resistance and unobserved, six companies of British troops at Mosjoen, Mo and Bodø. They were under Colonel Gubbins, and their object was to prevent the German advance on Narvik and, especially, prevent the Luftwaffe from establishing bases for operating against Narvik. When, on 9 April, the Colonel arrived at Mosjoen (the southernmost of these landing places), German pressure from the south was already so strong that he contemplated withdrawing to Mo or Bodø, the latter being considered the more important position. A coastal steamer transporting German forces to Ranan Fjord was spotted by British air reconnaissance, and Lord Cork sent *Calcutta* and *Zulu* to intercept her. They arrived too late to prevent the landing of the troops at Hemnes on the evening of 10 April, but after the landing the steamer was sunk.

This landing at a point 45 k.m. behind the British base at Mosjoen removed all doubt in the mind of Colonel Gubbins as to the necessity for evacuating the place, which he did on the following night, withdrawing his troops to Aalsten at the entrance to Ranan Fjord. On 12 May this force was taken to Mo, where three further companies had been landed, as the British intended to hold the place as long as possible. The disembarkation there was subjected to German air attacks, being the centre of attention, since the weak German forces at Hemnes now found themselves in a dangerous position. During the British transport movements in Ranan Fjord, Hemnes was fired on repeatedly by the ships, but no attempt was made to liquidate the place.

In the meantime the situation at Narvik underwent a radical change. The Foreign Legion troops at Ballangen were transported on the night of 13 May to Herjangs Fjord, naval forces acting in support, and the landing took place with only slight resistance. They occupied Bjerkvik at the end of the fjord, and Melby on the east bank. The troops at Bjerkvik joined with the Chasseurs-Alpins advancing from Elvenes, and the battalion landed at Melby occupied the coastal road at Elvegaard leading to Oyde Fjord. Elvegaard was occupied by the French who advanced under cover of naval forces along the north bank of Rombaks Fjord where they took up their positions on the south side of Narvik on the

Ankenes Peninsula. The British troops were relieved by Polish forces, who advanced to the eastward and established themselves on the south bank of Beis Fjord. The British troops were sent by sea to reinforce the Bodø position.

These extensive movements of troops resulted in hemming in the German positions at Narvik on three sides, and placing the Allies in a position for the final attack. But the daily increasing activity of the Luftwaffe caused Lord Cork and the new British Commander, General Auchinleck, to postpone the attack until it could be adequately supported by Allied air power. This did not occur until 26 May by which time the two landing grounds at Bardufoss, sixty miles north-east of Narvik, and Skoanland, on the east coast of Tjeldsundet, had been prepared and occupied by the R.A.F. It was then decided that the attack was to take place on 28 May.

From the middle of May the Luftwaffe had at its disposal a large number of Ju. 88's, which were based on Trondheim, and after a suitable intermediate landing ground had been found near Mosjoen. Stukas (Ju. 87's) were also available for the Narvik operation. Preparations could now be made for the laying of German mines from the air in the fjords, as requested by the Narvik Group. In the period between 14 and 26 May, the Luftwaffe succeeded in sinking or damaging a dozen enemy warships or transports, including the battleship *Resolution* which was damaged by bomb hits on 16 May in Tjeldsundet, and the A/A cruiser *Curlew* which was sunk in the same place on 26 May.

The transport *Chrobry* was also sunk by the Luftwaffe. This ship was due to bring the British troops from Ankenes to Bodø on 14 May. General Auchinleck considered that as the area Bodø–Mo was of vital importance, the former place must be held at all costs and the latter as long as possible. When the transport *Chrobry* with 700 troops was in Westfjord, still about thirty miles from her destination, she was attacked by Stukas round about midnight and set on fire; exploding ammunition killed a number of the troops and the remainder were evacuated and taken to Harstad. The ship was sunk by British aircraft, the guns and tanks were lost. In these operations the destroyer *Somali* was damaged and had to be sent home. When two days later the troops were being transported in warships from Harstad to Bodø, the cruiser *Effingham* ran on the rocks, had to be abandoned, and was torpedoed. With these reinforcements Colonel Gubbins' force in the Bodø area consisted of 4,000 men, with only four guns.

Meanwhile the head of the German Army column – 2nd Mountain Division, 181 Infantry Division – which was commanded by General Feuerstein, was approaching the area Mo–Bodø, having advanced from Namsos. After the British evacuation of Mosjoen on the night of 11 May, this column had occupied the place and a few days later fighting took place between it and Mo. Although both sides were about equal numerically, the Germans enjoyed support from tanks, artillery and the Air Force, and were thus able to force the withdrawal of the British to the north. On 18 May Mo was abandoned by the British and a week later, closely pursued by German troops, they reached the inner end of Salten Fjord. The main British position here was at Fauske on the north bank of the fjord, about 45 k.m. east of Bodø. On 28 May the German troops were advancing on Fauske, and the fighting here for the possession of Bodø would have become fierce if the Allied Supreme Command had not already decided on 24 May to liquidate the whole of the Norwegian operation. The basis of the decision was that after the German advance into Holland, Belgium and France the Allied troops in Norway were urgently required for the defence of the United Kingdom.

The evacuation orders resulted in the rapid removal to Bodø in destroyers and numerous small vessels of the troops that had been at Fauske, and embarkation for England commenced on the 29 May. There were several Luftwaffe attacks from Narvik, which did not materially interfere with the embarkation. On 30 May General Feuerstein's group was already 15 k.m. north of Fauske, and near Bodø, which was taken on 1 June. On the following day the German troops detailed for the advance on Narvik began their northward movement. They consisted of three special Alpine companies under Lieutenant Colonel van Hengl, and the journey was expected to take three weeks. Parts of the 2nd Mountain Division and of the 181 Infantry Division were left behind to protect the lines of communication. The German Navy was directed to arrange supplies from Trondheim to Bodø inside the fjords, as the poor roads permitted only small reinforcements by the land route. The occupation by the German Air Force of Bodø brought the great advantage that it was now possible to employ dive bombers at Narvik.

As the Germans were close upon the Allies at Bodø, evacuation commenced at once, but at Narvik the situation was different; the

German defence was in difficulties and the Allies had made all preparations for a successful attack and capture of the town. These plans were pursued to facilitate the eventual evacuation by achieving a decisive blow, also to damage the harbour installations and the ore railway, and to interrupt the ore traffic for as long as possible. The Allied intention to evacuate remained unknown to the Germans. The direct attack on Narvik by bombardment from British warships commenced shortly after midnight on 27/28 May. Twenty minutes later Norwegian and Foreign Legion troops, who had been brought from Oyde Fjord across Rombaks Fjord, were landed at Orneset on the south bank close to Narvik. As very few landing craft were available the first wave was weak. The arrival of the second wave was delayed because German guns were able to cover the embarkation points, but the landing of the troops was completed by 0400. Shortly afterwards the Luftwaffe attacked with thirty aircraft, and the British counter-attack from the air was hindered through fog on the landing ground at Bardufoss. The A/A cruiser *Cairo* was damaged by bombs, and the British ships had to concentrate on their own anti-aircraft defence. However, the landing was completed before the Luftwaffe operation, so the Allied troops could dispense with supporting gunfire from the ships.

Allied forces proceeded at once to penetrate into Narvik, and simultaneously French Alpine troops began to attack on the north bank of Rombaks Fjord, and Polish troops on the south bank of Beis Fjord. They advanced eastward to the inner fjords to prevent the retreat of the Germans into the mountains. Under these conditions Narvik could no longer be held. The country round the landing places was the scene of heavy fighting during the day, but in the evening the Allies were in undisputed possession of the harbour and town, and General Dietl withdrew into hilly country east of Narvik. Within two days the Polish troops reached the eastern end of Beis Fjord and the French troops, advancing on both banks of Rombaks Fjord, reached Stroemmen Narrows. On 31 May the German troops on the Narvik peninsula found themselves in a very serious position owing to a surprise advance of two Polish battalions coming from the east end of Beis Fjord to Sildvik. No German reinforcements were available to support the south flank, and the British used the destroyers in Rombaks Fjord and also their Air Force to prevent German troop movements. German aircraft had laid some mines in the Stroemmen Narrows but they were ineffective.

The following days were marked by particularly bad snowstorms and rain which affected the enemy's operation, but which also prevented air reinforcements and supplies from reaching the German troops. German intelligence indicated great shipping activity on 3 June in the Narvik area, and the German Naval Staff concluded that the enemy was seeking a rapid decision there since the situation in Belgium and France could not permit him to maintain such an effort in Northern Norway.

On 6 June fighting was resumed in the Narvik area. The enemy's destroyers again fired from Rombaks Fjord on the German positions, suffering no losses through the German mines. On 8 June it was known that the Norwegian King and Government were about to leave the country, and that the Norwegian Commander-in-Chief, General Ruge, had been told to enter into negotiations with the German High Command. From this the Naval Staff concluded that the British were about to evacuate the Narvik position, and on the following day German reconnaissance showed that the evacuation had begun. On the evening of 8 June General Dietl reported to the German Supreme Command that the enemy had evacuated the town and harbour, and that both were again in German hands. On the following day the Norwegians stopped fighting. Before leaving Narvik the British had thoroughly destroyed the dock installations, the power station and the ore railway for several kilometres. With these measures, and by blocking the harbour through the sinking of twenty ships, they had hoped to prevent any further transport of ore from Narvik for at least one year. Actually it was not until 8 January, 1941, that the first iron ore steamer could be sent from Narvik.

Extensive preparations had been made by the British for the return of the 24,500 troops, and for the protection of the transports. The main embarkation took place at Harstad, where Luftwaffe attacks were without material result. The last German air success was the sinking of the British armed boarding vessel *Vandyck* on 11 June, north of Harstad, at Andenes. The effect on the return journey of the eleventh-hour appearance of German Naval forces will be described in the next chapter.

Operation 'Juno'

Even at the time of the fighting for Trondheim, the German Naval Staff believed that operations by the German battleships in the area west of Stadtlandet up to Frohavet offered prospects for the relief of the situation on land. These plans were not put into force because of the serious loss of ten destroyers at Narvik, making it impossible to provide the necessary destroyer escort for the battleships.

From the middle of May, when the position at Narvik deteriorated, a supporting operation by the battleships became more necessary. In the meantime destroyers had become available as a minimum escort for these ships.

On 14 May the first discussion took place with the Chief of the Naval Staff on the proposed operation by the Fleet, and the Naval Staff's view was expressed in the following terms:–

> 'With the situation deteriorating at Narvik, it is considered necessary to provide some relief, and the situation of the enemy appears to offer prospects for action against the British naval forces there. A penetration into Westfjord up to the entrance to Narvik, and into Vaagsfjord up to Harstad, appears possible under prevailing navigational conditions in the channels. Trondheim, which must immediately be strengthened with antiaircraft defences, offers the best refuelling base for the ships engaged in this operation, which, in view of the situation at Narvik, should be launched as soon as possible.'

Raeder immediately ordered preparations for the attack. Two days later the operational plan was extended to conform to Hitler's orders that supplies by sea must be guaranteed for the Army Group Feuerstein, on its way to Narvik.[29] The Naval Staff considered that light naval forces alone, without support of heavy ships, would be insufficient. Since the operation would have to be protracted, with repeated sorties by the battleships, these would have to be based on Trondheim. On 27 May the Naval Staff decided to extend the operation, which received the cover name 'Juno', so as to include not only an attack on the enemy naval forces in the area Narvik–Harstad–Bodø, but also the protracted presence of naval forces in the North Norwegian operational area.

Army Group XXI, Luftflotte 5, and the Admiral Commanding Norway were instructed to take the necessary co-ordinating steps, and Admiral Boehm was ordered to move his headquarters from Oslo to Trondheim for the period of the operation. Group XXI was asked to indicate land targets in the operational area for bombardment by the ships, such as disembarkation points, encampments and artillery positions. The inadequate anti-aircraft defences of Trondheim were a worry to the Naval Staff, who succeeded in getting the Luftwaffe to move heavy batteries there from Oslo. The necessary tankers were sent to Trondheim, and the supply ship *Nordmark* was ordered to take up a position from 4 June in latitude 72° N., between 0° and 5° E. The supply ship *Dithmarschen* was ordered to take up a position from 6 June between 67° 40' N., 3° West, and 68° 30' N., 0° 40' W.

On 27 May the German 'Y' Service intercepted a most valuable British W/T message, which gave a clear insight into the organisation of the Northern Patrol to the south of Iceland. The Naval Staff regarded this intelligence as justifying an operation by the battleships from Trondheim.

In his directive of 29 May to the Commander-in-Chief of the German Fleet, Admiral Marschall, the Naval Group Commander, West (General Admiral Saalwächter) stated:–

The following instructions are issued in accordance with orders from the Naval Staff:–

(1) The first and principal task is penetration into And Fjord and Vaagsfjord for the destruction of enemy warships and transports there, and of his bases. According to available information most of our objectives are in this area. If reconnaissance reports indicate that penetration into Ofot Fjord, even up to Narvik, would be more

promising, then this will become the main task. A further task is the safeguarding of Army supplies on the route from Trondheim to Saltdal–Bodø–Mo. The latter task is to be carried out concurrently with the main task, or after the completion of the latter, and Trondheim is to be used as a base. To achieve surprise it is advisable to avoid entering Trondheim until the operation in the Narvik area has been completed.

(2) The operation will be carried out with the battleships *Scharnhorst* and *Gneisenau*, the cruiser *Hipper* and the destroyers *Galster*, *Lody*, *Steinbrink* and *Schoemann*. The sortie will take place from the Kattegat and Skagerrak.'

This directive was intended to show the Commander-in-Chief that his main task was the destruction of British naval forces and transports in the area Harstad–And–Vaagsfjord, but this is not apparent in the verbal discussion between Admiral Marschall and Raeder on 31 May, summarised in the War Diary of the Naval Staff as follows:–

'In accordance with the general directives of the Naval Staff and of Group West, naval operations are designed to meet the requirements of the situation on *land*. The Commander-in-Chief of the Fleet must make decisions on this basis, while taking into consideration any intelligence received from Group West, including air reconnaissance reports and 'Y' reports. Primarily the intention is to act against the allied naval forces and transports operating against the German Narvik Group, and secondly to afford relief to our land forces. In addition the continuous threats to our land communications by British naval forces must be eliminated by the repeated appearance of German naval forces at different points along the coast.

The control in detail of this operation cannot be undertaken by Group West, but must be under the Commander-in-Chief of the Fleet in consultation with Admiral, Norway.

'Major decisions will of course rest with Group West or the Naval Staff.'

It is necessary to mention these details, since an argument developed later as to whether the Commander-in-Chief of the Fleet had received a definite order for the task at Harstad, or whether the initiative had been left to him. On this question Group West and the Naval Staff expressed a divergent view from that held by the Commander-in-Chief.

At 0800 on 4 June, the Fleet left Kiel for Operation Juno, proceeding northward from the Great Belt, and reaching a position off Skagen at 0600 the following day. Air reconnaissance revealed nothing. Later, German 'Y' reports gave the following British naval forces in the North Norwegian area on 6 June:– *Valiant*, *Glorious*, *Ark Royal*, *Devonshire*, *Southampton*, *Vindictive*, *Coventry*, and about fifteen destroyers. Harstad was believed to be their main base, and as a result of Y information the main units of the Home Fleet were believed to be north-west of Scapa in the Northern Patrol area. At 2000 on 6 June the German Fleet was in position 68° N., 30' W., and during the night *Hipper* and the destroyers completed with fuel from the *Dithmarschen*. Admiral Marschall used radio-telephony to inform his ships of the intention to attack Harstad on the night of 9 June. Late that evening Group West informed the Commander-in-Chief that British radio traffic showed no unusual features, such as might have been expected if a sortie of the German ships had been spotted.

The following entry occurs in the War Staff Diary for 7 June:–

'From radio interception in the Harstad area, it appears that there is a British convoy rendezvous off the entrance to Tromsø. At 0700 German air reconnaissance sighted four ships and three escorts on a southerly course, about 360 miles north-west of Trondheim; convoy traffic between England and North Norway is particularly active at the moment.

Air reconnaissance in the area Harstad–Narvik spotted three groups of vessels between 1235 and 1355, about eighty miles north-west of And Fjord. They consisted of one light cruiser, two destroyers, two large ships on a westerly course, two destroyers to the north-west of these, and further to the north *Ark Royal*, *Glorious*, and one destroyer stopped. In the evening three patrol boats were sighted by air reconnaissance, 240 miles north-west of Trondheim, steering south-west. The only British heavy ship in the Narvik area was identified by Y as *Valiant*. Radio traffic between Narvik and England shows nothing unusual. The German battleship formation has not so far been spotted. Thus the prospects for our operation are good.'

The convoy mentioned as having been spotted at 0700 did not influence the movements of the German Commander-in-Chief, who assumed that these were empty transports; and he was anxious not to reveal his position prematurely, since this might spoil the surprise attack on Harstad, or even lead to cancellation of the operation.[30] The Commander-in-Chief continued to aim at an attack on Harstad on the night of 9 June, with support from the air if possible, but added the restrictive clause that it would occur 'when conditions at Harstad are better known and the time of attack can be more definitely stated'. In the evening of 7 June Admiral Marschall stated in his diary: 'Air reconnaissance in northern area is, as previously, not available.' The Commander-in-Chief collected his commanders onboard the flag-ship to discuss Operation Harstad. During the discussion an urgent message was received at 2055 from Group West as follows:–

> 'Air reconnaissance reports one cruiser, two destroyers, two large ships at 1325 in the northern entrance to And Fjord, proceeding west at medium speed, and two destroyers at 1345, twenty-five miles north of Andenes, on a northerly course. Also two aircraft carriers and two destroyers stopped at 1400, about forty-five miles north of Andenes.'

This much delayed reconnaissance report caused the Commander-in-Chief to review the position. The fact that many British units were at sea convinced him that major enemy movements were in hand, and that important targets would probably not be found within the fjords. Under these circumstances he believed that the danger of mines, nets, torpedoes and gun batteries while entering the fjords, did not justify the risk to his battleships. And there was no reconnaissance report of Harstad. The diary of the Commander-in-Chief states:–

> 'It occurs to me that the noticeable westward movement may indicate a British evacuation of Norway, and that the westward-bound convoys will now offer valuable targets.'

Admiral Marschall therefore decided to operate against the convoy that had been reported, and to await further intelligence before taking action in the Harstad area. He doubted whether pursuit of the aircraft carriers would achieve any result, since no up-to-date information was available as to their position.

At 0400 on 8 June the Commander-in-Chief informed the Admiral, Group West, of his intention to attack the convoy. The latter did not agree with this diversion from the main task to what he believed to be empty ships. At 0530 Group West therefore directed the Commander-in-Chief to use at least his battleships for the main task of attacking Harstad, unless there were other reasons not known locally, and to use *Hipper* and the destroyers for attacking the convoy. At this stage the Chief of Naval Staff intervened, as he considered the order to attack Harstad too binding for the Commander-in-Chief. Through the Chief of Naval Staff's intervention the Naval Group Commander, West, altered the wording of his instruction as follows:– 'The main objective is, as before, the destruction of enemy naval forces in the area Harstad–Narvik.'

Meanwhile the Fleet had come across the tanker *Oil Pioneer* (5,600 tons) and the accompanying trawler *Juniper* at 0600/8 in position 67° 20' N., 4° E. Both were sunk without being able to transmit W/T signals; and twenty-nine survivors were picked up. As these ships did not belong to the convoy that had been reported, the search for the latter was continued and for this purpose *Hipper*'s and *Scharnhorst*'s aircraft were launched. Very soon *Hipper*'s aircraft reported a convoy to the south, consisting of a cruiser and a merchant ship, and *Scharnhorst*'s aircraft to the north sighted a 12,000 ton armed merchant ship and a hospital ship. The Commander-in-Chief ordered *Hipper* to sink the merchant ship, while he searched in vain for the convoy. *Hipper* sank the British steamer which proved to be empty transport *Orama* (19,840 tons), carrying one hundred German prisoners. Two hundred and seventy-five survivors were picked up by *Hipper* and the destroyers. The hospital ship *Atlantis* was not molested.

The radio office in the *Gneisenau* successfully jammed the *Orama*'s effort to transmit an S.O.S. signal. Nevertheless, the German Commander-in-Chief considered that the British would very soon have wind of these events, and it appeared that *Hipper* and the destroyers would not have a second chance of undisturbed fuelling at sea. He therefore detached them to Trondheim to refuel and for subsequent protection of convoys between Trondheim and Bodø. He intended to continue operations with the battleships in the area Harstad–Tromsø. He still had no reconnaissance reports about Harstad, and was convinced that a penetration into Vaagsfjord offered no real prospects, but he hoped that it would be possible to attack the aircraft carriers north-west of Andenes, which had been identified by Y interception several times in the last few days. This hope was to be fulfilled within the next few hours.

At 1645 in position 69° N. 3° 30' E. a mast-head was sighted to the eastward, and an approach was made at full speed. It was soon identified as a large aircraft carrier with destroyer escorts; the formation was, in fact, the *Glorious* with the destroyers *Ardent* and *Acasta*. The radio interception unit in *Gneisenau* observed that the British ship was trying to make an enemy report. This British enemy report was transmitted on the Fleet short wave as well as on the northern area wave. The transmission on short wave was not received by any station, and that on the area wave was effectively jammed. Further German observation of British radio traffic gave no indication that the German Fleet had been reported.

The action with *Glorious* and the two destroyers lasted about one and three-quarter hours – from 1730 to 1912 – as the carrier tried to escape with maximum speed, and the accompanying destroyers very skilfully shrouded her in smoke, which made German observation of the fall of shot very difficult. The opening range was 25,000 metres. An hour after opening fire one destroyer capsized, the second was on fire, and the carrier was seen to have a heavy list. During the action the British destroyers made full use of their torpedoes, and several times forced the German battleships to take avoiding action. At 1840, when the range was about 14,000 metres, *Scharnhorst* was hit aft by a torpedo which put the after turret out of action, and a leak of water later made the centre and starboard main engines unusable, reducing her speed to 20 knots. The torpedo hit killed two officers and forty-six men. At 1912, the German Commander-in-Chief ordered cease fire as the carrier was in a sinking condition. The second destroyer attempted to escape to the west, and was pursued for a short time by *Gneisenau*. *Gneisenau* then turned back to join the damaged *Scharnhorst*, and the British destroyer sank shortly afterwards.

The German Commander-in-Chief received increasingly serious reports of the damage in *Scharnhorst* as the result of the torpedo hit, and decided to bring her to safety as soon as possible. Under these circumstances he had to give up the intention of rescuing the survivors of *Glorious*. After the action he first steered for Trondheim, but wanted to use the existing favourable situation to take *Scharnhorst* at once direct to a home port. When he reported this intention to Group West on the night of 8/9 June, the latter ordered him to enter Trondheim. The ships arrived there on the afternoon of 9 June, and left again without *Scharnhorst* on the morning of 10 June to continue the operations. This sortie had no result and was ended by the Commander-in-Chief on the night of 10/11 June, as he had concluded from the completion of the British evacuation of Northern Norway that no worthwhile targets remained. This cancellation of further operations accorded with the situation report from Group West, but did not meet with the approval of the Naval Staff, who attached great importance to persevering. On the morning of 11 June the ships entered Trondheim.

Immediately after the end of the action with *Glorious* the Commander-in-Chief sent a radio message giving the result to the Naval Staff and to Group West, followed by a short account of the battle which was taken to Trondheim by *Scharnhorst*'s aircraft. While the Naval Staff was much pleased with the result, it criticised the professional conduct of the whole operation.

When Y reports indicated that up to the morning of 8 June the British had no knowledge of the German operation, and that only *Valiant* was in the Harstad area, the Naval Staff as well as Group West considered that a penetration into this area offered great prospects. Both were disappointed when Admiral Marschall, who from conversations with Raeder had got the impression that he had complete operational freedom, reported his intention early on 8 June of attacking an enemy convoy, 150 miles west of the Lofoten Islands. In the view of the Naval Staff this operation could produce no relieving effect on the land situation. Moreover, the action proposed by the Commander-in-Chief, which could have been undertaken by light forces, involved a risk of revealing the position of the battleships before their main task of penetrating to Harstad had been carried out. It was disappointing that the heavy damage to *Scharnhorst* put her out of action for months. The

Naval Staff considered that her torpedo hit might have been avoided by a better tactical conduct of the action; also that the ships should not have entered Trondheim immediately after the action.

There is no doubt that the original satisfaction at the Commander-in-Chief's success was more justified than the criticism to which he was later exposed. The loss of a British aircraft carrier was a worthwhile object, since such a ship could have been more effective against land operations in the mountainous country than other types of warships. But the Naval Staff had a definite idea as to how the operation should develop, and was disappointed when the Commander-in-Chief acted differently. It is possible that the Naval Staff was influenced in its Harstad plans by the events at Narvik on 13 April, when *Warspite* was so successful. From the start Admiral Marschall was sceptical about the Harstad Operation, and saw his battleships endangered by the coastal batteries which the British could bring to bear on them in the narrow fjords. In his opinion, this was a risk not warranted by the results that could be expected. The danger was probably no greater than that incurred by *Warspite* on 13 April in Westfjord and Ofot Fjord, but the Harstad plan had a very different background. *Warspite* was one of many British battleships, whereas *Scharnhorst* and *Gneisenau* were the only German ones. Moreover *Warspite* had a dozen destroyers available as escort during the long approach through the fjords, and the Commander-in-Chief of the British Home Fleet, realising the danger, had himself considered it necessary to see to all the details of the operation.

It is doubtful whether on this occasion the German Naval Staff made the best possible use of its two battleships. The German Commander-in-Chief did not carry out these plans, hence the test could not be made. As things stood he would probably have suffered little in penetrating to Harstad, but his conclusion was right, and even a successful penetration would have brought no result, since the British warships and transports had already evacuated the place on the night of 8/9 June. When Admiral Marschall decided not to go for Harstad but to attack the convoy that had been reported he took the last chance that offered of operating against the withdrawing enemy.

The differences that occurred in Operation Juno between the Naval Staff, Group West, and the Commander-in-Chief of the Fleet have been mentioned in detail, because they illustrate, once an operation is launched, how difficult it is to harmonize the operational conceptions and intentions of two controlling centres ashore with those of the Commander-in-Chief afloat. These difficulties could not be cleared up after the operation; they led to the relief of Admiral Marschall as Commander-in-Chief, and his replacement by Vice-Admiral Lütjens.

Operation Juno had a further result in that it put an end for the time being to the desire of the Naval Staff to exert strong and continuous pressure in the area between Greenland and Norway by operating the Fleet from Trondheim.

Up to the morning of 9 June the British had no knowledge of the events of the previous day, thanks to the effective jamming activity of the radio office in *Gneisenau*. It was not until 9 June that the hospital ship *Atlantis* gave incomplete news of the losses. From 10 June the German Fleet was shadowed by British air and submarine reconnaissance. On the afternoon of 11 June, twelve British aircraft unsuccessfully attacked the German ships that had by then returned to Trondheim. A second attack by fifteen Skuas from *Ark Royal* occurred between 0200 and 0300 on 13 June. The aircraft claimed to have obtained at least one hit on *Scharnhorst*. This proved to be correct; the *Scharnhorst* was hit by one 500 lb. bomb which, however, glanced off the ship and fell into the water without exploding. Eight of the attacking aircraft were lost. The British submarines were more successful.

Although the Naval Staff pressed strongly for the continuation of operations in northern waters, the sailing of the Fleet was delayed until 20 June owing to the change in the command. At 1600 on that day Vice-Admiral Lütjens, the new Commander-in-Chief, proceeded with the *Gneisenau*, the *Hipper* and one destroyer into the area round Iceland. At the same time the damaged *Scharnhorst*, with destroyer and torpedo boat escort, began her journey home. After the *Gneisenau* Group had passed Frohavet, it was reported by a British submarine at 2330 in a position forty miles north-east of Halten Island. The submarine attacked, and *Gneisenau* was hit by a torpedo on the starboard side forward. This resulted in Admiral Lütjens breaking off the operation and returning to Trondheim. He did not consider the possibility of sending *Hipper* on alone. The return journey of the *Scharnhorst* Group was not without incident. The ships were spotted on the afternoon of 21 June by British air reconnaissance, and from 1600 onwards there were continuous attacks by torpedo-bombers and bombers, all of which were repulsed by the Germans without sustaining damage. From the ships it was observed that six aircraft were shot down by A/A guns, and seven by German fighters. As Y reports indicated that superior enemy naval forces were approaching to intercept *Scharnhorst*, the group was diverted into Stavanger for the night, continuing its journey on the following morning after the enemy had withdrawn. On the evening of 23 June the ships arrived at Kiel without interference.

Operation Juno marked the end of the German campaign in Norway. The operation had started under favourable auspices and had brought the Fleet some good results, but the end had been marred by the disabling of both battleships for several months. The strategic objective of providing relief for the German Army group had not been achieved. Action came too late, for the Allied withdrawal had already commenced.

Concluding Remarks

The occupation of Norway was a great military success for Germany. In the face of British naval superiority, the landing operation could only succeed if the intention remained concealed long enough to make allied counter-measures late and therefore ineffective. This was achieved. The Allies' delay, and their failure to act immediately on receipt of the first news of the German invasion, were contributory causes to the German success.

From the first the Franco-British counter-action was bound to fail because, while underrating the extent of the German effort in men and material, it was undertaken with insufficient forces. From the beginning it should have been clear to the British Command that no counter-action offered prospects of success unless the first German troops landed in Norway could be cut off from their home bases. The British succeeded in doing this locally at Trondheim and Narvik, but failed against the main stream of reinforcements and supplies on the sea route from Germany to Oslo. Along this route the British used only submarines, which could hinder but not stop the flow of supplies. Only the bold extension of British naval power into the Skagerrak and Kattegat could have achieved this. The British warships would have had to operate here for some days after the first German landings. It is probable that the destruction of the large troop transports then on their way to Oslo would have completely changed the course of events; not until these ships arrived at Oslo did the German troops there become operational. If they had failed to arrive, the British counter-landing in Central Norway would have held great prospects of success. It was probably because of the air menace that the British decided against using the Fleet in this way. The German Air Force exercised unconditional control of the air in these areas, which were well within the range of the German air bases, and there is no doubt that an extension of British naval action into the

Kattegat would have involved the British Fleet in very heavy losses. The whole situation was marked by a new factor, namely, that German air power had made it possible to eliminate Britain's sea power in a limited area in which Germany possessed no corresponding naval strength.

The Luftwaffe also took a major part in the defence against Allied counterattacks, particularly in the first days after the British landing. Yet here the German Army was the decisive factor, since it relied on supplies through Oslo to gain the necessary strength to deal with any enemy. Co-operation between the German Army and Air Force in this stage of the fighting was particularly close and effective. In the mountainous country the Luftwaffe was an indispensable aid to the advance of the Army, and the Army captured bases which the Luftwaffe required for its extensive operations. In the first phase of the campaign, up to the landing, the main burden was carried by the German Navy. It was used to the full, and in spite of heavy losses proved equal to the task. In the second phase, the Navy had necessarily to play a modest part. The Norwegian campaign was not only the first example of a large combined operation of all three Services, but in retrospect it can be said that all Services worked with the utmost understanding of each other, and that all demands on them were fully met.

This campaign, which had been so successfully carried out in the field, was a complete failure politically. During the occupation the contact with the Norwegian counsellor Quisling proved disastrous from the German point of view. He had raised the hope in the German Command that, with the help of his followers, the occupation could be achieved on a more or less peaceful footing. Actually his influence was small, and his personality was a complete obstacle to a peaceful understanding. The prospects of such an understanding had in any case diminished, when on the night of 9 April, as a result of premature disclosure to the Norwegian Government, both sides had exchanged blows; yet even after this there were political possibilities of a peaceful settlement, as had occurred in Denmark. These were not exploited and could have borne fruit only if Quisling, whom the King of Norway disowned, had been dropped. On the other hand, when later and with Hitler's approval Quisling tried to form an effective Government he failed to obtain either from the Reich Kommissar Terboven or from the German High Command and the Armed Forces the necessary support for his difficult task. It may not be known that Hitler, when sending Terboven to take up his post at Oslo, uttered the following parting words, 'Herr Reich Kommissar, you can do me no greater service than to make the Norwegians our friends.' It would have been difficult to find a personality less suited to this task than Terboven. His severe and unsympathetic administrative measures resulted in stifling the slight sympathy for Germany that existed among the Norwegian people, and he was not prepared to surrender any of his power to the idea of Norwegian self-government.

Raeder's protests, based on reports by Admiral Boehm in Norway, had no effect with Hitler, who although aware of dangerous developments, could not bring himself to drop Terboven, one of his old guard. Thus the higher historic purpose of German action in Norway – to gather the racially similar Norwegian people into the moral and spiritual orbit of the Germanic races – remained unfulfilled. The Norwegians' admiration of the success of the German armies, their disappointment over the failure of British help and, not least, their willingness to acknowledge the exemplary behaviour of German troops after the occupation, all helped to clear the way for an understanding, but the German leaders failed to use compromise or tact for exploiting the situation. Thus the association of Norway with Germany, born of military necessity, struck no roots in the Norwegian people, but remained a mere historical episode.

Endnotes

1. War Diary of the Naval Staff Part C. VII of 320.1239.
2. War Diary of the Naval Staff 18.1.40.
3. War Diary for 22.1.40.
4. War Diary C. VII for 21.2.40.
5. War Diary for 23.2.40.
6. War Diary for 29.2.40.
7. War Diary C.VII/40.
8. War Diary for 4.4.40.
9. Notation by General Gameline on 10 March, 1940 to Prime Minister Daladier; also to Corbin, French Ambassador in London on 21 February, 1940.
10. Battle Summary No. 17 The Conjunct Expeditions to Norway B.R. 1736 (10).
11. War Diary, Part A, April, 1940.
12. This was the Trondheim Group – *Hipper* and four destroyers – which was standing off the entrance to the fjord, as it was still too early to enter; if the ships were on a westerly course when sighted, this had no real significance.
13. *See* page 426.
14. *See* page 422.
15. Actually Admiral Layton had received orders for the night of 10 April 'to maintain a patrol of the entrance of Bergen, to prevent enemy forces from escaping.'
16. Action report by 1st Officer of *Blücher*.
17. War Diary of the Naval Attache, Commander Schreiber.
18. *See* page 427.
19. British report gives the opening range as 6,000 yards, and the German as 10,000 yards.
20. Recorded British and German times do not always accord; the following account uses German time, which is one hour later than British time.
21. *See* page 430.
22. *See* page 440.
23. *See* page 431.
24. *See* page 415.
25. War Diary IV/40.
26. *See* page 459.
27. British Battle Summary, Part 108.
28. *See* page 459.
29. *See* page 492.
30. War Diary of the Commander-in-Chief for 7.6.40.

495

Biographies

Admiral Lord Alan West of Spithead GCB DSC PC

Alan West joined the Royal Navy at Britannia Royal Naval College in 1965. He became Commanding Officer (CO) of the minesweeper HMS *Yarnton* in 1973, before qualifying as a Principal Warfare Officer (PWO) in 1977. He held specialist appointments in HMS *Juno* (*Leander*-class frigate), HMS *Ambuscade* (Type 21 frigate) and HMS *Norfolk* (*County*-class destroyer).

Promoted Commander in 1980 and appointed CO of the Type 21 frigate HMS *Ardent*, he took the ship to the Falkland Islands in 1982 and led the Amphibious Task Force into Falkland Sound to provide gunfire support, until sunk by a series of air attacks, being hit 17 times and having 22 dead from a complement of 199. He was last to leave his stricken ship and was awarded the DSC for his leadership.

West was subsequently appointed to the Directorate of Naval Plans in the MoD 1982–1984 and promoted Captain in 1984, becoming Assistant Director of Naval Staff Duties, also in the MoD, from 1985–1986. His appointment to the dual role of CO HMS *Bristol* and Captain of the Dartmouth Training Squadron in 1987–1988 led to a study on the future employment of women in the Royal Navy. He became Head of the Maritime Intelligence Directorate 1989–1992, before attending the Royal College of Defence Studies in 1992 and undertaking the Higher Command and Staff Course in 1993 prior to returning to the MoD as Director of Naval Staff Duties 1993–1994.

Promoted Rear-Admiral in 1994, West was Naval Secretary and Director General Naval Manning 1994–1996, before returning to sea as Commander United Kingdom Task Group/Commander Anti-Submarine Warfare Striking Force (COMUKTG/CASWSF) 1996–1997.

Promoted Vice-Admiral in 1997 as Chief of Defence Intelligence 1997–2000 and then to Admiral in 2000, when he was created a KCB he became Commander-in-Chief Fleet and EASTLANT and Commander Allied Naval Forces North 2000–2002. He held the most senior Royal Navy post as First Sea

Lord and Chief of the Naval Staff 2002–2006, during which time he inspired and led the RN Trafalgar 200 celebrations. He was created a GCB in 2004.

After retirement from the Royal Navy he became the first Chancellor of Southampton Solent University and in the same year was appointed to the board of the Imperial War Museum. From 2007–2010 he was Parliamentary Under-Secretary of State at the Home Office, with responsibility for Security and created a life peer. He sits in the House of Lords and is involved with a large number of charities, many concerned with the sea.

Dr Richard Porter

Hon. Curator at the Britannia Museum and an Associate Lecturer with the University of Lincoln at Britannia Royal Naval College. He joined the College in 1989 as a Senior Lecturer in the Department of Marine Environmental Sciences, having read Geology at the University of Sheffield. After completing his PhD, his career began in the museum world. He became Head of the Education Department at The Manchester Museum and was Assistant Keeper at Sheffield City Museums, prior to that, where he had been involved in the production of both permanent and temporary exhibitions.

At Dartmouth, he was instrumental in setting up a permanent museum at the College which opened in 1999. Since then, he had been Curator of the Britannia Museum, until 2014. In 2005, he co-authored, with Dr Jane Harrold, *Britannia Royal Naval College 1905–2005: One hundred Years of Officer Training at Dartmouth*. For this history of the College, they were awarded the Sir Robert Craven Trophy by the Britannia Naval Research Association, for their outstanding contribution to naval research. A revised, updated edition was published in 2007, re-titled *Britannia Royal Naval College Dartmouth: An Illustrated History*, reprinted in 2012.

Mike Pearce

Served with the Ministry of Defence (Navy) for almost 40 years, holding management and planning roles within many different fields of MoD activity and Royal Navy projects. He was on the staff of the Britannia Royal Naval College, Dartmouth for 12 years and is Vice Chairman of the Britannia Museum Trust. As a naval historian he is a series editor for the Britannia Naval Histories of World War II, has written introductions to several of the titles and acts as illustrations editor for the series.

Abbreviations

A/A Anti-aircraft
AP Shell Armour Piercing
A/S Anti-submarine
ASIS Ammunition Store Issuing Ship
AT Admiralty telegram
ACNS Assistant Chief of Naval Staff
CO Commanding Officer
CS Cruiser Squadron
DCNS Deputy Chief of Naval Staff
FAA Fleet Air Arm
FR French Ship
GC&CS Government Code and Cypher School
HMHS His Majesty's Hospital Ship
HMNoS His Norwegian Majesty's Ship,
HMS His Majesty's Ship
HMT His Majesty's Trawler, can also mean His Majesty's Troopship
HM Submarine His Majesty's Submarine
KMS Kriegsmarine Schiff or (German) Navy Ship
MNBDO Mobile Naval Base Defence Organisation
MS Merchant Ship, sometimes for Motor Ship. Identical to the MV prefix
NAS Naval Air Squadron
OIC Operational Intelligence Centre
ORP Polish Ship
RMS Royal Mail Ship
RNAS Royal Naval Air Station
SNO Senior Naval Officer
SS Steamship
TSDS Two Speed Destroyer Sweep
VT fuze Variable Time Fuze

Index

A

Aachen, SS (*f*52)

Aalborg 464

Aalesund 174–175, 189, 193–194, 219–221, 231, 233, 235, 239, 241, 247–248, 252, 462

Aalsten 476

Åndalsnes 103, 180, 187, 189, 193–194, 199, 202, 205–206, 208–209, 211, 217, 231, 233–252, 254, 272, 276–277, 459–463, 465–468, 470

Acasta, HMS (*f*111), 309, 311–313, 487

Acheron, HMS 237, 242

Aerial, Operation 93

Afridi, HMS (*f*95), 175, 224–225, 227, 243, 256–257, 468–469

Alacrity, HMS 308

Albatros, KMS Torpedo Boat 19, (*f*15), 127, 433, 435

Alfarnes 249

Alsace-Lorraine, Absorbed 26

Alsten Island 275

Alster, SS (*f*76), (*f*81), 154, 188, 453

Altmark, KMS Oiler and Supply 17, (*f*1), (*f*3), (*f*4), 386

Amazon, HMS 243

Amazone, FR Submarine 182

Angle, HMS 210

Ankenes (*f*53), 267, 270, 279, 284, 288, 291, 293, 311, 316, 474, 477, 485

Annesley, Capt John C 277

Antares, KMS 454

Antiope, FR Submarine 182

Anton Schmitt, KMS 20, (*f*38), (*f*62), (*f*63), 107, 145, 148, 438–439, 441–443

AP shell, 15-inch 21, (*f*73)

Arab, HMS 210

Arado 196, floatplane 19, (*f*18), (*f*27), (*f*28), 113

Arandora Star, SS (*f*120), (*f*123), 308

Arbroath, SS 308

Ardent, HMS (*f*) 88, 309, 311–313, 487

Arendal 106, 126

Arethusa, HMS 114, 124, 142, 180, 187, 203, 222, 236–238, 240, 249

Ark Royal, HMS 19, 22, (*f*17). (*f*69), 188, 197, 204–207, 246, 276–277, 279, 285, 287–288, 300, 309, 313, 315–317, 484, 490

Arrow, HMS 237, 242, 308

Ashanti, HMS 203, 226

Askholmene 127

Assmann, Vice Admiral Kurt 13, 379

Aston Villa, HMS 210

Atlantis, HMHS (f117), 283, 311, 314, 322, 486

Atlejarl, SS 216

Auchinleck, General CJE (f115), 277–279, 286–290, 292, 294, 296, 300, 302, 309, 477

Auckland, HMS 187, 208, 228–229, 232–235, 248, 250–252

Audet, General Sylvestre-Gérard 224, 228, 464

Auphan, Capt Gabriel P 201

Aurora, HMS 110, 137, 143, 161, 180, 187, 246, 261, 265, 268–270, 284–286, 291, 475

Aylmer, Capt Edward A 238

B

Bahia Castillo, SS 216, 457

Ballangen Fjord 149, 165

Bangsund 220–222

Bardufoss (f103), 206

Barenfels, SS 20, (f23), (f24), 188, 451, 453

Barham, HMS 187, 194, 231–232, 234

Baroy Island 164–165, 167

Basilisk, HMS 285

Batory, MS (f119), 161, 308, 322, 461, 471

Battalion, Chasseaurs-Alpins 252, 261, 267–268, 271, 273–274, 286, 288, 294, 474, 476

Battalion, Norwegian Army 290, 293, 297

Battalion, Polish 287–288, 291, 294, 302

Battle Summary No.17 100

Beagle, HMS 291, 293, 308

Bedouin, HMS (f39), (f40), (f74), 120, 165–166, 168–169, 444

Beis Fjord 479

Beitstad Fjord 224

Richard Beitzen, KMS 449

Beobachtungsdienst, (B-Dienst) 15

Bergen 16, 19, (f86), 105–106, 116–117, 126, 133, 136–137, 142, 151, 183, 188, 192, 199, 202, 207, 399, 401, 410–411, 420, 428–429, 431, 454

Bernd von Arnim, KMS Cover, 18, (f33), (f41), (f43), (f55) (f62), 107, 116, 128, 145, 149, 166, 415, 424–425, 441, 446–447

Berney-Ficklin, Major-General Horatio PM 198

Berwick, HMS 110, 124, 137, 144, 158, 180–181, 187, 204–205, 269, 411

Béthouart, General Emil A (f115), 286, 290, 292–295, 297, 302, 309

Bettinges, Costal Battery 462

Bickford, Capt Jack G 109–110, 154, 410

Biggs, Cdr Hilary W 166, 169

f – photograph

Birmingham, HMS 110–111, 114, 120, 175, 187, 203–204, 213–215, 222, 225, 229, 242–243, 251–252, 411, 418

Bismarck, KMS 322

Bison, FR (f94), 256–257, 468–469

Bittern, HMS 22, (f93), 187, 208–210, 232–233, 237, 252–253, 465

Bjerkvik 275, 277, 284–288, 292

Black Swan, HMS 187, 208, 232–233, 237–238, 248, 465

Blackburn Skua, dive-bomber 19, 20, 21, 22, (f16), (f17), (f19), (f20), (f23), (f24), (f86), 144, 206, 212, 317, 490

Blackheath, SS 308

Blake, Vice-Admiral Sir Geoffrey 201

Blenheim, Bristol Bomber 111, 207, 213

Bletchley Park 14–15

Blücher, KMS 18–19, (f12), (f13), (f14), (f29), 102, 122, 127, 396–397, 433–435, 437

Blue Star Line 93

Bockenheim, SS (f53)

Bodø (f88), 153, 192, 217, 271–274, 276–280, 288, 297–299, 453, 460, 469, 475–478, 487

Boehm, Admiral Hermann 401, 482, 494

Bofors, 40mm 24

Bolaerne, Islands of 19

Bommel Fjord 143

Bonte, Kommodore Friedrich (f34), 127, 148, 166, 188, 324–326, 396, 423–425, 438, 442

Borgund, DS 313

Bothnia, Gulf of 17, 104

Boyle, Admiral of the Fleet William 25

Boyle, Cdr Richard C 257

Bradman, HM Trawler (f92), 243

Brand, HMNoS Torpedo Boat 451

Brazen, HMS 265–266

Bremen, MS 466

Bremse, KMS 107, 126, 142, 428, 430

Brettingsnes 158

Bristol Pegasus III, Engine (f72)

Britain, Battle of (f104)

Britannia Royal Naval College 13

Brummer, KMS 21, (f84), (f85), 216, 457

Bruno Heinemann, KMS 107, 154, 450

Buddybet 237, 243, 251

Buenos Aires, SS 216, 457

Bulldog, HMS 214–215

Bulman, Paul W 'George' (f104)

Bygden 265

C

Cadart, Admiral Jean E 227, 253, 255–257

Cairo, HMS 175, 187, 222–223, 226–227, 276–277, 279, 284, 288, 291–293, 300, 429

Calcutta, HMS 114, 208, 226, 229, 248, 250–252, 256, 275, 476

Campbell, HMS 241

Carlisle, HMS 204, 208, 236–238, 252–255, 257

Carls, Admiral Rolf Hans Wilhelm K 400, 452

Carton de Wiart VC, General Adrian PG 180, 187, 194, 196, 221, 223, 225, 227, 229, 235, 240, 245, 252, 254, 256, 273, 322, 461, 466

Casus Belli 102

Cate B, SS (*f*52)

Cedarbank, BMM 186, 239

Chamberlain, Neville 16, 389, 469

Chaudiere, HMCS (*f*83)

Chrobry, MS (*f*118), 161, 175, 222, 225–227, 278–279, 288, 322, 461, 463, 471, 477

Churchill, Winston 16–17, 103, 105

Clarke, Rear-Admiral Charles P 291, 294

Clouston, Cdr James Campbell 158

Clyde, HM Submarine 182

Coastal Flying Squadron (No. 506) (Costal Command) 400

Codrington, HMS 143, 270, 320

Congreve, Cdr Geoffrey 299, 303

Copenhagen 108, 111

Cossack, HMS 17, (*f*1), (*f*2), (*f*4) (*f*37), (*f*83), 165, 168–169, 172, 174, 387, 444, 446–447

Couch, SS 308

Courageous, HMS (*f*105)

Coventry, HMS 279, 284, 291, 293, 302, 308–309, 484

Coxwold, SS 308

Creasy, Capt George E 270

Cromarty Firth, SS 308

Cunningham, Vice-Admiral Viscount Andrew Browne 121, 124, 158, 175, 180–181, 187, 219, 246, 253–256, 258, 269, 297, 309, 322, 411

Curacoa, HMS 208, 236–239, 465

Curityba, KMS 454

Curlew, HMS 22, (*f*96), 205, 223, 225, 227, 288, 300, 477

D

Darlan, Admiral François 201

de Salis, Capt Antony F 266, 268

Delight, HMS 293, 308

Denny, Capt Michael Maynard 235, 237, 241, 243, 247–250

Deptford, SS 17

Derrien, Admiral Edmond 124, 227, 253, 257–258

Deutschland, KMS (*f*28)

Devonshire, HMS 23, (*f*114), 110, 124, 137, 144, 158, 180–181, 187, 253–254, 256–257, 269, 309, 313–314, 322, 411, 484

Diana, HMS 251

Diego Suarez 103

Diesen, Admiral Henry E 250, 297

Diether von Roeder, KMS (*f*36), (*f*37) , (*f*44), (*f*49), (*f*52), (*f*64), 107, 166, 168

Dietl, General Eduard Wohlrat Christian 128, 288, 294, 299, 424, 448, 470, 472–473, 475, 479–480

Dithmarschen, KMS 310, 482, 484

f – photograph

Djupvik Bay 166–167
Dogger Bank 217
Dombaas 189–190, 193, 205, 231, 234, 236–238, 240, 244, 463, 466–467
Donibristle, RNAS (*f*16)
Dönitz, Admiral Karl 186
Dormer, Cecil HBM Minister to Norway 297
Dröbak, Narrows 18, 126–127, 160
Duchess of Athol, RMS 199
Duchess of York, SS (*f*123), 308
Duck, Operation 180, 211–212
Dunkirk 16
Durnford, Capt John W 180, 211–212
DX, Operation 205

E

Echo, HMS 77, 293
Eclipse, HMS 158, 161, 450
Edward-Collins, Vice-Admiral Sir George 109, 114, 123–124, 142, 180, 187, 203, 236–237, 240–242, 246, 249–251, 411
Effingham, HMS (*f*87), (*f*88), (*f*89), 226, 237, 269–270, 279, 285–286, 299, 477
Egersund 106
Eidsvold, HMNoS 20, (*f*32), (*f*33), 128, 145, 423–424
El d'Jezair, FR 227, 256–257
El Kantara, FR 227, 253, 256–257

El Mansour, FR 227, 253, 256
Electra, HMS 261, 270
Elvegaard 148
Elvegaardsmoen 471–472, 474
Elverum 189–190
Emden, KMS 122, 396, 433, 435
Emile Bertin, FR 114, 121, 124, 142, 226–227, 464–465
Empress of Australia, SS 161, 175, 222, 225
England, Operation 409
Enigma, Kriegsmarine Cypher 15
Enterprise, HMS 268–269, 276–277, 291
Erich Giese, KMS (*f*39), 107, 145, 148, 166–168, 443, 446
Erich Koellner, KMS (*f*40), (*f*73), 107, 145, 148, 165–167, 441, 443–445
Erich Steinbrinck, KMS 310, 483
Escapade, HMS 261
Escort, HMS 158
Eskimo, HMS 20, (*f*55), (*f*75), (*f*76), (*f*77), (*f*81), 120, 153–154, 165–169, 172, 174, 294, 444, 447
Europa, MS 466
Evans, Admiral Sir Edward 109, 411

F

Faeroes 160, 187, 301, 308, 313, 314, 322
Faksen shoal (*f*89)
Falkenhorst, General von 106
Fame, HMS 270, 285–286, 288, 291, 308
Faulknor, HMS 266
Fauske 300, 478
Fearless, HMS 204, 265

504

Fejeosen Fjord 136, 142

Fell, Acting-Cdr WR 279–280

Feuerstein, General Valentin 478, 481

Firedrake, HMS 291, 293, 308

Flamingo, HMS 187, 208, 232–233, 237

Fleetwood, HMS 208, 248, 276–277

Fleinvaer 153

Fleischer, General Carl G 181, 261, 277, 294

Fliegerfuehrer 468

Fliegerkorps X 394, 400, 426

Florida, SS 455

Flying Fish, SS (*f*20)

Focke-Wulf 200 (*f*123)

Forbes, Admiral Sir Charles 24, 109, 114, 120, 123, 133, 136, 142, 143, 174, 195, 198–199, 201, 227, 239, 245–248, 250–253, 272, 299–301, 314, 316, 324, 411, 420

Foresight, HMS 214

Forester, HMS (*f*82), 165, 168, 444

Fortune, HMS 204

Foudroyant, FR 278

Foxhound, HMS (*f*82), 165, 168, 172, 444, 446

Francklin, Lieutenant 292

Franconia, RMS 308

Fraser, Brigadier 277–278

Frauenlob, KMS 22, (*f*86)

Frederikshavn 189

Friedenau, KMS 455

Friedrich Eckholdt, KMS 107, 154–155, 449–450

Frohavet 158, 481

Furious, HMS 20, (*f*68), (*f*69), 123, 137, 142, 144, 154–155, 160–161, 164–165, 174, 181, 187, 196, 206, 289, 445–446, 450, 474

Fury, HMS 214

G

Galatea, HMS 114, 124, 142, 180, 187, 203, 222, 236–237, 241, 249, 391

Gallant, HMS 214

Gambier Bay, USS 22

Gdynia-America Line (*f*118), *f*119)

Geisler, Air General Hans-Ferdinand 400

Georg Thiele, KMS 20, (*f*54), (*f*55), (*f*56), 107, 149, 166–168, 424–425, 441, 443, 446–447

Georgic, MV 308

Gladiator, Gloster 21, (*f*102), (*f*103), 244, 303

Glasgow, HMS (*f*106), 110, 124, 136–137, 143, 174–175, 187, 204, 219, 221, 226, 241, 247–248, 411, 420

Glorious, HMS 11, 15, 21–22, 25, (*f*107), (*f*108), (*f*109), 188, 197, 204–206, 244, 289, 300, 303, 309, 311–314, 321–322, 467–468, 484, 487–488

Glowworm, HMS 11, 18, (*f*5), (*f*6), (*f*7), (*f*8), 110, 115–117, 120–121, 324, 411, 415, 417

f – photograph

Gneisenau, KMS 15, 18, 21–22, (*f* 26), (*f* 27), (*f* 110), (*f* 109), 107–108, 122, 128–129, 159, 310–312, 314, 316–317, 396, 419, 439, 448, 483, 486–487, 489–490

Goering, Reich Marshal Hermann 17

Government Code and Cypher School 14

Graf Spee, KMS 17, (*f* 4), 386

Gratangen 271

Gratangsbottem 472

Great Belt 111, 123, 399, 436, 484

Greenock 198, 204

Greif, KMS German Torpedo Boat (*f* 31), 432

Grenade, HMS 150, 254, 256–257

Greyhound, HMS 115, 150, 417

Griffin, HMS 242, 254, 256–257

Grom, ORP (*f* 97), 284, 475

Groven, Harald 61

Gubbins, Colonel Colin McVean 273–277, 279–280, 297

Gurkha, HMS 137, 143, 420

Gyren Shoal (*f* 15)

H

Haakon VII, King 19, 23, (*f* 114), 247, 297, 309, 322, 480, 493

Halsey, Admiral William Frederick 'Bull' 22

Halten Island 490

Hamar 190

Hamburg-America line (*f* 124)

Hamilton, Capt Louis HK 268, 284

Hamm, SS 457

Hammer, Operation 195, 197, 199, 201, 240

Hammond, HM Trawlers 243

Hamnes 144

Hamnesholm 165

Hans Lody, KMS (*f* 117), 310, 483

Hans Lüdemann, KMS 18, (*f* 44), (*f* 49–52), 107, 116, 145, 148–149, 166, 169, 439, 441–442, 446–447

Hansestadt Danzi, KMS 397

Hardy, HMS 20, (*f* 35), (*f* 41), (*f* 54), (*f* 58–61), 145, 148–149, 439–441

Harmattan, SS 308

Harpoon, Operation (*f* 74)

Harstad (*f* 89), 193, 206, 217, 261, 265–266, 279, 281, 283, 298, 301–302, 308–309, 311, 315, 321–323, 480, 484–489

Hartvig, Lake 287, 471

Hatston, RN Air Station 19–20, 137, 144, 198, 206–207, 212

Haugen 286

Haugesund, Norway (*f* 17), 183

Havant, HMS 180

Havelock, HMS 285–287, 291–292, 308

Havock, HMS (*f* 38), (*f* 41), (*f* 50), 145, 148–149, 213, 439–440

Hein Hoyer, SS (*f* 52)

Heinkel, He.60c (*f* 18), (*f* 27), (*f* 28)

Heinkel, He.111 (*f* 96–99), 420, 430, 450

Heligoland Bight 182, 412, 428

Hemnes 274–276, 476

Henry, Operation 175, 193–194, 217, 219, 221, 224, 226

Hereward, HMS 211, 213

Herjangs Fjord (*f*57), 145, 148, 167, 271

Hermann Künne, KMS (*f*45–49), 107, 148, 165–167, 439, 441–442, 444–446

Hermann Schoemann, KMS 310, 449, 483

Hero, HMS 58, 65, 73–74, (*f*80), 111, 165–169, 444

Hesperus, HMS 180, 276–277

Hewitt, Cdr John G 233, 235, 251

Heye, Capt Helmuth 18, 396, 426, 428, 449

Highlander, HMS 175, 225

Hipper, KMS 11, 18, 25, (*f*5–11), (*f*116), (*f*117), 107–108, 116, 121, 128, 154–155, 160, 310–311, 316–317, 324, 396, 415, 418, 420, 422, 426, 428, 449, 483–484, 486, 490

Hitler, Adolf 105, 383, 385, 387–388, 390–392, 394, 466, 481, 493–494

HN.25, Convoy 144

Hogg, Brigadier D 248–249

Holland, Rear-Admiral Lancelot E 187, 197–198

Hommelvik 197

Hood, HMS 187, 194, 231, 234–235

Horten, Naval Base 127

Horton, Vice-Admiral Sir Max 182

Hostile, HMS (*f*37), (*f*50), (*f*64), 116, 145, 148–149, 213, 215, 439–440

Hotblack, Major-General Frederick E 198

Hotspur, HMS (*f*62), (*f*65), 145, 148, 150, 439

Hudson, Lockheed 211, 213

Hunddalen 294, 300

Hunter, HMS 20, (*f*38) 51–52, (*f*41), (*f*54), (*f*62), (*f*65), 145, 148, 439–441

Hurricane, Hawker Mk.IIc (*f*104), 312

Hurricane, RAF Hawker 21, 303

Hyperion, HMS 111, 158, 213

Hysnes, Torpedo Battery 462

I

Icarus, HMS (*f*51), (*f*81), (*f*82), 154, 165, 168–169, 203, 241, 444

Ilex, HMS 158, 181

Imogen, HMS 158, 181

Imperial, HMS 257

Impulsive, HMS 203, 241

Infantry Division, 170 400

Infantry Division, 181 400

Infantry Division, 196 400

Infantry Division, 198 400

Infantry Division, 214 400

Infantry Divisions, 69 400

Infantry Divisions, 163 400

Infantry, King's Own Yorkshire Light 222, 225, 241

Inglefield, HMS 158, 181

Intrepid, HMS (*f*3)

Invergordon 187, 233

Irish Guards 268–269, 278, 282, 298–299

f – *photograph*

Iron-ore, Swedish 26
Isis, HMS 158, 181
Ivanhoe, HMS 173–174, 203, 241

J

Jackal, HMS 239, 247, 275–276
Jan Wellem, KMS 20, (*f*124–127), (*f*131), 148–149, 188, 398, 424, 438, 453
Janus, HMS (*f*93), 211, 213, 252, 273
Jardine, HMT 243
Jason, SS (*f*92)
Javelin, HMS 239, 247, 275–276
Jøssingfjord 17, (*f*3)
Jungingen 76
Juniper, HMS 310, 314
Junkers, Ju.87 (*f*100), 477
Junkers, Ju.88 (*f*101), 400, 420, 464
Juno, HMS 211
Juno, Operation 309, 321, 481, 484, 489–491
Jutland (*f*84), 111, 189, 394, 436, 455

K

K.G. 4, Bomber Group 400, 464
K.G. 22, Bomber Group 462
K.G. 26, Bomber Group 400, 420, 450, 464
K.G. 30, Bomber Group 400, 420, 462, 464

K.G. 100, Bomber Group 400, 464
Kaholm 127
Kaholm, Battery 434–435
Kandahar, HMS 213–215
Karl Galster, KMS 483
Karl Peters, KMS 107, 142, 428, 430
Karlsruhe, KMS 21, (*f*30), 183, 431–432, 451
Kattegat 106, 108, 122, 182–183, 201, 216–217, 393, 400–401, 437, 492
Kattegat, MS 188, 398, 453
Kaupisch, Air General Leonhard 400–401
Kelly, HMS 213–215, 254, 256
Kent, HMS (*f*78)
Keyes, Admiral of the Fleet Sir Roger 469
Kiel 34, 46, 122, 160–161, 310, 432, 451–453, 484, 491
Kimberley, HMS (*f*79), 120, 153, 154, 165, 168–169, 174, 213–214, 444, 446
King George V, HMS (*f*78)
King-Harman, Cdr Robert D 109
Kinnaird Head 124
Kipling, HMS 211
Kirkenes 104, 197
Kiruna, Sweden 14, 17, 28, (*f*130)
Kleikamp, Capt Gustav 436
Köenigsberg, KMS 19, 24, (*f*18–22), (*f*30), 107, 126, 142, 144, 206, 428, 430–431, 450, 452
Köln, KMS 107, 142, 428–431, 450
Kondor, KMS Torpedo Boat 435
Kongsmoen 272
Kongsvinger 189

Kors Fjord 136, 142, 216 429

Korsör 108

Kraagsvaag Fjord 426

Kristiansand (f 30), 106, 117, 126, 160, 183, 213, 389, 393, 396, 398, 401, 416, 432, 451, 464

Kroken 220

Kummetz, Rear Admiral Oskar 18, 127, 396, 432

Kvarven, Shore battery 20, 429, 451

Kya Light 175, 221, 253–254, 256

L

L'Indomptable, FR 213

Lambert, Lieutenant-Colonel HR 282

Lancaster, HMS 257

Lancastria, RMS (f 121), 308

Langeland Belt 122

Larwood, HMT 243

Lavangsfjord (f 96)

Layman, Cdr Herbert FH 150

Layton, Vice-Admiral Geoffrey 110, 114–115, 124, 136–137, 142, 151–152, 174–175, 180, 187, 203–204, 215, 221–222, 226–227, 229, 241–242, 246, 248, 250–251, 411, 420

le Luc, Admiral Maurice-Athanase 201

Le Malin, FR 213

Le Triomphant, FR 213

Legion, French Foreign 285, 287, 290, 292–293, 302, 479

Leipzig, KMS 25

Leopard, KMS Torpedo Boat 107, 450

Lesjaskog, Lake (know as Gladiator Lake) 205, 234, 240, 244, 463, 467

Lesjaskogvatnet (f 103)

Lesjaswick, Aerodrome 234

Lillehammer 190, 231

Lillesjona 222–223, 225, 266, 463

Lofoten Islands (f 74), (f 76), 128, 150, 154, 159–160, 164, 175, 180–181, 186–187, 193, 195, 202, 212, 219, 449, 488

London Naval Treaty, 1930 76

Longhope 213

Lord Cork, Admiral of the Fleet, William Henry Dudley Boyle 174, 180, 203–204, 206, 247, 261, 265–266, 268–269, 271–277, 279, 281, 285–286, 288–289, 292–293, 296–301, 309, 316, 321, 326, 474, 476–477

Lord Halifax, Edward Frederick Lindley Wood 409

Lubeck 464

Lueneburg 464

Lulea, Swedish port 17, 103–104

Lumley, Major H 235

Lütjens, Admiral Johann Günthe 159–160, 320, 402, 448–449, 490

Lützow, KMS 18–19, 21, (f) 46, 122, 160–161, 183, 396–397, 433, 435, 452

Lyster, Admiral Arthur L 281

f – photograph

M

M.1072, Minesweeper 455
M.1101, Minesweeper 455
M.1701, Minesweeper 455
Mackesy, General Pierse J 174, 261, 266, 268–269, 277, 286, 321, 326, 473
Malangen Fjord 247
Malaya, HMS (f72), 416
Manchester, HMS 114, 121, 136, 143, 175, 187, 203–204, 215, 222, 226–227, 242, 251–252
Maori, HMS 254, 468
Margot, SS 276
Marie Leonhardt, KMS 454
Marschall, Admiral Wilhelm 310–312, 315–316, 321, 402, 482–486, 488–490
Mashobra, SS 282, 303
Mashona, HMS 175, 224, 226–227, 250
Matabele, HMS 175, 221, 224, 279
Matapan, Battle of Cape 15
Maund, Captain Loben EH 261
Mauranger Fjord 142
Maurice, Operation 180, 193–194, 217, 221–222, 226–227, 240, 242, 247
Mausundvaer 158
Methil 114
Mewis, Vice-Admiral Raul 401
Middelfart 108
Milan, FR 288

Mjösa, Lake 189
Mo 278, 297, 460, 476, 478
Moen 122
Mohawk, HMS 175, 203, 214, 243, 273
Molde 220, 231, 234–237, 239, 241–242, 244, 246–251, 272, 462, 465
Monarch of Bermuda, RMS (f122), 161, 308
Monark, SS 216
Montcalm, HMS 253, 256–257
Moonsund, KMS 454
Moore, Group Capt Maurice 303
Morgan, Brigadier 180, 194, 222, 233, 234, 236, 244, 462–463, 466, 467
Moscow, Treaty of 16
Mosjoen 228, 252, 274–275, 460, 475–478
Motorised Rifle Brigade, 11th 400
Mountain Division, 181 Infantry Division 478
Mountbatten, Capt Lord Louis 213–215
Möwe, KMS Torpedo Boat 434
Muckle Flugga 114

N

Namsen Fjord 220–221, 223, 225–228, 253, 256
Namsos (f93–95), 103, 175, 180, 187–188, 193, 195, 199, 202, 205–206, 208–211, 217, 219–220, 222, 224–225, 227–231, 233, 242, 245–247, 252–256, 258, 260, 266, 270, 272–273, 275–277, 322–323, 459–461, 463–466, 468, 470, 478

Napier, Cdr Trevylyan M 275–276

Narvik 14, 16–17, 20–21, 25, 28, (*f*1), (*f*23), (*f*33), (*f*35), (*f*37), (*f*38), (*f*40–42), (*f*49), (*f*50), (*f*52–54), (*f*60), (*f*64), (*f*65), (*f*74), (*f*75), (*f*79–81), (*f*97), (*f*124), (*f*126), (*f*129), (*f*130), (*f*132), 100, 102–106, 108–111, 117, 120, 122–123, 127–128, 133, 143–145, 149–152, 155, 158, 160, 164–169, 172–174, 181, 186, 188–189, 191–192, 199–200, 203–204, 206, 217–218, 230, 246, 252, 260–261, 267–268, 270–271, 274, 278, 281, 284–285, 288–290, 292–296, 302, 317–318, 323–326, 388, 393, 398, 410–411, 413, 416–418, 420, 422–423, 425, 438–439, 442–446, 454, 457, 459–461, 471–472, 475–476, 478–481, 484, 486, 489

Narwhal, HM Mine Laying Submarine 216–217

Nations, League of 387

Naze 111, 186, 216–217

Nelson, HMS 187, 194, 231–232, 416, 419

Neuenfels, KMS 148

Newcastle, HMS 301, 314–315

Nicholson, Capt Randolph Stewart Gresham 177, 187, 220–222, *278*

Nordkapp, HMNoS 181, 453

Nordmark, KMS 482

Norge, HMNoS 20, (*f*33), (*f*41), 128, 145, 424

Normandy landings 26

Northern Foam, HMT 180

Northern Gem, HMT 303

Northern Sky, HMT 180

Nubian, HMS 203, 223–224, 226–229, 256

Nyborg 108

O

Odderöy Island 126

Oddery, Battery 431–432

Oerlikon, 20mm 24

Official Secrets Act 101

Ofot Fjord 20, 22, (*f*96), 145, 148, 152, 165–167, 268, 270, 275, 284, 288, 291, 302, 310, 323, 425, 442–443, 482, 489

Oijord 267

Oil Pioneer, SS 308, 310, 314, 486

Olav Tryggvason, HMNoS 127

Olav, Crown Prince 23, (*f*114), 190, 247, 309

Oleander, RFA 303

Oligarch, RFA 308

Operational Intelligence Centre 15

Orama, RMS (*f*116), (*f*117), 311, 313–315, 322, 486

Orion, RMS (transport) 180, 187, 199, 222, 237

Ormonde, SS 308

Oronsay, SS 199, 308

Orphée, FR Submarine 216

Orzel, ORP Submarine 116, 182–183, 416

f – *photograph*

Oscarsborg, fortress 18, 127

Oslo (*f* 84), 106, 108, 122, 126–127, 189, 231, 389, 399–401, 416, 420, 432, 435–437, 451–452, 454, 457, 464, 471, 482, 492, 494

Oslofjord 18–19, 37, 46

Oydejord 290, 292–293

P

Paget, Major-General Bernard C 240–241, 243–245, 248, 251

Paul Jacobi, KMS 107, 154, 450

Paul, Operation 17

Pearl Harbor 24

Pegram, Capt Frank H 143, 174–175, 219–221, 223, 248

Pelican, HMS 208, 465

Penelope, HMS 110, 114, 120, 123, 150, 152–154, 265, 272, 275, 281, 411, 418

Phillips, Admiral Tom Deputy Chief of Staff 260

Phoney War 16

Poland, Capt. Albert L 232–234, 248

Polarnoye 386

Porpoise, HM Submarine 217

Posidonia, SS 183

Pound, First Sea Lord, Admiral Sir Dudley 16, 201

Primrose, Operation 193–194, 211, 217, 231, 233–235, 238, 246–247, 251

Prinz Eugen, KMS (*f* 12)

Protector, HMS 265, 281, 285

Punjabi, HMS (*f* 40), (*f* 78), 120, 165, 167, 174, 444, 447

Q

Qu'Appelle, HMCS (*f* 82)

Quisling, Vidkund, Norwegian fascist 23, 190, 385, 392, 436, 493

R

Raeder, Grand Admiral Erich 16–17, 104, 106, 117, 323–324, 383–387, 391, 401, 481, 483, 488, 494

Ramnes 144

Ramsöy Fjord 155

Ranen, SS 299, 303

Rauenfels, KMS 165, 149, 188, 440

Rauöy, Battery 126

Ravenhill, Cdr Richard W 228, 256

Rawlings, Capt Henry B 301, 315

Reina del Pacifico, SS 161

Renown, HMS 18, (*f* 25), 44, 110, 115, 121, 128–129, 133, 150, 159, 161, 164–165, 174, 187, 197, 203, 212, 301, 314, 316–317, 410, 417, 419

Repulse, HMS 110, 114, 120–123, 133, 150, 161, 197, 203, 212, 247, 314–315, 411, 418–419, 444

Resistance, Norwegian 23

Resolution, HMS 197, 203, 247, 270, 284–285, 477

Rieve, Capt Friedrich 431–432

Rio de Janeiro, SS 116–117, 121, 182–183, 324, 416, 436

Roda, SS 432

Rodney, HMS 24, (*f*90), 110, 114, 121–123, 137, 144, 161, 164–165, 174, 187, 198, 203, 247, 314, 316–317, 411, 419–420

Roeder, KMS 438, 441–443, 446–447

Rombaks Fjord 21, (*f*41–43), (*f*46), (*f*47), (*f*51), (*f*55), (*f*92), (*f*97), 145, 167–169, 172, 266, 290–292, 294, 446–447, 474, 479–480

Romsdals Fjord 220, 250

Roope, Cdr Gerard Broadmead 11, 18, 115

Roros 189

Rosyth 109, 111, 114, 121, 123–124, 136, 161, 180, 187, 198–199, 203, 213–214, 227, 232, 237–238, 241–242, 323, 414

Royal Leicestershire Regiment 236

Royal Scotsman, HMS 274

Royal Ulsterman, HMS 273–274, 308

Rubis, FR Submarine 217

Rugard, KMS 397

Ruge, General Otto 190, 250–251, 277, 297, 480

Rupert, Expeditionary Force 181

Rupert, Operation 260, 268, 271

S

Saalwächter, General-Admiral Alfred 401, 482

Saegnes 292

Sag Fjord 261

Salangen 473

Salmon, HM Submarine 25

Salten Fjord 478

Sandnessjøen (*f*57), 275–276

Sao Paolo, SS 453

Saphir, SS (*f*52)

Saumur, HMS 210

Scapa Flow 15, 21, (*f*78), (*f*91), 109–111, 115, 121, 143, 151, 161, 174, 180–181, 187, 198–199, 202–207, 211–215, 226, 228, 242, 247–249, 251–252, 257–258, 276, 301, 314–317, 388–389, 411–412, 414, 428, 468, 471, 484

Scharnhorst, KMS 15, 18, 22, (*f*109–113), 107–108, 114, 128–129, 159, 310–312, 314, 316–317, 396, 413, 417–419, 439, 448, 455, 483, 486–491

Scheer, KMS 25, 316

Schenk, Rear-Admiral Otto 401, 432

Schlesien, KMS 398

Schleswig-Holstein, SMS 108, 397–398, 436

Schmundt, Rear-Admiral Hubert 142, 428, 430–431, 450

Scots Guards 261, 271, 275, 297–298

Sea Transport Division 430

Sea Transport Division, 1st 398, 402, 416, 430, 432, 454

Sea Transport Division, 2nd 108, 399, 452, 454

Sea Transport Division, 3rd 108, 399, 455

Seal, HM Submarine 125, 182, 211, 216–217

f – *photograph*

Sealion, HM Submarine 182–183, 217
Seawolf, HM Submarine 182, 216
Selven, Torpedo Battery 462
Severn, HM Submarine 182, 216
Shark, HM Submarine 182
Sheffield, HMS 114, 123, 136, 174–175, 187, 204–205, 215, 219, 221, 226, 241, 246, 249, 411, 416
Sherwood Foresters 236
Shetlands–Stadlandet line 108
Sickle, Operation 180, 193, 217, 234–235, 238–240, 246–247
Sikh, HMS 175, 203, 221, 224, 227, 243, 249
Sildvika 168, 294
Simpson, Colonel HW 232–235, 249, 462
Sirte, Battle of (*f*63)
Skagerrak 106, 108, 116, 122, 125, 159–160, 180, 182–183, 201–202, 213, 216–217, 389, 393–394, 400–401, 412, 429, 437, 457, 492
Skagerrak, MS 188, 398, 428, 453
Skaw 122
Skjel Fjord 150, 154, 173, 180, 226, 252, 261, 265, 279, 281
Skjelfjorden (*f*76), (*f*81)
Skjomenfjord 63
Skjorn Fjord 158
Skoltegrunnd Mole (*f*19)
Skomvaer Light 117, 128, 154, 174, 187
Skonvaer 417–418

Sleipner, HMNoS 188, 432, 453
Snaasen, Lake 466
Snapper, HM Submarine 182–183, 216
Sobieski, MS 199, 308
Sogne Fjord 216
Solfolla 207, 303
Sollum Voe 175
Somali, HMS 175, 187, 203, 223, 250–252, 277–278, 285–286
Sonsbukten 127
South Wales Borderers 270, 279, 284, 288, 298
Southampton, HMS (*f*115), 114, 121, 136–137, 161, 187, 246, 249, 261, 265, 269, 291, 294, 308–309, 420, 473, 484
Spearfish, HM submarine 19, (*f*29), 160, 182–183, 217, 452
Special Operations Executive (SOE) 23
Sprague, Rear Admiral Clifton 22
St Nazaire (*f*121)
St. Abbs Head 213
St. Magnus, MV 239
St. Sunniva, MV 239
Stadtlandet 114, 175, 231, 235, 481
Stannard, Lieutenant Richard B 210
Stavanger 16–17, (*f*22), (*f*91), 137, 142, 188, 196, 207, 234, 323, 399, 410–411, 420, 454, 464, 491
Stedingen, SS 416
Steinkjaer 190, 220, 228, 230, 466
Sterlet, HM Submarine (*f*84), (*f*85), 216
Stevens, Capt E Barry 287, 292
Storen 190, 244, 467

Stork, HMS 278, 292, 302, 308

Strandlokka 189

Strommen Bay 426

Stuka, Ju.87 22, (*f*93), (*f*95), (*f*100), (*f*118)

Sturges, Colonel Robert G 204

Suffolk, HMS 21, 78, (*f*91), 180, 187, 196, 200, 203, 211–213, 462, 465

Sullom Voe 143, 242

Sunfish, HM Submarine 122, 182–183

Sussex, HMS 301, 314–315

Svalbard II, DS 313

Swordfish, Fairey 17, 20, (*f*45), (*f*66–69), (*f*105), (*f*106), (*f*130), 161, 206, 207, 311, 445

Swordfish, Floatplane 21, (*f*48), (*f*57), (*f*72)

Sydney-Turner, Lieut-Cdr Patrick GO 164

T

Taarstad 165, 443–445

Taku, HM Submarine 217

Tank-Nielson, Admiral Carsten 220, 231

Taraldsvik 293

Taranto 24

Tarpon, HM Submarine 182

Tartar, HMS 203, 249–250

Telemark 23

Tennholm Fjord 153

Terboven, Josef Reichskommissar 23, 190, 493–494

Terschelling 215

Tetrarch, HM Submarine 216, 217

Teviot Bank, HMS 109, 114, 121, 411

Theodor Riedel, KMS 107, 154, 450

Theseus, HMS 308

Thistle, HM Submarine 182

Thorshavn 180

Tjeidøy 151, 153–154

Tjeldsundet 144, 151, 278–279, 282, 288, 477

Todd, Capt Percy 411

Tothill, Cdr John Anthony William 273

Tranøy 150–151, 153–154

Triad, HM Submarine 183, 216

Trident, HM Submarine 182–183, 416

Triton, HM Submarine 123, 182–183

Troldvik 167

Tromsø 22, (*f*114), 158, 174, 181, 187, 197, 223, 247, 251, 269, 284, 297, 301, 308–310, 317

Trondheim 16, 22, 105–106, 108, 111, 121, 126, 133, 136, 142, 151, 154–155, 158–160, 180, 183, 187–189, 191–192, 194–196, 199–200, 202–203, 205–206, 217, 220, 224, 231, 236, 240, 242, 244, 247, 257, 260, 311–312, 315–316, 325, 388, 393–394, 396, 398–399, 410–411, 418, 420, 422, 426, 428, 448–450, 453–454, 457, 459–462, 464, 466–470, 478, 482, 487–488, 490

Troubridge, Capt Thomas Hope 155, 158, 167

f – *photograph*

Truant, HM Submarine (*f*31), 125, 143, 182–183

U

U-4 183
U-26 462
U-29 85
U-43 462
U-47 93
U-49 282
U-51 166, 426
U-64 (*f*57), 166, 172, 282, 444
Ulster Monarch, MV 249–251, 308
Ulster Prince, MV 249–250, 273–274, 308
Ultra 15
Unity, HM Submarine 182, 216
Urundi, TS 455
Utsire 143, 412

V

Vaagsfjord 144, 161, 173, 175, 181, 187–188, 193, 203, 261, 265–266, 310–311, 459, 471, 481–482, 487
Vaernes, Aerodrome 197, 205, 257, 317, 466
Valiant, HMS 110, 114, 121, 123, 137, 144, 161, 175, 186–187, 197, 203, 205, 222, 246–247, 265, 301, 308, 313–315, 322, 411, 484, 488
van Hengl, Lieutenant Georg Ritter 478

Vandyck, HMS 308, 480
Vanoc, HMS 175, 225
Vansittart, HMS 241
Vardoe 413
Veblungsnes 249
Vefsen Fjord 272, 275, 277
Vemork Norsk Hydro plant 23
Verdalsoren 220, 230
Verma, Power Station 234
Vest Fjord (*f*118), 111, 115, 120, 127–128, 133, 149–151, 154, 158, 160, 166, 173–175, 180, 183, 192, 270, 288
Vian, Capt Philip (*f*2), 30
Victoria Cross 18, 20
Vigo, Spanish Port (*f*123)
Ville d'Alger, FR 229–230
Ville d'Oran, FR 227, 464
Vindictive, HMS 70, 175, 265, 269, 285, 298, 301–302, 309, 484
Virek (*f*) 63
Vivian, Rear-Admiral Algernon Walker-Heneage 238, 252, 254–256, 279, 284, 293, 302, 314
von Falkenhorst, General Paul N 400–401, 475
von Schrader, Vice Admiral Otto 401, 450

W

Walker, MV 249, 291
Walrus, flying boat 68, 90, 207, 211, 282, 303
Wanderer, HMS 249
War Pindari, RFA 223–224

Warburton-Lee, Capt Bernard Armitage 11, 110, 133, 144–145, 148, 158, 324, 326, 410, 439–440

Warspite, HMS 20–21, (f 39), (f 40) (f 48), (f 57), (f 70–73), 123, 144, 161, 164–169, 172–173, 186, 197, 203, 261, 265, 267, 269, 323, 444–445, 489

Wellington, Vickers Bomber 111, 414

Wells, Vice-Admiral Lionel V 188, 243, 246–247, 254, 317

Weserübung, Operation 105, 385, 388, 390, 392, 400

Westcott, HMS 249

Westerland 464

Westfjord 415–417, 423, 426, 439, 442, 444, 448, 453, 471, 477, 481, 489

Whirlwind, HMS 175, 225

Whitworth, Vice Admiral William 'Jock' 18, 20, 110–111, 115, 117, 120–121, 123, 128–129, 133, 145, 149–151, 153–154, 159, 161, 164, 165, 172–173, 186, 203, 222, 260, 266, 268–269, 301, 323–324, 326, 410, 417–419, 439, 444–445, 447

Wigbert, KMS 455

Wilfred, Operation 17

Wilhelm Heidkamp, KMS 20, (f 32), (f 34), (f 35), 107, 148, 424, 438, 441, 443

Wilhelmshaven (f 9), 398, 413, 428, 450

Windisch, General Alois 475

Wishart, HMS (f 106)

Witch, HMS 241

Witherington, HMS 243

Wolf, KMS 107

Wolfgang Zenker, KMS (f 42–44), (f 52), (f 55), 107, 148, 166, 441, 443, 446–447

Wolverine, HMS 278

Wren, HMS 285

Wright, Cdr John Piachavd 134, 149, 153

Wurttemberg, KMS (f 124)

X

X-24, Midget Submarine (f 24)

XXI, Army Group 189, 400, 425, 435, 461, 467, 469, 471, 475, 482

Y

Yates, Capt Gerald D 150, 152–154

York, HMS 110, 124, 137, 144, 158, 161, 226, 237, 242, 253–254, 256, 411

Z

Zulu, HMS 266, 269, 275, 476

f – photograph

Britannia Naval Histories of World War II

Historical material, newly commissioned commentary, maps, plans and first-hand accounts of specific battles. Each foreword is written by naval veterans of the highest order.

Never previously published in this format, World War II Battle Summaries are documents once stamped 'restricted' or 'confidential' and held in the archive of Britannia Royal Naval College in Dartmouth, South West England. They are unique records written up by naval officers during the conflict, and soon after 1945. Events are recorded in minute detail, accompanied by maps and plans drawn up during the period by serving officers. These historical texts have been reorganised into a contemporary format. The first-hand accounts are from worldwide sources and contain reactions, emotions and descriptions, making fascinating reading.

Introduction by
M J Pearce

Confronting Italy
Mediterranean Surface Actions in 1940. Exploding the Myth of Mussolini's 'Mare Nostrum'

Paperback
ISBN 978-1-84102-439-4
Hardback
ISBN 978-1-84102-442-4
ebook
Amazon B086M6J66F
Number of Pages
192 pages

Foreword
Admiral Sir John Cunningham Kirkwood 'Jock' Slater, GCB, LVO, DL. A former first Sea Lord and great-nephew of Admiral Sir Andrew Cunningham, Commander-in-Chief of the Mediterranean fleet during this period when the actions covered in this volume took place.

- Contains both an Italian and British first-hand account.
- Includes tracking maps drawn when the Battle Summary was compiled.
- Includes the supplement to the *London Gazette*.

Actions in the Mediterranean were fought when the Royal Navy was still evolving its use of naval air power and when radar at sea was primitive and fitted to only a few ships, while Italy's Regia Marina was handicapped by having access to neither.

Introduction by
M J Pearce

Dunkirk
Operation "Dynamo"
26th May – 4th June 1940
An Epic of Gallantry

Paperback
ISBN 978-1-83801-070-6
Hardback
ISBN 978-1-83801-071-3
eBook
Amazon B0888T89RY
Number of Pages
420 pages

Foreword
Admiral Sir James Burnell-Nugent KCB, CBE, MA. He became Second Sea Lord and Commander-in-Chief Naval Home Command with responsibility for all personnel matters. He flew his flag in HMS Victory, making frequent use of Nelson's Great Cabin.

- Declassified content records events in minute detail.
- Includes maps drawn when the Battle Summary was compiled.
- Unpublished photographs of the beaches, town, and harbour is included.

The Royal Navy achieved what it set out to do, despite grievous losses, in the teeth of determined opposition. The loss of the main British field army would have enfeebled the nation militarily and psychologically, potentially resulting in a negotiated peace with Nazi Germany.

Introduction by
G H Bennett

Rise of the Aircraft Carrier
Pacific Naval Strategy 1941–1945

Paperback
ISBN 978-1-83801-073-7
Hardback
ISBN 978-1-83801-074-4
eBook
ISBN 978-1-83801-075-1
Number of Pages
340 pages

Foreword
James Bergeron, Chief Political Advisor for NATO Maritime Command in Northwood, United Kingdom. Previously in support of NATO as a member of the US Government Service, he is considered to be one of NATO's most experienced foreign policy advisors in the fields of maritime operations.

- Declassified content records events in minute detail.
- Includes detailed maps drawn when the Battle Summary was compiled.
- 192 photographs of carriers and aircraft both USN, IJN and HMS included.

Unmatched US industrial capacity enabled the design and construction of large numbers of highly capable carriers, their escorts and new naval aircraft. Despite early losses, the USN swiftly outstripped the IJN in numbers and capability, leaving the Japanese to rely on converting aircraft carriers from all manner of other vessels.

Introduction by
G H Bennett

Fire & Ice
Arctic Convoys 1941-1945

Paperback
ISBN 978-1-83801-076-8
Hardback
ISBN 978-1-83801-077-5
eBook
ISBN 978-1-83801-078-2
Number of Pages
500 pages

Foreword
Vice-Admiral Sir Simon Lister KCB OBE. Commander, HM Naval Base Plymouth in 2005. In 2017 Lister took a sabbatical from his Royal Navy Career to lead the Aircraft Carrier Alliance delivering the nation's new Queen Elizabeth Class carriers.

- Declassified content records events in minute detail.
- Supplemented by a modern historical introduction and commentary.
- Enhanced by the inclusion of a large number of photographs.

With the massive campaign on Germany's Eastern front hanging in the balance in 1941 to 1942, the German Armed Forces deployed significant numbers of submarines, bomber and torpedo aircraft, together with *Tirpitz* and *Scharnhorst*, against the slow-moving Allied convoys of merchant ships and their escorting forces.

Introduction by
G H Bennett

Operation Neptune
D-Day Landings in Normandy June 1944

Paperback
ISBN 978-1-917152-04-4
Hardback
ISBN 978-1-917152-03-7
eBook
ISBN 978-1-917152-05-1
Number of Pages
544 pages

Foreword
Craig L. Symonds is Professor Emeritus at the United States Naval Academy where he taught naval history and Civil War History for thirty years. He has also won the 'Annie' Award in Literary Arts given by Anne Arundel County, Maryland.

- Includes the now declassified Battle Summary No 39, in minute detail.
- Supplemented by a modern historical introduction and commentary.
- Enhanced by a large number of photographs and an 180 page unpublished Appendix.

Operation "Neptune," the name given to the assault phase of Operation "Overlord," the general plan for the liberation of north-west Europe was indeed appropriate – because without in any way detracting from the magnificent work of the sister services, the Navy was necessarily bound to play the major part in the opening stages of convoy and transport.

www.ingramcontent.com/pod-product-compliance
Lightning Source LLC
Chambersburg PA
CBHW060828190426
43197CB00039B/2529